IRISH LITERATURE IN TRANSITION, 1700–1780

This volume examines eighteenth-century Irish literature, highlighting the diversity of texts, authors, and approaches that characterises contemporary studies of the period. Chapters consider the contexts of history, politics, language, philosophy, gender, sexuality, and the environment while situating Irish literature in relation to Ireland, Britain, Europe, and beyond. Well-known authors (Jonathan Swift, Edmund Burke, and Oliver Goldsmith) are read alongside less familiar writers (including Mary Barber, William Chaigneau, Frances Sheridan, and Samuel Whyte) and popular and ephemeral literatures take their place with formerly canonical texts. It demonstrates the exciting vitality and richness of eighteenth-century Irish literature – written and performed – as well as its complex intersections with different communities and traditions. This book will be a key resource to scholars and students of Irish eighteenth-century studies as well as readers generally interested in questions of Anglophone and Irish-language culture, representations of gender and sexuality, and national and transnational identities.

MOYRA HASLETT is Professor of English at Queen's University Belfast. Her first monograph – *Byron's Don Juan and the Don Juan Legend* (1997) – won the Rose Mary Crawshay Prize awarded by the British Academy. She is also the author of a popular general book on eighteenth-century literature: *Pope to Burney, 1714–1779: Scriblerians to Bluestockings* (2003). She is one of the general editors of the Early Irish Fiction, c. 1680–1820 series, and has co-edited a special issue of *Irish University Review* on the same topic (2011). She is also the Principal Investigator of the AHRC-funded Irish Song Project (www.irishsongproject.qub.ac.uk).

IRISH LITERATURE IN TRANSITION

General editors:
Claire Connolly, University College Cork
Marjorie Howes, Boston College

This six-volume series captures the dynamic energies transmitted over more than 300 years of the established literary landmarks that constitute Irish literary life. Ambitious in scope and depth, and accommodating new critical perspectives and approaches, Irish Literature in Transition captures the ongoing changes in the Irish literary canon. Each of the six volumes revises our understanding of established issues and texts and, simultaneously, introduces new questions, approaches, and authors. These volumes address periods of transition, but also periods of epochal upheaval and turning points of real significance. Each one of these books challenges in different ways the dominant approaches to a period of literature by shifting the focus from what happened to understanding how and why it happened. They elucidate the multifaceted interaction between the social and literary fields in the evolution of Irish literature until the present moment. Taken together, Irish Literature in Transition constitutes a new kind of literary history across centuries of intense cultural and literary creation. It offers a comprehensive analysis of the Irish literary experience, creating a new and dynamic version of literary history that highlights the significance of change as a lived, felt force.

Books in the series

1. *Irish Literature in Transition, 1700–1780* edited by Moyra Haslett
2. *Irish Literature in Transition, 1780–1830* edited by Claire Connolly
3. *Irish Literature in Transition, 1830–1880* edited by Matthew Campbell
4. *Irish Literature in Transition, 1880–1940* edited by Marjorie Howes
5. *Irish Literature in Transition, 1940–1980* edited by Eve Patten
6. *Irish Literature in Transition, 1980–2020* edited by Eric Falci and Paige Reynolds

IRISH LITERATURE
IN TRANSITION, 1700–1780

EDITED BY

MOYRA HASLETT

Queen's University Belfast

CAMBRIDGE
UNIVERSITY PRESS

CAMBRIDGE
UNIVERSITY PRESS

University Printing House, Cambridge CB2 8BS, United Kingdom

One Liberty Plaza, 20th Floor, New York, NY 10006, USA

477 Williamstown Road, Port Melbourne, VIC 3207, Australia

314–321, 3rd Floor, Plot 3, Splendor Forum, Jasola District Centre,
New Delhi – 110025, India

79 Anson Road, #06–04/06, Singapore 079906

Cambridge University Press is part of the University of Cambridge.

It furthers the University's mission by disseminating knowledge in the pursuit of
education, learning, and research at the highest international levels of excellence.

www.cambridge.org
Information on this title: www.cambridge.org/9781108427500
DOI: 10.1017/9781108689045

First published 2020

Printed in the United Kingdom by TJ International Ltd. Padstow Cornwall

A catalogue record for this publication is available from the British Library.

Library of Congress Cataloging-in-Publication Data
NAMES: Haslett, Moyra, editor.
TITLE: Irish literature in transition, 1700–1780 / edited by Moyra Haslett,
Queens university Belfast.
DESCRIPTION: Cambridge, United Kingdom ; New York, NY : Cambridge University Press,
2020. | Series: Irish literature in transition ; Volume 1 | Includes index.
IDENTIFIERS: LCCN 2019038267 (print) | LCCN 2019038268 (ebook) | ISBN 9781108427500
(hardback) | ISBN 9781108689045 (ebook)
SUBJECTS: LCSH: English literature – Irish authors – History and criticism. | English literature –
18th century – History and criticism. | Irish literature – 18th century – History and criticism. |
Literature and society – Ireland – History.
CLASSIFICATION: LCC PR8747 .I75 2020 (print) | LCC PR8747 (ebook) | DDC 820.9/9415–dc23
LC record available at https://lccn.loc.gov/2019038267
LC ebook record available at https://lccn.loc.gov/2019038268

ISBN 978-1-108-42750-0 Hardback

Contents

List of Illustrations   *page* viii
List of Contributors   ix
Series Preface   xiii
General Acknowledgements   xv

Introduction   1
Moyra Haslett

PART I   STARTING POINTS

1   Starting Points and Moving Targets: Transition and the Early
    Modern   31
    Marie-Louise Coolahan

2   'We Irish': Writing and National Identity from Berkeley to
    Burke   49
    Ian Campbell Ross

3   Re-Viewing Swift   68
    Brean Hammond

PART II   PHILOSOPHICAL AND POLITICAL FRAMEWORKS

4   The Prejudices of Enlightenment   91
    David Dwan

5   The Molyneux Problem and Irish Enlightenment   110
    Darrell Jones

6   Samuel Whyte and the Politics of Eighteenth-Century Irish
    Private Theatricals   129
    Helen M. Burke

PART III LOCAL, NATIONAL, AND TRANSNATIONAL CONTEXTS

7   Land and Landscape in Irish Poetry in English, 1700–1780   151
    Andrew Carpenter

8   The Idea of an Eighteenth-Century National Theatre   171
    Conrad Brunström

9   Transnational Influence and Exchange: The Intersections
    between Irish and French Sentimental Novels   189
    Amy Prendergast

10 'An Example to the Whole World': Patriotism and Imperialism
    in Early Irish Fiction   207
    Daniel Sanjiv Roberts

PART IV GENDER AND SEXUALITY

11 The Province of Poetry: Women Poets in Early
    Eighteenth-Century Ireland   227
    Aileen Douglas

12 Queering Eighteenth-Century Irish Writing: Yahoo, Fribble,
    Freke   244
    Declan Kavanagh

13 'Brightest Wits and Bravest Soldiers': Ireland, Masculinity,
    and the Politics of Paternity   263
    Rebecca Anne Barr

14 Fictions of Sisterhood in Eighteenth-Century Irish Writing   284
    Moyra Haslett

PART V TRANSCULTURAL CONTEXTS

15 The Popular Criminal Narrative and the Development of the
    Irish Novel   307
    Joe Lines

16 Gaelic Influences and Echoes in the Irish Novel, 1700–1780   324
    Anne Markey

17 New Beginning or Bearer of Tradition? Early Irish Fiction
    and the Construction of the Child   343
    Clíona Ó Gallchoir

PART VI RETROSPECTIVE READINGS

18 Re-Imagining Feminist Protest in Contemporary Translation:
    Lament for Art O'Leary and *The Midnight Court*   365
    Lesa Ní Mhunghaile

19 'Our Darkest Century': The Irish Eighteenth Century in
    Memory and Modernity   382
    James Ward

        Index   401

Illustrations

1   Andrew Boorde, *The Fyrst Boke of the Introduction of*   *page* 35
    Knowledge, 2nd edn (London, 1555), sig. C2v. © British
    Library (C.71.b.29)

2   *The Hibernian Magazine: Or Compendium of Entertaining*   139
    Knowledge (April 1778), facing p. 193. Mrs Gardiner as Lady
    Macbeth in Phoenix-Park. By permission of the Royal Irish
    Academy © RIA (C/8/2/E)

3   *The Hibernian Magazine: Or Compendium of Entertaining*   139
    Knowledge (May 1778), facing p. 249. Robert Jephson, Esqr in
    the Character of Macbeth. By permission of the Royal Irish
    Academy © RIA (C/8/2/E)

4   David Garrick, *The Fribbleriad* (London, 1761), Frontispiece.   253
    Illustration of 'Fizgig' (Thady Fitzpatrick). By permission of
    the Beinecke Rare Book and Manuscript Library, Yale
    University

5   William Chaigneau, *The History of Jack Connor*, 2 vols   276
    (Dublin, 1766), II, between pp. 232 and 233. Reproduced
    courtesy of the National Library of Ireland (LO 13227/2)

6   William Chaigneau, *The History of Jack Connor*, 2 vols   351
    (Dublin, 1766), I, Frontispiece. Reproduced courtesy of the
    National Library of Ireland (LO 13227/1)

Contributors

REBECCA ANNE BARR is University Lecturer in the Faculty of English at the University of Cambridge. Her research focuses on fictional form, masculinity, and sexuality in the eighteenth-century novel. In 2016 she was awarded a Lewis Walpole fellowship on *John Bull and Irish Bull: Representations of Irish Masculinity in Late Eighteenth-Century Visual Satire*. With Sylvie Kleiman-Lafon and Sophie Vasset, she is co-editor of *Bellies, Bowels and Entrails in the Eighteenth Century* (2018).

CONRAD BRUNSTRÖM is Senior Lecturer in English at Maynooth University. He is the author of two monographs, *William Cowper: Religion, Satire, Society* (2004) and *Thomas Sheridan's Career and Influence* (2011), and has also published on Samuel Johnson, Frances Burney, Frances Sheridan, and Matthew Prior.

HELEN M. BURKE is Professor Emerita of English at Florida State University. She is the author of *Riotous Performances: The Struggle for Hegemony in the Irish Theater, 1712–1784* (2003) and numerous articles on eighteenth-century theatre. Recent publications include 'The Catholic Question, Print Media, and John O'Keeffe's *The Poor Soldier* (1783)' in *Eighteenth-Century Fiction* (2015), and 'The Irish Joke, Migrant Networks, and the London Irish in the 1680s' in *Eighteenth-Century Life* (2015).

ANDREW CARPENTER is Emeritus Professor of English at University College Dublin and a Member of the Royal Irish Academy. Among his recent publications is an anthology, jointly edited with Lucy Collins, *The Irish Poet and the Natural World: An Anthology of Poems in English from the Tudors to the Romantics* (2014) and an edition of the manuscript poems of Olivia Elder (2017).

MARIE-LOUISE COOLAHAN is Professor of English at the National University of Ireland Galway. She is the author of *Women, Writing, and Language in Early Modern Ireland* (2010), as well as articles and essays about women's writing, early modern identity, and textual transmission. She is currently Principal Investigator of the ERC-funded project, *RECIRC: The Reception*

and Circulation of Early Modern Women's Writing, 1550–1700 (www
.recirc.nuigalway.ie).

AILEEN DOUGLAS is Professor in English at Trinity College Dublin. She has
co-edited Sarah Butler's *Irish Tales* and Elizabeth Sheridan's *The Triumph of
Prudence over Passion* for the Early Irish Fiction series (2010–) of which she is
a general editor. Her most recent publication is *Work in Hand: Script, Print,
and Writing, 1690–1840* (2017).

DAVID DWAN is a tutorial fellow and associate professor at Hertford College,
University of Oxford. He is the author of *The Great Community: Culture and
Nationalism in Ireland* (2008) and co-editor of *The Cambridge Companion to
Edmund Burke* (2012).

BREAN HAMMOND is Emeritus Professor of English Literature at the
University of Nottingham. Author of several books and papers on Swift,
his most recent book-length study being *Jonathan Swift* (2010), he has also
edited the 'lost Shakespeare play' *Double Falsehood* for the Arden
Shakespeare series (2010).

MOYRA HASLETT is Professor in Eighteenth-Century and Romantic Literature
at Queen's University Belfast. She has edited Thomas Amory's *The Life of
John Buncle, Esq.* (1756) for the Early Irish Fiction series, of which she is
general editor with Aileen Douglas and Ian Campbell Ross. In connection
with this project, the general editors have also co-edited a special issue of *Irish
University Review* (2011) on fiction in Ireland in the long eighteenth century.
She is currently editing (with Conor Caldwell and Lillis Ó Laoire) *The
Oxford Handbook of Irish Song, 1100–1850.*

DARRELL JONES teaches early modern and eighteenth-century literature at
Trinity College Dublin. He previously held an Irish Research Council
Government of Ireland Postdoctoral Fellowship in the Moore Institute at
the National University of Ireland Galway. He has published a number of
articles on Locke's reception in eighteenth-century literary culture and is
currently working on a book on early modern concepts of the blank slate.

DECLAN KAVANAGH is Lecturer in Eighteenth-Century Studies and Director
of the Centre for Gender, Sexuality, and Writing at the University of Kent.
He is the author of *Effeminate Years: Literature, Politics, and Aesthetics in
Mid-Eighteenth-Century Britain* (2017).

JOE LINES completed his PhD in English at Queen's University Belfast. He has
research interests in Irish fiction from the long eighteenth century. He has
recently published articles on masculinity in the work of Thomas Amory and
the Irish politics of Charles Johnston's fiction in *Eighteenth-Century Ireland*
and *Journal for Eighteenth-Century Studies.*

ANNE MARKEY is Literature Tutor in the Open Education Unit of Dublin City
University. As part of the Early Irish Fiction series, she edited *Children's*

Fiction 1765–1808 (2011), and co-edited *Vertue Rewarded; or, The Irish Princess* (2010) and *Irish Tales* (2010). Her current research focuses on the Edgeworths' *Harry and Lucy* series and on the poetry of Dominick Kelly.

LESA NÍ MHUNGHAILE is a lecturer in eighteenth- and nineteenth-century Irish-language literature and culture at the National University of Ireland Galway. She has published widely on contact and collaboration between Anglo-Irish antiquarians and Gaelic scholars and scribes and on Irish-language scribal culture, including scholarly editions of Charlotte Brooke's *Reliques of Irish Poetry* (2009) and Énrí Ó Muirgheasa's *Amhráin na Midhe* (2015). She is also the author of a monograph study of Joseph Cooper Walker, *Ré Órga na nGael* (2013), which was awarded the Foras na Gaeilge/ACIS Prize for Books in the Irish Language 2014.

CLÍONA Ó GALLCHOIR is a lecturer in English at University College Cork. Her research focuses on Irish writing in the long eighteenth century, particularly women's writing, and on children's literature. She is the editor, with Heather Ingman, of *A History of Modern Irish Women's Literature* (Cambridge, 2018), and the literature editor of the journal *Eighteenth-Century Ireland*.

AMY PRENDERGAST is Teaching Fellow in Eighteenth-Century Writing in the School of English, Trinity College Dublin. She is the author of *Literary Salons across Britain and Ireland in the Long Eighteenth Century* (2015), and has published articles on Maria Edgeworth, Elizabeth Griffith, and the salon hostess Lady Moira. Her current research focuses on women's diaries from eighteenth-century Ireland.

DANIEL SANJIV ROBERTS is Reader in English at Queen's University Belfast. He has edited Charles Johnston's *The History of Arsaces* for the Early Irish Fiction series, and works by Thomas De Quincey and Robert Southey for the major collected editions of these authors. His *Ireland's Imperial Connections, 1775–1947*, edited with Jonathan Wright, is currently forthcoming from Palgrave Macmillan.

IAN CAMPBELL ROSS is Emeritus Professor of Eighteenth-Century Studies at Trinity College Dublin. His work includes *Laurence Sterne: A Life* (2001), an edition of Sterne's *Tristram Shandy* (2009) and contributions to *The Cambridge History of Irish Literature* and *The Edinburgh History of Scottish Literature*. He is a general editor of the Early Irish Fiction series (Four Courts Press).

JAMES WARD teaches eighteenth-century literature at Ulster University. Work on Jonathan Swift appears in *Swift Studies, Eighteenth-Century Ireland, Irish University Review, Irish Studies Review*, and *The Cambridge Companion to Irish Poets*. A monograph study of the representation of the long eighteenth century in modern writing, art, and screen media is entitled *Memory and Enlightenment: Cultural Afterlives of the Long Eighteenth Century* (2018).

Series Preface

Irish Literature in Transition provides a new account of transitions between and across the centuries of Irish literature. Adopting varying frames and scales of reference, the series offers an original map of a territory too often navigated via the narrow channels of political history. Each of the six volumes revises our understanding of established issues and texts and, simultaneously, introduces new questions, approaches, and authors. Together, these books generate alternative genealogies across time and space and help readers to understand and interrogate the ways in which one period reimagines and remakes another.

Discussions of Irish culture have long focused on the close relationship between literature and history. For all the power of such narratives, however, the field has yet to develop a sufficiently dynamic sense of that relationship. Literary transitions do not 'reflect' historical change in any simple or straightforward way. Rather, the complex two-way traffic between these realms involves multiple and uneven processes such as distortion, selection, repression, embrace, and critique. The temporal relationships involved in such traffic include simultaneity, time lag, and anticipation.

The six books in this series track patterns of transmission and transformation across Irish culture. More specifically, they ask: what kinds of transitions are registered and provoked by literature and culture? What are the levers and mechanisms of change? How helpful are our current concepts of literary movements, time periods, and national traditions? What is the status of the literary in our literary histories and how do we understand the relations among form, genre, and chronology?

We consider these questions from our own location in a time of scholarly transition. The sheer weight of archival material now available is transforming our sense of both the past and present of Irish literature, while prompting us to produce new kinds of critical narrative. Older literary histories of Ireland are coming under pressure from new modes of reading, such as those attuned to ecocritical issues, affect theory, queer genealogies, questions of scale, and diasporic and transnational geographies. As the concept of the 'survey' itself comes under scrutiny in classrooms and universities, these volumes show how authoritative interpretations can be innovative, challenging, and enabling for future readers and writers. Each volume intervenes in continuing critical conversations about culture rather than summarising the field or closing down debate. At the same time, the series charts the contours of literary history across the centuries in ways that highlight the significance of change as a lived, felt force.

Transition: the term means passage from one well-defined period to another; it also helps to track subtle interconnections, contingencies, or modulations; and it will provoke questions about the definition of change itself. In adopting that term, Irish Literature in Transition seeks to provide insight into the future of Irish Studies as it reimagines the literary past and present.

CLAIRE CONNOLLY, *University College Cork*
MARJORIE HOWES, *Boston College*

General Acknowledgements

As General Editors of Irish Literature in Transition, we wish to record our thanks to everyone who helped bring this six-volume series to publication. Our fellow editors, Moyra Haslett, Matthew Campbell, Eve Patten, Eric Falci, and Paige Reynolds have worked tirelessly on books that make significant new contributions to our understanding of Irish literature across time and space. We also record our thanks to the many contributors who helped shape the intellectual identity of this series with their thoughtful and innovative chapters. Dr Ray Ryan of Cambridge University Press prompted us to rise to the challenge of shaping a new narrative of Irish literature in transition. We thank him for that opportunity, and for all his insight and support along the way. Thanks also to Edgar Mendez of the Press for his help and hard work in seeing the books through to publication.

The support of the President's Strategic Fund of University College Cork and the Irish Studies Program at Boston College is gratefully acknowledged here.

CLAIRE CONNOLLY *(University College Cork)*
MARJORIE HOWES *(Boston College)*
General Editors

Introduction

Moyra Haslett

William Dunkin's exuberant comic poem, *The Parson's Revels*, offers a useful starting point for this collection because it gives voice to something of the complexity of eighteenth-century culture in Ireland. The poem's setting is a Christmas-time feast held in the mid-1740s at Beauchamp Hall, near Athy, County Kildare.[1] Within the poem's fiction, the Rev. Richard Beauchamp gathers together a motley assembly of guests, whose rich diversity allows the poet to introduce a miscellany of historical and fictional characters: Captain Cudmore, a blustering soldier; Fr. Fegan, a Roman Catholic priest; Dennison, a Presbyterian; Oaf, a Puritan weaver; Dr Mackaway, a physician; Crab, a Quaker; and one Judge Jowler. All of these appear to be figurative types, whereas a number of identifiable contemporaries are also offered by the poem: the printer George Faulkner; the blind Irish harper Murphy; and a supporting cast of Trinity College graduates, neighbours from the county, and relatives of Beauchamp. Differences of occupation, religion, political views, temperament, and drinking habits comically collide when they gather together at the one feast:

> In equal wise the Parson had
> Some sober Folks, and many mad,
> Some humoursome, and some as sad
> > As Smedly.
>
> The World he knew from long Conviction,
> Was all made up of Contradiction,
> And so he chose without Restriction
> > A Medly.   (p. 73)

The language of the poem enacts these differences at the level of voice, as the diverse range of the characters' voices is registered through Hiberno-English, drunken stuttering, linguistic bulls or inadvertent puns, brogue-inflected English and Latin, and, occasionally, some macaronic Irish. The Catholic guests, Fegan and Murphy, speak with a heavily accented pronunciation

that, though vivid in performance, looks odd on the page. A certain condescension in reproducing Irish brogue on the page meets a relish for the
pungency of different voices and a revelling in the exuberance of language.

The social, class, cultural, and geographical diversity of *The Parson's
Revels* is shared by other literary works that have attracted recent attention.
The novel *Virtue Rewarded* (London, 1693), for example, features a cast of
characters which includes a German Prince and Commander in King
William's army and his English aide-de-camp, two gentlewomen of the
Anglo-Irish lower gentry, a native South American Antisuyan woman,
a Spanish conquistador, and, in an interpolated tale, a pre-Norman Irish
princess. Walk-on parts, no less significant for their brevity, are given to
a group of Jacobite rapparees, the Irish Jacobite commander Patrick
Sarsfield and King William himself.[2] In *The History of Mr. Charles
Fitzgerald and Miss Sarah Stapleton* (Dublin, 1770) by the Catholic doctor
Dominick Kelly, we encounter members of the rural gentry of County
Westmeath but also their servants, a Presbyterian physician and his
Catholic servant, a Catholic priest and an Anglican chaplain, and
a Dublin lawyer. Kelly's novel speaks to an Irish Catholic audience through
its explicit allusions to Catholic texts, but its readers would also have been
alert to its depiction of intermarriage, its satirical guying of Ascendancy
gentry and its mocking treatment of strategic religious conversion.[3]

In Dunkin's poem, the combination of a diverse cast given to quarrelling
and copious amounts of drink ensures that misunderstanding and insults
ensue. These involve not only the predictable clash between the
Presbyterian Dennison and the Catholic priest Fegan, but also heated
exchanges between Mackaway and Faulkner, with Faulkner accused first
of Jacobitism and then of political trimming. The images embroidered on
Captain Cudmore's belt and jerkin recall a career of drunken street brawl-
ing. But just as Cudmore's grotesque rampaging figures in the poem as art,
the poem everywhere transmutes the sectarian, political and personal
grudges and animosities into a rollicking paean to Irish hospitality. All
the various characters, whether Catholic priest or Puritan Protestant, blind
musician or unruly soldier, join together in enjoying the parson's generosity, in rounds of eating, drinking, dancing, singing, and noisily declaim-
ing toasts. The harper Murphy plays and sings of Irish heroes – Fionn mac
Cumhaill, Brian Boru, 'Red' Hugh O'Donnell and Shane O'Neill – before
finishing, 'though much against his Heart', with a song which retells
William's victory at the Boyne, while Fegan joins in with a general toast
to the health of the departing Lord Lieutenant, Chesterfield. The convivi-
ality of the host, the setting of a Christmas feast, and the high spirits of the

poem sweep its readers up in the heady noise of a moment in which differences are, if only temporarily, set aside.

There is much here that seems characteristic of literature of the period: the free abandon of the poem's linguistic word-play played off against its interlacing rhyme scheme, the sudden juxtapositions of the earthy and the learned, the combination of gravity and comedy. The work is eccentric, whimsical, and facetious, in a way reminiscent of many other literary texts of the eighteenth century: Jonathan Swift's *A Tale of a Tub*; the fiction of Thomas Amory and Laurence Sterne; Seán Ó Neachtain's satire, *Stair Éamuinn Uí Chléirigh*; and Brian Merriman's *Cúirt an Mheán Oíche* all come to mind.[4] A homage to Irish hospitality, it alludes openly at one point to Aodh Mac Gabhráin's famous poem, 'Pléaráca na Ruarcach', which also celebrates a Christmas feast and which had recently been set to music by the Irish harper Carolan and by the Dublin-based Italian composer Lorenzo Bocchi, and translated into English by Charles Coffey and by Swift. Irish hospitality, a motif of many poems, plays, and novels, is here celebrated as a confident synecdoche of the nation.

Some of this confidence may be due to the apparent stability of Protestant Ireland in the wake of the defeat of Jacobitism at Culloden in April 1746.[5] So, while the poem often expresses the undoubted sectarianism of eighteenth-century Ireland, it also satirises the various members of its cast, including the Protestant gentry, with something like equality. Cudmore and Oaf suffer the indignity of having 'tails' docked and are unceremoniously upended (Oaf has his wig catch fire when he falls asleep with pipe still clamped in his mouth); Crab, against his conscience, joins in the drinking; one of the Athy neighbours, Bradford, speaks with drunken, slurred speech. Fegan's pride in his descent from 'Sir Teague O Regan', meanwhile, is unexpectedly confirmed by Dunkin's note on O Regan as: 'An Irish gentleman of remarkable courage and conduct, allowed to be one of the best officers in King James's army' (p. 74). The prospect of revels at which Irish Anglicans, Dissenters, and Roman Catholics put aside their differences to enjoy rounds of drink, song, and feasting may be an obvious fiction, but the poem's high spirits resist older views of 'Anglo-Irish' culture as representing a static, and segregated, social order.

The poem's reference to Mac Gabhráin's 'Pléaráca' (p. 95) appears to suggest a tradition of Irish feasting shared by 'native' and 'settler' communities in Ireland. The hospitality of the Irish was, indeed continues to be, proverbial. ('Céad míle fáilte' is among the lyrics of one of the most popular Irish songs of the period – 'Eibhlín a rún'.)[6] But the exuberance of Dunkin's poem is in stark contrast to the work of poets such as Dáibhí Ó

Bruadair, Séamas Dall Mac Cuarta, and Aogán Ó Rathaille who more typically lament the lack of hospitality they endure, as poets without patrons in a country of dispossession.[7] The political causes of that change are usually made quite clear, as for example in the popular Jacobite song, 'Dromineann donn dílis' ('My dear Droimeann Donn'):

> Níl fearann, níl tíos agam, fíonta ná ceol,
> níl flaithibh im choimhdeacht, níl saoithe ná sló,
> ach ag síor-ól an uisce go minic sa ló
> agus beathuisce 's fíon ag mo naimhdibh ar bord.

> I've no land and no home, no music or wine,
> no princes to guard me, no scholars or troops,
> only water to drink every hour of the day
> with whiskey and wine on my enemies' table.[8]

Mac Gabhráin's 'Pléaráca', though composed in the early eighteenth century, celebrates a legendary sixteenth-century feast given by the Irish chieftain Brian na Múrtha Ó Ruairc in his family's castle in Dromahair, County Leitrim. Ó Ruairc was the last traditional ruler of the lordship of West Breifne, his lifetime of resistance against the English culminating in his being hung, drawn, and quartered at Tyburn in 1591, convicted of eight articles of treason.[9] Although the poem itself does not refer to Ó Ruairc's political resistance, the poem is inevitably a representation of a life and culture long past.[10] And given the sweeping changes in land ownership which the Williamite settlement effected – Catholic ownership of land had been around 59 per cent in 1641 but had dropped to at most 20 per cent by 1688 – celebrations of lavish Gaelic feasting were more likely nostalgic reminiscences, shot through with the melancholy of contemporary realities.[11]

Eighteenth-century Irish society can be characterised by its sociability and associationalism, by its linguistic variety and proliferating print cultures, its wit and brio. But the century is also marked by the experiences of famine, migration, religious oppression, economic crises, and rural agitation. In the famine of 1740–41, for example, up to 15 per cent of Ireland's population died; while the Penal Laws openly discriminated against Catholics in statutes drawn up between 1695 and 1756. For all the fun of Dunkin's poem, then, its 'exemplarity' also needs to be set against such contexts.

Historicising the Period

Older accounts of a society divided between 'settler' and 'native' have given way to a new history of a changing, heterogeneous nation. The confident

'Protestant Ascendancy' of previous studies is now viewed as troubled and riven, rather than complacent and secure, a cultural world fractured by the disjunction between authoritarian ambitions and complex contingencies. The evidence of bilingualism, the prominence of dissent, and the importance of a European dimension to the period's politics and culture are just some of the subjects of new studies. The turn to the history of ideas in Ireland, which includes the emergence of 'enlightened' philosophies which were held in tension with strongly upheld hegemonies of power and orthodoxy, has also led to a greater interest in ideological debates of various kinds and an awareness that the eighteenth century preceded the formation of ideas of racial or ethnic difference. In this context, the examination of beliefs, opinions, values, and feelings has much to tell us of the fine-grained experiences of eighteenth-century Ireland. And literary culture of the period – whether in print, manuscript, or performance – offers an unrivalled source for the specificities of lived experience, albeit one mediated and refracted through the conventions and traditions of the material cultures of print, coterie exchange, the theatre and the street, and of literary and popular genres.

Such terms as 'colony' or '*ancien régime*', around which late twentieth-century historical debates tended to revolve, are, of course, not always inappropriate: Ireland was undoubtedly experienced in these terms by significant numbers of its population during this time. As one contemporary historian of the period has noted, the two models are not mutually exclusive alternatives: 'In many ways Ireland had the outward appearance of a European kingdom; but the legacy of Tudor and Stuart conquests meant that Irish society was repeatedly conceptualised in terms of settlers and natives.'[12] A sensitivity to nuance and intersectionality in particular instances of class, gender, religion, and politics has meant that earlier generalisations and broad-brush distinctions are now difficult to sustain. New attention to the histories of Irish Dissent has ensured that binary models (of Protestant versus Catholic, or Irish versus English) can no longer claim the kind of explanatory power they once did. These reconceived historical frameworks undoubtedly influence, and are in turn shaped by, a renewed literary criticism. The broadening of critical interest beyond the formerly canonical (Swift, Oliver Goldsmith, Edmund Burke, and Richard Brinsley Sheridan, most obviously) has led to increased interest in women writers, popular writers, and genres beyond the narrowly literary ones of fiction, poetry, and drama. Many of these writers remained in Ireland – William Dunkin, for example – rather than turning to publication or performances in London. Irish writers were drawn to

London by the far superior economic prospects it offered to writers: the 1709 Copyright Act gave authors in England a share of any book's profits, unlike in Ireland, where the Act did not apply; and the custom of the author's benefit night disadvantaged dramatists in Dublin, where extended runs of plays were much less common. However, print editions of Irish fiction in the period show Dublin assuming increasing importance across the century: several key works of the early period are reprinted later in Dublin than elsewhere, while a number of later-century novels are printed in Dublin before their London editions.[13]

Similarly, where earlier work on Irish drama focused almost entirely on the careers of the famous dramatists who made their careers primarily in London – George Farquhar, Richard Brinsley Sheridan, Oliver Goldsmith – more recent studies have concentrated on theatre in Dublin, and, to a lesser extent, on regional theatre in Ireland.[14] Such critical work has paid particular attention to the ambivalences, equivocations, and ambiguities of texts and performances. William Philips depicts, in *Hibernia Freed* (1722), Irish victory over the Danes prior to the Norman Conquest but the play closes with a prophecy of the later conquest of Ireland; Robert Ashton's frequently performed *The Battle of Aughrim* (1728) appealed to both Catholic and Protestant audiences in combining a celebration of the victors with a lament for the vanquished. A greater attention to the totality of theatre – its specific production and performance histories – has also permitted a more inclusive understanding of Irish theatre. Farquhar's character Sir Harry Wildair, for example, was a role dominated by Irish actors on the London stage (Robert Wilks in the first performances, from 1701, then Peg Woffington, in breeches, from 1740). Attention to the 'pop-up' theatres of puppet, tumbling, and rope-dancing shows, Lilliputian troupes of child actors and musical performances, has broken the mono-poly of critical attention once enjoyed by the Theatre Royal, Smock Alley; while its theatre riots have been studied as forms of productions in themselves.[15]

The once near-exclusive axis of Dublin–London has thus been decisively fractured by more complex geographies. We might think here of the mapping in the following fictions: *Vertue Rewarded* (1693), Amory's *Memoirs of Celebrated Ladies of Great Britain* (1755), and Elizabeth Sheridan's *The Triumph of Prudence over Passion* (1781). All three novels avoid London almost entirely. The main plot of *Vertue Rewarded* takes place in Clonmel, Tipperary, in the summer of 1690, while its interpolated stories take us to latter-day Peru and to the south of Spain.[16] The characters of Amory's *Memoirs* travel from the north of England to the Hebrides to the Canary Islands. And the two heroines of *The Triumph of Prudence over Passion* travel out of Ireland to France, stopping in London, associated with vice and immorality, for as short a time as possible. It is noteworthy, then, that Toby Barnard opens his book on reading in Ireland, *Brought to Book* (2017), with the example of the sea-captain who, in the 1680s, carried books from Bristol and distributed them throughout Munster, which Barnard argues is typical rather than anomalous in terms of the distribution of books.[17]

Once the dominance of the Dublin–London relationships is qualified, the number and variety of writers is amended, and the underpinning framework of binary connection is broken, then the usefulness of that explanatory term 'Anglo-Irish' also comes under sustained pressure.[18] While 'Anglo-Irish' continues as a term in the essays which follow, it does so in specific contexts in which the power of the Anglican political establishment is invoked. In terms of literary studies, however, the term appears to fit fewer and fewer writers.

The Anglo-Irish?

Eighteenth-century literature in Ireland has long enjoyed an almost unrivalled claim on literary studies more broadly through the profile of Swift, Burke, Sheridan, and Goldsmith, central figures to any consideration of, say, satire, philosophy, theatre, and the professionalisation of writing in this period. Only the prominence of Yeats and Joyce within literary modernism can rival the importance of Irish writers to the literary history of the eighteenth century. For many previous literary critics, these eighteenth-century authors were more 'Anglo' than 'Irish' and their absorption within the canon of English literary studies was automatic. Within Irish studies, however, such writers were often 'insufficiently Irish'. In 1995 one critic used this phrase to defend the choice of 1800 as the starting point of his study of 'Anglo-Irish' writing. Only after the Act of Union, he argued, did the 'Anglo-Irish' become 'Irish enough for a viable literature to begin'. A consequence of such a decision, as poet and critic Bernard O'Donoghue noted in a review, was to cut Samuel Beckett's *Watt* off from Swift 'with whom it has more in common than with novelists from Edgeworth through to Bowen'.[19] The exchange gives us an immediate sense of the foreclosures that definitions and date parameters necessarily impose upon our choices of research interest, the direction of our scholarly debates, and the shaping of our readings.

Rather than re-orient a field in a manner comparable to later volumes in this series, this multi-authored study is the first book to offer a full account of Irish literature written between 1700 and 1780. Despite the excellent pioneering work by a number of scholars, no 'signature' book on all genres of writing has previously been attempted. It is perhaps ironic that the first attempt to assemble such a collection comes at a moment of awareness regarding the provisional nature of histories and surveys. Even a book containing nineteen chapters cannot do full justice to the diversity and richness of the literary cultures of this period, and exclusions or omissions may be immediately apparent to many readers. Equally apparent, however, will be the ways in which important changes within the disciplines of literary studies and history in particular have shaped its contours. Within literary criticism of the last twenty years we can point to the challenge to established canons of authors, the importance of historicist procedures in our reading of literary texts, and the consolidation or emergence of newer interests such as empire, the environment, transnational and transcultural crossings, and the figurings of gender and sexuality. Equally potent have been changes within contemporary histories of the period, in the recognition of the complexity of a country which might be seen to be both a British colony and an exemplar of a European *ancien régime* model of politics, which buttressed the power of an Anglican elite while both suppressing and negotiating with a numerically dominant population of Catholics and a significant population, particularly in the north, of Dissenters.

As well as generating adjustments to existing political narratives, these developments have also led to new studies of women authors; oral, manuscript, and popular cultures; theological debate and the Enlightenment; the hybridity and intersections of the languages of eighteenth-century Ireland (Irish and English, most obviously, but Ulster-Scots, Latin, and French too); public and private theatricals.[20] Particularly enabling for the recent expansion of the scope of the field have been new editions of primary work from the period.[21] Poets such as William Dunkin and Olivia Elder, novelists such as Thomas Amory and Charles Johnston are newly accessible and have begun to attract well-deserved attention. Bibliographical and theatre production resources have enabled the rediscovery of countless authors, texts, and performances once prominent though often long forgotten.[22] As mentioned above, the very term which for so long defined literature of this period – 'Anglo-Irish' – has become even more problematic as an identifier for writing in and of eighteenth-century Ireland as a result of this expansion. Whether used in its loosest sense, to signify, simply, writing in English, or in the narrower sense of writing by Irish Protestants, the term carries connotations of privilege and power which only sometimes reflect the realities of the lives of the authors so named. 'Anglo-Irish' may be used accurately to designate poetry by Olivia Elder, a Presbyterian minister's daughter living near Coleraine, the Jacobite romance *Irish Tales* by the unknown 'Sarah Butler' (1716), and the ballad operas of the shadowy Charles Coffey, with their tune-settings from popular Irish-language airs; to do so is, however, to diminish the descriptive and critical power of the phrase so as to make it simply equivalent to Anglophone writing. 'Anglo-Irish' also hides the complexity even of those authors seen as exemplary of the term: Swift's embittered battles with Whigs in power both in London and in Dublin; Burke's strong affiliation with and support for Irish Catholics; the critical considerations of empire in the work of Goldsmith and Sheridan, in addition to their families' histories of conversion and 'Old English' origin respectively. An eighteenth-century 'Ascendancy' class undoubtedly existed – what it itself referred to as 'the Protestant [implicitly Anglican] interest'.[23] But its authors were not always entirely of this class. Neither Swift nor Goldsmith, Sheridan nor Burke shared the kind of political and financial power and privilege enjoyed by the propertied elite. An Irish Ascendancy class, or the Anglo-Irish elite, may have enjoyed the compositions of Irish Anglophone culture, but they were not its principal creators. Their patronage supported many forms of cultural life – evident in book dedications, subscription lists, and theatre sponsorship – but they were not the only audience for literary works of this period. More complex, more subtle histories of the period make shorthand, unquestioning synonyms of 'Protestant', 'Anglo-Irish', and 'Ascendancy' impossible to sustain, at the same time as literary scholars seek out print ephemera, the vestiges of oral culture, the popular entertainments of the lower and middling classes, and define the terms of 'Irishness' more generously.

Irish Protestants living in London (or perhaps in Bristol, Bath, or Scarborough) remained always, if only partially or attenuatedly, 'Irish'. One of the ways in which they were demarcated as being different is particularly pertinent to literary studies: the versions of English spoken and written by them were often marked with the syntax and vocabulary of Irish, which might manifest itself in a 'brogue', a 'bull', verbal ingenuity, or self-consciousness. Friendships and collaborations were also often marked by shared Irish affiliations. Recent work has begun to recreate the condition of being Irish in London more fully, with the vast networks of friendship and enmity, of business and sociability within which Irish authors worked in London being recovered. Goldsmith did not leave

Ireland behind when he moved to England: the London which became his
home was filled with fellow Irishmen, including Edward Purdon, John
Pilkington, Samuel Derrick, and Paul Hiffernan. These friendships
ensured that Ireland was almost as present to him in London as it would
have been in Dublin.[24] Such recent critical trends as the heightened
attention to the 'archipelagic' and the 'transnational' suggest that we are
now working in an auspicious climate in which to reconsider the 'Irishness'
of English-language, London-based authors. Charles Shadwell's *The
Humours of the Army* (1713) and Charles Molloy's *The Half-Pay Officers*
(1720), for example, both respond to Shakespeare's *Henry V* in dramatising
soldier figures from Scotland, Wales, and Ireland. In invoking explicitly
archipelagic themes, both plays speak to current critical interests, and
simultaneously shift the focus of study.[25]

'Anglophone' literature of the period remains more widely accessible to
twenty-first-century readers than Irish as the forces of modern globalisa-
tion join earlier historical forces in restricting the numbers of Irish speakers. Latin literature of the period remains even less accessible than Irish
(and is arguably undervalued as a result).[26] Systematic discrimination
against Catholics entailed that print culture in Ireland in the period was
overwhelmingly in English rather than in the Irish in which they spoke,
recited, transcribed, and sung. Sensitivity to this requires that we are
mindful of the exclusions which a focus on print culture thus entails.
Irish oral and manuscript cultures are more obviously multilingual than
that of print. In all three domains, however – oral, manuscript, and print –
we find playful and strategic uses of hybridised language, evident in the
deployment of macaronic verse and Hiberno-English, and in the stereotypically Irish infelicity of linguistic 'bulls' and early instances of Ulster-
Scots.[27]

'Literature' is now generally understood as incorporating many diverse
kinds of artistic and cultural expression. The manuscript circulation or
oral recitation of poetry; private and regional theatrical performances;
broadsheet satires and other kinds of printed ephemera; popular fiction
and 'improving' pamphlets: all of these are increasingly the focus of our
studies, and thus are included in the chapters which follow. Texts and
performances are formed within and shaped by wider contexts of the
totality of creative expression (manuscript, song, ephemera), printed
materials of all kinds (including not only works of verse, prose fiction
or drama but also political pamphlets, histories, sermons, philosophical
works), and the totality of lived experience (the situatedness of class,
gender, sexuality, religious background, linguistic competency). Of all

writers of our period, Swift remains the most firmly canonical, his *Gulliver's Travels* the most celebrated and studied prose fiction. Challenges to canonical authority have not dislodged either this author or this text. But it is instructive to consider both how *Travels into Several Remote Nations of the World*, to restore to the work its original title, might be situated in Swift's own career and in modern and contemporary readings of it. Swift, we know, interspersed the writing of this fiction with his polemical interventions in the political crisis of the Wood's halfpence affair. And his visit to London in 1726 to arrange the publication of *Gulliver's Travels* also resulted in the publication of the Pope–Swift *Miscellanies* (1727–32), in which solemn works of political prose – such as *A Discourse of the Contests and Dissentions between the Nobles and Commons in Athens and Rome* and 'The Sentiments of a Church-of-England Man, with Respect of Religion and Government' – were reprinted alongside humorous and autobiographical poetry ('Cadenus and Vanessa', 'Mrs Harris's Petition', and poems addressed to Esther Johnson as 'Stella', for example). This volume captures a not dissimilar diversity in reading *Gulliver's Travels* in successive chapters as an intervention in key philosophical debates, as a queer text, as a fiction of empire, and in relation to Irish folktale, and in reading Swift as the friend of Mary Barber and Constantia Grierson, as the author of the Latin poem 'Carberiae Rupes', in terms of ideas of masculinity, and of how changes in our approaches to Swift's works reveal something of the shifts and cross-currents in the discipline of literary study. New approaches to *Gulliver's Travels* and to Swift obviously reflect back our own concerns as much as discover what might lie within the polished glass of his texts.

Attention to previously unregarded figures has a significant impact upon our sense of literary history. Thanks to the efforts of recent scholarship, we can now identify many compelling claims to literary 'firsts': the first Restoration theatre (the Theatre Royal, or Smock Alley, founded in 1662); the first regional novel (*Vertue Rewarded*, 1693); the first Catholic novel in English (Sarah Butler's *Irish Tales*, 1716); the first substantial collection of verse in English from Ireland (Matthew Concanen's *Miscellaneous Poems*, 1724); David Garrick's first performance as Hamlet (at Smock Alley in 1742); the first published Gothic novel (Thomas Leland's *Longsword*, 1762). Thomas Sheridan was the first theatre manager in the two islands to prohibit the privilege of 'freedom of the scenes' in which audience members could cross the stage to the wings and green room during a performance; the Dublin Musical Academy (founded 1757) was the first in the British Isles to admit ladies into its chorus.[28]

Equally of interest here are the aspects of literary culture which might be seen now to be distinctive to Ireland in this period. The most straightforward way in which to map such differences is to consider Ireland's exclusion from the London Acts of Parliament concerning copyright legislation (1709) and theatre licensing (1737). That Henry Brooke's play *Gustavus Vasa* (1739) had been banned in London was quickly made apparent, both in Faulkner's adroit marketing of his printed edition with the subtitle 'As it was to have been acted at the Theatre-Royal in Drury-Lane', and in the play's production, as *The Patriot*, in Aungier Street Theatre in Dublin (1741). Although theatre censorship existed in Ireland – Brooke's ballad-opera, *Jack the Giant-Queller* (1749) was banned because of its attack on Dublin's Lord Mayor and Alderman – its specific iterations were often different from those of London. (Faulkner again quickly exploited this opportunity by rushing into print *The Songs in Jack the Gyant Queller*.)[29] And audience expectations appear to have differed too. One explanation for Peg Woffington's loss of popularity on the Dublin stage is the notoriety of her conversion from Catholicism to the established church.[30]

Distinctively important literary genres in the eighteenth century include the Jacobite *aisling* poem, the sentimental novel, the comedy of manners, 'rogue' literature, the ballad, and the 'improving' pamphlet, all of which feature in the chapters which follow. And, as with the example of Swift's *Gulliver's Travels*, canonical authors and texts retain their force here too, in studies of Burke's participation in enlightenment debates and the question of his 'Irishness', in the situating of Goldsmith's *The Deserted Village* in the context of Irish landscape poetry of the period, and in contemporary reflections upon the politics of 'Enlightenment' in Ireland. While a notably diverse range of authors and texts is considered in this volume, the contexts within which these are read similarly indicate a widening of vision evident in recent literary-critical and historiographical approaches. Transitions within the eighteenth century alongside those of our present moment mean that a much wider range of optics is needed if we are to perceive Irish literary culture in its rich variety. The chapters gathered here offer a range of such perspectives. They ask questions, prompt new ways of reading and probe possible limitations to our current modes of thought.

Irish Literature in Transition, 1700–1780

Marie-Louise Coolahan's opening chapter immediately challenges the starting point of 1700 for this volume. If literature 'in transition' is the focus of the series, then an argument could be made for starting that history a century or so earlier, with Edmund Spenser's 'Mutabilitie Cantos' (?1597–98; pub. 1609) in particular. The literature of early modern Ireland exemplifies a complex form of transition in which languages, genres and political accommodations jostle for provisional and contingent forms of significance. Just as critical studies in the mid-1990s could dispense with Irish fiction prior to 1800 as being 'insufficiently Irish', our own exclusion of the earliest beginnings of literature in Ireland might shadow the account offered to readers here. These are challenges for future scholarship as well as present projects: as Coolahan notes, shifting interests and emphases will direct attention, in ways which we cannot predict.

Where Coolahan's chapter investigates the various meanings of being 'in transition', Ian Campbell Ross considers how complex the term 'Irish' could be in its eighteenth-century invocations. Many Protestant writers claimed both or either 'English' or 'Irish' identities, at a time when ideas of nationhood were not necessarily tied to religious or ethnic affiliations. Ross's probing of these ideas incorporates a wide range of contexts, proving that determining 'Irishness' is never simply a matter of an author's birth or place of residence, subject matter or religious or political affiliation. Thus, the perspectives of such varied elements as contemporary philosophical debate, the emergence of literary criticism as a discipline, the place of publication or performance, changes in the stereotypical Stage Irishman, and cultural shifts such as a growing interest in both antiquarianism and patriotic opposition, are all part of the framing of the question of Irishness. Henry Brooke emerges as a compelling 'exemplary' case study, even if representative 'in nothing but the confused and contradictory national identities he professed at various times of his life' (p. 62). In exactly these ways, Brooke is paralleled by the more famous Edmund Burke, who spoke of his concern for Catholic rights but defended British constitutionalism, who challenged British policy in India and Ascendancy powers in Ireland but also the revolutionary Jacobins, and whose childhood and upbringing were informed by Catholic, Anglican, and Quaker elements. Despite such complexities in the examination of individual authors, Ross ultimately detects a gradual receptiveness towards the idea of a national Irish identity which would thrive in the cultural and political climate of the 1790s. The eighteenth century emerges as the period in which the very idea of 'Irishness' is itself 'in transition', before settling into more secure national definitions which the nineteenth century would propose.

Brean Hammond shows how trends and shifts in approaches to Swift tell us much about the changing frames and parameters of our studies of this period more broadly: biographical work and developing interests in book history have both tended to coalesce with and confirm readings of Swift as an Irish writer, in such a way as to make statements such as Swift's 'Englishness' – a term he himself might have willingly owned and which was blithely imputed to him by generations of scholars – absolutely refutable. Perhaps it is enough to note that Swift spent roughly sixty-four of his seventy-eight years in Ireland, and, in a recent estimation, composed up to one hundred pamphlets and broadsheets on Irish affairs.[31] Hammond's argument is also an appeal to scholars to move beyond defending or arraigning Swift as a man, attempts which invariably lead only to entanglement and contradiction, ensnared by Swift's irony or the immoderation of his style. Hammond's Swift is no 'moderate' but a writer of extreme beliefs whose originality is a product of that very extremity. If we centre Swift in his Irish contexts, we are better placed to understand 'the structuring contradictions resulting from his unorthodox personality in collision with his circumstances' (p. 77).

Long considered not to have experienced an 'Enlightenment' as such, Ireland's distinctive accounts of progress have recently emerged as a significant dimension of the period's literary culture. This is evident not only in studies of an 'Irish Enlightenment', but also in recent studies of individual figures such as John Toland and Oliver Goldsmith, and of broader movements such as book history and elite women's culture.[32] Where such accounts tend to see enlightenment ideas as creating a conciliatory force in Irish thought and experience, dissolving problems of sectarianism and division, David Dwan takes a darker view.[33] His chapter, 'The Prejudices of Enlightenment', argues that ideals associated with European enlightenment thinking – the use of reason, the promotion of toleration, the impulse to improvement – are present in Ireland, but are inflected and sometimes distorted by that context. Debates about religious toleration, for example, were themselves riven with sectarian arguments and anxieties. Berkeley and Burke both wrote sympathetically of the position of Irish Catholics and opposed coercive attempts to make them conform. But both defended their opposition to compulsory conversion in terms of refusing a Catholic model of religious intolerance. The chapter takes its cue from Burke's particular responses to 'prejudice', which alternatively viewed it as something to be defended or feared. Prejudice might take the form of the Penal Laws, to which Burke was totally opposed, but it could also signify the prejudices of long-held, customary views or of instinctive, feeling responses which could be trusted. Such defences were themselves not unqualified: longevity creates a 'presumption or prejudice' in favour of a rule or practice but does not guarantee it absolutely; feelings could act as the limit-point for absolute rationality. It would be prejudicial in us to place too much faith in reason, for example. Prejudice, in Dwan's reading, is both the 'anti-self' and 'alter ego' of Enlightenment in Ireland.

Feeling and sight are given literal form in Darrell Jones's chapter on the famous crux of eighteenth-century Irish philosophy, the 'Molyneux problem': whether a blind man, suddenly able to see, would be able to detect the difference between a sphere and a cube by sight alone. This fictive blind man became historical in various empirical experiments in the period. Jones's tracing of the problem ranges through philosophical, literary, and scientific writings and adds to the list of well-known Anglican figures, works by French and Irish Catholic thinkers on the topic too. As the defining problem for eighteenth-century Irish philosophy and a pervasive motif in Irish fiction, Jones's chapter indicates how this thought experiment reveals the theological nature of the Irish Enlightenment. Dwan and Jones agree in seeing an Irish Enlightenment as ultimately shaped by religious or confessional debates rather than any secularising imperative. In their readings, ideas of enlightenment cleave to the domains of politics and history, culture and ethics, and thus provide frameworks for many of the chapters which follow.

Where the chapters by Dwan and Jones reflect upon how Irish philosophy is shaped by politics, Helen Burke's chapter on Samuel Whyte's involvement in private theatricals examines how Irish political debate was transformed by culture. Although Whyte sees himself as following Thomas Sheridan's legacy of accomplished political oratory, his class critique of the Irish elite is more overt. Whyte openly allied himself with the middle-class reformer Charles Lucas and the artisan and merchant class campaigns which he led, but his subtle attacks on the aristocracy – through choice of play and pointed messages in newly written prologues – also got caught up in attacking liberal support for Catholics. Whyte's politics begin to look much less radical once he articulates anxiety concerning the encroachments of lower 'vulgar', and Catholic, players and performances. Here too, 'prejudice' remains as important as 'toleration'.

Considerations of 'land' in an Irish context will always be political, and the disparate realities of life for the Anglo-Irish gentry and the rural Irish poor are among the important contexts for Andrew Carpenter's study of Irish poetry and the natural world. Poetry here gives voice to and shapes the broader ideologies which underpin its making. In Carpenter's terms, the right of the 'New English' to 'live in the countryside was consolidated by the apparent imposition of order on it' (p. 151). Such order might incorporate the impulses of a classical imitation or parody, or the celebration of the Irish country house, the reassurance that the Irish countryside was capable of improvement, or the relish of country pursuits of various kinds (hunting, boating, taking the waters at a spa-town). It could also register the horror of violent climatic events (in poetry on the Great Frost of 1740–41 or on tempestuous storms) and, more benignly, begin to romanticise wilder forces of nature as sublimely thrilling. But in all of these features, its difference from the English tradition was marked: the country-house poem flourished in Ireland a century after its English counterpart, while Irish georgic would require another century yet.

Conrad Brunström's chapter reads the intertwining of personal and public dynamics in the career of Thomas Sheridan, particularly in relation to his ambition to manage a 'National Theatre' in Ireland, one which would win fame throughout Europe and act as a platform for an evolving citizenry. Brunström has argued for a less conservative Thomas Sheridan than the figure who emerges in Helen Burke's work. Here he revisits the question of Sheridan's politics – whether he was a patriot or Castle politician – through the interconnected contexts of Sheridan's own temperament and contemporary perceptions of that personality, the pragmatics of theatre management, and Sheridan's over-riding commitment to an idealistic view of the stage in which actors in particular could cultivate the rhetorical skills which might propel a nation worthy of its citizens' loyalty into being. In the theatre, uniquely, civic policy could be treated in 'embodied terms'. Here, then, issues such as the nature of the public sphere and of public opinion, the politics and aesthetics of popular taste, and the emergence of a sense of national identity can be openly experimented with.

Frances Sheridan is the focus of Amy Prendergast's chapter, in which she considers the particularly transnational and intercultural dynamics of novels of sensibility, popular across Ireland, Britain, and France in the mid-eighteenth century. Readers from both elite and middling classes, in Ireland and in France, could demonstrate their cosmopolitanism and commitment to enlightenment principles through their enjoyment of sentimental novels. Sheridan's novel *The Memoirs of Miss Sidney Bidulph* (1761) in particular is situated as both a response to and an influence upon the equally popular fiction of Marie-Jeanne Riccoboni. Prendergast's chapter responds to recent calls, from within historical and literary studies, that Irish culture should be viewed beyond the binary axis of Dublin and London. Building upon earlier work on French books in Ireland, this chapter demonstrates how the work of Irish women writers such as Frances Sheridan and Elizabeth Griffith engages with ideas of a cosmopolitan Republic of Letters.

Daniel Roberts's chapter widens the geographical scope yet further – to the Americas, to India, and to fictional foreign territories – in his consideration of Ireland's implications within the discourses of imperial expansion. In particular, the shifting definitions of fiction and empire throughout the eighteenth century are charted in readings of three novels – *Vertue Rewarded* (1693), *Gulliver's Travels* (1726), and *The History of Arsaces* (1774) – as too, is the interweaving of ambition and uncertainty, of conflicted identities and allegiances, of political idealism and pragmatics in both the authors' stated positions and in their fictions. The chapter might be read as a response to more recent ways of thinking about patriotism in Ireland, seeing it not to be complacently secure but internally riven with tensions and anxieties. The readings in this chapter illustrate the ways in which patriot discourse as it was refracted through fiction combined confidence and defensiveness, assertion and self-questioning. The early novel's engagement with the experience of empire, in its representation of the dislocation and fracturing of the self in its encounter with foreignness and its tussle with the discourses of barbarism and civility, is particularly acute when articulated and imagined by writers whose self-identifications and perspectives are both Irish and British/English. In Roberts's phrase, these novels are 'many-angled' because of the contradictions of their historical and cultural moments, the experiences of their authors and the alternate exigencies and possibilities of fiction.

Although literary-historical and literary-theoretical work on gender and sexuality has been a dominant presence within English studies, reconsiderations of eighteenth-century Irish women's writing have been relatively few, and queer studies of the period scarcer still.[34] The readings in this section demonstrate how the framing of our studies of the period in terms of Irish female and gay experiences, representations and readings has the potential to challenge long-held certainties about the period. We know that at least sixty Irish women poets published books of verse in this period, for example, although relatively few of these have been studied.[35] Aileen Douglas extends our readings by focusing particularly on Mary Barber's volume, *Poems on Several Occasions*, published in 1735 (though the collection also included poems by other writers, including Barber's close friend, Constantia Grierson). The chapter considers the ways in which Barber and Grierson negotiated expectations of women's writing, drawing on gestures which cemented their poetic authority (writing poems on charitable giving, for example, or using ventriloquism as a form of perspectival sleight of hand) while ostensibly conforming to codes of feminine propriety. Their poems are read as acts of careful assertion in terms not only of their style and content, but in the manner of their printing and in their framing by significant paratexts. The ingenuity of their work, in which the same strategies which advance the modesty of their poems also promote them, is revealed: diffidence is the trope which, skilfully managed, allows Barber and Grierson to present confident, ambitious poetry.

New contexts of a different kind are invoked in Declan Kavanagh's reading of a queer eighteenth-century Ireland. His chapter examines the queer potential that inheres in the idea of transition, by focusing on characters and experiences in which gender and sexuality are equivocal, oblique, unsettling, and indeterminate. Historical accusations of sodomy are read alongside divergent texts: the voyage to Houyhnhnmland in Part IV of *Gulliver's Travels*; the mock-epic taunting of the Irishman in Charles Churchill's *The Rosciad*; and, pushing past the strict volume dates in order to catch queer resonances that sound in succeeding decades, the proto-transgendered figure of Harriet Freke in Maria Edgeworth's *Belinda*. These three texts offer different perspectives and challenges to the imperialising discourse of sexual normalcy; their foregrounding of emergent norms, otherwise largely hidden, permits them to expose and question heteronormativity and its attempt to fix identity. Kavanagh calls for a form of historicising queer studies which would resist the ahistoricism which occurs under the aegis of heterosexual assumptions about universalism. In the three texts under consideration, 'Irish' (or 'English' or 'Anglo-Irish') and 'queer' are possibilities rather than identities, 'overlapping, contradictory, and conflictual definitional forces', to borrow Eve Kosofsky Sedgwick's terms, rather than 'a coherent definitional field'.[36]

Among the denunciations of queer identity in the eighteenth century, as Kavanagh shows, is that of being 'neuter', neither one sex nor the other, with connotations also of sterility. In Rebecca Barr's chapter, the picaresque fiction of William Chaigneau's *The History of Jack Connor* (1752) is read in terms of patrilineal inheritance and a code of exemplary masculine conduct in which the Anglo-Irish can be idealised as – at least potentially – benevolent and improving landlords. As Barr's chapter demonstrates, the idealism is hard-won in a context in which models of masculinity are shifting, the status of the Ascendancy class can be experienced as fragile and uncertain, and negative models of effeminacy and of the uncouth Stage Irishman continue to circulate. The chapter also amplifies and illuminates the new significance accorded to the status of the soldier in studies of eighteenth-century Ireland.[37] Jack Connor, Barr argues here, offers an exemplary figure of Irish Whig sociability and serves to shore up the self-image of Protestant Ireland as honourable and well meaning. The bloodied face of the Shakespearean soldier Coriolanus, however, offers a presage of a much less quiescent politics yet to come, and reminds us that Chaigneau's celebration of the Irish gentleman was a product of a very particular mid-century moment.

In contrast to the pervasive trope of Ireland as female lover to England's suitor-husband – most evident in the genres of the *aisling* in Irish poetry and in the Anglophone national tale – Prendergast and Barr offer readings of mother–daughter and father–son relationships which also figure the relationship between Britain and Ireland. In my own chapter, female homosocial relationships are explored as confident articulations of female identity and as suggestive models of political governance. Despite widespread anxiety about female-only assembly and scepticism regarding the virtues of female friendship, women writers in this period evidently found friendship between women to be a theme in which they could articulate and explore a range of feelings and emotions not otherwise sanctioned by their culture. The chapter considers a range of poetry and fiction – by Charlotte McCarthy, Margaret Goddard, Olivia Elder, Frances Sheridan, and her daughter Elizabeth in relation to differentially situated ideas of 'sisterhood' before turning to the ways in which Ireland came to be figured as a 'sister' kingdom to Britain in the later century, thus shaping the proto-feminism of earlier traditions in new, national formations.

The popular culture which, Helen Burke's chapter argued, Samuel Whyte feared, is explored through the figure of the rogue in the chapter by Joe Lines. Drawing upon criminal narratives both fictional and biographical, published in London and in Dublin, and tracing their multiple editions and iterations, Lines demonstrates how the apparent anti-Irish or anti-Catholic elements of these narratives are made complex by the transnational traditions of picaresque fiction, in which hero-rogues move easily between and among different nations, adapting and assimilating as they go. While the titles of these characters obviously signal their Irish, often specifically Gaelic, nationality – the 'Irish Rogue', the 'indefatigable Tory' Redmond O'Hanlon, and the 'notorious cheat' Manus Mac Oneil, for example – such titles belie the ways in which the narratives themselves represent characters who are shown to be hybrid figures, as witty and clever as they are treacherous, whose exploits are both fearful and comic, and who can inspire admiration as well as unease. The complexity evident in these readings is opposed to the more unsubtle characterisations of early stage plays, such as those by Thomas Shadwell, and paves the way for a flourishing of fiction in the mid-century which, Lines shows, owes much to the earlier tradition of criminal narratives.

Influences of a different kind are traced in Anne Markey's chapter. Markey shows how a number of early Irish novels in English reveal a knowledge of or engagement with Gaelic literature, culture, and history. *Vertue Rewarded* (1693), *Irish Tales* (1716), *Gulliver's Travels* (1726), *The Life of John Buncle, Esq.* (1756–66), and *The Fool of Quality* (1765–70) are all shown to articulate a sympathetic, often celebratory, account of native Irish culture, borrowing from manuscript sources, folklore and legend, knowledge of Gaelic customs and practices, or oral forms such as the anecdote. The chapter acts as an important reminder that Irish was by far the most commonly spoken language across huge swathes of Ireland – an estimated 90 per cent of the population in Munster and Connaught were Irish-speakers as late as the 1770s – and that this context inevitably shaped English-language print culture.[38]

Clíona Ó Gallchoir's chapter shares with Markey's a sense of the importance of Irish social customs of fosterage and wet-nursing, and, more broadly, the relations between Anglican and Catholic communities. Ó Gallchoir reviews the sectarianism of the 'improving' discourses of the Irish establishment in her reading of Chaigneau's *The History of Jack Connor* and Brooke's *The Fool of Quality*. Both novels are shown to explore more nuanced attitudes towards Catholic Ireland than would be evident in their own authors' pamphlets. The primary context for the chapter is that of the formation of Charter Schools, a system designed to convert an otherwise intractable Catholic population by educating poor children in the ways of English literacy and Anglican faith. As Ó Gallchoir shows, the system was itself riven by tensions between colonial views of the Irish (in which conversion of adults was abandoned as futile and children could be callously separated from their parents) and enlightened principles of education (in which sentimental plots allow for wholesale transformation). The eighteenth century's fascination with the figure of the child as the 'bearer of a new tradition' transmutes Lockean principles of amelioration through education and Rousseauvian primitivism. In the context of Ireland, these influences push fiction in more progressive directions, and encourage more sympathetic views of religious toleration, the possibility of social mobility, and the exigencies of individual experience, buffeted by cycles of history beyond the individual's control.

The two chapters in the final section address some of the ways in which eighteenth-century Irish literature continues to resonate beyond its own moment of composition, performance, or printing. One key element has been the flourishing of English-language translations of Irish-language poetry from this period. In the late twentieth century alone, poets as varied as Moya Cannon, Seamus Heaney, Biddy Jenkinson, and Eiléan Ní Chuilleanáin translated poems from this tradition. Lesa Ní Mhunghaile's chapter gives a special place to the two most famous poems of the eighteenth century, Eibhlín Dhubh Uí Laoghaire's *Caoineadh Airt Uí Laoghaire* and Brian Merriman's *Cúirt an Mheán Oíche*, celebrated for their outspokenness and formal innovation both then and now, and transformed into the twenty-first century through the agency of translations by Vona Groarke (2008) and Ciaran Carson (2005). While historians of eighteenth-century Ireland have debated the extent to which Gaelic poetry of the period can be read as evidence of Jacobite allegiance, this chapter considers the poems not as reflections of their authors' beliefs or the cultural or political attitudes of their time, but rather in terms of how as aesthetic accomplishments their power and agency have been transmuted into contemporary concerns, idioms, and significances by these important new works.[39]

Yeats's famous idealisation of Swift, Berkeley, Burke, and Grattan as representatives of 'that one Irish century that escaped from darkness and confusion' reverses the imagery which Daniel Corkery had invoked six years earlier to describe his own attempt to 'light up' the period with a dazzling view of Gaelic poetry in *The Hidden Ireland* (1924).[40] James Ward's final chapter in this volume explores eighteenth-century claims and values through the prism of late twentieth- and early twenty-first-century responses to particular texts – Farquhar's *The Recruiting Officer* and Goldsmith's *The Deserted Village* – and to the broader issues of violence and memory raised by the texts, their performances and contexts. Eavan Boland's poetry, Thomas Keneally's novel *The Playmaker* (1987), and Timberlake Wertenbaker's play *Our Country's Good* (1988) are read as allegories of the making of memory, in which the act of exposing what has been erased is seen to be a central responsibility. For Boland, the central context is that of the values of Enlightenment in which Goldsmith's poetry was both originally written and in which it is invoked today. For Keneally and Wertenbaker, the 1789 convict production of Farquhar's play in colonial Australia is a performance in which the play's figurings of coercion and violence are restaged and remade.

Ward's focus on the act of framing – the way in which the 'memory-texts' re-contextualise their eighteenth-century predecessors through historic trauma, while also implicating them within it – offers a suggestive end point for the volume as a whole, with its reminder of the ways in which frames 'instrumentaliz[e] certain versions of reality'.[41] In ending with two essays on contemporary creative responses to eighteenth-century literature, the volume signals that its ultimate framing is that of our contemporary moment, in its attempt to engage sensitively with the historical realities of the eighteenth century, whether those take the form of cultural expressions or occlusions.

The contents of this present volume have been made possible by a contemporary openness to an expanded canon of authors and texts, to histories of ideas which range far beyond the canonical philosophy of Berkeley and Burke, and to a newly conceived past in which the experiences of war, religious conversion, migration, and agrarian and artisanal unrest are as important as the older focus upon the 'high politics' of Dublin Castle, the Irish parliament, and the constitutional issues of colonial nationalism. Yet these chapters all begin with the ability of imaginative and literary writing not only to reflect its own culture but also to offer multivalent perspectives on complex contingencies, to reveal hidden or suppressed elements of opinion or belief, or to shape its aspirations.

The complicated situation of Ireland in the eighteenth century, as described by one major historian, suggests why the literary imagination, with its nuanced particularities, might be best placed to reflect and refract the realities of its period:

> [Ireland was] too physically close and too similar to Great Britain to be treated as a colony, but too separate and too different to be a region of the metropolitan centre; inheriting an undoubted division between settler and native, yet without the racial distinctions that could make these absolute.[42]

Dunkin's poem, with which this introduction began, undoubtedly deserves to be studied in its full complexity, as do the works of many formerly unregarded authors considered in this volume. The contexts in which we might place Dunkin's poem include the author's life and career and the precision of the moment in which it is written: the departure of Chesterfield from Dublin and with him, the end of a period of political patronage of the arts, for example. The poem might be said to embrace the colonial stereotype of the 'Stage Irishman' with such exaggerated celebration that the stereotype is itself confounded in a riot of 'Irish English' verse. But it is also ghosted by contemporary Irish-language poems which lament the passing of the old world of Gaelic hospitality and is thus thrown into the dark politics of its own exuberance. It demands to be read in terms of the multiplicity of literatures and contexts within which it might be considered. The essays that follow attempt to show both why and how this needs to be done for a wider range of literary texts from our period than has previously been attempted.

Notes

1. William Dunkin, *The Parson's Revels*, ed. Catherine Skeen (Dublin: Four Courts Press, 2010). All subsequent quotations are taken from this edition and will be cited in the text.
2. For references to these last three, see *Vertue Rewarded; or, The Irish Princess*, ed. Ian Campbell Ross and Anne Markey (Dublin: Four Courts Press, 2010), pp. 115–16, 113–14, 110.
3. Ian Campbell Ross, '"Damn these Printers ... By Heaven, I'll Cut Hoey's Throat": *The History of Mr. Charles Fitzgerald and Miss Sarah Stapleton* (1770), a Catholic Novel in Eighteenth-Century Ireland', *Irish University Review* 48.2 (Autumn/Winter 2018), 250–64.
4. Note too, however, the fruitful comparisons which might be made between this work and earlier burlesques, such as Richard Stanihurst's verse translation of the *Aeneid* (Leiden, 1582), discussed in Marie-Louise Coolahan's chapter below; or the two Restoration travesties reproduced in Andrew Carpenter, ed., *Verse Travesty in Restoration Ireland:* Purgatorium Hibernicum *and* The Fingallian Travesty (Dublin: Irish Manuscripts Commission, 2013).
5. Skeen takes as her copy-text for the poem a manuscript dated 1746.
6. 'Eibhlín a rún' is attributed to the poet Cearbhaill Ó Dálaigh, date unknown. A printed song-sheet from *c.* 1740 shows its inclusion of the phrase 'Céad míle fáilte' ('a hundred thousand welcomes') which has come to embody Irish hospitality. See 'Ducatu non vanna. Aileen aroon. A Irish Ballad sung by Mrs Clive', available online at www.irishsongproject.qub.ac.uk/song/200 [accessed 16 April 2018].
7. See, for example, Seán Ó Tuama, ed., *An Duanaire, 1600–1900: Poems of the Dispossessed*, trans. Thomas Kinsella (1981; Dublin: Dolmen Press, 1994), pp. 116–17, 130–33, 142–45, 170–71, 310–11, 328–31. Historians of eighteenth-century Ireland remain divided over the question of how reflective of social realities the Gaelic poetic traditions of lament were. The debate began with Louis Cullen's challenge to Daniel Corkery's *The Hidden Ireland* and remains current: see Louis M. Cullen, *The Hidden Ireland: Reassessment of a Concept* (1969; Dublin: Lilliput Press, 1988); Breandán Ó Buachalla, *Aisling Ghéar: Na Stíobhartaigh agus an tAos Léinn, 1603–1788* (Dublin: An Clóchomhar, 1996); Éamonn Ó Ciardha, *Ireland and the Jacobite Cause, 1685–1766: A Fatal Attachment* (Dublin: Four Courts Press, 2002); S. J. Connolly, 'Jacobites, Whiteboys and Republicans: Varieties of Disaffection in Eighteenth-Century Ireland', *Eighteenth-Century Ireland / Iris an dá chultúr* 18 (2003), 63–79; Vincent Morley, 'The Continuity of Disaffection in Eighteenth-Century Ireland', *Eighteenth-Century Ireland / Iris an dá chultúr* 22 (2007), 189–205;

David A. Fleming, 'Affection and Disaffection in Eighteenth-Century Mid-Munster Gaelic Poetry', *Eighteenth-Century Ireland / Iris an dá chultúr* 27 (2012), 84–98; and Vincent Morley, *The Popular Mind in Eighteenth-Century Ireland* (Cork University Press, 2017).

8. Ó Tuama, *An Duanaire*, pp. 310–11. See also Diarmuid Ó Súilleabháin's poem in the same collection, in which the poet can only provide a gander for the table, but promises a 'whole fatted ox' should the French arrive in Ireland; pp. 170–71.

9. Darren McGettigan, 'O'Rourke (Ó Ruairc), Brian Ballach Moore', in *Dictionary of Irish Biography*, ed. James McGuire and James Quinn (Cambridge University Press, 2009): http://dib.cambridge.org/viewReadPage .do?articleId=a7029 [accessed 18 January 2018].

10. Ó Rathaille's 'Cúirt uí Cheallacháin' offers a relatively late description (1709) of lavish hospitality by a Gaelic landowner, and the novelist Thomas Amory offers one later yet (see Anne Markey's chapter below).

11. David Dickson, *New Foundations: Ireland, 1660–1800* (1987; Dublin: Irish Academic Press, 2000), pp. 4, 8, and S. J. Connolly, *Religion, Law, and Power: The Making of Protestant Ireland, 1660–1760* (1992; Oxford: Clarendon Press, 2002), p. 13. Irish Catholics did not have rights to lease and inherit land restored until 1778.

12. Ian McBride, *Eighteenth-Century Ireland: The Isle of Slaves* (Dublin: Gill and Macmillan, 2009), p. 14.

13. For novels republished later in Dublin, see, for example, William Congreve, *Incognita* (originally 1692; Dublin reprint 1743); Sarah Butler, *Irish Tales* (London, 1716; Dublin, 1735); Mary Davys, *The Reformed Coquet* (London, 1724; Dublin, 1763); Charlotte McCarthy, *The Fair Moralist* (London, 1745; Dublin, 1783); William Chaigneau, *The History of Jack Connor* (Dublin and London, 1752; Dublin, 1766). For Dublin first printings, see Charles Johnston's *The Reverie* (1762); Elizabeth Sheridan's *Emeline* (1780) and *The Triumph of Prudence over Passion* (1781).

14. Christopher Wheatley, *'Beneath Ierne's Banners': Irish Protestant Drama of the Restoration and Eighteenth Century* (University of Notre Dame Press, 1999); Christopher Morash, *A History of Irish Theatre, 1601–2000* (Cambridge University Press, 2002); Helen M. Burke, *Riotous Performances: The Struggle for Hegemony in the Irish Theater, 1712–1784* (University of Notre Dame Press, 2003); Christopher Morash, 'Theatre in Ireland, 1690–1800', in *The Cambridge History of Irish Literature*, ed. Margaret Kelleher and Philip O'Leary, 2 vols (Cambridge University Press, 2006), I, pp. 372–406; Conrad Brunström, *Thomas Sheridan's Career and Influence: An Actor in Earnest* (Lewisburg, PA: Bucknell University Press, 2011); John C. Greene, *Theatre in Dublin, 1745–1820*, 8 vols (Bethlehem, PA: Lehigh University Press, 2011). On regional theatre, see Helen Burke, 'Eighteenth-Century Theatrical Touring and Irish Popular Culture', in *Irish Theatre on Tour*, ed. Nicholas Grene and Christopher Morash (Dublin: Carysfort Press, 2005), pp. 86–107 and Michael Brown, *The Irish Enlightenment* (Cambridge, MA and London: Harvard University Press, 2016), pp. 234–37.

15. On Irish popular theatrical culture, see, for example, Grainne McArdle, 'Signora Violante and Her Troupe of Dancers, 1729–32', *Eighteenth-Century Ireland / Iris an dá chultúr* 20 (2005), 55–78. For the theatre riots of 1712, 1743, 1747, and 1754, see, in addition to the sources listed above, Susan Cannon Harris, 'Clearing the Stage: Gender, Class, and the "Freedom of the Scenes" in Eighteenth-Century Dublin', *PMLA* 119.5 (October 2004), 1264–78; the same author's 'Outside the Box: The Female Spectator, *The Fair Penitent*, and the Kelly Riots of 1747', *Theatre Journal* 57 (2005), 35–55; and Sonja Lawrenson, 'Frances Sheridan's *The History of Nourjahad* and the Sultan of Smock-Alley', *Eighteenth-Century Ireland / Iris an dá chultúr* 26 (2011), 24–50.

16. See Ian Campbell Ross, 'Mapping Ireland in Early Fiction', *Irish University Review* 41.1 (Spring/Summer 2011), 1–20.

17. Toby Barnard, *Brought to Book: Print in Ireland, 1680–1784* (Dublin: Four Courts Press, 2017), p. 15. Barnard's second example is of connections between Liverpool and Drogheda in 1683 (p. 17).

18. See also David Gray's challenge to the designation of 'Ulster-Scots' writing, since early and mid-eighteenth-century writing in this tradition was composed in and about Donegal and Dublin: '"Stemmed from the Scots"? The Ulster-Scots Literary *Braird* and the Pastoral Tradition', in *Eighteenth-Century Ireland / Iris an dá chultúr* 32 (2017), 28–43.

19. Julian Moynahan, *Anglo-Irish: The Literary Imagination in a Hyphenated Culture* (Princeton University Press, 1995), pp. 5, 6; reviewed by Bernard O'Donoghue in *Review of English Studies* 48.190 (May 1997), 281. Compare the note in the introduction to *The Field Day Anthology of Irish Writing* that 'nothing was excluded for being insufficiently Irish': Angela Bourke et al., eds., *The Field Day Anthology of Irish Writing*, Vols 4/5: *Irish Women's Writing and Traditions*, 2 vols (Cork University Press, 2002), IV, p. xxxiii.

20. Murroghoh O'Connor and Seán Ó Neachtain are notable examples of authors able to switch between English, Irish, and Latin.

21. See, for example, Andrew Carpenter, ed., *Verse in English from Eighteenth-Century Ireland* (Cork University Press, 1998) and the novels of the Early Irish Fiction series, published in Dublin by Four Courts Press since 2010.

22. See Rolf Loeber and Magda Loeber, with Anne M. Burnham, *A Guide to Irish Fiction, 1650–1900* (Dublin: Four Courts Press, 2006) and John C. Greene's 8-volume *Theatre in Dublin, 1745–1820*, which runs to 5,380 pages in total. Crucial too has been the continuing importance of the Eighteenth-Century Ireland Society, which was co-founded in 1986 by Ian Campbell Ross, Andrew Carpenter, and Alan Harrison, and promotes and sustains influential interdisciplinary and bilingual studies of the period through its annual conference and journal.

23. W. J. McCormack challenged the use of 'Protestant Ascendancy' to describe sectional interests prior to the 1790s in an essay in the 1989 issue of *Eighteenth-Century Ireland*, and the following year the journal published a counter-response by James Kelly. For a summary of this exchange, and of Joep

Leerssen's critique of 'Anglo-Irish', see Scott C. Breuninger, 'Berkeley and Ireland: Who are the "We" in "We Irish Think Otherwise"?' in *Anglo-Irish Identities, 1571–1845*, ed. David A. Valone and Jill Marie Bradbury (Lewisburg, PA: Bucknell University Press, 2008), pp. 104–25. As long ago as 1986, the Irish historian Louis Cullen critiqued what he called 'the reckless modern use of the term "Anglo-Irish", a meaningless concept which, when used in the eighteenth-century context, lumps together a wide variety of families whose backgrounds, evolution and outlook were quite distinct. [...] The term, except as one of convenience in literary study, is best avoided', in 'Catholics under the Penal Laws', *Eighteenth-Century Ireland / Iris an dá chultúr* I (1986), 23–36 (p. 28). With the expansion of the canon of authors studied, that convenience no longer holds, if, indeed, it ever did.

24. See Norma Clarke, *Brothers of The Quill: Oliver Goldsmith in Grub Street* (Cambridge, MA: Harvard University Press, 2016); and, for a historical focus on the lives of the Irish middling classes in London, see *Eighteenth-Century Life* 39.1, Special Issue: *Networks of Aspiration: The London Irish of the Eighteenth Century*, ed. David O'Shaughnessy (January 2015).

25. On archipelagic approaches, see John Kerrigan, *Archipelagic English: Literature, History, and Politics, 1603–1707* (Oxford University Press, 2008); on the two plays referred to here, see Helen Burke, 'Crossing Acts: Irish Drama from George Farquhar to Thomas Sheridan', in *A Companion to Irish Literature*, ed. Julia M. Wright, 2 vols (Malden, MA and Oxford: Wiley-Blackwell, 2010), I, 127–41.

26. For the first monograph on the topic, see Laurie O'Higgins, *The Irish Classical Self: Poets and Poor Scholars in the Eighteenth and Nineteenth Centuries* (Oxford University Press, 2017).

27. For the latter of these, see the selection from William Starrat in Frank Ferguson, ed., *Ulster-Scots Writing: An Anthology* (Dublin: Four Courts Press, 2008), pp. 59–61.

28. For a list of 'first genres' in early modern Ireland, see Marie-Louise Coolahan's chapter below. Note also the following: Katherine Philips's play *Pompey*, a translation from Corneille, was the first professional production in English of a play by a woman (at the Theatre Royal in Smock Alley, in February 1663).

29. See Kevin J. Donovan, '*Jack the Giant Queller*: Political Theater in Ascendancy Dublin', *Éire / Ireland* 30.2 (Summer 1995), 70–88.

30. Richard Allen Cave, 'Woffington, Margaret [Peg] (1720?–1760), actress', in the *ODNB*: www.oxforddnb.com/view/10.1093/ref:odnb/9780198614128 .001.0001/odnb-9780198614128-e-29820 [accessed 18 January 2018].

31. McBride, *Eighteenth-Century Ireland*, p. 294.

32. See for example: Michael Brown, *A Political Biography of John Toland* (London: Pickering & Chatto, 2012); *John Toland's Letters to Serena*, ed. Ian Leask (Dublin: Four Courts Press, 2013); James Watt, '"The Indigent Philosopher": Oliver Goldsmith', in *A Companion to Irish Literature*, ed. Julia M. Wright, 2 vols (Malden, MA and Oxford: Wiley-Blackwell, 2010), I, 210–25; Michael Griffin, *Enlightenment in Ruins: The Geographies of Oliver Goldsmith* (Lewisburg, PA:

Bucknell University Press, 2013); Amy Prendergast, *Literary Salons across Britain and Ireland in the Long Eighteenth Century* (Basingstoke: Palgrave Macmillan, 2015); Aileen Douglas, 'Women, Enlightenment and the Literary Fairy Tale in English', *Journal for Eighteenth-Century Studies* 38.2 (2015), 181–94.

33. For a contrasting view of Irish enlightenment thought which argues for its conciliatory force, in the mid-century at least, see Michael Brown, *The Irish Enlightenment* (Cambridge, MA: Harvard University Press, 2016).

34. On women writers and issues of gender, see Siobhán Kilfeather, 'Beyond the Pale: Sexual Identity and National Identity in Early Irish Fiction', *Critical Matrix* 2.4 (Fall 1986), 1–31; '"Strangers at Home": Political Fictions by Women in Eighteenth-Century Ireland' (unpublished PhD thesis, Princeton University, 1989); 'Origins of the Irish Female Gothic', *Bullán* 1.2 (Autumn 1994), 35–46; 'Look Who's Talking: Scandalous Memoirs and the Performance of Gender', *The Irish Review* 13 (Winter 1992/93), 40–49; Aileen Douglas, '"Whom Gentler Stars Unite": Fiction and Union in the Irish Novel', *Irish University Review* 41.1 (2011), 183–95; Douglas, 'Women, Enlightenment and the Literary Fairy Tale'; Gerardine Meaney, Mary O'Dowd, and Bernadette Whelan, *Reading the Irish Woman: Studies in Cultural Encounter and Exchange, 1714–1960* (Liverpool University Press, 2013), pp. 13–53; and Heather Ingram and Clíona Ó Gallchoir, eds., *A History of Modern Irish Women's Literature* (Cambridge University Press, 2018).

35. See Carpenter, *Verse in English from Eighteenth-Century Ireland*, p. 5.

36. Eve Kosofsky Sedgwick, *Epistemology of the Closet* (1990; Berkeley, CA: University of California Press, 2nd edn, 2008), p. 45, as cited in Kavanagh's chapter below.

37. See, for example, Burke, 'Crossing Acts'; Robert W. Jones, 'The Drama of Richard Brinsley Sheridan', in *A Companion to Irish Literature*, ed. Julia M. Wright, 2 vols (Malden, MA and Oxford: Wiley-Blackwell, 2010), I, pp. 243–55; and McBride, *Eighteenth-Century Ireland*.

38. See McBride, *Eighteenth-Century Ireland*, p. 61.

39. The debates regarding Gaelic poetry and history might be traced through the work of Louis Cullen, S. J. Connolly, Breandán Ó Buachalla, Éamonn Ó Ciardha, and Vincent Morley: see note 7 above.

40. W. B. Yeats, 'Introduction to *The Words upon the Window-pane*' (1930), in *Explorations* (London and New York: Macmillan, 1962), p. 345. Daniel Corkery, *The Hidden Ireland: A Study of Gaelic Munster in the Eighteenth Century* (1924; Dublin: Gill and Macmillan, 1984), p. 6.

41. The phrase is cited by Ward and is taken from Judith Butler, *Frames of War: When Is Life Grievable?* (London: Verso, 2009; rev. edn, 2016), p. xiii.

42. S. J. Connolly, 'Eighteenth-Century Ireland: Colony or *Ancien Regime?*' in *The Making of Modern Irish History: Revisionism and the Revisionist Controversy*, ed. D. George Boyce and Alan O'Day (London and New York: Routledge, 1996), pp. 15–33 (p. 26).

PART I

Starting Points

CHAPTER I

Starting Points and Moving Targets: Transition and the Early Modern

Marie-Louise Coolahan

Edmund Spenser's 'Mutabilitie Cantos', composed in Ireland at the end of the sixteenth century, ruminate on the relationships between transition, change, and permanence. The cantos tell the story of Mutability, descendant of the Titans, who rebels against Jove, claiming empire of the heavens on the basis of her Titanic birthright and opposing this to Jove's right by conquest. This opposition of birthright versus conquest, precedence versus power, stability versus innovation, is mapped onto Ireland. Mutability demands that their dispute be heard in court and adjudicated by Dame Nature. The venue for the trial is Arlo Hill, or Galtymore, the mountain close to Spenser's home at Kilcolman in County Cork. Thence, the narrative shifts to a story within the story, in which Spenser adapts Ovidian myth to allegorise the degeneration of the Irish landscape. The topographical specificity frames its account of historical transition in Irish terms. Irish history is metamorphosed. The goddess Diana, who would regularly hunt and bathe on Arlo, is betrayed by her nymph Molanna to the peeping Faunus, upon which Diana furiously punishes both and abandons the hill. Diana curses the land, the poem's speaker ruefully confirming her decree via first-hand experience, rooted in his sixteenth-century present:

> Since which those Woods, and all that goodly Chase,
> Doth to this day with Wolues and Thieues abound:
> Which too-too true that lands in-dwellers since haue found.[1]

The poem's lamentation of the landscape's degeneration from idyll to wasteland inevitably evokes the Munster rebellion and plantation; the cantos' legal proceedings limn the region's land disputes.

As the tale of Mutability's rebellion is resumed, the gods assemble on Arlo Hill to hear her case, which rests on the paradoxical yet persuasive argument that change is a permanent condition of existence:

> But *Times* do change and moue continually.
> So nothing here long standeth in one stay:
> Wherefore, this lower world who can deny
> But to be subiect still to *Mutabilitie*?[22]

Dame Nature's summary judgment – that all things retain their original state and thereby triumph over change – never holds sway over this fragmentary poem. Comprised of two cantos (disjointedly numbered six and seven), with a third two-stanza sliver numbered eight and declared formally 'vnperfite', these verses confound closure. Resolution and permanence are unattainable and radically undermined. The very open-endedness of this last *Faerie Queene* canto epitomises the idea of literature in transition and reflects the edgy sense of flux that is characteristic of writing and composition in early modern Ireland.

How do we define 'transition', and in which direction: from or to? The concept points to the transitive – to effects caused by change, from one thing to another thing. Following from this, it is the means by which we locate and attribute meaning to change. If literature in transition is about evolution, moving forward as change is processed, it should map ideally onto a period designation such as 'early modern', which is fundamentally rooted in teleology (of which more later). From an early twenty-first-century perspective, when English is by far the dominant language in Ireland (as well as globally) and Anglophone literary tradition has expanded to accommodate many voices, the starting point of transition in Ireland is undoubtedly the acceleration of Elizabethan policies in the later sixteenth century. But that eventual linguistic hegemony was not inevitable from the vantage point of transition, when everything was still to play for. Indeed, we could argue that the literature of sixteenth- and seventeenth-century Ireland is essentially transitional in quality, with no single tradition enjoying hegemony and all jostling for position. In terms of language, English migrants arrived into a multilingual space: Irish Gaelic was dominant outside the Pale, which itself was at least bilingual; Latin was the learned lingua franca; French and English were also spoken. Elizabethan policies pushed for immigration by Protestant, English-speaking planters and their families. These were the 'New English' in contemporary and subsequent shorthand, as opposed to the 'Old English' Catholic descendants of the Normans, and the 'Old' or 'native' Irish, Catholic and Gaelic-speaking. The late sixteenth century is the moment when competing forms of Englishness emerged in tension both against each other and established Irish identities, which were themselves historically fractured along regional and sept (clan) lines. State expropriations of land led to reiterated cycles of displacement and settlement. Ireland was a land of opportunity for adventurous English folk who could ignore the successions of insurgency and war. The poet Spenser was one of this number. He arrived in 1580 as secretary to Lord Deputy Grey and benefited from the Munster plantation, gaining land and building a castle at Kilcolman in Cork (where he composed *The Faerie Queene*). His pastoral poem *Colin Clouts Come Home Againe* dramatised the ambivalences of his community's identity, torn between attraction to the London court and a critical repulsion against metropolitan court politics that was unavoidably coloured by residence in Ireland. Spenser knew more than most about mutability and changing fortunes; he and his family were burnt out in October 1598.[3]

If political turmoil, linguistic contestation, and inter-community or ethnic strife are the drivers of literary innovation and decline, then early modern Ireland has an arresting claim to the paradigm of transition. Indeed, the scholarly appetite for understanding the effects of change as a process of transition underway in early modern Ireland is evident in the proliferation of riffs on 'Making Ireland …', kickstarted by Nicholas Canny's 2001 *Making Ireland British*, picked up eight years later by Jason Harris and Keith Sidwell's collection *Making Ireland Roman* (which includes a chapter on 'Making Ireland Spanish'), and most recently by Jane Ohlmeyer's 2012 *Making Ireland English*.[4]

The 'Mutabilitie Cantos', forever unresolved, are emblematic of the transitional qualities of literature in early modern Ireland. The poem's metaphysical concerns are explicitly worked through on its landscape. They are reflective of, and reflections on, the uncertainties of property and inheritance in that place at that time. The instabilities of identity for the New English settler class are played out in the dispute between Mutability and Jove. Legitimacy and stability were in dispute, which is why precedence and antecedence – the to and from of transition – were so contested. Jane Grogan has argued of these incomplete verses, that 'it is not just the prospect of mutability as decay, the agent of mortality, that challenges the idea of a constant world order […]: it is also the problem of becoming, of changefulness'.[5] Between becoming and changefulness, generation and extinction, lies another possibility for literature and transition. This chapter argues that late sixteenth- and seventeenth-century Ireland are crucial to understanding the roots and imperatives of subsequent transitions but it also acknowledges that the teleological lens privileges only one side of the story. Writing in a period of irreversible change generates genealogical firsts – precursors of what is to follow – but also genres specific to their own time. The chapter probes the relationship of literature with transition: as representing change, as its written record, as the document of response to a new world taking shape or of self-assertion in that world. Finally, it considers questions of perspective and the determining role of the end point in identifying beginnings.

Languages, Literature, and Transition

Linguistic pragmatism was characteristic of literary transition in the face of Anglophone conquest. As with the ambivalent identity explored in *Colin Clout*, linguistic transition was characterised by blurred lines and literary shifts. The realities of living on a small island ensured that the language and culture of different communities rubbed off on each other. Irish words were adopted into the English spoken on the island and vice versa. Travellers and soldiers could avail of the medical and travel writer Andrew Boorde's *Fyrst Boke of the Introduction of Knowledge* (1542). A compendium of European travel accounts, Boorde's third chapter on 'the naturall disposicion of an Irishe man, & of theyr money and speche' is illustrated by a woodcut of a couple, the man lying in his female partner's lap, embracing her with his arrow in hand (Fig. 1). It concludes with a phrasebook, 'If there be any man the which wyll lerne some Irysh', in which the Gaelic translation for numbers and such idioms as 'How do you fare' are provided phonetically: in this latter case, as 'Kanys stato' (*Conas atá tú?* in modern Irish).[6] The distinctly Irish sounds of English made it onto the English stage as early as 1599 in Shakespeare's *Henry V*, whose Captain Macmorris laments 'What ish my nation?'.[7] Ben Jonson's *The Irish Masque at Court* (1613) was performed in London at the wedding festivities for Robert Carr, Earl of Somerset and favourite of King James, and Frances Howard, former Countess of Essex, whose first husband led Queen Elizabeth's troops in Ireland in the closing years of the sixteenth century. It presents four Irish footmen (Dennis, Donnell, Dermock, and Patrick) who arrive apologising for the tardiness of their masters, Irish ambassadors. The latter figures play on stereotypes of the wild Irishman, dressed in Irish mantles and dancing to harp music and bardic song, finally revealing themselves as anglicised courtiers when their mantles are removed at the play's climax. The text is replete with such early experimentations with the sounds of Hiberno-English as Dennis's comic opening lines, 'For Chreesh's sake, phair ish te King? Phich ish he, an't be?', and the more politically barbed plea: 'Be not angry vit te honesht men for te few rebelsh and knavesh.'[8]

English words also found their way into Irish Gaelic texts. An elegy on Donnchadh Ó Briain (Donough O'Brien; 1581–1624), fourth Earl of Thomond, by Tadhg Mac Bruaideadha, for example, adopted the terms of English governance – *Coróin* ('crown'), 'President'.[9] Such cross-

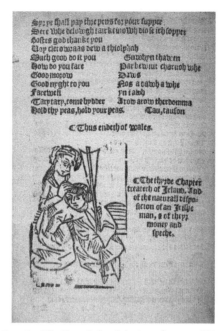

Fig. 1 Andrew Boorde, *The Fyrst Boke of the Introduction of Knowledge*, 2nd edn (London, 1555), sig. C2v. © British Library (C.71.b.29)

fertilisations were particularly appropriate in his case. The O'Briens had surrendered the Gaelic title for an English earldom. The fourth earl committed his military forces to English advancement and consolidation, but simultaneously maintained traditional Gaelic cultural activities such as patronage of Mac Bruaideadha, hereditary poet and historian to the Uí Bhriain.[10] As scholars such as Sarah McKibben, Lesa Ní Mhunghaile, Breandán Ó Buachalla, and Michelle O Riordan have shown, resilience and adaptability were key features of Gaelic literature undergoing this transition.[11] These were hybrid ethnic groups. Marc Caball, writing about early seventeenth-century Kerry, warns against 'retrospective determinism in attempts to discern self-conscious ethnic parameters in an area dominated over centuries by gaelicised Anglo-Norman elites'.[12] These regions were already mixed and had adapted to change.

Military incursion and land grabbing were the immediate and obvious effects of English policy; literary and cultural infiltration was incremental and sustained. The most obvious effect in cultural terms was the impact on Gaelic literary culture. The 'Classical Irish' period – so-called due precisely to its stability and the longevity of its artistic values – had flourished and extended over Ireland and Scotland since the early thirteenth century. Chieftains' courts were peopled by retinues of cultural arbiters: poets (*fileadha* and *ollamhain*), genealogists and chroniclers (*seanchaidhe*), judges (*breitheamhain*), harpists (*cruitirí*), and musicians. The rules, metres, and genres of poetry were complex and sophisticated; a properly trained *fileadh* would typically have spent at least seven years in training. He would have been male and a member of the social caste that produced poets.[13] But these were not artists operating in a bubble oblivious to outside influences. The overwhelmingly teleological narrative of bardic decline, while ultimately true, has lent itself in the past to indignant nationalist interpretation and partial historical accounts – most famously, perhaps, as articulated in Daniel Corkery's *The Hidden Ireland* (1924). However, as scholars such as Mícheál Mac Craith and Marc Caball have shown, Gaelic poets were resourceful and open to literary evolution. Mac Craith has traced the various routes by which Renaissance ideas and thinking penetrated sixteenth-century poetry and prose. Caball has demonstrated that poets could be pragmatic in the face of change, adapting to the new allegiances of patrons such as Cú Chonnacht Mág Uidhir of Fermanagh or Cormac Ó hEadhra of Sligo, writing them into traditional praise poetry.[14]

Transition was not only a matter of survival for Irish-language literature but also of accommodation – and accommodation extended to hitherto peripheral voices such as those of versifying women. As the established system came under pressure, scribes and families moved to preserve more vernacular forms of verse, including women's compositions. Fissures in the modes of cultural transmission facilitated the recording of non-elite agents whose compositions had predominantly circulated via oral culture. An excellent example of this is Caitilín Dubh (*fl.* 1624–29), whose five poems on members of the extended O'Brien clan of Thomond were included in the family's *duanaire* (poem-book), compiled in 1712 by Aodh Buí Mac Cruitín. Her elegy on the fourth earl (the aforementioned Donnchadh Ó Briain) demonstrates ready incorporation of her subject's Anglophile commitments in Gaelic terms, casting his military triumphs in the shape of a traditional *caithréim* (battle roll).[15] The form in which she composed, *caoineadh* (keen), illustrates the longevity of the oral tradition just as its manuscript preservation is a marker of transition. Although poems such as those by Caitilín Dubh or the sole surviving *caoineadh* by her contemporary Fionnghuala Ní Bhriain found their way into such prestigious manuscripts only in the eighteenth century, it is clear from a range of sources (most memorably the six-teenth-century Scottish poet Feidhlim Mac Dhubhghaill's irritable '*fuath liom cliar ara mbí bean*' ['I hate a poet-band that includes a woman']) that non-professional poetry composed by women had long existed.[16] It is the threat to elite Gaelic cultural practices that prompted the recording of more marginal voices.

The fact that such compositions began to be preserved by scribes in itself indicates recognition that the system was changing but also that silver linings, such as the trespassing of vernacular voices into elite literary culture, pertained. As Vincent Morley has outlined: 'Irish literature was still dominated by professionally trained poets in 1600, and the graduates of continental seminaries were prominent at mid-century, but by the 1690s the voice of the populace had become audible.' His *The Popular Mind in Eighteenth-Century Ireland* is pioneering in moving those voices centre stage.[17] And while Irish-language print culture failed to take off on the island of Ireland, it nevertheless played a profound role in the construction of the idea of a national identity that hinged upon Catholicism and the Irish language. The Franciscan order pursued an activist print agenda, founding St Anthony's College, Louvain, in 1607, an institution from which a steady stream of popular devotional works in the Gaelic vernacular were issued, targeted at audiences at home and in exile.[18]

The experience of exile, with its prompting to contemplation and assertion of identity, offers one route towards assessing what was distinc-tively Irish about transition. The range of exiled experiences has been garnering sustained attention from historians.[19] Such materials are ripe for consideration by literary scholars. To take women's writing as an example, Micheline Kerney Walsh signalled the survival of letters and accounts in two groundbreaking articles. Later work on Irish women's petitions to the Spanish state is indebted to the years Kerney Walsh spent gathering, transcribing, and copying the records of the Irish diaspora across France and Spain.[20] Ciaran O'Scea uses the documents of Spanish state bureaucracy to assess levels of literacy among the Irish diaspora, and has unearthed the records and documents of Irish women living as *beata* (lay nuns) in Galicia. Thomas O'Connor's study of the Spanish Inquisition uncovers women's and men's narratives of conversion and denunciation.[21]

Latin, the lingua franca of early modern Europe, remained a dominant elite medium of communication well into the eighteenth century, and Irish writing in Latin was as resourceful as that in Gaelic, as the work of the Centre for Neo-Latin Studies in Cork has shown. Jason Harris and Keith Sidwell's essay collection, *Making Ireland Roman*, alongside a series of parallel-translation editions, have reminded modern scholars of the transnational vitality and assertive polemic of Irish neo-Latin writing in this period. The competition over identity, government, and religion on the island was played out in Latin to an international audience in the battle for hearts and minds. For example, Richard Stanihurst, who contributed the account of Ireland to Holinshed's *Chronicles*, published in 1584 a history of Ireland that made the case for the pre-eminence of his own Old English community, *De Rebus in Hibernia Gestis*. On the other side of the religio-political divide, Philip O'Sullivan Beare's *Zoilomastix* was written to counter Stanihurst's work; his *Historiae Catholicae Iberniae Compendium* (Lisbon, 1621), a work of Counter-Reformation history addressed to an international Catholic audience, presented Tudor policies as heretical English persecution.[22] Latin was the language of choice for Gaelic chieftains in their dealings with the English state during the sixteenth century.

Observing that the fallout of the Reformation 'produced a divided Latin writing and reading community' in Ireland, Harris and Sidwell draw attention to the fact that 1,000 books in Latin were published by Irish authors between the sixteenth and eighteenth centuries, an embrace of print culture far more sustained and impactful than was achieved by the other language traditions on the island.[23] Among these was Dermot O'Meara's epic poem, *Ormonius* (1615), in which Queen Elizabeth's ally, 'Black' Tom Butler, tenth Earl of Ormond, is represented as a warrior hero loyal to the crown. But the poem also incorporates the Gaelic *caithréim* and the *aisling* form that was to dominate eighteenth-century Irish poetry: the dream-poem in which a female figure for Ireland appears to the poem's speaker. The anonymous manuscript *Poema de Hibernia* recounts the history of the Williamite wars. Its partisan perspective in favour of Richard Talbot, Earl of Tyrconnell, has led its modern editors to propose Thomas Nugent, Baron Riverston, as the author.[24] This capacity to absorb, incorporate, and extend points to resilience as the paradigm of literature in transition in early modern Ireland. Latin's shrinking from view is in great part a product of much later transitions, as economic, social, and political changes caused both alternative languages on the island of Ireland to lose currency in favour of English.

As the plantations and land policies took root, members of the settler class imported their versions of English and Renaissance literary culture. Those engaged in Anglophone literary production were careful to signal its wider resonance. Lodowick Bryskett, for example, whose *Discourse of civill life* was written in 1580s Dublin and published in 1606, projected a vision of the gentlemanly humanist coterie, conversing at the centre of the Irish Pale. An adaptation of the Italian Giambattista Giraldi Cinthio's *Tre dialoghi della vita civile*, Bryskett's account presented an apparently exemplary community of colonial administrators and military commanders debating the virtues of the contemplative over the active civic life. Anne Fogarty captures the politico-literary undertones of the project: 'Bryskett's Irish garden is transformed into a vista of Renaissance order, while conversely the discussion of the moral qualities of a civil society becomes implicitly a commentary on their absence in Ireland.'[25] Spenser was of this company; Bryskett has him relate the genesis of his *Faerie Queene*, in the process insisting on its context in Irish service. As we have seen, Spenser's time in Ireland was productive and prolific, if uneasy in terms of identity. The New English experience of immigration stimulated all kinds of poetry and prose. The poet Anne Southwell moved with her husband to Poulnelong, Cork, around 1603, where she used her poetry to build and maintain relationships among the settler class. Her fellow devotional poet, Francis Quarles, who served as secretary to Archbishop James Ussher during the 1620s, chose his time in Ireland to experiment self-consciously with secular romance, dating his dedication to *Argalus and Parthenia* to 4 March 1629, in Dublin. Autobiographical writing was prompted by the clash of cultures as, for example, in *The Vocacyon of Johan Bale* (1553). Arguably the first autobiography to be published in English, this work relates the experience of the newly appointed Bishop of Ossory, who had the misfortune to have been appointed by Edward VI only months prior to the accession of his Catholic sister, Mary. Life writing like Bale's was steeped in the turmoil of the period; indeed, recourse to writing was increasingly a means of processing the transitions entailed in migration, conflict, and settlement. The impetus to relate the narrative of one's own conversion, required for admission to the Independent churches, prompted many New English Protestant arrivals to formulate their experiences in prose.[26]

But it was not only among the New English that Anglophone literary production took hold. The Old English Westmeath author Richard Nugent published his sonnet sequence *Cynthia* in London in 1603. This recounts the speaker's failed courtship and subsequent exile, mourning not only the loss of romance but also the Irish landscape, with a number of the sonnets addressed to male friends. The title draws on the iconographic association with Queen Elizabeth, who died that same year, facilitating readings of the narrative as articulating an abandoned Old English loyalism. Another Old English writer, Richard Bellings, a lawyer trained at Lincoln's Inn, later Confederate secretary and chronicler of the 1640s wars, published his continuation to Philip Sidney's *Arcadia* in 1624. The commendatory poems hail Bellings as rejuvenating Irish writing. Those compelled to write in English for political rather than literary reasons show how elite accommodation could also figure as adjustment to the new reality. The petition-letters of Eleanor (née Butler) Fitzgerald, Countess of Desmond, for example, exhibit a command of persuasive language and rhetorical tropes framed as self-justification in language the Queen would understand. Desmond was driven to write to Elizabeth many times in a writing career that spanned her husband's rebellions, her widowhood, and re-marriage to another turbulent Gaelic lord. Such writing is evidence of more than accommodation; it demonstrates adjustment to the new political reality, and on its terms.

The hibernification of English literary modes such as the court masque worked both ways. While Jonson experimented with the language of English in Ireland in his *Irish Masque*, the form itself was adopted by settlers across the country. A masque was commissioned of George Wither in 1610, for example, to celebrate the wedding of Francis Willoughby and Cassandra Ridgeway.[27] Such examples are less innovative than conformist; rather than exploring the possibilities of the form as Jonson did, these performances demonstrate the signs of English court influence and the impulse to signal Anglophone convention. Drama in English enjoyed a series of peak moments in seventeenth-century Ireland. Theatrical productions occurred in Dublin, Kilkenny, and Londonderry. Lord Deputy Wentworth sought to establish Dublin Castle as a courtly centre in the 1630s, hiring James Shirley as playwright-in-residence. The climate produced such curiosities as *Landgartha*, the first Anglophone play by an Irishman (Old English Dubliner, Henry Burnell) to be staged. Overcome and stymied by Wentworth's execution and subsequent wars, Dublin theatre was revitalised at the Restoration, when Theatre Royal, Smock Alley was founded. Another moment of apparent flowering, this period was lit up by the Anglo-Welsh playwright and poet Katherine Philips, whose most successful year was spent in Dublin from 1662 to 1663.[28]

Restoration Dublin was – it appears from the extensive archival work of Andrew Carpenter – a vibrant poetic space. Three different versions of a verse travesty of Book VI of Virgil's *Aeneid* were published in 1670, 1686, and 1691, all reproducing the emergent Dublin, 'Fingallian', dialects and colloquialisms of Hiberno-English.[29] But the sounds of Dublin English had spilled into Anglophone print culture as early as 1582, when Richard Stanihurst (he of the Latin *De Rebus in Hibernia Gestis*, above) had his translation of the first four books of the *Aeneid* printed in Leiden. Its lexical exuberance and linguistic invention have led modern critics to see it in generic continuity with Joyce's *Finnegans Wake*; even as an expression of the colonised disruption of epic form. The act of translation, intrinsic to humanist ideals of civilisation, was just as much a preoccupation of aggressively colonial thinkers as defenders of the Old English Pale, argues Patricia Palmer. John Harington's translation of Ariosto's *Orlando Furioso*, composed while in Ireland as an undertaker in the Munster plantation, is interpreted as focused on military didacticism. The incomplete translation of Alonso de Ercilla y Zuñiga's Spanish tale of the conquest of Chile made by George Carew, Lord President of Munster, mined its original for ruthless martial ideas.[30] The diversity of approaches to translation, the variety of emerging new genres, the embracing and adaptation of humanist and Anglophone literary culture, all point to the dynamism of literature in transition in early modern Ireland. The little-acknowledged continuity of macaronic verse underlines the fact that English-language traditions were equally as adaptable and resilient as others on the island, expanding to accommodate Hiberno-English and Irish words and to articulate English experience of Ireland.[31]

Scholarship and Transition

On the one hand, then, we can argue that the later sixteenth century marks the beginning of transition in Irish literature, the early in the modern. On the other, we should acknowledge how the picture mutates. The canon of early modern Irish writing in English is far from fixed; rather, it has been enjoying wholesale reappraisal, as scholars bring new works to attention via modern editions. This reflects the mutability of scholarly concerns and imperatives, themselves always rooted in their own present and therefore processing the ebbs and flows of their own time. Highlights of recent editorial and translation work include the only known Irish sonnet sequence, Nugent's *Cynthia*, first printed in London in 1603. The 1641 printing of Burnell's *Landgartha* was prefaced by the only two known Latin poems by an Irishwoman of this period, his daughter Eleanora. The Latin, French, and English prose and poetry of Dubliner Walter Quin was completely unknown until edited in 2014.[32]

Scholarship has also been in transition. The expansion of writerly forms embraced as literature and the reconceptualisation of autobiographical and biographical writing as life writing have incurred fresh appraisals of prose forms such as the letter.[33] The body of texts known as the 1641 Depositions demonstrates the standalone, temporal specificity of genre, discontinuous with literary teleology. But its reception history blares out the perennially shifting sands of signification inherent in writing that attracts readers over time. These narratives are the product of the English state response to the 1641 Catholic rising. Protestants fleeing their homes were urged to make depositions to state commissioners, relating their losses and experiences of violence, as records for any future trials or compensation claims. These accounts are replete with hearsay and rumour as well as first-hand reports; their veracity has been debated throughout a critical history that ranges from outraged contemporary reproductions to revisionist interrogation, linguistic and literary analysis.[34] The 1641 Depositions illustrate another dimension of literature's relationship with transition: the genre that is produced by its historical moment.

The expansion in our categories of literature to include such textual forms is itself a product of our own time. From our perspective, we might use literature to probe the lived experience of transition, to explore how contemporary culture dealt and coped with upheaval. But the range of genres so considered – from deposition and conversion narrative to humanist dialogue – cannot efface our historical distance. Such texts are always constructions rather than unmediated, spontaneous witnesses to lived experience, a factor that is more easily recognised in a poem like the 'Mutabilitie Cantos' or *Colin Clouts Come Home Againe* than a documentary text like autobiography.

Having retrieved this writing for a fresh canon, how do we make sense in our present of such a diverse yet unsustained range of literature as that produced in Ireland during the sixteenth and seventeenth centuries? The canon is not settled, yet its evaluation requires a wider purview. Are the surviving texts exceptional or typical? Are we dealing with a literary culture that is characterised by adaptability, or by stops and starts, discontinuity and even ephemerality? The apparently unique *caoineadh* by Fionnghuala Ní Bhriain stands only with those of Caitilín Dubh in seventeenth-century Gaelic culture: were these the only such women composers or the only ones whose work was preserved (because of proximity to the O'Briens of Thomond)? These questions arise equally for male writers outside the Gaelic tradition, also newly (re)discovered. Is Richard Nugent's sonnet sequence a one-off, unique from an Irish literary perspective but behind the curve of English literary fashion? Or does it operate outside such generic chronologies, better understood as representative of a thriving coterie culture whose traces are now lost? Is literature in transition *by its transitional nature* patchy, solitary, isolated, without peers – or is it the nature of transformational change that literary production stutters, ceases, fails to gain momentum? Transition invokes questions about longevity and ephemerality, resilience, resourcefulness, and extinction. This range of resonance points to different aspects of the relationship between literature and change: literature that engages with change in the adaptive, resilient sense; literature that represents the lived experience of change in the documentary sense (albeit always constructed representations); literature that is produced only because of changed circumstances. When and where does 'transition' in Irish literature begin? Is the case to be made for transition and the early modern that the seeds of later literary genres begin in that period: the first sonnet sequence, the first play, the first recorded *caoineadh*, the first woman's Latin poem, the first novel? Or is it that this is the moment of irreversible change, the beginning of Anglophone penetration – and that this drives attention towards literary strategies of engagement with change, whether by resilience and adaptation, mimetic representation, or the creation of new, shortlived, and period-specific forms of writing?

The answers require that we switch from starting point to end points. The value of the term 'early modern' lies in its general embrace of that which resonates as 'modern' today – the printing press (notwithstanding its superseding by digital means of distribution), democracy, empirical science, imperial (and subsequently global) trade, the nation-state. Yet for all its summative value, it is reductive, flattening social, technological, and cultural features that do not fit the meta-narrative. Equally, and instructively, the starkness of the implied division between the medieval and the early modern has been under sustained attack by medievalists (at least since David Aers's deliciously titled 'A Whisper in the Ear of Early Modernists'), who rightly point to continuities as well as change.[35] This point is clarified by interrogation of the catch-all designation 'Renaissance' – often used as synonymous with 'early modern' – a term which misdirects us from its geographical and temporal artificiality. The Italian Renaissance is marked by Petrarch's vernacular love poetry in the mid-fourteenth century, whereas the English Renaissance picks up these cues only with Wyatt and Surrey in the late 1500s – and critics are divided as to whether Ireland can be said to fit a Renaissance paradigm at all.[36] Similarly, the associations of 'early modern' are contingent. The first printing press was in operation in Gutenberg in 1450 but Queen Elizabeth complained of the lack of a Gaelic printing press 117 years later.[37] Different 'rebirths' occurred at different times. Particular innovations had longer gestation periods in particular places due to a confluence of circumstances; the conditions for their being embedded were not the same everywhere. Perhaps this is what leads us to distinctively Irish forms of transition. Moreover, the line we draw from beginning to end may breach our periodisations. If the starting point of literary transition in Ireland is the 'early modern', we must interrogate both that 'early' and 'modern'. The teleological and aesthetic advantage implied in the designation – all roads lead to the modern; what is important are its precursory seeds – is both inescapably true and existentially frustrating for the literary historian. We produce the past by imagining it in our present; we cannot avoid present, current hermeneutic drives and priorities. But this can also blind us to what else is there, which may be (re)discovered by future scholars responding to, and writing in, different times.

If the past is produced by present remembrance, we reproduce that which chimes best with ourselves. We look for what we recognise: the antecedents of the novel, the seeds of literary genres and cultural practices that resonate today. The starting points for transition are always plural and determined by our vantage points in the present. We can see this most bluntly in developments of the later twentieth century: feminist scholars have sought female-authored works; modern education systems mean that Latin writers have receded; Anglophone hegemony means a smaller audience for Irish-language texts. Such locatedness is essential to the idea of 'transition', which is always about the process of change from one thing to another. Which lines of connection we draw are shaped by our own contexts. But these, too, are subject to change. The 'modern' is no monolith; its imperatives shift and jolt. What seemed irrelevant and even incomprehensible yesterday may acquire resounding insight tomorrow. This is exemplified at the present time of writing by a recent *Washington Post* article by political theorist Danielle Allen. Recounting many years teaching Cicero's 'On Duties', Allen wrote to explain how the Trump election had altered her interpretive perspective: the 'boring simplicity of [Cicero's] prose', in this new context, was revealed to be a deliberate and exemplary performance of stoicism in the face of political tumult.[38] We must remain open to the possibilities of future resonance. Continuity and longevity of genre or critical consensus are not preordained, nor immutable.

In the final analysis, points of transition are always moving targets. Where we choose to start depends on where we stand in the present. Juliet Fleming rightly emphasises the impossibility of apprehending the historical moment as it was:

> Nothing can irrupt from the past into the present as its former self since all forms of survival require that an entity fits into its new context, and continues to change with as it changes that environment. This, surely, is what we could call the polytemporal – not that the past survives to rock the present, but that all things are in a constant state of evolution in relation to their contexts.[39]

This is not to say that a directionless mutability predominates but that the relationships of literary scholars with their materials evolve. Such evolutions – shaped and formed by their own moment(s) – are not linear but plural, with beginnings and endings that wrap around themselves, disappear and re-emerge, all the time filtered through a present imagination.

Notes

1. Edmund Spenser, *The Faerie Qveene*, ed. A. C. Hamilton (London: Longman, 1977), p. 723.
2. Ibid., p. 732.
3. *Edmund Spenser: The Shorter Poems*, ed. Richard McCabe (London: Penguin, 1999), pp. 343–71. The most recent biography is Andrew Hadfield, *Edmund Spenser: A Life* (Oxford University Press, 2012). See also, *inter alia*, Jane Grogan, ed., *Celebrating Mutabilitie: Essays on Edmund Spenser's Mutabilitie Cantos* (Manchester University Press, 2010); Willy Maley, *Salvaging Spenser: Colonialism, Culture and Identity* (London: Macmillan, 1997); and Patricia Coughlan, 'The Local Context of Mutabilitie's Plea', *Irish University Review* 26.2 (1996), 320–41.
4. Nicholas Canny, *Making Ireland British, 1580–1650* (Oxford University Press, 2001); Jason Harris and Keith Sidwell, eds., *Making Ireland Roman: Irish Neo-Latin Writers and the Republic of Letters* (Cork University Press, 2009); Hiram Morgan, '"Making Ireland Spanish": The Political Writings of Philip O'Sullivan Beare', in *Making Ireland Roman*, ed. Harris and Sidwell, pp. 86–108; Jane Ohlmeyer, *Making Ireland English: The Irish Aristocracy in the Seventeenth Century* (New Haven, CT: Yale University Press, 2012).
5. Jane Grogan, 'Introduction', in *Celebrating Mutabilitie*, ed. Grogan, p. 9.
6. Andrew Boorde, *The Fyrst Boke of the Introduction of Knowledge*, 2nd edn (London, 1555), sigs C2v, G3r, C4r, respectively.
7. William Shakespeare, *King Henry V*, ed. T. W. Craik (London: Routledge, 1995), III, ii, l. 124 (repeated l. 126). See also, *inter alia*, Stephen O'Neill, *Staging Ireland: Representations in Shakespeare and Renaissance Drama* (Dublin: Four Courts Press, 2007); Andrew Murphy, *But the Irish Sea Betwixt Us: Ireland, Colonialism, and Renaissance Literature* (Lexington, KY: University Press of Kentucky, 1999); and Christopher Highley, *Shakespeare, Spenser, and the Crisis in Ireland* (Cambridge University Press, 1997).
8. *Masques of Difference: Four Court Masques by Ben Jonson*, ed. Kirsten McDermott (Manchester University Press, 2007), pp. 133, ll. 6–7; 138, ll. 119–20. See also later seventeenth-century examples of the rendering of Hiberno-English in verse, in Andrew Carpenter, ed., *Verse in English from Tudor and Stuart Ireland* (Cork University Press, 2003), pp. 495–96, 518–23, 563.
9. Brian Ó Cuív, 'An Elegy on Donnchadh Ó Briain, Fourth Earl of Thomond', *Celtica* 16 (1984), 87–105 (pp. 94–95, 97).

10. See also Richard McCabe, *Spenser's Monstrous Regiment: Elizabethan Ireland and the Poetics of Difference* (Oxford University Press, 2002), pp. 40–56. For the bond between Richard Boyle, first Earl of Cork, and the Gaelic poet Piaras Feiritéir, see Nicholas Canny, *The Upstart Earl: A Study of the Social and Mental World of Richard Boyle, First Earl of Cork, 1566–1643* (Cambridge University Press, 1982), pp. 127–28.

11. Sarah McKibben, *Endangered Masculinities in Irish Poetry, 1540–1780* (University College Dublin Press, 2010); Lesa Ní Mhunghaile, 'Bilingualism, Print Culture in Irish and the Public Sphere, 1700–c. 1830', in *Irish and English: Essays on the Irish Linguistic and Cultural Frontier, 1600–1900*, ed. James Kelly and Ciarán Mac Murchaidh (Dublin: Four Courts Press, 2012), pp. 218–42; Breandán Ó Buachalla, 'James Our True King: The Ideology of Irish Royalism in the Seventeenth Century', in *Political Thought in Ireland since the Seventeenth Century*, ed. D. G. Boyce, Robert Eccleshall, and Vincent Geoghegan (London: Routledge, 1993), pp. 7–35; Michelle O Riordan, *Irish Bardic Poetry and Rhetorical Reality* (Cork University Press, 2007).

12. Marc Caball, 'Culture, Continuity and Change in Early Seventeenth-Century South-West Munster', *Studia Hibernica* 38 (2012), 37–56 (p. 55).

13. See Eleanor Knott, *An Introduction to Irish Syllabic Poetry of the Period 1200–1600*, 2nd edn (Dublin: DIAS, 1966); Osborn Bergin, *Irish Bardic Poetry: Texts and Translations* (Dublin: DIAS, 1970).

14. Mícheál Mac Craith, 'Gaelic Ireland and the Renaissance', in *The Celts and the Renaissance: Tradition and Innovation*, ed. Glanmor Williams and Robert Owen Jones (Cardiff: University of Wales Press, 1990), pp. 57–89; Marc Caball, *Poets and Politics: Continuity and Reaction in Irish Poetry, 1558–1625* (Cork University Press, 1998).

15. Angela Bourke et al., eds., *The Field Day Anthology of Irish Writing*, Vols IV/V: *Irish Women's Writing and Traditions*, 2 vols (Cork University Press, 2002), IV, pp. 400–01, stanzas 8–16.

16. William J. Watson, ed., *Scottish Verse from the Book of the Dean of Lismore* (Edinburgh: Scottish Gaelic Texts Society, 1937), pp. 244–45. See also Máirín Ní Dhonnchadha, 'Courts and Coteries I, c. 900–1600' and 'Courts and Coteries II, c. 1500–1800', in *Field Day Anthology*, ed. Bourke et al., IV, pp. 293–303, 358–66.

17. Vincent Morley, 'The Irish Language', in *The Princeton History of Modern Ireland*, ed. Richard Bourke and Ian McBride (Princeton University Press, 2016), pp. 320–42 (p. 331); Morley, *The Popular Mind in Eighteenth-Century Ireland* (Cork University Press, 2017).

18. Mícheál Mac Craith, 'Literature in Irish, c. 1550–1690: From the Elizabethan Settlement to the Battle of the Boyne', in *The Cambridge History of Irish Literature*, ed. Margaret Kelleher and Philip O'Leary, 2 vols (Cambridge University Press, 2006), I, pp. 191–231 (pp. 197–214).

19. For example (and *inter alia*), Thomas O'Connor and Mary Ann Lyons, eds., *Irish Communities in Early Modern Europe* (Dublin: Four Courts Press, 2006)

and Declan M. Downey and Julio Crespo MacLennan, eds., *Spanish–Irish Relations through the Ages* (Dublin: Four Courts Press, 2008).

20. Micheline Walsh, 'Some Notes Towards a History of the Womenfolk of the Wild Geese' and 'Further Notes Towards a History of the Womenfolk of the Wild Geese', *The Irish Sword* 61 and 62 (1961–62), 98–106 and 133–45 respectively. Jerrold Casway, 'Heroines or Victims? The Women of the Flight of the Earls', *New Hibernia Review / Iris Éireannach Nua* 7.1 (2003), 56–74; Marie-Louise Coolahan, *Women, Writing, and Language in Early Modern Ireland* (Oxford University Press, 2010), pp. 128–39. Kerney Walsh's archive at the Cardinal Tomás Ó Fiaich Memorial Library, Armagh, offers a wealth of material for enterprising researchers.

21. Ciaran O'Scea, *Surviving Kinsale: Irish Emigration and Identity Formation in Early Modern Spain, 1601–40* (Manchester University Press, 2015), pp. 87–120; Thomas O'Connor, *Irish Voices from the Spanish Inquisition: Migrants, Converts and Brokers in Early Modern Iberia* (Basingstoke: Palgrave Macmillan, 2016), esp. pp. 179–96.

22. *Great Deeds in Ireland: Richard Stanihurst's* De Rebus in Hibernia Gestis, ed. John Barry and Hiram Morgan (Cork University Press, 2013); Philip O'Sullivan Beare, *The Natural History of Ireland*, trans. and ed. Denis O'Sullivan (Cork University Press, 2009); Morgan, '"Making Ireland Spanish"'; Clare Carroll, *Circe's Cup: Cultural Transformations in Early Modern Ireland* (Cork University Press, 2001).

23. Harris and Sidwell, *Making Ireland Roman*, pp. 4, 5.

24. *The Tipperary Hero: Dermot O'Meara's* Ormonius *(1615)*, ed. Keith Sidwell and David Edwards (Turnhout: Brepols, 2011); Pádraig Lenihan and Mark Stansbury, 'An Account of the Battle of Aughrim from the "Poema de Hibernia"', *Analecta Hibernica* 44 (2013), 51–76; *Poema de Hibernia: A Jacobite Latin Epic on the Williamite Wars*, ed. Pádraig Lenihan and Keith Sidwell (Dublin: Irish Manuscripts Commission, 2018).

25. Anne Fogarty, 'Literature in English, 1550–1690: From the Elizabethan Settlement to the Battle of the Boyne', in *The Cambridge History of Irish Literature*, ed. Kelleher and O'Leary, I, pp. 140–90 (p. 150).

26. See Coolahan, *Women, Writing, and Language*, pp. 228–37, for some examples.

27. Carpenter, *Verse in English*, pp. 135–38.

28. See Alan Fletcher, *Drama, Performance, and Polity in Pre-Cromwellian Ireland* (Cork University Press, 2000); Deana Rankin, *Between Spenser and Swift: English Writing in Seventeenth-Century Ireland* (Cambridge University Press, 2005).

29. Andrew Carpenter, ed., *Verse Travesty in Restoration Ireland:* Purgatorium Hibernicum *and* The Fingallian Travesty (Dublin: Irish Manuscripts Commission, 2013).

30. Thomas Herron, 'Pale Martyr: Politicizing Richard Stanihurst's *Aeneis*', in *Dublin and the Pale in the Renaissance, c. 1540–1660*, ed. Micheal Potterton and Thomas Herron (Dublin: Four Courts Press, 2011), pp. 291–318; Patricia

Palmer, *The Severed Head and the Grafted Tongue: Literature, Translation and Violence in Early Modern Ireland* (Cambridge University Press, 2013).

31. See the discussion in Andrew Carpenter, ed., *Verse in English from Eighteenth-Century Ireland* (Cork University Press, 1998), pp. 6–23.

32. Richard Nugent, *Cynthia*, ed. Angelina Lynch and Anne Fogarty (Dublin: Four Courts Press, 2010); Henry Burnell, *Landgartha: A Tragie-Comedy*, ed. Deana Rankin (Dublin: Four Courts Press, 2014); *The Works of Walter Quin: An Irishman at the Stuart Courts*, ed. John Flood (Dublin: Four Courts Press, 2014).

33. Most currently, Julie A. Eckerle and Naomi McAreavey, eds., *Women's Life Writing and Early Modern Ireland* (Lincoln, NE: University of Nebraska Press, 2019).

34. John Temple, *The Irish Rebellion* (London, 1646); Brian Mac Cuarta, ed., *Ulster 1641: Aspects of the Rising* (Belfast: Institute of Irish Studies, 1993); Canny, *Making Ireland British*, pp. 461–550; David Edwards, Pádraig Lenihan, and Clodagh Tait, eds., *Age of Atrocity: Violence and Political Conflict in Early Modern Ireland* (Dublin: Four Courts Press, 2007); Nicci MacLeod and Barbara A. Fennell, 'Lexico-Grammatical Portraits of Vulnerable Women in War: The 1641 Depositions', *Journal of Historical Pragmatics* 13.2 (2012), 259–90; Annaleigh Margey, Eamon Darcy, and Elaine Murphy, eds., *The 1641 Depositions and the Irish Rebellion* (London: Pickering & Chatto, 2012).

35. David Aers, 'A Whisper in the Ear of Early Modernists; or, Reflections on Literary Critics Writing the "History of the Subject"', in *Culture and History, 1350–1600: Essays on English Communities, Identities and Writing*, ed. Aers (New York: Harvester Wheatsheaf, 1992), pp. 177–202.

36. Thomas Herron and Michael Potterton, eds., *Ireland in the Renaissance, c. 1540–1660* (Dublin: Four Courts Press, 2007); Potterton and Herron, *Dublin and the Pale*; Kathleen Miller and Crawford Gribben, eds., *Dublin: Renaissance City of Literature* (Manchester University Press, 2017).

37. *Calendar of State Papers, Ireland, 1509–1573*, p. 356.

38. Danielle Allen, 'Cicero Used to Be Boring. With Trump Around, he's Breathtaking', *The Washington Post*, 4 January 2017: www.washingtonpost.com/opinions/cicero-used-to-be-boring-with-trump-around-hes-breathtaking/2017/01/04/02043c1e-d2a3-11e6-9cb0-54ab630851e8_story.html?utm_term=.1f4c5cd27bff [accessed 2 August 2017].

39. Juliet Fleming, 'Scraping By: Towards a Pre-Historic Criticism', *Postmedieval: A Journal of Medieval Cultural Studies* 3 (2012), 119–33 (p. 131).

CHAPTER 2

'We Irish': Writing and National Identity from Berkeley to Burke

Ian Campbell Ross

In the first decade of the eighteenth century, George Berkeley trenchantly rejected certain ideas in Lockean philosophy, and mathematics. 'We Irish men cannot attain to these truths ... I Publish this ... to know whether other men have the same Ideas as we Irishmen.'[1] Whatever Berkeley's meaning, these remarks famously influenced W. B. Yeats's engagement with writers of the Irish eighteenth century, helping shape his own understanding of Irish nationality.[2] Having formerly refused to consider Berkeley or Burke as 'Irish' at all, Yeats later seized on Berkeley's remarks as 'the birth of the modern Irish intellect', declaring that the philosophy of Berkeley and Burke might form the basis of 'the whole life of a nation'.[3] A quite different, though equally essentialist, view was expressed sixty years later when another Protestant Irishman, the distinguished historian J. C. Beckett, writing on 'Literature in English' in the magisterial *New History of Ireland: Eighteenth-Century Ireland, 1691–1800* (1986), dismissed the very notion of even an 'Anglo-Irish' literature, arguing that Irish-born writers of the eighteenth century were 'self-consciously English in tradition and culture'.[4] Just a year earlier, Richard Kearney, in the 'Introduction' to *The Irish Mind* (1985), recognised that 'The existence of an Irish mind has frequently been contested': a position his edited collection sought to redress.[5] In *A History of Irish Thought* (2002), Thomas Duddy confronted the similar objections he encountered – to the effect that 'there really is no such thing as Irish thought' – arguing that 'There is ... such a thing as Irish thought, but it cannot be characterised in imperially nationalistic terms, or in any terms that presuppose privileged identities or privileged periods of social and cultural evolution.'[6]

Any consideration of Irish writing and national identity between 1700 and 1780 must, in fact, recognise that the terminology used to describe the different cultural groupings on the island is of dizzying complexity. Older terms such as 'Old English', 'New English', or 'mere Irish' gave way to starker ethnic or confessional divisions: 'English' and 'Irish', 'Protestant' and 'Papist'. In the years following the Williamite settlement of 1691, the Anglican elite might speak of themselves as 'the true English people of Ireland' in opposition to the 'savage old Irish'.[7] Yet despite doubts that lingered throughout the century, English-speaking men and women, of English settler background, increasingly referred to themselves as 'Irish'.

That they could do so depended in part on the eighteenth century's broad understanding of what constituted a 'nation'. Ephraim Chambers's *Cyclopædia* (1728) reads: 'NATION, a Collective Term, used for a considerable People, inhabiting a certain Extent of Ground, enclosed within certain limits, and under the same Government'. First offered in England in 1728, and repeated in every edition of the *Cyclopædia*, the definition was translated verbatim into French in the *Encyclopédie* of Diderot and d'Alembert. Prestigiously diffused throughout Britain, Ireland, and Europe more generally, this definition strikingly makes no reference to ethnicity, language, or religion.[8]

In practice, recent literary studies of the eighteenth century have (silently) employed similarly broad definitions, with their possibilities for a pluralist understanding of the nation that became explicit with the United Irishmen in the 1790s and the Young Ireland movement of the 1840s.[9] Such studies are informed also by the challenge over recent decades to traditional understandings of literary canonicity, extending their subject matter far beyond the impoverished understandings of 'literature' that developed in tandem with Romantic nationalism. So, we see new or fresh emphasis on, for instance, philosophy, political discourse, history – including literary and book history – along with women's writing and popular literature, illuminated by diverse, though often conflicting, theoretical approaches, among which postcolonialism has been especially influential (and problematic). Irish writing has also been open to a linguistic pluralism that includes work in Irish, English, Hiberno-English, Anglo-Norman, French, Latin, and Ulster-Scots. Such work has benefitted massively from important revisionist – and counter-revisionist – historical investigations of eighteenth-century Ireland.

In 1982, David Berman offered a version of Irish thought that paradoxically stressed unity in diversity, arguing that writers of the early eighteenth century holding very different positions on a philosophical question with far-reaching religious and political consequences were simultaneously giving expression to a peculiarly Irish identity.[10] It was, Berman argued, the radical challenge posed by John Toland's *Christianity Not Mysterious* (1696) that brought about a Golden Age of Irish philosophy.

By denying religious mysteries – 'nothing ought to be call'd a Mystery, because we have not an adequate Idea of all its Properties, nor any at all of its Essence' – Toland divided contemporaries into competing Enlightenment and Counter-Enlightenment camps.[11] The latter included George Berkeley, William King, Peter Brown, Edward Synge the Elder, Philip Skelton, and Jonathan Swift, who all published replies to a work that struck at the heart of the confessional state in which they lived, since the privileging of Anglicanism over Roman Catholicism was significantly dependent on those religious mysteries whose very existence Toland sought to deny. Besides Toland, Enlightenment thinkers included the Presbyterian minister Francis Hutcheson and, later, the maverick Church of Ireland Bishop of Clogher, Robert Clayton. Subsequently, the idea of an Irish Enlightenment has attracted several scholars, most recently Michael Brown, whose *The Irish Enlightenment* (2016) offers a tripartite division of the eighteenth century into a religious enlightenment (1688–*c.* 1730), social enlightenment (*c.* 1730–60), and political enlightenment (*c.* 1760–98), while stressing infra-denominational disputes, social differences in the public and private spheres, and a political culture that concluded with an 'enlightened civil war'.[12]

After the Irish parliament ordered *Christianity Not Mysterious* to be burned, Toland spent most of his life in England or in continental Europe. Yet though his later concerns were in no way narrowly national – he gave 'Cosmopoli' as the supposed place of publication of one of his works – Toland remained imaginatively and personally engaged with Ireland. In *Nazarenus* (1718), he drew on his knowledge of early Irish language and culture to offer a provocative account of ancient Irish Christianity, supposedly characterised by the beliefs of the 'Keldees' (i.e. Culdees), an order of lay religious, as both deistical and anti-Roman, and in *An Account of the Druids* (1726) he argued that the ancient Irish were no more ignorant or barbarous than the ancient Greeks and Romans. Toland also showed a particular pride in his own Irish identity, in 1708 procuring from Franciscan friars of the Irish College in Prague a testimonial declaring him to have been born on the Inishowen Peninsula to an ancient, noble, and honourable family.[13]

George Berkeley, meanwhile, has been seen as representing a middle way between the extremes of Enlightenment and Counter-Enlightenment Irish philosophy.[14] Having composed his 'Philosophical Commentaries', while a Fellow of Trinity College in Dublin, where *A Theory of Vision* (1709) and *Treatise Concerning the Principles of Human Knowledge* (1710) were published, Berkeley spent some years in London, where *Three Dialogues between Hylous and Philonous* (1713) appeared. After an extended continental tour, he returned to Trinity College, taking his doctorate in divinity in

1721. Later, Berkeley spent time in Rhode Island, planning an ideal city with a university on Bermuda, returning to Ireland and becoming Bishop of Cloyne in 1734. It was during this period of his life, in which he wrote, besides much else, *Alciphron* (1732) and *Siris* (1744), that Berkeley revealed his continuing social and economic concern with Ireland. As a Church of Ireland bishop, he authored two addresses to clergy and people, and to the Roman Catholics, of his diocese, urging loyalty to the Hanoverian state at the time of the 1745 Jacobite Rebellion. As a Protestant Irish patriot and improver, Berkeley concerned himself over many years with the means by which Ireland's inhabitants might become more prosperous, producing *The Querist* (1735–37; final edn, 1752), which takes the form of a series of, eventually, over 900 questions, designed to provoke his fellow Irishmen and women into considering how to effect the economic improvement he and his contemporaries desired.[15]

Not all of Berkeley's contemporaries were so quick to refer to 'we Irish', and Berkeley himself later distinguished himself from 'our Irish natives' and 'the common Irish'.[16] In grappling with the question of eighteenth-century Irish writing and national identity, no figure has been more widely or more variously discussed than Jonathan Swift. Born, posthumously, to a father who had settled in Ireland less than a decade before his birth, Swift was capable of stating (untruthfully) that he was born in England and referring to his life as 'an obscure exile in a most obscure and enslaved country'.[17] Yet when, in the 1720s, Swift became the centre of Irish political and economic resistance to England, with *A Proposal for the Universal Use of Irish Manufacture* (1720) and *The Drapier's Letters* (1724–25), he was acclaimed as the 'Hibernian Patriot'. We may believe that had Swift obtained a 'Lean Bishoprick, or a fatt Deanery' in England, he might have abandoned Ireland, never to return.[18] Certainly, it is not necessary to believe, for a moment, that Swift seriously intended to foment a 'national' uprising against England when, in his *Proposal for the Universal Use of Irish Manufacture*, he urged his fellow countrymen and women to burn '*every Thing that came from* England, *except their* People *and their* Coals', though the inflammatory phrase he added – 'Nor am I *even yet* for lessening the Number of those Exceptions' – certainly played on English fears.[19] Likewise, one need not overemphasise the significance of Swift's addressing his fourth *Drapier's Letter* to 'The Whole People of Ireland', while recognising that the alleged debasement of copper coinage was among the few issues that might truly have united Irish men and women of all confessions and social classes: '*Money*, the great *Divider* of the *World*, hath, by a strange Revolution, been the great *Uniter* of a most *Divided* People.'[20]

The issue of whether Swift may be seen as a representative figure whose attitudes and beliefs typify his age and class has proved almost as contentious as the question of whether the Ireland in which he lived is best understood as part of the European *ancien régime* or a colony. Yet while Sean Connolly has argued that Swift displayed a 'confused and contradictory sense of national identity', Anthony Pagden and Nicholas Canny ascribed to eighteenth-century colonists everywhere an identity which was 'very uneven, always incomplete, and at times perilously fragile'. This is not to suggest it is a matter of indifference whether eighteenth-century Ireland is best understood as a kingdom (sharing a monarch with England, later Great Britain) or a colony, only that Swift's identity is equally precarious but no less importantly 'Irish'.[21]

Swift thought – or pretended to think – Irish politics could interest no one outside of the island. Writing to Alexander Pope, he dismissed his powerful *A Short View of the State of Ireland* (1728; reprinted as *Intelligencer*, 15), along with the nineteenth *Intelligencer* essay, on the Irish coinage, as containing 'only a parcel of facts relating purely to the miseries of Ireland, and wholly useless and unentertaining'.[22] Similarly, Swift disparaged his public role in Irish affairs, ending: 'And this is enough for Irish Politicks, which I only mention, because it so nearly touches myself – a tenderness that reveals itself as raw in the conclusion of *A Modest Proposal*, written in the same year, where Swift concludes that the Proposer's savage remedy to Irish poverty is calculated *'for this one individual Kingdom of IRELAND, and for no other that ever was, is, or, I think, ever can be upon Earth'*.[23]

Swift's relentless self-deprecation in his later years tends rather to confirm than deny his identification with Ireland. The example of patriotic engagement he set was quickly adopted by other Protestant Irishmen, including Thomas Sheridan, Samuel Madden, and Thomas Prior. Attempting to shame Irish landowners who spent most of their lives in England, Prior's *List of Absentees* (1729) was one of the most notable contributions to contemporary writing on Irish social and economic affairs. By the 1720s, those who had referred to themselves thirty years earlier as the 'Protestants of Ireland' or 'the English gentlemen of this kingdom' might call themselves 'Irish gentlemen', while remaining firmly attached to Protestant values.[24] For the most part, they believed their privileged position in Ireland to be dependent on the political, religious, educational, and professional subordination of Roman Catholics (and to a lesser extent Presbyterians). Attempts to secure Protestant ascendancy involved both the penal legislation enacted raggedly between 1695 and 1759 and (ineffectual) attempts to convert Roman Catholics, by means of the

Charter Schools movement that began in 1733. Even so, attempts at rapprochement between those of different confessions started at least as early as the 1720s, in the actions and writings of a benevolent Protestant such as Bishop Edward Synge, in his 1725 sermon on toleration, the Whig commonwealth man Robert Molesworth, or the Presbyterian James Arbuckle, whose arguments were advanced under the pointedly national name of 'Hibernicus'. Roman Catholics argued their case also, in Cornelius Nary's *The Case of the Roman Catholics* (1724) and Lord Delvin's ill-fated address of loyalty on the occasion of the accession of George II in 1727. It was only with the founding, by Charles O'Conor and John Curry, of the Catholic Committee in 1760 that Catholic voices began, and then only slowly, to be heard clearly, and the Committee only became fully active in the revolutionary decade of the 1790s. Though mostly in abeyance, the penal legislation was not completely dismantled until Catholic Emancipation in 1829.

Notwithstanding this deeply divided legal and political context, variously acknowledged or silently assumed, Protestant writers continued to assert a distinct Irish literary identity. Swift lamented the fact that Irish readers and audiences of the early decades of the century preferred the productions of English-born writers, however mediocre, and James Arbuckle reminded readers that many distinguished 'English' writers were, in fact, natives of Ireland. Early attempts to offer national histories of Irish writing can be seen in W. R. Chetwood's *A General History of the Stage (More Particularly the Irish Theatre)* ... (1749) and in Paul Hiffernan's *The Hiberniad* (1754), which praised the 'extraordinary talents' of Irish writers, including James Ussher, John Denham, Roscommon, Boyle, Congreve, Southerne, Steele, Farquhar, Berkeley, Parnell, Swift, Constantia Grierson, Mary Barber, Laetitia Pilkington, and Turlough O'Carolan. Though we can be sure that these eminent figures did not hold any shared sense of national identity, the list is remarkable for its breadth, and freedom from religious or gender prejudice. A much shorter list of Irish writers was advanced by the founder of comparative literature, the Italian Carlo Denina who, in his *Discorso sopra le vicende di ogni letteratura* (1760; 2nd edn, 1763), rejected the notion that the best writing in English could be found only in England, evidencing the eminence of contemporary Scottish literature, and suggesting that soon 'IRELAND might become the seat of literature and science', citing 'the example of USSHER, SWIFT, BERKELEY, HUTCHESON'.[25] In different ways, both the Catholic Hiffernan and the Italian priest proposed the literary merit of (mainly) Protestant writing in English as a source of 'national pride': a phrase that would circulate widely throughout Europe with the publication of the Swiss Johann Georg Zimmermann's *Von dem Nationalstolze* (1758; trans. *On National Pride*, 1771).

It has been the challenge to canonicity – aided more recently by access to proliferating databases – that has made the range of Irish writing 1700–80 increasingly visible. In the mid-eighteenth century, Irish-born writers were active in prose, poetry, and the drama, articulating distinctive, if frequently contradictory, forms of national identity. Irish verse of the eighteenth century is a case in point, for we have a greatly enhanced awareness of the extent to which Irish poets, male and female, writing in coteries or directly for publication, in magazine or book form, were concerned to present in verse Irish themes, places, and experiences for an Irish public.[26] This they did not only in English but, from William Starrat at the end of the first quarter of the eighteenth century to Samuel Orr, Samuel Thomson, and other radicals of its final decades, in Ulster-Scots also.[27] Such poetry, like that written in Hiberno-English, speaks vividly of writers' consciousness of working outside of the increasingly standardised English of England itself. Unsurprisingly, much eighteenth-century verse, drawing on classical forms or models – epic, satire, pastoral – follows, and some-times anticipates, English verse of the same period. But Swift's extensive body of poetry – comprehensively revalued in the late 1970s and early 1980s – suggests the author's divided identity. When in England at the end of Queen Anne's reign, he wrote successfully for a London readership, in *Description of the Morning* (1709) and *Description of a City Shower* (1710). In Ireland, as a young or much older man, he addressed himself to Irish readers: writing public verse, from *Ode to the King* to *The Legion Club* (1731), and private poems to friends such as Thomas Sheridan, Charles Ford, or the Achesons of Market Hill, besides such unexpected poems as *O'Rourke's Feast* (1720), after Hugh MacGauran's *Pléaráca na Ruarcach*.

Other poets wrote equally with an eye on classical or English models and Irish themes, as did William Dunkin in his comic poems *The Murphaeid* (1728), in Latin and English translation, and *The Parson's Revels* (written 1746), in Hiberno-English. The rural landscape is reflected in the much-reprinted *Hesperi-Neso-graphia; or, A Description of the Western Isle* (1716), Murrough O'Connor's 'A Description of the County of Kerry' (1726), and Dominick Kelly's 'Battle of the Chaunters, fought near Castleblakeney in the County of Galway, July 27th, 1767' (1770). The urban scene is evoked imaginatively in Swift's 'To Charles Ford, Esq. On his Birthday' (1723), with its recreation of London in Dublin, or described admiringly, as in Laurence Whyte's *A Poetical Description of Mr. Neal's New Musick-Hall in*

Fishamble-Street, Dublin (1740) or *On the Hospital for Lying-in-Women, erected in Dublin* (1749) by Henry Jones, the 'bricklayer poet of Drogheda'. If none of these has had the continuing appeal of the best-known poem of the eighteenth century by an Irish writer, Oliver Goldsmith's *The Deserted Village* (1770), then it has long been a matter of critical disagreement whether that poem should be understood to refer to the England of the 1760s when it was written or the Ireland of the 1730s of the author's boyhood. As eighteenth-century Irish verse has been made visible once more, women's writing has been brought out of the shadows in which it long lingered. From Mary Monck, writing as 'Marinda', or Mary Davys at the beginning of the century, through Constantia Grierson and Mary Barber in mid-century, to Dorothea du Bois and Olivia Elder, writing in the 1760s and 1770s, we find a substantial body of poetry that illuminates overlooked female experience – generally private rather than public – in eighteenth-century Ireland. Such experience has only in recent decades begun to be valued in poetry and contemporary doubts about the propriety of women writing, still less publishing their work – along with a more general tendency towards anonymous publication of verse – means that the identity of many female poets is altogether beyond recall.

Much the same could be said of prose fiction. Early works that assert an Irish identity include the anonymous *Vertue Rewarded; or, The Irish Princess* (1693) while *Irish Tales* (1716) – which draws material from Geoffrey Keating's *Foras Feasa ar Éirinn*, circulating only in manuscript – is ascribed to a Sarah Butler, whose own identity is obscure in the extreme. Both novels offer positive images of Irish past and present but do so in directly contrasting ways. The former, set in Clonmel in the summer of 1690, offers a positive Protestant vision of the approaching Williamite victory; *Irish Tales*, conflating episodes from ninth- and eleventh-century Irish resistance to Danish invasion, culminating at the Battle of Clontarf, is a Roman Catholic, Jacobite romance. Such national works were exceptional for their period, but as the 'new species of writing' blossomed in the mid-century, Irish writers began to offer overtly national works, in imitation of French as well as English and Scottish models. The hero of William Chaigneau's *The History of Jack Connor* (1752) is born of mixed Protestant and Catholic parentage – a fact crucial to his understanding of his own identity within Ireland – and when he leaves the country for England, he changes his name to Conyers, to avoid anti-Irish prejudice. Of Huguenot background, Chaigneau argued that Ireland could prosper through responsible landownership, agricultural improvement, and the work of the Irish Charter Schools. *Jack Connor* was well received in England as well as

Ireland, and one London reviewer praised Chaigneau's 'smart reprisals' against the English for their 'national' prejudices against the Irish.[28]

Less obviously characteristic of Irish or English literature is Thomas Amory's *The Life of John Buncle, Esq.* (1756–66), which creates a memorable fiction extolling the virtues of its author's Unitarian beliefs, from a patchwork of quotations from other writers. The work is held together by Buncle's first-person narrator who insists that his own identity can only be understood by considering that he was 'born in London, and carried an infant into Ireland, where I learned the Irish language, and became intimately acquainted with its original inhabitants'.[29] Buncle's experience cannot be taken as an accurate representation of Amory's but the novel contains vivid glimpses both of Dublin in the early decades of the eighteenth century and of the Gaelic world in Kerry. The personal identity of John Buncle could never be described as representative of his, or any other, age but Amory's national identity – was he English or Irish? – was debated at length as late as 1788–89 in the pages of the *Gentleman's Magazine*. More familiar, as sentimental fiction of the mid-century, is Frances Sheridan's *The Memoirs of Miss Sidney Bidulph* (1761–67), which offers a harrowing representation of female experience in a patriarchal society, and ends by revealing its protagonist caught between virtue and sentiment: the cold comforts of an unfaithful English husband and the warm attractions of the Irish admirer whom she loves. Like other Irish authors of the period, Sheridan was capable of writing in forms that do not speak directly of her Irish identity, and *The History of Nourjahad* (1767) is a much-admired example of the fashionable oriental tale. Orientalism, however, was increasingly important in burgeoning Irish antiquarian studies and *Nourjahad*'s subject – the just ruler – is also that of *The History of Arsaces, Prince of Betlis* (1774), by Charles Johnston. The Limerick-born Johnston remains best known for *Chrysal; or, the Adventures of a Guinea* (1760–65), whose 'it-narrator' derives from the work of the unorthodox Bishop Robert Clayton. Johnston's last fictions, *John Juniper* (1781) and *Anthony Varnish* (1786), portray their Irish protagonists both at home and abroad.

The engagement by authors of Gothic fiction with issues of confessional and national identity has been vigorously, though variously, argued by recent critics who emphasise the impact Sir John Temple's *The Irish Rebellion* (1646) – an account of the Catholic rebellion of 1641 with its attendant (though hugely exaggerated) massacres of Protestants – had on the Protestant imagination in the years following the foundation of the Catholic Committee. Thomas Leland's *Longsword* (1762) is now widely accepted as the first Gothic novel in English, while Elizabeth Griffith in the 1760s and 70s, and Anne Fuller and Anna Millikin in the 1780s, offer precedents for such successors as Regina Maria Roche and Charles Robert Maturin.[30] Elizabeth Sheridan's epistolary *The Triumph of Prudence over Passion* (1781), by contrast, combines the familiar form of the marriage-plot novel with an engagement with both national and gender politics on the part of its central character, Louisa Mortimer. The novel opens with a vivid portrayal of one of the best-known moments in recent Irish history: the gathering of the Volunteers on Dublin's College Green – between the Parliament House and Trinity College – on 4 November 1779, during the Free Trade debate that would terminate in 1782 with the granting of enhanced powers to the Irish parliament. Sheridan's fiction concludes with Louisa's determination to assert not only female rationality and the right of women to participate in political life but her own independence, when she defies the conventions of the marriage-plot novel by declining to marry the (amiable) admirer who has courted her throughout. When *The Triumph of Prudence over Passion* was published in London in 1783, it was misleadingly renamed *The Reconciliation* but given the revealing subtitle, 'An Hibernian Tale'. Later novels too, including *The Fair Hibernian* (1789) and *The Irish Heiress* (1797), would flaunt their national preoccupations, anticipating more famous works, such as Maria Edgeworth's *Castle Rackrent: An Hibernian Tale* (1800) or Sydney Owenson (Lady Morgan)'s *The Wild Irish Girl: A National Tale* (1812).[31]

In the mid-century, the literary tastes of Irish readers, though closely related to those of readers in England, were beginning to favour Irish authors, settings, and themes. One anonymous English Gothic novel, *The History of Amanda* (1758), was published (probably piratically) in Dublin two years later, retitled *The Adventures of Sophia Berkley*, and given Irish characters and settings. Tobias Smollett's praise of David Garrick's acting of his most notable role, Richard III, in *Sir Launcelot Greaves* (1760–61) was silently altered in the novel's Dublin edition to laud the Irish actor Spranger Barry's portrayal of his most celebrated role, Othello. Novels by William Chaigneau and Frances Sheridan, among others, were notably more popular in Ireland than in England – though both sold well and were critically praised there – and while the fact that the 1709 Copyright Act did not apply in Ireland meant that Irish booksellers often published English and Scottish fiction, with or without legal agreements, increasing numbers of novels were published in Dublin alone, so reflecting a situation that had long applied to Irish verse.

While prose fiction manifested authors' national identity in an uneven and sometimes oblique manner, the case of drama is different. The performance of Irish identity – in the persona of the untrustworthy, buffoon-like, brogue-ridden Stage Irishman – is one of most widely discussed features of eighteenth-century theatrical life, and the period 1700–80 represents a transitional moment between the hostile representations of the Restoration and the increasing subversion of the negative stereotype that became commonplace in the final decades of the eighteenth century. Indeed, the Stage Irishman was so well known in the eighteenth century that Irish characters in realistic fiction often find themselves exhorted to behave according to the stereotype, as happens to Jack Connor, the daughter of whose first London employer 'often insisted on his making *Bulls* and *Blunders*', while making fun of his Hibernicisms. Early examples of the Stage Irishman in Thomas Shadwell's *Teague O Divelly* (1681) or Farquhar's *The Beaux' Stratagem* (1707) were challenged even by Farquhar himself, in *Love and a Bottle* (1698), and again by Thomas Sheridan in *The Brave Irishman* (1743) and Charles Macklin in *Love à la Mode* (1759) and *The True-Born Irishman* (1762). Negative representations were slow to disappear, however, and Hugh Kelly and Richard Brinsley Sheridan, most notoriously with Sir Lucius O'Trigger in *The Rivals* (1775), were among later Irish dramatists to employ them. Other playwrights meanwhile, including Richard Griffith, Elizabeth Griffith, and John O'Keeffe, offered positive characterisations of Irish men and women on the London stage.

It was the cultural dominance of London within the archipelago that did most to shape dramatic representations of Irishness in the eighteenth-century theatre. For most of the period surveyed here, Dublin had only a single theatre – the Theatre Royal, Smock Alley – making it almost impossible for dramatists to make a career at home. The Aungier Street Theatre that opened in 1734 was soon merged with Smock Alley, long managed by Thomas Sheridan, and it was not until 1758 that Dublin acquired a second theatre, managed by Spranger Barry, in Crow Street. Both Sheridan and Barry were notable actors in different genres, but the Stage Irishman continued to be popular enough in England for certain actors such as John Moody and John Johnstone, known as 'Irish Johnstone', to make their names in performing their national identity for the benefit of English audiences.

The small number of Dublin theatres did not, however, mean a lack of a lively theatrical life or an absence of successful Irish dramatists. Sheridan and Goldsmith are remarkable as authors of some of the very few eighteenth-century plays in English never to have fallen out of the repertory, but Farquhar, Steele, Arthur Murphy, and Hugh Kelly all enjoyed contemporary theatrical success; between 1720 and 1745, Dublin performances of Farquhar's plays were exceeded only by those of Shakespeare and Colley

Cibber. William Philips asserted his *St. Stephen's Green* (1700) to be a play for 'our Irish stage' and, similarly expressing a preference for Irish scenes, Charles Shadwell set *Irish Hospitality* (1717/18) in Finglas. In mid-century, Thomas Sheridan declared that 'I look upon the Country where a Man is born to be the Place pointed out by Providence for his Scene of Action.'[32] Irish political plays were also occasionally produced. John Michelburne's *Ireland Preserv'd; or, the Siege of London-Derry* (1705) and Robert Ashton's *The Battle of Aughrim* (1728) recalled the Williamite wars to audiences and readers alike; there were sixteen editions of the latter published in the eighteenth century and ten editions of the former appeared between 1705 and 1774.[33] In the years surrounding the Declaratory Act (1720), Charles Shadwell's *Rotherick O'Connor* (1719) offered a (subdued) Hanoverian gloss on the Anglo-Norman invasions while William Philips's *Hibernia Freed* (1722) is a Catholic and Jacobite dramatisation of events previously represented in Sarah Butler's *Irish Tales*. The self-consciously 'patriotic' decades of the 1770s saw Gorges Edmond Howard's *The Siege of Tamor* (1773) and Francis Dobbs's *The Patriot King; or Irish Chief* (1774). It would be a mistake to imagine that only plays set in Ireland or with Stage Irishmen articulate any notion of Irish identity, coherent or divided. Just as the reading public's taste in prose fiction offers an indication of a shifting sense of identity so, as Helen M. Burke has shown, the theatre itself offered a stage on which both factional and national identities might be performed.[34]

Poetry, prose fiction, and drama all reveal the articulation of national identity in the period 1700–80 to have been uneven, uncertain, and often contradictory. The career of Henry Brooke, who contributed notably to writing in many forms, suggests as much. Brooke was born around 1703 into a clerical family in County Cavan. Taught as a boy by Thomas Sheridan the elder, and educated at Trinity College, Dublin, Brooke left Ireland in 1724 to study law. Having subsequently spent seven years as a lawyer in Dublin, Brooke returned to London where his literary career flourished, particularly with the publication of a long, ambitious philoso-phical poem in heroic couplets, *Universal Beauty* (1735), praised by Pope. Brooke also published an admired translation of the first three books of Tasso's *Gerusalemme Liberata* (1738). Renown turned to notoriety when Brooke commenced his career as a dramatist. His *Gustavus Vasa; or, the Deliverer of His Country* (1739) gained the dubious distinction of being the first play banned under the 1737 Licensing Act, designed to prevent the theatrical satirising of the Prime Minister, Robert Walpole. The very choice of subject was provocative on Brooke's part, for Gustavus Vasa, who was elected king of Sweden in 1523 after helping free his country from Danish rule, was already a familiar figure in eighteenth-century political thought as a champion of 'Liberty', notably recalled in Robert Molesworth's radical *An Account of Denmark, as it was in the year 1692* (1694), a work that, by describing arbitrary power in a Lutheran state, appeared nearly as subversive of Protestant ascendancy as *Christianity Not Mysterious*. Though it could not be staged in England – in published form, the text attracted almost 1,000 subscribers – *Gustavus Vasa* was performed in Dublin in 1740 under the provocative name of *The Patriot*, a title that managed to evoke the 'patriotic' criticism of Walpole's long tenure of power, in line with the thought of Opposition Whigs, and the national antagonism between Ireland and England. Following *Betrayer of his Country* (1742; published as *The Earl of Westmoreland*) and the highly successful *The Earl of Essex* (1753), Brooke's *Jack the Giant-Queller* (1749), a ballad-opera containing Irish airs, saw the author supporting the ambiguously national politician Charles Lucas in his bid to enter parliament in the 1749 election; the play lasted for a single performance before being banned.[35]

Brooke's complex political and cultural loyalties are evident in other writings too. He contributed 'Constantia, or the Man of Law's Tale' to the Wexford-born George Ogle's modernised Chaucer in 1741 and, two years later, published a proposal for *Ogygian Tales: or, A curious collection of Irish Fables, Allegories, and Histories from the Relations of Fintane the Aged*, following the research (which he apparently intended to plagiarise) of the Catholic antiquarian Charles O'Conor. In 1744, Brooke proposed another work that failed to materialise: a history of Ireland from its beginnings. Such interest in Gaelic materials and early Irish history did not prevent Brooke from publishing the fiercely anti-Catholic *The Farmer's Six Letters to the Protestants of Ireland* (1745–46) at the time of the Jacobite Rebellion, or *The Spirit of Party* (1753), which further cooled relations with Charles O'Conor. Yet though he continued to publish further *Farmer's Letters* at intervals, a rapprochement occurred eight years later, when Brooke wrote *The Tryal of the Roman Catholics of Ireland*, in which, stimulated by O'Conor's role in the founding of the Catholic Committee, he argued for a relaxation of the Penal Laws. Long permanently resident in Ireland, Brooke published the first volume of his best-known work, the much admired sentimental novel, *The Fool of Quality* (1765–70), in Dublin – though the work's success led to subsequent volumes being first published in London, where the 1709 copyright laws better protected authors' interests. As a transitional figure in a transitional age, Henry Brooke may appear representative of his time and social class – though it would possibly be truer to say that he is representative in nothing but the confused and contradictory national identities he professed at various times of his life, in response to the conditions and changing political moments of the countries, Ireland and England, in which he found himself.

Today, Henry Brooke is better known perhaps as the father of Charlotte Brooke. It was with her father's encouragement – and that of Charles O'Conor, Sylvester O'Halloran and other Gaelic scholars of his acquaintance – that Charlotte Brooke began to interest herself in Gaelic verse of all kinds, leading to the publication of *Reliques of Irish Poetry* (1789), which offered English translations of Irish materials, along with versions of the originals. Charlotte Brooke also contributed to the antiquarian Joseph Cooper Walker's *Historical Memoirs of the Irish Bards* (1786) and the pioneering Irish-language journal *Bolg an tSolair* in 1795. *Reliques of Irish Poetry* nevertheless remains the best-known and most influential literary example of Irish antiquarianism, conducted by Protestants such as Edward Ledwich and Thomas Campbell, and Roman Catholics like Sylvester O'Halloran and Charles O'Conor, that found expression throughout the eighteenth century. As early as the 1710s, John Toland had written on ancient Ireland in *Nazarenus* and *An Account of the Druids*. In 1723, Dermot O'Connor published, perhaps with Toland's assistance, a translation of the *Foras Feasa ar Éirinn* by Seathrún Céitinn (Geoffrey Keating) a seventeenth-century historian of Old English (i.e. Catholic, Anglo-Norman) background, whose view of Irish history made its way, as has been mentioned, into eighteenth-century prose fiction and drama alike. The antiquarian debate of the later eighteenth century reveals the way in which often wild early theorising about origin myths developed into complex debates of European significance, including orientalism and primitivism, while attempting to articulate a national identity in ethnic, religious, and linguistic terms. Such debates, not least in the fraught decade of the 1790s, responded to the political moment, while slowly fostering the interest of polite readers, such as the Dublin salon hostess, Lady Moira, patron of Joseph Cooper Walker.[36]

How complex issues of national identity might be in the late eighteenth century is reflected in the career of the best-known Irish writer of the latter part of the eighteenth century, Edmund Burke. After studying in Trinity College, Dublin, Burke moved to London to study law, and quickly made his name in the English capital, as author of *A Philosophical Enquiry into the Origin of Our Ideas of the Sublime and Beautiful* (1757). The national impulses of this work have been variously understood as exhibiting elements of Burke's youthful response to the turbulent political situation in which he grew up and of his adoption of the theological representationalism of William King, Peter Browne, and Edward Synge, along with a belief in the emotive power of language, as advanced by George Berkeley.[37] In 1761, he returned to Ireland as secretary to the Irish Chief Secretary, William Hamilton, before entering the Westminster parliament in 1766. Politically, he is remembered today, especially following the publication of *Reflections on the Revolution in France* (1790), as the 'father of modern conservatism' – an arguably ironic fate for a man who defended the American colonists in the 1770s; led the impeachment of Warren Hastings of the East India Company; and lost his seat as member of parliament for Bristol as the result of his advocacy of free trade for Ireland in 1780. Burke had been born to a Roman Catholic mother from the Nagle family in County Cork, some members of whom were implicated in the Whiteboy trials of prominent Catholics in the 1760s, and received some Catholic education, though he professed the Anglicanism of his (possibly convert) father, a lawyer. In the 1760s, he wrote the first of his works urging a relaxation of the Penal Laws, notably in a petition to George III he co-authored with John Curry, which inspired a similar work by the Catholic Committee. As a result, during the Free Trade agitation and calls for legislative independence between 1779 and 1782, Burke was pilloried in England as, in a celebrated cartoon by James Gillray, a potato-eating Irishman and superstitious covert Jesuit.[38] His later Irish writings, meanwhile, such as the *Letter to Sir Hercules Langrishe* (1792), are characterised by his advocacy of a relaxation of the Penal Laws in order to protect the established order and prevent rebellion.[39]

The conflicted identity asserted by, or ascribed to, Burke reflects centuries of similar experience of a hyphenated identity. In the twelfth century, one Anglo-Norman lamented that 'just as we are English as far as the Irish are concerned, likewise to the English we are Irish'.[40] When, in Charles Johnston's *The Adventures of Anthony Varnish* (1786), the impoverished Irish protagonist first arrives in London, two gamblers facetiously place bets as to whether he is a foreigner. When Varnish tells them he is Irish, both claim to have won:

> 'I knew I was right, by G—d.' — 'Right!' says the other, 'how can that be! — we all know that Ireland is but an extraneous part of England; — isn't it, sir?' says he, looking me full in the face. — 'Yes, sir', replied I, half dead with confusion.[41]

English assurance and Irish confusion. In London, in *The Englishman*, Richard Steele wrote confidently: 'I am an *Englishman* born in the city of

Dublin.'[42] Writing from Dublin, Swift grudgingly accepted that national identity was beyond his personal control: 'I happened indeed by a perfect Accident to be born here . . . and thus I am a Teague, [or] an Irishman, or what People please.'[43] By the 1780s, Protestant and Catholic Irishmen and women might seek shared identity in the distant past that was the subject of antiquarian inquiry, in demands for legislative independence, or desire for increased religious toleration. Irish writing between 1700 and 1780 could never erase ethnic, religious, and political difference, yet, widely surveyed, it can still be seen to have moved, in complex, uneven, and contradictory ways, towards the halting articulation of a national identity.

Notes

1. George Berkeley, 'Philosophical Commentaries', in *The Works of George Berkeley, Bishop of Cloyne*, ed. A. A. Luce and T. E. Jessop, 9 vols (London: Thomas Nelson and Sons, 1948–57), I, p. 47.

2. On the question of Berkeley's meaning, see, variously, J. M. Hone and M. M. Rossi, with an introduction by W. B. Yeats, *Bishop Berkeley* (London: Faber & Faber, 1931); Dennis Donoghue, *We Irish: Selected Essays*, Vol. I (Berkeley, CA and London: University of California Press, 1986), p. 17; Scott C. Breuninger, 'Berkeley and Ireland: Who Are the "We" in "We Irish Think Otherwise"?', in *Anglo-Irish Identities, 1571–1845*, ed. David A. Valone and Jill Marie Bradbury (Lewisburg, PA: Bucknell University Press, 2008), pp. 104–25.

3. See, for example, W. B. Yeats, 'Introduction', in *A Book of Irish Verse* (London: Methuen, 1900), pp. xviii–xix; 'The Child and the State', in *The Senate Speeches of W. B. Yeats*, ed. Donald R. Pearce (1960; repr. London: Prendeville, 2001), p. 160. See also Donald T. Torchiana, *W. B. Yeats and Georgian Ireland* (Evanston, IL and London: Northwestern University Press and Oxford University Press, 1966), esp. ch. 6. For a re-reading of Yeats's engagement with Berkeley, see W. J. McCormack, *'We Irish' in Europe: Yeats, Berkeley and Joseph Hone* (Dublin: UCD Press, 2011).

4. J. C. Beckett, 'Literature in English, 1691–1800', in *A New History of Ireland*, Vol. IV: *Eighteenth-Century Ireland, 1691–1800*, ed. T. W. Moody and W. E. Vaughan (Oxford: Clarendon Press, 1986), pp. 424–70 (pp. 426, 425).

5. Richard Kearney, ed., *The Irish Mind: Exploring Intellectual Traditions* (Dublin: Wolfhound Press, 1985), p. 7.

6. Thomas Duddy, 'Preface', *A History of Irish Thought* (London and New York: Routledge, 2002), p. xii. Discussions of 'national' identity continue, however, to engage writers working in many disciplines, as in Tom Inglis's *Are the Irish Different?* (Manchester University Press, 2014).

7. The last denomination was used by Swift in 1737; see *The Correspondence of Jonathan Swift, D.D.*, ed. David Woolley, 5 vols (Frankfurt am Main: Peter Lang, 1999–2014), IV, p. 445.

8. Ephraim Chambers, 'Nation', in *Cyclopædia; or, An Universal Dictionary of Arts and Sciences*, 2 vols (London, 1728), II, p. 616.

9. See Thomas Davis on 'a nationality which may embrace Protestant, Catholic and Dissenter, Milesian and Cromwellian, the Irishman of a hundred generations, and the stranger who is within our gates', in 'Prospectus' to *The Nation* (1842). For particularly influential modern literary studies, see Seamus Deane, Andrew Carpenter, and Jonathan Williams, eds., *The Field Day Anthology of Irish Writing*, 3 vols (Derry: Field Day, 1991); Angela Bourke et al., eds., *The Field Day Anthology of Irish Writing*, Vols IV/V: *Irish Women's Writing and Traditions*, 2 vols (Cork University Press, 2002); and Margaret Kelleher and Philip O'Leary, eds., *The Cambridge History of Irish Literature*, 2 vols (Cambridge University Press, 2006).

10. See David Berman, 'Enlightenment and Counter-Enlightenment in Irish Philosophy', *Archiv für Geschichte der Philosophie* 64.2 (1982), 148–65; Berman, 'The Culmination and Causation of Irish Philosophy', *Archiv für Geschichte der Philosophie* 64.3 (1982), 257–79; Berman, *George Berkeley: Idealism and the Man* (Oxford: Clarendon Press, 1994); David Berman and Patricia O'Riordan, 'Introduction', in *The Irish Enlightenment and Counter-Enlightenment*, ed. Berman and O'Riordan, 6 vols (Bristol: Thoemmes, 2002), I, pp. vii–xxiii, esp. vii–xviii.

11. *John Toland's* Christianity Not Mysterious, ed. Philip McGuinness, Alan Harrison, and Richard Kearney (Dublin: Lilliput Press, 1997), p. 58.

12. Michael Brown, *The Irish Enlightenment* (Cambridge, MA and London: Harvard University Press, 2016).

13. *A Collection of Several Pieces of Mr. John Toland*, 2 vols (London, 1726), I, pp. v–vi.

14. See Berman, 'Enlightenment and Counter-Enlightenment', pp. 148–65; Berman and O'Riordan, 'Introduction', I, pp. vii–xviii; Duddy, *A History of Irish Thought*, esp. pp. 124–43.

15. *The Querist* was published in three parts, 1735–37; Berkeley subsequently revised it in 1750 and a final edition appeared in his *Miscellany* in 1752, the year before his death.

16. *The Querist* (Dublin, 1750), pp. 5, 17; Queries 19, 132.

17. Swift to Charles Wogan [1735]; *Correspondence*, ed. Woolley, IV, p. 272.

18. Peterborough to Swift (18 [*O.S.* 6] April 1711); *Correspondence*, ed. Woolley, I, p. 342.

19. [Jonathan Swift], *A Proposal for the Universal Use of Irish Manufacture* (Dublin, 1720), p. 6; when the pamphlet was reprinted in Faulkner's 4-volume edition of Swift's *Works* in 1735, long after the political context had ceased to be directly relevant, the phrase was replaced by one less minatory.

20. [Jonathan Swift], *A Letter to the Whole People of Ireland* (Dublin, 1724), p. 13.

21. S. J. Connolly, 'Swift and Protestant Ireland: Images and Reality', in *Locating Swift: Essays from Dublin on the 250th Anniversary of the Death of Jonathan Swift, 1667–1745*, ed. Aileen Douglas, Patrick Kelly, and Ian Campbell Ross (Dublin: Four Courts Press, 1998), pp. 28–46 (p. 41); S. J. Connolly, *Religion, Law, and*

Power: The Making of Protestant Ireland (Oxford: Clarendon Press, 1992), pp. 2–4; Anthony Pagden and Nicholas Canny, 'Afterword: From Identity to Independence', in *Colonial Identity in the Atlantic World, 1500–1800*, ed. Canny and Pagden (Princeton University Press, 1987), pp. 267–78 (p. 271).

22. Swift to Pope (12 June 1732); *Correspondence*, ed. Woolley, IV, pp. 30–31.

23. [Jonathan Swift], *A Modest Proposal* (Dublin, 1729), p. 14.

24. Roy Foster, *Modern Ireland, 1600–1972* (London: Allen Lane, 1988), p. 178.

25. Carlo Denina, *An Essay on the Revolutions of Literature*, trans. John Murdoch (London, 1771), pp. 284–85.

26. See, for instance, Patrick Fagan, ed., *A Georgian Celebration: Irish Poets of the Eighteenth Century* (Dublin: Branar, 1989); Bryan Coleborne, 'Anglo-Irish Verse, 1675–1825', in *The Field Day Anthology*, ed. Deane, Carpenter, and Williams, I, pp. 395–499; Andrew Carpenter, ed., *Verse in English from Eighteenth-Century Ireland* (Cork University Press, 1998).

27. See Frank Ferguson, ed., *Ulster-Scots Writing: An Anthology* (Dublin: Four Courts Press, 2008); Carol Baraniuk, *James Orr, Poet and Irish Radical* (2014; London: Routledge, 2016); Jennifer Orr, *Literary Networks and Dissenting Print Culture in Romantic-Period Ireland* (London: Palgrave Macmillan, 2015).

28. *The Monthly Review* VI (June 1752), 447.

29. Thomas Amory, *The Life of John Buncle, Esq.*, ed. Moyra Haslett (Dublin: Four Courts Press, 2011), p. 46.

30. Jarlath Killeen, *The Emergence of Irish Gothic Fiction: History, Origins, Theories* (Edinburgh University Press, 2014); Christina Morin, *The Gothic Novel in Ireland, c. 1760–1829* (Manchester University Press, 2018).

31. See also *Irish University Review* 41.1, Special Issue: *Irish Fiction, 1660–1830* (Spring/Summer 2011), *passim*; Aileen Douglas, 'The Novel before 1800', in *The Cambridge Companion to the Irish Novel*, ed. John Wilson Foster (Cambridge University Press, 2006), pp. 22–38.

32. Thomas Sheridan, 'Appendix', in *An Humble Appeal to the Publick, Together with Some Considerations on the Present Critical and Dangerous State of the Stage in Ireland* (Dublin, 1758), p. 40.

33. See Christopher Morash, 'Theatre in Ireland, 1690–1800', in *The Cambridge History of Irish Literature*, ed. Margaret Kelleher and Philip O'Leary, 2 vols (Cambridge University Press, 2006), I, pp. 372–406 (p. 395).

34. See Helen M. Burke, *Riotous Performances: The Struggle for Hegemony in the Irish Theater, 1712–1784* (University of Notre Dame Press, 2003), *passim*.

35. For Lucas and national identity, see Seán Murphy, 'Charles Lucas, Catholicism and Nationalism', *Eighteenth-Century Ireland / Iris an dá chultúr* 8 (1993), 83–102; for *Jack the Giant-Queller*, see Burke, *Riotous Performances*, pp. 159–65, 196–97.

36. See Clare O'Halloran, *Golden Ages and Barbarous Nations: Antiquarian Debate and Cultural Politics in Ireland, c. 1750–1800* (Cork University Press, 2004); Lesa Ní Mhunghaile, 'Anglo-Irish Antiquarianism and the Transformation of Irish Identity, 1750–1800', in *Anglo-Irish Identities, 1571–1845*, ed. David A. Valone and Jill Marie Bradbury (Lewisburg, PA:

Bucknell University Press, 2008), pp. 181–98; and Amy Prendergast, *Literary Salons across Britain and Ireland in the Long Eighteenth Century* (Basingstoke: Palgrave Macmillan, 2015), ch. 4.

37. Luke Gibbons, *Edmund Burke and Ireland: Aesthetics, Politics, and the Colonial Sublime* (Cambridge University Press, 2003), esp. pp. 6, 23–24; Berman and O'Riordan, 'Introduction', I, p. xix.

38. Nicholas K. Robinson, *Edmund Burke: A Life in Caricature* (New Haven, CT and London: Yale University Press, 1996), pp. 35–40.

39. See, for example, David Bromwich, *The Intellectual Life of Edmund Burke* (Cambridge, MA: The Belknap Press for Harvard University Press, 2014); Richard Bourke, *Empire and Revolution: The Political Life of Edmund Burke* (Princeton University Press, 2015).

40. Gerald of Wales, *Expugnatio Hibernica: The Conquest of Ireland*, ed. A. B. Scott and F. X. Martin (Dublin: Royal Irish Academy, 1978), p. 81.

41. Charles Johnston, *The Adventures of Anthony Varnish*, 3 vols (London, 1786), II, pp. 187–88.

42. Richard Steele, *The Englishman*, ed. Rae Blanchard (Oxford: Clarendon Press, 1955), p. 184.

43. Swift to Francis Grant (23 March 1733–34); *Correspondence*, ed. Woolley, IV, p. 229.

CHAPTER 3

Re-Viewing Swift

Brean Hammond

In order to re-view Swift, we must first view him. I take as my vantage point my own first serious view of Swift. When I was an undergraduate at Edinburgh University, the book most highly recommended by my tutors was Kathleen Williams's *Jonathan Swift and the Age of Compromise* (1958).[1] What view of Swift did Williams afford my callow former self? Although Williams claims on her first page that Swift is 'after all very like ourselves: ambitious, self-doubting, sometimes despondent and sometimes assertive and cheerful, and all these only in the common degree', just two pages later Williams notes that 'Swift was not that rare creature, the normal man' (pp. 1, 3). Disconcerted by this inconsistency, the young Hammond nevertheless read on and found the first mention of the 'middle way', which Swift, it seems, 'advocates in so many aspects of social and personal life' (p. 10). The extremes between which Swift was negotiating a middle way include those of deism and scepticism, championed by Shaftesbury and Mandeville. For Swift himself, though, religious faith itself was never in question, according to Williams. Acceptance of revealed religion is the only means at human disposal to counter the limitations of our nature and prompt us to act morally.

A similar spirit of compromise, expressing a desire to steer between opposite extremes, characterises Swift's attitude to politics: 'he seems never to have been a passionate party man' (p. 100), a statement swallowed whole by the young Hammond, but one that would now have to be masticated thoroughly. He is not a 'diehard Tory' and there is 'no sign in him of the Jacobitism which existed in the Tory ministry itself' (p. 101). In Williams's view, Swift's politics were founded upon venerating individuals such as Harley and not upon embracing ideologies such as those that distinguished Whigs from Tories. Men behaving badly, whether they be monarchs, noblemen, or commoners, affects the balanced constitution required by the smoothly functioning state. Swift perceives philosophical and political compromises to be necessary because human nature itself is complex and confused; and to make the best of what we have as human beings, we need to avoid the extremes of our own nature. Swift's satirical writings are conceived to teach us to do that. They have therefore a didactic function despite their apparent complexity. The *Tale of a Tub*, for example, instructs us to avoid both superficiality, which turns us into fools; and depth, which turns us into knaves. Thus the way is prepared for a 'soft' reading of *Gulliver's Travels,* according to which the Yahoos are not humans and the Houyhnhnms are not 'perfected human beings whom man should try to copy' (p. 177); but rather, human beings are, or can be at best, an 'acceptable and vital compromise between two sterile extremes' (p. 178). Williams concludes that 'Swift's careful selecting and adjusting among opposite systems brings him, time and again, to his one certainty in the traditional teachings of his church and the morality which they support' (p. 209).

For the purposes of re-viewing, the Williams account of Swift, enduring and influential in the continuing view of Swift as a mediating compromiser, an orthodox Anglican, is valuable for what it does *not* say about him. We can map the geography of our current view and assess our current state of knowledge by attending to what is omitted in the Williams construction. Nowhere in her account does Williams mention that Swift was an *Irish* writer who lived and worked in Ireland for the entirety of his life post-1714. She has no sense of 1714 as a watershed year for him. Swift's peers, artistically, are Sidney, Spenser, Dryden, and Pope; intellectually, they are Plato, the Stoics and Epicureans, Montaigne, Hobbes, Locke, Temple, Shaftesbury, Mandeville, and Bolingbroke – the last a particular target of Williams's vilification for his anti-religious, satirical brand of deism, which she believes to have had a corrosive influence upon Swift. Breathing this rarefied air, her Swift does not get down and dirty with English foreign policy during the last years of the French war. So eager is Williams to construct Swift as an orthodox, not-over-pious churchman that she simply cannot account for the ferocity and ardour of his attack on Dissenters and, to a lesser extent, on Roman Catholics. She seldom evinces curiosity about how Swift's words arrived on the page that she reads. How much did Swift himself have to do with the words that appear under his name? What relationships did he make with the printers who were, several of them, prosecuted for transmitting his ideas into print? What kind of a writer was he?

Williams also makes no use whatsoever of the *Journal to Stella* or of *The Intelligencer*, precious little of *The Examiner*, bravely reads the scatological poems though appears to consider the early Odes more significant than

Cadenus and Vanessa and *Verses on the Death of Dr. Swift* (the latter not discussed), makes a single passing reference to *The Drapier's Letters* and reads the tracts written in and about Ireland sparingly and selectively. Indeed, the account of Swift that she produces can be sustained only by an absence of bibliographical inquisitiveness and by restricting so drastically the canon of Swift's writing to which she will attend. The thrust of her argument renders Swift's famous *saeva indignatio* an embarrassment to her. At times, she is almost poignantly unequal to the task of writing about Swift, such as when she says of the proposal in *A Modest Proposal* that it is 'not only economically sound, it is humane, the only form of practical helpfulness left' (p. 132). The castrated Swift who emerges from Williams's literary surgery is the acceptably moderate writer and thinker that our canon-makers then wanted their featured authors to be – a faith-based moralist whose significant works sought to inculcate that morality in his readers.

My purpose is not to arraign the book at the bar of history and to gloat about how much more we now understand about Swift. Implied in the preceding paragraphs are three areas of Swift scholarship in which our current views can be calibrated against those of previous generations of readers: biography, Irish studies, and book history, to which I will now turn.

Biography

The challenge faced by Swift biographers is still that indicated by Ben Jonson in the 'Epistle To the ... Two Famous Universities' with which he prefaced *Volpone* in 1607, when he wrote of 'the impossibility of any man's being the good poet without first being the good man'.[2] Since the earliest accounts by Deane Swift, Lord Orrery, and Thomas Sheridan, biographers have disagreed as to whether Swift was a good man; *parti pris* on this moral question have conditioned literary judgments. Irvin Ehrenpreis's magisterial three-volume biography, completed in 1983, remains the one to which Swift scholars are most indebted.[3] The overall effect of his monumental work, however, has been to bolster the timid understanding of his subject that we have already observed in the Kathleen Williams approach. Ehrenpreis Freudianised his subject, to provide a (pseudo-) scientific understanding of Swift's personality, proving that actions seemingly not virtuous would appear so, or would at least be defensible, when the deep root causes of them were brought to light. As a later biographer, Leopold Damrosch, objects, this resulted in a formulaic identification of behavioural patterns, and the suppression of information inconvenient for the Freudian family romance:

> [Ehrenpreis] insisted that Swift's thinking and life were massively conventional – his views on religion, politics, and love were all tepidly middle of the road ... An older man – even if just a few years older – must be a father figure, or else resented for not being one. A woman Swift's age or older is a mother figure. And, inevitably, a younger woman is a daughter figure.[4]

Unsurprisingly, therefore, some Swiftian scholars considered that the job of writing Swift's biography needed to be redone the moment Ehrenpreis recorded his final full stop. How does one use a 2000-page biography? How does one recommend it to students and readers not hopeful of immortality? Ehrenpreis had produced a reference book, not a biography. Only two years later, in 1985, Oxford University Press published David Nokes's *Jonathan Swift, a Hypocrite Reversed* – a 'critical biography' that reviewers considered lived up to its name. Nokes did not write in direct opposition to Ehrenpreis. Indeed, his desire to understand Swift also results in the retention of much Freudian paraphernalia: 'The repeated reminder [in 'When I come to be Old'] to avoid falling in love with a young woman is the cry of a damaged sensibility that wishes to draw attention to its own damage.'[5] His approach is characterised, rather, by an apparent *dislike* of his subject. Contrary to Ehrenpreis, Nokes's psychological plumbing of Swift's depths disinters a personality with which his biographer has little sympathy. In part, the impact of Nokes's biography derived from a (selective) return of the repressed. Ehrenpreis had closed academic ranks upon biographical work done in the 1950s and 60s by Irish writers who did not hold university positions, their claims dismissed by him as the stuff of legend.[6] The story of Swift's secret marriage to Esther Johnson, for example, makes a triumphant return under Nokes's sponsorship (although he does not endorse the even more plausible idea that Esther Vanhomrigh was in a sexual relationship with Swift). Where Nokes makes his most potent contribution to Swiftian biography is in his conception of how hypocrisy signifies in accounting for the way Swift lived his life. His subtitle, 'a hypocrite reversed', borrows an aperçu from Bolingbroke: that Swift was so terrified of being thought a hypocrite, one who feigned and made a parade of his good qualities, that he concealed them and made himself appear much worse than he was. Going beyond this, Nokes's analysis of the *Argument [against] the abolishing of Christianity* voices a suspicion that may be of some significance:

> The evidence suggests that Swift's ambivalence towards father-figures in his
> life extended also to God, and inhibited him from truly believing in the
> personal love, for him, of God the Father. His instinct for playing the
> hypocrite in reverse may well have been an attempt to project outwards
> a deep sense of hypocrisy that he felt within himself. (p. 101)

'With friends like Nokes', one might say . . . but Nokes is here on the verge
of articulating the deep structural reasons for some of the difficulties and
paradoxes that Swift's writings present, as he is again when, for instance, he
writes that 'as a political demagogue, Swift was seriously limited by his
complete lack of faith in the Irish people to whom, ostensibly, he appealed'
(p. 296); and again when he discusses Swift's shuttling between liberal and
authoritarian approaches to the conditions of socio-political existence. In
the final analysis Nokes's biography remains bounded by the ethical
question of construing Swift's motives and evaluating his actions: was he
a good man, or was he not? In my view, we need to escape the limitations of
the ethical question to understand Swift adequately, a point to which I will
return.

Post-Nokes, a slow distillation of new knowledge has augmented our
understanding of Swift's ancestry and his dealings with the print industry in
particular, without radically transforming our view of him. We know more
about Swift's forebears – about, for example, his veneration for his Royalist
grandfather that is one crucible of his implacable hatred of dissenting
sectaries, and about his relationship with his mother. Occasionally, seemingly small additions to knowledge have had a surprisingly seismic effect,
as for example when we learn about Richard Coleire, the Man who Was
Gulliver (possibly); or note that the resonant name Gulliver may have been
a very late addition to the 1726 text, possibly deriving from a Banbury
innkeeper, Samuel Gulliver of The Dolphin.[7] David Woolley's re-edition
of Swift's letters, in publication since 1999 and completed with an index in
2014, makes the most significant contribution to biographical knowledge.[8]
This edition has rendered necessary and simultaneously enabled new assessments of Swift's life, work, and writing. Those have come in the form of
major biographies by Leopold Damrosch and Eugene Hammond, as well as
one that concentrates on Swift's politics, David Oakleaf's *A Political
Biography of Jonathan Swift*. Dustin Griffin's study of the relationship
between Swift and Pope, though specialised, is much more than
a biographical footnote.[9] All of the above draw on Woolley's notes, which
are less familiar to specialists than are the Harold Williams glosses. This
imparts freshness to studies for which the letters are the single most important source.

Damrosch goes further than Nokes in re-introducing what we might term the 'Dubliners' Swift' of the 1950s and 60s. According to Damrosch, Swift's name should really be Jonathan Temple, because he was the bastard son of Sir John Temple, for whose son Sir William (therefore his half-brother) he worked as a secretary between 1689 and 1699. Jonathan Temple/Swift *was* secretly married to [H]esther Johnson, whom he called 'Stella'. Since she was Sir William's illegitimate daughter, Swift was married to his own niece by whom he was rumoured to have had a bastard son. For at least fifteen years of his adult relationship with Stella, he conducted an explicitly sexual relationship with the woman he called 'Vanessa', Esther Vanhomrigh, by whom he was also rumoured to have had a bastard son. The story of Swift's having precipitated her death in 1723, when he informed her of his marriage to Stella, so vividly imagined by Sybil le Brocquy, is revived by Damrosch.[10] Bastardy runs through this account; indeed, readers might be tempted to consider Swift a bastard in the less technical sense. Damrosch, surprisingly perhaps, does not appear to think any the worse of him, denying that Swift was a misogynist and even more inconsistently, holding the line that Swift was an entirely orthodox Church of Ireland Protestant believer.[11] If he was, he was a supreme example of psychological compartmentalisation – of keeping one's private and public life in separate spheres – or worse, of hypocrisy. So Nokes's condemnatory term enters again through the back door. Damrosch finds himself defending the indefensible.

Eugene Hammond's two-volume biography published in 2016 returns us in some respects to Ehrenpreis's 'laundry-list' approach. Indeed, he outdoes Ehrenpreis in his seeming ambition to document every single day for which we have evidence of how Swift lived it. His account profits immensely from the Woolley edition of Swift's letters, which he reads with great sensitivity and intelligence. Yet his life of Swift is fissured by the fault line that we have observed to bedevil biographical writing. Hammond's Swift conducts himself in a fashion less inconsistent with his being an orthodox and devout Church of Ireland clergyman and believer than does Damrosch's Swift. This Swift was not married to Stella, nor was his parentage doubtful. But he was having a consummated affair with Esther Vanhomrigh, certainly after 1719, and the notorious references to coffee-drinking in the letters are indeed code for carnal sex. Yet Hammond expends much effort in getting Swift off hooks, demonstrating that his intentions were usually moral, or at the very least, excusable. Here, we might consider a small case study. In 1721–22, Swift wrote a poem entitled 'The Storm; or Minerva's Petition', attacking Josiah Hort, Bishop of Ferns, who had the reputation of being a whore-mongering atheist. One couplet reads: 'Since *Burnet*'s Death, the bishops' Bench, / 'Till Hort arriv'd ne'er kept a Wench'. Citing this, Hammond mildly comments: 'what Swift was thinking about his own recent practice with Hessy [Esther Vanhomrigh] remains a mystery'.[12] He does not cite Archbishop King's letter to Hort of 23 February 1723, in which King writes: '[Swift] most solemnly protests, that he has no concern in it and I verily believe him.' As Stephen Karian comments, Swift's is 'an artful and entirely false denial'.[13] Hammond is everywhere uneasy with the lengths to which Swift's malfeasance could go. He prefers to believe that Swift did not write 'The Life and Genuine Character of Dr. Swift' (1733) than that his denials of authorship were false. In deprecating the flatness of this poem's lines, Hammond appears to have fallen victim to the hoax.

Originality, Hammond asserts, is what keeps readers returning to Swift, and few would disagree: 'Swift's originality is to this day the most foundational reason for his still being remembered and enjoyed as a writer, and it is what he liked about himself as a writer. For much of his life, he disdained the ordinary way of doing anything' (II, p. 675). This astonishingly original and unconventional *oeuvre* has been produced, however, by a man whose behaviour, values, and beliefs were all normative:

> I do not share [with past biographers] the suspicion that most of Swift's enmities were politically motivated. I do not feel critical of him because he was often fastidious with his money. I do not think he was insincere about his religious faith. His pride, his sexual interests, his often shocking or uninhibited language, his instinct for revenge ... were all fundamental elements of his being, but elements that he either used for rhetorical effect, or that he tried to keep in check, and that he felt religion helped him to keep in check. (I, p. xix)

This threatens to return Swift to middle-of-the-road moderation, with Hammond's instinct leading to a sentimentalisation that compromises the radical originality of Swift's writing. Nowhere is this more clearly demonstrated than in his account of the work that so signally defeated Kathleen Williams: *A Modest Proposal*. This is 'so ethically minded' and 'so ethically admirable' (II, pp. 504, 505) that its satirical force simply cannot be directed at the Irish poor. Readers in search of a more bracing view should consult the opening chapter of Claude Rawson's *God, Gulliver, and Genocide*, where the case is powerfully argued that Swift's angle of vision created by his deployment of the cannibalism trope is wide enough to embrace all sections of society, including the Catholic poor, in its satirical overview.[14] On a similarly sentimentalised plane, Hammond offers a softer-than-soft reading of *Gulliver's Travels* resulting in statements such as 'Gulliver's inhumanity to his long-suffering wife is unutterably painful' (II, p. 383) which is plausible only if *Gulliver's Travels* is written to engage such empathetic identification, which in my view it is not. *That* it is not is an aspect of its originality. It stands in the way of developing models of absorptive reading that would make the novel a vital, but in Swift's view dangerously populist, cultural force. Nowhere does Hammond resemble Kathleen Williams more closely than in his vitriolic hatred for Bolingbroke, whom he stigmatises as a glozing hypocrite, ultimately seen through by Swift. Nothing hypocritical, though, in Swift's advising his cousin Honoria to tell her daughter, who has run away, that 'when she is ruined, as will certainly be the case . . . you will never see her'. Swift's behaviour towards the two Esthers brought them both to the brink of ruin; but this downright hypocritical advice is said by Hammond to be 'loving but shockingly strict' (II, p. 647).

My own study of Swift published in 2010, though not primarily a biography, had a biographical hypothesis to which I remain committed: Swift's originality is the *result* of, rather than being conceived *in despite of*, the extremism of his personality and beliefs.[15] Swift several times reiterates the view that individuals are entitled to hold whatever opinions they like, but they are not entitled to express them if they may lead to social disturbance or to non-compliance with the law of the land. In *Gulliver's Travels*, the King of Brobdingnag 'knew no Reason, why those who entertain Opinions prejudicial to the Publick, should be obliged to change, or should not be obliged to conceal them' – a formulation encapsulating in an almost oxymoronic clench the Swiftian nexus of libertarianism and authoritarianism.[16] So strongly did Swift subscribe to this principle that he even approved of similar sentiments when expressed by Oliver Cromwell: in 'Thoughts on Religion', Swift quotes approvingly Cromwell's reply to the governor of the Irish town of New Ross, who sought for liberty of conscience in his articles of surrender:

> I meddle not with any man's conscience. But if by liberty of conscience you mean a liberty to exercise the mass, I judge it best to use plain dealing, and to let you know, where the Parliament of England have power that will not be allowed of.[17]

Be a Catholic in your conscience, but do not attempt to make public observance of that faith if it is illegal. Biographers are slow to take on the consequences of such an intellectual article of faith. At worst, this means that we cannot derive any certain idea of what Swift really believed from what he wrote, because he held his true beliefs under a reservation similar to the Jesuit concept of equivocation. In a passage found only in Orrery's copy of 'On Poetry: A Rapsody' (1733), Swift scathingly attacks unbelieving bishops: 'What tho' they don't believe in Christ / Deny them Protestants – thou ly'st.'[18] From this, it would be natural, but unsafe, to assume that Swift therefore *does* believe in Christ. This scrupulously qualified doctrine on free expression could have created the existential circumstance, apprehended by Nokes, that Swift lived his life in fear of the charge of hypocrisy. His conviction that freedom of expression must be limited partly accounts for the absurdity, to him, of the forms of 'freethinking' that he satirised so relentlessly. Further, it meant that his own life was not lived in conditions of ideal liberty – ironic when his lasting Irish reputation is as an outspoken defender of freedom – and that it was lived in the dark shadow of hypocrisy.

If Swift was able to 'reverse' hypocrisy, throwing the accusation back in the accuser's face, he could not have ignored his fear of it – the anxiety that as a churchman he might have been in bad faith. His near-fanatical desire to keep up appearances, which was responsible for some of the worst actions of his life, is explicable as a behavioural parallel to the intellectual position referred to above. It is not only in respect of Swift's personal relationships and deeply held beliefs that the accusation of hypocrisy has been levelled. Sean Moore's *Swift, the Book, and the Irish Financial Revolution*, a prize-winning monograph, makes the argument that Swift and other members of the Anglican and Church of Ireland elite, created and pursued an economic interest through banking services, lending money to the state to service Ireland's national debt and seeking to influence Irish economic policy thereafter – policy that they knew to be detrimental to the Irish poor.[19] On this reading of them, some of Swift's Irish pamphlets were creating the ideological superstructure for the economic advantage of the *Monti* (the name Moore confers on this Anglican group whose 'bank' did nothing but service debt), while others, such as *A Modest Proposal,* were crying crocodile tears. Assuredly, Moore's position is not one that many Swiftian scholars have endorsed and some have questioned its evidentiary basis.[20] Defending it against criticism, Moore has called himself 'a disciple of the "hard school" of Swift studies, notably espoused by Claude Rawson, in that I see that Swift had ambivalence, if not outright antipathy, towards the Irish poor as manifest in such works as *A Proposal for giving Badges to the Beggars*'.[21] Swift's 1737 proposal for identifying beggars by yellow badges is judged by Eugene Hammond to be humane: 'his sense of responsibility towards [beggars] ... suffuses his *Proposal*'.[22] Such is the polarity of discussion generated by Swift.

We need not share Ben Jonson's requirement that a good writer be a good man. It seems unlikely, though, that strikingly original writing such as Swift produced was the output of the conventional, moderate, middle-of-the-road thinker on social, religious, or political issues to whom Kathleen Williams introduced me decades ago. To explain Swift's life and conduct adequately, we need to abandon the assumption that he thought entirely as other similarly stationed men of his time did. We should concentrate less upon the ethical problematic of Swift's goodness and more upon the structuring contradictions resulting from his unorthodox personality in collision with his circumstances.

Irish Studies

Where the biographies of Swift have tended to concentrate on the personality, the developing work of giving an adequate account of the Irish context of his life and work is central to understanding those circumstances. No reader of Hammond's biography could come away with the impression that the people most important to Swift after his move to Ireland were the Scriblerians. Among Hammond's most penetrating aperçus is the observation that Swift's farewell to English hopes did not happen, as is conventionally argued, in 1714, but actually in 1718 when he finally accepted that Lord Oxford would not invite him to England to collaborate on the political history of the years 1710–14. After that, he gave himself to Ireland and his causes became Ireland's causes. The people with whom he associated were obscure Irish gentry-folks who would have left little mark on history were it not for their association with Swift. The assumption made on literary grounds that Swift's closest intellectual companions continued to be Pope, Gay, and Bolingbroke therefore needs some revision.

Discriminating and nuanced analysis of Swift's relationship with Pope by scholars such as Dustin Griffin and James McLaverty suggests that the older thinking about Swift and Pope, that has them standing together as representative of Augustanism, emblematising the values of eighteenth-century neoclassicism and pre-Enlightenment rationality, is wide of the mark.[23] Indeed, the epistolary exchanges that preceded the publication of *Gulliver's Travels* make crystal clear the philosophical and temperamental chasm that separated Swift from Pope.[24] That chasm is embodied in the four volumes of *Miscellanies in Prose and Verse* (1727–32), ironically constructed to promote their solidarity and to depict them marching down hand in hand to posterity. In the event, the volumes became a dumping

ground for second-rate Pope propped up by some first-rate Swift, though
not actually the first-rate Swift that Swift himself wanted to publish, since
Pope would not print the *Libel on Dr. Delany*. This poem is an epitome of
the differences over poetic form and content that separated the two writers
for much of the 1730s. Both published verse autobiographies – Swift's
Verses on the Death of Dr. Swift and Pope's *Epistle to Dr. Arbuthnot* – that
are in subtle opposition to one another, as are the rival publications of
complete works in 1735.

The matrix for this is Swift's Irish experience, recent analysis of which
has done a great deal to characterise the nature of Swift's partisan affiliations. Kathleen Williams was right, in a sense, to say that Swift was not
a party man; though in saying that he was not 'passionate' about party, she
misleadingly implies that he was equally agnostic – which he was not,
about anything ever. Since the publication of J. A. Downie's landmark
Jonathan Swift: Political Writer in 1984, the closest we have come to
a consensus about Swift's political allegiance is that his self-description
formulated in conversation with Lord Somers gets it exactly right: 'I found
myself much inclined to be what they called a Whig in politics . . . But, as
to religion, I confessed myself to be an High-churchman.'[25] This verdict is
endorsed by David Oakleaf, whose *A Political Biography of Jonathan Swift*
(2008), while acknowledging that Swift's name has been annexed to almost
every available ideological affiliation in the period from Jacobite Tory to
republican Whig, itself presents a Swift who was a lifelong defender of the
Revolution Settlement and of Hanoverian legitimacy.[26] The only mud in
the water here is Swift's intense dislike of particular monarchs, including
William III – which could give the impression that he had Jacobite
sympathies. Oakleaf's work is particularly valuable in arguing that fear
and hatred of war were fundamental to Swift's political understanding –
derived from seventeenth-century English and Irish history. He provides
a powerful account of the three major Irish wars and the ways in which
those shaped the sectarian society into which Swift was born and within
which he lived his last three decades. Swift's ferocious defence of the
Church of Ireland and consequent attack on Dissenters and Catholics,
was the direct result of the anomalous and beleaguered position of the
Anglo-Irish minority for whom he spoke. Continuity and consistency in
Swift's ideological and partisan thinking are created by his support for the
Test Act, for the position of the less-elevated clergy and for the land- and
rent-based arrangements that provided them with a living. Latterly, the
colonial-style exploitation of Irish economic conditions apparently represented by William Wood's bid to control and profit from Ireland's copper

currency, and the English attempt to recruit Englishmen to all leadership positions in Ireland, gave Swift's views a coherence that transcends party labels altogether in conferring upon Ireland its earliest sense of a national identity.

Doubts about the Downie–Oakleaf consensus continue to resurface. What is at issue here is the question of Swift's *extremism*. Oakleaf draws an interesting distinction: 'Swift's *emotional* and *rhetorical* extremism can also encourage readers to assume that he belongs to an ideological extreme. Although he rejected extreme positions intellectually, he reveled in extreme statements.'[27] I am one such reader, duly encouraged. My own book on Swift has this opening sentence: 'Jonathan Swift . . . was a great writer because he was an extremist.'[28] To Oakleaf, Swift has Kathleen Williamsesque moderate things to say; it's just that he says them with great vehemence. In a series of brilliant publications, however, Ian Higgins has continued to argue that, even in Swift's seemingly most time-transcendent writings such as *Gulliver's Travels*, he is embroiled in the pamphlet wars of his time and leans towards extreme ideological positions. In an essay entitled 'Jonathan Swift's Political Confession', Higgins attends seriously to the imputations levelled by Swift's freethinking opponent Anthony Collins, that Swift took his place in a Royalist and High Church polemical tradition of violent ironical invective.[29] Here and elsewhere, Higgins's work challenges Oakleaf's assumption that a viable distinction can be drawn between matter and manner in Swift's writing: Swift's brand of ironic writing, he would counter, has its own built-in politics. Thus, in an essay entitled '"Killing No Murder": Jonathan Swift and the Polemical Tradition', Higgins demonstrates Swift's familiarity with satirically extreme pamphlets of the seventeenth century, arguing that such writing is palimpsestically present even in his greatest writing.[30] Edward Sexby's 1657 *Killing Noe Murder*, the pamphlet in which Cromwell is invited to accept the tribute of assassination and members of the army are urged to carry that out, is argued to be behind Swift's various recommendations of king-killing and other extreme suggestions of Scots Presbyterians. A rhetoric characterised by Higgins as comprising 'black humour, blatant exaggeration, and elision of homicidal rhetoric with actual menaces' (p. 39) culminates in the argument about a final solution to the Yahoo problem in *Gulliver's Travels*. An earlier essay by Roger Lund had argued that Swift's very deployment of irony in the *Tale of a Tub* was regarded as ipso facto evidence of godlessness because it was widely considered that only an atheist could write about religious matters in such a manner.[31] I have myself argued that the allegorical sections of the

Tale are not as clearly readable as is often thought, and that there are problems with any analysis of the *Tale* that represents the character of Martin as a purely benevolent mediator between the excesses of Peter and Jack.[32] Why 'Martin'? If Martin is Martin Luther, why should he be Swift's authorial surrogate? If there is no *raissoneur* figure, the way is left open for the extremist view that the Church of England does not have any monopoly on good clerical practice.

The most thorough investigation of Downie–Oakleaf has been undertaken recently by Ashley Marshall, who examines the topic from the vantage point of Swift's obsession with writing history.[33] To regard Swift as a wholesale and enthusiastic supporter of William III and the Revolution Settlement is, she believes, a serious distortion of the evidence, more dangerous than is the stretching of it to create Swift as a crypto-Jacobite. The closest she comes to Swift as a Jacobite is her examination of Swift's marginalia on his copy of Gilbert Burnet's *History of His Own Time*, an issue that had already become contentious between Oakleaf and myself. Where I had said that 'many of Swift's marginalia are Jacobite in sympathy, reverential towards Charles I and implacably hostile to William III', Oakleaf does not construe Swift's anti-monarchical sentiments as sympathetic to Jacobitism.[34] Marshall thinks, with Higgins and myself, that Swift would have welcomed a regent in 1688 in preference to the disruption of legitimacy implied in William's coup, but she points out that the comments are made very late in Swift's life and do not necessarily represent a lifetime commitment.[35] Marshall's key insights include her insistence that Swift was an authoritarian, not a defender of liberty in any fashion that we would now recognise – no defender of personal freedom or universal human rights. Swift's politics changed drastically after 1714, she argues, when his instinctive authoritarianism and suspicion of populism was challenged by hatred for the Hanoverian authority he came to live under, especially in regard to its consequences for Ireland.

What is emerging is that the question of what label to affix to Swift's politics, whether 'old Whig', 'radical Whig', 'moderate Tory', or 'Jacobite Tory', is less intriguing than the underlying question of how it is that such different labels can be generated. The answer, again, lies in Ireland and its quasi-colonial situation. Political parties on the English model developed later in Ireland than in England, post-1703. From the first, they were more narrowly focused than in England, concentrated around matters of religion, with the Tories perceiving the Catholics as largely a spent force, while Protestant Dissenters were dangerous enemies who needed to be controlled by the Sacramental Test Act (1704); and the Whigs reversing those polarities. Following the 1713 election, the Whigs were in the ascendant in the Irish House of Commons, rendering Irish soil as barren of advantage to Swift as England under the Hanoverian Whigs would soon become.[36] After Swift set up shop in Ireland, his political mission became less a matter of espousing either party and more of exerting constant vigilance upon English political 'undertakers' who might try to disadvantage the Church of Ireland and its clergymen. The perspective that credits Swift with being a proto-nationalist due to his *Drapier's Letters* campaign of the mid-1720s, the watchman for the entire Irish nation, is not immune to irony.

Although one might agree with David Oakleaf that through this campaign, Swift articulated the aspirations of an imagined Irish national community in response to an external threat, it is apparent that he did so while simultaneously adopting positions that both espoused and vehemently opposed the colonial basis upon which relations between Ireland and England stood post-1720.[37] Recent scholarship has been progressively analysing into its separate components the ideological superstructure through which Swift gave imaginative entity to an Irish nation, which has meant perceiving that it was to a degree deceptive and disingenuous. S. J. Connolly, who has been prominent in arguing that Ireland is not properly considered a colony during Swift's period, points to a moment in Swift's writing when he appears more than usually conscious of the real demographic complexity of the society in which he lived. His Irish-inflected pamphlet of 1733 (published 1738) *Reasons Humbly Offered to the Parliament of Ireland for Repealing the Sacramental Test*, adopts an Old English persona, that of an English Catholic who helped in the original conquests of Gaelic Ireland and who, though Catholic, remained loyal to the English Crown until forced by subsequent ill-treatment – as if they were native Irish – to rebel. This enables the distinction to be made between the 'savage' Irish aboriginals, the more civilised later English Catholics, and the current Protestant landed class, whom Swift wrongly claimed to be the landed beneficiaries of fanatic Civil War Protestant regicides.[38] Another important postcolonial analyst of Swift's Ireland, Robert Mahony, has argued that of two possible narratives, (1) that Swift was a founder of Irish nationalism and (2) that he was not concerned at all with native Irish interests, the latter is much closer to the mark.[39]

Book History

If biographical and Irish contextual studies of Swift have been more an eddy than a progress, approaches based on bibliography and textual studies and on the history of the book are relatively linear in adding to our understanding – unsurprisingly, perhaps, since the proliferation in online databases and search capabilities has transformed possibilities for surrounding the textual object with relevant print. When Swift features on 'major authors' courses and is studied in conjunction with other great writers, misconceptions can be generated: such as that Swift's career was primarily literary and that he was in any simple sense an 'author', that he was English, that he was joined at the hip with Pope, that his manifest destiny was to write *Gulliver's Travels*, and that this work is adequately described as a novel. All of Swift's masterpieces are conceived in dialogue with other books, both with their contents and with their physical formats; and a fuller understanding of Swift's relationships with the print industry has been one of the major achievements of recent scholarship because it challenges some of the assumptions of the 'great tradition' approach to his writing.

Two major editions have been important sources of new knowledge. *The Library and Reading of Jonathan Swift: A Bio-Bibliographical Handbook* compiled in four volumes by Dirk F. Passmann and Heinz J. Vienken, collects all printed materials not only known to be in his library but also known to have formed part of his reading.[40] *The Cambridge Edition of the Works of Jonathan Swift* will eventually issue in eighteen volumes, and those published thus far – including editions of the *Tale of a Tub*, *Gulliver*, and of Swift's various parodies and hoaxes – have already nuanced our understanding of Swift.[41] As an example, Valerie Rumbold's account of what exactly Swift is doing in the Bickerstaff hoax brings to light comic strokes dimmed to us but resplendently bright to contemporaries. The object of Swift's parody, Partridge the almanac-maker, is not the harmless confidence-man we might take him to be: he is a firebrand Whig radical, whose political postures Swift never forgets in framing Bickerstaff's mockpredictions. Thus Bickerstaff predicts that in 1708 the entire house of Bourbon will die, with the exception of Louis XIV's grandson, Philip V of Spain – the one person whom the English *needed* to die to solve the international crisis over which the War of the Spanish Succession was being fought.[42] In the understanding of Swift's poetry, too, new things are happening. The *Swift Poems Project* sets out to inventory and transcribe all texts of all poems by or related to Swift into the early nineteenth century.[43] New attributions have been made by James Woolley: hitherto unknown poems such as 'A Wicked Treasonable Libel' (1718) and 'An Excellent New Panegyrick on Skinnibonia' (1728) are now part of Swift's poetic canon.[44] Stephen Karian makes the argument that we should regard Swift primarily as a manuscript-based poet – a poet who typically writes not for print publication and its largely unknown readership, but for manuscript circulation among a small group of readers or for oral delivery to a select audience.[45] His book *Jonathan Swift in Print and Manuscript* has shown how post-1714, the diversity of manuscript forms in which Swift's poems circulated created a tension between greater poetic freedom and a loss of control over reception and consumption.[46]

The growing contribution being made by book history to the understanding of Swift was marked by an important collection of essays published in 2013: *Jonathan Swift and the Eighteenth-Century Book*.[47] As Paddy Bullard and James McLaverty argue in their introduction, Swift was a 'nebulous' author. It is not merely that Swift satirised every aspect of bookmaking in his writing, but also that

> he left behind him a major body of writing in which textual complications are deeply entangled with material expression. It is the intelligence with which that entanglement has been contrived by the author himself that makes his work a compelling subject for historians of the book. (p. xii)

Marcus Walsh's essay in the volume sheds direct light on how the material expression of the *Tale* – its asterisks, blanks, dashes, and booklists – serves to interrogate 'the ways in which modern books present evidence, and organise and make claims to knowledge'.[48] Although the *Tale*'s satirical thrust might suggest hostility towards books and libraries, Bullard puts a case that Swift was not, as I and others have argued, an 'adversarial' reader, but rather that his bibliographical engagements were an aspect of his sociability, exerting control over the 'bristling antagonisms' of his satirical embodiments of libraries. Sociability is also, for Stephen Karian, an aspect of Swift's literary identity becoming primarily that of the poet post-1728, when his visits to the Achesons of Market Hill generated a body of verse that was family-based entertainment devised for private consumption.

Several essays in the volume extend our understanding of Swift's involvement with the print industry. Through James McLaverty's essay, we understand more about how the Faulkner edition of Swift's works sought to present him, what advantages it offered over earlier printed works, the erupting rivalries between Dublin and London publishers (a topic covered in detail by Adam Rounce) and the unsystematic editorial contribution that Swift himself made to the collection and presentation of his complete works. Ian Gadd and Pat Rogers cover Swift's relations with the London book trade, Rogers's essay suggesting that despite his denials and repudiations, it is likely that Swift personally assisted Curll in assembling his supposedly pirated 1710 *Miscellanies*.[49] Here again, hypocrisy and double-dealing are an aspect of Swift's *modus operandi*.

Swift's writing career spanned a period during which the printing and publication of imaginative writing was only just beginning to gain professional respectability. Whereas to Pope his printers resembled indentured labourers, Swift made enduring relationships and personal friendships with a series of publishers, some of whom were prepared to risk their livelihoods and liberty for him – even if it is another question whether he *should* have put them to such hazard. Benjamin Tooke Jr, John Barber, Edward Waters, John and Sarah Harding, Benjamin Motte, George Faulkner . . . it is arguable that these are the names that should echo through Swift studies on equal terms with those of his friends, guardians, and relations: the Grattans, the Rochforts, Dan Jackson, Thomas Walls, John Worrall, Anthony Raymond, Peter Ludlow, Patrick Delany, Thomas Sheridan, Robert Cope, Mary Barber, Laetitia Pilkington, the Achesons, Mrs Brent, Martha Whiteway, Richard Helsham, John Lyon. In the last analysis, these lists may be more significant than that of the great writers and thinkers provided by Kathleen Williams.

Notes

1. Kathleen Williams, *Jonathan Swift and the Age of Compromise* (Lawrence, KS and London: University of Kansas Press, 1958).
2. Quoted from Ben Jonson, *Three Comedies*, ed. Michael Jamieson (1966; Harmondsworth: Penguin, 1969), p. 42.
3. Irvin Ehrenpreis, *Swift: The Man, His Works, and the Age*, 3 vols (London: Methuen, 1962–83).
4. Leopold Damrosch, *Jonathan Swift: His Life and His World* (New Haven, CT and London: Yale University Press, 2013), pp. 4–5.
5. David Nokes, *Jonathan Swift, A Hypocrite Reversed: A Critical Biography* (Oxford University Press, 1985), p. 42.
6. See Denis Johnston, *In Search of Swift* (Dublin: Hodges Figgis, 1959); Sybil le Brocquy, *Cadenus: A Reassessment in the Light of New Evidence of the Relationships between Swift, Stella and Vanessa* (Dublin: Dolmen Press, 1962).
7. Hermann J. Real, 'The Dean's Grandfather, Thomas Swift (1595–1658): Forgotten Evidence', *Swift Studies* 8 (1993), 84–93; Michael Treadwell, 'Swift, Richard Coleire, and the Origins of *Gulliver's Travels*', *Review of English Studies* 34.135 (1983), 304–11; Christopher J. Fox, 'Getting Gotheridge: Notes on Swift's Grandfather and a New Letter from Thomas Swift', *Swift Studies* (2005), 10–29.
8. *The Correspondence of Jonathan Swift, D.D.*, ed. David Woolley, 5 vols (Frankfurt am Main: Peter Lang, 1999–2014).

9. Eugene Hammond, *Jonathan Swift: Irish Blow-In* and *Jonathan Swift: Our Dean* (Newark, NJ: University of Delaware Press, 2016). I refer to these hereafter as volumes I and II; Dustin Griffin, *Swift and Pope: Satirists in Dialogue* (Cambridge University Press, 2010).

10. Le Brocquy, *Cadenus*, ch. 9.

11. Damrosch, *Jonathan Swift*, pp. 427ff.

12. E. Hammond, *Jonathan Swift*, II, p. 222.

13. Stephen Karian, *Jonathan Swift in Print and Manuscript* (Cambridge University Press, 2010), p. 84.

14. Claude Rawson, *God, Gulliver, and Genocide: Barbarism and the European Imagination, 1492–1945* (Oxford University Press, 2001).

15. Brean Hammond, *Jonathan Swift* (Dublin: Irish Academic Press, 2010).

16. *The Cambridge Edition of the Works of Jonathan Swift*, Vol. XVI: *Gulliver's Travels*, ed. David Womersley (Cambridge University Press, 2012), Part II, ch. 6, p. 187. See also Womersley's Long Note 21 on this topic, pp. 524–26.

17. *The Prose Works of Jonathan Swift*, Vol. IX: *Irish Tracts, 1720–1723, and Sermons*, ed. Herbert Davis (Oxford: Blackwell, 1948), p. 263.

18. Quoted from *The Poems of Jonathan Swift*, ed. Harold Williams, 3 vols (Oxford: Clarendon Press, 1937), II, p. 658. The lines are ll. 7–8 in an eight-line passage added in Orrery's hand in the margin of a first edition of the 1733 London edition, at l. 190. They are also provided by Scott in his second edition of Swift's *Works* (1824). See Williams, *Poems of Jonathan Swift*, II, p. 639.

19. Sean Moore, *Swift, the Book, and the Irish Financial Revolution* (Baltimore, MD: Johns Hopkins University Press, 2010).

20. See, for example, the review of the book by Salim Rashid in *Eighteenth-Century Ireland / Iris an dá chultúr* 27 (2012), 197–200.

21. Sean Moore, 'Response: Occupy Eighteenth-Century Ireland, or, Bishop Berkeley's Slaves and the Irish Anglican Enlightenment', *Eighteenth-Century Ireland / Iris an dá chultúr* 27 (2012), 200–04 (p. 201).

22. E. Hammond, *Jonathan Swift*, II, p. 732.

23. Griffin, *Swift and Pope*; James McLaverty, 'George Faulkner and Swift's Collected Works', in *Jonathan Swift and the Eighteenth-Century Book*, ed. Paddy Bullard and James McLaverty (Cambridge University Press, 2013), pp. 154–76.

24. See B. Hammond, *Jonathan Swift*, pp. 159–63.

25. J. A. Downie, *Jonathan Swift: Political Writer* (London: Routledge, 1984); *The Prose Works of Jonathan Swift*, Vol. VII: *The History of the Four Last Years of the Queen*, ed. Herbert Davis and Harold Williams (Oxford: Blackwell, 1951), p. 120.

26. David Oakleaf, *A Political Biography of Jonathan Swift* (London: Pickering & Chatto, 2008), pp. 79, 149ff.

27. Ibid., p. 154.

28. B. Hammond, *Jonathan Swift*, p. 1.

29. Ian Higgins, 'Jonathan Swift's Political Confession', in *Politics and Literature in the Age of Swift: English and Irish Perspectives*, ed. Claude Rawson (Cambridge University Press, 2010), pp. 3–30.

30. Ian Higgins, '"Killing No Murder": Jonathan Swift and Polemical Tradition', in *Swift's Travels: Eighteenth-Century British Satire and Its Legacy*, ed. Nicholas Hudson and Aaron Santesso (Cambridge University Press, 2008), pp. 39–54.

31. Roger Lund, '*A Tale of a Tub*, Swift's Apology and the Trammels of Christian Wit', in *Augustan Subjects: Essays in Honor of Martin C. Battestin*, ed. Albert J. Rivero (Newark, DE: University of Delaware Press, 1997), pp. 87–109.

32. B. Hammond, *Jonathan Swift*, pp. 64–66.

33. Ashley Marshall, *Swift and History: Politics and the English Past* (Cambridge University Press, 2015).

34. Brean Hammond, 'Swift's Reading', in *The Cambridge Companion to Jonathan Swift*, ed. Christopher Fox (Cambridge University Press, 2003), pp. 73–86 (p. 78); Oakleaf, *A Political Biography*, p. 151.

35. Marshall, *Swift and History*, pp. 37, 175.

36. See David Hayton, *Ruling Ireland, 1685–1742: Politics, Politicians and Parties* (Woodbridge, Suffolk: Boydell, 2004), chs 7 and 8.

37. Oakleaf, *A Political Biography*, p. 179.

38. S. J. Connolly, *Religion, Law, and Power: The Making of Protestant Ireland, 1660–1760* (Oxford: Clarendon Press, 1992); S. J. Connolly, 'Old English, New English and Ancient Irish: Swift and the Irish Past', in *Politics and Literature in the Age of Swift: English and Irish Perspectives*, ed. Claude Rawson (Cambridge University Press, 2010), pp. 255–69.

39. Robert Mahony, 'Jonathan Swift and the Irish Colonial Project', in *Politics and Literature in the Age of Swift*, ed. Rawson, pp. 270–89.

40. Dirk F. Passmann and Heinz J. Vienken, *The Library and Reading of Jonathan Swift: A Bio-Bibliographical Handbook, Part 1: Swift's Library*, 4 vols (Frankfurt am Main: Peter Lang, 2003).

41. *The Cambridge Edition of the Works of Jonathan Swift*, Vol. I: A Tale of a Tub and Other Works, ed. Marcus Walsh (Cambridge University Press, 2010); Vol. II: *Parodies, Hoaxes, Mock Treatises: Polite Conversation, Directions to Servants and Other Works*, ed. Valerie Rumbold (Cambridge University Press, 2013); Vol. VIII: *English Political Writings, 1711–1714: 'The Conduct of the Allies' and Other Works*, ed. Bertrand A. Goldgar (Cambridge University Press, 2008); Vol. XIV: *Irish Political Writings after 1725: A Modest Proposal and Other Works*, ed. David Hayton and Adam Rounce (Cambridge University Press, 2017); Vol. IX: *Journal to Stella: Letters to Esther Johnson and Rebecca Dingley, 1710–1713*, ed. Abigail Williams (Cambridge University Press, 2013); Vol. XVI: *Gulliver's Travels*, ed. Womersley.

42. Valerie Rumbold, 'Burying the Fanatic Partridge: Swift's Holy Week Hoax', in *Politics and Literature in the Age of Swift*, ed. Rawson, pp. 81–115.

43. The *Swift Poems Project* is housed by the Skillman Library at Lafayette College, Easton, Pennsylvania, edited by the late John Irwin Fischer, James Woolley, and Stephen Karian: digital.lafayette.edu/collections/spp [accessed 12 August 2019].

44. James Woolley, 'Writing Libels on the Germans: Swift's "Wicked Treasonable Libel"', in *Swift, the Enigmatic Dean: Festschrift for Hermann Josef Real*, ed. Rudolf Freiburg, Arno Löffler, and Wolfgang Zach, with the assistance of Jan Schnitker (Tübingen: Stauffenberg, 1998), pp. 303–16; James Woolley, 'Swift's "Skinnibonia": A New Poem from Lady Acheson's Manuscript', in *Reading Swift: Papers from the Fifth Münster Symposium on Jonathan Swift*, ed. Hermann J. Real and Helgard Stöver-Leidig (Munich: Wilhelm Fink, 2008), pp. 309–42.

45. Karian, *Jonathan* Swift, p. 31.

46. Ibid., p. 71.

47. Paddy Bullard and James McLaverty, eds., *Jonathan Swift and the Eighteenth-Century Book* (Cambridge University Press, 2013).

48. Marcus Walsh, 'Swift's *Tale of a Tub* and the Mock Book', in *Jonathan Swift and the Eighteenth-Century Book*, ed. Bullard and McLaverty, pp. 101–18 (p. 102).

49. James McLaverty, 'George Faulkner and Swift's Collected Works', pp. 154–76; Adam Rounce, 'Swift's Texts between Dublin and London', pp. 119–213; Ian Gadd, 'Leaving the Printer to his Liberty: Swift and the London Book Trade, 1701–1714', pp. 51–64; Pat Rogers, 'The Uses of the Miscellany: Swift, Curll and Piracy', pp. 87–100: all in *Jonathan Swift and the Eighteenth-Century Book*, ed. Bullard and McLaverty.

PART II

Philosophical and Political Frameworks

CHAPTER 4

The Prejudices of Enlightenment

David Dwan

The 'Irish Enlightenment' no longer looks like a good idea that never happened. However the phenomenon is cast – as an epoch, ideal, or project – its history is now being written, producing one of the more significant transitions in recent scholarship on eighteenth-century Ireland.[1] The aim of this essay is to sketch out some of the main contours of enlightenment in an Irish context, outlining some of its key debates and most intractable problems. I want to bring some shape to this very wide discussion by focusing on the idea of prejudice – a notion that could be cast as both the counter-force and alter ego of enlightenment across eighteenth-century Europe. Charles O'Conor spoke for many in Ireland when he requested that the 'long *Night* of *Prejudice* give way to the *Lights* held forth by *Nature*'.[2] But enlightenment, as we shall see, was also accused of nursing prejudices of its own, not least its prejudice against prejudice itself, and it would trigger an interesting set of debates on the nature and limits of reason in religion, politics, and moral life.[3]

Before considering these issues in depth it is worth considering two basic prejudices of interpretation that derive in part from the enlightenment itself but have also constrained our understanding of what it entailed. The first assumes that Ireland (for social, political, and religious reasons) was deeply inimical to enlightenment; the second and related presumption is that the enlightenment is an aggressively secular phenomenon. Both views have been challenged, but not entirely outgrown, partly because their roots extend into the eighteenth century itself. It was, after all, a settled prejudice of enlightened Europe that Ireland was poor terrain for enlightenment. Key luminaries from David Hume to Voltaire regarded the Irish as 'a rude people' – too mired in religious superstition and barbarism to serve as hosts to the new learning.[4] Some of Ireland's subsequent *illuminati* perpetuated the view. Conor Cruise O'Brien – a self-declared 'child of the Enlightenment' – was liable to come across as a proud orphan in his native land.[5] Ireland had been 'little touched by the Enlightenment' in O'Brien's eyes, although the place was sufficiently exposed to its glare to generate a fierce reaction against it that would continue to O'Brien's day.

Ireland's anti-Enlightenment credentials for O'Brien were borne out by the fact that the country remained a 'theocracy', albeit a democratic one.[6] Here O'Brien tended to assume that enlightenment was an intrinsically secularising force – a position shared by many of his contemporaries and predecessors alike. According to the nineteenth-century historian W. E. H. Lecky, for instance, the progress of rationalism (Lecky's term for 'enlightenment') was reflected and sustained by the 'secularisation of politics' across Europe.[7] Unfortunately, Lecky's own country bucked the trend: 'Ireland is now the only civilised country', he complained, 'where public opinion is governed not occasionally, but habitually, by theological considerations.'[8] Here national pride and national interest were often sacrificed to an ugly form of sectarianism.

Lecky was right about the obduracy of religious conflict in Ireland, but the relationship between enlightenment and faith was always a more complicated one than his own secularisation thesis allowed. After all, enlightenment in Ireland (and elsewhere) was conditioned by the wars of religion of the sixteenth and seventeenth centuries. Advocates of enlightenment certainly feared the revival of the old religious animosities. They duly stressed the dangers of enthusiasm – or what William Molyneux identified as 'a religious sort of madness' – and preached the virtues of reasonableness and toleration.[9] But toleration, as Edmund Burke made clear, should not be confused with 'infidelity and indifference'.[10] In Burke's eyes, at least, toleration was 'a part of [. . .] religion' – an extension of Christian charity – not its outward limit (WS, II, p. 387). On the other hand, irreligion was no guarantee of moderation and mutual forbearance. Atheism, Burke maintained, could generate a fundamentalism of its own. 'The enthusiasts of this time', he reported in the 1790s, 'like their predecessors in another faction of fanaticism, deal in lights.' Confronted with the blaze of this atheistic enlightenment, Burke would famously choose for himself the 'sober shade of the old obscurity' (WS, IV, p. 431).

Burke has been understandably cast as a critic of enlightenment (while his rhetoric certainly contributed to impressions that it marched hand in hand with atheism), but he can equally be seen as one of its key exemplars.[11] 'Sapere aude' ('dare to know') – the Horatian motto that Kant famously applied to enlightenment – was Burke's credo too, though he insisted that knowledge should also dare to know its limits.[12] He was an advocate of rational reform in politics and economic life and stressed the social dividends of 'ingenuous science' (*WS*, II, p. 322). Here he promoted the virtues of empiricism – or 'a more extensive and perfect induction' – over the metaphysical subtleties of scholasticism (*WS*, I, p. 190). Indeed, if 'the Enlightenment begins', as Ernst Cassirer once suggested, 'by breaking down the older form of philosophical knowledge', then Burke and Bishop Berkeley are clearly part of that process.[13]

Berkeley was a fierce critic of the 'sophistry of the Schoolmen'.[14] And while he rued the fact that 'in these free-thinking times, many an empty head is shaken at Aristotle and Plato' – he was a brilliant practitioner of the new philosophical learning that had issued from Descartes and Locke (*W*, V, p. 151). An able critic of both of these modern thinkers, he ultimately used an empirical philosophical method to critique the very idea of matter itself. Berkeley's pronouncements on science, from his critique of mechanistic explanations to his theory of vision, to his fixation with tar-water, have aged less well than his philosophy; nonetheless, he was clearly fascinated by modern science. He also contributed to the emergent discipline of political economy – often cast as the paradigmatic science of enlightenment – producing interesting theories on banking and the circulation of money.

The intellectual careers of Berkeley and Burke emphasise the dangers of associating enlightenment with secularism *per se*. In the eyes of both men religion was a condition of genuine enlightenment, not its benighted antithesis. As Berkeley's Crito declared: 'Under the Christian religion this nation hath been greatly improved. From a sort of savages, we have grown civil, polite, and learned' (*W*, III, p. 217). Berkeley was for this reason obsessed by the social costs of the new atheism: it would trigger a 'relapse into the same state of barbarism which over spread the northern nations before they were enlightened by Christianity' (*W*, VII, p. 205). While Berkeley was keen to defend the faith, it is worth noting that he also conceded to a secular method of argument: 'I intend not to build on the authority of Holy Scripture, but altogether on the principles of reason common to all mankind' (*W*, VI, p. 17). This appeal to common reason may reflect his subscription to an enlightened philosophical style, but Berkeley was in no doubt that 'the being of a God is capable of clear proof, and a proper object of human reason' (*W*, III, p. 327).

Burke entertained a less strident sense of proof when it came to religious matters. Pledged to a strongly empirical conception of knowledge, he was acutely aware of our cognitive limits. As he put it in 1757: 'That great chain of causes, which linking one to another, even to the throne of God himself, can never be unravelled by any industry of ours. When we go but one step beyond the immediate sensible qualities of things, we go out of our depth'

(*WS*, I, p. 283). But he was confident that the effects of religion could be known; indeed, its great utility was a 'proof of its divinity'.[15]

Burke later presented religious faith as a natural prejudice – belief in God lacked exhaustive demonstrative grounds, but it was basic to human animals (or at least the well-adjusted ones). Yet he was also aware that religion in his own country had been expressive of prejudice in a more pejorative sense. Catholics and Dissenters, for instance, had long been subject to a form of religious persecution held in place by 'Gigantick prejudice'.[16] But disentangling good from bad prejudice was not a straightforward matter – for Burke, or indeed, for many of the *illuminati* – and it would become one of the defining problems of enlightened reform in Ireland. Indeed, enlightenment seemed to spawn three forms of paradox: according to its critics, at any rate, its concept of reason was unreasonable, its toleration was intolerant, and its sense of improvement was morally regressive. It is hard to know if these criticisms were themselves expressions of enlightenment (producing more self-reflexive forms of it), but they also exposed its practical and theoretical limits in an Irish context.

The Prejudices of Reason

Few enlightened thinkers were more vigorous in the campaign against prejudice than the philosopher and controversialist John Toland. In his *Letters to Serena* (1704) he produced an elaborate philosophy of error, outlining the origins and mechanics of prejudice. 'We no sooner see the Light', he proclaimed, 'but the grand Cheat begins to delude us from every Quarter.'[17] The problem was exacerbated by formal education ('The University is the most fertile Nursery of Prejudice').[18] People were further buttressed in their prejudices by priests. Toland would remain a critic of priestcraft – namely, spurious forms of authority – in politics and religion all his life ('All Friends of Priestcraft, Foes of Mankind are').[19] In contrast to the bad dependencies generated by custom and prejudice, Toland extolled the moral, political, and epistemic virtues of 'independence'. But such independence was hard to come by in the world. Indeed, Toland's critique of prejudice could sometimes stoke a kind of paranoia in which 'all the Men in the World are join'd in the same Conspiracy to deprave the Reason of every individual Person'.[20]

But what was reason in Toland's eyes? After all, in *Christianity Not Mysterious* (1696) he complained that even the word reason had become 'as equivocal and ambiguous as any other'.[21] Toland took pains, therefore, to define what he meant by the term, producing a distinctly Lockean rendition of reason and of knowledge (Locke, for Toland, was 'the greatest philosopher after Cicero in the Universe').[22] Thus reason presupposed simple and distinct ideas as its ground and depended on the internal consistency – or *'Agreement or Disagreement'* – of those ideas for its operation.[23] But while Locke allowed for a distinction between knowledge, on the one hand, and faith on the other (faith, he explained, 'is the Assent to any Proposition, not [...] made out by the Deductions of Reason'), Toland effectively merged the two.[24] *'Faith'*, he insisted, 'is *Knowledg'*.[25] Thus, for Toland, all genuine religion rested on entirely rational foundations. This would lead him to the notorious assertion that there was nothing in religion that was either contrary to or above reason. After all, we cannot *'adore what we cannot comprehend'* – or so Toland insisted.[26] 'To be confident of any thing without conceiving it', he concluded, 'is no real *Faith* or Perswasion, but a rash Presumption and an obstinate Prejudice.'[27]

So Toland attacked the concept of divine mystery and seemed to undermine the need for revelation in religion. He did not deny the existence or indeed, truth-content of revelation, but he insisted that it was a form of information that was subordinate to reason. Revelation relied upon reason to make its content fully intelligible; moreover, its disclosures were subject to canons of rational justification. As Toland put it: *'Reason* is the only Foundation of all Certitude; and [...] nothing reveal'd, whether as to its *Manner* or *Existence*, is more exempted from its Disquisitions, than the ordinary Phenomena of Nature.'[28] There was nothing in the Gospels, he added, contrary to reason. According to Peter Browne (a fellow of Trinity College, Dublin), this was to make revelation redundant and to remove the grounds for faith. Here Browne distinguished between knowledge and faith and defended the latter as a legitimate form of belief. Moreover, faith, he insisted, often involved an implicit trust in the authority of another ('That which constitutes the formal act of *Faith* as it is distinct from Knowledge, is an *Assent upon the Authority of another Person'*).[29] Toland effectively undermined this investment in the authority of another – or so his critics alleged – and in his railing against priestcraft pretended that 'the *Priests of all Religions are the same'*.[30] This was particularly vexing to members of the Anglican establishment in Ireland.

One of the most vocal defenders of this order was Jonathan Swift – a scathing critic of so-called freethinkers like Matthew Tindal, Anthony Collins, and, of course, John Toland ('the great oracle of the Anti-Christians').[31] 'It is an old and true Distinction', Swift insisted, 'that Things may be above our Reason, without being contrary to it' (*PW*, IX, p. 164). The mystery of the Trinity or the relationship between the soul and the body were incomprehensible to human beings; here we were called upon by God 'to believe a Fact that we do not understand' (*PW*, IX, p. 168). For Swift, there was nothing very mysterious about mystery since we were surrounded by it all our lives: 'How little do those who quarrel with Mysteries, know of the commonest Actions of Nature! The Growth of an Animal, of a Plant, or of the smallest Seed, is a Mystery to the wisest among Men' (*PW*, IX, p. 164). Swift was in many respects a sceptic about knowledge. 'Truth', as he put it, 'lives in the Bottom of a Well' and was not readily accessed (*PW*, I, p. 247). Like other sceptics before him, he suggested that the tacit acceptance of surface verities was generally more prudent than an arbitrary rigour ('so far preferable is that Wisdom, which converses about the Surface, to that pretended Philosophy which enters into the Depth of things'). According to this self-cancelling type of scepticism, 'Credulity' was superior to 'Curiosity' (*PW*, I, p. 109). Indeed, he was highly critical of those who would try to dislodge 'fundamental opinions' in religion and politics in the name of a higher understanding (*PW*, IX, p. 261). 'Some Men, under the Notions of weeding out Prejudices', he complained, 'eradicate Religion, Virtue, and common Honesty' (*PW*, IX, p. 243). Instead of the moral and epistemic independence glorified by freethinkers, Swift emphasised our 'mutual subjection' (*PW*, IX, p. 139).

George Berkeley had aspirations to an independence that he mocked in freethinkers: 'I do not pin my faith on the sleeve of any great man. I act not out of prejudice & prepossession. I do not adhere to any opinion because it is an old one, a receiv'd one [or] a fashionable one' (*W*, I, p. 58). Though he declared himself free of prejudice, he also condemned a total war against it. Here Berkeley differentiated 'prejudice' from simple 'irrationality' or falsehood. 'The not distinguishing between prejudices and error is', he proclaimed, 'a prevailing oversight among our modern free-thinkers' (*W*, VI, p. 205). Prejudices, he explained, are notions or opinions which the mind entertains without knowing the grounds. This did not necessarily make them untrue – indeed, deliberation may show them to be perfectly valid. To strike against prejudice in the name of enlightenment, however, is to undermine enlightenment itself, for it seemed to overlook the social basis of all learning. We all learn from others, and at some point we will all defer – implicitly or otherwise – to the authority of another. This dependency is particularly true of young learners: they do not attempt to establish the grounds for their principles but take them on trust. Yet such 'trust' is also a basic feature of social life: shopkeepers take the rules of mathematics for granted; sailors depend on pre-established ideas of geometry and geography to sail a ship. Here and elsewhere 'there are and must be prejudices, that is, opinions taken upon trust' (*W*, VI, p. 206). To declare an absolute prohibition on prejudice is to undermine trust and this, for Berkeley, has potentially disastrous consequences; it erodes the social framework and alienates people from their own moral personalities: 'if you strip men of their [...] prejudices, with regard to modesty, decency, justice, charity, and the like, you will soon find them so many monsters, utterly unfit for human society' (*W*, VI, p. 204).

If Berkeley believed 'the age of monsters is not far off' (*W*, VI, p. 221), Burke ultimately concluded that the age of monsters had arrived – largely in the form of the French Revolution. Burke issued many salvoes against this epochal event – but he would also find himself compelled to defend what David Hume called the 'moral prejudices' against those who would campaign against all prejudice.[32] Burke could speak of 'prejudice' in highly pejorative ways: yet, he also clung fast to it. (Defending his stand on the pacification of America in 1777, he announced: 'I could not at once tear from my heart prejudices which were dear to me, and which bore a resemblance to virtues'; *WS*, III, p. 322). He expanded on the theme in the *Reflections on the Revolution in France* (1790): here he coarsely maintained that he cherished prejudices because they were prejudices; yet he also proclaimed to esteem them because they were reasonable and just. Burke's concept of a justified or rational prejudice clearly begged the question; it could also seem like a basic contradiction in terms. As Mary Wollstonecraft later argued: 'A prejudice is a fond obstinate persuasion for which we can give no reason; for the moment a reason can be given for an opinion, it ceases to be a prejudice though it may be an error in judgment.'[33] But prejudice for Burke often seemed to mark the limit of rational justification itself and he had an acute sense of these limits from the very inception of his literary and political career.

It is worth recalling that for thinkers like John Toland all authority needed to be grounded on reason: 'What Dominion is not founded on Reason', Toland declared, 'is unreasonable, and consequently Tyrannical.'[34] But Burke seemed to think that it was unreasonable to ask reasons for everything: 'what would become of the World if the Practice of all moral Duties, and the Foundations of Society, rested upon having their Reasons made clear and demonstrative to every Individual' (*WS*, I, p. 136)? For Burke, there were both practical and theoretical limits to rational justification. He often cast feeling as this limit point. As he put it in the 1750s, for instance: 'Metaphysical or Physical Speculations neither are, or ought to be, the Grounds of our Duties, because we can arrive at no certainty in them. They have a weight when they concur with our own natural feelings; very little when against them' (*N*, p. 71). Some practices, Burke argued, are just *felt* to be wrong; asked why they are

wrong we simply point to our feelings as evidence that they are so. This
position would be roundly mocked by his critics (Coleridge, for instance, later
produced a scoffing summary of Burke's outlook: 'God has given us Feelings,
and we are to obey them! and the most absurd Prejudices become venerable,
to which these Feelings have given Consecration').[35] Yet feeling, for Burke,
was both a condition and a limit of moral rationality: we are alarmed into
reflection when our feelings are aroused, but we cannot always get outside our
feelings in order to justify them. Indeed, Burke suggested that it might be
disastrous to try. He worried about those who would seek to transcend their
feelings in the name of a spurious objectivity. As he put it in the 1790s: 'The
moral sentiments, so nearly connected with early prejudice to be one and part
of the same thing, will assuredly not live long under a discipline, which has for
its basis, the destruction of all prejudices' (*WS*, IV, p. 469). Morality needed its
presuppositions and these lacked exhaustive demonstrative grounds.

'It might be some consolation for the loss of our old regards', Burke
declared in 1777, 'if our reason were enlightened in proportion as our honest
prejudices are removed', but this was not necessarily the case (*WS*, III, p. 301).
Reason, he believed, was a 'precarious' faculty and easily led us astray (*WS*, I,
p. 268). As Burke concluded in the 1750s: 'A man who considers his nature
rightly, will be diffident of any reasonings that carry him out of the ordinary
roads of Life' (*N*, p. 90). If Toland deemed custom a 'Tyrant', Burke generally
regarded it as a wise mother.[36] As he noted to himself: 'There is some general
principle operating to produce Customs, that is a more sure guide than our
Theories. They are followed indeed often on odd motives, but that does not
make them less reasonable or useful' (*N*, p. 90). Long-standing practices were
not infallible and Burke had little time for those who would defend 'the
inheritance of absurdity, derived to them from their ancestors' (*WS*, III,
p. 491). However, the longevity of a particular rule or practice created
a presumption or prejudice in its favour. Burke was an advocate of rational
reform in politics, but he also maintained that rulers needed to execute their
duties 'without wounding the prejudices of the people' (*WS*, III, p. 152). This
had not happened in America – and it led to war; nor had it occurred in
Ireland. Here the religious beliefs of the vast majority of the population were
subject to legal penalty. In Burke's eyes, it had yielded one of the worst
schemes of 'religious persecution' in Europe (*WS*, IX, p. 452).

The Prejudices of Toleration

'The constitution of these kingdoms', Berkeley noted in 1738, 'hath been
one while overheated by the indiscreet zeal of one set of men. We have

alternatively felt the effects of superstition and fanaticism' (*W*, VI, p. 217). Berkeley cast his own Anglican faith as the best *via media* between the extremes of Catholic superstition and Protestant fanaticism. However, he would also preach the importance of respect and good neighbourliness between schisms. There were, of course, significant limits to Berkeley's brand of tolerance: 'whatever conduct common sense as well as Christian charity, obligeth us to use towards those that differ from us in religion, yet the public safety requireth that the avowed contemners of all religion should be severely chastised' (*W*, VI, pp. 70–71). Blasphemy, he insisted, should be punished with the same severity as treason. Many enlightened commentators – from Charles O'Conor to Edmund Burke – would follow Berkeley's footsteps in abjuring atheism while promoting toleration. Yet toleration in Ireland was expressive of the wars of religion as much as it was an attempt to mitigate their effects. We don't need to tolerate those we love; we tolerate those to whom we object. A basic animus or prejudice, therefore, would appear to be built into the very concept of toleration itself.

Of course, many in Ireland felt that there were good grounds for their prejudices and this would lead them to query the very idea of toleration. The vicar of Naas, Stephen Radcliffe, rejected Edward Synge's proposals for a limited toleration of Catholics in Ireland on these grounds: one was morally obliged to 'Recover the Papists from their Errors, and bring them to the Knowledge of the Truth.'[37] Indeed, toleration, it was argued, required people to relinquish their hold on truth in the name of a dogmatic scepticism. This was the charge that the Anglican clergyman Jonas Proast made against Locke's plea for toleration in the 1690s: Locke may have declared that there was 'only one true religion' but he baulked on this conviction in his own commitment to tolerance – or so Proast claimed.[38] Locke's case apparently rested on a sceptical claim: all religions are equally uncertain and therefore have an equal right to be tolerated. For Proast, however, this was tantamount to conceding that there is no 'true Religion'.[39] Clearly, Proast thought that there was one and one was morally obliged to enforce it: if some people were 'so stiff in their Prejudices' that they insisted on taking the wrong road, then thorns and briars should be put in their way.[40] Similar arguments would be proposed in Ireland: here that resonant line of Luke's – 'Compel them to come in' (Luke 14: 23) – would do the rounds, although what constituted compulsion would be much debated.[41]

Like many enlightened figures, Locke had railed against prejudice. As he announced in *Of the Conduct of the Understanding*, 'shake off this great and dangerous imposter prejudice, who dresses up falsehood in the likeness of truth, and so dexterously hoodwinks men's minds as to keep them in the dark with a belief that they are more in the light than any that do not see with their eyes'.[42] But in his response to Proast he seemed to adopt a more nuanced position. A Turk's confidence in the truth of his religion may be 'a prejudice', he argued, but a Turk would think the same of a Christian's. Faith for many Christians is a matter of 'unquestionable principle' – which Locke identified as another word for prejudice.[43] According to Locke, not everyone can proceed in the manner of Descartes, doubting everything until they arrive at certainty, particularly with regard to religion. Here the pursuit of certainty is misdirected and demands knowledge where there can only be faith. Proast's brand of certainty is dogmatic as is his prejudice against prejudice: his demand that we should lay aside our prejudices in the name of true religion would undermine religion itself. So Locke's 'Third Letter' may be viewed as a plea for toleration in the name of prejudice, not against it.

Of course, Locke's letters on toleration are arguably a defence of prejudice in a different and more pejorative sense – Catholics were to be extended no toleration at all. Locke did not argue that Catholic worship was intolerable because it was 'idolatrous' – this was no ground for persecution: rather, it was for their attachment to a foreign prince. He also suggested that reciprocity was a condition of toleration and that Catholics were too intolerant to honour this demand. Consequently, they should receive no toleration themselves. All of Locke's arguments would be recycled in Ireland. John Toland put the case pithily in 1701: '*Papists* ought not to be tolerated in any free State, because they not only deny Liberty to all others, and pronounce 'em eternally damn'd; but also because they are Subjects to a foren Head whose Authority they prefer to that of their native Magistrats.'[44] Toland repeatedly criticised religious persecution on enlightened grounds (by prohibiting the free expression of opinion, it inhibited 'all progress in *knowledge* or advancement of *Learning* and *Sciences*' and engendered 'a brutal barbarity').[45] In *Nazarenus*, he provided a sympathetic account of Mosaic Judaism, primitive Christianity and early Islam. Moreover, in 1714 he defended Jews from the 'vulgar prejudices' launched against them and called for their full naturalisation as citizens under the Crown.[46] Nonetheless, he continued to insist that no toleration should be extended to the intolerant: 'Papists never grant a Toleration to others', so should receive none.[47]

The scholar and Catholic activist Charles O'Conor repeatedly argued that Protestants had little to fear from their Catholic countrymen ('The Dangers of *Popery* to this Kingdom', he proclaimed, 'are none at all').[48] O'Conor was

a self-consciously enlightened critic of the Penal Laws: they were the rem-
nant of darker days and reflected a deeply anachronistic fear of internal
dissension and papal conquest (Catholics, he argued, had demonstrated their
loyalty to the constitution for almost seventy years). The various strictures
against Catholics – denying them the right to vote, to hold public office, to
practice law, to be educated abroad, or to enjoy unrestricted ownership of
land – were not rigorously enforced; and Catholics had found many ways
around them. Nonetheless, O'Conor argued that the popery laws betrayed
basic traditions of constitutional liberty; they also violated all concepts of
natural justice and public utility. Denied proper security in land, Catholics
were discouraged from improving themselves or their country. Such persecution, moreover, connived against public morals. (Drawing on
Montesquieu, O'Conor argued that however false, religion was '*the best
Security we can have for the Probity of Men*'.)[49] O'Conor thus longed for
'the happy emancipation from Prejudices, which hath already taken place on
several countries of the continent', but he also realised that this was liable to
take some time in Ireland.[50] 'Prejudices against the Roman Catholic
Religion', he reported, 'run still very high.'[51]

Many in Ireland would continue to see Catholicism as a persecuting
faith. Memories of the terrible massacre of Protestants in Ireland in 1641 –
which even in Voltaire's *Treatise on Toleration* is discussed in grim detail –
would keep this idea alive. As the Rev. John Rogers put it in a sermon in
1780, 'Popery is of a persecuting spirit, and has always marked her steps,
wherever she trod, with blood.'[52] Even those who wanted to adopt a more
forgiving approach to Catholicism – like Bishop Berkeley – still tended to
cast it as a deeply intolerant religion. Berkeley deeply disapproved of calls
to compel Catholics to conform: was not such compulsion 'the worst thing
in Popery, and consequently to copy after the Church of Rome therein,
were not to become Papist ourselves in the worst sense!' (*W*, VI, p. 160). In
his pleas for the toleration of Catholics in the 1720s, Edward Synge would
argue the same: Protestants resembled Jesuits in their arguments for
persecution except they were a lot less subtle.[53] Edmund Burke would
also adopt this line: he had no time for those who would 'oppose to Popery
another Popery' (*WS*, III, p. 640). So, sectarianism could inform the very
idiom of toleration itself. Indeed, in Toland's eyes toleration was a 'truly
Protestant principle'.[54]

Toleration, according to Burke, was a relatively new virtue in Europe,
but it was indissociable from the rise of enlightenment: 'as mankind has
become enlightened', Burke explained in the 1760s, 'the idea of religious
persecution, under any circumstances, has been almost universally

exploded by all good and thinking men' (*WS*, IX, p. 465). Burke was a defender of the established church, but believed this was entirely compatible with toleration: as he argued in 1773, 'tolerate all kinds of consciences'; this, he believed, was the best foil to those who have none – namely, atheists and epicureans (*WS*, II, p. 87). He repeatedly called for the relaxation of restrictions against Dissenters and Catholics and was a particularly furious critic of the penal code in Ireland. It was, he declared in 1792, 'a machine of wise and elaborate contrivance; and as well fitted for the oppression, impoverishment and degradation of a people, and the debasement, in them, of human nature itself, as ever proceeded from the perverted ingenuity of man'. Burke tended to exaggerate the systematic character of religious persecution in Ireland – it was as he put it, 'a complete system, full of coherence and consistency' (*WS*, IX, p. 637). In other contexts, he was prepared to admit that the laws were 'every day fading into disuse' (*WS*, IX, p. 566), although he also worried that attempts to reform them might in fact revive their force, adding new insult to longstanding injury.

Burke's response to the popery laws revealed the dual nature of prejudice in his thought. In Ireland people found themselves 'attacked by prejudices which aim to intrude themselves into the place of Law' (*WS*, IX, p. 458). The aggressive partiality of the penal code, he maintained, was at odds with all the rules of equity. Yet he also believed that prejudicial laws violated all the 'powerful prejudices of human nature'. Prejudice, it seems, was both the villain and victim in Ireland. A common theme between his critique of the penal laws and his later defences of prejudice in the *Reflections*, however, is his emphasis on custom or 'the stable prejudice of time' (*WS*, IX, p. 467). A veneration for the beliefs of one's forefathers, Burke argued, was natural to the human mind and was basic to political order. But the popery laws penalised this moral psychology and connived against the very order it pretended to vouchsafe. Indeed, Burke would later argue that all the religions of Europe were prescriptive religions: in other words, their longevity was their main sanction; they had 'a train of legitimate prejudices' as their main stay (*WS*, IX, p. 662). Each of these religions should be respected. As he put it in 1773, 'There is reasonable worship in them all' (*WS*, II, p. 388).

Seven years later, Arthur Young struck a gloomy note about the prospects for reconciliation in Ireland: 'The Enlightened spirit of Toleration, so well understood and practised in the greatest part of Europe, is making progress every day, save in Ireland alone.'[55] The relaxation of the Penal Laws in 1778 (which removed the most severe restrictions on the ownership of land) and 1782 (which removed constraints on Catholic worship) gave succour to some – the 'Spirit of Liberality', Burke reported, 'begins to gain Ground in Ireland', although he would soon resume his polemic against prejudice and persecution in Ireland.[56] Of course, the problem may have had something to do with the concept of toleration itself – according to Kant, it could present itself as an 'arrogant' virtue, expressing the very contempt it pretended to transcend.[57] Burke, for instance, condemned measures to reform the Penal Laws in 1782 as an exercise in 'contempt' as much as 'indulgence' – not least because they explicitly retained many of the old prohibitions (Catholics were not allowed to sit in parliament nor exercise the franchise, nor hold office under the Crown, nor be permitted to practise as barristers or attorneys). The spirit of toleration, Burke told Hercules Langrishe, should 'be tender and large', not suspicious and begrudging (*WS*, IX, p. 605). Moreover, it should dwell on the good of others, not bite its tongue at their evils. Catholicism, he informed William Smith, should be cherished as a good, albeit not 'the most preferable good'. It should certainly not be regarded as an 'inevitable evil' (*WS*, IX, p. 663).

And yet this points towards a broader prejudice within enlightenment itself. After all, for many of its ambassadors in Europe (Montesquieu, Voltaire, Diderot, Helvétius) and Ireland (Toland, Molyneux, Berkeley, Hutcheson) enlightenment was indistinguishable from the rise of Protestantism: as Charles O'Conor seemed to acknowledge, the Reformation was the paradigm-case of the mind's emancipation from '*Popish darkness* and *Popish Superstition*'.[58] But this presumption had also made 'the Reformation in a degree noxious' to many of Ireland's inhabitants – or so Burke would claim (*WS*, IX, p. 468). Thomas Leland seemed to annoy Protestants and Catholics alike when he suggested that the Reformation in Ireland amounted to little more than 'the impositions of English government on a prejudiced and bigotted people'.[59]

Of course, it was an established theme of enlightened thought that a 'conquest can destroy harmful prejudices, and ... can put a nation under a better presiding genius'. Montesquieu had made this case in *The Spirit of the Laws*, although he also suggested that it was wise for conquerors to respect the established mores of a subject people.[60] In *A System of Moral Philosophy* Francis Hutcheson suggested that if a prudent legislator, armed with sufficient power, can impose enlightened policies on 'a stupid and prejudiced people', however loath they may be to receive them, then it was legitimate for him to do so.[61] But many commentators queried the wisdom of such an approach in Ireland. Here, 'the spirit of a fierce people was *irritated* against lawful authority, instead of being *won to it*, by any composition with their manners, or any prudent concessions to their prejudices'.[62] Governments, Burke insisted, should avoid bad collisions between power and opinion and should accommodate popular beliefs in the interests of peace. Here he stressed the duty and policy of conforming 'to the prejudices of a whole people, even where the foundation of such prejudices be false or disputable' (*WS*, III, p. 263). He made these remarks in reference to America, but, as I have suggested above, they had a bearing on his native country, Ireland.

The Prejudices of Improvement

Enlightenment, as we have seen, was expressive of religious animosity as much as it was an attempt to mitigate its effects. Nonetheless, many enlightened commentators would attempt to put aside their religious differences in the name of peace and economic prosperity. Indeed, as Toby Barnard, James Livesey, and Michael Brown have argued, Ireland produced a remarkable amount of improvement literature in the 1720s, 1730s, and beyond.[63] Note, for instance, Sir John Browne's *Seasonable Remarks on Trade* (1728), Thomas Prior's *List of the Absentees of Ireland* (1729), and Arthur Dobbs's *Essay on the Trade and Improvement of Ireland* (1729–31). But it is worth stressing that even on the technical question of improvement a controversial set of religious assumptions could prevail. Charles O'Conor would attack the Penal Laws for their pernicious economic effects; indeed, Burke claimed the laws were reducible to the simple injunction: 'Thou shalt not improve' (*WS*, IX, p. 477). But Berkeley would sometimes wonder if the cause of backwardness lay with Catholicism itself. As he confided to a Catholic priest: 'Many suspect your religion to be the cause of that notorious idleness which prevails so generally among the natives of our island' (*W*, VI, p. 247).

Berkeley was obsessed with Ireland's 'innate hereditary sloth' (*W*, VI, p. 235) and wondered, 'whether it not be a sad circumstance to live among lazy beggars' (*W*, VI, p. 134). However, he also proposed a variety of creative measures to increase industry and labour, believing them to be the source of all wealth. In this regard, he was an inveterate 'improver' and twinned the country's enlightenment with its economic well-being. But it is also worth noting Berkeley's deep misgivings about the spread of luxury (as he wrote in 1742, 'luxury seems the original root of those evils under which we groan'; *W*, VIII, p. 262). His objections to luxury had an economic basis: he speculated that a fine gentleman was a 'public nuisance' and a woman of fashion a 'public enemy' because they contributed nothing to the production of wealth. But he also worried that luxury was indicative of a broader moral decline: 'we are the first to have become wicked on principle' he gloomily concluded (*W*, VI, p. 84). The background text here was Mandeville's *Fable of the Bees* – a work that had famously averred that private vices had public utility. The covetousness of some fostered the industry of others. As Mandeville put it: 'Fraud, Luxury, and Pride must live / Whilst we the Benefits receive.'[64]

In many respects, Mandeville was a severe moralist – his account of universal hypocrisy relied on this – but Berkeley insisted that his intention was simply to promote vice and to undermine civic virtue. Hutcheson was also a Mandeville-basher. Wealth and well-being, he contended, did not depend on vice, but were usually undermined by it. If Mandeville stressed the power and ubiquity of self-interest, Hutcheson emphasised the fact of disinterested benevolence. Men, he suggested, were naturally disposed to serve the 'Publick Good' regardless of their own welfare ('Virtue is not pursued from the Interest or Self-love of the Pursuer, or any Motives of his own Advantage').[65] Nonetheless, Berkeley – and many modern Catos – were concerned that this type of virtue was on the wane. In Berkeley's eyes, Mandeville had proclaimed public spirit to be an 'idle enthusiasm, which seizeth only on weak minds' (*W*, III, p. 52). This was another exaggeration, but Mandeville had maintained that the public interest was often better served by the pursuit of self-interest than by the promotion of self-sacrificing virtue. He thus seemed to question the direct link between the good polity and the good citizen and removed the moral basis for the execution of virtue. 'Pubic spirit, that glorious principle of all that is great and good', Berkeley declared, 'is become ridiculous in this enlightened age' (*W*, VI, p. 79).

Indeed, civic virtue and economic improvement could appear to contradict each other in an enlightened age. Berkeley and Hutcheson would insist upon their compatibility – at least when wealth and virtue were rightly conceived – as would later bands of commercially minded republicans. Swift, too, was a notable improver – advocating the building of roads, the drainage of bogs, and the cultivation of tillage in Ireland – but he questioned the moral presumption behind the very concept of advancement.[66] His modest proposal, famously recommending the sale and consumption of children, exposed the prejudices of certain projectors or their dangerous lack of them. Such absolute open-mindedness, Swift suggests, is a type of moral insanity. Indeed, *A Tale of a Tub* (written for the 'universal improvement of mankind') contains recommendations for the 'Improvement of madness *in a Commonwealth*' (*PW*, I, p. 102). And the Academy of Lagado in *Gulliver's Travels* pokes further fun at the idea of improvement itself. The notion that the progress of science or commerce necessarily fostered virtue was, for Swift, a bad presumption. An enlightenment so hostile to prejudices, he suggests, should take time to study its own.

So prejudice, as I have argued, was the great theme and limit point of enlightenment in Ireland. It was condemned by the *illuminati* as a source of misunderstanding and intolerance, but tolerance, as we have seen, could foster prejudices of its own. And yet the aim of transcending prejudice was sometimes judged to be one of the most dangerous prejudices at all. Many, of course, would continue to share Toland's dream of a total emancipation from benighted traditions and inherited errors. In 1791, the *Belfast Newsletter* called for the destruction of the 'empire of prejudices, that empire of gigantic shadows, which are only formidable while they are not attacked'.[67] But for philosophical as much as for political reasons, such an empire was not likely to disappear any day soon.

Notes

1. See, in particular, Ultán Gillen, 'Varieties of Enlightenment: The Enlightenment and Irish Political Culture in the Age of Revolutions', in *Peripheries of Enlightenment*, ed. Richard Butterwick, Simon Davies, and Gabriel Sánchez Espinosa (Oxford University Press, 2008), pp. 163–82; Ian McBride, *Eighteenth-Century Ireland: The Isle of Slaves* (Dublin: Gill and Macmillan, 2009), pp. 51–99; Michael Brown, *The Irish Enlightenment* (Cambridge, MA: Harvard University Press, 2016).
2. Charles O'Conor, *The Case of the Roman-Catholics of Ireland. Wherein the Principles and Conduct of That Party Are Fully Explained and Vindicated* (Dublin, 1755), p. 78.
3. In the 1960s, Hans-Georg Gadamer declared that the 'fundamental prejudice of the Enlightenment is the prejudice against prejudice itself'. As we shall see, enlightened views were more complicated than Gadamer allowed. See Hans-Georg Gadamer, *Truth and Method*, trans. Joel Winsheimer and Donald G. Marshall, 2nd rev. edn (London: Continuum, 2004), p. 273.
4. On Irish rudeness, see David Hume, *The History of England, from the Invasion of Julius Caesar to the Revolution in 1688*, 8 vols (London, 1778), VI, p. 400. On Hume's views of Ireland, see David Berman, 'David Hume on the 1641 Rebellion in Ireland', *Studies* 65.258 (1976), 101–12. On Voltaire, see Graham Gargett, 'Voltaire's View of the Irish', in *Ireland and the French Enlightenment, 1700–1800*, ed. Gargett and Geraldine Sheridan (Houndmills: Palgrave Macmillan, 1999), pp. 152–70.
5. Conor Cruise O'Brien, *On the Eve of the Millennium: The Future of Democracy Through an Age of Unreason* (New York: Simon and Schuster, 1994), p. 29.
6. Conor Cruise O'Brien, in *Irish Times*, 1 March 1977. For a more sustained discussion of such opposition, see David Berman, 'The Irish Counter-

Enlightenment', in *The Irish Mind: Exploring Intellectual Traditions*, ed. Richard Kearney (Dublin: Wolfhound Press, 1985), pp. 119–40.

7. W. H. Lecky, *History of the Rise and Influence of the Spirit of Rationalism in Europe*, 2nd edn, 2 vols (London: Longmans, Green, and Co., 1865), II, pp. 106–249.

8. Ibid., II, pp. 7–8.

9. William Molyneux to John Locke (26 March 1695); *Some Familiar Letters Between Mr. Locke, and Several of His Friends* (London, 1708), p. 106.

10. *The Writings and Speeches of Edmund Burke*, ed. Paul Langford et al., 10 vols (Oxford: Clarendon Press, 1981–2015), II, p. 388. Further references to this edition are given in the text after the abbreviation *WS*.

11. See Richard Bourke, 'Burke, Enlightenment and Romanticism', in *The Cambridge Companion to Edmund Burke*, ed. David Dwan and Chris Insole (Cambridge University Press, 2012), pp. 27–40.

12. *A Notebook of Edmund Burke*, ed. H. V. F. Somerset (Cambridge University Press, 1957), p. 95. Further references to this edition are given in the text after the abbreviation *N*.

13. Ernst Cassirer, *The Philosophy of the Enlightenment*, trans. Fritz C. A. Koelln and James P. Pettegrove (Princeton University Press, 1951), p. vii.

14. *The Works of George Berkeley, Bishop of Cloyne*, ed. A. A. Luce and T. E. Jessop, 9 vols (London: Thomas Nelson and Sons, 1948–57), III, p. 202. Further references to this edition and are given in the text after the abbreviation *W*.

15. Edmund Burke, *Pre-Revolutionary Writings*, ed. Ian Harris (Cambridge University Press, 1993), p. 198.

16. *The Correspondence of Edmund Burke*, ed. Thomas Copeland et al., 10 vols (Cambridge University Press, 1958–78), III, p. 457.

17. *John Toland's* Letters to Serena, ed. Ian Leask (Dublin: Four Courts Press, 2013), pp. 2–3.

18. Ibid., p. 7.

19. John Toland, *Clito: A Poem on the Force of Eloquence* (London 1700), p. 16.

20. *Toland's* Letters to Serena, p. xxiv.

21. John Toland, *Christianity Not Mysterious . . .*, 2nd edn (London, 1696), p. 8.

22. John Toland, *The Life of John Milton . . .* (London, 1699), p. 147.

23. Toland, *Christianity Not Mysterious*, p. 11.

24. John Locke, *An Essay Concerning Human Understanding*, ed. Peter H. Nidditch (Oxford: Clarendon Press, 1975), p. 689.

25. Toland, *Christianity Not Mysterious*, p. 145.

26. Ibid., p. 24.

27. Ibid., p. 132.

28. Ibid., p. 6.

29. Peter Browne, *A Letter in Answer to a Book Entitled, Christianity Not Mysterious . . .* (London, 1697), p. 143.

30. Ibid., p. 169.

31. See *The Prose Works of Jonathan Swift*, ed. Herbert Davis et al., 14 vols (Oxford: Blackwell, 1939–74), II, p. 37. Further references are to this edition

and are given in the text after the abbreviation '*PW*'. On Swift's attitudes to atheism and deism, see Daniel Carey, 'Swift among the Freethinkers', *Eighteenth-Century Ireland / Iris an dá chultúr* 12 (1997), 89–99.

32. See David Hume, 'Of Moral Prejudices', in *Essays: Moral, Political, and Literary*, ed. Eugene F. Miller (New York: Cosimo, 2006), pp. 573–78.

33. *Mary Wollstonecraft: Political Writings*, ed. Janet Todd (London: William Pickering, 1993), p. 197.

34. John Toland, *An Apology for Mr Toland* ... (London, 1697), p. 15.

35. S. T. Coleridge, *The Friend*, ed. Barbara E. Rooke, 2 vols (London: Routledge, 1969), II, pp. 123–33 (p. 124).

36. *Toland's* Letters to Serena, p. 15.

37. Stephen Radcliffe, *A Letter to the Reverend Mr. Edward Synge* ... (Dublin, 1725), p. 29.

38. See *Locke on Toleration*, ed. Richard Vernon (Cambridge University Press, 2010), pp. 8, 65.

39. Ibid., p. 112.

40. Ibid., p. 58.

41. See, for instance, Edward Synge, *The Case of Toleration Consider'd with Respect Both to Religion and Civil Government* (London, 1726), pp. 13–14, 27, 36; Edward Synge, *A Vindication of a Sermon Preach'd before the Honourable House of Commons of Ireland* ... (Dublin, 1726), pp. 5, 11; Radcliffe, *A Letter to the Reverend Mr. Edward Synge*, p. 4; Stephen Radcliffe, *A Serious and Humble Enquiry whether It Be Lawful, Prudent, or Convenient, that a Toleration of Popery Should Be Enacted* ... (Dublin, 1727), p. 5.

42. John Locke, *Some Thoughts Concerning Education: And, Of the Conduct of the Understanding*, ed. Ruth W. Grant and Nathan Tarcov (Indianapolis, IN: Hackett, 1996), p. 186.

43. *Locke on Toleration*, p. 154.

44. John Toland, *Anglia Libera* ... (London, 1701), pp. 101–02.

45. John Toland, *The Memorial of the State of England* ... (London, 1705), p. 48.

46. John Toland, *Reasons for Naturalizing the Jews in Great Britain and Ireland* ... (London, 1714).

47. John Toland, *The State-Anatomy of Great Britain* ..., 3rd edn (London, 1717), p. 21.

48. O'Conor, *Case of the Roman-Catholics*, p. 70.

49. Ibid., p. 67.

50. Ibid., p. 15.

51. Ibid., p. 77.

52. See James Kelly, 'Inter-Denominational Relations and Religious Toleration in Late Eighteenth-Century Ireland: The "Paper War" of 1786–88', *Eighteenth-Century Ireland / Iris an dá chultúr* 3 (1988), 39–67 (p. 42).

53. Synge, *A Vindication*, p. 47.

54. Toland, *State-Anatomy of Great Britain*, p. 21.

55. Arthur Young, *A Tour of Ireland with General Observations Made on the State of That Kingdom*, 2 vols (London, 1780), II, p. 146.

56. *Correspondence of Edmund Burke*, III, p. 458.

57. Immanuel Kant, *Practical Philosophy*, ed. and trans. Mary Gregor (Cambridge University Press, 1996), p. 21.

58. Charles O'Conor, *Seasonable Thoughts Relating to Our Civil and Ecclesiastical Constitution* (Dublin, 1753), p. 14. On this point, see McBride, *Eighteenth-Century Ireland*, p. 84.

59. Thomas Leland, *The History of Ireland from the Invasion of Henry II . . .*, 3 vols (Dublin, 1773), II, p. 201.

60. Montesquieu, *The Spirit of the Laws*, trans. and ed. Anne Cohler, Basia Miller, and Harold Stone (Cambridge University Press, 1989), p. 142.

61. Francis Hutcheson, *A System of Moral Philosophy*, 2 vols (Glasgow, 1755), II, p. 231.

62. John Curry and Charles O'Conor, *Observations on the Popery Laws* (Dublin, 1771), p. 21.

63. Toby Barnard, *Improving Ireland? Projectors, Prophets and Profiteers, 1641–1786* (Dublin: Four Courts Press, 2008); James Livesey, *Civil Society and Empire: Ireland and Scotland in the Eighteenth-Century Atlantic World* (New Haven, CT and London: Yale University Press, 2009), pp. 54–89; Brown, *The Irish Enlightenment*, pp. 186–206.

64. Bernard Mandeville, *The Fable of the Bees*, 6th edn, 2 vols (London, 1729–30), I, p. 12.

65. Francis Hutcheson, *An Inquiry into the Original of Our Ideas of Beauty and Virtue*, ed. Wolfgang Leidhold (Indianapolis, IN: Liberty Fund, 2004), p. 102.

66. On Swift as an improver, see D. W. Hayton, 'Swift, the Church and the "Improvement of Ireland"', in *Reading Swift: Papers from the Sixth Münster Symposium on Jonathan Swift*, ed. Kirsten Juhas, Hermann J. Real, and Sandra Simon (München: Wilhelm Fink, 2013), pp. 325–38.

67. *Belfast Newsletter* (8 July 1791), p. 1.

CHAPTER 5

The Molyneux Problem and Irish Enlightenment

Darrell Jones

Towards the end of the seventeenth century, the Irish natural philosopher William Molyneux (1656–98) wondered what might happen if a man who had been blind from birth was suddenly enabled to see.[1] Over the course of the next hundred years, the 'Molyneux problem', as the resulting thought experiment eventually came to be known, occupied the minds of many of the most brilliant and progressive intellectuals both in Ireland and further afield. Yet while the problem's contribution to European philosophy is well established, its role in the history of Irish ideas has proved more difficult to assess. Much of that difficulty is closely related to the deceptively nebulous concept of 'Enlightenment'. A generation ago, David Berman argued that eighteenth-century Irish philosophy was largely defined by the rise to dominance of 'Counter-Enlightenment' forces; in this context, Berman described Molyneux's puzzle as 'the most important Irish philosophical problem', and its protagonist, the blind man, as 'the root metaphor' of eighteenth-century Irish thought.[2] Since then, however, both of Berman's claims have at times been called into question, while the relationship between them remains to be fully explored. On the one hand, Thomas Duddy and Daniel Carey have acknowledged the influence of Molyneux's problem on eighteenth-century Irish intellectual history, while resisting the temptation to interpret either in terms of a contest over Enlightenment.[3] On the other, Ian McBride has explicitly declared that 'the Enlightenment in Ireland began with [Molyneux's] thought experiment', whereas Michael Brown in *The Irish Enlightenment* makes no mention of the problem at all.[4] One way or another, the Molyneux problem has something to reveal about the meaning of 'Enlightenment' in eighteenth-century Ireland. The following chapter attempts to discover what that is.

Molyneux's Problem

The Molyneux problem first appeared in print in London in 1694, in the second edition of John Locke's *An Essay Concerning Humane Understanding*. This is how Locke described the scenario, in a passage that he added to his chapter '*Of Perception*':

> I shall here insert a Problem of that very Ingenious and Studious pro-moter of real Knowledge the Learned and Worthy Mr. *Molineux*, which he was pleased to send me in a Letter some Months since; and it is this, *Suppose a Man born blind, and now adult, and taught by his touch to distinguish between a Cube, and a Sphere of the same metal, and nighly of the same bigness, so as to tell, when he felt one and t'other, which is the Cube, which the Sphere. Suppose then the Cube and Sphere placed on a Table, and the Blind Man to be made to see. Quære, Whether by his sight, before he touch'd them, he could now distinguish, and tell, which is the Globe, which the Cube.*[5]

A simple enough question, it might be thought. Yet it has often been observed that the Molyneux problem is philosophically ambiguous.[6] One way of identifying and addressing its ambiguities is to examine the early development of the problem in context. The letter from Molyneux to which Locke referred was sent in the spring of 1693. In fact, this was the second occasion on which Molyneux had attempted to draw Locke's attention to his query. Five years earlier, the Dubliner had written to Jean Le Clerc's *Bibliothèque universelle et historique* with 'A Problem Proposed to the Author of the Essai Philosophique concernant L'Entendement', a French abridgment of Locke's forthcoming *Essay* having recently been published in Le Clerc's journal. Presumably inspired by the *Essai*'s distinc-tion between simple ideas belonging to single and to multiple senses, Molyneux submitted to its mysterious author a version of his scenario that also included a second question about the blind man, the sphere, and the cube: 'Whether he Could know by his sight, before he stretchd out his Hand, whether he Could not Reach them, tho they were Removed 20 or 1000 feet from him?'[7]

Locke was initially reticent about the problem that Molyneux proposed. Having received and endorsed an unsolicited letter, he evidently declined to respond. Molyneux, by contrast, was invested in his problem for reasons that were personal, intellectual, and social. Husband to a woman who had lost her sight through illness within months of their marriage in 1678, Molyneux dropped conflicting hints at possible solutions to his problem in isolated passages of his treatise on optical lenses, *Dioptrica nova* (1692). In relation to questions of depth perception, Molyneux maintained that 'the Estimate we make of the *Distance* of Objects' is 'rather the Act of our *Judgment*, than of *Sense*'. As he explained, '*Distance* of it self, is not to be perceived; for 'tis a Line (or a Length) presented to our Eye with its End towards us, which must therefore be only a *Point*, and that is *Invisible*.'[8] Elsewhere, however, Molyneux denied that 'use and custom' are the only means by which objects are judged erect when 'perceived by an *inverted* Image on the Fund of the Eye'. Citing the hypothetical case of 'an adult Person, who has been blind from his Birth, and now suddenly restored to his Sight', he posited that the person 'is not prejudiced by custom, and yet (doubtless) would judge as usual' (p. 212). Underlying speculations such as these was a crucial distinction that Molyneux drew in 'the manner of the Visive Faculties *Perception*'. As he observed: ''tis not properly the Eye that *sees*, it is only the Organ or Instrument, 'tis the *Soul* that *sees* by means of the Eye' (p. 105). Suggestive though this was, Molyneux was writing as an optical physicist who only occasionally alluded to the cognitive and psychological aspects of vision. Enquiries of that nature more properly lay within the philosophical province of Locke's *Essay*, which Molyneux singled out for special praise in his dedication of *Dioptrica nova* to the Royal Society of London (p. [iv]).

Shortly after his book was published, Molyneux sent Locke a complimentary copy, and a seminal correspondence began. The two authors had been exchanging letters for a period of about six months before Molyneux deemed it proper to return to the 'jocose problem' that Locke had previously ignored. This time, Molyneux replaced his second question about distance with a counter-intuitive answer to his primary query. He also explicitly submitted to Locke that he 'may find some place', in the forthcoming edition of his *Essay*, for a discussion of his hypothetical scenario. Initially without further comment, Locke replied that his friend's 'ingenious problem will deserve to be published to the world'.[9] The following year, he duly inserted it, in almost verbatim quotation, at a relevant location in his text.

To the question of whether the blind man made to see would be capable of distinguishing between the metal sphere and cube, Locke reported that Molyneux had answered:

> *Not, For though he has obtain'd the experience of, how a Globe, how a Cube affects his touch; yet he has not yet attained the Experience, that what affects his touch so or so, must affect his sight so or so; Or that a protuberant angle in the Cube, that pressed his hand unequally, shall appear to his eye, as it does in the Cube*[.]

Locke, for his part, supported Molyneux's solution:

> I agree with this thinking Gent. whom though I have never had the happiness to see, I am proud to call my Friend, in his answer to this his Problem; and am of opinion, that the Blind Man, at first sight, would not be able with certainty to say, which was the Globe, which the Cube, whilst he only saw them: though he could unerringly name them by his touch, and certainly distinguish them by the difference of their Figures felt.

And he continued:

> This I have set down, and leave with my Reader, as an occasion for him to consider, how much he may be beholding to experience, improvement and acquired notions, where he thinks, he has not the least use of, or help from them: And the rather, because this observing Gent. farther adds, that *having upon the occasion of my Book, proposed this to divers very ingenious Men, he hardly ever met with one, that at first gave the answer to it, which he thinks true, till by hearing his reasons they were convinced.* (II.9.8)

As ready and willing as it appears, Locke's acquiescence to Molyneux's request must have involved an uncomfortable process of tacit negotiation. In the first place, Locke set the problem in the context of a chapter that Le Clerc had omitted from the French abridgment by which Molyneux had originally been inspired.[10] Given Locke's argument in the proximal paragraphs that the experience of instantaneous perception is an illusion caused by the 'settled habit' of judgment, Molyneux's distinction in *Dioptrica nova* between the judgment of the soul and the prejudice of custom remained to be clarified and secured. In the second, Locke felt able to support the proposed solution only to the extent that the man 'at first sight' would be unable 'with certainty' to identify the sphere and cube. Indeed, the length of time and the range of perspectives that the man might need in order to respond with certainty were questions on which Molyneux and Locke would never explicitly agree.[11] In the absence of such a consensus, Molyneux's man soon set out on a storied life of his own among contemporary Irish philosophers and theologians.

The Blind Man and the Anglicans

Within eighteen months of the appearance of his problem in print, Molyneux enclosed in a letter to Locke an alternative solution recently put forward by Edward Synge (1659–1741), an Anglican clergyman from County Cork who would later be appointed Archbishop of Tuam in County Galway. Although he described Synge as 'an ingenious man', Molyneux told Locke that he would 'easily discover by what false steps this gentleman is lead into his error'.[12] As with Locke, the circumstances of Synge's encounter with Molyneux's problem are worth consideration. Having heard an account from his colleague Francis Quayle on a visit to the home of another fellow clergyman, Benjamin Lukey, Synge immediately became fixated on solving the puzzle. Since Quayle, who later forwarded the results to Molyneux, seems tactically to have kept his friend uninformed of the answer on which Molyneux and Locke had agreed, Synge, unlike Locke, approached the problem from a personally unbiased position.

The double basis of Synge's affirmative solution was a terminological distinction that Locke might usefully have adopted and a first conditional that he was evidently inclined to reject. Having first established that 'I call every notion of any thing which a man entertains, an *Idea*', but that the 'notion only, which a man entertains of a visible thing, as it is visible, I call an *Image*', Synge proceeded to develop an argument whose hypothetical terms he tellingly repeated:

> And if immediately, upon the sight of the globe and cube, there be grounds enough for such a person clearly to perceive the agreement, and the difference between his pre-conceived *ideas* and newly conceived *images* of those figures, then may he be able to know which is the globe, and which the cube, without touching them again after he has seen them.
>
> For the agreement which he may find between his *idea* and his *image* of a globe, and the difference of the *idea* of a globe from the *image* of a cube *(& sic vice versâ)* will be a sufficient direction to him. (If I say, there be sufficient ground immediately to perceive the said agreement and difference.)[13]

Synge went on to elaborate his answer by enumerating the geometrical properties of spheres and cubes. Nevertheless, Locke, like Molyneux, immediately concluded that the rector from Cork was effectively engaging in tautology, and was therefore begging the essential question that the problem was designed to address. As Locke wrote to Molyneux early in 1696: 'I see by Mr. S's answer to that which was originally your question, how hard it is, for even ingenious men to free themselves from the anticipations of sense.'[14]

Despite its rejection by Molyneux and Locke, Synge's response gave an early indication that future attempts to solve Molyneux's problem would be required to operate at multiple levels of enquiry. Moreover, whereas Molyneux had originally conceived his scenario for purely philosophical purposes, it ultimately emerged from Lukey's Anglican symposium replete with theological implications. In *An Appendix to A Gentleman's Religion* (1698), Synge recounted a conversation that he claimed to have had with a man who was 'blind from his Infancy', and explained that a simple experiment, in which people at a distance would perceive and describe his movements, had convinced the man of the existence of light and colours. For Synge, the blind man's abstract knowledge of vision was a valuable example of 'representative Conception', and he saw no reason 'why we should not believe the Doctrines of the Trinity, and Incarnation, upon the Testimony of the Holy Scriptures, as well as the blind Man did the Existence of Light and Colours, upon the Testimony of other Men'.[15]

As his references to two of the established Christian mysteries suggest, Synge's *Appendix* constituted part of a semi-official Anglican response to the *enfant terrible* of Irish theology, John Toland (1670–1722), whose immediately notorious *Christianity Not Mysterious* had been published two years before.[16] If Synge's approach differed in its admittedly dubious basis in a first-hand account of an informally experimental procedure, then the physical plausibility of Molyneux's scenario was another question with theological repercussions for writers on either side of the debate. In his second edition, Toland maintained that 'an able *Physician* do's sometimes restore Sight to the Blind', and that a miracle occurs only if the cure is effected 'without the ordinary Time and Applications'.[17] For William King (1650–1729), Archbishop of Dublin, however, an observation such as Toland's cut both ways. In a sermon delivered at Christ Church Cathedral in May 1709, King suggested that a blind man who had been told about light and colours would readily 'endure Labour and Pain, and submit to the most difficult and tormenting Operations of *Physick* or *Chirurgery*, in order to obtain the use of Eyes', before pointedly presenting his valiant subject as an exemplar of spiritual faith. 'And then will not he rise up in Judgement against us, and Condemn us?', King demanded, 'since he endures so much to obtain sight, on the imperfect Representations of it, that are made to him by other Men, whilst we will not believe and endure as much for Eternal happiness on the Testimony of God'.[18]

The blind man as a metaphor for the human spiritual condition remained current in Irish Anglican theology throughout the eighteenth century.[19] By the time King's sermon was printed, however, a far-reaching philosophical exploration of Molyneux's scenario had been published by a junior clergyman from County Kilkenny who later became Bishop of Cloyne in County Cork. A decade earlier, the fifteen-year-old George Berkeley (1685–1753) had entered Trinity College, Dublin, at a formative time in the history of Irish philosophy. Largely due to Molyneux's advocacy, Locke's *Essay* was by that time firmly established on the Trinity undergraduate curriculum; simultaneously, an experimental culture was flourishing, despite occasional lapses in the activities of its institutional body, the Dublin Philosophical Society, which Molyneux had founded in 1683, and which his son Samuel, a college friend of Berkeley's, later revived.[20] Indeed, by the time he began work on *An Essay towards a New Theory of Vision* (1709), Berkeley had already been obsessing about the Molyneux problem for years.[21]

Taking as his starting point Molyneux's axiom that distance in itself is imperceptible, Berkeley dealt in turn in his *Essay on Vision* with the distance, magnitude, and situation of tangible objects in order to demonstrate that none of these ideas is immediately perceptible by sight. In each case, Berkeley had recourse to a carefully devised variation on the theme of Molyneux's problem, the first of which already amounted to a preliminary statement of an ultimately immaterialist ontology:

> From what hath been premis'd, it is a manifest Consequence, that a Man Born Blind, being made to see wou'd at first, have no *Idea* of Distance by Sight. The Sun and Stars, the remotest *Objects* as well as the nearer wou'd all seem to be in his Eye, or rather in his Mind. The *Objects* intromitted by Sight, wou'd seem to him (as in truth they are) no other than a new Set of Thoughts or Sensations, each whereof is as near to him, as the Perceptions of Pain or Pleasure, or the most inward Passions of his Soul.[22]

To say the least, Berkeley's parenthetical assertion that the objects of sight have no independent existence stood in need of rigorous justification. To that end, Berkeley set out to develop his thesis that visual ideas, consisting only of light and colours, are '*specifically Distinct*' from their tactile counterparts, so that no idea or kind of idea is '*common to both Senses*', despite the misleading effects of linguistic convention.[23] Accordingly, when he finally turned to the Molyneux problem itself, Berkeley proposed that the scenario presents its subject with a semiotically incomprehensible task. As he explained:

> the *Ideas* of Sight are all new Perceptions, to which there be no Names annex'd in his Mind; he cannot, therefore, understand what is said to him concerning them. And to ask, of the two Bodies he saw placed on the Table, which was the Sphere, which the Cube? Were, to him, a Question down right Bantering and Unintelligible: Nothing he sees being able to suggest to his Thoughts, the *Idea* of Body, Distance, or, in general, of any thing he had already known.[24]

In Berkeley's radical analysis of Molyneux's problem, the blind man's experience of enlightenment is fundamentally bewildering and disconcerting. Given time, however, Berkeley's subject would ultimately find that visual ideas are arbitrary, constant, and universal signs on whose habitual relationship with tactile ideas he could rely. To Berkeley, this hidden state of perceptual affairs spoke eloquently and emotively of a profound metaphysical truth: that 'the proper Objects of Vision constitute the Universal Language of Nature'; and that reflection on its 'wonderful Art and Contrivance' can 'give us some Glimmering, Analogous, Prænotion of Things, that are placed beyond the certain Discovery, and Comprehension of our present State'.[25] In fact, Berkeley's theory of vision was only a subtle step or two away from the comprehensively immaterialist ontology that he was soon to publish in *A Treatise Concerning the Principles of Human Knowledge* (1710). Unsurprisingly, then, Berkeley's *Essay on Vision*, and the radical interpretations of the Molyneux problem on which it was largely based, quickly met with problems and objections.

Experimental Developments

One obvious question that immediately arose concerned the amenability of Berkeley's conjectures to empirical or experimental proof. An unlikely opportunity seemed to have arrived within months of the publication of the *Essay on Vision*: in a supplementary appendix to his second edition, Berkeley referred to '*a Man somewhere near* London [who] *was made to See, who had been Born Blind, and continued so for about Twenty Years*'. The man in question was almost certainly William Jones, who had reportedly been cured of blindness by the oculist Roger Grant at Newington in June 1709. Encouraged though he was, Berkeley expressed concern for '*proper Interrogatories*' on the case, which may have been a comment on the dubious account that the Dublin-born journalist Richard Steele (1672–1729) had recently published in the *Tatler*.[26] In any event, the episode was quickly exposed as fraudulent by an anonymous pamphleteer, who demonstrated that Jones had been neither blind nor cured, and that crucial details of Steele's impressionistic report had been fabricated. In fact, the anonymous writer cast serious doubt not only on Grant's credentials and expertise, but also on the prospect of any human being having the capacity to perform a genuine cure. As he put it, in apparent contradiction of Toland: 'from the Beginning of the *World* to our Saviour's Time, no *Man* ever *open'd the Eye of one that was born Blind*; and from our Saviour's Time to this Day, no man but Mr Grant ever did the like Miracle'.[27]

Around the same time that this apparent opportunity disappeared, Berkeley's distinction between visual and tactile ideas came under pressure from the popular hypothesis that certain blind men could identify colours by their sense of touch. Reported observations on one such man, John Vermaasen of Maastricht, had first been published in 1664 by the Irish natural philosopher Robert Boyle (1627–91), who speculated that Vermaasen's remarkable ability must have derived from his unusual sensitivity to the forms and degrees of 'Asperity' in coloured bodies.[28] Since then, the alleged phenomenon had drawn theoretical support from the materialistic optics advanced by Isaac Newton, while its currency was secured by William Derham's Robert Boyle lectures on natural theology, which were first published in 1713 and frequently reprinted throughout the century.[29] Even so, Boyle had readily accepted that the process of feeling colours was far more painstaking than immediate, and that even a true adept was liable to err on occasion. Neither observation was lost on Jonathan Swift (1667–1745), who typically satirised the absurdity of the purported skill, along with the credulity of its promoters, in Part III of *Gulliver's Travels* (1726):

> There was a Man born blind, who had several Apprentices in his own Condition: Their Employment was to mix Colours for Painters, which their Master taught them to distinguish by feeling and smelling. It was indeed my Misfortune to find them at that Time not very perfect in their Lessons; and the Professor himself happened to be generally mistaken: This Artist is much encouraged and esteemed by the whole Fraternity.[30]

A more direct set of objections to Berkeley's so-called heterogeneity thesis was made by the Ulster philosopher Francis Hutcheson (1694–1746) in a letter to William Mace in September 1727. Stating categorically that 'Messrs. Locke and Molyneux are both wrong about the cube and sphere proposed to a blind man restored to sight', Hutcheson presented a series of arguments in order to demonstrate that 'visible and tangible extension' are 'really the same idea'. While the first relied on the reasonable assumption that pure perceptions of colour are essentially impalpable, others invoked bizarre experimental conditions that might have been conceived by Swift's virtuosi in the laboratories of the Academy of Lagado. However, since all of Hutcheson's hypotheses were ultimately derived from the observable fact that 'blind men may understand mathematics', it is possible to reconstruct Berkeley's likely response from the sections of his *Essay on Vision* that deal with geometry.[31] Whereas Hutcheson understood mathematical propositions to be arguments about visible objects, Berkeley had posited that visible figures are only as useful in geometrical reasoning as words, 'neither of them being any otherwise concern'd therein, than as they represent or suggest to the Mind the particular Tangible Figures connected with them'. For Berkeley, then, blind men may indeed understand mathematics, but an 'Unbody'd Spirit', who *'cou'd see, but not feel'*, could have no comprehension of geometry.[32] Accordingly, Hutcheson's blind man's knowledge of extension was irrelevant to his earliest impressions of light and colours.

Whereas Berkeley's opinion of Hutcheson's objections can only be inferred from his *Essay on Vision*, a closely contemporary and complementary critique soon provided the basis for a public defence of his theory. Appearing anonymously in London's *Daily Post-Boy* in September 1732 and reprinted by Berkeley the following year in *The Theory of Vision . . . Vindicated and Explained*, these new objections dared to go where Hutcheson had seemingly feared to tread. Imagining a man with 'an exquisite Sense of feeling', the anonymous critic supposed that 'a little Experience would make him feel a Colour in the Dark', and that 'one common Cause' must therefore produce the various sensory ideas, which consequently 'have a necessary Connexion with it'. However, as Berkeley maintained in his response, 'my Theory no where supposeth, that we may not justly argue, from the Ideas of one Sense to those of another, by Analogy and by Experience: On the contrary, this very Point is affirmed, proved, or supposed throughout'.[33] For Berkeley, it was only by positing the absence of at least one sensory faculty that the analogical and yet arbitrary nature of normal sensory experience could be conceived.

Berkeley's vindication provided a usefully brief synopsis of the often elaborate arguments of his earlier *Essay on Vision*, though with two important differences. In the first place, following the previous year's third edition of his *Essay on Vision*, Berkeley now invested his theory with explicitly theological significance by identifying vision as *'the Language of the Author of Nature'* (§38). In the second, Berkeley concluded his argument with a lengthy citation of a long-awaited piece of apparently supporting evidence. In 1728, the pioneering surgeon William Cheselden had published a report in the *Philosophical Transactions* of the Royal Society of a two-part operation on the eyes of a teenage boy who had been 'blind', on account of cataracts, at least from his infancy. Berkeley's extract from Cheselden's report relates to the boy's experiences of vision after only one of his cataracts had been couched:

> When he first saw, he was so far from making any Judgment about Distances, that he thought all Objects whatever touched his Eyes (as he expressed it) as what he felt did his Skin; and thought no Objects so agreeable as those which were smooth and regular, though he could form no Judgment of their Shape, or guess what it was in any Object that was

pleasing to him. He knew not the Shape of any thing, nor any one thing from another, however different in Shape or Magnitude: but upon being told what things were, whose Form he before knew from Feeling, he would carefully observe that he might know them again: but having too many Objects to learn at once, he forgot many of them: And (as he said) at first he learned to know, and again forgot a thousand Things in a Day. Several Weeks after he was couched, being deceived by Pictures he asked, which was the lying Sense, Feeling or Seeing? He was never able to imagine any Lines beyond the Bounds he saw. The Room he was in, he said, he knew to be but Part of the House, yet he could not conceive that the whole House could look bigger. He said every new Object was a new Delight, and the Pleasure was so great that he wanted Ways to express it. (§71)[34]

Although Cheselden's report left plenty to be desired as a study in the philosophy of perception, Berkeley, like many of his contemporaries, was immediately convinced that Molyneux's scenario had now been adequately investigated, and that the negative solution to his hypothetical problem was therefore sufficiently proved.

French Connections

Among Berkeley's more unlikely supporters was the French Newtonian, Lockean, and deist, Voltaire. Having lived in England in the late 1720s, Voltaire was instrumental in establishing a close relationship between contemporary Anglophone optical theory and a developing culture of Enlightenment. In his *Letters Concerning the English Nation* (1733), the Frenchman observed that '*Des Cartes* gave Sight to the Blind', but that it was Newton, who 'saw Light so perfectly', who best represented both the scientific achievements and the rational aspirations of the age.[35] Later, in his *Élemens de la philosophie de Neuton* (1738), he further maintained that the 'new Philosophy' was directly opposed to the hypothetical conjectures of 'the Ancients', who in treating 'Physicks without the light of Experiments, have been only the Blind explaining the Nature of Colours to the Blind'. Indeed, Voltaire's assent to Berkeley's theory of vision was entirely dependent on Cheselden's empirical evidence. Having sum-marised the theory in a digressive chapter of the *Élemens*, Voltaire con-ceded that 'all this could only be explained, and made incontestable by some Person born blind, and restored to the Sense of Sight', before insisting that Cheselden's adolescent patient had achieved precisely that.[36]

Voltaire may have subscribed to the received Anglo-Irish wisdom, but some of his more radical compatriots were unconvinced. In the 1740s, the materialist Julien Offray de La Mettrie and the sensationalist Étienne Bonnot de Condillac questioned the validity of Cheselden's evidence on both physiological and methodological grounds.[37] Later, Denis Diderot went further still. In his ground-breaking *Lettre sur les aveugles* (1749), Diderot exploited interviews and reports of more or less questionable veracity in order to reconstruct with enticing empathy the subjective experiences of the blind. Most significantly, the *Lettre* culminated in an innovative solution to a carefully modified version of Molyneux's problem, which Diderot considered as two independent queries. In the first place, Diderot followed Condillac in arguing that a patient whose cataracts had very recently been couched was in no condition to undergo visual testing. Drawing attention to the effects of light on highly sensitive eyes, Diderot maintained that time was required 'for the whole ball of the eye to accommodate itself to all the necessary dispositions', and that touch was redundant to the process of learning to see. In the second, since he accepted that depth perception requires experience, Diderot substituted a circle and a square for Molyneux's three-dimensional figures, and proposed that various kinds of newly sighted people would approach their identification in entirely different ways. At one extreme, an untrained subject such as Cheselden's naïf could only resort to guesswork. At the other, an extra ordinary individual like Nicholas Saunderson, the famously blind former professor of mathematics at the University of Cambridge, would logically and successfully apply his expertise in the determination and practical demonstration of geometric properties.[38]

Intriguingly, Diderot claimed that his knowledge of Saunderson was partly derived from an Irish publication: an undiscovered *Life and Character* of the 'late Lucasian Professor', purportedly written by one William Inchclif and printed in Dublin in 1747 (p. 66). According to Diderot, Inchclif had recorded a remarkable conversation on the existence of God that had apparently unfolded as Saunderson lay dying in 1739. Responding to his vicar's ill-conceived rendition of the argument from perceptible design, Saunderson objected that the 'spectacle' of nature is fundamentally inaccessible to the blind, then argued that the sighted are equally in the dark about the origins of the universe and its species (pp. 56–65). Both its atheistic cosmology and its absence from the historical record strongly suggest that the Dublin *Life* of Saunderson was Diderot's mischievous invention.[39] Even so, its ostensibly Irish provenance remains instructive. For decades, Berkeley had been developing and applying his thesis that vision is the language of God. Yet the Saunderson that emerges from Inchclif's account is a wise, innocent, and virtuous illiterate in the lexicon and grammar of the divine. Having already rejected Berkeley's idealism as an absurdity born of 'blindness' (p. 49), Diderot, through Inchclif, tacitly cast aspersions on the character of a deity who had refused to communicate with one of his most exemplary and deserving children.

The debate in France added new dimensions to Molyneux's perceptual and conceptual problem. Whereas Berkeley and Voltaire saw the Cheselden case as the realisation of a hypothetical scenario, Diderot and his contemporaries were quick to observe that cataract surgery had physical implications, and that a test was invalid if it failed to take these into account. Similarly, whereas Berkeley and Voltaire viewed Cheselden's patient as a living specimen of Molyneux's abstract man, Diderot suspected that a teenage boy was less representative of humanity in general than any of his predecessors had imagined, and that a valid test required multiple newly sighted individuals. Both of these insights were influential in continental Europe, where the results were occasionally extreme. In Paris in 1762, the oculist Jacques Daviel used an alternative method of cataract extraction to obtain new findings that further supported Molyneux's original prediction; in Berlin in the 1770s, the Swiss philosopher Jean-Bernard Mérian called for the establishment of a public laboratory in which artificially blinded children could be trained as experimental subjects.[40] In Ireland, however, the case was different. Voltaire was a major author in the homeland of Molyneux and Berkeley, whereas Diderot and his colleagues were dismissed as infidels when their existence was acknowledged at all.[41] Consequently, if the questions that arose from the French debate were also to be asked in Ireland, they would have to emerge either spontaneously or indirectly.

Unlikely though it seems, one potential avenue of transmission was Irish Catholic education, which was typically conducted abroad. A year after Diderot's *Lettre* was published, the twenty-one-year-old surgeon Sylvester O'Halloran (1728–1807), recently returned from Paris to Limerick, explored in detail the physiological implications of standard ophthalmological practices in *A New Treatise of the Glaucoma, or Cataract*. Drawing on his extensive reading and experience, O'Halloran set out to describe and explain the common post-operative problems of obstructed vision, restricted ocular movement, and inflammation, all of which he claimed could be avoided by adopting a modified procedure of his own invention. Although he referred primarily to continental sources, he also briefly cited Cheselden, Boyle, and Molyneux's brother Thomas, author of a case study of 'a Soldier of *Kilmainhim*' who had been couched for cataracts around 1720 before succumbing to 'an *Inflammatory-Fever*'.[42] Even so, O'Halloran registered no specific interest in the facility of the formerly blind with cubes and spheres. Anatomical and surgical precision, rather than philosophical or psychological accuracy, were his aims. Even in his later critiques of Daviel's extractive method, which was practised with partial success in Dublin from the 1750s, O'Halloran strictly limited himself to technical and procedural observations.[43]

One Irish writer who would have been curious about O'Halloran's more general findings was Thomas Amory (*c.* 1691–1788), enigmatic author of the fictional autobiography, *The Life of John Buncle, Esq.* (1756–66). An avowed Lockean and '*Christian deist*', Buncle exhibits a broad range of interests in contemporary optical cultures that are partly reflected in his striking inversion of the traditional Anglican analogy: 'the majority of the clergy continue to blind the human understanding, and instead of couching the cataract, darken the souls of the people with a suffusion of mystery'.[44] More directly concerned with the psychologies of vision and blindness was Edmund Burke (1730–97), author of *A Philosophical Enquiry into the Origin of Our Ideas of the Sublime and Beautiful* (1757). Extensively influenced by Locke, Burke's *Enquiry* offers tantalising glimpses of an aesthetic solution to the Molyneux problem that it never explicitly reveals. Having already entertained the almost century-old speculation that blind men might feel colours, and having also described Cheselden's adolescent patient as 'particularly observing, and sensible for one of his age', Burke turned his attention towards the end of his *Enquiry* to a pair of more contemporary examples of blind men dealing successfully with visual ideas.[45] The first concerned the Scottish poet Thomas Blacklock, whose remarkable ability to describe 'visual objects' with uncommon 'spirit and justness' had recently been attributed by the critic Joseph Spence to his painstaking deductions about the emotional effects of light and colours on the visually unimpaired (V.5.133).[46] Burke's second example was Saunderson, the Cambridge mathematician whose likely response to the Molyneux problem Diderot had outlined in his *Lettre*. Recalling that Saunderson 'gave excellent lectures upon light and colours', Burke observed that both names and perceptions are functional signs of 'degrees of refrangibility', and that the professor could therefore 'reason upon the words' as easily as if he had been 'fully master' of the 'ideas' of 'red, blue, and green' (V.5.134).

Burke was almost as attentive as Diderot to the complex variety of blind subjective experience. Possibly, he was familiar with the Frenchman's work. Either way, one 'Irish' contemporary who knew Diderot personally was Laurence Sterne (1713–68), Church of England clergyman and celebrity author of *The Life and Opinions of Tristram Shandy, Gentleman* (1759–67).[47] Sterne met Diderot at the Baron d'Holbach's *salons* in Paris in 1762, and there are reasons to imagine that blindness and vision were among the subjects that they discussed. For one thing, Daviel's experimental results had been published in the city in the earlier part of that year. For another, Sterne had already subtly registered his interest in Molyneux's philosophical problem. In volume I of his *Life and Opinions*, Sterne's autobiographer presents an article from his mother's marriage settlement in which her maiden name is given as '*Elizabeth Mollineux*'.[48] Since names are invariably significant in *Tristram Shandy*, and since Locke was a conspicuous influence on its narrator, a plausible construal of Tristram's genealogy identifies William Molyneux among his maternal forebears.[49] Assuming that this analysis is correct, a new perspective begins to emerge on the enigmatic 'moral' of Tristram's marbled leaf: the 'motly emblem of [his] work' that appears in volume III (I, III.36.268–70), and which he explicitly relates to the 'many opinions, transactions and truths' that lie hidden beneath the black page of volume I (I, I.12.37–38). If Tristram, the Lockean son of 'Mollineux', is a student of the problem to which his eminent Irish ancestor gave his name, then to turn from the black to the marbled page is to enter the perception of the blind man made to see, and to find, like Berkeley's baffled subject or Cheselden's disoriented patient, that visual ideas are only light and colours until experience yields the habit of instant judgment. Moreover, since each original marbling was unique to a single copy, so too, for Tristram's early readers, was every process of enlightenment individual.[50]

Coda

In the 1790s, Anglican theologians developed a thesis about one of Christ's most enigmatic miracles that elegantly encapsulates some of the dominant characteristics of Irish Enlightenment thought. At Bethsaida, Jesus had spat and laid hands on a blind man, and asked him:

> Seest thou aught? And he looked up, and said, I see men; for I behold them as trees, walking. Then again he laid his hands upon his eyes; and he looked stedfastly, and was restored, and saw all things clearly. (Mark 8: 25)

According to James Drought (1738–1820), professor of divinity at Trinity College, Dublin, the blind man at Bethsaida had suffered from congenital cataracts. He offered his colleague Thomas Elrington (1760–1835) a gloss on the man's first perceptions: "'I see several objects round me, some moving, others at rest; my knowledge of the place and circumstances in which I am makes me suppose the latter to be trees, the former men; but I am not able to describe the distinctions in their form.'" For Elrington, this was an 'ingenious conjecture', and it proved the divinity of Christ. Alluding to Berkeley, and citing Cheselden, he argued that the separate parts of the miracle 'were the physical and mental cure, though perhaps it may not be so certain which of them was first performed'. Either way, Elrington maintained that 'it is not in that age nor in that country we are to look for men sufficiently acute to decide questions which seventeen centuries afterwards exercised the abilities of the most subtle metaphysicians, and received not a satisfactory decision till conjecture was confirmed by experience'.[51] Only in the era of Molyneux's problem could this aspect of Christ's divinity have been revealed. For Elrington, as for Berkeley, Enlightenment was a process that leads to God.

Notes

1. Research for this chapter was partly funded by an Irish Research Council Government of Ireland Postdoctoral Fellowship.
2. David Berman, 'Enlightenment and Counter-Enlightenment in Irish Philosophy', *Archiv für Geschichte der Philosophie* 64.2 (1982), 148–65; reprinted in David Berman, *Berkeley and Irish Philosophy* (London: Continuum, 2005), pp. 79–105 (pp. 81, 87).
3. See Thomas Duddy, *A History of Irish Thought* (London and New York: Routledge, 2002), pp. 74–78; Daniel Carey, 'Intellectual History: William King to Edmund Burke', in *The Princeton History of Modern Ireland*, ed. Richard Bourke and Ian McBride (Princeton University Press, 2016), pp. 193–216 (pp. 194, 196).
4. Ian McBride, *Eighteenth-Century Ireland: The Isle of Slaves* (Dublin: Gill and Macmillan, 2009), p. 63; Michael Brown, *The Irish Enlightenment* (Cambridge, MA: Harvard University Press, 2016).
5. John Locke, *An Essay Concerning Humane Understanding*, 2nd edn (London, 1694), II.9.8. Further references are to this edition and will be cited in the text.
6. See Marjolein Degenaar, *Molyneux's Problem: Three Centuries of Discussion on the Perception of Forms*, trans. Michael J. Collins (Dordrecht: Kluwer, 1996), pp. 127–29; Michael Bruno and Eric Mandelbaum, 'Locke's Answer to Molyneux's Thought Experiment', *History of Philosophy Quarterly* 27.2 (2010), 165–80 (pp. 174–75).
7. *The Correspondence of John Locke*, ed. E. S. De Beer, 8 vols (Oxford: Clarendon Press, 1976–89), III, pp. 482–83 (7 July 1688).
8. William Molyneux, *Dioptrica nova: A Treatise of Dioptricks* (London, 1692), p. 113. Further references are to this edition and will be cited in the text.
9. *Some Familiar Letters between Mr. Locke, and Several of His Friends* (London, 1708), pp. 37–38 (2 March 1693), p. 43 (28 March 1693).

10. See Martha Brandt Bolton, 'The Real Molyneux Question and the Basis of Locke's Answer', in *Locke's Philosophy: Content and Context*, ed. G. A. J. Rogers (Oxford: Clarendon Press, 1994), pp. 75–99 (p. 77).

11. See Laura Berchielli, 'Color, Space, and Figure in Locke: An Interpretation of the Molyneux Problem', *Journal of the History of Philosophy* 40.1 (2002), 47–65 (pp. 62–64).

12. *Some Familiar Letters*, p. 133 (24 December 1695).

13. Ibid., pp. 135–37 (6 September 1695).

14. Ibid., p. 146 (30 March 1696).

15. Edward Synge, *An Appendix to A Gentleman's Religion* (London, 1698), pp. 11–21.

16. See Peter Browne, *A Letter in Answer to a Book Entitled, Christianity not Mysterious* (Dublin, 1697), pp. 50–53, 121–22.

17. John Toland, *Christianity not Mysterious*, 2nd edn (London, 1696), p. 145.

18. William King, *Predestination and Fore-knowledge, Consistent with the Freedom of Man's Will* (Dublin, 1709), pp. 17–18.

19. See especially, Peter Browne, *Things Divine and Supernatural Conceived by Analogy with Things Natural and Human* (London, 1733), pp. 216–21.

20. See Molyneux to Locke (22 December 1692), *Some Familiar Letters*, p. 17; K. Theodore Hoppen, *The Common Scientist in the Seventeenth Century: A Study of the Dublin Philosophical Society, 1683–1708* (London: Routledge, 1970).

21. See George Berkeley, *Philosophical Commentaries*, ed. George H. Thomas, notes by A. A. Luce ([Alliance, OH]: [Mount Union College], 1976), pp. 129–30 n. 27.

22. George Berkeley, *An Essay towards a New Theory of Vision* (Dublin, 1709), §41.

23. Ibid., §127.

24. Ibid., §135.

25. Ibid., §§147–48.

26. George Berkeley, *An Essay towards a New Theory of Vision*, 2nd edn (Dublin, [1710]), pp. 197–98; see Donald F. Bond, ed., *The Tatler*, 3 vols (Oxford: Clarendon Press, 1987), I, pp. 384–89 (16 August 1709).

27. *A Full and True Account of a Miraculous Cure, of a Young Man in Newington, That Was Born Blind, and Was in Five Minutes Brought to Perfect Sight* (London, 1709), p. 14.

28. See Robert Boyle, 'Experiments and Considerations touching Colours', in *The Works of Robert Boyle*, ed. Michael Hunter and Edward B. Davis, 14 vols (London: Pickering & Chatto, 1999), IV, pp. 3–201 (pp. 40–45).

29. See William Derham, *Physico-Theology: Or, a Demonstration of the Being and Attributes of God, from His Works of Creation*, 2nd edn (London, 1714), p. 144 n. 2; also *The Philosophical Works of the Honourable Robert Boyle Esq.*, ed. Peter Shaw, 3 vols (London, 1725), II, p. 11 n.

30. *The Cambridge Edition of the Works of Jonathan Swift*, Vol. XVI: *Gulliver's Travels*, ed. David Womersley (Cambridge University Press, 2012), p. 262.

31. *The European Magazine and London Review* 14 (September 1788), 158–60 (p. 159). An extract from the letter is reproduced from this source in David Berman, 'Francis Hutcheson on Berkeley and the Molyneux Problem', *Proceedings of the*

Royal Irish Academy: Archaeology, Culture, History, Literature 74 (1974), 259–65 (pp. 263–65); reprinted in Berman, *Berkeley and Irish Philosophy*, pp. 138–49 (pp. 143–46).

32. Berkeley, *Essay on Vision* (1709), §§152–55.

33. George Berkeley, *The Theory of Vision, or Visual Language, Shewing the Immediate Presence and Providence of a Deity, Vindicated and Explained* (London, 1733), pp. 60–64; §27. Further references are to this edition and will be cited in the text.

34. For William Cheselden's report in full, see 'An Account of Some Observations Made by a Young Gentleman, Who Was Born Blind', *Philosophical Transactions* 35 (1727–28), 447–50.

35. Voltaire, *Letters Concerning the English Nation*, trans. [John Lockman] (London; reprinted Dublin, 1733), pp. 104, 127.

36. Voltaire, *The Elements of Sir Isaac Newton's Philosophy*, trans. John Hanna (London, 1738), pp. 2, 63–64.

37. See Degenaar, *Molyneux's Problem*, pp. 65–73.

38. Denis Diderot, *An Essay on Blindness, in a Letter to a Person of Distinction*, trans. [anon.] (London, 1773), pp. 90, 97–102. Further references are to this edition and will be cited in the text.

39. See Kate E. Tunstall, *Blindness and Enlightenment: An Essay* (New York: Continuum, 2011), pp. 45, 115–19.

40. See Degenaar, *Molyneux's Problem*, pp. 89, 78–83.

41. See Geraldine Sheridan, 'Irish Literary Review Magazines and Enlightenment France, 1730–1790', in *Ireland and the French Enlightenment, 1700–1800*, ed. Graham Gargett and Geraldine Sheridan (Basingstoke: Macmillan, 1999), pp. 21–46 (pp. 43–44).

42. Sylvester O'Halloran, *A New Treatise of the Glaucoma, or Cataract* (Dublin, 1750), pp. xxii, 47–48, 96–97.

43. See Sylvester O'Halloran, *A Critical Analysis of the New Operation for a Cataract* (Dublin, 1755), pp. 32–33; 'A Critical and Anatomical Examination of the Parts Immediately Interested in the Operation for a Cataract', *The Transactions of the Royal Irish Academy* 2 (1788), 121–41.

44. Thomas Amory, *The Life of John Buncle, Esq.* (1756), ed. Moyra Haslett (Dublin: Four Courts Press, 2011), pp. 57, 263 n. 44, 241.

45. Edmund Burke, *A Philosophical Enquiry into the Origin of Our Ideas of the Sublime and Beautiful*, ed. Paul Guyer (Oxford University Press, 2015), III.24.98, IV.15.115–16. Further references are to this edition and will be cited in the text.

46. See Joseph Spence, 'An Account of the Life, Character, and Poems of the Author', in Thomas Blacklock, *Poems*, 2nd edn (London, 1756), pp. i–liv (pp. xxxiii–liv).

47. See David Clare, 'Under-Regarded Roots: The Irish References in Sterne's *Tristram Shandy*', *Irish Review* 52.1 (2016), 15–26; Ian Campbell Ross, *Laurence Sterne: A Life* (Oxford University Press, 2001), pp. 276, 285.

48. Laurence Sterne, *The Life and Opinions of Tristram Shandy, Gentleman*, ed. Melvyn New and Joan New, 2 vols (Gainesville, FL: University Presses of

Florida, 1978), I, I.15.42–47. Further references are to this edition and will be cited in the text.

49. See Darrell Jones, 'Locke and Sterne: The History of a Critical Hobby-Horse', *The Shandean* 27 (2016), 83–111; Eric Rothstein, *Systems of Order and Inquiry in Later Eighteenth-Century Fiction* (Berkeley, CA: University of California Press, 1975), p. 70 n. 12.

50. Sterne went to considerable lengths to ensure that the marbled leaves for the first edition of *Tristram Shandy*, volumes III–IV (London: Dodsley, 1761), were produced according to his particular specifications: see Peter de Voogd, 'The Compleat Marbler', *The Shandean* 20 (2009), 69–82. In the author's absence, publishers of contemporary Irish editions, whether legitimate or piratical, were forced to come up with alternative solutions. An advertisement in the *Dublin Courier* (4 March 1761) informed potential customers that the first Irish edition (Dublin: Chamberlaine and Smith, 1761) included 'a curious emblematical Marble Leaf'; these unpaginated insertions, which may have been manufactured locally, exist in some surviving copies of the edition but are lacking in others. Less satisfactorily, though also more innovatively, the second and third Irish editions (Dublin: Saunders, 1761 and 1765) featured hand-painted versions of one side of the marbled leaf in pink, blue, and yellow watercolours. Thanks to Philip Maddock, Peter de Voogd, and Helen Williams for their assistance on these points.

51. Thomas Elrington, *Sermons Preached in the Chapel of Trinity College, Dublin, in the Year 1795* (Dublin, 1796), pp. 263–65, 122.

CHAPTER 6

Samuel Whyte and the Politics of Eighteenth-Century Irish Private Theatricals

Helen M. Burke

Samuel Whyte's involvement with eighteenth-century Irish private theatricals was well known to his contemporaries. The poet, Thomas Moore, who, by his own account, was one of this schoolmaster's 'favorite *show* scholars' in the 1790s, noted, for instance, that when private plays began to be staged at Carton, Castletown, Marlay, and other great houses near Dublin in the 1760s and 70s, his old master was usually on hand to assist. 'In most instances, the superintendence was intrusted [sic] to Mr. Whyte', Moore wrote, 'and in general the prologue, or the epilogue, contributed by his pen.'[1] The tendency of later nineteenth-century commentators to see this movement through the lens of the Grattanite myth, however, all but erased this schoolteacher's contribution from history. This can be seen, for example, in accounts of a specific production at Marlay, a performance of *The Masque of Comus* that took place at the Rathfarnham estate of the powerful Dublin banking family, the La Touches, in 1776. As we know from the section entitled 'Bon Ton Theatricals' in Whyte's *A Collection of Poems, on Various Subjects* (1792), the actors on this occasion were the numerous La Touche children, many of whom were Whyte's pupils; and as he was wont to do in plays which he put on with his students, this teacher not only wrote and delivered the prologue but also played the title role. In addition, he acted as the historian for the production by publishing the literature that it generated, a body of texts that included the *Comus* playbill, Whyte's own prologue, and an epilogue written by the patriot leader, Henry Grattan.[2] The fact that the 'ever-glorious Grattan' (as Moore termed him) contributed to this Marlay performance, however, overshadowed all other details in the minds of later nineteenth-century commentators and, as the Grattanite myth took hold, this political leader's role was enlarged at the expense of Whyte's.[3] Such elisions and exaggerations occur, for example, in *The Dublin University Magazine*'s overview of the 'age of theatricals' in 1850. While noting that Grattan wrote the epilogue for the

Marlay performance, the magazine writes inaccurately that he and fellow patriots, Hussey Burgh and Gervase Bushe, also acted in this performance, while omitting any mention of Whyte.[4]

To restore this Dublin schoolteacher to his former place in the world of Irish private theatricals, then, is not only to dispel more of the 'Grattan mystique' but also to demonstrate the inadequacy of a still-prevailing type of private theatrical historiography, one that sees this form of drama as expressing solely the interests, tastes, and values of an elite (patriotic or otherwise).[5] As the Marlay example shows, the elite required the assistance and expertise of people outside their own social circle in order to help stage and publicise their theatricals, and that dependence, as we will see, opened a space for Whyte's kind of social subject – one that, in his case, came from the ranks of the increasingly assertive Dublin Protestant middle class – to inject their moral, cultural, and political values into this form of theatre. To provide a context for that reading, however, it is necessary to look first at the relationship that 'Sam White' of Grafton Street had with the two reformers, of different kinds, mentioned in the following account of his school:

> it is impossible to give a better Idea of the Bustle, upon reforming our Language, than an Advertisement which appears every Day in the *Journal*: Whereby you are informed, that Mr. *Sam White*, in *Grafton-street*, teaches *English* in a Method approved by *Mr. Sheridan. Risum teneas?* One cannot be angry at *such* a Clamourer against Abuses, and *such* an Undertaker to remedy them. Does it not put you in mind of mad *Lucas* bellowing out the Disorders of the Constitution [...] in order to have a hand in reforming them?[6]

The first of these connections is the more obvious of the two, the man who, as this text suggests, provided Whyte with his educational 'methods': the actor/manager, educational theorist, and elocutionist, Thomas Sheridan.

Whyte's Grafton Street School and the Sheridan Legacy

Most likely the natural son of Richard Whyte, a younger brother from a County Down landowning family, Whyte began life in 1734 without a name or a country he could legitimately call his own. His unnamed mother died giving birth to him aboard a ship going from Dublin to Liverpool, and he spent his early life in a similarly unsettled state, moving between Ireland and England. By his own later admission, he had nearly hit rock bottom financially when his first cousin, Frances Sheridan (née Chamberlaine),

Thomas Sheridan's wife, stepped in to help him, and with her assistance and that of her husband, Whyte set up his 'English Grammar School' at 75 Grafton Street in 1758.[7] Sheridan also intended Whyte to head up the English department in the innovative type of Irish educational institution that the actor/manager was attempting to open up at that time as he looked for ways to repair his fortune after the disastrous 1754 Smock Alley riot.[8] These plans ultimately failed but they nevertheless provided Whyte with the blueprint for his own highly successful educational venture – one built around the idea of performance.

Sheridan's educational plan, which he presented in two orations before an assembly of the Irish nobility and gentry in the fall of 1757 and spring of 1758, envisioned the establishment of a new kind of school for Irish boys, one that, with the aid of Whyte's scholarship and the actor/manager's theatre experience, would emphasise the teaching of written and spoken English. As when he had argued earlier for the reform of the Dublin stage, Sheridan framed his intervention as a matter of the survival of the established church and state. As long as there were no good schools in Ireland, he argued, the nobility and gentry would keep sending their children to England, and the resulting absenteeism would ultimately cause the country to relapse into the 'Poverty, Misery, and Barbarism' in which it found itself prior to 1 July 1690.[9] On a more pragmatic note, Sheridan pointed out that the 'vitiated Pronunciation' of Ireland's youth prevented them from 'making such a Figure in publick Assemblies, as their Talents, Knowledge, and Literature would intitle them to', but that with the kind of education he was proposing – one in which 'English and the Art of Speaking would be systematically taught' – that 'Defect' could be eliminated and better social and career prospects would open up for all (pp. 14–15). The interest with which Sheridan's plans were initially received by the nobility and gentry indicates that they struck a chord. As Tony Barnard has pointed out, the desire to 'make a grand figure' was a preoccupation of the Irish elite throughout the century, and they were only too aware that their stigmatised speech was an obstacle to that ambition.[10] The idea, nevertheless, of having an actor educate their children struck many as unacceptable and that anti-theatrical prejudice, coupled with the hostility that Sheridan had engendered during his long reign as sole manager of Theatre Royal, Smock Alley, forced him to abandon this scheme. Though a Hibernian Academy organised along his principles briefly came into existence in 1759, it was short lived, and Sheridan turned to England and Scotland to spread his elocutionary and educational ideas.[11]

At Whyte's school on Grafton Street, however, the Sheridan legacy lived on, albeit in a structure that was privately rather than (as Sheridan had hoped) publicly supported. Advertisements in the *Dublin Journal*, as noted in the quotation above, informed the public when this school first opened that its pupils would be taught 'English in a Method approved by Mr. Sheridan', and in the printed tracts on education and elocution that Whyte himself wrote in the years that followed, he cited copiously from Sheridan's *British Education* (1756) and his *Course of Lectures on Elocution* (1762).[12] Following a co-educational principle that Sheridan had laid down in these *Lectures*, Whyte also began accepting young girls as his pupils and, as his mentor had done, he advertised his ability to teach a form of English that was 'perfectly free from any brogue or provincial taint'.[13] Performance, too, became the means both of delivering this elocutionary training and show-casing its results. Whyte revived a tradition established by Sheridan's father, Dr Thomas Sheridan, in the 1720s and 30s of having his students perform a play as part of public examinations at the end of each school year, and by the 1760s, he was himself acting in, and writing for, the plays that he staged with his students in the grand country houses of their parents.[14] In the 1770s, he also began the practice of including prologues and cast lists from these theatricals in his publications, thereby expanding the audience for these elocutionary talent shows beyond their original one. In 1769, for instance, he wrote a prologue for Aaron Hill's tragedy *Zara* which he had staged with three of his female pupils at Waterstown House, County Westmeath, then the residence of the Earl of Louth. That text and the cast list for this performance were then subsequently published in *The Shamrock, or Hibernian Cresses* (1772), along with a footnote stating that this whole entertainment was designed for the 'improvement in Elocution' of Mr Whyte's pupils.[15] From the list of subscribers attached to *The Shamrock* it is clear, too, that by the 1770s, his methods (both educational and promotional) had gained him a considerable following among the Irish nobility and gentry. This list reads like a 'Who's Who' of the Irish establishment at this time, and as noted on it, many of the children of these subscribers were Whyte's pupils.

By the mid-1770s, Whyte was also touting the benefits of his educational system to those who were destined 'for the Counting-house and mercantile Avocations', and the number of less famous names in the subscription list above suggests that, by then, he was also drawing from the city's merchant and trading classes.[16] They, like the elite, it would seem, were well aware of the social value of acquiring the type of polite eloquence that Whyte was teaching. But for the freemen (i.e. Protestant) subsection of that population in particular, it was also because, as the above quotation hints, Whyte was seen as a social reformer and patriot in the mould of Charles Lucas, the apothecary-turned-politician who had led the fight against oligarchical privilege and the 'old deference-based politics' during the middle decades of the century.[17] Similar reforming impulses, as we will see, run through Whyte's poetic writing and they surface in a more oblique way in his 'Bon Ton Theatricals'.

'Bon Ton Theatricals' and Lucasian 'Principles'

As Whyte's son later noted, Whyte made his first foray into the world of letters in 1750 to defend Lucas after he had been denounced as an 'enemy of his country' in the late 1740s, and that passionate poetic 'Reply Contemptuous', his son related, engendered a friendship between the two men that lasted throughout Lucas's lifetime.[18] While Whyte was visiting Waterstown in 1770 (presumably to stage a private theatrical), he completed a second, longer poetic 'Letter' to Lucas. By then, the reformer was nearing the end of his life and, conscious of that fact, Whyte strikes a more eulogist note in this piece, reflecting back on Lucas's significance not only for his country but for himself personally. Lucas stood alone against an 'impious Race of Men' who had sold the people's 'Rights and Freedom', Whyte writes, and in so doing, he set a patriotic example that others, including the schoolteacher himself, are now attempting to follow:

> Might I, without a Boast, that Honour claim,
> I would avow our Principles the same [...]
> Be it my Glory, as 'tis thine, to hate
> Each Tool of Faction, and each Pimp of State;
> To drooping Worth a fostering Hand to lend;
> And in whatever State, be Virtue's Friend,
> And, though thy Heights I not presume to reach,
> To live the Example of the Truths I teach.[19]

In passages like the following, in which he describes the indignities that traders and merchants had suffered at that hands of the gentry, Whyte channels the same kind of resentments that Lucas had tapped into when, for example, he sided with Sheridan against the 'Gentlemen' at Smock Alley in 1747.[20] As is clear from these lines, he identified with those tradesmen and their grievances. 'Pension'd Gamblers, Knaves, and Minions' were then the 'Prime Rulers of the State', Whyte writes, and under their regime, the people and the arts suffered:

> Stripp'd of our Birth-right, vainly we complain'd,
> For Tyrants once, perpetual Tyrants reign'd;
> Sunk in luxurious Sloth, their Bills unpaid,
> Meanness, and Penury debas'd our Trade;
> And Arts, and Learning all their Vigour lost.   (p. 308)

The prologues and epilogues that Whyte spoke at the homes of his wealthy patrons suggest that he saw this battle against elite tyranny and decadence as an ongoing one and, as Lucas's tracts had done, his texts highlight the social and political importance of his class of social actor. Though these theatrical texts generally begin by offering flattering remarks to Whyte's patrons, they also emphasise the deficiency of their class as a whole and, by circling back to the schoolmaster himself (as they inevitably do), they tend to suggest that those from the middling ranks of society, rather than the aristocracy or gentry, are the true guardians of the country's political and cultural heritage.

Such Lucasian 'principles' inform the above-mentioned Waterstown prologue, a text that Whyte wrote in the same location and at the same time as the Lucas 'Letter'.[21] The prologue begins by condemning the taste of the 'sickening town' that has caused the Dublin playhouse to abandon Shakespeare and the serious drama in favour of farce and rope-dancing.[22] And as it develops this theme, it generates an image of a vice-ridden upper class that, in the pursuit of pleasure and money, is also neglecting the interests of the country:

> Nobles and sharpers, one promiscuous throng,
> Night after night their anxious vigils keep;
> And Basto, not Macbeth, now murders sleep:
> While guzzling statesmen o'er their bottle drone,
> And greatly quit all interest, but – their own.   (p. 51)

Waterstown, the site of the weeping tragedy *Zara*, is then ostensibly held out as a counter to this raucous and debauched city scene, and Whyte's hosts are complimented both by a flattering comparison to the 'wise Athenians' (p. 51) and by allusion to the antiquity and purity of the Bermingham family's Anglo-Norman bloodline. But even as Whyte sets up this opposition between a corrupt town aristocracy and a virtuous country one, he also undermines it in the closing lines of the prologue by drawing attention to the weakness of his young charges (two of whom were daughters of the Earl). However lovingly delivered, this plea for sympathy for his young pupils shifts the focus away from the Earl and his family to himself. It is now the schoolmaster, rather than the Earl of Louth, who appears as the idealised father figure, and it is his virtuous sensibility that takes centre stage as Whyte pleads on behalf of his noble but 'weak' charges:

> For the dear objects of my pleasing care –
> I own, I feel paternal fondness there;
> Their modest tremors, sympathizing, read;
> And for their weak attempts indulgence plead –
> Though noble Osman in expression fail, […]
> And warmly pleading in the cause of Heaven,
> Be gentle Selima's slight faults forgiven.   (p. 52)

This autobiographical turn can be read as another instance of Whyte's endless efforts at self-promotion, his way of representing himself, in this case, as the kind of sympathetic father figure that, in the aftermath of Rousseau's educational writing, prospective wealthy clients might like to see in their children's teachers. But this ending, whereby Whyte displaces the Earl as the protector figure, also speaks to that supersessionist strain that, as Michael McKeon has noted, has historically been part of middle-class consciousness; and it brought into focus the sensibility, benevolence, and sociality that served as the ethical basis of that class's claim to equal power with the aristocracy.[23] Like his hero Lucas, who claimed to pity the oppressed Irish peasantry as much as the oppressed city freeman, Whyte represents himself here as the exemplary man of feeling, and this representation, according to the prevailing norms of the culture of sensibility, make him the exemplary social and political leader.[24]

Whyte's choice of plays for this and other private theatricals reveals his bias, too, for English drama that had this reforming and moralising bent. Aaron Hill's *Zara*, the tragedy chosen for the Waterstown performance, was a translation of Voltaire's play and characteristically used an orientalist tale as a vehicle for denouncing monarchist tyranny and intolerance: Sultan Osman succumbs to a fit of jealousy and kills his innocent Christian slave, Zara, because he has not adequately learned the lessons of rationality and moderation that this suffering lady provides. To perform such a play at the seat of an Earl was to bring home these enlightenment lessons to the Irish aristocracy and to suggest, in however veiled a fashion, that such instruction was still required. A similarly reformist message, it could be argued, was conveyed by *Comus* when it was staged at Marlay, the home of the La Touches. Milton's masque had originally been performed at Ludlow Castle in 1634 to celebrate the arrival of the Earl of Bridgewater as Lord President of the Council of Wales, and in this performance, as in the one at Marlay, the principal parts were played by the children of the house and their teacher. In his prologue, Whyte explicitly connects his own production with its original seventeenth-century one, in calling upon the Muse to inspire him with the 'celestial fire' of Milton so that he can do for Marlay what this great English poet had done for Ludlow.

Milton's masque, which centres on the contest between a virtuous 'Lady' and the lewd and wine-loving Comus, however, was not unambiguously celebratory in its tribute to his noble patron and the Ludlow family. The central temptation to intemperance and luxury takes place in Comus's residence at court, thus at the heart of aristocratic power, and Comus's ultimate escape suggests that the negative energies that he and his court represent are never totally defeated. Aristocratic vice, with its deceptive and seductive shows, Milton's masque suggests, remains as a force that has to be resisted. The Marlay masque sounded a similar warning note even if, as seems likely, the version that was used was George Colman's 1773 adaptation. To invoke Milton at the home of the La Touches, a Huguenot family that had come to Ireland initially to escape religious persecution, was to remind this powerful and wealthy family of its religious, social, and political roots – roots that linked it to a history of resistance to aristocratic power.

On occasion, too, Whyte appropriated the sharper reforming rhetoric that was the legacy of the commonwealth republican tradition, and when he did, his dramatic speeches began to resonate even more closely with the 'addresses' and 'letters' that Lucas had used to mobilise the Dublin artisan and merchant class some decades earlier. The prologue that Whyte wrote for the benefit performance of Joseph Addison's *Cato* at Crow-Street in 1772 is a case in point. This *Cato*, Whyte's own notes tell us, had been first staged by his male pupils before a private gathering of the boys' friends at the little theatre in Capel Street, and it became an even more fashionable occasion when, at the Duke of Leinster's suggestion, it was restaged at Crow Street as a benefit in aid of the debtors at the Marshalsea prison. The Duke, the Marquis of Antrim, and the Earl of Bellamont acted as stewards; two captains from the army stood sentry on the stage; and 'the three Graces' – the three Montgomery sisters who, a year later, were painted in fetching neoclassical poses by Sir Joshua Reynolds – provided decoration.[25] Like other such theatrical benefits, this benefit would have had a political as well as a philanthropic purpose: it was a way of demonstrating that the Irish elite had the benevolence and virtue of an authentic aristocracy.

The prologue that Whyte had voiced by Master Holmes, his seven-year-old pupil, however, worked against this effort at image management. It begins by noting that, in school as in the world, few succeed in their roles, and it blames this failure both on the unruly children themselves (compared here to 'wild gantlopes' [p. 54]) and their ignorant, indulgent, and prejudiced parents. The doting mothers who overlook these faults in their children, in particular, are mimicked and satirised – 'We cannot err – dear mothers, a'n't it true? / We are all perfection, or all blindness you' – and the pain that they and their offspring inflict is graphically illustrated in an anecdote about a schoolmaster who is unfairly discharged on the word of a deceitful and resentful child:

> Young Sulky by his tutor once reprov'd
> Swelled with revenge, and vow'd he'd be remov'd;
> And lo! a miracle! to make it good,
> A bottle of red ink is turn'd to blood!
> He smear'd his shirt, and Abigail, his friend,
> Alarm'd Mama! And so he gained his end;
> And every tea-table throughout the nation
> Branded the tyrant's name, and tore his reputation! (p. 55)

In part, of course, this story serves to mock the indulgence of the fine lady, a commonplace focus of satire throughout the eighteenth century. But it also articulates the outrage felt by those who, like Whyte, depended on the gentry for their livelihood and who were thus subject to their abuse. As noted above, Lucas had similarly capitalised on those feelings when he championed Sheridan against the 'Gentlemen' during the Smock Alley disturbances in 1747, and he published many other examples of gentlemanly abuse of citizens in *The Censor*, often described as Ireland's first radical newspaper.[26] In choosing Addison's *Cato* for this occasion, too, Whyte picked a play that preached the kind of civic republican virtue espoused by Lucas and other middle-class reformers during this period, and he signalled his support for 'great Cato's sentiments' in the apology that was delivered by the young boy who spoke the prologue:

> We plead our years too – I am sirs, only seven,
> Our Marcia's nine, her father scarce eleven;
> But with great Cato's sentiments impress'd,
> Honour and filial reverence fill each breast.
> Lead you the way, throw prejudice aside,
> Let candour judge, and cool discretion guide;
> Show, by example, more than precept can,
> What forms the great, the virtuous happy man. (p. 56)

Little people can teach the big people of the world the virtue that they are lacking, the seven-year-old's words suggest, if the great would only throw aside their 'prejudice'.

By the end of the 1770s, however, the tensions over the Catholic question that would lead Dublin freemen to embrace the concepts of Protestant Ascendancy and Unionism in the closing decade of the century were already beginning to surface in Irish public discourse.[27] Those tensions also surface in *The Theatre*, the long poem that, Whyte noted, he wrote in 1779 but then laid aside until 1790.[28] Subsequent commentators have generally assumed that the schoolmaster wrote this poem to respond to criticism that his emphasis on performance was inculcating a dangerous love of the theatre in some of his pupils.[29] And certainly much space is devoted to describing both the propriety of Whyte's form of private theatrical and the dangers and pitfalls of life on the public stage. But in contrasting a proper with an improper form of theatricality, Whyte may, in addition, have been attempting to distance himself from what was arguably the most publicised but also most politically controversial 'Bon Ton Theatrical' of the decade: the *Macbeth* that was staged at Luke Gardiner's private theatre at the Ranger's Lodge in Phoenix Park in January 1778. The star of that performance was one of the above-named 'Graces', the beautiful and talented Elizabeth Gardiner née Montgomery. And, as all of Dublin would have known, she was one of Whyte's past pupils.

Shakespeare in the Park and Irish Politics in the late 1770s

The Phoenix Park *Macbeth*, like most eighteenth-century productions with that name, was most likely some version of Davenant's operatically enhanced version of Shakespeare's tragedy, particularly as the published commentary on this play refers to singing witches, music, and an orchestra. Though a private entertainment, this event received press coverage usually reserved for a major new stage production. Detailed and glowing accounts of the two first performances quickly appeared in Dublin newspapers, and London newspapers published extracts from a similarly laudatory account that appeared in the January issue of *The Hibernian Magazine*.[30] That magazine also tantalised its readers with other titbits of information in subsequent issues. In April, it featured an image of Mrs Gardiner, striking a tragic pose as Lady Macbeth in one of the elaborate dresses described below (Fig. 2). Complementing this visual depiction was a poem lavishing praise on her for having 'charm[ed]' her audience in a 'thousand ways' with that performance. In May, it showed an image of Robert Jephson in a similarly heroic pose in the role of Macbeth (Fig. 3).[31]

It seems likely that Whyte supplied the epilogue that Mrs Gardiner spoke on that occasion. When published in *Collected Poems*, it is listed as

Fig. 2 *The Hibernian Magazine: Or Compendium of Entertaining Knowledge* (April 1778), facing p. 193. Mrs Gardiner as Lady Macbeth in Phoenix-Park. By permission of the Royal Irish Academy © RIA (C/8/2/E)

Fig. 3 *The Hibernian Magazine: Or Compendium of Entertaining Knowledge* (May 1778), facing p. 249. Robert Jephson, Esqr in the Character of Macbeth. By permission of the Royal Irish Academy © RIA (C/8/2/E)

being spoken by one of his pupils, and it contains the same kind of critique of fashionable entertainments that we find in his other theatrical texts. Operas, ridottos, pantomimes, balls, card-playing routs, and masquerades are all denounced as 'modern, modish things' by a speaker who claims instead to prefer the 'mourning muse' and the more rational pleasures of Shakespeare and Jonson (pp. 67–71). Such a moralising tone would have been consistent, too, with the portrait that Whyte drew of the Montgomery sisters in 'The Lyceum', a poem which he supposedly wrote after seeing these sisters and other female past pupils attending a lecture on the optic nerve in Dublin in 1771. In this poem he invites the 'supercilious Great' to lay aside their love of 'Fashion, Pomp, and State' and gaze instead on these feminine examples of 'true desert'.[32] He then gives a verbal sketch of each of these ladies that complements this picture of feminine virtue, even as it hints that its source is Whyte and his school. The passage describing the merits of his 'Belov'd Eliza' (identified in a footnote as Elizabeth Montgomery), for example, ends with the lines: 'This Praise is hers – and proud to tell, / I have known her long, and know her well.'[33] Thomas Moore would later observe that the 'Miss Montgomerys […] were among those whom my worthy preceptor most boasted of as pupils'.[34]

The stage machinery, scenery, dresses, and decorations on this occasion, however, were not the work of Whyte but rather of the popular Dublin comedian, screen-painter, and theatre manager, John Vendermere; and they were designed to support precisely that kind of show of 'Fashion, Pomp, and State' that the schoolmaster so frequently deplored.[35] The viceroy and his lady attended on alternate nights and, as had occurred on 'government nights' at the Dublin theatre in the earlier part of the century, their presence generated a competitive display of wealth and glamour among the Irish elite: as the *Hibernian Magazine* reported, all were 'vying with each other in Magnificence'.[36] Luke Gardiner, who was at that time pressing the administration for a title, undoubtedly hoped that this costly entertainment, like the costly Reynolds portrait of the 'Three Graces' which he had commissioned just before his marriage to Elizabeth, would forward that ambition; and, as she had done when she sat for that painting, Mrs Gardiner played a part in displaying her husband's wealth, as well as her own fashionable taste, on her body.[37] She made four dress changes during the evening's entertainment, each of which was more elaborate and costly than the previous one. While the dress that she wore as queen was made of 'gold ground silk, ornamented with artificial and silver flowers and with diamonds to the amount of 100,000 pounds', for instance, the one that she wore while she spoke the epilogue, was 'a pink satin Venetian night-gown with a most elegant blossom-coloured petticoat wrought by herself and trimmed with gauze flowers and jewels'.[38] These costume changes would have added a 'tongue-in cheek' quality to her epilogue's condemnation of 'smart coquettes' who flaunt their 'towering plumage' at fashionable assemblies (p. 68). Indeed according to one account, she enhanced this effect by her comic mimicry of these flirtatious ladies: a newspaper correspondent signing herself 'Lady Townly' remarked that the faces of the audience during the delivery of this epilogue could best be imagined by remembering 'Hogarth's print of an audience laughing at a pantomime entertainment'.[39]

Not all Dubliners, however, were charmed by the beautiful Mrs Gardiner and her fellow thespians, as became apparent from subsequent letters to the Dublin press. This negative reaction took its meaning, at one level, from the patriot/Castle conflict that had been deepening since the early 1770s. Jephson, the Macbeth of this production, for instance, had written witty pamphlets in support of Townshend's administration in the early 1770s, and was a backer of the government at the time of this performance.[40] The satiric letter from a 'Lover of the Drama' to the 'Thane of Cawdor' that appeared in *The Hibernian Journal* in February 1778 takes issue with him for these offences, as well as commenting disparagingly on Jephson's recent playwriting efforts. He is mocked for being the 'established Jester' of the Townshend court, writing 'French plays', and acting for hire in the senate.[41] The letter that appeared the following month, addressed 'To my Lord Macduff' (thus, to Luke Gardiner who had played that role in this production), strikes a similarly critical note, as Gardiner and the 'Great Vulgar' who attended his Phoenix Park entertainment are even more roundly denounced for their decadence and subservience to the administration. Gardiner is personally ridiculed for his 'foreign fopperies, gaudy liveries and […] fantastic equipage', and he and other Irish MPs are chastised for endangering the livelihood of stage actors, pandering to a 'theatrical viceroy', and neglecting their duties to their constituents. Finally, they are lambasted for encouraging 'declamatory Talents' in their female relatives. 'Well-bred Women already possess a Masculine confidence', this correspondent notes, and do not need to be further encouraged to make 'these public and obstreperous Exhibitions of themselves'.[42]

To be a Castle supporter at this time, however, was also to take the liberal side in the question of Catholic relief that had resurfaced in the late 1770s.[43] In denouncing this Phoenix Park performance for its foreignness, showiness, and female immodesty – all qualities associated with the

Catholic aristocracy of France and Italy – these critics may also have been
taking aim at these leaders' perceived religious perfidy. Jephson had delivered a famous speech in parliament in favour of Catholic relief in 1774, and
he remained so reliably on the Catholic side that in September 1777, four
months before this performance, Charles O'Conor, the founder of the
Catholic Committee, gave him some of his tracts to distribute at court.[44]
Gardiner was known to have pro-Catholic sympathies, and two months
after the 'Macduff' letter appeared, he introduced the heads of the first
Catholic relief bill into parliament. This bill and the second Catholic relief
act of 1782 would go down in history as Gardiner's Relief Bills.

One does not have to think that Whyte was personally bigoted – the
evidence suggests that he was not – to think that he would have wished to
differentiate his brand of private theatricals from this contentious form of
theatre, one that, moreover, brought into question his own well-known
practice of encouraging young ladies to perform in private plays.[45] The
process of articulating this difference, however, as can be seen in *The
Theatre*, brought into relief the confessionalism which, as Hill has noted,
had always been a feature of Dublin civic republicanism, and it exposed
that sense of cultural superiority that would underpin the support for
'Protestant Ascendancy' in the following decades.[46] The subtitle of the
1790 edition of *The Theatre* is *A Didactic Essay Including an Idea of the
Character of Jane Shore as Performed by a Young Lady in a Private Play*, and
from the 'Preliminary Advertisement' and attached cast list, the reader
learns that the actors were a party of 'Ladies and Gentlemen' at the Cuffe
Street home of a 'worthy friend' in Dublin in 1779 (p. v). At first view, too,
it might seem that this poem was simply reiterating at greater length the
public stage/private stage distinction that Whyte had been using to flatter
private theatrical hosts since early in his career. As in the Waterstown
prologue discussed above, the Dublin public stage is characterised as a
'wild' space where only 'nonsense' and 'folly' reign, while the private
theatrical arena is where 'Pathos', 'Taste', 'Genius', and 'the feeling soul'
find a 'secure retreat' after having been driven off the public stage (p. 4).

In this poem, however, the blame for the debased state of the stage, and
by analogy of Irish culture more generally, is laid not on the 'Great Vulgar'
but rather (more safely) on the class at the other end of the social spectrum:
the 'herd' (p. 2), emanating from the Dublin street, who are now introducing their values and tastes into the theatre. In an effort to please that
demographic, the poem suggests, tragic heroines now 'strut and strain' in
their roles, and they 'disgust' and 'grate' the ear with their 'mangled meters'
and 'uncultur'd idioms' (pp. 1, 2). In his elocutionary tracts, however,

Whyte (and before him Sheridan) had characterised the speech of the Irish Catholic masses in similar terms, and it is their 'acting' not only in the theatrical but also in the political arena that is obliquely disavowed here.[47] In giving the name 'Paddy' to the newsboy who reads the play's puffs to his 'unletter'd comrades' (p. 3) on the street and thus promotes their interest in the stage, Whyte makes the ethnic and religious valence of his critique more clear, even as he hints at what may have been a more personal, professionally related kind of anxiety. This newsboy, who is derisively mocked as a 'second Stagyrite'(p. 3) conjures up the image of that rival Catholic literate class that, under the leadership of scholars like O'Conor, were then challenging Anglican cultural hegemony (and by implication Whyte's own livelihood) by their interventions into the realm of letters.

The identifiers attached to the 'Ladies and Gentlemen' who acted the exemplary private play would no less clearly have defined the religious and class orientation of those performers, even as these markers would have worked to distinguish their social class both from the 'Great Vulgar' in Phoenix Park and the vulgar proper in the Dublin public theatre. The site of this performance was the Cuffe Street home of the Dublin LeFanus, a family that by that time was solidly middle class and Protestant. The cast for the evening also reflected that demographic. Among the players, for instance, were Whyte himself; the Rev. Peter LeFanu, a Church of Ireland clergyman; Joseph LeFanu, a clerk in the Irish Customs Office; Henry LeFanu, an army captain; and Richard Guinness who came from the banking line of the Guinness family.[48] The description of the performance of the 'Young Lady' mentioned in the poem's subtitle would also have served to define the values of this group, while at the same time differentiating Whyte's brand of theatrical both from the showy type of performance exemplified by Mrs Gardiner at the top end of the social scale, and by the 'buskin'd dames' (p. 15) who strutted their stuff on the public stage at its lower end. As Whyte reminded readers in a footnote, this exemplary actor was Alicia Sheridan, the daughter of Thomas Sheridan and she, along with her two more famous brothers, Charles and Richard, were past pupils of his school (p. 19). From the poem's detailed account, it is also clear that Alicia's performance of Jane Shore was meant to exemplify that 'sentimentalized mode of polite elo-quence' that Whyte, following Sheridan, had been promoting since the mid-century.[49] Alicia spoke '[w]ith every power and every grace of speech / which feeling can suggest, and art can teach' (p. 18), we are told, and in so doing, she aroused in her listeners those socially productive passions that both Sheridan and Whyte associated with good oratory. Those who witnessed her perfor-mance wanted to 'assert her cause', and engage, on her behalf, in a 'glorious strife' against 'proud oppression' and 'despotic laws' (p. 18). As Jean Marsden and others have noted, however, the qualities exemplified by Jane Shore – submissiveness, passivity, and a seemingly endless capacity for suffering – were also those associated with properly domesticated femininity in middle-class culture at that time.[50] It is that kind of 'character', as well as Nicholas Rowe's Whiggish brand of politics, Whyte implies, that he is teaching in his school. As his Irish readers would have known, the 'glorious strife' against 'despotic laws' in another one of Rowe's plays, *Tamerlane*, had long been used to signify the Williamite struggle that established Protestant hegemony in Ireland.

To look at the discourse emanating from, and about, eighteenth-century private theatricals, then, is to realise that, like public theatre discourse during the same period, it provides a window into the social, political, and religious tensions that lay beneath the surface of Irish life. This is in no small part because private theatricals were, in point of fact, rarely 'private'. Thanks to literati like Whyte, the productions of this form of theatre entered the public sphere where, like their counterparts from the commercial stage, they contributed to the larger contentious conversations on politics, society, and religion in eighteenth-century Ireland. Whyte's body of work on private theatricals takes its meaning from that ongoing conversation even if, as is generally the case in his texts, this schoolmaster translates political questions into cultural ones.

Notes

1. *The Poetical Works of Thomas Moore*, 10 vols (London: Longman, Orme, Green, & Longmans, 1841), I, pp. x–xi.
2. Samuel Whyte, *A Collection of Poems, on Various Subjects, Including The Theatre, a Didactic Essay, in Which Deluded Adventurers Are Inevitably Exposed*, ed. Edward Athenry Whyte, 2nd edn (Dublin, 1792), pp. 60–66.
3. *Poetical Works of Thomas Moore*, I, p. xi.
4. *The Dublin University Magazine* 35 (January–June, 1850), 714–16.
5. See Gerard O'Brien, 'The Grattan Mystique', *Eighteenth-Century Ireland / Iris an dá chultúr* 1 (1986), 177–94.
6. *A True History of the Scheme for Erecting a New Seminary for Education upon the Several Causes of Its Rise and Progress; and an Impartial Examination of All Its Purposes in a Letter to William *******, Esq* (Dublin, [1759]), p. 6. The 1769 date of the title page is mostly likely a printer's error since the date for the 'Letter' in the text itself is 1759 and its content also suggests the earlier date.
7. Patrick Fagan, 'Samuel Whyte', in *The Oxford Dictionary of National Biography*: www.oxforddnb.com.proxy.lib.fsu.edu/view/article/29342 [accessed 5 May 2017]; J. T. Gilbert, *A History of the City of Dublin*, 3 vols (Dublin, 1859), III, pp. 199–200.

8. Gilbert, *A History of Dublin*, I, p. 201. For the 1754 riot, see Helen M. Burke, *Riotous Performances: The Struggle for Hegemony in the Irish Theater, 1712–1784* (University of Notre Dame Press, 2003), pp. 209–40.

9. Thomas Sheridan, *An Oration, Pronounced before a Numerous Body of the Nobility and Gentry, Assembled at the Musick Hall in Fishamble-Street*, 2nd edn (Dublin, 1757), p. 7. Further references are given after quotations in the text.

10. Toby Barnard, *Making the Grand Figure: Lives and Possessions in Ireland, 1641–1770* (New Haven, CT and London: Yale University Press, 2004).

11. See Esther K. Sheldon, *Thomas Sheridan of Smock-Alley, 1719–1788* (Princeton University Press, 1967), pp. 272–76.

12. See, for example, Samuel Whyte's *Modern Education, Respecting Young Ladies as Well as Young Gentlemen* (Dublin, 1775), pp. 13, 54; and his *An Introductory Essay on the Art of Reading and Speaking in Public*, ed. Edward Athenry-Whyte (Dublin, 1800), pp. 38, 136. This second tract, according to Whyte's son, was written in 1759.

13. See Thomas Sheridan, *A Course of Lectures on Elocution: Together with Two Dissertations on Language* (London, 1762), p. 225; and Whyte, *Introductory Essay*, p. 44.

14. For the annual school performances, see Sheldon, *Thomas Sheridan*, pp. 6–9.

15. Samuel Whyte, *The Shamrock, or Hibernian Cresses. A Collection of Poems, Songs, Epigram, Etc. Latin as well as English, the Original Production of Ireland. To Which Are Subjoined Thoughts on the Prevailing System of School Education, Respecting Young Ladies as Well as Gentlemen, with Practical Proposals for a Reformation* (Dublin, 1772), pp. 53–55.

16. See the advertisement for Whyte's school in L. M. Stretch, *The Beauties of History*, 2 vols (Dublin, 1775), II, p. 384.

17. Jim Smyth, review of Jacqueline Hill, *From Patriots to Unionists*, in *Albion* 31.1 (Spring 1999), 183.

18. Samuel Whyte, *Poems on Various Subjects, Ornamented with Plates, and Illustrated with Notes, Original Letters and Curious Incidental Anecdotes*, ed. Edward Athenry Whyte (Dublin, 1795), p. 143.

19. Whyte, *The Shamrock*, p. 307. Further references to this poem are given after quotations in the text.

20. The 'Gentlemen's Quarrel' of 1747 (also known as the 'Kelly riots') began when a drunken Galway man named Edmund Kelly attempted a sexual assault on an actress behind the scenes of Smock Alley, and Sheridan responded by beating him and questioning his gentility. In three published 'Letters' and in an address delivered in the theatre itself, Lucas characterised this behaviour as an instance of native Irish aristocratic barbarity, and he urged the 'Free Citizens of Dublin' to resist not only their tyranny but that of all gentlemen who threatened tradesmen or ordinary citizens. See Burke, *Riotous Performances*, pp. 159–66.

21. Whyte states that he began the Lucas 'Letter' in 1768 and completed it in Waterstown in 1770: see Whyte, *The Shamrock*, p. 305.

22. Whyte, 'Bon Ton Theatricals', in *A Collection of Poems, on Various Subjects*, p. 50. All future references to Whyte's prologues or epilogues are to this edition and will be given after quotations in the text.

23. Michael McKeon, *The Origins of the English Novel, 1660–1740* (Baltimore, MD: Johns Hopkins University Press, 1987), pp. 174, 150–59; G. J. Barker-Benfield, *The Culture of Sensibility: Sex and Society in Eighteenth-Century Britain* (University of Chicago Press, 1992), pp. 214–86.

24. See Seán Murphy, 'Charles Lucas, Catholicism and Nationalism', *Eighteenth-Century Ireland / Iris an dá chultúr* 8 (1993), 83–102 (pp. 87, 88).

25. Whyte, *A Collection of Poems*, p. ii.

26. See, for example, the anecdote about the shopkeeper who is horsewhipped by the country squire in his own shop because he trusted that gentleman's tailor: *The Censor* (17 June 1749).

27. See Jacqueline Hill, *From Patriots to Unionists: Dublin Civil Politics and Irish Protestant Patriotism, 1660–1840* (Oxford University Press, 1997).

28. Samuel Whyte, *The Theatre: A Didactic Essay Including an Idea of the Character of Jane Shore as performed by a Young Lady in a Private Play, Etc. Etc.* (Dublin, 1790), pp. v, x. Further references to this work are given after quotations in the text.

29. See Gilbert, *A History of Dublin*, I, p. 209.

30. *The Hibernian Journal* (21–23 January 1778); *Saunders's News-Letter* (29 January 1778); *The Hibernian Magazine* (January 1778), 61–62; *The Morning Post and Daily Advertiser* (2 February 1778).

31. *The Hibernian Magazine* (April 1778), 193; and (May 1778), n.p.

32. Whyte, 'The Lyceum', in *The Shamrock*, p. 274.

33. Ibid.

34. *Poetical Works of Thomas Moore,* I, p. x.

35. See *Saunders's News-Letter* (29 January 1778).

36. *The Hibernian Magazine* (January 1778), 62.

37. For the Reynolds portrait and Gardiner's interest in the arts, see John Coleman, 'Luke Gardiner (1745–98): An Irish Dilettante', *Irish Arts Review* 15 (1999), 160–68.

38. *The Hibernian Magazine* (January 1778), 62.

39. *Saunders's News-Letter* (29 January 1778).

40. Frances Clarke, 'Robert Jephson', in *Dictionary of Irish Biography*, ed. James McGuire and James Quinn: http://dib.cambridge.org/viewReadPage.do?art icleId=a4272 [accessed 30 May 2017].

41. *The Hibernian Journal* (16–18 February 1778).

42. *The Hibernian Journal* (6–9 March 1778).

43. The effort to conciliate Catholics was connected to the British government's desire to recruit Irish men for the American war. See Thomas Bartlett, '"A Weapon of War yet Untried": Irish Catholics and the Armed Forces of the Crown, 1760–1830', in *Men, Women and War*, ed. T. G. Fraser and Keith Jeffery (Dublin: Lilliput Press, 1993), pp. 66–85.

44. *The Letters of Charles O'Conor of Belanagare*, ed. Robert E. Ward, John F. Wrynn, and Catherine Coogan Ward (Washington, DC: Catholic University of America Press, 1988), p. 349.

45. The testimony of both Thomas Moore and Thomas Dermody speaks to Whyte's religious tolerance (see the poetic tributes published in Whyte's *Poems on Various Subjects*, pp. 270–72). Whyte's notes on the poem 'Ode to British Freedom', however, suggest that he held the same views on the Catholic religion and the established state as most of his co-religionists. He described 1688, for instance, as the year when 'our Great Deliverer', acting on the 'united Wishes of a Free People' delivered Ireland from 'the Tyranny of Romanist Superstition' (*The Shamrock*, p. 214).

46. Hill, *From Patriots to Unionists*, p. 134.

47. For the increased participation of Irish Catholics in Dublin theatres at this time, see Burke, *Riotous Performances*, pp. 241–80.

48. For the LeFanu background, see Anna M. Fitzer, '"Feeling and Sense Beyond All Seeming": Private Lines, Public Relations and the Performances of the LeFanu Circle', *Nineteenth Century Theatre and Film* 38.2 (Winter 2011), 27–28. Both Richard Guinness and the sons of the brewer, Arthur Guinness, were past pupils of Whyte's school: see Patrick Guinness, *Arthur's Round: The Life and Times of Brewing Legend Arthur Guinness* (London: Peter Owen, 2014).

49. Paul Goring, *The Rhetoric of Sensibility in Eighteenth-Century Culture* (Cambridge University Press, 2005), p. 96.

50. Jean I. Marsden, *Fatal Desire: Women, Sexuality, and the English Stage, 1660–1720* (Ithaca, NY and London: Cornell University Press, 2006), pp. 60–61, 159–67.

Local, National, and Transnational Contexts

Land and Landscape in Irish Poetry in English, 1700–1780

Andrew Carpenter

The redistribution of land after the Battle of the Boyne brought to an end the bitter disputes which had surrounded land tenure in seventeenth-century Ireland. The English-speaking Protestants who took up residence east and south of the Shannon after 1690 set about consolidating their physical presence in the countryside: they adapted older buildings to create elegant houses, they formed terraces and flower gardens, they planted trees, they built long walls around their properties and they created vistas in landscapes they could look out on and call their own. Their right to live in the countryside was consolidated by the apparent imposition of order on it. Protected by the Penal Laws, Church of Ireland landowners leased land to tenant farmers who might be Catholics (in the southern parts of the island) or Presbyterians (in Ulster).[1] The countryside looked peaceful, and English-speaking poets often maintained that it was so – thus closing their eyes to the plight of those forced off the land; however, the experiences and aspirations of the dispossessed are clearly seen in Irish-language verse of the period.[2] From time to time, underlying tensions between the different communities led to considerable agrarian and sectarian violence. However, by the time the Romantic revolution swept over the middle-class, English-speaking world, poets visiting Ireland were seeking out the wild and potentially 'sublime' landscapes of County Wicklow, the lakes of Killarney, and the Giant's Causeway rather than admiring landscapes of pastoral plenty; even the poets who sought to ingratiate themselves with the owners of big houses by extolling them and their property reserved particular praise for gardens from which one could catch a glimpse of wild, untamed mountains. The people living outside the walls of the demesne were seldom afforded a mention.

Natural or Contrived?

Poets did, however, often mention themselves and their ability to appreciate both natural and contrived landscapes. The Dubliner James Ward, for instance, admired the landscaping that was being undertaken in the newly enclosed Phoenix Park on the outskirts of Dublin at the beginning of the century, and urged poets to praise the way humans imposed order on wildness and crafted nature to create pleasing 'views':

> What scene more lovely, and more form'd for Bliss,
> What more deserves the Muse's Strain than this?
> Where more can boundless Nature please, and where
> In Shapes more various, and more sweet appear?
>
> Now when the Centre of the Wood is found,
> With goodly Trees a spacious Circle bound,
> I stop my wandring – while on ev'ry Side,
> Glades op'ning to the Eye, the Grove divide,
> To distant Objects stretch my lengthen'd View,
> And make each pleasing Prospect charm anew.[3]

Ward and other Anglo-Irish poets – Mary Monck, for instance, and those whose work was included by Matthew Concanen in his 1724 anthology *Miscellaneous Poems, Original and Translated* – based their way of writing about the Irish countryside on models from Renaissance Italy and France, or on the work of Horace, Ovid, and the Virgil of the *Georgics*.[4] Echoes of the classics rang in the ears of the readers of poetry in the eighteenth century, and many poets played on the connection. However, when the countryside was used as a realistic backdrop in Irish poetry of the time, it was usually to heighten the contrast between the green open spaces and urban life, as in this passage from another poem by Ward in which he described how one city-dweller visiting a fair in the Dublin hinterland reacted to the view of countryside:

> The Butcher's soggy Spouse amid the Throng
> Rubb'd clean, and tawdry drest, puffs slow along: . . .
> Long to St Patrick's filthy Shambles bound,
> Surpris'd, she views the rural Scene around,
> The distant Ocean there salutes her Eyes,
> Here tow'ring Hills in goodly Order rise,
> There fruitful Valleys long extended lay,
> Here Sheaves of Corn, and Cocks of fragrant Hay.
> While whatso'er she hears, or smells, or sees
> Gives her fresh Transports, and she dotes on Trees.

> Yet, (hapless Wretch) the servile Thirst of Gain
> Can force her to her stinking Stall again.[5]

A more typical response was that of Swift's protégée, Mary Barber, who wrote to a friend who had invited her to visit her in the country:

> How gladly, Madam, would I go,
> To see your Gardens, and Chateau;
> From thence the fine Improvements view,
> Or walk your verdant Avenue;
> Delighted, hear the Thrushes sing,
> Or listen to some bubbling Spring;
> If Fate had giv'n me Leave to roam!
> But Citizens must stay at Home. . . .
>
> Whilst lovely Landscapes you survey,
> And peaceful pass your Hours away,
> Refresh'd with various blooming Sweets,
> I'm sick of Smells, and dirty Streets,
> Stifled with Smoke, and stunn'd with Noise.[6]

As well as being symbolic of an unconstricted, clean way of life, the Irish countryside provided the context for poems about real activities – football, smock racing, and feasting, for instance. The English-speaking readers of poems describing such pastimes could smile, condescendingly, as they enjoyed the mock-heroics of Ward's 'The Smock-Race at Finglas', Nicholas Browne's 'A North-Country Wedding', and Matthew Concanen's 'A Match at Football'.[7] These poems were all set in the countryside in the east or north of Ireland, though the last of these consciously burlesqued Virgil's *Aeneid* in its opening line: 'I sing the Pleasures of the Rural throng', so pointing up the absurdity of the classical echo. If the human participants in these poems were given names suggesting Irish Catholic origin – Paddy, Oonagh, Felim, or Shevan (Siobhán) – they would be seen as belonging to the tradition of the 'Stage Irishman'; if they were given traditional classical names such as Strephon and Chloe, the satire was that of urban sophisticates laughing at country bumpkins. The rural poor do not appear in these poems; nor, of course, do speakers of the Irish language, though there are regular references to the provision of music by blind pipers as well as occasional references to harpers.

The West

A poet clearly inspired by the classics – though not inclined to parody or burlesque them – was a Protestant tenant farmer from Kerry who called himself Morrough O'Connor. His extraordinary 1719 poem, 'Eclogue in Imitation of the first Eclogue of Virgil', takes the form of an extended dialogue between the poet and a friend detailing his disagreements with his landlords, the Provost and Fellows of Trinity College, Dublin. O'Connor's patriotism and his evident love of the land and of farming are unusual enough for the time: but, in a further gesture of affection for Ireland, O'Connor appended to the 1726 printing of his eclogue a remarkable poem praising the unimproved, natural landscape of Kerry:

> Sure there are poets who did never dream,
> On Brandon hill, nor taste the gentle stream,
> Which from the glitt'ring summit daily flows:
> And the bright pebbles in its fair bosom shews;
> From thy clear height I take my lofty flight,
> Which opens all the country to my sight:
> Both rocks and woods are from thy prospect seen,
> Blake in the winter, in the summer green:
> Where e'er I turn my eyes new scenes appear,
> Adorn'd with all the blessings of the year.[8]

The first lines of this poem are a direct copy of the opening of Sir John Denham's famous meditative and topographical poem 'Cooper's Hill' (1642): 'Sure there are poets which did never dream / Upon Parnassus, nor did taste the stream / Of Helicon.' O'Connor's readers would have detected the echo and were probably surprised to see this model applied to a real, specific, Irish landscape. As the poem progressed, the poet meditated on the beauty of the landscape and reminded himself and his readers of the past glories of the lords of Kerry, and of the quality of the produce of the 'kingdom' – such as, for example, its marble:

> Rome in her grandeur, never cou'd produce
> Such stones as we in common houses use;
> Her Gothick structures and her marble domes
> Were far inferior to our Kerry stones.

What is more, the poet asserted that living in the midst of the landscape of Kerry could only induce an awareness of the good things of life:

> Plenty and peace in ev'ry house abound,
> Such happiness can no where else be found;
> I who desire to live an easy life,
> Absent from faction and remote from strife,
> In Kerry only must expect to find
> Those lasting blessings sought by human kind.

O'Connor's poem is remarkable not only for its articulation of the idea that life in the depths of the Irish countryside was desirable for a reader well-versed in the classics, but also for its praise of the sweeping vistas of the west of Ireland and its obvious affection for an unimproved landscape. It is unusual for an early eighteenth-century poet to use such words as 'gentle', 'fair', and 'adorn'd with blessings' of anywhere in Ireland, and extraordinary to see them (as they are in this poem) applied to west Kerry – an area notoriously full of anti-British feeling and one which, before the age of railways and mass tourism, inspired fear and foreboding in many English speakers.[9]

At roughly the same time, Jonathan Swift – a man usually indifferent to landscape – described a ferocious storm lashing the coastline of West Cork. His poem, 'Carberiae Rupes', was influenced by the classical poems he – and every schoolboy of the time – had read, and was written in Latin. It was soon translated into English by his friend William Dunkin and published in Swift's works of 1735:

> Lo! from the Top of yonder Cliff, that shrouds
> Its airy Head amidst the azure Clouds,
> Hangs a huge Fragment; destitute of props
> Prone on the Waves the rocky Ruin drops.
> With hoarse Rebuff the swelling Seas rebound,
> From Shore to Shore the Rocks return the Sound.[10]

What sets Swift's poem apart from the landscape poems of his contemporaries is its imaginative power and the sense that nature's force is far greater than that of man: the wild winter winds raised 'raging Billows' that rolled 'o'er the craggy Steep without Controul' – sending the terrified fisherfolk scurrying for shelter. This may be more of a classical storm than an Irish one – but its setting was firmly Irish.

The World of the Landlord

By the 1720s, poets of varying competence were writing about Irish country houses and their estates, praising the elegance of the landscaping round a house, the abundance of its farm and garden produce, the architecture of the house itself, the generosity and humanity of its owner, and, of course, the beauty and potential fecundity of his daughters. In most cases, such poems were not published by subscription but dedicated to the owner of the house, who was expected to provide the poet with some tangible reward.

There are many such poems, though one of the best known of them is a joke – Thomas Sheridan's mocking praise of 'Delville', the miniature estate set up by Swift's friends Dr and Mrs Delany at Glasnevin near Dublin. Though the Delanys were ridiculously proud of their landholding, Sheridan could not resist making fun of it:

> You scarce upon the Borders enter,
> Before you're at the very Centre.
> A single Crow can make it Night,
> When o'er your Farm he takes his Flight;
> Yet in this narrow Compass, we
> Observe a vast Variety;
> Both Walks, Walls, Meadows and Parterres,
> Windows, and Doors, and Rooms, and Stairs,
> And Hills, and Dales, and Woods and Fields,
> And Hay, and Grass, and Corn it yields;
> All to your Haggard brought so cheap in,
> Without the Mowing or the Reaping.
> A Razour, tho' to say't I'm loath,
> Wou'd shave you and your Meadows both."

Laetitia Pilkington, another member of Swift's circle, wrote a more serious poem about 'Delville':

> Hail, happy Delville! blissful Seat!
> The Muses's best belov'd Retreat!
> With prospects large and unconfin'd;
> Best Emblem of their Master's Mind!
> Where fragrant Gardens, painted Meads,
> Wide op'ning Walks, and twilight Shades –
> Inspiring Scenes! – elate the Heart!
> Nature improv'd, and raised by Art,
> So Paradise delightful smil'd,
> Blooming, and beautifully wild.¹²

Most eighteenth-century Irish poems on this theme took grander houses and estates as their subject matter, however. Several celebrated the larger Irish demesnes which had survived the chaos of the seventeenth century and were being actively developed in the eighteenth – places like Carton, Castletown, and Powerscourt, where 'art' was improving on 'nature'. Praising Bellisle in County Fermanagh, William Balfour Madden wrote:

> All hail Bellisle, unrivall'd Mansion hail!
> Woods, Lawns and circling Waters, Hill and Dale!
> On thee has partial Nature pour'd her Store

So fondly lavish Art can add no more. . . .
Oh! might I hope with simulating Grace,
To emulate the Wonders of thy Place.
Wide as thy fair Expanse of Waves to flow,
Bright as thy Scenes of varying Tints to glow.
High as thy cloud-capt Mountain to ascend,
Rich as thy flow'ry Vallies to extend.
Then should Bellisle surpass Arcadia's Plains,
Or Cowper's-Hill in Denham's epic Strains;
And e'en aspire with Windsor to engage,
That lives to Fame in Pope's eternal Page.[13]

The conscious link with England's great pastoral poets, Denham and Pope, was designed to affirm the view that the Irish landscape should be seen as equal in beauty with any to be found in the country which many poets still thought of as 'home'. This 'political' dimension to Irish topographical and country-house poetry – the implicit questioning of 'Irishness' and its relationship to 'Britishness' or 'Englishness' – lay behind many such poems.

Some poets listed all the features designed to amplify the pleasure of viewing the land and landscape around an Irish country house; Wetenhall Wilkes, having praised the house, the waterworks, the flower gardens, and the parterres in the recently refurbished estate of the Fleming family in County Cavan, describes a curious artifice designed to deceive the eye of the country-house guest and make the 'designed' views around the house seem even more attractively 'artificial':

Just at the Southern End of this Canal
And at the head of a delightful Mall,
A Grotto stands, adorn'd with various Shells,
In whose deep hollow list'ning Echo dwells;
Here curious Works and Busts amuse; and here
Large Sheets of pannel'd Looking-Glass appear;
Which to false views the entring Eyes invite,
And most agreeably deceive the Sight.[14]

The poem goes on to explain that, above the grotto, is a 'Pleasure Room' from which house guests might 'view the Glories of the rip'ning Year' before repairing to a circular bowling green 'Near fifty Foot diameter', where they can sit on a 'decent, mossy seat' listening to the 'superfluous Bubbles' descending over a waterfall. All the senses are to be gratified – even by 'false views'. Such mechanical ways of amplifying the effects of a natural phenomenon – waterfall or vista – were typical of an aesthetic

sensibility shifting from the classical to the romantic. Wilkes's description
of the Flemings' estate moves from the near and middle view to the distant
prospect of 'an huge Mountain' boasting with 'Romantic Pride', its 'bul-
ging Brows' rising in 'wildest order', 'rude' and 'chaos-like', and its
'spangled Rocks' reflecting 'an awful Glance'. If, on a 'Cloudless day',
the house guests are tempted to venture out into this dangerous wildness
and climb the mountain, they will be rewarded with tremendous views –
prospects that will tire their 'wandring Eyes':

> Hills peep o'er Hills, and mix with distant Skies;
> But as they sharpen in th'ethereal hight,
> Their rudeness lessens to our distant Sight.

Whatever the reality of rural life, the poets describing the landscape as
seen from a high place near a demesne usually allowed the vista to include
some apparently neat cottages or a thriving village near the big house –
suggesting that the countryside was settled and peaceful and the generous
landlord universally loved. Those actually living in the country – the
dispossessed subsisting in hovels at the roadside, for instance – might
disagree: but the description of peaceful communities and contented
rustics was meant to reassure readers that Ireland was a safe place to
visit and to live in, a place that, on the whole, welcomed the imposition of
British civility. The desolate mountains around Killarney were, for the
poet Joseph Atkinson writing of the area, softened by the sight of 'the
spacious park and mansion' of Lord Kenmare, their 'lordly owner';
equally attractive to the poet was the expanding town of Killarney, the
'rural neatness' of which added to the perfection of 'the prospect' he was
describing. Atkinson, like another prolific landscape poet John Leslie,
employed all his skill to persuade readers that the Irish countryside, with
its mixture of the cultivated and the wild, was to be admired and enjoyed,
not feared.[15]

One of the ways in which city dwellers might enjoy the countryside was
by visiting a spa – of which there were many in eighteenth-century Ireland.
Some, like Templeogue near Dublin, spawned their own poetic circles and
publications: others were just celebrated in verse.[16] The waters and the
surroundings were invariably praised, as were the various entertainments
available – music of all kinds often provided by Irish harpers and pipers,
and romantic walks by the riverside following lively meals and preceding
sexual high-jinks.[17] Boat trips on lakes also provided copy for poets, some
of whom described the landscape through which the boats passed with
great care:

> On ev'ry Hand, to our admiring Eyes,
> New Prospects open and new Scenes arise. . . .
> With sudden Inlet and with new Delight,
> Long watry Vistas stretch before the Sight
> Nor give a Limit to the wondring Eye
> Save by black Mountains, or cerulean Sky.[18]

According to William Balfour Madden, individual islands in Lough Erne exhibited different characteristics:

> These in chaotic Rocks, of monstrous Size,
> And Figures of romantic Wildness rise:
> In Robes of Russet Tincture these are seen,
> These clad in Groves of everlasting green,
> While others with Autumnal Foliage glow,
> Dipt in the Colours of the show'ry Bow.

It was not just the lakes of Ireland that were favoured poetic subjects but also the rivers. They could be praised for their beauty but could also remind poets of the heroic battles that had taken place on their banks and of those who had been inspired by them.[19] In almost all such poems, the poet was very specific about the place being celebrated; it was clear that admiring a Hibernian landscape was an appropriate pastime for landlords and their guests.

The World of the Labourer

Others were, of course, working the land and so less inclined to stand back and admire the landscape. When released, on Sundays and holydays, from their back-breaking labour, country dwellers were often described enjoying themselves. A schoolmaster from County Meath, Bernard Clarke, described 'Paddy' and 'Tom', 'Jugg' and 'Nell' repairing to the woods on days when they were 'relieved from labour' to take part in 'sport and nutting'. The lads would display to the girls 'their rustic Parts' which encouraged the lasses to 'resign to them their Hearts'. The rising ground on which all these activities took place:

> Commands a Prospect of the Country round,
> Shews the fair Landskip in a charming View,
> Beset with Gall'ries of tall Ash and Yew,
> Hills, Woods, and Groves, Springs, Rivulets, and Streams,
> Rivers, and Meadows, were, my Muse, my Themes.[20]

The setting sounds bucolic enough though many poems about life on the land are quite explicit that, during their time off, labourers and their

partners indulged in heavy drinking and all-night debauchery. Such behaviour was not, of course, uniquely Irish – and many of the descriptions
were exaggerated – but these poems helped build the stereotypical view
that those living in the Irish countryside used the festivities surrounding
weddings or saints days, as well as excursions to fairs or markets, as excuses
to get drunk and violent.[21] Even descriptions of country festivities frequented by the middle class suggest high levels of alcohol consumption in
the Irish countryside during the eighteenth century.[22] The stereotype was
reinforced by John Anketell, a country clergyman from Monaghan who,
after describing a happy day of festivities honouring a local saint, wrote
that, under a glorious sunset, the tents selling drink to the pilgrims were
doing a brisk trade: 'Around they ply with whiskey, rum and beer, / While
cyder, wine and brandy join the cheer.' Later in the evening, 'To blows and
furious combat they proceed: / Friends fall by friends, and sons by fathers
bleed.'[23]

There are many poems like this that, whether intentionally or not, fed
the anti-Irish and anti-Catholic prejudices of those living in England. It is
not surprising that by the nineteenth century the view that those living in
the Irish countryside were barely civilised creatures given to heavy drinking
and faction fighting was comparatively widespread.

The culture of those with a limited ability to read English was supplied
by chapbooks; surprisingly, hundreds of these small folded sheets printed
cheaply on coarse paper containing the songs that were sung at fairs and in
lanes have survived, and they give a good indication of how those with little
education saw the world around them. In many cases, songs recounted
events that occurred in particular places or told of love-sick bachelors
wandering through a landscape dear to them:

> You lads and lasses I pray attend,
> And draw near a while until I relate,
> It is concerning a lovely river,
> Whose worthy praises I will relate,
> Where the pink and violet are gently blowing,
> The Duck and Mallard in flocks do go,
> The kids and the lambs on the plains are sporting,
> Down by the banks of the sweet Barrow.
>
> Near to this river lies my habitation,
> Where I'm convenient to each pretty lass,
> As they are dancing of a summers evening,
> Near to a place call'd the Old Pass,
> Where the pretty fishes are nimbly sporting,

> The silver streams they do gently flow,
> From that sweet brook to the chrystal fountain,
> Down by the banks of the sweet Barrow.[24]

Many songs exhibit pride in the beauty of the local area and list, with relish, the names of townlands or market towns. In general, however, it was not the landscape that occupied the minds of the anonymous writers of these songs as much as the activities of those living in the country – and the behaviour described would not always have been condoned in more polite societies.

A country activity frequently mentioned in poetry and song is the hunting of stags, foxes, or hares. In such work, there is usually a brief description of the landscape before a more detailed account of the (often named) hounds pursuing and killing the unfortunate animal. However, in Killarney, according to the poets, the captured stag would be tethered and its antlers garlanded with flowers by local girls. The animal would then be released to be chased and captured on another occasion.[25] This side of country life became a form of tourist spectacle designed to enhance the pleasure experienced by city dwellers who went, in increasing numbers as the century progressed, to the wild places of Ireland to look at the people who lived there as well as to admire the landscape.

Some poets sought to describe conditions on farms and in gardens. Henry Jones wrote 'On a fine Crop of Peas being spoil'd by a Storm' (1749), and there are several poems in which farm animals appear rather as they do in eighteenth-century landscape painting – placidly munching or cropping in well-enclosed fields.[26] The main poetic exceptions to this pattern seem to have their origin in the Irish midlands, in the work of Oliver Goldsmith and Laurence Whyte. The latter, who moved from County Westmeath in about 1710 to become a teacher of mathematics in Dublin, wrote vividly of the farm life he had known as a young man. His most substantial poem, 'The Parting Cup, or The Humours of Deoch an Doruis' (1740), recounts the fortunes of a tenant farmer in County Westmeath during the first decades of the eighteenth century. The farmer and his wife lived sparingly on local produce and brought up their children to work hard on the farm:

> He taught his *Sons* to hold the Plow,
> To sow the Seed, to reap and mow;
> To take the *Area* of a Field,
> Before it was manur'd or till'd.[27]

Pat, the eldest son, went to do business at fairs and markets 'But never chas'd a *Fox* or *Hare*, / Nor kept a *Racing Horse* or *Mare*'.

However, rural Ireland was changing: international trade barriers, the practice of increasing enclosure, and the raising of rents to support often non-resident landlords put Irish rural life under almost intolerable pressure. Life within the walls of a demesne might be easy enough, but Whyte presented life on a Westmeath farm as growing constantly more difficult:

> Now *Wooll* is low, and *Mutton* cheap,
> Poor *Graziers* can no Profit reap . . .
> And were it not for foreign Wheat,
> We now shou'd want the Bread we eat.

The end for the farmer in Whyte's poem comes when the landlord decides that 'Deoch an Doruis' and his wife have improved the land so much that their rent is now too low; and so it is doubled and then doubled again:

> They had their choice to run away,
> Or labour for a Groat a Day,
> Now beggar'd and of all bereft,
> Are doom'd to starve or live by Theft,
> Take to the *Mountains* or the *Roads*,
> When banish'd from their old *Abodes*;
> Their native *Soil* were forc'd to quit,
> So *Irish Landlords* thought it fit,
> Who without Cer'mony or Rout,
> For their *Improvements* turn'd them out. . . .

In this poem, it is not foreigners who are the villains, but 'Irish landlords', greedily seeking excessive returns from the land. The social cost of their actions is at the heart of Whyte's poem. Those trying to live on the land are victims of those seeking merely to enjoy the landscape. This poem presents life in rural Ireland as bitterly unrewarding – however pretty the landscape might appear to a visitor.

Such a view of Irish life also lies behind 'The Deserted Village', the work of another poet from County Westmeath, Oliver Goldsmith. Whether the 'Auburn' of that poem was a village in England or not, the depopulation and increasing destitution of much of the Irish midlands that Goldsmith witnessed in his youth in the 1720s and 30s were undoubtedly at least in the back of his mind when he wrote his stinging attack on luxury and enclosure:

> Sweet smiling village, loveliest of the lawn,
> Thy sports are fled, and all thy charms withdrawn; . . .
> Sunk are thy bowers, in shapeless ruin all,
> And the long grass o'ertops the mouldering wall.[28]

There are many poetic visions of the land and landscape of eighteenth-century Ireland, but Goldsmith's vision of one from which 'the bloomy flush of life is fled' remains one of the most haunting.

The Effects of Weather

Violent climatic events also produced poems in which the devastated landscape could be seen as one of real horror. The extended frost of 1740–41, 'malign, twice gliding o'er Hibernia's coasts', was a 'harbinger of death and desolation':

> The hoary winter, beldame of the year
> Unteeming, inly binds the frigid womb
> Of all-productive earth. In frequent bands
> The cattle perish . . . [29]

Those trying to work the land could not even sink a spade into the icy soil, rivers and waterfalls were frozen solid and corpses could not be buried:

> . . . In gardens, though immur'd,
> Or hedg'd, the pear, and apple-tree, late wont
> From summer-beams to yield a shady dome
> To noon-tide swain, and to the thirsty lip
> Nectareous draughts, and blush with orient gold
> Promiscuous dye . . . [30]

Birds, wild beasts, bees, and human beings were all frozen: carriages were driven on ice over what should have been flowing rivers. Even the sea froze over and 'The woolly Flock plunge in the treach'rous snow; / The bellowing ox for food his pastures blow.'[31]

When the snow finally disappeared and the ice melted, the countryside was overtaken by floods in which farm animals drowned and country dwellers were found dead in their houses, frozen alive. The following excerpt from a poem by Thomas Delamayne offers a glimpse of the catastrophe:

> Now the bared fields a ghastly scene disclose
> Of Herds and Herdsmen, Flocks and Trav'llers froze:
> Who, lost in pathless snows and sunk in death,
> Seem still in various attitudes to breathe;
> Like monumental statues of the fate
> They and their Race once felt in Nature's state![32]

There are many poems about the appalling state of the countryside during and after the frost of 1740–41; the fact that – as in the famines of the late 1720s – the

infrastructure of Ireland was totally unable to cope with the situation persuaded
many of those thrown off the land that their only option was emigration.[33]

Luckily, however, not all winters were as lethal and not all storms as
ferocious as those of 1740–41. The Ulster poet Olivia Elder described the
effects of a severe storm on the landscape near Aghadowey, just south of
Coleraine, in 1770:

> The trees that yesterday in beauty shone,
> Now mourn in rags their verdant honours gone;
> And roots of Oaks, the tallest in the Wood,
> Possess the places where their branches stood.[34]

Corn, uprooted by the wind, as well as branches of furze and briar, ended
up on the horns of cattle in fields nearby: nature was upside down. But
sometimes it seemed to poets that after the flashing lightning, the awe-
inspiring thunder, and the drenching rain of a summer storm, the Irish
landscape was more beautiful than ever. After such a storm, James
Delacourt wrote:

> So have I seen the florid rain-bow rise,
> In breded colours o'er the wat'ry skies,
> Where drops of light alternate fall away
> And fainting gleams in gradual dyes decay;
> But thrown together, the broad arch displays,
> One tide of glory, one collected blaze![35]

Looking at Landscape

Despite the willingness of many Irish poets to see their land and landscape
as beautiful, the perception that Ireland was a sombre and dangerous place
lingered stubbornly, particularly in the minds of those who had never
visited the country. A not untypical view is to be found in a poem by
Christopher Smart:

> In Ireland's wild, uncultivated plains,
> Where torpid sloth, and foggy dulness reigns,
> Full many a fen infests the putrid shore,
> And many a gulph the melancholy moor.
> Let not the stranger in these regions stray,
> Dark is the sky, and perilous the way;
> Beneath his foot-steps shakes the trembling ground,
> Dense fogs and exhalations hover round,
> And with black clouds the tender turf is crown'd.[36]

To some extent, the landscape was here being made to bear the hostility that many metropolitan English people felt for Ireland, a place they perceived as wild, ungovernable, and violent. After about 1760, however, as Romanticism swept through Europe, the wildness of the Celtic fringe of the British Isles became more appealing and exciting, particularly for those seeking 'the sublime'. Myth and ancient Irish history became subjects worth studying and the landscape in which great deeds were said to have taken place became significant. Even the Irish language was rehabilitated and its poetry translated into English.[37] The ruins that studded the Irish countryside became objects of veneration and, where possible, were integrated into man-made landscapes around big houses. Travel writers and poets dwelt on the thrilling mysteries supposedly associated with the 'gothic' ruins of Ireland and retold the stories with ever magnified drama. The Giant's Causeway became famous as a physical manifestation of some great and inexplicable event of the past, and places where wild nature could be seen not far from civilisation – such as the Dargle valley in County Wicklow – became much frequented. Engravings of the wild places of Ireland became popular and some poets tried their hand at describing them in words. Patrick Delany, for instance, wrote of a deep valley in County Tyrone, 'Where Mountains over Mountains tow'ring high / With pleasing Horror fill the distant Eye'.[38] Walter Chamberlayne's verbal description of the waterfall at Powerscourt prefigures the famous painting of the scene by George Barret (1764):

> Lo! down the Rock which Clouds and Darkness hide
> In wild meanders spouts a Silver Tide;
> Or sprung from dropping Mists or wintry Rills,
> Rolls the large Tribute of the Cloud-topp'd Hills;
> But shou'd the damp-wing'd Tempest keenly blow
> With whistling Torrents, and descending Snow,
> In one huge Heap the show'ry Whirlpools swell,
> And deluge wide the Tract where first they fell
> 'Till from the headlong verge of yon black Steep,
> A tumbling River roars intense and deep;
> From Rock to Rock its boiling Stream is broke,
> And all below, the Waters fall in Smoak.[39]

Earlier in the poem, Chamberlayne had dismissed the 'liquid landskips' of Versailles as inferior to the 'Pure Scenes of Nature' (such as the Powerscourt waterfall) which 'delight us most'. Nature's 'rudest Prospects bid the Fancy start, / And snatch the Soul beyond the Works of Art'.

Powerscourt was one of the demesnes that had survived the seventeenth century and into which money was being poured. Others, such as the landscapes surrounding Carton and Castletown, also attracted poets such as Samuel Shepherd and William Balfour Madden. The river at Leixlip – later made famous by Francis Wheatley in his much-reproduced painting of naked nymphs (improbably) bathing in the river Liffey there – was described in detail by Shepherd:

> [. . .] with unresisted Force
> The rapid Torrent pours his headlong Course,
> Foaming he sweeps along; the frighted Shore
> Groans as he passes; and the Caverns roar. ...
> Smooth for a while he laves the neighb'ring Grounds,
> Nor seems to murmur at his narrow Bounds,
> Then bursts at once, and gives a Loose to Rage;
> No Force can stop it; and no Art asswage:
> So he, with double Fury pouring o'er,
> Breaks thro' the Gates; and swells along the Shore:
> Where'er the Rocks their craggy Summits shew,
> *There* his Foam thickens; *there* his Surges grow.[40]

The landscape around the river is described in detail – but the river remained at the centre of what is, in effect, a poetic landscape attempting to portray the drama of the countryside just as a painter would seek to dramatise a view and give it focus and energy.

Looking Forward

From some points of view, eighteenth-century Ireland could be seen as a place of beauty and romance. Here, for instance, is how the English poet, George Crabbe, saw the Irish countryside in a poem written when his patron, the Duke of Rutland, was travelling to Ireland to become Lord Lieutenant:

> To Rutland health! Where'er his way he takes –
> By Ireland's frowning Hills or simple lakes;
> By Shannon's spacious current, spreading wide
> His aged banks, or Allo's tumbling Tide;
> By Barrow's Deeps, where Silver Salmon play;
> Or where stout Nore winds on his waters grey;
> By sedgy Lee, and Bandon's Woods among,
> Or Spenser's Mulla, where he wept and sung –
> Health to the Muses' Judge, the Muses' friend,
> The last and meanest of her vot'ries send.[41]

Since Crabbe never visited Ireland, it seems that imagination rather than observation lay behind his description of the hills as 'frowning', the Shannon as 'spacious' and the Lee as 'sedgy'. But Crabbe had read the work of Edmund Spenser, whose works describe features of the Irish landscape with considerable specificity and accuracy – and Spenser, after all, had been resident in Ireland for many years at the end of the sixteenth century. For a poet like Crabbe, living outside the country, the idea of Ireland had been formed at least partly by his reading of travel guides and epic poetry, but how he presented the country depended more on what he thought his patron wanted to hear than anything else. The land and landscape could be described as sublime or beautiful, welcoming or threatening, depending on whom the writer sought to impress.

The question facing Crabbe and most poets writing about the land or landscape of eighteenth-century Ireland was partly a political one. The big houses were intended to impress on all who saw them the power and superiority of their owners, despised by the previous owners of the land though they might be.[42] Demesne walls were to keep out the dispossessed, and there was much discontent, hardship, and suffering in the land. But how to write about this when confronted with a 'beautiful' view? The Irish countryside could never be – in the way the English countryside could be said to be – a place of peaceful, agricultural productivity, a northern landscape in which happy peasants sang cheerful songs and behaved like the workers in the *Georgics*.[43] Scotland, the country of origin of the quintessentially British Georgic poet James Thomson, was politically and commercially part of Great Britain, as was Wales; but Ireland was a separate kingdom, the inhabitants of which were prone to kick, noisily, against the pricks of British rule. So though the Irish countryside might be perceived as beautiful and potentially bountiful, and though mid-century prose writers such as Charles Smith and John Bush proclaimed its beauty and utility, it was not until after the Act of Union that Irish poets embraced the Georgic, using verse to instruct readers how to farm on Irish soil with Irish weather conditions.[44]

It seems, therefore, that social and political changes in attitudes towards Irish land were, throughout the eighteenth century, reflected in the English-language poetry that included land or landscape in its subject matter. Increasingly, looking at the land of Ireland – perceiving it as sublime, beautiful, or threatening – replaced a sense of the significance of owning it or working it. Everything would change radically within twenty years of Grattan's parliament of 1782, of course: Ireland would cease to be a mysterious, semi-independent island on the Celtic fringe. Its land and its landscape would become merely part of the United Kingdom.

Notes

1. See Ian McBride, *Eighteenth-Century Ireland: The Isle of Slaves* (Dublin: Gill and Macmillan, 2009), p. 286.

2. See Seán Ó Tuama, ed., *An Duanaire, 1600–1900: Poems of the Dispossessed*, trans. Thomas Kinsella (Dublin: Dolmen Press, 1981), and Alan Harrison's section, 'Literature in Irish, 1600–1800', in *The Field Day Anthology of Irish Writing*, ed. Seamus Deane, Andrew Carpenter, and Jonathan Williams, 3 vols (Derry: Field Day, 1991), I, pp. 275–326.

3. James Ward, '*Phoenix* Park', in *Miscellaneous Poems, Original and Translated by Several Hands . . . published by Mr [Matthew] Concanen* (London, 1724), pp. 383–84. This, the first substantial anthology of verse in English from eighteenth-century Ireland, contains work by Jonathan Swift, Patrick Delany, Thomas Parnell, Nicholas Browne, James Ward, Joseph Sterling, Matthew Concanen, and others of Irish extraction. Hereafter, dates are given for the first known publication of the poems discussed, unless otherwise noted.

4. Mary Monck's idealised pastorals in *Marinda: Poems and Translations on Several Occasions* (London, 1716) were translations from the Italian poets Giovanni della Casa and Giambattista Marino. There are scores of examples of eighteenth-century Irish poets translating or imitating the classics.

5. James Ward, *A New Miscellany of Poems and Translations* (Dublin, 1716), p. 2. The butcher's stall was in the market attached to the slaughterhouse near St Patrick's Cathedral.

6. [Mary Barber], *Poems on Several Occasions* (London, 1734), p. 132.

7. See Andrew Carpenter, ed., *Verse in English from Eighteenth-Century Ireland* (Cork University Press, 1998), pp. 79–80, 90–98, 128–34. All were first published in Concanen's 1724 collection, *Miscellaneous Poems*.

8. 'The County of Kerry. A Poem' (1726). See Andrew Carpenter and Lucy Collins, eds., *The Irish Poet and the Natural World: An Anthology of Verse in English from the Tudors to the Romantics* (Cork University Press, 2014), p. 164: 'blake' means 'bleak'.

9. Luke Gibbons, 'Topographies of Terror: Killarney and the Politics of the Sublime', *South Atlantic Quarterly* 95.1 (Winter 1996), 23–44.

10. [Jonathan Swift], *The Works of J.S., D.D., D.S.P.D. in Four Volumes* (Dublin: Faulkner, 1735), II, p. 479.

11. Thomas Sheridan, 'A Description of Doctor Delany's Villa', in *Miscellaneous Poems* (1724), pp. 239–40. For a modernised text, see *The Poems of Thomas Sheridan*, ed. Robert Hogan (Newark, DE: University of Delaware Press, 1994), pp. 130–31.

12. *Memoirs of Laetitia Pilkington*, ed. A. C. Elias Jr, 2 vols (1748; Athens, GA: University of Georgia Press, 1997), I, pp. 24–25.

13. William Balfour Madden, 'Bellisle: A Poem' (1761), in Carpenter and Collins, *The Irish Poet and the Natural World*, p. 258.

14. Wetenhall Wilkes, 'Bellville: A Poem' (1741), in Carpenter and Collins, *The Irish Poet and the Natural World*, p. 198. A 'mall' was a tree-lined walk. 'Echo' was a wood-nymph in Greek mythology.

15. Carpenter and Collins, *The Irish Poet and the Natural World,* pp. 269–78, 284–90, and 393–405.

16. See [Richard Pockridge], 'The Temple-oge Ballad' (Rathfarnham, 1730). Other similar texts are described by Bryan Coleborne in his PhD thesis, 'Jonathan Swift and the Dunces of Dublin' (National University of Ireland, 1982), pp. 161–219. For a representative sample of texts, see Carpenter, *Verse in English from Eighteenth-Century Ireland,* pp. 307–10.

17. See, for example, George Sackvill Cotter, 'Epistles from Swanlinbar', in *Poems, consisting of Odes, Songs, Pastorals . . .,* 2 vols (Cork, 1788), I, pp. 181–224; *The Ulster Miscellany* ([Dublin?], 1752), pp. 342–44; and 'The Farewell: A Pastoral Ballad' [to Mallow], in Samuel Whyte, *The Shamrock, or Hibernian Cresses . . .* (Dublin, 1772), pp. 421–23.

18. Carpenter and Collins, *The Irish Poet and the Natural World,* p. 261.

19. See, for example, 'To the River Slany', in John Ball, *Odes, Elegies, Ballads, Pictures, Inscriptions, Sonnets, Partly taken from the Faded Flowers . . .* (Dublin, [1772?]), pp. 51–55.

20. Bernard Clarke, *A Collection of Poems upon Various Occasions* (Dublin, 1751), p. 20.

21. [Jonathan Swift], 'The Description of an Irish-Feast', in *The Poems of Jonathan Swift,* ed. Harold Williams, 2nd edn, 3 vols (Oxford: Clarendon Press, 1958), I, pp. 243–47, and Clarke, *A Collection of Poems,* pp. 23–28.

22. William Dunkin, *The Parson's Revels* (1734), ed. Catherine Skeen (Dublin: Four Courts Press, 2010), *passim.*

23. John Anketell, *Poems on Several Subjects* (Dublin, 1793), pp. 209–18.

24. 'The River Barrow', in an untitled chapbook (Limerick, [1785?]).

25. John Atkinson, *Killarney. A Poem* (Dublin, 1798), p. 13. See also William H. A. Williams, *Creating Irish Tourism: The First Century, 1750–1850* (London and New York: Anthem Press, 2010), pp. 136–37.

26. Carpenter and Collins, *The Irish Poet and the Natural World,* pp. 228–29.

27. *The Collected Poems of Laurence Whyte,* ed. Michael Griffin (Lewisburg, PA: Bucknell University Press, 2016), pp. 105–34.

28. Carpenter, *Verse in English from Eighteenth-Century Ireland,* p. 348. 'Humble cottages': here probably the huts made of sods in which landless labourers lived.

29. William Dunkin, 'The Frosty Winters of Ireland' (1741), in Carpenter and Collins, *The Irish Poet and the Natural World,* p. 209.

30. Ibid., p. 210.

31. Thomas Hallie Delamayne, 'To Francis Bindon, Esq.' (1742), in Carpenter and Collins, *The Irish Poet and the Natural World,* p. 214.

32. Ibid., p. 217.

33. See David Dickson, *Arctic Ireland: The Extraordinary Story of the Great Frost and Forgotten Famine of 1740–41* (Belfast: White Row Press, 1997); Cormac Ó Gráda and Diarmaid Ó Muirthe, 'The Famine of 1740–41: Representations in Gaelic Poetry', *Eire-Ireland* 45.3/4 (2010), 1–22; and Lucy Collins, 'The Frosty Winters of Ireland: Poems of Climate Crisis, 1739–41', *Journal of Ecocriticism* 5.2 (July 2013), 1–11.

34. *The Poems of Olivia Elder*, ed. Andrew Carpenter (Dublin: Irish Manuscripts Commission, 2017), p. 27.

35. James Delacourt, 'To Mr Thomson, on his Seasons' (1734), in Carpenter and Collins, *The Irish Poet and the Natural World*, p. 185.

36. Christopher Smart, 'The Temple of Dulness', trans. Francis Fawkes, in *Poems on Several Occasions* (London, 1752), pp. 153–57.

37. See, most prominently, Charlotte Brooke, ed., *Reliques of Irish Poetry* (Dublin, 1789).

38. Patrick Delany, 'On Longford's Glin' (1732), in Carpenter and Collins, *The Irish Poet and the Natural World*, p. 177.

39. Walter Chamberlayne, 'A Poem occasion'd by a view of Powers-court House, the Improvements, Park etc' (1741), in Carpenter and Collins, *The Irish Poet and the Natural World*, p. 203.

40. Samuel Shepherd, 'Leixlip' (1741), in Carpenter and Collins, *The Irish Poet and the Natural World*, pp. 205–07. For Wheatley's painting, see Francis Wheatley, 'The Salmon Leap at Leixlip with Nymphs Bathing' (1783) (Yale Center for British Art, Paul Mellon Collection).

41. George Crabbe, 'To His Grace the Duke of Rutland' (composed 1782), in *Poems*, ed. A. W. Ward, 3 vols (Cambridge University Press, 1905–07), III, p. 493.

42. See Seamus Deane's argument that 'The Anglo-Irish were held in contempt by the Irish-speaking masses as people with no blood, without lineage and with nothing to recommend them other than the success of their Hanoverian cause over that of the Jacobites', in his *Celtic Revivals: Essays in Modern Irish Literature* (London: Faber & Faber, 1985), p. 30.

43. See the anonymous poem 'An Elegy on seeing some Irish Hay-Makers at work in England' published in *Felix Farley's Bristol Journal* (12 August 1782), in which the haymakers bewail Ireland's 'woe' as a land conquered by Britain: 'From your luxurience', say the wretched, exiled mowers, 'all our sorrows flow.'

44. The first original Irish Georgic (in the sense of a poem set in Ireland and containing advice about Irish farming conditions) is Charles Boyd's 'A Georgic of Modern Husbandry' of 1809 (see Carpenter and Collins, *The Irish Poet and the Natural World*, pp. 370–72). Although there was an Irish readership for classical and English Georgic in the period (translations of Virgil's *Georgics* were available in Ireland from the 1740s, and there are about twenty Irish printings of Thomson's *Seasons* before 1780), the Georgic mode was not adapted to Irish soil and weather until after the Union.

CHAPTER 8

The Idea of an Eighteenth-Century National Theatre

Conrad Brunström

In 1758, Thomas Sheridan, controversial manager of the Theatre Royal, Smock Alley, Dublin, published a lengthy appeal on behalf of the suggestion that Dublin should have just one officially sanctioned theatre. This appeal, like so many of his published appeals, soon became a personal plea of self-justification. The future of a rational and national theatre, a theatre that was 'good' for the people of Ireland, became one and the same with the future of Thomas Sheridan himself:

> It is generally thought that a Man cannot have a great number of Enemies, without being in some degree blameable. But History, Antient and Modern, abounds with innumerable Proofs to the contrary. Whenever Party-rage has been let loose in a Country, whenever the Cry of the Multitude has been thought the Voice of Justice and Reason; the best and most excellent of Men have ever had the greatest number of Enemies, and have been most persecuted. The History of the popular Government of *Athens* affords as many Instances, as there are produced in it great and eminent Characters of this Truth, exemplary Virtue, eminent Services done to their Country, and the highest Spirit of Patriotism, not only were sufficient Reasons for, but almost infallibly did occasion the Death, or Banishment of all those who were possessed of such distinguished Merit. Nor did *Rome* in some Instances fall short of the ingratitude of *Athens* in that Respect. The very naming *Theomistocles*, *Aristides*, *Socrates* and *Cicero*, will make it needless to say more on this Head.
>
> Here no doubt, the Manager's Enemies will exultingly cry out, what Pride! What Arrogance! to compare himself with such illustrious Names![1]

The manager's enemies did indeed cry out in such terms. Sheridan's exaggerated reassertions of national importance had been attracting enemies ever since 1743 when, as a young actor, a dispute over a thwarted costume change had brought him into conflict with the equally controversial Theophilus Cibber. The almost liturgical recitation of these names from classical antiquity gives a good indication of the kind of historical claim Sheridan wants to make for his stint as theatre manager, as well as his sense of the centrality of theatre to a healthy commonwealth.

Like Julius Caesar, Sheridan is prone to 'illeism': many of his most personal appeals are delivered in the third person. It is surely not coincidental that one of Sheridan's choice roles was that of the hero in his own adaptation of *Coriolanus*, Shakespeare's sombre study of a public figure unable to avoid alienating the public.[2] A note of despair informs much of his prose and at times he suggests that his chief ambition is to serve as an exemplary failure to inspire subsequent generations. He praises his own managerial legacy thus:

> This was an Aera, which they who frequented the Theatre at that Time will not readily forget. They will often give Accounts of it to their Children and Grand-children, when the Stage shall probably be relapsed into it's former Barbarism, when those Accounts shall be considered as the fond Tales of Age, and the Relators only smiled at as, *Laudatores temporis acti.*[3]

Sheridan's idea of a national theatre is to give Dublin a theatre with a European reputation; to have Dublin listed and referenced approvingly whenever an international comparison of theatres is made.[4] At various points in this short book, the beginnings of a careful argument for a single state-patronised national theatre are hinted at, but repeatedly, the sense of personal grievance overwhelms that case. Although the tediousness of Sheridan's endless self-justification can have its own perverse fascination, this chapter will suggest that the 'idea' of a national theatre cannot be excised from highly personalised politics, and that public discussion of arts funding always tends to place individuals in tragic situations.

A pamphlet published in response to Sheridan's *Appeal*, titled *The Case of the Stage in Ireland* (1758), attempts to describe the arguments of the pro- and anti-Sheridan parties at this point. While the pamphlet claims to offer a fair and balanced view of the controversy, the anti-Sheridan case is given considerably more space and detail than the opposing one, and this suggests that the pamphleteer is sympathetic to Spranger Barry's bid to open a theatre in Crow Street. The anti-Sheridan section of the pamphlet denies that two theatres will necessarily ruin one another and pours scorn on the notion that the stage is the forum in which a virtuous and active young citizenry is nurtured. In addition, the pamphleteer takes some pleasure in reducing the actual role of a theatre manager to a prosaic list of practical responsibilities, deflating the august civic leadership role that Sheridan aspires to. The final duty of a manager is, apparently, as follows:

> As the principal End of the Manager's Duty is to please the Public, he should be strictly careful to avoid giving the least Offence. If he should be so unfortunate, he should be furnished with a sufficient Degree of Humility, to make public Attonement for his Misconduct; nor should he, through Pride or Obstinacy, reject the Advice of his cool and sensible Friends on any such Occasion.[5]

Sheridan's closest friends could not have claimed on his behalf that Sheridan satisfied this requirement. While claiming to be the public's faithful servant, Sheridonian humility displays a peculiar grandiloquence that fails to convince neutral readers or audiences. Moreover, Sheridan was arguably unfortunate in his choice of enemies. As a lexicographer he found himself in opposition to Samuel Johnson and as an orator he provoked the contempt of Edmund Burke. The young Edmund Burke attacked Sheridan repeatedly in his paper *The Reformer* (1748), written at the height of the supposedly blessed 'aera' of Sheridan's complete theatrical sovereignty. The following paragraph is both spirited and representative:

> Nothing can be more ridiculous than the Presumption with which Men promise things, that so far from being able to perform 'tis evident from their Practice they don't understand. The Manager of the Theatre after having, for the most part, entertained the Town with the worst chosen Plays; promised in a pompous Speech to raise the Irish Stage to an equal Eminence with any in Europe. What Steps he has hitherto taken to this great End are pretty apparent. He has cleared the Stage of that Mob of Spectators which was indeed a Disgrace to it: he has taken Pains with the Actors to make them diligent in getting their Parts; and their Entries and Exits are now more regular; he has put a Stop to the bad Practice of admitting for odd Money, a Set of wild Fellows who generally came flustered from Taverns, to the Disturbance of the more orderly part of the Audience; he has been expensive in procuring Scenes for the Embellishment of the Stage (those for the Harlequinades, Men of Taste will not thank him for, when they see such Provision made for Buffooneries, they have long wish'd banished it). In short, he has done all but the most material; namely, the acting good and moral Plays, which, and which only, could have intitled him to the Name of a Stage Reformer.[6]

It should be noted that Burke nowhere quarrels with Sheridan's formal and disciplinary reforms. Burke's objection to Sheridan (here and elsewhere) concerns the latter's choice of plays. The teenage Burke evidences a remarkable degree of what can only be described as squeamishness in *The Reformer*, objecting to onstage kissing, and despising the comedies of George Farquhar in terms which do no great credit to the young Burke's reputation as a dramatic critic. However, Burke's subsequent reputation has helped ensure that Sheridan's managerial high-mindedness has always been challenged, both in his own day and in recent times.

There are two main extended contemporary eighteenth-century sources for the story of Sheridan's stewardship of Smock Alley Theatre, both written by colleagues of Sheridan. One is broadly sympathetic to Sheridan and the other is extremely sympathetic to Sheridan.[7] The first of these is Robert Hitchcock's invaluable *An Historical View of the Irish Stage* (1788).[8] Hitchcock opens his account with an important defence of his credentials, as former prompter at Smock Alley, but as such, he cannot pretend to objectivity. (Frequently the prompter would be the only person in possession of a complete copy of the play, and their repeated overview of performances in any case makes their perspective an interesting one.)[9] Besides, there can be no such thing as an 'objective' account of dramatic practice in this period, as any account that pretended to objectivity could only be too far from the real action to be of any significant interest. Hitchcock declares the importance of his subject in terms which his leading 'characters' – such as Thomas Sheridan – would have applauded:

> in the very zenith of Greek and Roman greatness, the ablest lawgivers of those days have ever carefully cultivated the drama, convinced that it gave life to their institutions, and formed an essential ingredient in the portion of public happiness and liberty. The mutual connexion, indeed, between the success of the stage, and the welfare of the state, have more than once been visible, and it has with justice been remarked, that the political and theatrical prosperity of a nation have gone nearly hand in hand.[10]

This kind of high-minded civic awareness illustrates the fact that theatre is the place where private enterprise and public policy come together, where commercial opportunism and legislative policy grapple with one another, and where naked self-interest often comes dressed as a form of social welfare.

Selfish and social interests, however, may sometimes be legitimately congruent. The question of whether or not Dublin should have one 'national' theatre is never detached from the question of who is to run that theatre. Sheridan, denying that a theatrical duopoly is sustainable in Dublin, asserts that the real question is the nature of whichever theatre is not destroyed by the contest:

> Mr Barry and Mr Sheridan stand Candidates for the sole Property of the Irish Stage. Mr Barry's Pretensions are, that as soon as he had made any tolerable Progress in his Profession he set out for London, entered into foreign Service, there has remained for ten Years, during which Time he

never revisited his native Country, but one Season that he was compelled to it; and by his own Acknowledgement he does not now mean to fix here, but now and then, either in Summer or Winter, to pay Dublin a Visit, according as his Affairs are circumstanced, and bring others with him, in order to fill their Purses, carry as much Money away with them as they can, and add one more to the many Drains which keep this poor Country so low. Whilst Mr Sheridan remained at home, and with infinite Pains and Cost was the first who established a Theatre in this Kingdom, worthy of the Name. He did it at the frequent Hazards of his Life, to the Ruin of his Constitution, and hitherto with considerable Loss.[11]

Sheridan treats Barry, his Crow Street rival, as an absentee landlord. Aware that a patriot party regards him as a courtier, he makes his own case for authentic patriotism, based on continuous residency and personal suffering. Eventually, Sheridan puts forward an actual proposal for a theatre that is fully integrated into national policy, if not a 'National Theatre' in the modern sense, then certainly a nationalised theatre.

> After much Thought on the Subject, as well as much Experience, Mr *Sheridan* thinks that he can lay down this as a maxim.
>   That the Dublin Stage *never will remain long in a flourishing Condition whilst it is the Property of a private Person.*
>   That the Constitution of the Stage of *Paris*, where the Theatre is the Property of the Public, and gives a certain Portion of the Profits to charitable Uses, seems to him the only one that would place that of *Dublin* on a good or durable Foundation.[12]

Sheridan, in other words, would cheerfully surrender ownership, or shares in a private theatre, in order to become the chief salaried employee in a public one. Sheridan looks to Paris rather than to London, in large part because France, unlike England, has long given state backing to its own cultural heritage.[13]

   Sheridan's rather florid style was shared by his second in command at Smock Alley, Benjamin Victor, author of the 'extremely sympathetic' account, the satisfyingly hefty *History of the Theatres of London and Dublin* (1761). Victor was an even closer associate of Sheridan's than Hitchcock: he served as treasurer and deputy manager of the Smock Alley Theatre (1746–59), having previously been employed in the linen trade.[14] Both Hitchcock and Victor give disproportionate space to Sheridan in their surveys, treating his triumphs and disasters as the real interest of their respective books. Given their close professional association with Sheridan, Victor and Hitchcock are perhaps at their most interesting when they feel compelled to discuss Sheridan's failings. One point on which they were agreed was that Sheridan allowed the wage bill to get out of hand. Hitchcock observes that Sheridan's greatest error was 'his engaging to give larger salaries to particular performers than the theatre could then afford. And though these engagements were all punctually fulfilled, yet he left precedents which his successors have found very difficult to imitate.'[15] Victor makes the same point more colourfully:

> The Manager, at this Expedition, instead of bringing over a profitable Freight as before, this Trip overloaded his Vessel, even to the Danger of sinking. He engaged Mr. and Mrs *Macklin*, Mrs *Vincent*, Mrs. *Bland*, (now *Hamilton*) Miss *Minors*, Mr *Mozeen*, and Mr *Storer*; and in the musical Way, Mr. *Lampe* and Wife, Signior *Pasquali*, Mr. *Sullivan*, Mr. *Howard*, Mrs. *Storer*, and Mrs. *Mozeen*. All this musical Party were articled for two Years. [...] I attended carefully to the Product of this musical Bargain; and the Profits did not amount to the Sum paid for the Article of writing the Score for their Performances, which was over one hundred and Fifty Pounds! So that the Tot of their Salaries, which was near fourteen hundred Pounds a Year, was a dead Loss to the Manager.[16]

Whatever else Sheridan bequeathed the Dublin theatre, both Victor and Hitchcock agree, he entailed the fatal legacy of star power. Not only did he fail to budget adequately to pay for the stars he engaged, but he set a fatal precedent for subsequent generations of managers and treasurers, since actors could not be prevailed upon to commit for less than what they knew others had secured in previous seasons. This wage inflation exacerbated what was already a high-risk enterprise. Illness, unexpected unpopularity, or (as in the case of Theophilus Cibber) drowning on the way over the Irish Sea (thus literalising Victor's metaphor): all could wipe out these significant investments. Furthermore, a focus on star actors, actors who are already well known to the public, had an additional effect: to reinforce a very familiar (and English) theatrical canon at the expense of any new plays which might have an Irish setting. Familiar actors are easier to advertise in familiar roles and it is harder to persuade established stars to attempt new roles which they are less confident about triumphing in.

In contrast to the star power of English actors, formed on the London stage, we need to recall the intimacy of eighteenth-century Dublin. Smock Alley's physical proximity to the parliament in College Green (with Trinity College adjacent) as well as to Dublin Castle, helps to explain the tense triangulation of loyalties within which the theatre functioned. Helen Burke and Susan Cannon Harris have argued persuasively just how closely Sheridan became associated with the Protestant Castle elite in opposition to a disruptively persistent Gaelic aristocratic interest.[17] While these associations were certainly made and were politically potent, Sheridan's own motives are less easily plotted politically, particularly when his theatrical agenda is considered alongside his elocution writings and lectures. These latter commitments formed part of an attempted phono-centric pedagogic revolution that was even more significant for Sheridan than theatre management. Sonja Lawrenson offers a more nuanced, careful, and imaginative reading of the colonial dynamics of theatre dispute than Harris or Burke, although she still deploys terms like 'the ideological struggle between Thomas Sheridan and the Connaught Gentlemen', thereby assuming that this struggle was conscious and acknowledged.[18] Sheridan's struggles were many and varied and could not be contained by the repressive policies of Dublin Castle. Obsessed as he was with phonocentrism, Thomas Sheridan regarded oratorical culti-vation as 'the one thing needful' for Ireland, Britain, or any other self-respecting nation. No political cause, no political or economic 'objective' could be judged independently of its capacity to stimulate or inhibit oratory. Indeed, reactionary measures and oppressive policies might tend ultimately towards the common good insofar as they sponsored, by accident or design, a reinvigorated sense of eloquence.[19]

The issue of a 'national theatre' provokes the necessary question of whether Ireland possessed a sufficient number of devolved institutions to qualify as a nation. Given Ireland's anomalous colonial status, does support for any colonial institution represent a form of collaboration, or is Ireland's nationality something that can be reinforced using existing institutions? As Christopher Murray has noted: 'Managers were pragmatists and went with the historical flow.'[20] Challenging vice-regal authority would have been an almost oxymoronically impossible exercise for a Theatre Royal manager. Meanwhile, the most astute (and sometimes astutely ruthless) of Lords Lieutenant sought to disrupt opposed categories of courtier and patriot by representing themselves (with varying degrees of success) as patriots them-selves. Key to this process was the long-established practice of 'undertaking', that is, finding willing Irish parliamentarians to 'undertake' the political agenda of the Lord Lieutenant himself. However, Lords Lieutenant were seldom appointed for more than five years at a stretch. Most of them regarded their vice-regal term of office as a stepping stone to some other, British, political appointment. Thus, satisfying the Westminster political establishment was invariably their ultimate political agenda, no matter what pressure was exerted from various patriot parties in Dublin, whether from the College Green parliament or from the effervescent electoral politics of Dublin's trade guilds.

At the beginning of the eighteenth century, Dublin's population was mainly Protestant. At the end of the nineteenth century, it was not. The exact demographic tipping point is hard to determine, chiefly because Protestants had no political (or psychological) interest in facing up to any such trauma. Historians of Irish patriotism in the eighteenth century have first to acknowledge that the most anti-Catholic of patriots provided the dominant and most energetic strand of patriotism for most of the century. The assertion of Irish self-governance derived from the endlessly quoted ur-text of Irish self-government, William Molyneux's *The Case of Ireland Stated* (Dublin, 1698) which based its claims not upon Irish cultural difference but rather upon co-religion and common identity with England. Molyneux-inflected patriots sought parliamentary sovereignty based on their 'British' identity and a supposed English predisposition towards representative modes of government.

The fact that a jealously Protestant nation-within-a-nation with a garrison mentality could have evolved, by the 1780s, into a patriotism newly invigo-rated with Grattanite ecumenism, provides perhaps the single most inter-esting issue within Irish eighteenth-century studies. This rhetorical process is accomplished not by repudiating sectarian rhetoric but by reinterpreting it and by assimilating material that ought to be incapable of assimilation into what becomes, with hindsight, a mainstream of nationalist assertion. Sheridan himself, championed by Lucas in the 1740s, championed Grattan in turn in the 1780s. Is a 'Theatre Royal' an institution that cannot help but promote loyalty to a foreign power, or is it a public institution that can incubate the kind of civic consciousness out of which a future nationality can emerge?

One of Sheridan's favourite roles was the title role in Henry Brooke's tragedy, *The Earl of Essex* (performed 1750). Like Sheridan himself and like Charles Lucas, Brooke was a perplexing patriot. Brooke managed to combine anti-Catholic fervour with sympathetic pro-Gael imagery and rhetoric, and his attitude to the Penal Laws was similarly complex.[21] Sheridan played the tragic Elizabethan courtier in both Dublin and London. Essex, of course, was undone following his inability or unwillingness to put down a rebellion in Ireland, and his story, though set in England, not only offers an impossibly romantic relationship with England's most storied Queen, but a way of staging conflicts between the two nations. Essex is also implicitly and injudi-ciously praised by the Chorus at the beginning of Act V of Shakespeare's *Henry V*, and Shakespeare's own sponsor, the Earl of Southampton, would go to his death as an ally of Essex, provoking a contentious discussion of Shakespeare's own loyalties. For any Irish author to stage this story in

Ireland is to activate a variety of fascinating controversies. The prologue, spoken by Sheridan, runs thus:

> Much more should you from freedom's glorious plan,
> Who still inherit all the rights on man;
> Much more should you with kindred sorrows glow
> For your own chiefs, your own domestic woe;
> Much more a British story should impart
> The warmest feelings to each British heart.[22]

Both Brooke and Sheridan are Irishmen who assert their political rights in terms of their sense of being 'British'. By 1761, Irish actor Thomas Sheridan, driven out of Ireland as a result of violent insurrection, plays the Earl of Essex, who is returning from Ireland following violent insurrection. Brooke's play uses the suitably Machiavellian figure of Robert Cecil as its initiative villain, spreading dangerous rumours regarding the negotiations between Essex and the native Irish so as to remove a dangerous rival and ingratiate himself with Essex's spurned lover, the countess of Nottingham. Hannah Pritchard's Queen Elizabeth initially rejects the very notion of impeaching Essex, in lines which sound less like a sixteenth-century despot than an eighteenth-century politician:

> ... Dare not then
> To dictate to me farther; I'm a Briton –
> I was born free as you, and know my privilege.
> Henceforward you shall find that I'm your queen,
> The guardian and protectress of my subjects;
> And not your instrument to crush my people:
> No passive engine for cabals to ply,
> No tool for faction – I shall henceforth seek
> For other lights to truth; for righteous monarchs,
> Justly to judge, with their own eyes should see;
> To rule o'er freemen, should themselves be free.[23]

Elizabeth bases an anachronistic sense of 'right' on being a 'British citizen' rather than an absolute Tudor monarch. Essex, in the meantime, defends himself against the charge of having been unnecessarily conciliatory with the Irish aristocratic rebels. The heroic Essex is a viceroy who has, in his own conception and estimation, the discretionary power to treat with the Gaelic aristocracy and to make peace on his own terms. The fall of Essex illustrates, for Brooke, the logistical problems of both time and distance which separate those charged with decision-making in Ireland from those with ultimate sovereign control over Ireland, and the consequences of these problems:

namely, that there is no fair or objective perspective from which to judge whether or not a particular negotiation is 'justified'. As a consequence, even national decision-making comes down to a clash of personalities and the question of who to trust. Sheridan himself habitually assumed a kind of vice-regal status and demanded the same broad commission in the exercise of his authority that Essex had asserted. Unlike Essex, however, Sheridan felt unable to sign a treaty with rebellious Irish audiences.

What constitutes audience 'rebellion' also requires some consideration. Continual low-level disturbance is a feature of virtually all theatrical performance between the 1660s and 1820s, when there are no such things as dimmer switches and the auditorium is kept fairly bright throughout the performance. The most disruptive audience members are frequently to be found among the aristocracy, who do not recognise any sanction that can be placed upon them by mere 'players'. Equally troublesome are the foot-men of rival aristocrats who have been dispatched to secure adequate seating for their employers. The ambivalent status of players (and the eighteenth century was at least blessed with a gender-neutral term with which to describe male and female actors), adds to what we would now regard as a disruptive atmosphere. For centuries, players (like gladiators in ancient Rome) have been regarded as both stars and slaves, names to conjure with and headlined on posters, yet essentially trapped within a servile 'profession'. The theatrical career of Thomas Sheridan is bound up with the story of decisive attempts to assert the gentility of the stage. The extent to which this very gentility makes the stage an accomplice of entrenched genteel interests continues to be the subject of protracted debate.[24]

Thomas Sheridan incited his first set of Dublin riots in 1743 when he refused to appear on stage as Cato without the costume which he had been promised. As a slight young man below average height (though taller than Garrick), Sheridan believed that this particular robe was essential to give him the presence and gravitas to sustain the famous role of Cato. In the seventeenth and eighteenth centuries, theatres were commonly dependent upon the generosity of private individuals to lend particular garments, and it seems that this robe had been prematurely reclaimed by its owner. When Sheridan declined to go on stage without the robe he had counted on wearing, Theo Cibber, as theatre manager of Smock Alley, declared that he could play the part himself, which incurred Sheridan's severe resentment.

Cibber, replying to Sheridan's own published justification, pulled no punches: 'I must have Recourse to his Vocabulary, e'er I can find Words low enough to paint him.'[25] Cibber refers to Sheridan repeatedly as 'Tommy', a sneering diminutive that would be employed time and time again by Sheridan's many enemies for the next decade and a half. He also addresses him as 'thou egregious Mock Monarch', enforcing a vision of Sheridan as a deluded and ludicrous potentate, one whose head has been turned by the experience of wearing cardboard crowns on stage.[26]

Sheridan's second set of riots (the 'Kelly riots' of January 1747) were far more significant and controversial, and concerned the drunken behaviour of Edward Kelly, a 'gentleman' from Galway whose loud and lecherous comportment led to his expulsion from the theatre. As Kelly reappeared in the theatre and resumed his disruptive behaviour, Sheridan felt compelled to break character so as to announce that 'I'm as good a gentleman as you', a statement that provoked riots, a pamphlet war, and legal proceedings. As a result of winning the war of words (within Dublin at least), Sheridan was empowered to govern Dublin's only theatre with unprecedented authority (effective broadly from 1747 to 1754), reinforcing his unaffectionate nickname of 'King Tommy' in the process. An ally (supposedly unexpected and unsolicited) of Sheridan's in this crisis turned out to be the 'Patriot' civic leader Charles Lucas. The fact that Lucas's brand of patriotism was Williamite and ultra-Protestant has served to further taint the reputation of Sheridan for future generations of historians, despite the fact that Seán Murphy has demonstrated that Lucas's sectarianism is far less clear and far less consistent than has long been assumed.[27]

Sheridan, using the intriguing mask of a 'Plebeian', made a special appeal to 'the ladies' of Dublin, suggesting that a sense of injured femininity should transcend traditional class-based contempt for players and that sexual assault on a female player encourages sexual assaults more generally. 'The Safety of the Player's Person, and the Preservation of his Rights, as a Subject, in their full extent is as much the concern of the Laws, is as much the Object of the Publick Care, as the Safety of the Gentleman's Person is, or the Preservation of his Rights.'[28] Regarding the issue of legal rights, it might be noted that the Sheridans themselves were Old Irish rather than Anglo-Irish or planter Irish and Thomas Sheridan was descended from a renegade Catholic priest. In the same pamphlet, Sheridan makes it clear that he is all too aware that the context of the Kelly riots has been configured as an attack on the 'Old Irish' aristocracy and rejects this construction: 'As to the Milesian Race, we are not without our O's of our Side the Question, and some O's that are a Credit to us too.'[29] For Helen Burke, this 'Milesian' heritage was troubling for Sheridan, forcing him into an exaggerated posture of colonial loyalism. Yet Sheridan's only original work for the stage is the affectionate farce *The Brave Irishman* (1754), in which an open-hearted 'O' (Captain O'Blunder) is allowed to triumph over prejudice and narrow-minded London duplicity.

The third set of riots, which proved disastrous not only for Sheridan but the entire Sheridan family, were the so-called Mahomet Riots of 1754. Sheridan had become increasingly identified by his many enemies with the court party, and had meanwhile alienated and offended one of his chief players – West Digges. Dublin had been absorbed by the so-called 'Money Surplus' controversy. On the rare occasions when the Irish Exchequer showed an annual surplus, this surplus was required to be formally remitted to Britain. This same surplus might be 'generously' handed back to Ireland, but the legal requirement was itself a humiliating reminder of the subservience of the College Green to the Westminster parliament. During a run of Voltaire's orientalist melodrama *Mahomet*, the Patriot party had strategically appropriated a particular speech delivered by Digges in the role of Alcanor, one pertinent to a mood of national resistance to the humiliating terms of the surplus requisition:

> . . . If, ye powers divine!
> Ye mark the movements of this nether world,
> And bring them to account, crush, crush those vipers,
> Who, singled out by a community
> To guard their rights, shall for a grasp of ore,
> Or paltry office, sell 'em to the foe.[30]

On the night of one particular performance, Sheridan addressed the cast to express his distaste for encores and their disruptive effect on the flow of the play. According to Victor's account, he did not actually prohibit an encore, but when the speech was delivered and an encore demanded at that point, Digges gestured behind him and announced that he was unable to comply with the audience's demands. Riot ensued.[31]

Though a friend of Sheridan's, Victor took the view that if Sheridan had not been destroyed by the Mahomet Riots, he would have been destroyed sooner or later by an audience that had decided that Sheridan was of the courtier party:

> I am clearly of Opinion, as the celebrated *Beef-Steak Club* had so much disgusted the *Anti-Courtiers*; and as the Manager was so universally con-demned by the Town for being the sole Supporter of it, if that Night had not determined his Fate, it would not have been postponed much longer; for they intended to *Encore* him the first Opportunity, and his Refusal would have produced the very same Consequence; and therefore, this Misfortune must be attributed to the Unhappiness of being unwarily drawn into that

Snare by *Wit* and good *Company*, which have destroyed the ablest and wisest Men from the Beginning of the World.[32]

Thus, in Victor's view, if Sheridan and/or Digges had behaved differently that night, a major riot would only have been postponed rather than averted. Notably, Victor does not suggest that Sheridan was the prisoner of a political party, still less an ideology, but was rather seduced by wit and good company. Even if he was not unfaithful to his wife with Peg Woffington, there was something about the enjoyment of the Beef-Steak Club over which she strangely presided that he found irresistible, and refused to give up to placate the perceptions of the wider public. As always, Sheridan managed to combine protestations of commitment to a 'public' stage with a habitual contempt for public opinion.

Discussion of eighteenth-century Irish theatre has, ever since the period itself, been disproportionately focused on the personality and motives of Thomas Sheridan. Here I would take the view that 'motives' are impossible to prove one way or another, but that taking Sheridan at face value, which includes taking his civic and political agenda seriously, results in more interesting conversations than does dismissing his rhetorical efforts out of hand as mere window dressing for the Castle establishment. When Thomas Sheridan finally reconciled with Richard Brinsley Sheridan prior to the former's death in 1788, the remarkable applause and acclaim which the younger Sheridan had earned following his speech during the Hastings trial in Westminster Hall is often considered a major reconciliatory factor. It is clear that less significant from Thomas's point of view than the nature of British misrule in India, or Hastings's specific culpability within such structures of oppression, was the rhetorical power on display from a member of the Sheridan family. Although Thomas Sheridan often complained of the state of the stage and declared his preference for formal oratory, throughout his life he regarded the stage as the only means of cultivating the rhetorical skills required to create an active and responsible citizenry.

Although any rigorous definition of political science looks for longer and more structured causes than 'personality politics', theatre history (perhaps inevitably) finds it difficult to extricate itself from prolonged discussion of the clash of dramatic personalities. When Sheridan campaigns on behalf of his version of a Theatre Royal, he is not merely exhibiting a version of personal hubris but a much larger tendency to treat civic policy in embodied terms. He cannot merely describe the conditions for a virtuous stage, he has to play the part himself. Theatre in the eighteenth century cannot be defended in uninvolved or objective terms, but only in theatrical and tragic terms, and elevated public drama necessarily demands the spectacle of a great man in distress. Victor notes that only an actor can understand other actors:

> And from all this, I stand convinced of this *Truth*, (and from the best Proof that can be obtained, EXPERIENCE) *that no Man, let his theatrical Knowledge be ever so great, can be a Gainer by being the Manager of a Theatre, unless he is, at the same Time, the* FIRST IN THE PROFESSION OF AN ACTOR; *or* CONNECTED WITH ONE WHO IS. The Reasons are obvious; those Performers to be employed, that have Power, from their Reputation in the World, to draw Audiences, know that Power, and how to set a due Value on it; and after their Worth is properly rated, the Accidents that follow, such as ill Health, and the like, are to be Draw-backs from the expected Profits of the Manager. (I, p. 145)

Victor is convinced that the source of theatrical revenue is the reputation of individual actors. Imprudent generosity on Sheridan's part has made tapping this source an increasingly expensive operation, but he is aware of no other source which would be quite so lucrative. The reason why people go to the theatre is to see great performances from celebrated actors – a fragile phenomenon but the only profitable one. Victor repeats himself so as to emphasise this essential point: 'no Man that is not a CAPITAL ACTOR, or *in Partnership with one*, can be a successful *Manager* of a *Theatre-Royal*, where great Entertainments must be exhibited, and consequently, great Engagements must be entered into, and Dangers encountered' (I, p. 149).

Victor qualifies this managerial desideratum, however, by referring specifically to theatres 'royal', allowing for the possibility that cheeky alternative venues of the kind managed by Henry Fielding at the Haymarket prior to 1737 might be able to turn a profit without star power. But a theatre that claims some kind of official title requires 'great Entertainment' and star power is the measure of greatness. Audiences come to see Garrick, Sheridan, Mossop, and Barry, not plush curtains, statuary, and pyrotechnics. Sheridan's final Dublin theatre disaster causes Victor to wax lyrical:

> But alas! our Misfortunes began from this very Period; Fate was against us; to see the Changes of this sublunary World; where fortunate Circumstances arise to some from the Miseries and Destruction of others. After a very dreadful stormy Night, a Rumour prevailed, that the Ship called the *Dublin*, Captain *White*, from *Parkgate*, full of passengers, was lost. (I, p. 190)

Victor may have started out as a linen merchant, but his long association with theatre soon gave him a very dramatic turn of phrase and a sense of

Aristotelian peripeteia. The ship commanded by Captain White becomes a sort of Norman 'White Ship' whose wreckage dashes the hopes of a theatrical posterity, including of course the infamous but profitable Theo Cibber: 'Poor *Cibber*! He had long felt the Blasts of Adversity; his Life was tempestuous, and his Fate to end it in a Storm!' (I, p. 191). Alas poor Cibber – I knew him, declares Victor, before concluding the first volume of his history with an elegiac farewell to Ireland. Victor himself was not Irish, but lived in Ireland for long enough to develop a sense of a place he called Ireland ('the Land of HOSPITALITY and true BENEVOLENCE') which was distinct from England and cherishable on account of those distinctions (I, p. 208).

The drowning of Cibber and associated disasters may resemble a kind of Swiftian parable on the dangers of over-dependence on imported luxury goods. The parallel with Ireland's various trade disqualifications does not quite hold, however, since many of the imports from London to Dublin were in essence re-imports and if English actors triumphed on the Dublin stage they were proportionately balanced by the numbers of eminent Irish actors who triumphed on the London stage.[33] It is certainly the case, however, that the eighteenth-century theatrical economy was over-dependent on a relatively small number of 'big names' going back and forth across the Irish Sea on a regular basis, and the wreck of White's ship was an example of putting all one's eggs in one basket with calamitous economic consequences.

In the wake of the Dublin disaster and Sheridan's refusal to return to Dublin, the Smock Alley Theatre lost its status as the official Theatre Royal following a tug of war with Barry's Crow Street theatre. For Sheridan, the maintenance of a national theatre for Dublin meant the maintenance of just one theatre, which also entailed a personal monopoly. To accuse Sheridan of being motivated by personal greed demands greater evidence of fiscal prudence than either Victor or Hitchcock is inclined to credit him with. If he was not a public benefactor, he was personally impractical.

Few contemporary philosophers have been treated to such a withering empirical critique as Jürgen Habermas, whose coffee-inflected notion of 'The Public Sphere' as a distinctively early eighteenth-century phenomenon has been coolly dissected by those with a more detailed sense of political participation and its limitations in the early eighteenth century.[34] If the coffee house is de-privileged as a unique site within which to stage arguments about what is public and what is private, then it is possible to argue that the stage itself 'stages' such debates far more effectively. To what extent is a theatre a public space and to what extent is it a private concern? Such arguments rarely consistently applied, and for a manager like Thomas Sheridan, the stage is a public space when it suits him to enforce a legal monopoly and a private space when it comes to demands to make himself accountable to any real and present versions of 'the public'. Can anyone seek to control the public in the public interest?

At the heart of the Dublin theatre controversies of the 1740s and 50s is the question of whether such a patriotic cultural initiative should function independently of Castle patronage. Should such a theatre cater for popular taste or should it function 'in advance' of prevalent opinion? Such issues are difficult enough in the context of a twenty-first-century independent state, but in a colonised nation that retains some of the trappings of autonomy without actual self-government, such issues are inflammatory. The idea of a 'National Theatre' foundered, and in some ways continues to founder, on a recurring paradox. If theatre is popular enough to reflect the wishes of a national 'general public', then why should it receive state sponsorship or protection? Is theatre intended not for the nation that is, but the nation that might be, a more elevated, refined, and aesthetically mature nation, to whose interests, less evolved contemporary nations might have to be sacrificed?

Notes

1. Thomas Sheridan, *An Humble Appeal to the Public, Together with Some Considerations on the Present Critical and Dangerous State of the Stage in Ireland* (Dublin, 1758), p. 8.
2. Esther K. Sheldon, *Thomas Sheridan of Smock Alley, 1719–1788* (Princeton University Press, 1967), p. 177.
3. Sheridan, *An Humble Appeal*, pp. 21–22. The Latin might be translated as 'Praisers of past times'.
4. Ibid., p. 11.
5. *The Case of the Stage in Ireland: Containing the Reasons for and against a Bill for Limiting the Number of Theatres in the City of Dublin* (Dublin, 1758), p. 38.
6. *The Reformer* 2 (4 February 1748), in *The Writings and Speeches of Edmund Burke*, Vol. I: *The Early Writings*, ed. T. O. McLoughlin, James T. Boulton, and William B. Todd (Oxford: Clarendon Press, 1997), p. 72.
7. There are plenty of anti-Sheridonian writings to be negotiated also, which consist largely of short pamphlets, satirical poems, and squibs, fascinating on their own account. See, for example, *The Buskin and Sock, Being Controversial Letters Between Mr. Thomas Sheridan, Tragedian and Mr. Theophilus Cibber, Comedian, just published in Dublin* (Dublin, 1743); *A Letter to the Admirers of Mr. S—* (Dublin, 1749); *The Stage or Coronation of King Tom. A Satyr* (Dublin, 1753); and *The Signs and Groans of Mr. Sh—, with A Full Account of a Comical Farce That Was Acted Last Saturday Night at the Theatre in Smock-Alley, and the Occasion Thereof. Also, an Account of the Manager's Rude Behaviour to the Audience at the Play of Mahomet* (Dublin, 1754).

8. Robert Hitchcock, *An Historical View of the Irish Stage: From the Earliest Period Down to the Close of the Season 1788* (Dublin, 1788).

9. See Tiffany Stern, *Rehearsal from Shakespeare to Sheridan* (Oxford University Press, 2007).

10. Hitchcock, *An Historical View of the Irish Stage*, p. 11.

11. *The Case of the Stage*, p. 72.

12. Ibid., p. 86.

13. See D. Maclaren Robertson, *A History of the French Academy, 1635–1910* (New York: G. W. Dillingham, 1910).

14. Victor's original commercial endeavour was an attempt to import refined Irish linen into the English market, a venture that Jonathan Swift himself might have applauded. See W. P. Courtney, 'Victor, Benjamin (d. 1778), theatre manager and writer', in *Oxford Dictionary of National Biography* online [accessed 13 December 2017].

15. Hitchcock, *An Historical View of the Irish Stage*, p. 274.

16. Benjamin Victor, *A History of the Theatres of London and Dublin from 1730 to the Present Time*, 2 vols (Dublin, 1761), I, pp. 108–09. Further references to this work are given after quotations in the text.

17. Helen Burke, *Riotous Performances: The Struggle for Hegemony in the Irish Theater* (University of Notre Dame Press, 2003); Susan Cannon Harris, 'Clearing the Stage: Gender, Class, and the Freedom of the Scenes in Eighteenth-Century Dublin', *PMLA* 119.5 (October 2004), 1264–78.

18. Sonja Lawrenson, 'Frances Sheridan's *The History of Nourjahad* and the Sultan of Smock-Alley', *Eighteenth-Century Ireland / Iris an dá chultúr* 26 (2011), 24–50 (p. 44).

19. See Conrad Brunström, *Thomas Sheridan's Career and Influence: An Actor in Earnest* (Lewisburg, PA: Bucknell University Press, 2011), esp. ch. 5, 'An Actor for Ireland' (pp. 101–28).

20. Christopher Murray, 'Encore "What ish My Nation?": Irish Theatre and Drama in the Eighteenth Century Irish Theatre", *Eighteenth-Century Ireland / Iris an dá chultúr* 27 (2012), 185–191 (p. 190).

21. See Kevin Donovan, 'The Giant-Queller and the Poor Old Woman: Henry Brooke and the Two Cultures of Eighteenth-Century Ireland', *New Hibernia Review / Irish Éireannach Nua* 7.2 (Summer 2003), 107–20.

22. Henry Brooke, *The Earl of Essex. A Tragedy. As It Is Now Acting at the Theatre-Royal in Drury Lane* (Dublin, 1761), p. 4.

23. Ibid., p. 16.

24. The fullest account of Sheridan's theatrical career remains that of Esther Sheldon, *Thomas Sheridan*. Her sympathetic account is countered in Burke, *Riotous Performances*.

25. Theophilus Cibber, *A Proper Reply to a Late Scurrilous Libel, entitled, Mr Sheridan's Address to the Town* (Dublin, 1743), p. 2. For Sheridan's own pamphlet, see *Mr Sheridan's Address to the Town* (Dublin, [1743]).

26. Cibber, *A Proper Reply*, p. 13.

27. Seán Murphy, 'Charles Lucas, Catholicism and Nationalism', *Eighteenth-Century Ireland / Iris an dá chultúr* 8 (1993), 83–102.

28. A Plebeian [Thomas Sheridan], *An Humble Address to the Ladies of the City of Dublin* (Dublin, 1747), p. 10.

29. Ibid., p. 18.

30. James Miller, *Mahomet the Imposter. A Tragedy by Mons. Voltaire* (Edinburgh, 1759), p. 2.

31. For a brief and spirited account of the riots from a 'Patriot' perspective, see *The Sighs and Groans of Mr Sheridan* (Dublin, 1754).

32. Victor, *A History of the Theatres*, I, pp. 139–40.

33. In addition to Sheridan himself, notable Irish actors who triumphed at Covent Garden and Drury Lane included George Anne Bellamy, Peg Woffington, James Quin, Spranger Barry, Henry Mossop, and Charles Macklin.

34. See, for example, Brian Cowan, 'Mr. Spectator and the Coffeehouse Public Sphere', *Eighteenth-Century Studies* 37.3 (Spring 2004), 345–66.

CHAPTER 9

Transnational Influence and Exchange: The Intersections between Irish and French Sentimental Novels

Amy Prendergast

Eighteenth-century Ireland was linked with France, culturally, socially, and politically. The beginning of the long eighteenth century saw contingents of French soldiers sent to Ireland, while the Treaty of Limerick (1691) resulted in the transport of many Irish forces to France, with numerous military exiles forging careers there. Jacobites and soldiers were joined by doctors, clergymen, and intellectuals, as the Irish in France encompassed people from a variety of backgrounds. Elite Irish men and women travelled to France to explore its culture; young men ventured there as part of the grand tour, some attending the country's famous salons, such as those hosted by Mesdames Geoffrin or du Deffand; while other men and women settled there and established their own literary gatherings, Anastacia Fitzmaurice and Mary Bridget Plunket, for example. Ireland meanwhile welcomed France's Protestant refugees following the Revocation of the Edict of Nantes (1685), with communities becoming established in Dublin, Waterford, and Cork, as well as the unique Huguenot settlement in Portarlington in Queen's County (now County Laois) where the French represented the majority of the local population.

In addition to these significant movements of people was the circulation of texts. The number of eighteenth-century Irish booksellers engaged in publishing and selling French texts is indicative of their popularity within the country, with over fifty Irish booksellers publishing material in French over the course of the century.[1] The publication of French translations was not limited to Dublin, as Cork and Belfast also increasingly printed French texts from the 1760s onwards, while distribution in the late 1770s of the *Magazin à La Mode* – a French-language periodical printed and published in Dublin – indicates an interested readership in Derry, Limerick, Kilkenny, and Waterford.[2] French publications that were imported, translated, and reprinted in Ireland, included books on education, key works of the French Enlightenment, and, as this chapter will show, French fiction. In terms of both the movement of people and the circulation of ideas, then, intense influence and cross-fertilisation between Ireland and France were especially evident in the eighteenth century.[3]

This chapter aims to move beyond Anglo-centric considerations of the Irish novel, through a focus on the cross-cultural transfers in existence between Ireland and France, as evidenced in the specific form of the sentimental novel. The popularity of Laurence Sterne's *Tristram Shandy* (1759–67) and *A Sentimental Journey Through France and Italy* (1768) in France and of Oliver Goldsmith's *The Vicar of Wakefield* (1766) in Germany and France has long been recognised. But beyond these writers is the cultural exchange of a significant number of women writers who, through the popularity of sentimental fiction in the 1760s and 70s, may be said to have altered the geography of reception for Irish fiction. Sentimental novels, with their emphasis on interiority, on personal experiences, and emotional responses, extended beyond national borders, and were themselves influenced by developments afoot elsewhere. Intersections between Irish and French sentimental novels from this period thus reveal much about literary influence and intertextuality.

French sentimental fiction found a receptive audience in Ireland. Works by writers such as Pierre de Marivaux, Antoine-François Prévost (Abbé Prévost), Françoise de Graffigny, and François de Baculard d'Arnaud, were purchased and consumed alongside works by Irish writers of sentimental fiction such as Anne Burke, Henry Brooke, and Hugh Kelly.[4] Echoes, connections, and dialogues between writers in France and Ireland were recognised by early twentieth-century scholars, who noted, for example, how the traumatic experiences of Frances Sheridan's eponymous heroine, Sidney Bidulph, echoed the misery described in Prévost's works: 'Faulkland and Sidney are wrung like Prévost's sufferers, and pour out their misery in similar accents.'[5] Sustained analysis and detailed comparative work reveals that there are many parallels observable in sentimental novels from France and Ireland, including those written by female authors from both countries.

A focus on sentimental writing indeed allows for the exploration of the particular importance of women writers in the eighteenth century, for although written by both men and women, sentimental writing became increasingly identified with female authorship in the mid-eighteenth century. In England in the 1760s, writers such as Sarah Scott and Frances Brooke embraced the genre, while in Ireland, Elizabeth Griffith and Frances Sheridan were to the forefront of a comparable wave of popularity.

The identification of sentimental writing with women writers had become explicit by 1773, with *The Monthly Review* noting that 'this branch of the literary trade appears, now, to be almost entirely engrossed by the ladies'.[6] The value allocated to sensibility afforded women some degree of power and authority. The 1760s and 70s also coincided with the rise of Bluestocking salons and literary salons more broadly in England and Ireland, with male and female participants offering women writers approbation and encouragement, as well as the possibility of patronage and financial support.[7] This chapter focuses on two case studies, looking at the careers and literary work of Frances Sheridan (1724–66) and Marie-Jeanne Riccoboni (1713–92) in particular. It will explore their writings; their engagements with the world of translation; and the reception of their work. Translators acted as cultural intermediaries in literary exchange and they played a significant role in the reception of the sentimental novel in both Ireland and in France. This chapter suggests that transnational comparisons are essential to any understanding of 'national' traditions.

Franco-Irish Cultural Encounters: The Novels of Marie-Jeanne Riccoboni and Frances Sheridan

The surname of Sheridan's foremost heroine, Sidney Bidulph, from her novel of 1761, announces itself in the fourth letter of Riccoboni's *Juliette Catesby* (1759), spelled thus in Brooke's translation and as Bidulf in the French – a Miss Bidulph has accepted a marriage proposal from Sir George Humble, after Henrietta's refusal of his hand. In addition to the numerous thematic and stylistic similarities which will be explored in this section, this immediately signals the possibility of a link between Riccoboni and Sheridan and of a sympathy between the two novelists.

Frances Sheridan (née Chamberlaine) was born in Dublin to a clergyman father who denigrated female education. Her childhood learning was fortunately orchestrated by obliging brothers, particularly Walter, who provided the young Frances with reading material and taught her to write. Sheridan spent the first two decades of her life in Ireland's capital, where she met her husband Thomas, a theatre manager and actor. The family, with four surviving children, including the writers Richard Brinsley, Alicia, and Elizabeth (or 'Betsy'), shared their time in Ireland between their town house on Dorset Street, and their home in Quilca, County Cavan. By all accounts, Sheridan was a sociable character, hosting single-author salons in Quilca House, and later in London. Several of the Sheridan family had moved to London for financial reasons in 1754, although they returned to Ireland in

1756 for two years. As a playwright, author, and salon hostess, Sheridan engaged with different genres: her successful sentimental novel, *The Memoirs of Miss Sidney Bidulph* (1761), was followed by two plays, *The Discovery*, which ran for seventeen nights at Drury Lane in 1763, and *The Dupe*, performed later that year, and she also wrote poetry, including 'Ode to Patience' and 'The Owls'. The final years of Sheridan's life saw the family travel to Bristol, Bath, London, and Scotland, before relocating to Blois, along the river Loire, for the final months of her life, where Frances composed two novels, *The History of Nourjahad* (1764) and *Conclusion of the Memoirs of Miss Sidney Bidulph* (1767), as well as the comedy *A Journey to Bath*.[8]

Originally an unsuccessful Parisian actress, Marie-Jeanne Riccoboni (née de Heurles de Laboras) is better known as the admired author of sentimental novels, including *Lettres de Mistress Fanni Butlerd* (1757), *Histoire de M. le marquis de Cressy* (1758), and *Lettres de Milady Juliette Catesby* (1759), all published anonymously in Paris, although listed as Amsterdam.[9] After retiring from the theatre in 1761, Riccoboni published under her own name: *Histoire de Miss Jenny* (1764), *Histoire d'Ernestine* (1765), *Lettres d'Élisabeth-Sophie de Vallière* (1772), and *Lettres de Milord Rivers* (1777). By this point, she had become a prominent member of the Republic of Letters, participating in salon gatherings, including that of the Baron d'Holbach, and exchanging correspondence with literary celebrities such as Denis Diderot, Pierre Choderlos de Laclos, David Garrick, and David Hume.[10] Unlike Sheridan, Riccoboni was unhappily married and childless, and, after having left her husband, she spent four decades of her life cohabiting with an actress and living by her pen. As with many female writers in the late eighteenth century, Riccoboni combined novel writing with translation, publishing French translations of both novels and plays.

Both writers' works were widely read, and the publication histories of the two women's novels reveal the extent of their popularity: *Sidney Bidulph*, for example, went into second editions in both London and Dublin within its first year (1761). Literary currents and the popularity of the novel meant that there was also an appetite in Ireland for sentimental writing by French authors. The widespread reprinting of French novels indicates an extensive readership for these across the country, while there was also a large audience for French novels in translation.[11] Works by Prévost, Marivaux, and Graffigny in particular found an interested audience in Ireland, before the later popularity of Riccoboni. Prévost's *Manon Lescaut* (1731) offers an early example of a successful French sentimental novel which was still being printed in Dublin in 1767 as *The History of the*

Chevalier des Grieux, written by himself.[12] Its mixing of realism and romance in the yearning of the eponymous des Grieux for the courtesan Manon was widely praised beyond France, while Prévost's writings also include Irish protagonists, such as the Dean of Coleraine, in his popular *Le Doyen de Killerine* (1735).[13] This novel's publication in translation led to a public debate regarding the merits, or more specifically the flaws and blunders, of two translations vying for an Irish readership.[14] Françoise de Graffigny's *Lettres d'une Peruvienne* (1747), translated as *Letters of a Peruvian Princess* (Dublin, 1748), was also a 'best-seller of the time'.[15]

Riccoboni's novels found an incredibly receptive audience both in France and abroad. Such was the popularity of her first novel, *Fanni Butlerd*, that it had gone through thirty-two editions by 1832.[16] Her third novel, *Lettres de Milady Juliette Catesby à Milady Henriette Campley, son amie* was so popular that it was second only to *La Nouvelle Héloïse* in terms of editions and re-editions of French works in this period.[17] Frances Brooke's translation of *Juliette Catesby* was particularly popular in Ireland, appearing in four Dublin editions between 1760 and 1780.[18] *The History of Miss Jenny Salisbury* was also successful, appearing in two Dublin editions in 1764. The *Dublin Mercury* advertised the work as being 'translated from the French of the celebrated madam Riccoboni'.[19] Correspondence also attests to the popularity of the novel among the elite in Ireland, with copies being sent from family members in England: Lady Holland wrote to her friend the Marchioness of Kildare, 'You shall have *Mlle. Jenny* sent you – 'tis very pretty', while Emily Fitzgerald, the Duchess of Leinster, noted: 'Mlle Jenny is a better wrote book [than *Madame Blemon*]; 'tis by the author of Lady Catesby.'[20]

The influence of eighteenth-century French authors on sentimental writing in Ireland is immediately discernible. François de Baculard d'Arnaud's *Les Époux Malheureux, ou histoire de Mr et Mme de Bédoyère* (1745) includes a preface in which the author sets out his intention to write 'a succession of dramas each more touching and more devastating than the last', and such dramas might be seen to prefigure the trials and terrors suffered by Sidney Bidulph.[21] An especially significant influence on writers of sentimental fiction from the 1760s and 70s was of course Jean-Jacques Rousseau, particularly *La Nouvelle Héloïse*, which was published the same year as Sheridan's *Sidney Bidulph* (1761).[22] Both fictions describe a woman marrying out of obedience, rather than love or passion, and forsaking the true object of her affection. Marivaux's *La Vie de Marianne* (1731–41) is another text whose impact on novelists of sensibility cannot be overstated. The parallels with Samuel Richardson's *Pamela* (1740),

including the attempted seduction of the innocent and unprotected protagonist, have formed a large part of debates concerning literary influences
on Richardson's novel since the eighteenth century.[23] Three English translations of *Marianne* existed by the 1740s, and the novel's focus on female
intuition and vulnerability is obvious in many texts, including, certainly,
Sheridan's *Sidney Bidulph* and many of Riccoboni's novels, particularly her
1751 continuation, *Suite de Marianne*.

In *Sidney Bidulph*, unlike in earlier novels such as *Vertue Rewarded*
(1693) or *Pamela*, virtue is decidedly not rewarded. Reason, prudence,
and the repression of passion are not enough to ensure a happy or even
a non-suffering life: 'I was born to sacrifice my own peace to that of
other people; my life is become miserable', declares the pitiful Sidney in
volume one.[24] Writing to her 'dear and ever beloved Cecilia' after being
reunited with her cheating husband, Mr Arnold, Sidney identifies the
human emotion at the core of the sentimental novel: 'how exquisite are
the pleasures and pains that those of too nice feelings are liable to! You,
whose sensibility is as strong as mine, know this' (p. 283). Most of the
pains experienced by the eponymous heroines of both *Sidney Bidulph*
and *Juliette Catesby* arise from the protagonists finding themselves
betrayed by lovers who have fathered illegitimate children with other
mistresses. *Juliette Catesby* opens with Juliette herself abandoned by her
beloved lord d'Ossory with no explanation. Much later, she learns that
this abandonment was due to his having forced himself on a friend's
younger sister after consuming too much alcohol. Regretting his actions,
he then views himself as forced to forsake the woman he loves in order to
rectify his mistake or 'misfortune' by marrying this innocent.[25] In
Sheridan's novel, a letter received before the anticipated wedding reveals
that Sidney's beloved fiancé, the impetuous Orlando Faulkland, is also
to be the father of another woman's child. Unlike d'Ossory, Faulkland
feels no obligation to marry the woman, for a variety of reasons later
explained to the reader, including her duplicity. Having 'no will of my
own', Sidney follows her mother's urgings and refuses to marry
Faulkland, leading to a tragic chain of events, which leave her temporarily 'neglected, forsaken, despised' (pp. 117, 171). Both Juliette and
Sidney eventually marry their beloveds, although Sidney's marriage,
forming part of a long life of woe despite exemplary female conduct,
is inevitably extremely short. The tale ends with Faulkland's suicide and
his bestowal of his child, also called Orlando, into Sidney's care, where
his story will be played out in the *Conclusion* alongside that of Sidney's
two daughters, Cecilia and Dolly.

Both *Sidney Bidulph* and *Conclusion*, as well as *Juliette Catesby* and many other novels by Riccoboni, are primarily set in England, rather than the writers' countries of birth. Riccoboni's Anglophilia has previously been recognised, but it is important also to view these novels' settings explicitly in terms of the mode of sentimental writing.[26] For many Irish writers in England, and indeed for English novelists more generally, 'home was not understood as a geographical point of origin, but as a particular kind of non-localised space for the exploration of subjectivity and power'.[27] This is especially true of sentimental fiction, with its focus on the inward life, on emotional developments, responses, and collapses. Although easy divisions between the public and private have long since been eroded in both historicist and theoretical work on the period, the sentimental novel does engage primarily with ideas of privacy and intimacy in its commitment to portraying the effects of personal circumstances on its protagonists. Thus, the geographical setting for the sentimental novel is frequently less significant than in other kinds of fiction.[28] *Sidney Bidulph*'s references to Kent, London, Bath, Wiltshire, and Putney, principally form only a background for the main narrative of distress and betrayal.

Ireland, however, does feature in the fiction of Sheridan and Riccoboni in a myriad of ways, beyond references to locale. Several of the names of characters in Riccoboni's *Juliette Catesby* (1759), for example, have unambiguously Irish resonances, including titles of well-known members of the aristocracy. These names appear to be decided upon by the author due to the degree of prestige and international recognition associated with them: the Comtesse de Rannalagh, lord d'Ossory, and lord d'Ormonde in *Juliette Catesby*, for example. Rather than purporting to present information about their namesakes' characters in the manner of a *roman-à-clef*, these names act primarily to enable readers to gain access to an imagined foreign setting, allowing them admission to a world of privilege. Riccoboni's later novel, *Histoire de Miss Jenny, écrite et envoyée à milady, comtesse de Roscomonde, ambassadrice d'Angleterre à la cour de Dannemark* (1764), is also dedicated to an Irish aristocrat, the Countess of Roscommon. Although there is no such lady of that title at the time of the novel's appearance, inclusion of the name again establishes exotic overtones, allowing readers to consume a work ostensibly connected to the Anglo-Irish elite.[29]

Ireland is present in *Sidney Bidulph* also, most obviously through the presence of Orlando Faulkland, portrayed as an Anglo-Irish absentee landlord, or, at the very least, as a figure strongly associated with Ireland both through possession of Irish land and temperament. He embodies many characteristics associated with the Irish national character, including the hot-headedness of the Stage Irishman: 'when he is provoked, no tempest is more furious'.[30] His name also evokes that of Henry Cary, Viscount Falkland, who served as Lord Deputy in early seventeenth-century Ireland, was associated with political misjudgments, and whose wife converted to Catholicism during the term of his Irish office.[31] Ireland also features as the site of unregulated passions in the novel, with Mrs Faulkland's marital infidelity and the subsequent attempted murder of her by her husband both occurring there. The two-generational structure employed by Sheridan allows the author to explore ideas of national identity and the complicated relationship between Ireland and England, through that of Sidney and her mother Dorothy.[32] The metaphor of the extended family extends into the *Conclusion* also, raising questions of posterity and the repetition of past sins with Sidney recounting her own troubled life to her daughters as a forewarning. The difficult matrilineal relationships and the pathetic circumstances of the marriage of Sidney and Orlando, 'that wild man', are quite different to the more harmonious unions of Irish and English characters in later Irish novels, such as Sydney Owenson's *The Wild Irish Girl* (1806), which themselves develop elements of sensibility as part of 'the national tale'.

Irish writers' espousal of the sentimental novel reveals much about their different aspirations and understandings of identity. Given the associations of sensibility with French culture, adopting the form of the novel of sentiment could demonstrate their cosmopolitanism and their commitment to a larger Enlightenment project. They could also explicitly align themselves with the eighteenth century's increasing commitment to philanthropy, and the cult of sensibility in particular, which found a natural outlet in the novel form. Through their portrayals of suffering and resistance, of challenges met with fortitude as well as emotion, novelists in Ireland could demonstrate that those on the fringes of Europe were also capable of feeling 'delicate distress', as Elizabeth Griffith entitled her 1769 novel.

One way for women such as Griffith to demonstrate their commitment to cosmopolitanism was to insert themselves into the Republic of Letters through epistolary exchanges. The importance of letters to women in Ireland and France in maintaining their role in the public sphere cannot be overstated. Letters played an integral role in their literary lives, and allowed them both an emotional outlet as well as an avenue for performance of the self, and a means of publicly communicating their thoughts and perspectives. There is an obvious synergy discernible between letter writing and the mode of sensibility, and this is clearly applicable in the case of the women writers discussed here, who often consciously draw upon sentimental motifs in epistolary communications. Offering an emotional outlet, their letters include detailed recordings of the writer's state of mind or response to personal afflictions. Rather than simply containing information about their activities, the letters enable the writers to develop a public authorial persona. The participants in these epistolary networks often supported such personas or performances of the self, either accepting or aiding in manufacturing them. The Bluestockings, for example, constructed the Irish salon hostess Elizabeth Vesey as an otherworldly being, particularly susceptible to melancholia and an excess of feeling. She is described in letters both to and about her as a sylph, or sylph-like: 'Beings of your sylphish composition may live without sleep, and think and act without relaxation.'[33] Vesey is frequently associated both with various emotional states and the imagination, especially figured in relation to her perceived isolation in Ireland while residing at her Lucan estate. The Bluestocking letters thus reveal particular connections being made between femininity, sensibility, and Ireland.

The key role letters played for women at this time is reflected in the epistolary format being embraced by many female authors, including Riccoboni and Sheridan. Six of Riccoboni's eight novels are in letter form; Sheridan's *Conclusion* too appears as a series of letters; while *Sidney Bidulph* is written as journal entries addressed to the protagonist's beloved friend Cecilia, who receives them at intervals. This general espousal of an epistolary format is just one of the many echoes between the novels of Riccoboni and Sheridan, as similar ideas and themes are addressed by both writers, who challenge their heroines and exploit their readers' emotions. These echoes and acts of cultural transfer between France and Ireland, and French and Anglophone texts, are repeated in the two authors' navigation of the networks surrounding the dissemination of such texts through the agency of translation, as the next section demonstrates.

Great Alterations: Mid-Eighteenth-Century Translation and Cultural Exchange

Early Irish fiction was predominantly published in London and Dublin, and the few titles that were translated tended to be into German and Dutch. However, the European popularity of the novel of sentiment, particularly in France, changed the geography of reception. Oliver Goldsmith's *The Vicar of Wakefield* almost immediately appeared in both German and French, as *Der Landpriester von Wakefield* (Leipzig, 1767) and

Le Ministre de Wakefield (London and Paris, 1767), the latter attributed to Mme de Montesson.[34]

Riccoboni often claimed that some of her texts were 'traduit de l'anglais', translated from English, when they were in fact original works, such as *Histoire de M. le marquis de Cressy* (1758). In contrast, other works are indeed 'translations' of English-language novels or plays, although these often domesticate the foreign elements, and repurpose the work for a French audience. Having published *Fanni Butlerd*, *Histoire de M. le marquis de Cressy*, and *Lettres de Milady Juliette Catesby* anonymously, Riccoboni affixed her name to her adaptation of Henry Fielding's *Amelia*: *Amélie. Roman de Mr. Fielding* (1762). Her involvement with translation also led her to engage with material by two Irish writers, Roscommon-born Arthur Murphy and Kerry-born Hugh Kelly in her project, *Le Nouveau Théâtre Anglois* (Paris, 1769), which translates five Anglophone comedies for a new, Francophone audience.[35] Murphy's *The Way to Keep Him* (1760), now appearing as *La Façon de fixer*, was presented alongside Kelly's *False Delicacy* (1768), Edward Moore's *The Foundling* (1748), George Colman's *The Deuce Is in Him* (1763), and *The Jealous Wife* (1761). Riccoboni's publication has much to tell us about the tastes of English and French theatre-goers, and particularly emphasises the importance of comedy in England (no translations of tragedies are offered).

Riccoboni's undertakings for this project provide considerable information on cultural exchange and encounter, as well as the practice of translation. A letter from Riccoboni to Garrick in which she outlines her task reveals much about her approach and methodology, as well as her interpretation and understanding of the process and craft of translation:

> You will find a great alteration in the dialogue, I should warn you that I took fierce liberties. The two English authors will charge me with ineptitude, with ignorance, they will say that they were not listened to. They will be right in London, but they will be wrong here. I have not claimed to correct, but to render their work more likely to please my compatriots. My friend, the tastes of all nations conform on certain points. Nature, truth, sentiment interests the Englishman, the Frenchman, the Russian, and the Turk, in equal measure. However, spirit, banter, wit, the tone of good jokes, change name in changing location. That which is lively, light, and gracious in one language, becomes cold, heavy, insipid, and rude in another. [...] That which raises a burst of laughter in France could occasion booing in London or in Vienna.[36]

Riccoboni's emphasis on altering the work for new audiences supports the view that eighteenth-century translations are often better understood as creative, original works, rather than primarily copies or imitations. She has taken obvious liberties in her engagement with the work, altering the material to make it more pleasing to a French audience, supporting the idea that 'The thrust, in the eighteenth century, is towards taming foreign fiction, rather than attempting to preserve the "foreignness" for which modern translation theorists like Lawrence Venuti have argued.'[37] Eighteenth-century translation's move towards transnationalism, its becoming 'an instrument of nationalized literary exchange', is borne out in this example, which moves away from the idea of providing a 'pure' counterpart, and aims instead to capture the spirit of the original.[38]

Knowledge of French in Ireland was widespread, and was important for both scholarship and business, as well as embodying the 'fashionable attainment' of earlier association. Access to the French language tended to be associated with three diverse groups in Ireland: the Huguenot community, Catholics who were educated abroad, and the Ascendancy elite.[39] It is interesting to note also that Trinity College, Dublin was to the fore in introducing two chairs of modern language (French and German, Italian and Spanish) in the period under discussion, thereby offering public recognition of these languages. Although reading French works was generally thought an appropriate activity for elite Anglo-Irish women, the topic of the material chosen for translation could lead to disapproval. Such was the case with the translation undertaken by Catherine Maria Bury, later Lady Charleville, of Voltaire's *La Pucelle*. Although the extent of her role in the translation of the poem was unclear, Dr Thomas Barnard, the Bishop of Limerick, expressed his disapproval of the linking of Lady Charleville in any way with the translation in the following reported conversation with Lady Sarah Napier:

> 'Why, that Pucelle: it was not *right*: no woman should have lent her aid – indeed few women could; and, if you set aside the principle which ought to have prevented it, the verse is to her praise.' I immediately said I grant you that I wish her name never had been in question as it does not suit the delicacy of a woman's character – but consider the work was read to her forever and she was applied to as a judge of the French only.[40]

Thus, while proficiency in French could be a useful attainment for a woman in Ireland, knowledge of the language was to be carefully applied to sanctioned projects, in order to avoid the taint of impropriety. Sentimental fiction was certainly a safer choice for a woman to translate than Voltaire and this goes some way to explaining the vogue for such translations in this period. The publication of English translations of French works in Ireland reached its highest point in the 1760s.[41] Elizabeth Griffith worked diligently as a translator while she lived in Ireland between 1759 and 1764, translating various works, including *The Memoirs of Ninon d'Enclos* (1761).

A focus on eighteenth-century Irish writing in an exclusively Anglophone context occludes evidence of influence from beyond arbitrary linguistic boundaries.[42] Bridging linguistic and national frontiers via translation enables a clearer sense of the development of writing across Western Europe. The circulation of texts in both original and translated editions from disparate countries permitted the spread of ideas and influence. Projects such as Riccoboni's *Nouveau Théâtre Anglois* or Elizabeth Griffith's fascinating 1777 publication *A Collection of Novels*, which includes two of her own translations from the French alongside novels by earlier English women writers, reveal much about women's agency, their contribution to canon formation, and their dissemination of literary developments independently of national considerations.

While associated primarily with women, who often used the activity as a means of entering the public sphere of print culture without making any claims to originality, many men also engaged in translation, and this is true of several translators of works by Sheridan.[43] The manuscript of a French translation of Sheridan's play, *The Discovery*, exists as *La Découverte* (*c.* 1764), presented from 'a young male author to a young lady', and signed 'M. de B**'.[44] The translator presents the text to Sheridan, stating, 'From the moment I knew that the full translation of this comedy would be agreeable to you, I dedicated myself to the task with all the zeal I could be capable of possessing.'[45] *Sidney Bidulph* and *Conclusion* were also both translated into French within their first years of publication. Prévost was more famously the translator of the works of Samuel Richardson, and, like Riccoboni, is another example of a novelist-translator. His translation of *Sidney Bidulph, Mémoires Pour Servir à l'Histoire de la Vertu, Extraits du Journal d'une Jeune Dame* (1762) found enormous popularity in France, being described as 'le livre du jour', or the book of the moment, by Louis Petit de Bachaumont, and being praised in *L'Année Littéraire* and the *Mercure de France*.[46] Although often described as a free translation, Prévost's *Mémoires* is much more faithful to Sheridan's original than the writings of many other contemporary translators. The text does make certain changes to accord with national sensibilities, as we have seen is typical also of Riccoboni's approach. This is particularly evident when Faulkland and Mrs Gerrarde are depicted in France, when Prévost makes strategic alterations to the reference to the 'poor wine drunk in France'.[47] J. B. R. Robinet offered a second translation of *Sidney Bidulph*, with the imprint of Amsterdam, in 1762, while *The History of Nourjahad* was translated by Madame de Sérionne.[48] In addition to these translations of her novels, the high reputation of Sheridan's work in France is also discernible from the later success of Louis-Sébastien Mercier's *L'Habitant de la Guadeloupe: Comédie en trois actes* (1785), which engages with the character of Mr Warner, Sidney's wealthy cousin who arrives in England from the West Indies.

Examples such as these indicate the impact of translation on the dissemination of both early Irish fiction and theatre, significantly increasing the audience for these works, and ensuring a continued tradition of influence, emulation, and exchange. Close studies of the translations mentioned in this chapter reveal significant differences in methodological approaches. These various infidelities and alterations have much to tell us about the changes afoot in translation, with an overall movement away from metaphrase, described by Dryden in 1680 as 'turning an Author word by word, and Line by Line, from one Language into another'.[49] They are also reflective of the tastes and cultural sensibilities of the receiver countries, which the translators seek to incorporate into their works, as in the cases of Riccoboni aiming to render jokes more hilarious for a French audience or Prévost not wanting to offend his reader. Rather than aiming for strict literal fidelity, these translators hope to offer what they deem the most suitable version or adaptation of the source text for the new target audience, ostensibly increasing the latter's enjoyment and appreciation of the foreign cultural production.

Conclusions

In order to change how we perceive early Irish writing, we must go beyond Anglo-centric interpretations of the novel. In addition to its English influences, most obviously Samuel Richardson and Henry Fielding, the Irish novel is also clearly informed by writing emerging from France in the eighteenth century. Novels by French authors had a significant presence in Ireland, in both original form and translation, London reprint and Irish commission, throughout the eighteenth century. The audience in Ireland for sentimental writing was extensive, and works by Marie-Jeanne Riccoboni were particularly in demand. A comparative reading of the novels of Frances Sheridan and Mme Riccoboni reveals links in themes and style, form and emphasis, while also offering evidence for parallels in the two women's experience of translation as a force of transnationalism. Cultural connections between France and Ireland are readily apparent, and recognising the intersections of Ireland and the continent in the popularity of the sentimental novel does much to advance the sense of the novel's universality in the mid-eighteenth century.

This universality and the flow of adaptations, translations, and creative original works demonstrate a wave of exchange between source and receiver countries, as various writers incorporate different elements into their literary works. Through linking Ireland with the greater world and recognising such writers' cosmopolitanism and engagement with European literary trends, one can also identify an emerging field of writing by Anglophone Irish writers. Sentimental writing is an important aspect of early Irish fiction, and by inserting Ireland into the larger narrative regarding the development of both this genre and the novel generally, we change our perception of this genre of writing, of its geographies of reception, as well as of the degree of cultural influence and exchange between readers and writers in both Ireland and France, with implications for those in Britain too. By moving away from an exclusive focus on Anglo-French, or cross-Channel, considerations of exchange and translation, Ireland's contribution to the development of the sentimental novel both within and beyond the island of Ireland can be more easily observed and more readily celebrated.

Notes

1. See particularly the work of Máire Kennedy, including: *French Books in Eighteenth-Century Ireland* (Oxford: Voltaire Foundation, 2001); 'Nations of the Mind: French Culture in Ireland and the International Booktrade', in *Nations and Nationalisms: France, Britain, Ireland and the Eighteenth-Century Context*, ed. Michael O'Dea and Kevin Whelan (Oxford: Voltaire Foundation, 1995), pp. 147–58; and, with Geraldine Sheridan, 'The Trade in French Books in Eighteenth-Century Ireland', in *Ireland and the French Enlightenment, 1700–1800*, ed. Graham Gargett and Geraldine Sheridan (Basingstoke: Macmillan, 1999), pp. 173–96 (p. 190).

2. Kennedy and Sheridan, 'The Trade in French Books', p. 193. Máire Kennedy, 'The Distribution of a Locally-Produced French Periodical in Provincial Ireland: The *Magazin à La Mode*, 1777–1778', *Eighteenth-Century Ireland / Iris an dá chultúr* 9 (1994), 83–98.

3. For studies of Irish–French relations, see, for example, Graham Gargett and Geraldine Sheridan, eds., *Ireland and the French Enlightenment, 1700–1800* (Basingstoke: Macmillan, 1999); Jane Conroy, ed., *Franco-Irish Connections: Essays, Memoirs and Poems in Honour of Pierre Joannon* (Dublin: Four Courts Press, 2009); Thomas O'Connor, ed., *The Irish in Europe, 1580–1815* (Dublin: Four Courts Press, 2001); Mary Ann Lyons and Thomas O'Connor, *Strangers to Citizens: The Irish in Europe, 1600–1800* (Dublin: National Library of Ireland, 2008); and Marie Léoutre, 'Député Général in France and in Exile', in *The Huguenots: France, Exile, Diaspora*, ed. Jane McKee and Randolphe Vigne (Brighton: Sussex Academic Press, 2013), pp. 146–54.

4. Works by Marivaux can be found in twenty-five collections of Irish private libraries; Prévost in nineteen: see Kennedy, *French Books*.
5. Ernest A. Baker, *The History of the English Novel*, 10 vols (1924–39; repr. New York: Barnes and Noble, 1950), V, p. 143.
6. *The Monthly Review* 51 (1773), 154, review of *The History of Pamela Howard*. For analysis of sentimental novels of the 1780s and 90s, see Melissa Sodeman, *Sentimental Memorials: Women and the Novel in Literary History* (Stanford University Press, 2014).
7. For a specifically Irish context for Bluestocking activities, see Amy Prendergast, *Literary Salons across Britain and Ireland in the Long Eighteenth Century* (Basingstoke: Palgrave Macmillan, 2015).
8. For more detail on the life of Sheridan, see Alicia LeFanu, *Memoirs of the Life and Writings of Mrs. Frances Sheridan* (London, 1824); Conrad Brunström, 'Frances Sheridan', *The Literary Encyclopedia*: www.litencyc.com [accessed 8 September 2016]; Ian Campbell Ross, 'Frances Sheridan', *Oxford Dictionary of National Biography*: https://doi.org/10.1093/ref:odnb/25365 [accessed 8 September 2016]; and Heidi Hutner, 'Introduction', in Frances Sheridan, *The Memoirs of Miss Sidney Bidulph* (Toronto: Broadview, 2011), ed. Hutner. For an interesting discussion of Sheridan as playwright, and the failure of *The Dupe*, see Elizabeth Kuti, 'Rewriting Frances Sheridan', *Eighteenth-Century Ireland / Iris an dá chultúr* 11 (1996), 120–28.
9. For work on Riccoboni, see, in particular, publications by Marijn S. Kaplan, including 'Riccoboni's 1768 Letter to the *Mercure de France*: Reclaiming a Woman Writer's Literary Legacy', *Women in French Studies* 19 (2011), 24–36; 'Marie Jeanne Riccoboni's *Lettres d'Élisabeth Sophie de Vallière*: A Feminist Reading', *Women in French Studies* 13 (2005), 25–36; and *Translations and Continuations: Riccoboni and Brooke, Graffigny and Roberts* (London: Routledge, 2011). *Fanni Butlerd* is later spelled *Fanny Butler*.
10. See *Mme Riccoboni's Letters to David Hume, David Garrick and Sir Robert Liston: 1764–1783*, ed. J. C. Nicholls (Oxford: Voltaire Foundation, 1976) and 'Correspondance de Laclos et de Madame Riccoboni au sujet des Liaisons dangereuses', in *Laclos: Oeuvres complètes* (Paris: Gallimard, 1959).
11. Kennedy, *French Books*, pp. 66–91.
12. Antoine-François Prévost, *Histoire du chevalier des Grieux et de Manon Lescaut* was the last volume of seven from Prévost's *Mémoires et aventures d'un homme de qualité qui s'est retiré du monde* (1728–31).
13. For more, see Éamon Ó Ciosáin, 'Attitudes towards Ireland and the Irish in Enlightenment France', in *Ireland and the French Enlightenment*, ed. Gargett and Sheridan, pp. 129–51.
14. Geraldine Sheridan, 'Warring Translations: Prévost's *Doyen de Killerine* in the Irish Press', *Eighteenth-Century Ireland / Iris an dá chultúr* 14 (1999), 99–115.
15. Graham Gargett, 'Voltaire's View of the Irish', in *Ireland and the French Enlightenment, 1700–1800*, ed. Gargett and Sheridan, pp. 152–71 (p. 170).

16. For full details of these editions, their different page-lengths, titles, and formats, see Joan Hinde Stewart, 'Introduction' to Marie-Jeanne Riccoboni, *Lettres de Mistriss Fanni Butlerd*, ed. Hinde Stewart (Geneva: Librairie Droz, 1979), pp. xxxiii–xxxv.

17. Kaplan, *Translations and Continuations*, p. x.

18. Rolf Loeber and Magda Loeber, with Anne M. Burnham, *A Guide to Irish Fiction, 1650–1900* (Dublin: Four Courts Press, 2006); Gargett and Sheridan, eds., *Ireland and the French Enlightenment*, p. 270. This novel bears the imprint of both London and Dublin publishers (Dodsley and Potts), suggesting a collaborative agreement.

19. *Dublin Mercury* 387 (15–18 April 1769).

20. Lady Holland to Marchioness of Kildare (13 August 1764), in Emily Fitzgerald, *The Correspondence of Emily, Duchess of Leinster*, ed. Brian Fitzgerald, 3 vols (Dublin: Stationery Office, 1949–57), I, p. 403. Emily Fitzgerald famously educated some of her twenty-two children in accordance with the principles of Rousseau, after reading his *Emile* (1762), and unsuccessfully attempted to recruit the writer himself to act as tutor.

21. James R. Foster, 'The Abbé Prevost and the English Novel', *PMLA* 42.2 (1927), 452–53.

22. Copies of Rousseau are included in at least sixty-seven library catalogues of named Irish owners, being within the top ten French authors in Irish private libraries, behind Voltaire, Montesquieu, and Molière, as well as dictionaries, grammars, and *La Sainte Bible*. Kennedy, *French Books*, pp. 183–84.

23. See, for example, James S. Munro, 'Richardson, Marivaux, and the French Romance Tradition', *Modern Language Review* 70.4 (1974), 752–59.

24. Frances Sheridan, *The Memoirs of Miss Sidney Bidulph*, ed. Heidi Hutner (Toronto: Broadview, 2011), p. 166. Further references to this novel will be cited in parenthesis.

25. Brooke in her translation criminalises d'Ossory's actions: 'lui apprendre mon malheur' is translated as, 'I thought sometimes of going to Montford, of confessing my crime'; Kaplan, *Translations and Continuations*, p. 200.

26. Ibid., p. xi.

27. Aileen Douglas, 'The Novel before 1800', in *The Cambridge Companion to the Irish Novel*, ed. John Wilson Foster (Cambridge University Press, 2006), pp. 22–38 (p. 34).

28. More unusual in this regard is *The Triumph of Prudence over Passion* (1781) by Sheridan's daughter Elizabeth, which continues Sheridan's commitment to sensibility and personal trials and tribulations, particularly in the figure of Emily, but introduces distinctly contemporary, political, and even patriotic contexts, with references to the Irish Volunteers, occurrences in France, political events, and public virtue.

29. Robert Dillon, the ninth Earl of Roscommon, died unmarried in 1770, having succeeded to the earldom in 1746. John Debrett, *Debrett's Peerage of England, Scotland, and Ireland* (London, 1840), p. 623.

30. Sheridan, *Memoirs of Miss Sidney Bidulph*, p. 54.

31. Siobhán Kilfeather, '"Strangers at Home": Political Fictions by Women in Eighteenth-Century Ireland' (unpublished PhD thesis, Princeton University, 1989), p. 213.

32. Ibid., pp. 165–256.

33. Elizabeth Carter, *A Series of Letters between Mrs. Elizabeth Carter and Miss Catherine Talbo*t . . . 4 vols (London, 1809), III, p. 313.

34. Another French translation of *The Vicar of Wakefield*, entitled *Le Curé de Wakefield*, was also later published in London (1796) and Dublin (1797).

35. Irish playwrights found a hugely responsive audience for their works in London in the mid- to late eighteenth century. Frances Sheridan's son, Richard Brinsley, found particular success with *The School for Scandal* (1777), the most performed play in London for the next twenty-five years. For more on Irish playwrights in London, see David O'Shaughnessy, ed., *Eighteenth-Century Life* 39.1, Special Issue: *Networks of Aspiration: The London Irish of the Eighteenth Century* (January 2015).

36. 'Marie Jeanne Riccoboni to David Garrick: Saturday, 20 August 1768', *Electronic Enlightenment Scholarly Edition of Correspondence*, ed. Robert McNamee et al., Vers. 3.0. University of Oxford (2016) [accessed 8 September 2016]. Translation is mine. Part of this letter is also reproduced by Riccoboni in her introduction to *Le Nouveau Théâtre Anglois* (1769), pp. xi–xii.

37 For Anglo-French cultural exchange and translation, see the work of Gillian Dow, including: *Translators, Interpreters, Mediators: Women Writers, 1700–1900* (Bern: Peter Lang, 2007); 'Criss-Crossing the Channel: The French Novel and English Translation, 1660–1832', in *The Oxford Handbook of the Eighteenth-Century Novel*, ed. J. A. Downie (Oxford University Press, 2016), pp. 88–104; and 'Translation, Cross-Channel Exchanges and the Novel in the Long Eighteenth Century', *Literature Compass* 11.11 (2014), 691–702.

38. Mary Helen McMurran, 'Eighteenth-Century Translation', in *The Spread of Novels: Translation and Prose Fiction in the Eighteenth Century* (Princeton University Press, 2010), pp. 1–27 (p. 21).

39. Kennedy, *French Books*, p. 166 and *passim*. Máire Kennedy, 'Huguenot Readers in Eighteenth-Century Ireland', in *The Huguenots*, ed. McKee, pp. 173–94. Of course, Irish rather than English was the language of the majority of the population in mid-eighteenth-century Ireland and continued to increase until the Famine. See Niall Ó Ciosáin, 'Languages and Literacy', in *Print and Popular Culture in Ireland, 1750–1850* (Basingstoke: Macmillan, 1997), pp. 154–69.

40. Papers and Correspondence of Charles Brinsley Marlay of Westmeath, Ireland and his family, University of Nottingham Manuscripts and Special Collections, MY 72.

41. Kennedy and Sheridan, 'The Trade in French Books', pp. 178–79.

42. For a discussion of translation and Irish Studies in a nineteenth-century context, see Anne O'Connor, 'The Languages of Transnationalism: Translating, Training, and Transfer', *Éire-Ireland* 51.1/2 (Spring/Summer 2016), 14–33. By

that century, French novels were deemed 'too risqué' to be translated and consumed by an Irish audience (p. 28).

43. Dow, *Translators, Interpreters, Mediators*, pp. 98–99.

44. *La découverte: comedie*, MS. 1996.001, inscribed 'Un jeune auteur à une jeune dame', Los Angeles, Clark Library, UCLA.

45. Ibid.

46. S. P. Chew, Jr, 'Prévost's *Mémoires Pour Servir à l'Histoire de la Vertu*', *Modern Language Notes* 54.8 (1939), 592–97 (p. 593).

47. Other differences, including some mistakes, and some minor alterations are identified in Chew, 'Prévost's *Mémoires*'.

48. For discussion of *Nourjahad*, see Sonja Lawrenson, 'Frances Sheridan's *The History of Nourjahad* and the Sultan of Smock-Alley', *Eighteenth-Century Ireland / Iris an dá chultúr* 26 (2011), 24–50.

49. John Dryden, 'Preface Concerning Ovid's Epistles', in *The Poems of John Dryden*, ed. John Sargeaunt (Oxford University Press, 1913), p. 508.

CHAPTER 10

'An Example to the Whole World': Patriotism and Imperialism in Early Irish Fiction

Daniel Sanjiv Roberts

Imperial analogues appear frequently in the political and fictional imagination of Anglophone writers in Ireland over the course of the eighteenth century. Such writers were typically of the Protestant Ascendancy, which, as historians have shown, increasingly came to see its interests as being in opposition to England's, developing thereby a sense of patriotism with regard to their separate identity.[1] In his classic work of Irish patriotism, *The Case of Ireland Stated* (1698), William Molyneux inveighed against the view that 'some raise against us [. . .] that *Ireland* is to be looked upon only as a *Colony* from *England*'.[2] For Molyneux, the idea that Ireland could be regarded as a colony was to be firmly resisted in favour of an assertion of its legislative independence based on the due recognition of Ireland's position as a sister kingdom to England. Nevertheless, his repudiation of the idea only served to raise the spectre of its corollary, that the colonial model was the standard. Colonial metaphors, often drawing on historical and classical parallels in the imaginations of the enlightened Protestant order, came readily to mind during an era which succeeded the plantation of Ireland, and, from the early seventeenth century, witnessed the establishment – and subsequent loss – of the American colonies in the west, followed by the foundation of a burgeoning empire in the east. These major regional and global developments crucially involved, in interconnected ways, the growth and protection of British military and maritime powers, the claiming and safeguarding of commercial and trading rights, and the development through migration of settler colonies over newly discovered areas of the world that were coming under – and sometimes resisting – imperial influence. Such developments left their mark, unsurprisingly, on the fictional imagination of Anglophone writers of the period.

Most famously, this was revealed in Jonathan Swift's satirical fantasy of other worlds, *Gulliver's Travels* (1726), or, as first published, *Travels into Several Remote Nations of the World*. This was a work that was clearly indebted to, and parodic of, the immensely popular genre of European travel writing, a mode that, along with other imperial practices, was productive of what Mary Louise Pratt has described as 'a Eurocentred form of global [. . .] or "planetary" consciousness'.[3] Swift's reputation as the pre-eminent Anglo-Irish writer of the period and the canonical status of his satirical and fictional masterpiece have led his work to be often read somewhat in isolation as a work of monumental and idiosyncratic genius. While Swift's undoubted immersion in the religious, political, and intellectual culture of his time has been much studied – and has informed the many rewarding readings we have of *Gulliver's Travels* – his place as an Irish writer within a longer narrative of fictional and discursive evolution with regard to empire has been considerably less so. This chapter will attempt to address this lacuna and to open up the field to further investigation by reading *Gulliver's Travels* in relation to other works of fiction with significant imperial analogues, in particular the anonymously published *Vertue Rewarded; or, The Irish Princess* (1693) and Charles Johnston's *The History of Arsaces, Prince of Betlis* (1774).[4] In doing so, it will suggest a complex imbrication of colonial and imperial concerns with other, better-recognised, issues of civility, ethnicity, and identity pertaining to Ireland that are embodied in these fictions, with particular regard to the growing sense of patriotism emerging amongst the Protestant Ascendancy at this time.

It is important to clarify at the outset that we are dealing here with shifting relations and changing terminology through a crucially formative period not only of British colonial politics and ethnic identities, but also of the novel as a genre. Problematic aspects of these categorical issues can be gleaned from the title pages of the works of fiction here selected; while the earliest of these, *Vertue Rewarded; or, The Irish Princess*, was described on its title page as a 'novel', *Gulliver's Travels* was presented to its first readers as a work of travel writing, and *Arsaces* proclaimed itself in the manner well-established of novels by the mid-eighteenth century as a 'history'. Furthermore, while the 'Irish Princess' of *Vertue Rewarded*'s first-published title might have correctly signalled elements of a romance, the unfolding of the narrative, as we shall see, would involve not only a legendary native princess of Ireland, but also an English-speaking heroine, from a cultured but relatively humble Protestant settler family, who would become a princess only through marriage. The newer associations of ethnicity attached to Irishness in this novel are integral to a radical transformation of generic mode from romance to realism, even as the Protestant order associated with the rise of the novel consolidated its power and control in Ireland.[5] As I shall argue, Gulliver's discovery of new lands and Arsaces's assumption of royal authority over his subjects may be seen to repeat and solidify this developing theme over the longue durée of this period, even as historical exigencies complicate and add fine grain to the picture.

A common feature in all these works of fiction is undoubtedly their engagement with colonial societies and paradigms, imagined variously in time, location, and proximity to their contemporary moment. And integral to these variously imagined engagements is the concern, broadly indebted to early modern and Enlightenment modes of thinking, with the distinction between civility and barbarity, marked out at this time as visibly inherent in the difference between Europe and its others, the latter denoted especially by the 'savage' peoples of the New World and of Africa as reported to educated readers through the literature of travel. A complicating factor in this broad distinction of Enlightenment thinking though, is the anomalous place granted to Ireland within it, akin in many ways to the savagery associated with non-European others. In their own ways, each of the major primary texts under discussion in this chapter can be seen to respond to, complicate, and challenge these unpalatable charges which were still prevalent amongst contemporaries, especially in England. As such, they are an expression of what has been termed Protestant patriotism, a growing sense of pride coupled with awareness of Ireland's distinctness from and potentially conflicting interests with Britain. As Protestant settlers laid claim to Ireland in the eighteenth century, fitfully sinking differences with Catholics and increasingly identifying as Irish themselves in the development of a patriotic identity associated with land ownership, the distinctions between barbarism and civility in Ireland, as these fictions show, were significantly compromised, troubling the imaginations of their authors.

Vertue Rewarded; or, The Irish Princess (1693)

While the Williamite wars of 1690–91 mark a definitive moment in modern Irish history and obviously secured the political framework for English Protestant rule over Ireland in the eighteenth century, it is worth recalling that this famous victory – too often remembered in anachronistically nationalistic and narrowly sectarian terms today – bore larger European and global dimensions during an era in which Britain was rapidly expanding both westwards and eastwards.[6] From the continental point of view, the Williamite wars could be seen to be part of the longer-standing power struggle from 1688 between the League of Augsburg led by William of Orange and the France of Louis XIV. And, within this European competition for imperial stakes, the Protestant settlement of Ireland with its discordant Catholic connections to other imperial players on the continent, constituted, as Jane Ohlmeyer has put it, 'the *sine qua non* for English expansion'.[7] These wider European and global aspects of the conflict are very much in evidence in *Vertue Rewarded*, set in Clonmel during the military campaign, and published with remarkable rapidity in the wake of the Williamite wars. The primary plot concerns the romance between a European prince of a small principality leading the Williamite forces into Clonmel and a young lady of the town named Marinda. She proves to be in her own countrified way, witty, accomplished, and cultured, but she is of no great consequence in lineage or wealth. Though the Prince is struck by her beauty and pursues her with ardour, he initially has no intentions of marrying her. Her principled refusal of his suit brings him around to a full and proper appreciation of her virtue as much as of her beauty, predictably resolving the romance and elevating her to the position of a princess. Interpolated with the primary story are two other narratives, the first, of a holy well, based on supposedly ancient Irish folklore (though exposed by its modern editors to be 'fakelore'), and the other, a tale of the Spanish conquest of Peru which draws on Paul Rycaut's 1688 translation of Garcilaso de la Vega's *The Royal Commentaries of Peru*.[8] (Rycaut, it might be further noted, had been Chief Secretary in Ireland between 1685 and 1687, by which point he had already established a European-wide reputation as an authority on empire, as author of *The Present State of the Ottoman Empire*, 1666.) These interpolations cohere with the principal narrative of Marinda's virtue, extending its implications both historically and geographically, and hybridising its generic composition considerably.

Clearly, the primary narrative of *Vertue Rewarded*, with its descriptions of interactions between the gentry and the Williamite forces in Clonmel, is drawn from close knowledge of provincial Ireland in this period. It is evident that the small-town but cultured world that welcomes the foreign Prince comprises the English-speaking Protestant order of Ireland. Though the action of the novel is not centrally concerned with battle, warfare and conquest offer significant metaphors for the development of the romance, in keeping with the military ethos of the major male characters. On the edges of the narrative we hear of attacks by rapparees (or Irish irregulars) who live up to the standard view of Irish uncouthness, molesting women and behaving with barbarous insolence against the civilised order of the country. The Prince's intervention in one such instance, when he rides to the rescue of a gentlewoman under attack – her status attested by the maid accompanying her – quickly reveals the disparity between the chivalrous code of honour observed by the Prince and the rude behaviour of the Irish countrymen intent on harming the woman. The Prince's attempt to intercede is immediately met by 'a short Answer in *Irish*' and the thrust of a pitchfork, which, missing its target, injures his horse. The Prince's response is to return 'the *Irishman's* Complement with a shot', killing his adversary on the spot, and soon disbanding the unruly Irish who are made to flee.[9] It is the superior weaponry of the Prince, a technological advantage, even more than his strength or valour, that wins the day. A twist in the tale is soon apparent when it emerges that the young woman in question is Marinda; however, she shows little gratitude to the Prince, as, at this point in the narrative, she is convinced that the Prince, despite his professions of love, is in fact secretly married, thus rendering his intentions somewhat less than honourable. Her belief in the Prince's perfidiousness moreover is the result of a somewhat devious plot engineered by the Prince's confidant Celadon, and approved by the Prince, to ascertain whether the Prince might not enjoy her favours without actually marrying her. Hence, his rescue of her is met with cold rebuff. Marinda's resolve, however, not to entertain the Prince's suit under such circumstances only proves her virtue beyond a doubt, guiding the now fully enamoured Prince towards the only course by which he might satisfy both honour and passion: to disabuse her of Celadon's falsehood, and to seek her hand in marriage sincerely.

The patriotism of the Irish settler community keen to assert its good faith – symbolised here by the virtuousness of its women – is interestingly paralleled in the inset tale of Cluaneesha, daughter of the King of Munster. Cluaneesha, under suspicion of dishonour from the swelling of her belly, vindicates herself by drinking from a holy well associated with the power of disclosing virtue. Her virtue is rewarded by the restoration of her health, and her return to royal, as well as popular, favour. Marinda's assumption into royalty when she marries the Prince by the end of the novel only points to the parallel suggested by the interpolated tale of her alter ego from an earlier era, the 'real' Irish princess, Cluaneesha, whose virtue is also rewarded, and whose higher aristocratic birth foreshadows the aspirations, and, in the wake of the Williamite wars, confidence, of the Protestant propertied elite who were already busily replacing the native aristocracy and legitimising their rule in Ireland. The use of settler 'fakelore' silently displacing the folklore of Ireland bespeaks in literary form the supplanting tendencies of the settler group, even as it asserts the civility and virtue of a bygone era in Ireland which the debased native population of Ireland had failed to properly represent.

Perhaps a more complex, and unsettling, representation of colonial occupancy and legitimacy may be seen in another significant inset narrative, 'The Story of Faniaca', set in Peruvian South America under progressive colonisation by the Spanish. Here, the Spanish encounter the Incas and another indigenous group, the Antisuyans, a cannibalistic, though nobly savage, tribe, who had resisted incursions by the Incas. Drawing in detail on Garcilaso's *Royal Commentaries*, which depict the Spanish conquest, despite its pretensions of civility, as a treacherous and avaricious enterprise waged against the naiveté of the South American peoples, this story involves yet another romance, this between Faniaca, the daughter of an Antisuyan priest, and a Spanish conquistador, Astolfo. The stark contrast of civilisational values involved in this encounter, between the superior military organisation and firepower of the Spaniards (aided by their colonial subjects, the Incas) and the barbarity of the cannibalistic Antisuyans, bears subtle parallels with the deeper undercurrent of the novel, contrasting the guile and sophistication of the Williamite order represented by the Prince and Celadon with the crude resistance displayed by the native Irish. The 'covetousness' of the Spanish for gold matches the Prince's 'passion' for Marinda, while the honourable nature of the Antisuyans finds its correlative in the bravery of the Irish resistance, notwithstanding the attack on Marinda (p. 113). These unsettling depictions of imperial honour and morality trouble any simplistic opposition between barbarity and civility, rendering the text both complex and conciliatory. Details of the cannibalistic habits of the Antisuyans drawn from the *Royal Commentaries* (which was also an influence on Swift's *A Modest Proposal*) would remind readers familiar with stereotypes of the 'wild Irish' of their legendary cannibalism, playing into this long-standing tradition, though also complicating it.[10] Although Faniaca admits 'a secret horrour in myself' at the cannibalism of her people (p. 80), it is clear from her account that their practice was bound together with notions of honour, so much so that the bravest of their victims who showed no signs of pain were later deified and became through their implacable death the object of Antisuyan veneration. Comparably, the novel's depiction of native Irish resistance to the Williamite forces mingles ideas of savagery with those of honour, typified by the novel's partially admiring portrayal of the Irish hero Patrick Sarsfield's raid at Ballyneety. Though we learn that Sarsfield 'surprized the Convoy, and, cutting them to pieces, burnt them, their Carriages and Provisions [. . .] to ashes', his 'unusual Bravery' in penetrating the countryside under English control to mount his attack is equally commended by the narrator (p. 113).

A similarly provisional view with regard to ideas of imperial superiority may be found in the primary source text for the South American elements of the narrative of *Vertue Rewarded*. Garcilaso's evidently mixed feelings regarding the Spanish conquest of the American Indians derives no doubt from his own mixed racial identity – signalled by his nom de plume, in Rycaut's translation, of 'the Inca Garcilasso de la Vega' – as the son of an Inca princess, Isabel Suárez Chimpo Ocllu, and a Spaniard.[11] Furthermore, publishing details of the translation by Rycaut – who may have had a part to play in the composition of *Vertue Rewarded*, as its editors have specu-lated – suggest awareness of a comparably transitory allegiance to any particular royal power. Rycaut's translation of Garcilaso's *Commentaries* reproduces its Spanish source only to be dedicated in 1688 to James II, whose dominions were, as Rycaut noted, 'adjacent' to those of the Spanish, making him obviously 'a Party concerned in the Affairs of the New World'.[12] Prior to the work's publication, however, by 1687 Rycaut had been relieved of his post as Chief Secretary to Ireland by the Catholic Earl of Tyrconnell, James's viceroy, as a result of his programme of Catholicisation, and Rycaut's dedication of the volume to James may have been an attempt to seek or regain the monarch's favour. Moving forward into 1693 however, we see details of Rycaut's work enter into the anonymous narrative of *Vertue Rewarded*, now playing into a decidedly Williamite slant. The reworking of the Spanish historical materials to satisfy divergent national and monarchical preferences suggests the malle-ability of the narrative to suit imperial intentions that are unsurprisingly common to the major Catholic and Protestant ruling interests of Europe.

European imperialism in this world view was but a necessary mode of advancement, undertaken in competition with other European powers playing for the same stakes. Returning to the narrative of *Vertue Rewarded* in this light, we may note the apparently anomalous recruitment of the Catholic Spaniard Astolfo to the Protestant forces of William of Orange, which is the reason for his presence in Ireland, along with the Williamite troops. As historian Ian McBride has noted however, William himself was a pragmatist and displayed religious tolerance. Despite Orangist propaganda that his war would deliver England from 'the tyranny of popery', he allowed Catholic officers in his army and promised the rulers of Austria and Spain that Catholics in Britain and Ireland would be free to practice their faith.[13] By falling foul of Spanish law for the honourable crime of killing his sister's betrayer, Astolfo is forced into fleeing his own country. Taking advantage of the Dutch recruitment of troops on the continent, as he later explains, 'for some design they had not yet divulged' (p. 129), he enters into a pragmatic and yet principled allegiance to William, raising the possibility by his example, in the context of a religiously divided settlement, that religious differences might be overcome after all. In the denouement of the novel, Faniaca's tracking down and reclamation of Astolfo in Clonmel frees Marinda's rich cousin Diana from his suit (she is evidently uncomfortable with his Catholicism as much as his Spanishness, though her father favours the match), allowing her to marry the English Protestant officer, Celadon.[14] The ending of this multi-layered novel with its several inter-communal, inter-religious, and inter-ethnic romances brought to the successful conclusion of matrimony, suggests the ambition of its fictional world to elide complex religious and cultural differences, and envisage the successful integration of hitherto disparate elements within the promised harmony of the Williamite settlement.

Travels into Several Remote Nations of the World (1726)

The historical experience of the early decades of the eighteenth century seemed, however, to offer a far more sombre view of Ireland's status under English rule than that suggested by the happy ending of Vertue Rewarded. What was evident to Jonathan Swift certainly by the first decade of the century was that, far from harmonising relations and ushering in an age of peace and prosperity, English rule had considerably damaged Ireland's economic prospects and resulted in an impoverished populace and an alienated ruling order. An early representation of Ireland's abandonment in Swift's extensive pamphleteering oeuvre appears in The Story of the Injured Lady (written 1707, first published 1746), a tale that offers in its allegory a neat antithesis of the moral of Vertue Rewarded. Here, the injured lady who represents Ireland sacrifices her virtue credulously, resulting in her lover 'affecting on all Occasions to shew his Authority, and to act like a Conqueror'.[15] The lover's shameful treatment of his lady and his exploitation of her estate offer obvious parallels with colonial practices, while the advice offered by the lady's friend in The Answer to the Injured Lady asserts in strict allegorical form the key elements of a coherent patriotic and anti-colonial stance, namely, constitutional equality, freedom of trade, liberty to develop resources, and the rejection of absenteeism. While these cardinal points, as Joseph McMinn has shown, would characterise Swift's political attitude throughout his career as an Irish patriot, it is the lady's moral imperfection – she is undone 'half by force, and half by consent' – that offers us the nearest clue to the perpetual ambivalence regarding Ireland which would inform Swift's works.[16]

Swift's most ambitious and unsettling exploration of such views appears, however, in *Gulliver's Travels*. Framed as a travel narrative, its four parts – and the strange lands they describe – provide a parodic and many-angled view of social and political relations both locally and globally. Though Gulliver is admittedly an Englishman, and there is little explicit mention of Ireland in the work, it is evident that Swift's Irishness informs many of the text's most trenchant observations on colonialism, most famously in Gulliver's ringing denunciation towards the end of Part IV:

> Natives are driven out or destroyed, their Princes tortured to discover their Gold; a free Licence given to all Acts of Inhumanity and Lust; the Earth reeking with the Blood of its Inhabitants: And this execrable Crew of Butchers employed in so pious an Expedition, is a *modern Colony* sent to convert an idolatrous and barbarous People.[17]

While this description of colonialism as a form of plunder, particularly of gold, is more obviously indebted to the 'black legend' of the Spanish conquest of the Indies than to Anglophone perceptions of British imperialism, other elements of the description, in particular its emphasis on the dispossession of natives and the conversion of 'an idolatrous and barbarous People', could apply quite obviously to the Irish example. Along such lines, a further distinction could be drawn between the English and Scottish occupiers of Ireland, implying a finer degree of irony with regard to the antagonism of dissenting Protestants (mainly the Scots Presbyterian settlers) to Irish Catholics, both being deluded in Swift's orthodox Anglican view, and savage to boot. Yet Swift's indignation at England's treatment of Ireland as a colony was largely limited to his perception of metropolitan perfidiousness with regard to the English settlers with whom he identified, while the deeply damaging effects of the Penal Laws on native Irish Catholics were overlooked, and English favour shown to the Presbyterian settlers on the basis of their shared Protestantism seemed misguided. At one level then, Gulliver's unsubtle attempt in the paragraph that follows to dissociate Britain from such criticisms and to commend the British as 'an Example to the whole World for their Wisdom, Care, and Justice in planting Colonies' (p. 441) is a masterstroke of irony, involving Swift's Irish patriotism to the full, even as it is now played out in a vastly expanded global critique of empire. At another though, it reflects an uneasy light on Swift's own highly ambivalent position as an English settler in Ireland, intent on the preservation of the Protestant, specifically Anglican, power within its legislative order.

Other aspects of British domination over Ireland are evident throughout *Gulliver's Travels*, for instance in the descriptions in Part III of the control exerted by the kingdom of Laputa over the Barnibarbians, while the 'interleaved' description, unpublished in Swift's lifetime, of the Lindalinian rebellion and plot to kill the king is an even more daring reference to the Irish resistance to Wood's coinage and the foiled Jacobite plot of 1722 to kill George II.[18] Swift's personal involvement in the campaign against Wood's infamous copper coinage through the publication of his *Drapier's Letters* had constituted his most celebrated work of patriotism, indicating further continuities between his stance as an Irish patriot and his critique of empire, particularly in its economic aspects, in *Gulliver's Travels*. Yet the excision of such material from *Gulliver's Travels* suggests a much broader, less particularised, framework of interpretation envisaged for the work as a whole. Comparing the specific focus of Swift's pamphleteering with the wide-angled and multi-dimensional view of *Gulliver's Travels*, one is struck by the extent to which the latter absorbs and transcends his earlier political thinking, assimilating such views within an expanding global order of European imperial domination led by Britain even as it insisted on the probity and integrity of its own supposedly civilising mission. While *The Story of the Injured Lady* offers a neat allegorical representation of colonial relations between England and Ireland (with Scotland, synecdochically representing her Presbyterian settlers in Ireland, appearing as Ireland's violently ill-tempered though higher-favoured rival for English affections), Gulliver's reference in the passage cited above to the gold-lust of colonial endeavour recalls the (English) stereotypical view of Spanish imperialism – a trope evident too in *Vertue Rewarded* – and his commendation, in defence of British colonialism, of 'the most vigilant and virtuous Governors, who have no other Views than the Happiness of the People over whom they preside' (p. 442), extends his critique, through its heavily laden irony, to virtually all forms of European colonialism since the discovery of the New World. Such universalising critiques of empire arguing that European colonialism was at its heart duplicitous and savage had, of course, strongly emerged in early Enlightenment thinking from Bartolomé de las Casas and Michel de Montaigne onwards, underpinned by the Lockean view of social contract whereby coercive government was held as necessarily invalid.[19]

Historians and literary critics have debated the views of the Anglo-Irish with regard to their own place as colonialists in Ireland. The historian

David Hayton insists, for instance, that 'members of the propertied elite in eighteenth-century Ireland did not regard themselves as a "colonial" caste', yet Swift's depiction of the Yahoos, as numerous critics have pointed out, includes several elements of the still-prevailing view of the 'wild Irish' in racial and behavioural terms.[20] Swift's suspicion of Catholicism and dissent, his despair with the wretchedness of the Irish populace, and his failure to champion the dispossessed native Irish, have resulted with some justice in the view of Swift's patriotism as primarily an Anglo-Irish phenomenon.[21] Nevertheless, I wish to argue here that Swift's use of ironic and fictional forms – most notably of course in *Gulliver's Travels* – enables conflicted and self-questioning modes of significance that transcend the merely personal elements of his world view. This is not to detach his works from a basis in historical understanding, but rather to acknowledge what is inherently unstable and ultimately unresolvable in the genres that he worked with, not least that of realism. What distinguishes Swift's irony in *A Modest Proposal* (1729) from mere hyperbole is the verisimilitude it achieves on many levels, including the shocking fact of cannibalism as a practice long associated with the Irish. The Irish had endured a cannibalistic reputation deriving from their legendary Scythian origin and revived in early modern writings such as those of Fynes Moryson, while Garcilaso's descriptions of the Antisuyans in Rycaut's influential translation of the *Royal Commentaries*, as noted above, offered an historical parallel to Ireland that had been explored in earlier fictional work.[22] Furthermore, the insistence of Swift's projector on the moderate and practical nature of his scheme is completely consistent with the tone of colonial authority bent on 'improvement', his very civility in attempting to alleviate Irish poverty leading him with irrefutable logic to the barbarity that he suggests.

Such aspects of realism – shared with the emerging genre of the novel in many ways – certainly added piquancy and bite (with no pun intended) to Swift's satire. Despite the amount of critical ink spilt on interpretations of *A Modest Proposal*, however, Swift's aims in the work are fairly obviously focused. The full title of the first edition of the pamphlet specified that the proposal aimed to prevent 'the children of poor people from being a burden to their parents or country, and for making them beneficial to the public', an irony that identifies its target squarely enough, in a way that the opening and title pages of the various early editions of *Gulliver's Travels* do not, leaving generations of critics puzzling over the nature and precise target of Swift's satire in his most famous work.[23] It is of course the multiplicity of meanings potentially generated in novelistic fiction through

its varied readership and locations of publication that operate most powerfully here, militating against any particular allegorical interpretation of the
text, however convincing, as definitive. Though *Gulliver's Travels* remains
in many ways an untypical example of the novel, standing the conventions
of realism on their head by playfully drawing its human protagonist
through distortions of reality and fantasy worlds in its successive parts,
its use of verisimilitude typified by Gulliver's precise observations and
measurements throughout is very much in keeping with the genre, just
as its rapid publication and dissemination through varied readerships
ensured the fecund generation of its significance well beyond the control
of its author or publishers. Swift's teasing immersion in the spirit of the
new genre which mimicked reality – including the manipulation of
Gulliver's image in the frontispiece in successive editions in relation to
his own portraits – suggests his willingness to allow the work to play on his
own self-image in ways that could be self-parodying, reflecting a self that
might confront itself with disconcerting accuracy. Gulliver's gradual recognition of himself as a Yahoo in Part IV of *Gulliver's Travels* – prompted by
the responses of Houyhnhnms and Yahoos alike, and in spite of his
eagerness to be accepted by, and mimicry of, the Houyhnhnms – seems
oddly to be resembled by Swift's evidently grudging admission in a letter of
1734 to the Scottish economist, Francis Grant, that he was, by virtue of his
birth in Ireland, 'a Teague, [or] an Irishman, or what People please', even
as he contended that this circumstance was a 'perfect Accident', and that
'the best Part' of his life had been spent in England.[24]

The History of Arsaces, Prince of Betlis (1774)

Born at Carrigogunnell in County Limerick of reputedly Scottish aristocratic descent, the author and barrister Charles Johnston registers in his
novels a Swiftian satirical influence which he applied to issues of public
morality, often in relation to empire.[25] Mostly remembered for his hugely
successful *Chrysal, or the Adventures of Guinea* – first published in 1760
though revised and extended through the several editions that quickly
followed – he published a series of other novels (as well as a poem and
a play) though none met with quite the same success. A caustic satirist of
the scandalous lives and histories of his age, and aptly dubbed by Walter
Scott as a 'prose Juvenal', his works display a remarkable awareness of the
growth and interconnectedness of empire during the period through their
geographical and historical reach.[26] Here, we will examine briefly the novel
he published in the febrile atmosphere leading to the American

Revolution, *The History of Arsaces, Prince of Betlis* (1774), a work that demonstrates a Swiftian inheritance, played out in the public context of heated discussions in Britain regarding the rebelliousness of American colonists in the west and the rapacious behaviour of Indian 'nabobs' (usually East India Company officials) in the east, who had reduced the populous and fertile region of Bengal to abject famine by 1770. Within this context events in America had notably revived patriotic sentiments in Ireland, significantly informing the intricate plot of Johnston's novel.

Set in an expansive east, and including in its sprawling narrative historical details of the founding of Carthage in the ninth century BCE and of the Muslim incursions of the seventh century into North Africa, amongst other instructive parallels, *The History of Arsaces* has been described as Johnston's 'most thoughtful treatment of empire and colonialism'.[27] The novel commences with the protagonist, an Arab youth named Selim, leaving the sheltered life of his home to wander the world. His various adventures give him an insight into a wide range of societies before he realises his true identity as Arsaces, the Prince of a small but fiercely resistant kingdom named Betlis, under siege by the emperor whom he regards as his master, Temugin (Genghis Khan). His reconciliation with the King of Betlis, his father, Astyages, on the battlefield touches the heart of Temugin, resulting in the restitution of Astyages's kingship, and the fulfilment of Arsaces's destiny as Prince of Betlis and heir to the kingdom. The overarching narrative is clearly then a loyal and conciliatory one in relation to the American context, though Astyages's acceptance of Temugin's imperial dispensation echoes patriotic arguments regarding legislative independence which had long been aired in Ireland:

> 'Conqueror of the world,' answered Astyages, 'it ill befitteth me to make terms with him into whose power I have willingly surrendered myself. If thou wilt permit me to study the happiness of my people; and preserve them in the enjoyment of those laws, which their fathers have handed down to them, we will render thee, with fidelity, all the services which can be expected from men who are free.'[28]

Despite Astyages's promise of fidelity here, the recognition of his people's freedom and of his own monarchical duty to them, renders his surrender a qualified one, its legalistic implications, echoing Molyneux's claims for Ireland, carefully framed by the barrister Johnston.

Though prudently distanced from contemporary events through spatial and temporal means, thereby avoiding possible suppression, *Arsaces* unmistakably refers to recent occurrences both in America and India, such

coincidences being linked by implicit reference to the global activities of
the East India Company. Selim's story frames the inset narrative of yet
another imperial tale, that of his spiritual father, Himilco, the sole survivor
of the imperial city state of Byrsa, modelled on Carthage. Himilco's travels
into India (which he recounts to Selim) confront him with a scene of
devastation which contemporaries would have recognised as descriptive of
the Bengal famine of 1769 to 1770 that had claimed around ten million lives
(around a quarter of the population), a disaster recalling analogously for
Irish readers experiences of the major famine of 1740 which Johnston
would have remembered from his student days in Dublin. The abject
deprivation of the people leads them into the most dehumanising forms
of moral depravity: 'Virgins offered themselves to violation in the streets,
for a mouthful of food. The son sold his father into slavery. The mother
devoured the infant which sucked her breast. The living were not able to
bury the dead' (p. 112). Such descriptions in which pity is mingled with
disgust at the utter depravity to which people are reduced by poverty and
hunger, including acts of cannibalism, recall the wretched condition of the
poor in early modern portrayals of Ireland, which had fed into Swift's Irish
pamphlets such as *A Short View of the State of Ireland* (1728) and *A Modest
Proposal*.[29] Confronted by such horrors, Himilco gains an insight into the
causes of the country's rapid decline through the explanation provided by
a Brahmin, a representative of the elite native order within the emerging
colonial order of eighteenth-century India, who reveals that their hardy
oppressors had arrived from the west 'in want and wretchedness', but
quickly 'taking advantage of our pusillanimity and weakness' had so
reduced the rulers and the industry of the people through their exploitative
trading practices that the country had been utterly destroyed (pp. 103–04).
Though the savagery and rapaciousness of the colonialists are castigated,
there is acknowledgement too of the deficiencies of the East Indians who
lack the wit or courage to resist them. Yet the Brahmin notes presciently
that the wickedness of these adventurers would not go unpunished, 'heaven, by a signal instance of its justice, hath made them avenge our wrongs,
upon their own heads' (p. 108). Alluding to the charges of corruption
brought against East India Company officials such as Robert Clive, and the
widespread protests against trading monopolies in Ireland and America
from the early 1770s, the Brahmin's premonitory words suggest here
a providential turn of justice that would consume the perpetrators of
such iniquities despite their present wealth and arrogance.

Like Swift's however, Johnston's powerful satire of imperial hubris
cannot be read without qualification as a critique of empire *per se*.

Though he saw deeply into the global workings of empire and warned his age uncompromisingly of its moral failings, his own loyalist and providential views shape his understanding and limit the extent of his critique. His historical vision, though encompassing a wide range of earlier societies, is yet circumscribed by his loyal view of the perfection of monarchical government, though betrayed as he saw it in his own times by the interests of commercial empire and a corrupt political order.[30] Though it has not been possible within this chapter to examine in detail the many iterations of empire that are explored in the vast historical and geographical perspective provided by *Arsaces*, we may conclude with a specifically Gulliver-inspired moment of imperial fantasy which suggests as well the distance that Johnston has travelled from his predecessor.

Departing from Himilco's directions along his travels, the redoubtable Selim (as he still regards himself) enters a land in which he encounters a race of tiny creatures, no more than two cubits in height, whose naively comical reactions of fear and surprise on seeing him closely recall the Lilliputians' response to Gulliver. Their lives, however, are soon threatened by a hideous creature, more slender and taller than any man, with a 'tawny skin [...] thinly shaded with hair of the same colour'. Though Selim immediately recognises the creature as 'one of those animals which make the middle link between the brute and human natures in the chain of life', the resemblance of 'his flat visage' to the human face brings 'shame and horror' to him (p. 148). Slaying the horrid creature which preys on the little creatures, Selim is regarded as their saviour and given shelter in their subterranean city. Without any curiosity regarding the outside world and knowing no passion whatsoever, their simple underground lives represent a form of savage contentment of which Selim soon tires: 'convinced of the contemptible ignorance of those torpid visionaries', he leaves them without regret (p. 153). Selim's untroubled destruction of the humanoid being – even though it is suggestive of proto-evolutionary views of humanity – and his firm affirmation of passion and knowledge, represent therefore a determinate moral choice rejecting the contentment of a savage state. His final discovery of his destiny as a Prince is fully in keeping with his acceptance of a divine political order ensuring a notion of human freedom that is properly secured through imperial and royal prerogatives. Johnston's exploration of other worlds, comparable to Swift's, reveals a fuller understanding of the insidious workings of empire, and yet a more comfortable and stable view of European superiority.

Conclusions

Surveying early Irish fiction from *Vertue Rewarded* to *Arsaces* via Swift, we see how colonial metaphors and debates regarding legislative independence for Ireland are gradually altered through history into a global understanding of imperialist practices through arms, intrigue, and commerce. These representations were implicated in the steady transformation of genre over the period, as idealised views of empire – exhibited in the spread of civility, learning, and enlightenment – were revealed through the passage of time as the unpalatable truths of imperial plunder and conquest. Nevertheless, such a realisation was not achieved through a sudden process of historical illumination. Rather, the transformation of genre and of historical understanding involved here carried within itself the seeds of its own recognition, as the heroic ideals of the classical world, far from representing a monolithic and glorious edifice of the past, were ever open to reinterpretation and actualisation as educated writers of the eighteenth century knew well. The savagery and primitivism of the humanoid creature slain by Selim in *The History of Arsaces* are met by his discovery, within the same desert, of the ruins of ancient empires reminiscent of Rome and Carthage, the images of imperial hubris counterposing those of mere barbarity, and now satirically directed towards British attitudes to its American colonies. Though each of the authors I have discussed above wrote to different historical and political moments and worked within a genre that was both rapidly changing and solidifying, the three fictions display remarkable continuities in their grapplings with the savage implications of empire and its precarious grasp on civility. Though largely incipient and embryonic in this period, such insights into the nature of empire would develop, over the course of the following century, into the ideas of nationhood that would come to shape Ireland's postcolonial destiny.

Notes

1. For rewarding historical discussions of this phenomenon, see Nicholas Canny and Anthony Pagden, eds., *Colonial Identity in the Atlantic World, 1500–1800* (Princeton University Press, 1987), pp. 159–212; Colin Kidd, 'The Weave of Irish Identities, 1600–1790', in *British Identities before Nationalism: Ethnicity and Nationhood in the Atlantic World, 1600–1800* (Cambridge University Press, 1999), pp. 146–84; and David Hayton, 'Anglo-Irish Attitudes', in *The Anglo-Irish Experience, 1680–1730: Religion, Identity and Patriotism* (Woodbridge, Suffolk: Boydell & Brewer, 2012), pp. 25–48.

2. William Molyneux, *The Case of Ireland Stated*, ed. J. G. Simms (Dublin: Cadenus Press, 1977), p. 115.

3. Mary Louise Pratt, *Imperial Eyes: Travel Writing and Transculturation* (London: Routledge, 1992), p. 5.

4. *The Cambridge Edition of the Works of Jonathan Swift*, Vol. XVI: *Gulliver's Travels*, ed. David Womersley (Cambridge University Press, 2012); *Vertue Rewarded; or, The Irish Princess*, ed. Ian Campbell Ross and Anne Markey (Dublin: Four Courts Press, 2010); and Charles Johnston, *The History of Arsaces, Prince of Betlis*, ed. Daniel Sanjiv Roberts (Dublin: Four Courts Press, 2014). Further quotations from these works will be from these editions and will be cited in the text.

5. The significance of Protestantism for the development of the novel was argued by Ian Watt in *The Rise of the Novel: Studies in Defoe, Richardson and Fielding* (London: Chatto and Windus, 1957), and although aspects of his work have been challenged, many of its arguments continue to influence our ways of thinking about the novel.

6. See Ian McBride, *Eighteenth-Century Ireland: The Isle of Slaves* (Dublin: Gill and Macmillan, 2009), pp. 159–93.

7. Jane Ohlmeyer, 'A Laboratory for Empire?: Early Modern Ireland and English Imperialism', in *Ireland and the British Empire*, ed. Kevin Kenny (Oxford University Press, 2004), pp. 26–60 (p. 58).

8. For a discussion of the novel's 'fakelore', see *Vertue Rewarded*, p. 17.

9. Ibid., p. 116.

10. Ian Campbell Ross, '"A Very Knowing American": The Inca Garcilaso de la Vega and Swift's *Modest Proposal*', *Modern Language Quarterly* 68.4 (2007), 493–516.

11. Rycaut's full title for the work *The Royal Commentaries by the Inca Garcilasso de la Vega* follows Garcilaso's own practice and the various Spanish editions of his work; see Ross, '"A Very Knowing American"', p. 510.

12. El Ynca Garcilaso de la Vega, *Royal Commentaries of Peru*, trans. Sir Paul Rycaut (London, 1688), n.p.

13. McBride, *Eighteenth-Century Ireland*, p. 160.

14. The *OED* records Diana as the first self-identifying '*Irish*-woman' (albeit from fiction), quoting her concerns regarding marriage to Astolfo: 'those on the continent make such saucy domineering Husbands, that no free-born *Irish*-woman will endure their slavery' (*Vertue Rewarded*, p. 104). See 'Irishwoman, n.', *Oxford English Dictionary Online* [accessed 15 August 2019].

15. *Swift's Irish Writings: Selected Prose and Poetry*, ed. Carole Fabricant and Robert Mahony (New York: Palgrave Macmillan, 2010), pp. 4–5.

16. Joseph McMinn, 'A Weary Patriot: Swift and the Formation of an Anglo-Irish Identity', *Eighteenth-Century Ireland / Iris an dá chultúr* 2 (1987), 103–13 (p. 105).

17. Swift, *Gulliver's Travels*, p. 441.

18. Ibid., pp. 741–43; see also pp. 643–46 and 721–24 for a discussion of the ambiguous textual status of this manuscript passage (in his friend Charles Ford's hand) amongst other supposed errors and omissions from early editions of the work. For a critical discussion of its political implications, see Ian Higgins, 'Jonathan Swift and the Jacobite Diaspora', in *Reading Swift: Papers from the Fourth Münster Symposium on Jonathan Swift*, ed. Hermann J. Real and Helgard Stöver-Leidig (München: Wilhelm Fink Verlag, 2003), pp. 87–104 (p. 98).

19. Claude Rawson, *God, Gulliver, and Genocide: Barbarism and the European Imagination, 1492–1945* (Oxford University Press, 2001), pp. 17–91, and Emer Nolan, 'Swift: The Patriot Game', *British Journal for Eighteenth-Century Studies* 21 (1998), 39–53.

20. Hayton, 'Anglo-Irish Attitudes', p. 27.

21. See, for example, McMinn, 'A Weary Patriot'.

22. For the tradition of associating the native Irish with various kinds of barbarism, including cannibalism, see Rawson, *God, Gulliver, and Genocide*, pp. 69–91.

23. That the pamphlet concerned 'poor people in Ireland' was a gloss added to the title page of the first London edition, unnecessary for the Irish readership to which the pamphlet was first addressed. I am grateful to Ian Campbell Ross for drawing this to my attention.

24. *The Correspondence of Jonathan Swift, D.D.*, ed. David Woolley, 5 vols (Frankfurt am Main: Peter Lang, 1999–2014), III, p. 730.

25. See the biographical note in my edition of Johnston, *The History of Arsaces*, pp. 224–33.

26. Daniel S. Roberts, 'A "Teague" and a "True Briton": Charles Johnstone, Ireland and Empire', *Irish University Review* 41.1 (2011), 133–50. It might be noted that while Johnston's name has been spelt with a concluding 'e' for over a century and a half – ever since the publication of Walter Scott's influential memoir of his life and works – more recent critical practice, subsequent to the article cited here, has reverted to the spelling that appears most commonly in his own work and amongst his contemporaries.

27. Aileen Douglas, 'The Novel before 1800', in *The Cambridge Companion to the Irish Novel*, ed. John Wilson Foster (Cambridge University Press, 2006), pp. 22–38 (p. 33).

28. Johnston, *The History of Arsaces*, p. 206.

29. Rawson, *God, Gulliver, and Genocide*, pp. 232–37.

30. In this regard, the positioning of Johnston here might be compared with that of Oliver Goldsmith in Michael Griffin, *Enlightenment in Ruins: The Geographies of Oliver Goldsmith* (Lewisburg, PA: Bucknell University Press, 2013).

Gender and Sexuality

PART IV

Gender and Sexuality

The Province of Poetry: Women Poets in Early Eighteenth-Century Ireland

Aileen Douglas

Mary Barber begins her 'Preface' to *Poems on Several Occasions* (1735) by remarking, 'I am sensible that a Woman steps out of her Province when she presumes to write for the Press', and then immediately mitigates any perceived transgression by insisting that she began writing poetry to aid the education of her children and for charitable purposes.[1] To an extent, Barber's claim is indeed borne out by the volume, containing as it does several poems exhorting readers to charitable acts or concerned with the education of the young. At the same time, other evidence suggests that the 'Preface' gives an incomplete account of Barber's poetic ambitions. For *Poems on Several Occasions* is a fine material object: an expensive, handsome quarto, adorned with many ornaments, clearly designed to be noticed. Additionally, and significantly in terms of the publication of poetry in the first half of the eighteenth century, the book includes one of the most impressive subscription lists of that period.[2] Subscribers to the publication would have paid a certain amount up front – thereby funding the volume – and paid the remainder once copies were available. Generally regarded as a 'half-way house between dependence on a single patron to underwrite a book and reliance upon sales', publication by subscription required on the author's part forwardness, or connections, or both, to be successful.[3] Even as *Poems on Several Occasions* draws attention to Barber's modest, decorous beginnings as a writer, the volume manifests ambition and a desire for recognition.

To speak of Barber's collection is, in fact, a simplification. Mary Barber writes the preface to the volume and the majority of the poems are hers, but the volume also contains poems by five other individuals, including some poems by Barber's son Constantine, and six poems by Constantia Grierson.[4] One of the most frequently used of early eighteenth-century titles, 'Poems on Several Occasions' (or slight variations thereof) afforded considerable flexibility. In this particular volume, poems are occasioned by the sociability of the places in which they were written: Dublin, and, on the other side of the Irish Sea, the fashionable spa towns of Bath and Tunbridge Wells. Slight events such as dinners and outings occasion some poems, but others respond to profound experiences of illness and loss. Such thematic and tonal variety can be disconcerting to modern readers. Then there are poems that take as theme the occasions of their creation and original exchange, and therefore recreate in printed form a version of the specific form of sociability from which they emerged: that of scribal circulation.[5] An effect of this disarming strategy is to suggest the poems, albeit now appearing in the special form of the commercial, printed volume, were not presumptuously written 'for' the press. Rather, the volume presents many of its occasional poems as relatively mundane objects privately exchanged, often between women, and enacts a decorous sociability shared by the sexes but in which women are predominant. Given these features, *Poems on Several Occasions* might be considered one of those 'intermediation points' described by Betty A. Schellenberg, in this case, a place where the genres and conventions of scribal production are adapted to 'serve the ends of the print medium'.[6]

Guided by the pattern of assertion and apologia initiated by Barber's 'Preface', this chapter considers *Poems on Several Occasions* so as to tease out a variety of ways – thematic, rhetorical, and material – through which women poets in early eighteenth-century Ireland might negotiate readers' expectations of gender, and of poetry, in publishing their work. In her 'Preface', Barber emphasises that the poet merely continues the work of the mother, and vindicates the publication of poems written 'to form the Minds of Youth' (p. xxv). Those poems by Barber featuring her son, Constantine, are among her best known, possibly because they have been regularly anthologised. Less familiar is the other major thematic vindication the volume offers: the poem as prompt to the exercise of charity. If poetry is to be thought of as enabling specific acts of charity then the poem's readers come dramatically into focus, not as impersonal purchasers of a printed commodity, but rather as members of a local, particular, social grouping. More intimate bonds enable the volume's most inventive poetic strategy: that of ventriloquism. Taking voices other than her own, especially the voice of her son Con, allows Barber modestly to deflect attention from her own person, while also, as shall be seen, engaging in quite assertive rhetorical acts.[7] A parallel process of assertion and deflection is embodied in the material aspect of the volume. As an expensive book and desirable object, *Poems on Several Occasions* makes a statement. At the same time, the act of reading encourages awareness of a pre-existing and rather different material context: the ordinary world of things. Poems 'on several occasions' are also poems – literally – on several things: on fans, on rings, on books, on seaside rocks. Awareness of the layers of materiality within *Poems on Several Occasions* allows sight of poetry as an extended hinterland, marked by various formations and manifestations, of which the printed volume is only the most visible.

Poems on Several Occasions is a transitional, hybrid work, both in terms of gender and nation. Built around the figures of Constantia Grierson and Mary Barber, the volume is suspended between modes of female author-ship that are familiar, modest, and sociable and those that are newer, assertive, and individual. In regard to national identity, the settings and themes of the poems manifest what might be called a flexible differentia-tion. Dublin is vividly realised in the poems of both women, but so too are English settings in the poems of Barber. Barber participates in the fashion-able life of English spa towns, but announces herself 'A Native of *Hibernia*' (p. 147). Signs of patriot economics are found in the poems of both women, Barber celebrating Swift as Drapier and Hibernia's 'Patriot', and Grierson bemoaning the flow of Irish gold to Albion (pp. 71–72, 139). Significantly, though, such sentiments did not exclude canvassing for English subscribers or militate against the volume's London publication, facts suggesting 'national' identification to be partial, as well as flexible.

Prior to the publication of *Poems on Several Occasions*, Barber, the wife of a linen draper, had published individual poems, anonymously, in both Dublin and London. Grierson was a midwife by training, but she also worked alongside her printer husband, George, in the family business. Acquiring subscribers for *Poems on Various Occasions* – it is only the third example of a woman publishing a volume of poetry this way – was Barber's work.[8] In the book's substantial preface she gives significant attention to the history of the subscription (possibly in the way of self-defence, as the publication had been delayed owing to her illness). In contrast, the figure of Grierson, whose poetry appeared in the volume posthumously, and who set 'so little Value' on her poems 'that she neglected to leave Copies behind her but of very few' represents an apparently self-effacing version of the female poet (p. xxvii). The absorbing dynamic of the volume, in which the poetic representations of Grierson and Barber at times contrast dramatically but at others blend sympathetically, is first established in the volume's rich paratextual material. This includes a letter by Jonathan Swift, a 'Dedication' and 'Preface' by Barber, and a set of commendatory prefatory verses by Grierson addressed to Barber. It offers a complex apologia for female publication, one that intimates how female poets can alter the poetic land-scape through the inclusion of new subject matter and perspectives.

Mary Barber's first publications, appearing in 1725, consisted of three anonymous poems. One of these was addressed to Lord Carteret, the well-regarded and cultured Lord Lieutenant of Ireland, with the others being addressed to his wife and daughter respectively. In the later 1720s Barber became part of a literary circle that included Jonathan Swift, Dean of St Patrick's Cathedral and at the time the city's pre-eminent literary figure, and his friend and fellow poet and churchman Patrick Delany, who was Barber's neighbour in Glasnevin, just to the north of the city.[9] Other members included Elizabeth Sican, none of whose writings are known to survive, the clergyman Matthew Pilkington (who published his own *Poems on Several Occasions* in 1730), and his wife Laetitia, as well as Constantia Grierson. Writing to Alexander Pope in 1730, Swift used the poetic activities of Barber, Sican, and Grierson to promote Dublin's cultural claims over those of the metropolitan centre, asking rhetorically: 'Can you shew such a Triumfeminate in London?'[10] According to Laetitia Pilkington's *Memoirs* (1748–54), the driving force behind the circle was in fact Dr Delany, who often held a '*Senatus Consultum*' to correct the group's poems, 'at which were present sometimes the Dean, (in the Chair) but always Mrs. *Grierson*, Mr. *Pilkington*, the Doctor, and myself'.[11] Rendered confident by the reception her poems met within this group, Mary Barber had, by 1730, decided to mount a subscription campaign in England and for this purpose went to fashionable Tunbridge Wells, where she contributed a number of poems, again anonymously, to an anthology, *Tunbrigialia*.[12]

It is probable that Constantia Grierson was introduced to this group of writers by Laetitia Pilkington. From a very modest background in Kilkenny, Grierson had in the early 1720s trained as a midwife with Laetitia's father, the obstetrician Jan van Lewen, and had lived in the Van Lewen home. Despite meagre schooling, Grierson gained a reputation for formidable learning and was esteemed for the editions of Terence (1727) and Tacitus (1730) on which she worked with her husband.[13] That Constantia was named alongside George Grierson in petitioning for the patent of the King's Printer is Ireland is an important recognition of her significant role in the family enterprise.[14] At the same time, Constantia remained reticent regarding the publication of her poetry and prior to *Poems on Several Occasions* only one of her poems had appeared, anonymously, in print.[15]

Opening *Poems on Several Occasions*, however, the reader encounters neither Barber nor Grierson, but Jonathan Swift. Addressing himself to 'the Right Honourable John, Earl of Orrery', Swift first delivers his 'Opinion' on the propriety of Barber dedicating her poems to the nobleman before then sketching out an image of the virtuous Orrery such as Barber might design in the 'Dedication' to come. Briefly commending Barber as a woman of wit, good sense, humility, and gratitude, Swift concludes that she '*seemeth to have a true poetical Genius, better cultivated than could well be expected, either from her Sex, or the Scene she hath acted in, as the Wife of a Citizen*' (p. vii). Only when Swift has prepared the way, does Barber herself address Orrery as a patron. Swift's letter, addressed to another elite male figure, and recommending to his protection the poems that follow, might be seen as containing female creativity within elite homosociality. That is, however, only part of the picture. As Swift himself makes clear, it is Barber who is the instigator here: she who wrote to Swift requesting his intervention, and she who has not only asked for a copy of his address to Orrery but also for permission to make it public. In this light, Emily O'Flaherty's contention that Barber's significance lies in her achievement as a 'woman poet who attracted an impressive list of sub-scribers, and also in her development of sophisticated strategies in order to garner that support', rings true.[16] Barber, in her 'Dedication', manages to combine praise of Orrery with compliments to Swift, so putting her own stamp on Swift's letter and drawing attention to its value: 'Those who know how fearless Dr. SWIFT hath ever been in *satirising Vice* in the highest Stations, will never suspect his *Praise* of the Great to proceed from any thing, but the Desire of doing Justice to uncommon, unsullied, Merit' (p. x).

Barber's further praise of Orrery is deliberately offered in terms of a female perspective on virtue: 'A good Son, and a good Husband, are Characters that include whatever is most amiable in human Nature; at least, if Mothers and Wives, may be allowed for Judges' (p. xii). The validity of a female perspective is further buttressed in the 'Preface' when Barber confronts the idea that the 'Publick' can have little to do with verses written between mother and son. '*[N]othing can be of more Use to Society than the taking early Care to form the Minds of Youth*', she asserts, making the further claim that such concerns are '*the best Apology a Woman could make for writing at all*' (pp. xxv–xxvi). The first half of the 'Preface' details Barber's debts to her patrons, the encouragement of her publication by her social betters, and identifies a particular set of themes that vindicate female publication.

Subsequently, Barber turns away from her own poetry to provide a eulogy on the life and work of her fellow poet, Constantia Grierson, virtuous, learned, and tragically dead at the age of twenty-seven: '*it is a Pleasure [. . .] to think that [the poems] written by other Hands, will always make this Collection of Value*' (p. xxvi). It was primarily through Barber's brief biographical account of Grierson – often excerpted or paraphrased in subsequent publications – that later eighteenth-century knowledge of Grierson and her works was diffused.[17]

From the late sixteenth and into the early eighteenth centuries, posthumous publication of both male and female writers was a well-established practice, of particular import for women. There is no more complete representation of the modest female poet than she who, having no interest in fame, receives a posthumous publication at the hands of a relative.[18] In 1716, the Irish landowner and diplomat, Robert Molesworth, publishing the poems of his daughter, Mary Monck (1678–1715), presented them as:

> the Product of the leisure Hours of a Young Gentlewoman lately Dead, who in a Remote Country Retirement, without any Assistance but that of a good Library, and without omitting the daily Care due to a large Family, not only perfectly acquired the several Languages here made use of, but the good Morals and Principles contain'd in those Books, so as to put them in Practice, as well during her Life and languishing Sickness, as at the Hour of her Death.[19]

Dedicating the volume to Caroline of Ansbach, the Princess of Wales, Molesworth said the poems were 'as we found most of them in the Scrittore after her Death, written with her own Hand, little expecting, and as little desiring the Publick shou'd have any Opportunity either of Applauding or Condemning them'.[20]

The practice of posthumous publication made familiar the trope of the modest female poet indifferent to fame, whose material legacy was only secured by the intervention of others. Where *Poems on Several Occasions* deviates from such earlier examples as those of Anne Killigrew and Mary Monck is that the role of compiler, there the preserve of a male relative, is taken not only by a woman, but by a woman poet. In addition, that woman poet is herself a subject in the verse. In the 'Preface', Barber refers to poems in her own favour written by Grierson as proof that women may 'endeavour to raise the Character of each other', and this underlines the significance of female address and support throughout the volume. That Grierson is said in the 'Preface' to have set little value on her own fine poems in English, also gives added point to the poem with which *Poems on Several Occasions* opens, '*To Mrs.* Mary BARBER, *under the Name of* SAPPHIRA: *Occasion'd by the Encouragement She met with in* England, *to publish her Poems by Subscription*'. Prominent in the volume's paratextual materials, this poem sets up a dialogue with Barber's own 'Preface' and ensures that the elite male homosociality of Swift and Orrery is paralleled by female-authored commentary on women poets and publication.

Dated 5 January 1732, the year of Grierson's death, 'To Mrs. Mary Barber' describes Barber's virtues as a woman and a poet and endorses her efforts towards publication. In the course of the poem, Grierson directly addresses possible subscribers: 'These Works, which Modesty conceal'd in Night, / Your Candor, gen'rous BRITONS, brings to Light.' Whereas the themes of love and war have dominated poetry, Barber, Grierson asserts, will offer 'Themes, in themselves, alike sublime, and new' and she proceeds to give as an example 'Beneficence', or charity, a theme 'almost unknown to Song' (pp. xlv–xlvi). The very title of 'To Mrs. Mary Barber, under the Name of Sapphira' brings together two overlapping poetic worlds: the world of the Dublin-based coterie in which manuscript poems circulate and in which Grierson and Barber participate, and the world of publication by subscription in which Barber appears as an author under her proper name. The poem is one of six poems by Grierson in *Poems on Several Occasions*, although a further two poems and a fragment were subsequently to appear embedded in Laetitia Pilkington's *Memoirs*.[21] Critics have commented that both Barber and Pilkington, each of whom had to contend with some notoriety, sought to benefit by association with Grierson and her 'unimpeachable reputation' for piety and domestic propriety.[22] There is something to this notion. In 1731, Barber had been involved in a murky incident involving forged letters on the state of Ireland purportedly by Swift presented to Queen Caroline, letters which warmly praised Barber's poetry. In 1732, she had also been briefly imprisoned for importing seditious material (this time actually by Swift) into England.[23] Pilkington, by the time she published her *Memoirs*, had separated in scandalous circumstances from her husband and been excluded from the Dublin circle. Indeed, her *Memoirs* were written in part to justify her conduct.[24] Notwithstanding these circumstances, the textual evidence of Grierson's 'To Mrs. Mary Barber' suggests that it is wrong to think of the relationship between Barber and Grierson simply in terms of appropriation. Grierson, as her direct address to the 'gen'rous BRITONS' who are the putative subscribers to Barber's volume demonstrates, was happy to have her own work read beyond the restricted circulation of a Dublin coterie so as to promote her fellow female writer in English print culture.

Both Grierson and Barber justify the publication of *Poems on Several Occasions* through the poems' novel encouragement of 'beneficence', and in the volume the exercise of charity is a recurring theme, significantly given a variety of treatments. 'To the Right Honourable the Lady Dowager Torrington' and 'Written for a Gentlewoman in Distress. To her Grace,

Adelida, Dutchess of Shrewsbury' are part of a group that presents poetry as instrumental in exciting women's charity to other women, and the poet as the crucial intermediary in the process. Addressing the Lady Dowager Torrington, Barber comments that her own circumstances do not permit her to exercise charity as she would like, but that she feels 'Delight' when she can inspire such action in others:

> From giving Wealth, my Hands are ty'd;
> That great Felicity's deny'd.
> Yet have I, sometimes, the Delight,
> To help a Wretch, by what I write;
> To make some happier Bosoms melt,
> And heal the Woes, they never felt.   (p. 34)

It was with precisely this kind of poem that Barber began her public poetry in 1725, with 'The Widow Gordon's Petition', written on behalf of an officer's widow and presented to Lady Carteret, the Lord Lieutenant's wife. This highly eloquent poem, also included in *Poems*, begins with the widow speaking of her impoverishment and inability to feed her children, before she turns to 'Fair CARTERET', addressing the noblewoman as one who 'never hears the Wretched sigh in vain'. The poem ends with a powerful reversal in which the widow imagines herself and Carteret now before the 'last Tribunal'. In this image, however, the poor widow no longer petitions Carteret, but rather intercedes on behalf of her benefactor: 'That she, who made the Fatherless her Care, / The Fulness of Cœlestial Joys may share' (pp. 4–5). In its ventriloquism and ability to unsettle power relationships even as it invokes them, 'The Widow Gordon's Petition' is characteristic of some of the best of Barber's writing. Speaking in the Widow Gordon's voice, Barber makes something out of nothing and moves from a position of abjection to one of power. Here, the poet is apparently absent, her authority masked by her assumption of the voice of the impoverished woman. In such poems the female poet assumes a voice not her own to petition more fortunate women, 'ye Daughters, who at ease recline' on behalf of female indigence. The poems both generate and record a kind of female virtue, projecting a feminocentric society in which the poet is vindicated by the worthy role she plays. Barber used an intermediary, Thomas Tickell, to bring the anonymous poem to Lady Carteret's attention. The 'Preface' to *Poems on Several Occasions* gives the further history of what happened, recording not only that Lady Carteret interested herself in raising a 'considerable Sum' for the Widow, but also that her determination to 'find out the Author' of the poem eventually led to Barber gaining 'the Protection of that whole Noble

Family' (pp. xviii–xix). The episode was clearly important to Barber's sense of herself as a poet, and a decade later she was proudly referring to it in verse. To be successful as it was, gaining Barber patrons and the Widow Gordon relief, the petition had first to be read in a social context that permitted direct contact between the subject of the poem, its author, and the aristocratic woman to whom it was addressed.

In a contrasting, smaller group of poems, Barber uses satire and astringent wit to chastise the hypocrisy and self-deception of those who are in a position to be charitable, but are not. 'An unanswerable Apology for the Rich', begins with Castalio on bended knees asking heaven when he will have power to 'raise up Merit in Distress'. To this the poem expostulates: 'How do our Hearts deceive us here! / He gets Ten Thousand Pounds a Year.' The poem offers a witty inventory of Castalio's ever-increasing wants for brocade, jewels, lace, paintings, plate, and china before concluding: 'Wou'd Heav'n but send Ten Thousand more, / He'd give – just as he did before' (p. 19). Castalio deceives himself that he will ever aid distressed Merit because all his resources, no matter how extensive, are absorbed by his own conspicuous consumption. The failure of the wealthy to be charitable is also the subject of a second satiric poem, addressed 'To the Reverend Dr. L—'. The occasion is one of the most common, and fashionable, forms of eighteenth-century philanthropy: a sermon to raise funds for the children of a charity school. This particular case, a sermon in support of Charity-Children at Tunbridge Wells, is, however, one '*where the Collection was small*'. The poem comes to a withering conclusion:

> 'Tis said, *Hibernia* boasts a Flood,
> Famous for petrefying Wood:
> Tunbridge, thy Min'ral Streams, we know,
> A stranger Transformation show:
> Their dire effects the Wretched feel;
> Thy Waters turn the Heart to Steel. (p. 141)

The Hibernian flood famous for petrifying wood was Lough Neagh in Ulster, which had been the subject of investigations of the Dublin Philosophical Society in the 1680s.[25] As a fashionable spa town, Tunbridge Wells depended on the reputation of its mineral waters, here cleverly represented as bringing not health but hardened, steely, hearts. Unlike the generalised account of Castalio, this second poem is placed in a very specific place and time, and was one of a group of poems Barber originally published in *Tunbrigialia*.

Barber's poems on charity should feature prominently in more general discussions of her relationships with her readers. Of the fifty-six people Barber addresses directly in her 117 poems fifty were subscribers, and critics speculate as to whether her desire to please patrons 'severely compromised the quality of her poetry'.[26] Two points should be made here. 'The Widow Gordon's Petition' and 'To the Reverend Dr. L—' are very different in tone, and demonstrate Barber's flexibility and versatility in the manipulation of poetic voice. She can write ingratiatingly so as to 'melt' the bosoms of such well-born patrons as 'fair CARTERET' in poems that work through indirection and masking. She is also capable, however, of sharply applying the satiric lash to her fashionable readers, and attacking 'hypocrisy and injustice with a strong and individual voice'.[27] Such variations are easy enough to observe. What is less immediately apparent to a modern reader, encountering Barber's poems in a rare book room or, more likely, on a database, is just how diluted our experience of these poems on charity necessarily is. In their initial, local, context these poems could actually excite aid for the Widow Gordon, or force recognition of the reader's charitable failures. Outside that context, the reader is exempted from action, as it were, and is consequently less likely to realise just how serious a vindication of Barber's poetry was her treatment of 'Beneficence'. Print publication removes poems from the events that originally occasioned them. In Barber's case this can have dramatically varied effects: the potential of the poems on charity is diminished, but the possible sycophancy of poems addressed to patrons is amplified.

Just as Barber's poems on charity yield new kinds of public acknowledgement, so too do her poems on domestic relationships. Praising Orrery in her 'Preface', Barber had drawn attention to the importance of *male* domestic virtues if 'mothers and wives may be allowed for judges'. In *Poems on Several Occasions*, Barber, as wife and mother, does judge. That poetry provides a proper vehicle for the assertion of rational maternal authority is an important principle in the volume and one voiced in witty and unexpected ways. '*Written for my Son, and spoken by him in School, upon his Master's first bringing in a Rod*', opposes the 'Instrument of Tyranny' through which the school master expresses his power with Lockean precepts that involve teaching through play:

> TAKE my Advice; pursue that Rule:
> You'll make a Fortune by your School.
> You'll soon have all the Elder Brothers,
> And be the Darling of their Mothers.   (p. 37)

In '*An Apology written for my Son to his Master, who had commanded him to write Verses on the Death of the late Lord*———', Barber insinuates her own poetic and maternal authority into the schoolroom by having her son voice Barber's own objections to inauthentic and deceptive panegyric:

> I Beg your Scholar you'll excuse,
> Who dares no more debase the Muse.
> My Mother says, if e'er she hears
> I write again on worthless Peers,
> Whether they're living Lords, or dead,
> She'll box the Muse from out my Head.   (p. 50)

The 'short impish' line here is, as Margaret Doody observes, most likely a model influenced by Swift. Entirely without pretension, colloquial, and comic, it nonetheless permits Barber to assert herself as an authority – 'My Mother says' – and as the protector of the muse.[28]

Comedy and ventriloquism allow the female poet to upend hierarchies and position herself as the defender of 'the Muse', but it is exclusion from traditional forms of learning and expression that are ventriloquised in one of Constantia Grierson's poems. Spoken as by one of Con's schoolfellows, the poem treats of Con's poor performance in Latin. Having long admired Con's facility in '*English* Verse', his 'undeceiv'd Companions' now realise by his failure to perform so well in Latin that his achievements are not his own: 'The Muse, thy Mother, only speaks in thee.' In a rather stolid fable, the schoolfellow then advises Con that the gifts heaped by the Muses on his mother excited the jealousy of Phoebus who, determined to contain the achievements of Barber, denied to her Latin, the 'universal Tongue' of great poetry (pp. 87–89). Recalling that Grierson had apparently taught herself not only Latin but also Greek and possibly Hebrew, one might speculate if Grierson is indirectly drawing attention to her own competence here. Be that as it may, Grierson's poem extends the ventriloquising play within the volume, as the poems spoken by the boys draw attention to the proper uses of poetry and the restrictions faced by women seeking a public voice.

The assertion of the domestic scene and domestic relationships as proper poetic themes is brilliantly executed in '*The Conclusion of a Letter to the Rev. Mr. C—*', which begins:

> 'Tis Time to conclude; for I make it a Rule,
> To leave off all Writing, when *Con.* comes from School.   (p. 58)

Con dislikes what his mother has already written and advises that she send the Rev. Mr C '*a poetical* Letter', thereby initiating a passage in which

Barber ventriloquises the latter's hostility to women's writing and his desiderata for a wife as upper servant. This in turn is broken off:

> THUS far I had written – Then turn'd to my Son,
> To give him Advice, ere my Letter was done.   (p. 60)

The letter then concludes with advice to Con on the qualities he should seek in a wife, as well as on his own conduct in matrimony:

> WHEN you gain her Affection, take care to preserve it;
> Lest others persuade her, you do not deserve it.   (p. 61)

Lively, informal, and deceptively simple, 'The Conclusion of a Letter' concerns an everyday domestic event – a boy coming home from school – and the ensuing conversation between mother and child. Having ventriloquised Mr. C—'s demeaning perspectives on wifely duties, the poem then turns the tables by articulating, through the authoritative voice of a mother, the domestic virtues that are required in a husband. Especially creative and appealing is the poem's performance of apophasis, whereby the poet continues to do what she says she is going to leave off. The entire feint of the poem is that it takes place in the space of *not* writing. The poet is prepared to leave aside her letter in order to care for her child, only to discover that the proper fulfilment of her duties requires that she write after all. In the process, a small domestic incident becomes an appropriate poetic subject.

If many of *Poems on Several Occasions* find new spaces, literal and rhetorical, for the woman writer, others submerge the poem as object in a quotidian world of things. Critics have tended to understand the early eighteenth-century 'thing-poem' as an aspect of commercial modernity.[29] A volume such as *Poems on Several Occasions* rather differently encourages the reader to see its processes of exchange and circulation as a foregrounding of the bonds of sociability that engendered the poems in the first place. Particularly notable here is the group of poems written on, or to accompany, books: addressed to named women readers, these poems use the material object of the book, as it moves between hands, to assert female virtue and the intangible and immaterial values of female sociability.[30] Barber's 'To *Mrs.* Anne Donnellan, *with the fourth* Essay *on* MAN' addresses a woman who has been called an 'Irish proto-Bluestocking' and who enjoyed a considerable reputation as a singer and amateur musician.[31] Published in January 1734, the final epistle of Pope's *Essay on Man* discusses human happiness as resulting from virtue and self-knowledge. In the poem, Donnellan appears as Philomela, the nightingale of Roman myth, and Barber presents Pope's poem as a fitting and adequate gift for a woman of such virtue and talent:

DEAR *Philomela*, oft you condescend,
With Notes Seraphic, to transport your Friend:
Then in Return, let Verse your Soul rejoice,
Wise, as your Converse, rapt'rous as your Voice. (p. 180)

Grierson's brief poem '*To the Honourable Mrs.* Percival, with Hutcheson's *Treatise on* Beauty *and* Order' is addressed to Martha Percival, Anne Donnellan's mother, a patron of the arts and salon hostess on both sides of the Irish Sea.[32] The poem accompanies Francis Hutcheson's *An Inquiry into the Original of our Ideas of Beauty and Virtue; in Two Treatises* (1725). Written in Dublin, Hutcheson's work argued for an internal moral sense, analogous to the other senses, and giving human beings an instinctive sense of right and wrong. Hutcheson, like Barber and Grierson, was part of a circle surrounding the Lord Lieutenant, Lord Carteret. The poem, however, excludes Hutcheson from Percival's conversation, and, in an elegant compliment, suggests that her exemplary conduct could have saved him the effort of writing the book in the first place:

O were our Author with thy Converse blest,
Could he behold the Virtues of thy Breast;
His needless Labours with Contempt he'd view;
And bid the World not read——but copy you. (p. 155)

Although dependent on major works of eighteenth-century writing by Pope and Hutcheson, neither of these poems assumes a subordinate position. Compressed and economic, the poems characterise both book and recipient, lightly turning the reader's attention towards the lived virtues of the woman to whom the books and poems travel. Books enjoy a privileged status as ready sources of intertextual resonance, but here they appear alongside a range of everyday objects, including a cap, a fan, and seaside rocks, that feature in the volume, either as the subject of poetry, or as the material on which the poem is written. *Poems on Several Occasions* manifests two complementary movements: poetry takes its place among the objects of everyday life, and everyday scenes become the subjects of poetry.

Play between thing and poem, art and life, is also present in Barber's '*On sending my Son, as a Present, to Dr.* Swift, *Dean of* St. Patrick's *on his Birthday*'. Written in the immediate aftermath of the Wood's halfpence affair, the poem acknowledges Swift as the Drapier, and plays with ideas of commemorating him through an animate statue. Rather than such a costly, precious object, Barber sends Swift the 'RICHER Present' of her son, 'A finish'd Form, of Work divine, / Surpassing All the Pow'r of Art.' Kings, the poem concludes, could not send a nobler gift, 'A *meaner* were unworthy *Swift*'

(p. 72). Most obviously, this poem displaces art in favour of nature, and in so doing foregrounds maternal power. Yet, Barber's 'Present' only makes sense, and its true value is only revealed, by virtue of the glossing poem: so art, this time collaborating with the maternal, is re-asserted.

Poems on Several Occasions opens and closes with poems on the business of getting books out into the world: Constantia Grierson's laudatory poem on Barber being encouraged to publish initiates the volume, while Barber's own comic poem addressed '*To a Lady, who commanded me to send her an Account in Verse, how I succeeded in my* Subscription' brings it to an end. In its medley of voices, jaunty rhythms, and deprecating account of the female poet, 'To a Lady' clearly owes something to Jonathan Swift's 'Verses on the Death of Dr. Swift, D.S.P.D.' (1739), a poem Swift 'probably completed' at the end of 1731 and is known to have shown to his intimates prior to publication.[33] Much of the effect of the poem comes from the way in which voice quickly follows voice, as the poet's mainly female acquaintances are imagined declining to subscribe for a variety of reasons:

> I know a Woman cannot write;
> I do not say this out of Spite;
> Nor shall be thought, by those who know me,
> To envy one so much below me.   (p. 277)

Alongside female incapacity, the commentators speculate on the volume's delayed appearance, and doubt the issue of the subscription: 'Besides, I oft have heard it hinted, / Her Poems never will be printed.' Finally, the 'High-born Belinda' who prides herself on her critical powers, gets to twist the knife:

> Call it not *Poetry*, she says;
> No – Call it *Rhyming*, if you please:
> Her Numbers might adorn a Ring,
> Or serve along the Streets to sing[.]   (p. 280)

Whereas the earlier voices rehearse common prejudices concerning gender and writing, Belinda's apparent judiciousness makes her dismissal more forceful. Invoking a hierarchy of material written forms, Belinda condescendingly views Barber's rhymes as either cheap print, ballads to be sung on the street, or as purely decorative mottoes for a ring.[34] Of course, as Belinda's supposed put-down of Barber's poetry appears printed in the very kind of lavish volume she thinks impossible, her words are decisively undercut. Also, it is worth pointing out, Belinda's charge has already to some extent been anticipated and deflected by those poems in the volume that announce their own implication in an ordinary life of things.

'I am sensible that a Woman steps out of her Province when she presumes to write for the Press.' *Poems on Several Occasions* is self-conscious as to gender and nation. On occasion, Grierson and Barber write as Hibernians addressing specifically Irish matters, but the London publication of the volume signals the containment of these ideas within a metropolitan idea of cultural production. Several features of the collection serve to ameliorate any sense of unseemly female presumption: the adoption of a child's voice, the use of comic and unpretentious rhyme and rhythm, the implication of poetry in everyday acts of exchange and sociability. These strategies disarm, but they also contribute to what *Poems on Several Occasions* asserts: that a woman's 'Province' is a legitimate subject for poetry.

Notes

1. [Mary Barber], *Poems on Several Occasions* (London, 1734), p. xvii. The title page gives the incorrect date of publication; it was in fact 1735. Further references to this volume are given after quotations in the text.
2. The list includes 918 names, subscribing for 1,106 copies. See Emily O'Flaherty, 'Patrons, Peers and Subscribers: The Publication of Mary Barber's *Poems on Several Occasions* (1734)' (PhD thesis, NUI Galway, 2013) and Adam Budd, '"Merit in Distress": The Troubled Success of Mary Barber', *Review of English Studies*, New Series 53.210 (2002), 204–27.
3. W. A. Speck, 'Politicians, Peers, and Publication by Subscription, 1700–1750', in *Books and Their Readers in Eighteenth-Century England*, ed. Isabel Rivers (New York: Leicester University Press and St Martin's Press, 1982), pp. 47–68 (pp. 47–48).
4. The other contributors were John Boyle, fifth Earl of Orrery (1707–62), the writer Elizabeth Rowe (1674–1737), and the Bath poet William Ward (1708–47).
5. On the continuing importance of social modes of female authorship in the early eighteenth century, see Sarah Prescott, *Women, Authorship and Literary Culture, 1690–1740* (Houndmills: Palgrave, 2003), pp. 1–38.
6. Betty A. Schellenberg, *Literary Coteries and the Making of Modern Print Culture* (Cambridge University Press, 2016), p. 3.
7. Christopher Fanning sees the central critical problem with Barber's poetry as 'the value attached to indirection as a technique in writing'; in 'The Voices of the Dependent Poet: The Case of Mary Barber', *Women's Writing* 8.1 (2001), 81–98 (p. 83).
8. O'Flaherty, 'Patrons, Peers and Subscribers', p. 101; the first volume of poetry by a woman to be published by subscription was Mary Masters, *Poems on Several Occasions* (London, 1733).
9. See *The Poems of Patrick Delany*, ed. Robert Hogan and Donald C. Mell (Newark, DE: University of Delaware Press, 2006).

10. *The Correspondence of Jonathan Swift, D.D.*, ed. David Woolley, 5 vols (Frankfurt am Main: Peter Lang, 1999–2014), III, p. 279.

11. *Memoirs of Laetitia Pilkington*, ed. A. C. Elias, Jr, 2 vols (1748; Athens, GA: University of Georgia Press, 1997), I, p. 283. For a consideration of this circle as literary coterie, see Christine Gerrard, 'Senate or Seraglio? Swift's "Triumfeminate" and the Literary Coterie', *Eighteenth-Century Ireland / Iris an dá chultúr* 31 (2016), 13–28, and A. C. Elias, Jr, '*Senatus Consultum*: Revising Verse in Swift's Dublin Circle, 1729–1735', in *Reading Swift: Papers from the Third Münster Symposium*, ed. Hermann J. Real and Helgard Stöver-Leidig (Munich: Wilhelm Fink Verlag, 1998), pp. 249–68.

12. *Tunbrigialia: or Tunbridge Miscellanies, For the Year 1730* (London, 1730).

13. A. C. Elias, Jr, 'A Manuscript Book of Constantia Grierson's', *Swift Studies* 2 (1987), 33–56.

14. See Lisa Marie Griffith, 'Mobilising Office, Education and Gender in Eighteenth-Century Ireland: The Case of the Griersons', *Eighteenth-Century Ireland / Iris as dá chultúr* 22 (2007), 64–80 (pp. 69–70).

15. *The Goddess Envy to Doctor D[e]l[an]y* ([Dublin], 1730); see Elias, 'Manuscript Book', p. 52.

16. O'Flaherty, 'Patrons, Peers and Subscribers', p. 16.

17. Ibid., p. 76.

18. Margaret Ezell, 'The Posthumous Publication of Women's Manuscripts and the History of Authorship', in *Women's Writing and the Circulation of Ideas: Manuscript Publication in England, 1550–1800*, ed. George L. Justice and Nathan Tinker (Cambridge University Press, 2002), pp. 121–37.

19. [Mary Monck], *Marinda: Poems and Translations upon Several Occasions* (London, 1716), n.p.

20. On the publication of *Marinda* and Molesworth's motivation for publication, see Gillian Wright, *Producing Women's Poetry, 1600–1730* (Cambridge University Press, 2013), pp. 192–238.

21. *Memoirs of Laetitia Pilkington*, ed. Elias, I, pp. 18–20, 228.

22. Gerrard, 'Senate or Seraglio?', p. 26; Elias, 'Manuscript Book', p. 53.

23. See John Irwin Fischer, 'The Government's Response to Swift's *An Epistle to a Lady*', *Philological Quarterly* 65 (1986), 39–59.

24. See Norma Clarke, *Queen of the Wits: A Life of Laetitia Pilkington* (London: Faber & Faber, 2008).

25. K. Theodore Hoppen, *The Common Scientist in the Seventeenth Century: A Study of the Dublin Philosophical Society, 1683–1798* (London: Routledge & Kegan Paul, 1970), p. 137.

26. Budd, '"Merit in Distress"', p. 210; Prescott, *Women, Authorship and Literary Culture*, p. 137.

27. Andrew Carpenter, ed., *Verse in English from Eighteenth-Century Ireland* (Cork University Press, 1998), p. 198.

28. Margaret Anne Doody, 'Swift and Women', in *The Cambridge Companion to Jonathan Swift*, ed. Christopher Fox (Cambridge University Press, 2003),

pp. 87–111 (p. 107); see also the same author's 'Swift among the Women', *The Yearbook of English Studies* 18 (1988), 68–92.

29. See, for example, Barbara M. Benedict, 'Encounters with the Object: Advertisements, Time, and Literary Discourse in the Eighteenth-Century Thing-Poem', *Eighteenth-Century Studies* 40.2 (2007), 193–207.

30. An exception in this regard is the most solemn of these poems, Barber's 'Written for my Son, in a Bible that was presented to him'. Conventionally enough, this poem concludes that any ambition, including that of the poet, is inconsequential when seen against a proper concern with eternity (*Poems*, p. 82).

31. Patrick Kelly, 'Anne Donnellan: Irish proto-Bluestocking', *Hermathena* 154 (1993), 39–68 (p. 39).

32. On Martha Percival, see O'Flaherty, 'Patrons, Peers and Subscribers', pp. 89–99.

33. Stephen Karian, *Jonathan Swift in Print and Manuscript* (Cambridge University Press, 2014), p. 175.

34. On mottoes or posies written for rings, see Juliet Fleming, *Graffiti and the Writing Arts of Early Modern England* (London: Reaktion Books, 2001), pp. 138–43.

CHAPTER 12

Queering Eighteenth-Century Irish Writing:
Yahoo, Fribble, Freke

Declan Kavanagh

In his chapter 'Searching in the Dark' (2006), Chris Mounsey examines male–male relationships in early modern and eighteenth-century
Ireland by focusing on two specific cases of Irish homosexuality.[1] The
first involves the sodomy trial in 1631 of Mervin Touchet, Baron
Audley and second Earl of Castlehaven, which, in terms of both the
trial itself and its lurid afterlife, has 'never been out of print' (p. 1).
Touchet was brought to trial, largely through the machinations of his
son, for the crimes of engaging in sodomy with four of his servants and
assisting in the rape of his wife and his son's wife. The second case
centres on the accusations of sodomy which were drummed up by Irish
patriots such as Henry Boyle in 1754, and levelled against George
Stone, the English Primate of Ireland, and George Sackville, the son
of Lionel Sackville, Viceroy of Ireland. In examining these two cases,
Mounsey aims to shed light upon 'a current methodological argument
about how to study Irish homosexuality', namely the tension between
essentialist and social constructionist approaches to queer history (p. 1).
In discussing the Touchet case, he focuses his reading upon two
contrasting scholarly interpretations of the trial: Rictor Norton's
Mother Clap's Molly House: The Gay Subculture in England, 1700–1830
(1992) and Cynthia Herrup's *A House in Gross Disorder* (1999).[2]
Mounsey argues that 'what distinguishes these accounts of the case is
that Norton's methodology is based in his unswerving essentialism,
while Herrup concentrates her version on the overlapping discourses of
government and the law, typical of the social constructionist' (p. 4). As
a consequence of these theoretical allegiances, the differences between
the two approaches to Touchet's sodomy scandal pivot on the issue of
whether or not Touchet can be properly interpreted as a seventeenth-
century homosexual. For Norton, Touchet was a homosexual, first and
foremost, whilst for Herrup, the question of Touchet's homosexuality
becomes less about affirming any sort of proto-homosexual identity in

the past and more about the complex deciphering of how the accusation of sodomy is itself embedded in discourses which circulate and shape seventeenth-century Ireland, such as class, religion, and the realities of English colonialism for the Irish.

Mounsey's reading of homosexuality in the Irish past focuses solely on male homosexuality. Early surveys in Irish lesbian and gay studies are often characterised by such a gender divide, with the publication of discrete essays on the topics of male homosexuality and lesbianism being commonplace. In *The Field Day Anthology of Irish Writing, Volume IV* (2002), for example, Emma Donoghue notes that 'fictions about love between women have remained on the margins of Irish literature as it is published and taught'.[3] Sidestepping the issue of essentialist or social constructionist approaches to lesbian history, Donoghue selects from a wide range of texts that are 'lesbian in content not necessarily in authorship' (p. 1090). Eighteenth-century women excerpted by Donoghue include Eleanor Butler and Sarah Ponsonby, Charlotte MacCarthy, and Maria Edgeworth. In bringing together texts by these authors, Donoghue envisages the further development of an emancipatory lesbian scholarship in Irish studies: 'we are beginning to create a grammar of lesbian connection, complex yet clear enough to free us from the self-hatreds of the closeted past' (p. 1091). The recent publication of a study of Butler and Ponsonby, Fiona Brideoake's *The Ladies of Llangollen* (2017), beautifully fulfils Donoghue's earlier vision for scholarship that would engender a 'grammar of lesbian connection'.[4] Work of this kind is currently making us reimagine the contours of eighteenth-century Irish culture with decisive consequences.

In reassessing the current state of Irish queer studies, this chapter offers examples of what reading queerly might reveal in the context of Irish eighteenth-century literature and culture. The chapter begins with a reading of Jonathan Swift's Yahoo as both a *queer* and *queering* textual depiction in *Gulliver's Travels* (1726), before offering an overview of some of the recent methodological approaches to the queer past. I will then examine two texts, Charles Churchill's *The Rosciad* (1761) and Maria Edgeworth's *Belinda* (1801), in order to read the nuanced ways in which these authors queered eighteenth-century Ireland in their writings. Whereas Charles Churchill is treated as a relatively minor poet in eighteenth-century literary history, Maria Edgeworth's novels and treatises have garnered sustained critical attention.[5] More particularly, Edgeworth's novel *Belinda* has become a staple text for gay and lesbian studies readings of the period, at least since Lisa L. Moore's monograph, *Dangerous Intimacies: Toward a*

Sapphic History of the British Novel (1997), opened up the critical debate to considerations of sapphic relationships between the novel's triumvirate of female characters: Lady Delacour, Belinda, and Harriet Freke.[6] In this chapter, the queerness of Freke is placed within the contours of queer readings of Swift's Yahoo and of Churchill's rendering of the Irish actor Thaddeus Fitzpatrick as a 'fribble'. Swift's Yahoo, Churchill's fribble, and Edgeworth's Mrs Freke: each one manifests as indeterminately troubling, serving to upset dominant tropes of normative gender and sexuality, and thus these texts bring into sharp relief the very contingency of normalcy itself.

To examine queerness in the context of eighteenth-century Ireland is, in Mounsey's phrase, to search in the dark, but what our grasping hands can touch is very much up for discovery. A queer reading may well be bound up with issues of sexuality, but this is not necessarily always the case. The Irish feminist and psychoanalytic critic Noreen Giffney defines queer theory as denoting:

> a collection of methods all devoted to examining desire and its relationship to identity. Queer theorists interrogate the categorization of desiring subjects (that is, the creation of identities based on desire), while making visible the ways in which some desires (and thus identities) are made to pass as normal, at the same time that others are rendered wrong or evil.[7]

Queer theory, then, interrogates the formation of desiring subjects along the fault line of the binary between normative, or heteronormative, cross-sex desiring subjects and supposedly non-normative same-sex desiring subjects. Reading a character like Harriet Freke as queer has the potential to bring into sharp relief the complex ways in which a novel like *Belinda* works, albeit precariously, to make the binarised heterosexual and cis-gendered normalcy of characters like Clarence Hervey and Belinda Portman visible and privileged to the reader; whilst simultaneously ensuring that characters who do not 'pass as normal', to use Giffney's phrase, are, by the end of the novel, either reformed and made to pass, like Lady Delacour, or finally rendered invisible, like Freke. When I read Freke, or Churchill's fribble, as queer or queering, I am *not* anachronistically ascribing a queer identity to these past figures in literature, rather, I am instead proffering readings that attend to the complex ways in which such portrayals of gendered indeterminacy served, not to queer, but to anchor, emergent norms in their own time.

As Ana de Freitas Boe and Abby Coykendall argue in the introduction to their collection *Heteronormativity in Eighteenth-Century Literature and*

Culture (2014), 'the eighteenth century, in reconfiguring what counts as sex and sexuality, prescribed not only how, but with whom, people may have sex, bringing about a discursive regime from which not every subject benefits equally'.[8] The period in question, in bequeathing to us our modern regime of sex and gender, concomitantly produced the very discourses which underwrote the legitimacy of this heteronormative regime. In queering eighteenth-century culture, readers who apply this lens will quickly discover that eighteenth-century Anglophone culture is already inherently queer, a condition that is no more strongly felt than in its most intimately hybridised form: namely, Anglo-Irish culture. In her important study, *The Gothic Family Romance: Heterosexuality, Child Sacrifice, and the Anglo-Irish Colonial Order* (1999), Margot Gayle Backus argues that 'the eighteenth-century Anglo-Irish were frequently confronted with disturbing reminders of their contested position in Ireland'.[9] In Backus's view, much Anglo-Irish literature can be seen as charting 'the struggle of eighteenth- and early-nineteenth-century Anglo-Irish colonial elites to position themselves within a chaotic environment in which a clear and stable set of ethnic or culturally based class divisions had yet to emerge' (p. 81). In reading the staunchly English Churchill's fribble and the Anglo-Irish Edgeworth's Freke, I do so within this context of instability in emergent Anglo-Irishness. For the English Churchill, Ireland and Scotland appear as England's alien Celtic fringes, as that which is not English and which, following the promotion of Ossian in the 1760s, troubles conceptions of a discrete English cultural hegemony. Following Backus's reading, the Irish fribble becomes the site of Otherness against which the emergent norm of Englishness can define itself. For Edgeworth, an English-born woman, who settled in County Longford with her father after 1782, the category of Anglo-Irishness must have been grappled with; it was undoubtedly an identity that Edgeworth felt to be taking shape. First, however, I will turn to an earlier iteration of the queerness of Anglophone Ireland, coded within the century's most famous prose fiction.

Yahoo

In Jonathan Swift's *Gulliver's Travels* (1726), it is Lemuel Gulliver himself who best instances the troubling ways in which normative English male identity can be rendered queer. At the start of Part IV, Gulliver embarks upon his final voyage, only to suffer a mutiny at the hands of a sodomitical crew, who quickly offload him upon the shore of Houyhnhnmland.[10] In what is already a remarkably queer narrative, the fourth journey emerges as the queerest by far. In attempting to understand the strange inhabitants of Houyhnhnmland, Gulliver is confronted with the binary of reason versus passion; two divergent positions that are embodied by the horse-like Houyhnhnms and the Yahoo creatures, respectively. Much of the drama of this voyage arises from Gulliver's attempt to repudiate the Houyhnhnms's troubling identification of him as a Yahoo. It is perhaps telling that the reader is informed, as an aside, that Gulliver's wife is left 'big with Child', as it is precisely this emphatic and 'factual' heterosexuality that is implicitly queered by the Houyhnhnms's alignment of him with the libidinous Yahoos. In his first encounter with the Yahoos, Gulliver relates how he is 'discomposed' by their 'singular, and deformed' physicality (p. 207). Filled, almost instantly, with a 'strong Antipathy' towards the Yahoos, Gulliver nevertheless takes the 'Opportunity of distinctly marking their Form' (p. 207). In first observing the male Yahoos, Gulliver curiously focuses his description on the anus: 'They had no Tails, nor any Hair at all on their Buttocks, except about the *Anus*; which I presume Nature had placed there to defend them as they sat on the Ground' (p. 207). The anus also features in Gulliver's differentiation of the male from the female Yahoos, who possess hair 'about the *Anus*, and *Pudenda*' (p. 207). Perhaps because Gulliver's later embrace by the female Yahoo has become such a famous scene in modern readings of the book, this initial attention to Yahoo anality has been entirely overlooked, despite its coming so quickly after the sodomitical 'debauchery' of his crew. It is tempting to read anal eroticism into Gulliver's account of his own 'Contempt and Aversion' at the sight of the Yahoos, since on this, his first encounter, it is the anus that distinctly marks Yahoo form (p. 207). If anal eroticism is implicit in his professed contempt for the Yahoo, such an erotic potential nevertheless gets 'stifled', when the Yahoos literally 'discharge their Excrements' onto Gulliver's head from the tree branches above.

It is clear that part of Gulliver's strong revulsion towards the Yahoos centres on their anality. His forceful dis-identification with the Yahoos manifests in his decision to remain fully dressed in the presence of the Houyhnhnms. Gulliver goes as far as to conceal 'the Secret of [his] Dress, in order to distinguish [himself] as much as possible, from that cursed Race of *Yahoos*' (p. 217). For much of the fourth part, Gulliver remains in the closet, so to speak, at least until his master's valet, the Sorrel Nag, discovers him in a state of undress one morning and outs him as a Yahoo. Gulliver is at pains to remain in the closet and pleads with his Houyhnhnm master 'that the Secret of my having a false Covering to my Body might be known to none but himself' (p. 218). Yet, Gulliver's undressing, and subsequent outing, troubles his own dis-identification with the Yahoos. In attempting to identify instead with the civilised and reasoned Houyhnhnms, Gulliver narrates the history of his own country, England, which is received unfavourably by his master. It is precisely his own sense of identity as a rational, Protestant, and English traveller that gets deconstructed throughout the fourth part. In repudiating his Yahoo nature, Gulliver notably rejects the 'libidinous and mischievous' energies of the Yahoos, which he observes in the '*Red-haired* of both Sexes' (p. 241). Rejecting Yahoos means, in part, suppressing his own erotic desires in favour of the manifest asceticism of the Houyhnhnms. Having been at pains to avoid touching the Yahoos, when Gulliver finally leaves Houyhnhnm country, it is in a canoe that he has fashioned from Yahoo skins. In this chilling scene, the potential intimacy of anal eroticism is exchanged for a violent intimacy with bodies that once disconcerted him. Ironically, in the gruesome act of stitching together Yahoo skins, Gulliver also pulls apart his own humanity.

Swift's representation of the Yahoo is both queer and queering. Like Churchill's fribble and Edgeworth's Mrs Freke, the Yahoo figures as queer because of its unsettling indeterminacy; it is a being that is neither fully human nor fully animal. As I have argued, Yahoos also serve to queerly upset Gulliver's own discrete sense of himself as a reasoned and controlled English man. In many ways, the Yahoo is the queer example *par excellence* in eighteenth-century Irish writing in English.

In reading *Gulliver's Travels* queerly, I do not suggest that Lemuel Gulliver, nor indeed Jonathan Swift, is secretly homosexual. Reading *queerly* may well involve a search for precursors to our contemporary lesbian, gay, bisexual, transgender, and queer identities, but it is also, more broadly speaking, about interrogations of the 'normal'. In writing of Gulliver's repudiation of the Yahoo, Swift queerly interrogates the emergent norm in early eighteenth-century Britain of the English, Protestant, male traveller. Since the publication of Mounsey's essay and Donoghue's *Field Day* contribution, approaches to interpreting the queer past have moved beyond questions of essentialism and social constructionism. However, the category of the homosexual remains the fulcrum for historical and theoretical methods which seek to embrace anachronism, queer temporalities, and the very destabilisation of the relationship between the past and the present. For those working within historicist methodologies and contexts, queering the past is often met with the scholarly anxiety of others working in the period, who erroneously (or correctly) imagine such projects to result in the anachronistic misattribution of homosexual identity to authors in the past. In the first volume of *The History of Sexuality: The Will to Knowledge* (1976), Michel Foucault locates the emergence of the category of the 'homosexual' in the West in the 1870s:

> As defined by the ancient civil or canonical codes, sodomy was a category of forbidden acts; their perpetrator was nothing more than the juridical subject of them. The nineteenth-century homosexual became a personage, a past, a case history, and a childhood, in addition to being a type of life, a life form, and a morphology, with an indiscreet anatomy and possibly a mysterious physiology.[11]

From the sodomitical, a category that figured a range of sexual and social transgressions, emerged the homosexual as a species. Importantly, the Foucauldian project demonstrated the cultural and historical contingency of all sexual identity. In another sense, however, it unwittingly engendered an unproductive analytic preoccupation with the modelling of all pre-nineteenth-century sexualities, with such work invested in tracing how one newer sexual descriptor (for example, the molly) supervenes upon the existing sexual descriptor (the catamite).

Madhavi Menon has argued that the project of gay and lesbian historiography – which has done so much to denaturalise conceptions of sexuality – is nevertheless bound to heterotemporality, a historicism that deploys difference as history.[12] In response, Menon offers the framework of homohistory as a way of enacting historical readings that posit resistance to sexuality as historical difference. Attending to desire as opposed to sexuality, Menon aims to disrupt the hetero logic of historicism through an unhistoricism that considers 'neither past nor present' as 'capable of a full and mutually exclusive definition'.[13] Defending a genealogical approach to the queer past, Valerie Traub cautions that 'to fail to specify the terms of queer's historicity is to ignore desire's emergence from distinct cultural and material arrangements of space and time, as well as from what psychoanalysis calls libidinal predicates'.[14] In surveying this confrontational dialogue between historicist and unhistoricist scholars, Chris Roulston suggests that 'scholars doing queer history appear to be falling into two camps; those who continue to see the value in historicizing and analyzing queer relations as historically contingent, and those who aim to deconstruct the very notion of the historical, perceiving it as normalizing, heterosexualizing, and teleological'.[15] As I have argued in *Effeminate Years: Literature, Politics, and Aesthetics in Mid-Eighteenth-Century Britain* (2017), an anachronistic 'presentism' risks buttressing the normativity of heterosexuality even further:

> Whether a queer reading of the past is invested in recovering *queers in history* or in *queering history*, a shared corollary of these important endeavors should

be the forceful unsettling of the ahistoricism that underwrites heterosexuality and serves to naturalize its universalizing tendencies.[16]

To read eighteenth-century men and women as gay, lesbian, bisexual, or transgender is also to suggest that our own contemporary experience of sexualities is entirely understood; or as Eve Kosofsky Sedgwick puts it, it is to risk a reading which 'underwrite[s] the notion that "homosexuality as we conceive of it today" itself comprizes a coherent definitional field rather than a space of overlapping, contradictory, and conflictual definitional forces'.[17] For all their care and attention, essentialist readings of the queer past, as Sedgwick tells us, 'risk reinforcing a dangerous consensus of knowingness' about contemporary sexualities.[18] Reading queerly then is not the same as an essentialist mining of the past for the discovery of our gay forefathers and foremothers. Tracing the queerness inherent in eighteenth-century texts is not necessarily anachronistic; queerness is not imposed upon the past, it is instead already present in the text, and, by extension, in the discourse of the age in which the text was written.

In the remainder of this chapter, I attend to Churchill's fribble and Edgeworth's Mrs Freke as instances of queer figures in Irish writing in the long eighteenth century. In doing so, I examine representations that are carefully, though variously, constructed by Churchill and Edgeworth as liminal, or what might be called transitional. If some of us are still searching in the dark for homosexuality in history (and, perhaps, we always will be), then searching for queerness might shed light on the history of normalcy, not homosexuality; it is from the history of normalcy that the queer subject might be touched through its own period-specific deviant transitions.

Fribble

An ambient xenophobia, together with a persistent anti-effeminate attitude, characterised the work of Charles Churchill (1731–64), more, perhaps, than any other English eighteenth-century satirist. If representations of the fop figured the threatening luxurious excesses of urban society, Churchill's portrayal of an effeminate Irish fribble diverts this anti-effeminate satire away from the metropolis. In order to understand this reversal, some clarification of the term 'fribble' is required. In his *Dictionary* (1755), Samuel Johnson defined a 'fribbler' as a trifler 'who professes rapture for the woman, [but] dreads her consent'.[19] As Johnson details, the fribble can attract and even seduce women, but ultimately he cannot sexually perform. While Philip Carter has shown how the fop is ridiculed for his social rather than sexual misdeeds, satire on the fribble hinges more pointedly on the issue of gender ambiguity.[20] Whereas the fop is an effeminate and affected man, the fribble is indeterminately gendered. As we will see, *The Rosciad* further conflates Irish men in particular with this fribblish gender ambiguity.

The most coherent example of this anti-effeminate satire in Churchill's corpus comes in a passage in his poem *The Rosciad*, which centres on the Irish actor Thady 'fribble' Fitzpatrick. This extensive portrait was added to the eighth edition of the poem following Fitzpatrick's quarrel with David Garrick over the Fitzgiggio riots at Drury Lane and Covent Garden in January 1763.[21] These riots were prompted by the enforcement of full-price admittance rates for audience members regardless of when they arrived for the performance. However, the feud between the two actors can be traced back to the late 1740s when Garrick satirised Fitzpatrick as a fribble in his farce *Miss in her Teens* (1747). Fitzpatrick retaliated thirteen years later in *An Enquiry into the Real Merit of a Certain Popular Performer* (1760), which discredited Garrick's acting in the service of 'rectifying the corrupt taste of the public'.[22] Garrick's acting is unfavourably contrasted in gendered terms with that of the Irish actors James Quin and Henry Mossop: Garrick's 'languor' and 'sluggishness' in his role of Pierre in *Venice Preserved* is distinguished from the celebrated 'manliness of expression' of Quin and Mossop. Notably, 'the little great man', as one contributor dubs him, cuts an 'insufficient figure' in the stage (p. 3). In a reversal of the pederastic binary of dominant/man and passive/boy, Fitzpatrick makes this effeminate subjection explicit when he notes how Garrick is 'a person exhibiting himself a spectacle to every 'prentice boy, who, with a shilling in his pocket, accepts the invitation, promulgated in the play-bills, and asserts the in-disputable right of signifying his approbation or dissatisfaction' (p. 20). Most alarmingly then, Garrick's presence on the stage leaves him vulnerable to the objec-tifying and penetrating male gaze.

In response to this *Enquiry*, Garrick recast Fitzpatrick in his verse-satire *The Fribbleriad* (1761) in the role of a fribble simultaneously named 'Fizgig' and 'X, Y, Z?' (Fig. 4).[23] In the preface, Garrick mockingly describes the poem as 'an *Iliad* in a *nutshell*', with Fizgig amounting to the Achilles of the piece (p. vii). Garrick portrays Fitzpatrick as a hack scribbler who disseminates 'falsehood, malice, envy, spite' (p. 1), which become his distinguishing marks:

> A *Man* it seems – 'tis hard to say –
> A *Woman* then? – a moment pray –

FIZGIG.

Fig. 4 David Garrick, *The Fribbleriad* (London, 1761), Frontispiece. Illustration of 'Fizgig' (Thady Fitzpatrick). By permission of the Beinecke Rare Book and Manuscript Library, Yale University

> Unknown as yet by sex or feature,
> Suppose we try to guess the creature;
> Whether a *wit*, or a *pretender*?
> Of *masculine* or *female* gender?
> Some things it does may pass for either,
> And some it does belong to neither:
> It is so fibbing, slandering, spiteful,
> In phrase so dainty and delightful;
> So fond of all it reads and writes,
> So waggish when the maggot bites:
> Such spleen, such wickedness, and whim,
> *It* must be *Woman*, and a *Brim*.
> But then the Learning and the Latin!   (p. 2)

Garrick's portrait of Fitzpatrick as a fribble is not simply of a
womanly man, but can be more properly described within the one-
sex model as the image of a being falling away from the masculine ideal
towards feminine defectiveness. Rather than elaborating Fizgig as a
womanly man, Garrick refuses gender coherence by deploying indeterminate terms such as ''tis hard to say' and 'Unknown'. Significantly,
the fribble's behaviour may 'pass for either' or 'neither', while female
immorality undercuts the masculine 'Learning' and 'Latin' of a fribble's
conversation.[24] But here the flux between the one- and two-sex models
in this period is at play, for what is most monstrous about Garrick's
fribble is its unintelligibility within an emerging hetero logic of incommensurability between the sexes. The persistent use of the question
mark together with the purely alphabetical classification ('X, Y, Z?')
extends this gendered indeterminacy into a questioning of the very
humanity of the fribble, emphasised by the description of the fribble as
a non-human 'creature'. More tellingly we are told that wounding the
pride of the 'Lady-fellow' scribbler causes 'male' and 'female' to vanish
into 'malice, rage and fear' (p. 5).

In The Rosciad, Churchill draws on Garrick's satiric portrayal of Thady
Fitzpatrick. Rather than the effeminate body being locatable at the metropole, as John Brown, for instance, emplaces it in An Estimate of the Manners
and Principles of the Times (1757), Churchill specifies that fribbles are Celtic
in origin.[25] In fact, the fribble's explicitly 'Irish growth' is the only certainty
in a description that is otherwise freighted with ambiguity:

> A Motley Figure, of the FRIBBLE TRIBE,
> Which Heart can scarce conceive, or pen describe,
> Came simp'ring on; to ascertain whose sex
> Twelve sage impannell'd Matrons would perplex.
> Nor Male, nor Female; Neither, and yet both;
> Of Neuter Gender, tho' of Irish growth;
> A six-foot suckling, mincing in his gait;
> Affected, peevish, prim, and delicate;
> Fearful it seem'd, tho' of Athletic make,
> Lest brutal breezes should too roughly shake
> Its tender form, and savage motion spread
> O'er its pale cheeks the horrid manly red.[26]

Tellingly, a definitive sex is something to ascertain rather than being clearly
indicated by the fribble's body or self-presentation. In line with the one-sex
model, the fribble, we are told, is not male or female, but 'both', a
description that again presents 'sex' in terms of a single continuum.

Moreover, Churchill specifies fribbles as an Irish 'TRIBE'. As Nicholas Hudson argues, within the pressures of a homogenising discourse of imperial expansion at mid-century, non-European populations were classed as tribes on the basis that they lacked the cultural and political requirements to justify the honorific title of 'nation'.[27] Thus, Churchill's depiction of the Irish as a fribblish 'tribe' serves to undermine rhetorically any possibility for Irish political or cultural participation in the modern British nation. This xeno-effeminophobic depiction of an Irish fribblish tribe in *The Rosciad* anticipates later deployments of the term within imperialist discourse to denote non-Europeans. The adoption of 'tribe' as a common descriptor functioned in slave rhetoric to erase the distinctive cultures and traditions of those trafficked from the African continent. Churchill's use of 'tribe' operates in a similar way, levelling the distinctions of Irish and Scottish, which facilitate an English xenophobic and anti-effeminate metropolitan queering of Britain's Celtic fringe as distinctly non-European and uncivilised. Whereas Alexander Pope's *Epistle to Dr Arbuthnot* (1735) casts Lord Hervey as the castrated Sporus, a figure of contemptible subordination, Churchill's fribble is unique in its explicit conflation of androgyny with ethnicity through Celtic tribal classification: 'Of *Neuter* Gender, tho' of *Irish* growth' (l. 146).

The caesural pressure in this line comes from the unresolved illogic of connecting 'neuter gender' with a specifically Irish 'growth'. How can sterility produce growth? Arguably, such sterile growth can only become intelligible when considered within the logic of an imperialist discourse at mid-century that zoned the Celtic periphery as both economically unproductive and sexually non-reproductive. Whereas Fitzpatrick's sexed body is unintelligible in Garrick's *The Fribbleriad*, Churchill articulates an '[a]ffected, peevish, prim, and delicate' body that is nonetheless still legibly masculine, being 'six-foot' and 'of Athletic make' (l. 149). Crucially, the satire gains its force from this queer spectacle of incongruity, from the disconnection between a body that is sexed as male and that which remains indeterminately gendered. The depiction of the strong physicality of the athletic fribble signals an anxiety of unrealised potential; the fribble has the raw material and energy to be manly, but chooses not to harness it.

Churchill's anti-Irish and anti-effeminate satire centres on the dissonance between male bodies that are normatively sexed as male yet are seemingly incapable of performing the prescribed masculine role: 'A six-foot suckling mincing in its gait' (l. 147). Read in terms of Judith Butler's theorising of gender, the Irish fribble lacks a crucial stabilising concept of masculinity and is thus prohibited from accessing the sort of normative British middle-class identity that drives imperialist logic at mid-century.[28] More complexly, Garrick's performing of a hegemonic bourgeois masculinity in *The Rosciad* necessitates a binarised imagining of the female players as natural and incommensurable counterparts. Churchill's consistently positive commentary on women seems all the more striking when we recall how female players were routinely denounced as prostitutes and courtesans. As Kristina Straub notes, an actress's public profession complicated the assumption that feminine sexuality was the private and passive opposite of masculinity.[29] The diatribe against the Italian opera in the final section of *The Rosciad* brings into sharp relief an ideological framing of the natural female body as a synecdoche for a healthy and productive body politic. Specifically, the critique of Italian opera is interesting for what it suggests about the sort of pleasures that are appropriate to the British stage and to its people:

> But never shall a Truly British Age
> Bear a vile race of EUNUCHS on the stage.
> The boasted work's call'd NATIONAL in vain,
> If one Italian voice pollutes the strain.
> Where Tyrants rule, and slaves with joy obey,
> Let slavish minstrels pour th'enervate lay;
> To Britons, far more noble pleasures spring,
> In native notes, whilst BEARD and VINCENT sing. (ll. 721–28)

The enjambed closed couplet at the beginning of this verse paragraph formally secures the incommensurability of 'true' British pleasures with the queer and non-reproductive pleasures of the Italian eunuchs. Positioned as foreign and therefore perversely un-British, the appearance of the Italian castrati on the London stage threatens to enact a reversal of 'Kind Nature's first decrees' (l. 719). Cross-sex complementarity, in contrast, is implicit in the poem's linking of the natural performances of 'native singers' John Beard and Mrs Vincent, from which 'far more noble pleasures spring'. This two-sex framing of Beard and Vincent works to foreground gendered incommensurability as a feature of the British stage, and, by metaphoric extension, as integral to the (re)productive nation. The final couplet connects 'noble pleasures spring' with 'native notes'; however, the reader is told in the previous lines that the more troubling indeterminacy, of the 'vile race of EUNUCHS', remains a possibility, 'If one Italian voice pollutes the strain'. The stanza ultimately presents a gendered complementariness that is always subject to a queer undoing.

Freke

'Him!' said Percival.
'I protest it is a woman!' said Vincent.
'No, surely,' said Belinda: 'It cannot be a woman!'
'Not unless it be Mrs Freke,' replied Mr Percival.[30]

In Maria Edgeworth's first English society novel, *Belinda*, published forty years after *The Rosciad*, it is the indeterminately gendered character of Harriet Freke who signals queer possibilities. Mrs Freke emerges like the simpering fribble onto the novel's densely populated theatrical stage, laughingly exclaiming, 'Who am I! only a Freke!', an ontological question that is presented to the reader rhetorically as exclamatory and defensive (p. 250). Both underscore the ontological instabilities engendered by the character's unsettling presence throughout the novel. Mrs Freke is introduced through Lady Delacour's narration of the tragic events that have (mis)guided her away from the aristocratic norms of domestic and public propriety, and the social dictates of wifely/motherly duty, towards the self-destructive patterns of hate-fuelled competitive behaviour towards her rival Mrs Luttridge. Lady Delacour attempts to best her rival in, among other things, her conspicuous consumption of luxury and in her prioritising of vapid social engagements over the more meaningfully feminine labour of maintaining a private and familial domestic space. Encouraged by the rakish behaviour of her friend, Mrs Freke, Lady Delacour's competition with Mrs Luttridge manifests itself in the distinctly masculine competitive arena of the duel. Lady Delacour and Mrs Luttridge are attended at the duel by their seconds, Mrs Freke and Miss Honour O'Grady, and, although O'Grady behaves just as 'manfully' as Freke, she is nonetheless described by Lady Delacour as conducting 'herself not only with the spirit, but with the good nature and generosity characteristic of her [Irish] nation' (pp. 56–57).

O'Grady is a minor character, who disappears entirely from the novel after the traumatic duel and once Mrs Freke betrays the wounded Lady Delacour to become her rival's confidant. Yet O'Grady acts as a double for Mrs Freke, who ultimately only develops in the novel by usurping, off-stage, O'Grady's role as Mrs Luttridge's intimate female friend. In lesbian and gay studies' interpretations of Harriet Freke, this mirroring of Freke and O'Grady has been unremarked upon, but it is particularly suggestive for a reading of the Irish queer, given the open identification of O'Grady with Irishness. O'Grady is last mentioned in Lady Delacour's history at the very moment before she narrates the 'blow' on her breast, which she apparently self-inflicts through her own misfiring, but which might also, possibly, be the result of her second's misguidance. In this pivotal scene, Freke's gauche handling of the duel is implicitly contrasted with the trustworthiness of O'Grady.

Freke's rupturing of her ties with Lady Delacour finds a more material analogue in Delacour's ruptured breast. As Lisa L. Moore incisively points out, Lady Delacour's wound is 'a wound to her femininity, the moral consequence of her gender transgression in the duel'.[31] Moore goes further in her reading to suggest how Lady Delacour's wound is in fact caused by Freke's own freakishness:

> Freke is represented as a catalyst rather than as an agent. She is the remote cause of the duel and the wound as opposed to a wounded duellist herself. Thus, in this scene she is never the victim of her own freakishness, that she is spared indicates another of the novel's ambiguities about the pleasures and powers of Harriet Freke's unnaturalness. It is her intimate friend Lady Delacour, who receives the mark of Harriet Freke's gender and social transgressions on her own body.[32]

The wounded breast, kept hidden by Lady Delacour and only revealed in her private closet to her servant Marriott and, eventually, to Belinda, becomes the occasion for the formation of 'unnatural' bonds between women. In Edmund Burke's famous aesthetic treatise on the sublime and the beautiful (1757), a woman's breasts are aestheticised as the most beautiful part of the female body, noting in particular 'the smoothness; the softness; the easy and insensible swell'.[33] Men's experience of beauty is then described by Burke as a social experience in that it gives rise to social bonds; through experiencing beauty, men learn to mix love with lust, and to fix their choice on certain women in order to generate families. Extending Moore's reading of the wounded breast as a material analogue for Freke's gender and sexual transgressions into the domain of eighteenth-century aesthetics, we might also note how Lady Delacour's wounded breast in its secret monstrosity is, perhaps, the most queer representation in *Belinda*. Lady Delacour's sublime wound perverts a Burkean aesthetics of the body, and the normative gendering of feminine beauty and masculine sublimity that subtends it, through its reconstruction of the very corporeality of feminine beauty, and the maternal – a woman's breasts – as queerly sublime.

Queer possibilities in *Belinda* thus centre on ways in which Edgeworth renders Lady Delacour's wound sublime, while also presenting Freke as sublimely indeterminate in terms of gender. However, the intense and secret female intimacies that Delacour cultivates with those women who know about her deformity, and Freke's, possibly sapphic, cross-dressing are possibilities which are ended with the novel's abrupt reassurance to the reader that such things never really existed. In a late chapter appropriately entitled 'A Spectre', the cancerous threat of Lady Delacour's wound is disproven by Dr X, who penetrates the private bonds of the women by casting his male gaze upon the wound to discover 'the real state of the case' (p. 314). The authoritative diagnosis of cancer of the breast as a false alarm renders Lady Delacour's terrors, and the sapphic sublime engendered by her naked breasts, wholly unfounded. In the same chapter, significantly, Freke voyeuristically threatens to usurp the place of male suitors and literally gets caught in a man's trap. Not only is the sapphic sublime banished by the surgeon's pronouncement on Lady Delacour's illness, the medical gaze also 'solves' the problem of Mrs Freke's fribblish indeterminacy:

> Mrs Freke's leg was much cut and bruised; and now that she was no longer supported by the hopes of revenge, she began to lament loudly and inces-santly the injury that she had sustained. She impatiently inquired how long it was probable, that she should be confined by this accident; and she grew quite outrageous when it was hinted, that the beauty of her legs would be spoiled, and that she would never more be able to appear to advantage in man's apparel. (p. 312)

Whose voice it is who argues that Freke will no longer be able to wear male attire is left unclear at this point. Perhaps, since the conversation is framed in terms of confinement and convalescence, Freke is speaking with the surgeon. Freke's almost fribblish beauty, the showing of athletic legs, is spoilt by disfigurement. The beauty that Freke possessed, and which was troubling for its unmistakable manliness, is now a spectacle of sublime terror, forever to be hidden under heavy petticoats. It would seem as if the queerness of Freke's indeterminacy and of Lady Delacour's sublime breasts are finally banished. Yet Lady Delacour, in a meta-fictional turn, queerly calls the reader's attention to the transitional nature of all narratives by providing the conclusion to *Belinda* herself: '"And now, my good friends," continued Lady Delacour, "shall I finish the novel for you?"' (p. 477).[34] While Delacour's ending is imagined as the successful culmination of the novel's heterosexual marriage plot, readers are nonetheless quickly reminded that Clarence Hervey's kissing of Belinda's hand in the final tableau is enforced as 'the rule of the stage' (p. 478). The union of Hervey and Belinda is thus presented as a stage convention, rather than as an inevitable or natural outcome of the novel's proceedings. The cross-sex couplings which populate the scene are joined together upon an entirely conditional basis. Given the queer possibilities in *Belinda*, it is hard not to think of Lady Delacour's theatrical ending as being unconvincingly choreographed. If nothing else, the queerly provisional nature of the novel's ending gestures towards the absences of the fribblish Freke and Honour O'Grady, who, if allowed onstage, would undoubtedly offer other plot possibilities to Lady Delacour, ones that refused such easy narrative closure.

Queer approaches to eighteenth-century Irish literature in English aim to uncover such possibilities. Whilst the search for historical precursors to our contemporary (and shifting) identities of LGBT continues to exercise some scholars, the queering of Enlightenment literature is a much more capacious endeavour. As I have argued in this essay, early Irish literature in English is already inherently queer and queering, a fact that is manifest in works as different from each other as Swift's satirical fiction, Churchill's mock-epic poem, and Edgeworth's Regency novel.

Notes

1. Chris Mounsey, 'Searching in the Dark: Towards a Historiography of Queer Early Modern and Enlightenment (Anglo) Ireland', in *Queer Masculinities, 1550–1800*, ed. Katherine O'Donnell and Michael O'Rourke (Houndmills: Palgrave, 2006), pp. 1–17. Further references are given after quotations in the text.

2. Rictor Norton, *Mother Clap's Molly House: The Gay Subculture in England, 1700–1830* (London: Gay Men's Press, 1992) and Cynthia B. Herrup, *A House in Gross Disorder: Sex, Law, and the 2nd Earl of Castlehaven* (Oxford University Press, 1999).

3. Emma Donoghue, 'Lesbian Encounters, 1745–1997', in *The Field Day Anthology of Irish Writing*, Vols IV/V: *Irish Women's Writing and Traditions*, ed. Angela Bourke et al., 2 vols (Cork University Press, 2002), IV, pp. 1090–137 (p. 1090). Further references are given after quotations in the text.

4. Fiona Brideoake, *The Ladies of Llangollen: Desire, Indeterminacy, and the Legacies of Criticism* (Lewisburg, PA: Bucknell University Press, 2017).

5. For work on Charles Churchill, see Adam Rounce, 'Charles Churchill's Anti-Enlightenment', *History of European Ideas* 31.2 (2005), 227–36, and Declan Kavanagh, '"Hercules, Turn'd *Beau*": Charles Churchill's Satire', in *Effeminate Years: Literature, Politics, and Aesthetics in Mid-Eighteenth-Century Britain* (Lewisburg, PA: Bucknell University Press, 2017), pp. 1–36. Critical work on Maria Edgeworth is wide ranging, but see, in particular, Clíona Ó Gallchoir, *Maria Edgeworth: Women, Enlightenment and Nation* (University College Dublin Press, 2005).

6. Lisa L. Moore, *Dangerous Intimacies: Toward a Sapphic History of the British Novel* (Durham, NC and London: Duke University Press, 1997).

7. Noreen Giffney, 'Quare Theory', in *Irish Postmodernisms and Popular Culture*, ed. Wanda Balzano, Anne Mulhall, and Moynagh Sullivan (Houndmills: Palgrave Macmillan, 2007), pp. 197–209 (p. 200).

8. Ana de Freitas Boe and Abby Coykendall, 'Introduction', in *Heteronormativity in Eighteenth-Century Literature and Culture* (Farnham: Ashgate, 2014), pp. 1–22 (p. 14).

9. Margot Gayle Backus, *The Gothic Family Romance: Heterosexuality, Child Sacrifice, and the Anglo-Irish Colonial Order* (Durham, NC and London: Duke University Press, 1999), p. 79. Further references are given after quotations in the text.

10. Jonathan Swift, *Gulliver's Travels*, ed. Christopher Fox (Boston and New York: Bedford Books of St Martin's Press, 1995), p. 205. Further references are given after quotations in the text.

11. Michel Foucault, *The History of Sexuality*, Vol. I: *The Will to Knowledge*, trans. Robert Hurley (London: Penguin, 1998), p. 43.

12. Madhavi Menon, *Unhistorical Shakespeare: Queer Theory in Shakespearean Literature and Film* (Houndmills: Palgrave Macmillan, 2008), p. 1. See also Jonathan Goldberg and Madhavi Menon, 'Queering History', *PMLA* 120.5 (October 2005), 1608–17.

13. Menon, *Unhistorical Shakespeare*, p. 3.

14. Valerie Traub, 'The New Unhistoricism in Queer Studies', *PMLA* 128.1 (January 2013), 21–39 (p. 33).

15. Chris Roulston, 'New Approaches to the Queer Eighteenth Century', *Literature Compass* 10.10 (2013), 761–70 (p. 762).

16. Kavanagh, *Effeminate Years*, pp. xxi–xxii.

17. Eve Kosofsky Sedgwick, *Epistemology of the Closet* (1990; Berkeley, CA: University of California Press, 2nd edn, 2008), p. 45.

18. Ibid.

19. Samuel Johnson, *A Dictionary of the English Language* ... (London, 1755), p. 860.

20. Philip Carter, 'An "Effeminate" or "Efficient" Nation? Masculinity and Eighteenth-Century Social Documentary', *Textual Practice* 11.3 (1997), 429–43 (p. 433).

21. See *The Poetical Works of Charles Churchill*, ed. Douglas Grant (Oxford: Clarendon Press, 1956), 'Notes to the Poems', p. 460. Further quotations from Churchill's poetry will be cited in the text and are taken from this edition.

22. Thaddeus Fitzpatrick, *An Enquiry into the Real Merit of a Certain Popular Performer* (London, 1760), p. 27. Further references are given after quotations in the text.

23. David Garrick, *The Fribbleriad* (London, 1761), p. vii. Further references are given after quotations in the text.

24. Nathan Bailey's *Dictionarium Britannicum; or a More Compleat Universal Etymological English Dictionary than any Extant* (London, 1736) defined 'brim' as 'a common Strumpet' (n.p.).

25. John Brown, *An Estimate of the Manners and Principles of the Times* (London, 1757). In the advertisement, Brown warns his readers that a much more extensive work is planned but that the nation is at present experiencing a crisis 'so important and alarming' that immediate intervention is needed, a crisis described as the erosion of England's moral fabric at the hands of a 'vain, luxurious, and selfish Effeminacy', which is centred in London (pp. 12, 20).

26. *Poetical Works of Charles Churchill, The Rosciad*, ll. 141–52.

27. Nicholas Hudson, 'From "Nation" to "Race": The Origin of Racial Classification in Eighteenth-Century Thought', *Eighteenth-Century Studies* 29.3 (1996), 247–64 (p. 257).

28. According to Butler, all identity is fixed through the stabilising concepts of sex, gender, and desire. See Judith Butler, *Gender Trouble: Feminism and the Subversion of Identity*, 2nd edn (New York: Routledge, 2006), p. 23.

29. Kristina Straub, *Sexual Suspects: Eighteenth-Century Players and Sexual Ideology* (Princeton University Press, 2006), p. 89.

30. Maria Edgeworth, *Belinda*, ed. Kathryn Kirkpatrick (Oxford University Press, 2008), p. 250. Further references are given after quotations in the text.

31. Moore, *Dangerous Intimacies*, p. 96.

32. Ibid., p. 98.

33. Edmund Burke, *A Philosophical Enquiry into the Origin of our Ideas of the Sublime and Beautiful*, ed. Adam Phillips (Oxford University Press, 1990), p. 105.

34. For the prominence of meta-fictional endings in eighteenth-century Irish fiction, see Aileen Douglas, '"Whom Gentler Stars Unite": Fiction and Union in the Irish Novel', *Irish University Review* 41.1 (2011), 183–95.

CHAPTER 13

'Brightest Wits and Bravest Soldiers': Ireland, Masculinity, and the Politics of Paternity

Rebecca Anne Barr

Appraising William Chaigneau's *History of Jack Connor* (1752) shortly after publication, *The Monthly Review* noted its author's origin in 'a neighbouring kingdom, famous for having produced some of the brightest wits and bravest soldiers in the modern world'.[1] Chaigneau's picaresque countered anti-Irish stereotypes with a narrative which united morality with pleasure, and which would prove helpful for 'the education of youth, especially young gentlemen', inculcating 'politeness, humanity ... the art of acquiring the respect, and the love of mankind'.[2] An affable, cosmopolitan, and urbane comic novel, *Jack Connor* is most commonly compared to Henry Fielding's *Tom Jones*, that benchmark of eighteenth-century masculine style. The dedication to Henry Fox, as Secretary at War, provides a decidedly martial context for the author to position himself as an equal in a polite public exchange, fashioning himself as 'a gentleman', that slippery term of esteem.[3] He is independent, free from the servility of patronage: 'this Address expects no pecuniary Indulgence', the dedication notes.[4] Such claims to autonomy might seem conventional, yet this manly independence is crucial in legitimating *Jack Connor*'s critique of English 'prejudice against their brethren of *Ireland*'.[5] This dedication, the novel's debates on politics and religion, and later paratextual additions of works on war and manufacture corroborate these assertions of active civic virtue. While readers who bound *Jack Connor* with 'low' works on highwaymen and pirates were providing one possible taxonomy, the novel's barrackroom declaratives are arguably part of the novel's fashioning of a loyal, independent, public-spirited Irish masculinity.[6]

Chaigneau's claim to wit and martial masculinity is an instance of the ways in which Irish writers attempted to countervail the dominance of the Stage Irishman.[7] Feckless, ignorant, passionate and proud, full of plausible empty speech, of uncertain rank or capital, and lacking the emotional continence that was increasingly crucial for masculine status, the Stage Irishman caused cultural cringe. Even Irish writers accepted the national stereotype as inherently risible: 'an Irishman is always comic' noted Richard Steele, ruefully.[8] If the power of the 'Englishman' on stage lies in his 'strategic withdrawal from scrutiny', such unmarked masculinity contrasts with that of the Irishman who, as Elizabeth Cullingford has noted, 'is always marked as different, as Irish, even by his own countrymen'. On the Irish, as much as on the English stage, 'Englishness was synonymous with masculinity' with Irishness connoting femininity.[9] If, however, eighteenth-century theatrical representations of the Irishman are painfully legible, his novelistic counterparts have frequently been understood as dramatic imports or lowlife variants. Many histories of national character understandably focus on performance: studies by Joep Leerssen and David Hayton find 'national' characteristics primarily in plays, ethnographic or travel accounts of Ireland produced for English readers, or in the visual culture of satirical print.[10] In these accounts the novel (usually posited as the rising force of eighteenth-century literature) becomes a mere ancillary to the cultural construction of Irish manhood. Novels produced by writers who we might now characterise as Irish (being born in the country or with considerable connection to the island) are likewise sidelined. So, while the theatre has been widely recognised as one of the most important sites of cultural exchange for Irish culture both in Ireland and elsewhere, enabling a vital transfer of talent and ideas, the comparable work of eighteenth-century fiction has been less visible.

This chapter uses *Jack Connor* as a case study to examine how Irish fiction in this period represents men and normative masculinity, negotiating the way in which the 'Irish' prefix complicates gender norms increasingly defined by English imperialism. If Irish fiction struggled with the assertion of gentlemanly status, other authors were strategically opaque about national identity, avoiding censure through what Roy Foster has called 'the necessary stratagems of irony, collusion and misdirection'.[11] As Seamus Deane observes, 'the Irish novel, partly because of its diasporic writers and audiences, poses the question of the national in such a manner that it can neither be affirmed or denied in any of the orthodox ways'.[12] Likewise, in the flux of political subordination and professional expedience, gender too becomes 'unorthodox', so that in novels such as *Tristram Shandy* or *The Vicar of Wakefield* strains of 'Irishness' can be read in the subversion of dominant or 'hegemonic' masculine forms. What, after all, could be more unorthodox than retired soldier Uncle Toby's war games and gently queer homosociality? If normative heterosexual masculinity often seems both 'omnipresent and invisible', decentred and marginal forms displayed by 'proximate others' can 'make visible' latent codes of behaviour.[13] The depiction of gender, as Joan Scott has argued, often functions as 'a primary way of signifying relationships of power' in litera-ture.[14] As gender is itself both historical and relational, Ireland is best understood in terms of antagonistic or imagined kinship, of disputed affiliations. As Joseph Valente argues, 'Irishness' is 'forged historically in an ineluctable if impossible relation to Britishness', emerging as 'an iden-tity that is "not one" or "not quite"'.[15] In terms of power and subordina-tion, then, Ireland's self-conception has long been mediated by political and cultural ties affinal and elective.

The uses of feminisation, and of rhetorical cross-dressing in the name of political articulation, have a long – and problematic – tradition in Irish writing in both Irish and English. The gendering of Ireland as wronged woman, for instance, in genres as diverse as Gaelic *aisling* and Swiftian prose (in 'The Story of the Injured Lady') demonstrates that writers understood sex and gender as a means of articulating political relations: the shame of colonisation, a rape; the union of nations, a happy marriage.[16] While the figuration of 'Mother Ireland' as female has been much analysed, 'Irish masculinities remain a chronically understudied area'.[17] Yet Ireland-as-woman was no isolated trope but implicitly 'functioned at once as ... a shameful reproach, and a possibility of transformation' for masculinity.[18] As Sarah McKibben's work on Irish-language poetry of the seventeenth century has shown, 'powerfully gendered and sexualised imagery was central to early modern colonial rhetoric of election, obligation, and destiny'.[19] Irish language bards of the 1600s and 1700s contested colonisa-tion as a penetration which endangered 'elite male character, prerogatives, patrimony, and even bodies ... threatening the very identity and cultural continuity of Ireland itself'. This 'gendered crisis' is 'metaphorised in potent terms of emasculation, penetration, and dissolution'. Masculine norms are thus deployed as part of a gendered rhetoric of protest and resistance on behalf of Catholic Gaelic culture. Yet by the eighteenth century significant colonial transculturation had occurred, leading to 'mutual transformation of socio-cultural forms'.[20] As McKibben's coda on Brian Merriman's racy *Cúirt an Mheáin Oíche* (*The Midnight Court*) makes clear, cultural hybridisation was in full swing by mid-century. Merriman's carnivalesque poem, which arraigns Irish manhood in a court of women, makes a merit of the specifically *Irish* form of inadequacy castigated by Gaelic poets and mocked by English dramatists. In *Cúirt an Mheáin Oíche*, 'Irish manhood is systematically compromised and comi-cally uncertain. By celebrating bastardy and questioning the sexual basis of men's domination of women, the text at once celebrates and mocks a defiantly unmasterful and culturally hybrid Irish manhood.'[21]

Anglophone Irish literature likewise bears traces of the ways in which Ireland's uncertain political and national position problematised gender norms. In Sarah Butler's Jacobite romance, *Irish Tales* (1716), for instance, heroic Irish masculinity is traduced and betrayed by invading Danes, but is also fatally undermined by dysfunctional familial power dynamics. The romantic hero Murchoe is no match for the rapacious sexual appetite of Turgesius, a Danish king intent on ravishing Murchoe's beloved Dooneflaith. Nor can he withstand the internecine masculine competition between his father and Dooneflaith's. The combination of colonial and native politics effectively robs Murchoe of autonomy and agency, so that it is Dooneflaith who assumes the masculine role: challenging would-be rapists, defying corrupt patriarchs, and spurring on resistance to the Danes. Indeed, the heroine's martial capacity causes her lover to lament that 'how inglorious have you made my Name!' by successfully dispatching the vile usurper herself.[22] 'Something less than the stalwart masculine hero', as Lucy Cogan notes, Murchoe is notable for 'displays of excessive emotion … usually coded as feminine.'[23] Since 'Jacobite culture was centred … on the absence of a strong male hero', Stuart resignation under Hanoverian rule redistributed gender attributes, with Dooneflaith embodying a politicised form of female masculinity.[24]

Yet 'effeminate' forms are not the sole provenance of the dispossessed Gaelic elite or the increasingly resigned Irish Jacobites. Ireland's planter classes; the Protestant refugees fleeing religious oppression in Europe; the politically marginalised dissenters; even the incontrovertibly privileged Ascendancy class, are all increasingly understood as fraught minority populations. While some Protestant writers attempted to distinguish their own autonomy and masculine control from others, all did so with the awareness of compromised agency and self-conscious hybridity. As Samuel Madden observed, the Irish gentleman was an 'amphibious animal', and Irish gentlemen were 'envied as Englishmen in Ireland, and maligned as Irish in England'.[25] The fraught terms of the Williamite settlement, Ireland's increasing financial and political subordination to England, the dramatic dispossession of vast swathes of Catholic nobility, and the entrenchment of a self-conscious Ascendancy minority as governing power in Ireland, rendered English forms of gentlemanly autonomy, independence, and self-possession problematic for Irish authors. Hegemonic or dominant masculinity was therefore even more of an evanescent ideal for most Irish authors. Masculinity in that hybrid form, the novel, reflects how the discontinuities of nation and genre impacted on claims to, and representations of, masculinity. Chaigneau's assertion of gentlemanly status is therefore a tendentious rhetorical claim for an

embattled minority: independent manliness a performance aimed at assert-
ing similarity and disabling British condescension.

The discomfiting disjunction between the co-ordinates of masculine
authority, Ascendancy privilege, and political subordination coincides with
a series of European-wide shifts in masculinity. As Michèle Cohen, Philip
Carter, and Thomas A. King (amongst others) have discussed, the eighteenth century saw a period of intense refashioning of English masculinities.[26]
All link this change to the consolidation of the Hanoverian succession: a
nation state in a process of dynastic legitimisation whose own identity (and
that of its subjects) was shaped by international relations. For Cohen, the
newly minted mercantile man of Whig commerce was linguistically defined
against Francophone 'effeminacy', displaying a morally authentic taciturnity
instead of a labile, 'feminine' performance. For Carter, England's ground
war in Europe and decline of the court promoted forms of masculine
autonomy which likewise rejected 'servile' courtliness. In King's account,
the waning of the Stuart court was accompanied by the collapse of what he
terms 'pederastic' models of male identity in which power was bestowed by
proximity to, or favour from, sovereign power. King shows that the post-
Revolutionary 'gentleman' eschewed ostentatious display of martial valour,
erotic conquest, and finery, but gained esteem via polite and rational self-
restraint, and a concomitant investment in the private spaces of domesticity
and interior subjectivity. Heterosexual marriage as companionate union and
sombre, rather than ostentatious, dress were both hallmarks of the new
masculinity.[27] Thus, 'the privatized, social, subjective body depended
upon the negation of the passionate, "natural", subjected body'.[28] Archaic
forms of masculinity associated with elite courtiers were subject to redescrip-
tion as defective, effeminate, or 'queer'.

King's analysis of the ways in which asymmetric power relations shaped
the conduct and behaviour of male bodies is crucial to reading Irish
masculinities. As Ian McBride has shown, 'Ascendancy Ireland was marked
by cultural instability and the reality or expectation of outside intervention
was a recurrent preoccupation': its position was always contingent upon
external powers.[29] Such dependence – whether on the English throne, or
on continental Jacobites or Rome – exposed the mechanisms of subjection.
Cultural necessity bound Irishmen to other powers, resulting in an
increased reliance on the proofs of obedience (bravery in service, for
instance). The theatrical braggadocio of the Stage Irishman is the literary
symptom of a political subjection: dependence repackaged as comic inept-
ness.[30] As modes of masculinity throughout the period became increasingly
'attached to a naturalized, "inborn" subjectivity … performative, socially-

contingent means of securing masculine prestige' fell 'into disrepute as inauthentic or, as mere play-acting', as that which could 'serve as an alibi for misconduct'.[31] The very ubiquity of the Stage Irishman reflects the depreciated, subordinate status of the Irish in a period in which allegations of national effeminacy were a crucial means of delegitimising political claims.[32]

Swift, Subordinated Masculinity, and the Irish Gentleman

If Swift is the self-hating behemoth of Anglo-Irish literature, his clerical persona and analysis of the Irish situation illuminate the contradictions of Ascendancy masculinity. Irrespective of his birthplace, Swift's ambition focused on the London metropole. His failure there, and subsequent exile to Dublin, generated a definitive combination of frustration, impotence, and resentment which was channelled into a perhaps compensatory Anglo-Irish constitutionalism. As a Church of Ireland minister, Swift's moral position was ostensibly spiritually authoritative. Yet his personal and cultural history underscores the precariousness of the authority of the Protestant church in Ireland and the sense of escalating moral collapse. Having witnessed the influx of Scottish Presbyterians in his first parish of Kilroot, near Belfast, he believed conformist Protestantism in Ireland was threatened not only by the clear and present danger represented by the Papist majority but by the proliferation of sects. As Clíona Ó Gallchoir argues in a seminal essay on gender in eighteenth-century economic writing, the Ascendancy's 'governing masculinity' was a tenuous performance at its very foundation, its ruling elite reliant on external power and beset by anxiety about its ability to control successfully an unruly populace. Its ideology of governance necessitated 'ongoing legitimation', she asserts, 'not least because the economic crises of the 1720s undermined the faith of Anglo-Irish "improvers" in "the superiority of the culture" and thus their mission to spread civility and progress in Ireland'.[33] Such crises of confidence were expressed through the symbolic language of male sterility, impotence, and failure.

In the ninth issue of *The Intelligencer*, Swift provides a lacerating analysis of the Irish peerage. Written following a debate in the Irish Lords over whether to limit the parliamentary privilege which protected members from being arrested for debt, Swift charges that the aristocracy's right to rule is undermined by their neglect of learning.[34] For Swift, the roots of Irish corruption are found in England. Irish gentlemen emulate the English 'whose Manners we affect to follow most' (p. 118). Yet the

English nobility offer no viable model of governance, their masculine vigour sapped by dynastic crisis, their power supplanted by self-interested '*New-men*':

> very few of those Lords remained, who began, or at least had improved their Education, under the happy reign of King *James*, or King *Charles* I, of which Lords the two principal were the Marquis of *Ormond*, and the Earl of *Southampton*. The Minors had, during the Rebellion and Usurpation, either received too much Tincture of bad Principles from those Fanatick Times; or coming to Age at the Restoration, fell into the Vices of that dissolute Reign. (p. 118)

Here Swift's 'portrait of elite masculinity is shaped by ... a Restoration grammar that is ... a politically authorising fantasy of a return to order'.[35] Identifying the Stuart courts as gentlemanly nurseries for stable, governing masculinity, Swift might seem almost nostalgic for archaic Jacobite rule. Yet his classical royalism carries a different valence in its Irish context. As Deana Rankin notes, 'the halcyon days *of Ireland* under James I and Charles I' was a staple of Anglo-Irish histories such as Sir John Temple's *The Irish Rebellion* (1646) so that this elegiac tone does not necessarily represent Jacobite sympathy.[36] Swift's critique conjures a golden age when aristocrats were scholarly and urbane, before the grubby self-interest of the Hanoverians, and the flamboyant Catholicism of James II. This gentlemanly ideal is of a distinctively literary and scholarly cast, his self-possession contrasted against the 'feminine' theatricality of modern education. 'Ancient' manliness inculcates humility and reserve, whereas the '*whole Duty of a Gentleman*' is now 'to Dance, Fence, speak *French*, and know how to behave your self among great Persons of both Sexes' (pp. 119–20).

Like noble youths on their grand tour, 'worthies of the Army' acquire the varnish of continental travel: returning from the War of the Spanish Succession they become 'Dictators of Behaviour, Dress and Politeness' in 'Chocolate-Coffee-Gaming-Houses'. 'A Colonel with his Pay, Perquisites, and Plunder' can there 'outshine many Peers of the Realm; and by the influence of an *exotick* Habit and Demeanor' become the template for manners (p. 120). For Swift, the soldier is a subspecies of the fop: his martial cosmopolitanism a specious form of gentlemanliness. He stages a coffee-house debate on education between a clergyman and an Officer whose swearing and sentiments ironise his assertion that '*the Army is the only School for Gentlemen*' (p. 120). *The Intelligencer* presents the Officer's braggadocio as an aspect of hyper-masculine ignorance, his overwhelming machismo a sign of 'unmanly' want of breeding. The juxtaposition of the shabby clergyman with the daring, but uncouth, Captain is also rehearsed in Swift's 'The Grand Question Debated', composed around the same time. In that poem, which discusses the merits of turning a cattle-fold into either a malthouse or a barracks, female desire for the finely dressed, sword-brandishing, and foul-mouthed Captain is parcelled up with a critique of Ireland's accommodation and subsidising of Britain's standing army. Fawning over military glamour is a sign of the country's thraldom to showy and morally empty forms of power. The solider (who robbed a parson while fleeing from a man whose wife he had seduced) encapsulates the unsuitability of military figures for moral law. If Lady Acheson's desire for a neighbourhood barracks is partly libidinal (suggesting perhaps her husband's incapacity), it also represents the Ascendancy's reliance on brute power to govern a kingdom unsubdued by other means.[37] Lord Acheson's refusal to countenance a barracks might be seen as an instance of enlightened landlordism: a masculine idealism which eschews the financial self-interest that would be served by housing soldiers whose dissolute ways would corrode domestic morality and the local patriarchy.

Failed manhood represents a serious problem when read in the context of Anglo-Irish relations. This is a generational and relational issue, an inability to successfully model and transmit powerful modes of masculinity. Education, which fills young minds with an 'Inclination to Good, and an Aversion to Evil', is neglected by corrupt patriarchs whose own models of loyalty, nobility, and manliness were impugned by their failure to defend their king and contaminated by the profligacy of the court. Nearly a decade after the Declaratory Act of 1720 made Ireland a subordinate Kingdom, Swift's essay concludes with a scarcely veiled hint at the ultimate outcome of English rule of Ireland:

> The Father grows rich by Avarice, Injustice, Oppression; he is a Tyrant in the Neighbourhood, over Slaves and Beggars, whom he calls his Tenants. Why should he desire to have qualities infused into his Son, which himself never possessed ... The Son bred in Sloth and Idleness, becomes a Spendthrift, a Cully, a Profligate, and goes out of the world a Beggar ... Thus, the Former is punished for his own Sins, as well as for those of the latter ... so many great Families coming to an end by the Sloth, Luxury, and abandoned Lusts, which enervated their Breed thorough every Succession, producing gradually a more effeminate Race, wholly unfit for Propagation. (pp. 123–24)

If Ireland's shameful beggary is the offspring of English vice, Swift's critique of a corrupt nobility culminates in a vision of extinction, where patrilineal transmission of effeminacy breeds sterile bloodlines.

If subordination emasculates Irish manhood, the creeping barrenness of England's great houses powerfully metaphorises the ramifications of such father–son relationships, confirming Ó Gallchoir's argument that Protestant Irish writers are 'profoundly uncertain as to their capacity to function as "fathers of the nation"', trapped in a succession which both legitimates their limited power and symbolically infantilises them.[38]

Martial Cosmopolitanism and Improving Masculinity

If Swift laments the effects of toxic paternity on Irish sons, Chaigneau's *The History of Jack Connor* likewise invokes patriarchy and paternity to explore, and ramify, the bonds between the two nations. Swift's mistrust of professional soldiers partly stems from their undermining of the 'manly independence' of Ireland's citizenry. Military ubiquity in Ireland can only have aggravated his sense of the ill effects of such power. In garrisoned Ireland the army was a common destination for both Protestant second sons as well as indigent Catholics, notwithstanding prohibitions on their joining. As a remunerative and potentially meritocratic masculine employment, the soldier was a common and (sometimes worryingly) attractive agent of cosmopolitanism. If Swift's scholar-gentleman is a corrective for improving Ireland, the Whiggish Chaigneau deploys the Irish soldier as a figure whose fluency in the world at large, and experience of combat, grant him status in the British nation state.

The vigorous offspring of the Irish servant, Dolly Bright, and Sir Roger Thornton, an Ascendancy landowner, Jack possesses plenty of the characteristics associated with the roguish Irishman while being an 'improved' hybrid. Dolly Bright, one of the very few Catholic figures in the novel, conveys the inherent possibilities of the populace. Literate, lively, fecund, she is hastily married off to an elderly Williamite soldier, Jeremiah Connor, in order to disguise the baby's illegitimacy. Dolly is not a natural 'termagant', the novel insists, but unsurprisingly her relationship with her elderly husband is unhappy and fractious. Sir Roger's rapid exit from Ireland and his failure to adequately provide for his natural son clearly critique the destabilising effects of English absenteeism on Ireland's moral and social order. Without the support of Sir Roger, the couple fall into arrears on their farm, Jeremiah is blinded and the whole family makes 'the *natural* and common' transition to begging.[39] Now destitute, Dolly succumbs to the sexual consolation of a Catholic priest who persuades her to abandon her son. As both an illegitimate son and, now, a foundling, Jack must become a 'self-made' man.

It is literacy that makes Jack. After his mother sells the family Bible, Jack reads intensively from Richard Allestree's influential *The Whole Duty of Man*. This devotional conduct book is foundational to his character, acting as a prophylactic against maternal popery and proving his very Protestant virtues. As an infant he read this work 'so frequently that at last he was very *expert*, and began to relish the subject' (p. 49). The book proves a talisman to the abandoned boy whose reading from it acts as his passport into the enlightened Ascendancy society of Lord Truegood and his family (p. 54). Jack learns from this book that '*The Calamities and Miseries that befall a Man, be it Want or Sickness ... also come by the Providence of God, who raiseth up and putteth down, as seems good to Him.*'[40] This intertextual admonition binds Ireland's misfortunes and Jack's picaresque into a providential pattern, aligning it with the many conduct books designed for fashioning the gendered identity of men in the period, laying down guidance for pious, polite, and civilised behaviour which fuses the spiritual and worldly aspects of manly life.

Chaigneau's focus on the formative power of literacy and education is confirmed by his references to John Locke's *Some Thoughts Concerning Education*. Both Allestree and Locke are central to eighteenth-century codes of masculine decency: depreciating models of manliness based on worldliness and rank, constructing instead forms of sober manliness and discreet virtue based on inner worth. As Locke noted:

> He that is a good, a vertuous and able Man, *must be made so within*. And therefore, what he is to receive from Education, what is to sway and influence his Life, must be something put into him betimes; Habits woven into the very Principles of his Nature; and not counterfeit Carriage, and dissembled Out-side, put on by Fear, only to avoid the present Anger of a Father, who perhaps may disinherit him.[41]

The contrast between authentic virtue and 'counterfeit' performance corroborates King's thesis on the rise of masculine subjectivity. Yet Locke's faith in the ballast of education also reveals an unease: that civil obedience is an expedience derived from fear, that the dutiful son does not love his subordination but only 'dissembles' in order to ensure the security of his property. Such anxiety had special bite in Ireland.

Chaigneau therefore labours to make Jack a pleasant and grateful son, to ensure the palatability of his 'reprizals against the English'.[42] Jack is passionate, handsome, and impetuous in his bravery in defending those he loves: a compendium of Fieldingesque 'good nature' with an Irish flavour. 'A master of drollery', he has a '*genteel* and *easy* Turn of Language', speaks fluent French and is pronounced a '*joli homme*' by enamoured girls (pp. 86–87). This quasi-continental *sprezzatura* co-exists with an energetic heterosexuality. His affair with his schoolmaster's daughter precipitates his exile from Ireland and his re-baptism as the anglicised Jack 'Conyers'. Advised to cloak the remnants of his '*common Irish* Manner of speaking', linguistic neutrality allows Jack to pass in England, endeavouring 'to speak like the people you live with, which will prevent your being *laugh'd* at and *ridicul'd* by the *Ignorant* and *Vulgar*' (p. 93). Contrasting Jack's initial '*Bulls* and *Blunders*' in London with the more egregious *franglais* of his Huguenot employer Mr Champignon, Chaigneau represents an inclusive and metropolitan Britishness, capable of accommodating national differences through humour but also suggesting the superiority of Irish adaptability (p. 99). Jack's nominal conversion merely accelerates his internal transformation. The letter from John Kindly, Lord Truegood's steward, that accompanies him on his journey acts as another catechism of polite manliness. Kindly (one of Jack's many substitute fathers) reiterates the necessity of loyal Protestantism, sociable cheerfulness, the conformity of outward propriety and inward integrity (pp. 95–97). Jack's experience of *English* liberty is formative. His '*amicable Collision*' polishes off roughness, his 'Trial and Experience' of the world creates the conditions for 'Refinement in Manners ... and Politeness of Style': he becomes, in effect, an Irish exemplar of Whig sociability.[43] Yet importantly the novel also works to renovate 'the deceptively familiar and conveniently fluid genre of the gentleman' from '*the inside*, enabling the emergence of an altogether new type of ruling male': an Irishman worthy of participating in British power.[44]

Jack's adaptability is characteristic of Irish masculinity, and Irish identity, throughout this period: its mobile and malleable self-presentation, the deployment of strategic opacity in the service of necessity. Lest such quicksilver capacity may seem untrustworthy, the novel secures it through companionate union, patriotic service, and validation by patriarchal authority. While Jack's amatory exploits occupy much of the first volume, by the second volume these 'sexual energies necessary to full masculinity' are 'assimilated smoothly ... into the politer self-discipline of the gentleman'.[45] Chaigneau makes Jack the romantic choice of the older Mrs Gold, parodying the Irish fortune-hunter narrative so popular in English fictions. Effectively purchased as a male object of desire for private (if reciprocal) pleasure, Jack's marriage raises the comic spectre of the impecunious Irishman whose lively virility is a prime commodity on the English marriage market. Yet Chaigneau compensates for Jack's passive felicity with the opposite sex by counterbalancing it with his participation in a homosocial club whose members (including the patriotic Colonel Manly) exemplify the improving sociability of an idealised public sphere. The almost allegorical union with Gold is instrumental in guaranteeing Jack financial stability, sexual continence, and social status: 'His *Fortune*, the *faithful* and *agreeable Companion* … and the *Love* and *Respect* of all, were the rewards of his *honest* intentions to all *Mankind* … he deserv'd the honourable Title of a *Man*' (p. 196). Yet this union is brutally circumscribed. Mrs Gold miscarries at news of the Jacobite Rebellion of 1745, dying shortly after her infant son, a crisis of politics and patrimony which propels Jack into soldiery. Once Jack's heir is dead, the narrative has no further need for his wife. Nuptial bliss is abandoned in favour of masculine militarism, as if Gold's superior finances and sexual maturity risk diminishing the protagonist's manly independence. Instead, the novel returns to its core romance: the love affair between Jack and the British state. The Forty-Five enables him to compensate for the loss of his son through renewed patriotic valour. Grief's devastation is cancelled by the active principle of patriotic loyalty, thus minimising the solipsistic possibilities of private emotion. Mere words are 'unmanly and imprudent', to fight for king and country 'requires not a moment's hesitation' (p. 196). Unlike the Young Pretender (a legitimate but unsuitable heir), Jack's career is a military success: he fights at Culloden in 1746, and then serves the Crown with distinction during the War of the Austrian Succession. These loyal exploits are reminders of Ireland's quiescence during the Jacobite Rebellion and of the importance of Irish soldiers in defending the British state against Catholic European powers. Jack's story, like that of his author, illuminates the ways in which the eighteenth-century warfare state drove transfers of people and power across Ireland and the continent.[46] The novel's investment in Irish career soldiers reflects contemporary statistics, since 'by 1760 it is estimated that somewhere between a quarter and a third of officers in the British Army were Irish Protestants'.[47] As the polemic of the United Irishmen would later claim, 'British power depended on Irish manpower'.[48] In the context of mid-century imperial belligerence, anxieties about luxurious degeneration, and allegations of effeminacy levelled against English manhood, the novel suggests that Irish military might provides an invaluable '*Strength* and a *Support* to the *British Government*' (p. 195).

Yet *Jack Connor* does not depict a merely warlike character or an archaic hyper-masculine hero. Committing itself to the new disposition created by the Williamite wars, the novel deconstructs the heroic mode of glamorous violence as a means of deflating and delegitimising Jacobitism, making the Irish soldier an ambassador of British civility. Chaigneau's hero is quite the contrary of the vainglorious Captain of 'The Grand Question Debated', who dismisses scholars as emasculated and sexually timid and asserts that

'To give a young Gentleman right Education, / The Army's the *only* good School in the Nation', while he whores and brawls his way through life.[49] As an agent for many Irish regiments, Chaigneau has a clear vested interest in promoting the British army as a civilising force that offers advancement to Irishmen of merit, and training in socially authoritative manliness. Indeed, in Colonel Manly's letter to the new Captain Conyers, the novel incorporates a set of behavioural strictures for officers. Manly's common-sense precepts stress the role of '*Common Sense*, and the deportment of a Gentleman': the sense of religious responsibility to King and Country (p. 199). Rank is preserved by an officer's fairness, kindness, respect, sobriety, and propriety of speech: values conspicuously absent in Swift's braggart Captain. Jack 'reads his Letter many Times, and compared it with the Instructions of Mr. *Kindly*' (p. 201). Like Kindly's letter, and Allestree's conduct book, Manly's paternalist advice is self-consciously inculcated by intensive reading and reflection.[50] Jack's military experience is depicted as active, fraternal, and underpinned by gentlemanly reading. Despite his bravery, Jack's combat at Culloden is confined to a few brief sentences, eschewing personal glory and the glamour of violence. Instead he expresses the nationwide happiness at the King's victory and praises the monarch's magnanimity in dealing with those '*Children* who betray the best of *Parents*' (p. 203). This idealised William is a 'merciful' father rather than a vengeful patriarch, one who unites and cares for his fractious and disobedient subjects.[51] Rather than a chivalric hero, then, Jack's self-effacing masculinity evinces what Elaine McGirr has identified as a 'new Georgian aesthetic': a 'contractual' form which enshrines a renovated 'Georgian hero – practical, reasonable, plausible, Protestant and patriotic'.[52] And, crucially, Irish.

Jack's military career on the continent reconnects him to his origins. At the Battle of Laffeldt, he intervenes to save a wounded Lieutenant surrounded by three chevaliers. Jack 'manfully defends' (p. 209) the prostrate youth, who is revealed to be Lord Thornton's legitimate son and, thus, his half-brother. While Chaigneau's text glorifies the martial protection provided by the Irish soldier, the 1766 Dublin edition provides an illustration which extrapolates the scene's power dynamics and its loyalist permutations (Fig. 5). In the illustration, Jack dominates the visual field: his back turned to his defeated adversaries and to the battlefield; his English brother mounted on a horse on the right. Though raised above Jack, Lieutenant Thornton bows his head towards his saviour, smiling sweetly. The exchange of the phallic sword between the two signifies trust and the transfer of martial power. As the Lieutenant reaches down to grasp the sword's hilt, its blade

Fig. 5 William Chaigneau, *The History of Jack Connor*, 2 vols (Dublin, 1766), II,
between pp. 232 and 233.
Reproduced courtesy of the National Library of Ireland (LO 13227/2).

points towards Jack's groin, emphasising both his vulnerability and their status as comrades-in-arms. The Irishman's honour creates a corresponding obligation in the English nobleman, expressed by the reciprocal gaze between the two soldiers: grateful on Thornton's side, sombre on Jack's. Chaigneau's text bears out the affective dimensions of this fraternal bond, as Jack tenderly cares for the wounded and bed-bound Lieutenant. Solicitude and care, as much as military service, are catalysts in the protagonist's development into Irish gentleman and full British subject. While socialising with exiled Irish Jacobites (who are represented as genial fellow soldiers rather than popish others), Jack is reunited with his mother, Dolly Bright, now the wife of a Captain Magragh in Cadiz. Jack's *Spectator*-reading mother, now thoroughly chastened and reformed, unveils his true Ascendancy origins, revealing the hero's father as Lord Roger Thornton rather than the humble Jeremiah Connor.

Maternal improvement and forgiveness; a comrade-in-arms revealed as a half-brother; childhood companions and adoptive parents pulled out of the hat as Jack befriends Lord Truegood (now Lord Mountworth) and falls in love with his daughter: the conclusion of the novel produces a system of total filiation for its 'illegitimate' son. To be 'applauded and regarded by Men of Sense and Knowledge, is the highest Honour a Man can have' (p. 226). If Jack's trials and rewards – military laurels, travel, noble friendship, and capital – enable him to successfully occupy the status of an Englishman, only a return to Ireland can unite these values with his national origins. Married to Lady Harriot Mountworth, and resident in Mountworth's Irish seat of Bounty Hall, Connor is *still* 'Conyers', acting as an Englishman. It is only the sight of the shack he lived in as a destitute child that prompts a crisis of self-recognition. Overwhelmed by memories of his lowly past, Jack faints and wakes weeping (p. 236). At this moment of feminised collapse, Mountworth offers support, 'not merely as a *Father*, but as a *Friend*' (pp. 236–37), a combination of support and solidarity which aids agency. Begging forgiveness, Jack names Mountworth his '*Father* … [whose] *Bounty* rais'd me; – [whose] humanity supported my infant weakness; [whose] *Virtues* formed my Soul' before he reveals his deception. His surrogate patriarch's recognition unites Connor with Conyers: the poor child become a gentleman. Mountworth's ecstatic confirmation, 'you are now my Son more than ever', contrasts with his caution that Jack forbear telling Sir Roger, since that father's misplaced '*Pride*' would only reject this worthy son.

A supportive Anglo-Irish patriarch thus supplants the deficient father whose refusal to recognise his Irish son would depreciate both his son's character and manhood. The novel's politics of legitimacy thus suggest that dynastic alignments can, like the 'Glorious Revolution', be matters of choice and election: not necessarily bound to past precedent and prejudice. Mountworth's paternal affirmation aligns him with the nurturing patriarchy urged by that 'Protestant Architect', William, who acts as 'the Common Father of all [his] People' demanding they put aside 'Parties and Divisions ... [recognising] no other Distinction ... but for those who are for the PROTESTANT RELIGION and PRESENT ESTABLISHMENT' (p. 188). The apotheosis of affectionate alliance between Ireland and England, Mountworth's affirmation metaphorises a fantasy of indulgent paternalism: 'so far from being asham'd of your Alliance, I glory in it', he tells Jack (p. 238). Paternity is produced and performed when issues of Irish patrimony and property are pressing. About to become a father and take possession of an estate in Waterford, Jack's allegiance to Mountworth, the representative of a moral Ascendancy, reforms the relation between patriarchal power in England and Ireland. Jack is an Irish Georgian hero whose heterosexual amours, martial gentility, and polite Protestantism embody a mid-century manliness. Chaigneau's picaresque promotes the patriarchal authority of Ireland's governing masculinity.

Jack, then, has benefited from the 'radicalised social mobility' of the natural son or foundling.[53] As Catríona Kennedy has noted, in Ireland 'marriage and the family were deeply implicated in the consolidation of protestant hegemony': increasing restrictions on intermarriage between Catholics and Protestants resulted in a 1745 law annulling all such unions contracted after 1746 and de-legitimising any offspring.[54] Yet Chaigneau's fiction raises the progressive potential of religious intermixing. Jack's birth suggests the moral inefficacy of proscription and hints at the wider moral dispossession caused by self-interested laws designed to prevent Catholic land inheritance. As in Merriman's *Midnight Court*, the bastard represents rejuvenation and a productive compromise between competing groups. Negligent Anglo-Irish landlords damage Ireland's familial structure, undermining domestic patriarchy. If Jack's picaresque is propelled by paternal neglect, his increasingly legible merit calls for renewed paternal affection and a concomitant transfer of masculine power to Ireland. Rather than a 'Protestant fantasy of transforming the natives', *Jack Connor* argues on behalf of a Protestant minority for Ireland as an orphan state: claiming merit through martial masculinity, and arguing for affinity through an expanded political family capable of recognising its natural sons.[55]

Conclusions

Chaigneau's fiction deploys the representational practices of masculinisation in order to legitimise the authority and potency of Irish Protestants, creating an imaginative dynastic filiation between the father state and Ireland, its son. Eschewing the rhetoric of feminisation that characterised much writing on the relationship between Ireland and England, *Jack Connor* uses a masculinist crucible to articulate its vision of national relations. Its rambling hero thrives despite defective paternity, electing a worthy father who is sensible of his virtues and rights and reproaching patriarchal failings of care and authority. Appealing to homosocial bonds and military necessity, rather than chivalric codes of complaisance, *Jack Connor* interpolates Irish masculinity into a transnational system of politeness, male privilege, and Protestantism. Manly's speech parallels personal reputation and national honour:

> in our private Capacities we must keep our Honour and preserve our Reputation, even sometimes at the Hazard of our Lives ... A *Nation* in this, is as a private Man. – We ought to acquire *Reputation* but be careful to *keep it*. – We must make ourselves *respected*, but, by good Conduct, preserve that Dignity. – We ought to love *Peace*, but by a constant readiness for *War*, be able to maintain the *one* with Honour, or pursue the *other with Justice and Glory.* (p. 186)

On the brink of the Seven Years War, Chaigneau's articulation of the utility of Irish manliness to the warfare state makes the soldier a patriotic symbol capable of restoring honour. Yet the novel closes with lines from Shakespeare's *Coriolanus*: a drama of war, soldiery, and the state which is intimately concerned with the 'disposition and legitimation of power through an entire social order' and whose performance history in Ireland maps onto moments of political struggle.[56] In the month before *Jack Connor* was published, Sheridan staged his version of *Coriolanus* at Theatre Royal, Smock Alley in Dublin. As an enthusiastic supporter of the theatre, Chaigneau would have been aware of the performance, staged partly to raise funds for a statue of the 'Patriot' Dean Swift. Sheridan's production ran for five nights, its popularity fuelled by its Whig rhetoric of virtue, manhood, and liberty at a time when Irish opinion was rankling against the appointment of Englishmen in government posts and the channelling of Irish revenue to England.[57] The lines with which Chaigneau closes his novel ('I have done, as you have done; That's, what I can; / ..., for my Country'; ll. 721–22) may seem like patriotic self-deprecation, but they are spoken by a hero whose face is bloodied from fresh combat.[58] The state arms the soldier but, as *Coriolanus* shows, his manly liberty may exceed the government's aims and bounds. In the context of rising dissatisfaction at British corruption and abuse of power in Ireland, the novel's closing lines convey a discontent that unsettles the narrative's affable loyalism. Chaigneau's fiction thus anticipates the rhetoric of masculinisation which would characterise the growing political patriotism of the 1770s.

Notes

1. *The Monthly Review* VI (June 1752), 447.
2. Ibid., p. 448.
3. Ibid., p. 447.
4. William Chaigneau, *The History of Jack Connor*, ed. Ian Campbell Ross (Dublin: Four Courts Press, 2013), p. 37. Future references are to this edition and are cited in the text.
5. *The Monthly Review* VI (June 1752), 447.
6. For the connection to popular biographies and novels, see Ian Campbell Ross's introduction to *Jack Connor* and the same author's 'Novels, Chapbooks, Folklore: The Several Lives of William Chaigneau's Jack Connor, now Conyers; or, John Connor, alias Jack the Batchelor, the Famous Irish Bucker', *Eighteenth-Century Ireland / Iris an dá chultúr* 30 (2015), 62–90.
7. For the definitive survey, see G. C. Duggan, *The Stage Irishman: A History of the Irish Play and Stage Characters from the Earliest Times* (Dublin: Talbot Press, 1937) and, more recently, Joep Leerssen, *Mere Irish and Fíor-Ghael: Studies in the Idea of Irish Nationality, Its Development and Expression Prior to the Nineteenth Century*, 2nd edn (Cork University Press, 1996), pp. 77–150.
8. Richard Steele, *The Spectator*, ed. Donald Bond, 5 vols (Oxford: Clarendon Press, 1965), I, p. 87.
9. Elizabeth Butler Cullingford, 'National Identities in Performance: The Stage Englishman of Boucicault's Irish Drama', *Theatre Journal* 49.3 (1997), 287–300.
10. Leerssen, *Mere Irish and Fíor-Ghael* and David Hayton, 'From Barbarian to Burlesque: English Images of the Irish, c. 1660–1750', *Irish Economic and Social History* 15 (1988), 7–31.
11. Roy Foster, *The Irish Story: Telling Tales and Making it Up in Ireland* (London: Allen Lane, 2001), p. 3.
12. Seamus Deane, 'Foreword', in Rolf Loeber and Magda Loeber, with Anne M. Burnham, *A Guide to Irish Fiction* (Dublin: Four Courts Press, 2006), pp. xvii–xxii (p. xxi).
13. Stefan Dudink, Karen Hagemann, and Anna Clark, 'Historicizing Male Citizenship', in *Representing Masculinity: Male Citizenship in Modern Western Culture*, ed. Dudink, Hagemann, and Clark (London: Palgrave Macmillan, 2008), pp. ix–xv (p. ix).

14. Joan Scott, 'Gender: A Useful Category of Historical Analysis', in *Gender and the Politics of History*, rev. edn (New York: Columbia University Press, 1999), pp. 28–50 (p. 42).

15. Joseph Valente, 'Self-Queering Ireland', *Canadian Journal of Irish Studies* 36.1 (2012), 25–43 (p. 27).

16. For a discussion of the ways in which Irish writers understood political governance in gendered terms, see Clíona Ó Gallchoir, '"Whole Swarms of Bastards": *A Modest Proposal*, the Discourse of Economic Improvement and Protestant Masculinity in Ireland, 1720–1738', in *Ireland and Masculinities in History*, ed. Rebecca Anne Barr, Sean Brady, and Jane McGaughey (London: Palgrave, 2019), pp. 39–65.

17. Catríona Kennedy, 'Women and Gender in Modern Ireland', in *The Princeton History of Modern Ireland*, ed. Richard Bourke and Ian McBride (Princeton University Press, 2015), pp. 361–81 (p. 361). Relatively few works explicitly address masculinity and Ireland in the period, though see Padhraig Higgins, *A Nation of Politicians: Gender, Patriotism, and Political Culture in Late Eighteenth-Century Ireland* (Madison, WI: University of Wisconsin Press, 2012); Declan Kavanagh, *Effeminate Years: Literature, Politics, and Aesthetics in Mid-Eighteenth-Century Britain* (Lewisburg, PA: Bucknell University Press, 2017); and Barr, Brady, and McGaughey, eds., *Ireland and Masculinities in History*.

18. Sarah McKibben, *Endangered Masculinities in Irish Poetry, 1540–1780* (University College Dublin Press, 2010), p. 67.

19. Ibid., p. 2.

20. Ibid., p. 10.

21. Ibid., p. 11.

22. Sarah Butler, *Irish Tales: or, Instructive Histories for the Happy Conduct of Life*, ed. Ian Campbell Ross, Aileen Douglas, and Anne Markey (Dublin: Four Courts Press, 2010), p. 56.

23. Lucy Cogan, 'Sarah Butler's *Irish Tales*, a Jacobite Romance', *Eighteenth-Century Fiction* 29.1 (Fall 2016), 1–22 (p. 16).

24. Ibid., p. 4.

25. Samuel Madden, *Reflections and Resolutions Proper for the Gentlemen of Ireland* (Dublin, 1738), pp. 95–96.

26. Michèle Cohen, *Fashioning Masculinity: National Identity and Language in the Eighteenth Century* (London: Routledge, 1996); Philip Carter, *Men and the Emergence of Polite Society: Britain, 1660–1800* (Harlow: Pearson Education, 2001); Thomas A. King, *The Gendering of Men, 1600–1750*, Vol. I: *The English Phallus* (Madison: University of Wisconsin Press, 2004). See also Kathleen Wilson, *The Island Race: Englishness, Empire and Gender in the Eighteenth Century* (London: Routledge, 2003).

27. See David Kuchta, *The Three-Piece Suit and Modern Masculinity: England, 1550–1830* (Berkeley, CA: University of California Press, 2002).

28. King, *Gendering of Men*, p. 149.

29. Ian McBride, *Eighteenth-Century Ireland: The Isle of Slaves* (Dublin: Gill and Macmillan, 2009), p. 26.

30. Leerssen, *Mere Irish and Fíor-Ghael,* argues that 'stage Irishmen became more sentimental and sympathetic in direct proportion to the extent to which political fears for gaelic Jacobitism dwindled after 1745' (p. 97).

31. Erin Mackie, *Rakes, Highwaymen, and Pirates: The Making of the Modern Gentleman in the Eighteenth Century* (Baltimore, MD: Johns Hopkins University Press, 2009), p. 9.

32. See Kavanagh, *Effeminate* Years, *passim.*

33. Ó Gallchoir, '"Whole Swarms of Bastards"', quoting Toby Barnard, *Improving Ireland? Projectors, Prophets and Profiteers, 1641–1786* (Dublin: Four Courts Press, 2008), p. 13.

34. See Jonathan Swift and Thomas Sheridan, *The Intelligencer*, ed. James Woolley (Oxford: Clarendon Press, 1992), p. 116. Future references are to this edition and are cited in the text.

35. Jason Solinger, *Becoming the Gentleman: British Literature and the Invention of Modern Masculinity, 1660–1815* (New York: Palgrave Macmillan, 2012), p. 16.

36. Deana Rankin, *Between Spenser and Swift: English Writing in Seventeenth-Century Ireland* (Cambridge University Press, 2005), p. 73; my emphasis.

37. See Ivar McGrath, '"The Grand Question Debated": Jonathan Swift, Army Barracks, Parliament and Money', *Eighteenth-Century Ireland / Iris an dá chultúr* 31 (2016), 117–36.

38. Ó Gallchoir, '"Whole Swarms of Bastards"', p. 43.

39. Chaigneau, *History of Jack Connor*, p. 45.

40. Richard Allestree, *The Whole Duty of Man* (London, 1658), p. 252.

41. John Locke, *Some Thoughts Concerning Education* (1693), ed. John W. Yolton and Jean S. Yolton (Oxford University Press, 1989), p. 110; my emphasis.

42. *The Monthly Review* VI (June 1752), p. 447.

43. Anthony Ashley Cooper, third Earl of Shaftesbury, *Characteristicks of Men, Manners, Opinions, Times,* ed. Philip Ayers, 2 vols (Oxford University Press, 1999), I, pp. 64, 10.

44. Solinger, *Becoming the Gentleman*, p. 3; my emphasis.

45. Mackie, Rakes, *Highwaymen, and Pirates*, p. 9.

46. Ian Campbell Ross, 'Chaigneau, William (1709–1781)', *Oxford Dictionary of National Biography* (Oxford University Press, 2004): www.oxforddnb.com/ view/article/5018 [accessed 4 April 2017].

47. McBride, *Eighteenth-Century Ireland*, p. 44.

48. Ibid., p. 45.

49. Jonathan Swift, 'The Grand Question Debated', in *Jonathan Swift: Major Works*, ed. Angus Ross and David Woolley (Oxford University Press, 1984), p. 500, ll. 180–81; my emphasis.

50. Ian Campbell Ross notes that Manly's letter is incorporated into Thomas Simes, *The Military Medley, Containing all the most Necessary Rules and Directions for Attaining a Competent Knowledge of the Art* (Dublin, 1763), p. 153: see Chaigneau, *History of Jack Connor*, p. 261.

51. This clemency towards Stuart rebels is in stark contrast to Irish legislation after the Treaty of Limerick, in which many of the generous terms promised by King William were broken by an Irish Protestant minority keen to suppress Jacobite Catholics; see McBride, *Eighteenth-Century Ireland*, p. 5.

52. Elaine McGirr, *Heroic Mode and Political Crisis, 1660–1745* (Newark, DE: University of Delaware Press, 2009), p. 205.

53. Wolfram Schmidgen, quoted in Lisa Zunshine, *Bastards and Foundlings: Illegitimacy in Eighteenth-Century England* (Columbus, OH: Ohio State University Press, 2005), p. 15.

54. Kennedy, 'Women and Gender', p. 362.

55. Aileen Douglas, 'The Novel before 1800', in *The Cambridge Companion to the Irish Novel*, ed. John Wilson Foster (Cambridge University Press, 2006), pp. 22–38 (p. 29).

56. John Kerrigan, *Archipelagic English: Literature, History, Politics, 1603–1707* (Oxford University Press, 2008), p. 18.

57. See John Kerrigan, 'Prologue', in *Celtic Shakespeare: The Bard and the Borderers*, ed. Willy Maley and Rory Loughnane (Aldershot: Ashgate, 2013), pp. xv–xli.

58. Shakespeare, *Coriolanus*, I, ix, ll. 18–20.

CHAPTER 14

Fictions of Sisterhood in Eighteenth-Century Irish Writing

Moyra Haslett

'A knot of ladies, got together by themselves, is a very School of Impertinence and Detraction; and it is well if those be the worst.'[1] Swift's comment, offered as advice to a 'very young lady on her marriage', might be taken as axiomatic for his period, in which representations of female assembly are so often derogatory, whether these are of the *mná caointe* of Irish funeral tradition, the market women who congregate on Ormond Quay, or the more 'polite' ladies of urban tea-tables.[2] And the suspicion of female assembly often extends to the disparagement of female friends and of sisters too. A classical tradition of writings on friendship, extending from Plato, Aristotle, and Cicero to Montaigne, routinely excluded women from the bonds of friendship enjoyed by elite men, and suggested that women were incapable of friendship towards each other.[3] Demands by husbands that their wives relinquish former female friends appear to have increased across the century. Certainly, suspicion of the intensity of female–female bonds was widespread. The father of the young Frances Sheridan, for example, refused to allow her to learn to write, lest she exchange love letters with a suitor or engage in 'the scarcely less dangerous interchange of sentiment in the confidential effusions of female correspondents'.[4]

Negative portrayals of literal sisters become less surprising in such a context. Eighteenth-century novels, for example, commonly explored the tensions between sisters. In Sarah Fielding's *The Adventures of David Simple* (1744) the hero encounters five successive sets of sisters, all characterised by mutual envy and avarice. In Samuel Richardson's *Clarissa, or the History of a Young Lady* (1747–48), the heroine's sister, Arabella, exemplifies 'unsisterliness' which, together with 'unsisterly', are cited by the *Oxford English Dictionary* as receiving their first documented uses in the novel. And many novelists dramatised the moral differences between women by representing a contrasting pair of sisters, as for example in Sarah Scott's *Agreeable Ugliness* (1754) and Charlotte Lennox's *Sophia*

(1762). Sisters were more likely to be depicted as rivals for a husband than comrades-in-arms. Meanwhile the word 'lesbian' makes an early appearance as an insulting word in a scandalously vituperative poem *The Toast*, published first in Dublin in 1732 as part of its author's campaign to recover a loan of several thousand pounds.[5]

In misogynistic satire and in conduct-oriented literature, then, female assembly, female friendship, the kinship of sisters, and the love of what we would now call lesbian women have clearly existed within a spectrum of undifferentiated female homosociality. This chapter focuses on representations of female friendship in printed texts of this period, but in thinking of friendship as a form of 'sisterhood', it addresses the political dimensions of those representations. Primarily used of prostitutes and nuns, and occasionally applied to groups of female servants and religious enthusiasts, women writers, fictional female club members, and – later in the century – to spinsters, pejorative uses of the word 'sisterhood' certainly predominate in our period. A search for 'sisterhood' among Dublin-printed texts confirms the catalogue of negativity: sisterhoods of nuns, prostitutes, 'tiplers', waiting maids, female prisoners, reformed prostitutes, and gossiping and censorious dowagers can be found, none of them depicted as commendable.[6]

However, more positive uses of the word 'sisterhood' are at least imaginable in this period too. In a poem published in 1730, 'The Basket' (possibly written by Samuel Wesley), the term is used in something like its modern sense of loyalty and solidarity between women. Two women, indignant on behalf of a grocer's wife who has been beaten by her husband, are described by the poet as a 'sisterhood'. In Sarah Scott's sympathetic depiction of an all-female community, the novel *A Description of Millenium Hall* (London, 1762; Dublin, 1763), the worthy women of the community are described as a 'sisterhood'.[7] And while pejorative representations of, and attitudes towards, female assembly continue throughout the period, an increase in female-authored printed material undoubtedly tilts the balance towards more favourable views of female friendship, although, as the examples noted above show, those derisive of and sympathetic to female attachments are not drawn exclusively along the axes of sex.

By thinking about female friendship in the overtly social and political domain of ideas of 'sisterhood', this chapter revisits Adrienne Rich's famous, but also much criticised, theory of a 'lesbian continuum', first given published form in 1980.[8] The concept has been challenged from a variety of feminist perspectives: as being overly inclusive in suggesting a graduated scale encompassing both friendship and lesbianism, as diminishing the importance of the sexual and the erotic within lesbianism, as assuming that female–female relations were inherently feminist, or that they subverted male privilege, for example.[9] However, the idea of the continuum reflects the ways in which derogatory attitudes towards female homosociality in this period created exactly these kinds of blurring.[10] If we combine attention to the historicised discourse of sisterhood in all of its inflections with the recent trend within feminism to see gender in terms of performance rather than identity, then a reading of printed, imaginative literature must be central to our understanding of the period, one in which ideological discourses and fictive imaginings are both part of the recovery of lived experience and its necessary supplement. The chapter thus considers female friendship as it is explored in a range of texts, poetic and fictional, by Irish women writers, before turning towards the ways in which 'sisterhood' began to be used as a particularly explicit political term to celebrate Ireland's equivalency with her sister-nation, England.

Poems of Female Friendship

Poems addressed to female friends, or on the topic of female friendship, became increasingly prominent in writing by women poets in the eighteenth century. One explanation for this popularity can be found in the figure of Katherine Philips, whose ardent, rapturous poems addressed to female friends, particularly to 'Rosania' (Mary Aubrey) and 'Lucasia' (Anne Owen), did not prevent her from being cited as a 'spotless' model for later women writers to emulate.[11] Philips spent just over one year in Dublin (June 1662–July 1663), accompanying her friend Anne Owen, now married to the Viscount of Dungannon, and seeing to financial affairs of her own. While there, in addition to her translation of Corneille, *Pompey*, performed at Theatre Royal, Smock Alley in February 1663, she wrote a number of poems addressed to Irish elite women: the Countess of Cork and her three daughters, and Lady Mary Butler, daughter of the Duke of Ormond. As Marie-Louise Coolahan has noted, these poems often circle around the question of whether friendship between social unequals is possible, and may have been motivated primarily by the access these women offered to more powerful male relatives.[12] However, among the praise offered to Philips by the anonymous 'Philo-Philippa', remains that of her reputation for friendship. It was friendship to Lucasia which brought Philips (here, 'Orinda') to Ireland, despite the dangers of the sea-crossing:

That noble friendship brought thee to our Coast,
We thank *Lucasia*, and thy courage boast.
Death in each Wave could not *Orinda* fright,
Fearless she acts that friendship she did write:
Which manly Vertue to their Sex confin'd,
Thou rescuest to confirm our softer mind;
For there's requir'd (to do that Virtue right)
Courage, as much in Friendship as in Fight.
The dangers we despise, doth this truth prove,
Though boldly we not fight, we boldly love.[13]

In seeing loving friendship as a badge of honour as great as that of any soldier, 'Philo-Philippa' makes the 'softer mind' of conventional femininity a hollow device, striking us as inappropriate in its context.

Although there were no Dublin editions of Philips's poetry, a number of sources testify to her continued fame in Ireland: copies of her books appear in Dublin sale catalogues, references to her occur in reprinted poems by Cowley and Roscommon and in histories of theatre in Ireland, and a number of writers and readers record their esteem.[14] In her *Memoirs* (1748) Laetitia Pilkington, for example, declares Philips one of her two favourite woman authors and summarises something of the way in which Philips could write rapturously, even ecstatically about female intimacy, while retaining a reputation for modesty: 'Love she has wrote upon with Warmth, but then it was such as Angels might share in without injuring their original Purity.'[15]

Although individual poems articulating friendship between women are to be found in all published work by women in this period, they are a particularly notable feature of published collections by Mary Barber, Charlotte McCarthy and Margaret Goddard. Barber's *Poems on Several Occasions* (London, 1735), as Aileen Douglas notes in her chapter in this volume, can be characterised by its celebration of female sociability, not only in its inclusion of poems by Constantia Grierson and poems on the exchange of books as gifts to other female friends, but also in its framing through the female networks of charitable giving and of poetry subscription itself. Female friendship poems sit alongside poems to actual or potential female patrons and enfold these pleas into the broadly sketched ethic of female support. The triangulation of many poems' address is evident in a number of the titles, and points to the extraordinarily feminocentric dynamic of the collection overall: 'To Mrs Newans, encouraging her to draw Lady Killmorey's Picture'; 'Written for a Gentlewoman in Distress. To her Grace Adelida, Dutchess of Shrewsbury'; and 'To the Right Honourable the Lady Kilmorey with a Letter, which was written by the late Lady Roydon, of the Kingdom of Ireland, just before her death', for example. In the following example, the dedication is made part of the title and thus extends its female network even more insistently: 'Occasion'd by reading the Memoirs of Anne of Austria, written by Madam de Motteville. Inscrib'd to the Right Honourable the Countess of Hertford'.[16] Patronage itself is explicitly cast as an act of friendship, while poems of whimsical self-deprecation suggest an audience of implicitly female friends who will recognise the manoeuvre.[17]

   McCarthy's poems were published with her novel *The Fair Moralist* (London, 1745; expanded edition 1746) and share with that narrative the theme of female affection.[18] Although Goddard's volume, *Poems on Several Occasions* (Dublin, 1748), reflects the mixed company she entertained as a respectable Dublin widow – with poems by Edmund Burke, Richard Shackleton, and other Trinity College friends included – it also includes sixteen poems which are either addressed to female friends or on the topic of love between women. Although the poems by both women are often written in a conventionalised idiom, in the generic language of classical pastoral, for example, the female intimacy which is their characteristic subject effects a reworking of the tradition.[19] A number of poems in both collections openly ventriloquise the perspective of a male admirer: McCarthy's 'Written on St Valentine's Day, for a Gentleman to send his Mistress', for example, and Goddard's 'On the New Star, 1737', in which Pope's *Rape of the Lock* is rewritten in the poet's desire to wear a lock of hair belonging to her friend, Bellamira.[20] In others, the perspective of a lover is implied. In one poem by McCarthy, 'Sylvia' is reassured of the poet's affection: though she does not write poetry in her praise, true honour is evident in her gazing at, or sitting with her all day long.[21] And female beauty can be celebrated in daringly sensuous fashion. One poem by McCarthy invokes Samuel Croxall's 'warm' poem *The Fair Circassian* (1720), a poetic rendering of the Song of Solomon which Croxall published anonymously. And in Goddard's song, 'On four ladies bathing, by Robin Good-Fellow, Poet Laureat to Oberon King of the Faries [sic]', Robin is figured as Actaeon, disturbing Diana and her nymphs.[22] Even when the poetry is rather conventional, then, the perspective of female homosocial affection twists and queers the convention.

   Female intimacy is more skilfully explored in the poetry of Olivia Elder (1735–80), the daughter of a Presbyterian minister who lived in Aghadowey, near Coleraine. Elder appears to have been preparing her poems for print before her death and a fair copy volume of these poems survives in a manuscript in the National Library of Ireland which has been recently edited and published by Andrew Carpenter.[23] Verse epistles to female friends stand out as a particularly prominent feature in the collection, and suggest that Elder almost certainly thought of herself as writing within a community of female friends although their verses to her in return have not survived. These friends remain as felt presences, however, within the poetry. Many of the poems claim to be written extempore, and the ease and good humour of 'talking on paper' are evident throughout. An especially good example of this is the poem 'To Miss M[argaret] B[lair] at C[oleraine] Novbr 13th 1769'. Missing the company of her friend, Elder imagines how she would advise her to 'use her imagination': "Tis true, you'll say I have the air, / And I may go build castles there.' The Muse is then whimsically personified as 'her Ladyship' with whom Elder has quarrelled and as a cuckoo who might return in spring, and her poem compared to a pickle lacking the classical savour of 'Attick salt'. Much genial fun is had with classical puns, tags, and quotations, and the vision of her pages being recycled from tea-sheets or returning to toilet paper. The comic facetiousness throughout the poem is exemplified in the outrageous use of the colloquial Hiberno-Irish 'puke' (for vomit) as the end rhyme for some transliterated Greek (pp. 35, 37). Other poems suggest 'in jokes' between friends: Margaret Blair is teased with being fat and reminded of a mutual friend with a remarkable proficiency in boxing (pp. 46–48); another epistle conjures the vision of Elder and her friend as unhappily married to two brothers of the neighbourhood, one a drunkard, the other finically proud (pp. 83–87).

The important female tradition which all of these poems exemplify – of effusive articulations of love and sensuality between women – was given the term 'romantic friendship' by Lillian Faderman in her book, *Surpassing the Love of Men* (1981), and defined as coming into public view through the poetry of Katherine Philips.[24] Harriette Andreadis, among a number of other critics, has written of the cost incurred by this designation to women identified as openly lesbian, as 'romantic friendship' permitted a separation of the discourses of forbidden lesbian sexuality and relations between 'respectable' women. Andreadis notes how:

> in the eighteenth century, unnamed erotic and possibly transgressive behaviors were to be institutionalized and made acceptable in the convention of 'female romantic friendship'. Thus, the work and life of Katherine Philips furnished an example that made possible the expression as well as the acceptance of eroticized friendships between women as a respectable alternative to the spectre of unnatural vice.[25]

The idea of the 'romantic friendship' potentially overwrites, and thus suppresses, erotic and sexual feelings between women as a safe form of 'politeness'. But the reception of these poems in the eighteenth century itself also permits this kind of double inscription, and to that extent, the modern theory of romantic friendship reflects historical reception.

The tradition of 'romantic friendship' would find its most famous embodiment in the events of 1778, when Sarah Ponsonby and Lady Eleanor Butler defied their parents' attempts to separate them and left Ireland together. Their home in Wales would give them their popular name – the 'Ladies of Llangollen' – and became a popular destination for visitors and correspondence. Anna Maria Edwards's story of their 'elopement' is told in the poem 'Female Friendship. A Tale. Founded on Fact', published in Dublin within ten years of their flight.[26] Edwards's conclusion is that their story testifies to how much stronger 'friendship' is than 'love'. But all of these poems suggest that heterosexual love is being refracted in importantly homosocial or sapphic terms. The contribution of fiction to these ideas would be to situate female affective bonds in relation to heterosexual relationships even more insistently, as depictions of female friendship are positioned within the narrative plot conventions of courtship and ensuing marriage.

Fictional Sisterhoods

In publishing her poetry as a supplement to her novel *The Fair Moralist*, Charlotte McCarthy constructed something of a compendium of romantic friendship.[27] In the conclusion of the novel, the heroine, the orphaned and destitute Emilia, refuses an advantageous and romantic marriage to the reformed libertine, Philander, and instructs him rather to prove his reformation by marrying Melissa, whom he had seduced before attempting the virtue of Emilia. Emilia's steadfast fidelity to Melissa, her childhood friend, is arguably sublimated in marriage to Melissa's brother, Theodore, and the narrative's resolution of a double-wedding binds Emilia and Melissa as closely as it does the married couples. This convenient transference of desires reflects the crossings of sex and gender throughout the narrative: disguised as a man, Emilia has been the object of desire for many women, and attended Philander as his closest ('male') confidante (pp. 34–36, 40–41, 46–47, 54–55); Melissa has pretended that Emilia is a new (male) lover (pp. 15–16); Philander has wooed Melissa as a proxy for Emilia (p. 20); and Emilia has been struck by the 'male' beauty of Melissa disguised as a man (p. 65). Had Philander not proved, finally, faithful to Melissa, the two female friends had resolved to 'both together sweetly share their Fortunes' in the retirement of a convent (p. 67), a resolution which would have completed the celebration of their friendship which is the one constant throughout. In these switches of desire and cross-dressing, the distinction between (homosocial) friendship and (heterosexual) love is repeatedly questioned.

McCarthy's novel is characteristic of early eighteenth-century fiction in its emphasis upon plot. Relatively little attention is given to the feelings of its characters, in contrast to the poetry which accompanied the novel in its London printings. Frances Sheridan's first attempt at fiction – *Eugenia and Adelaide*, written when she was possibly only fifteen (*c.* 1739) – is similarly plot-driven. Eugenia is betrayed by her mother, Adelaide by a female cousin, both of them acting as rivals to the girls' preferred suitors, but the two friends remain loyal to each other. And, like *The Fair Moralist*, the novel explores homosexual desire through cross-gendering: both Eugenia and her mother fall in love with the Spanish nobleman 'Don Clement' who turns out, retrospectively, to have been his twin sister Clementina in disguise. In order to meet clandestinely with Eugenia at a crucial point, Clementina, disguised as 'Don Clement', disguises himself (really, herself) as Donna Aurora. While Eugenia will eventually marry Clementina's brother, the Marquis, her attraction to 'Don Clement' is an important element of the narrative, wrong-footing the reader and suggesting sapphic potentialities at the very moment of refusing them. And the narrator's attempt to make this crossing of desire explicable hardly settles the matter in conventional terms: 'Indeed, the resemblance was so perfect between this amiable brother and sister, that it could hardly be called a change in Eugenia's heart.'[28] The Marquis's affection for 'Don Clement' (alias Clementina) is also made explicit only once heterosexuality is claimed: 'How often have you boasted to me of the freedom of your heart; and that you would not exchange the sweets you enjoyed in my friendship for the love of the greatest Princess upon earth!'[29] But the suddenness of the revelations ensures that these transferences of desire are sites of disruption and provocation.

These two novels, *The Fair Moralist* and *Eugenia and Adelaide*, thus mirror the open experimentation with gender and sexuality which is characteristic of the poetry of the 1740s by McCarthy and Goddard, and the potentially unsettling possibilities of female bonds. At the end of that decade, the publication of Richardson's *Clarissa* would have a hugely significant impact on fictional representations of female friendship in fiction, not least an increase in the number of such fictions in the second half of the eighteenth century. At its broadest level, this increase is inspired by the mode of sensibility, with its focus on feeling and emotion, itself a result of the phenomenal popularity of all three of Richardson's novels. But it was *Clarissa* in particular in which intense bonds between women are most insistently affirmed and idealised, as the affection and support between Clarissa Harlowe and her closest friend Anna Howe is figured as stronger than the ties of family. Although the novel remains most famous for the rape and martyrdom of its heroine, it also depicts an agonistic struggle between the affirmative, loving friendship of Clarissa and Anna and the sexual libertinism of Lovelace. In the very first letter of the novel, Anna announces, 'I love you, as never woman loved another.'[30] In the repellent view of Lovelace, in contrast, friendship between women is only ever a substitute for sex, hastily discarded once married: 'the word [friendship] is a *mere* word, the thing a mere name with them; a cork-bottomed shuttlecock, which they are fond of striking to and fro, to make one another glow in the frosty weather of a single state'.[31] Countering such a view is the evidence of the letters exchanged by Clarissa and Anna which, for many readers, then and now, have represented the most affirming element of the novel. Sarah Fielding, for example, has her male character Bellario reflect upon the depiction of friendship as one of the novel's highlights: 'True and false Friendship was never more beautifully displayed than in this Work; the firm, the steady Flame that burns in the fixed Affection between *Clarissa* and Miss *Howe*.'[32]

Richardson's novel was as popular in Ireland as it was elsewhere. Reprinted by George Faulkner within eighteen days of the novel's first London edition, a second Dublin printer, William Sleater, published an abridgement in 1756, the earliest abridgement to retain the epistolary form. Published with the support of many of Ireland's elite families, the work was dedicated to Elizabeth Ponsonby, wife of the first Commissioner of the Revenue who became, in 1756, Speaker of the House of Commons; drew more than a quarter of its subscriptions from women; and included an advertisement for the printing of ladies' visiting cards.[33] Surviving correspondence evidences how deeply felt *Clarissa*'s reception was in Ireland, from Catherine Bagshawe, a soldier's wife who beguiled her time while he was absent by reading the novel, to Lady Echlin living in Rush, whose eight-year correspondence with Richardson included the draft of an extensive alternative ending in which Clarissa was not raped and Lovelace died penitent.[34]

Like Elizabeth Echlin, Frances Sheridan responded to *Clarissa* creatively and Richardson himself played a key role in getting that response – her novel, *The Memoirs of Miss Sidney Bidulph* (1761) – published. Although the relationship between Sidney and her mother dominates this novel, as Amy Prendergast's chapter in this volume demonstrates, that between Sidney and her childhood friend is the one which frames the novel throughout: the novel consists of Sidney's candid letters to Cecilia and concludes with Cecilia's brief account of events.[35] Sheridan was encouraged to write the novel by Richardson after he had read *Eugenia and Adelaide* in manuscript. And in both novels it is the female friend as interlocutor, and as an implied presence throughout, who enables female expression and advocacy.

Sidney addresses Cecilia throughout as 'sister' and the strength of their friendship recurs throughout the narrative, including these reflections when Sidney returns to her childhood home:

> Our names, our virgin names, I find cut out on several of the old elm trees: this conjures up a thousand pleasing ideas, and brings back those days when we were inseparable. But you are no longer Rivers, nor I Bidulph. Then I think what I have suffered since I lost that name, and at how remote a distance you are from me; and I weep like a child.[36]

When the novel begins, Cecilia is on a tour with her family on the continent, but the separation becomes permanent when she marries and settles in Vienna. The plot's dramatic closing events – in which Sidney weds Orlando Faulkland in an unintentionally bigamous marriage after the supposed murder of his adulterous wife – also see Sidney attempting to arrange to meet with Cecilia in Holland (p. 455). That reunion happens instead in England, as Cecilia hastens to return to her friend after Sidney's final letters end on an abrupt note of despair: 'tell me if I ought to live any longer', 'nothing but my death should close such a scene as this' (pp. 456, 457).

Throughout the novel, Sidney writes openly of her feelings and thoughts, insofar as she can. Articulations of love and desire, as a number of modern critics have noted, are discouraged by Sidney's culture, but Cecilia is often in advance of Sidney's own self-knowledge and interprets the letters for coded articulations of what Sidney cannot admit even to herself (pp. 27, 78, 333–34). Sidney's account veers disconcertingly from every day, commonplace accounts of domestic life to the high-stakes emotional life of courtship and marriage, with Sidney repeatedly apologising to her friend for the triviality of her letters:

> You who are surrounded by the gaieties of a splendid court, had need of the partiality which I know you have for your Sidney, to desire a continuation of her insipid narrative. But, I suppose, if I were to tell you, that on such a day

> my white Guiney-hen brought out a fine brood of chickens, you might be as
> well-pleased with it, as I should be to hear from you of the birth of an arch
> duchess. (p. 270)

The account with which the novel ends, a continuation of Sidney's story as
told by Cecilia, hints that Cecilia gives up the life of a European court for
domestic retreat with her friend: 'Before I accompany Mrs Arnold into her
solitude . . .' (p. 465). And although Cecilia's life as the wife of an
Englishman abroad is not included within the frame of the novel, it exists
as an alternative possibility, beyond the limitations of Sidney's entrapment
within domestic plots and conventions.

   The relationship between public and private affairs in the lives of female
friends is more insistently explored in a novel by Frances Sheridan's
daughter, Elizabeth: *The Triumph of Prudence over Passion* (1781).[37] This
novel, too, is an epistolary fiction told by female friends, beginning with
letters exchanged by Louisa Mortimer in Dublin and Eliza Fitzgerald in
rural Cavan. But although they, like their counterparts in *Sidney Bidulph*,
occasionally apologise for the inconsequentiality of their accounts, they
also congratulate each other on being able to talk of politics as well as of
'trifles' (p. 88). The friends' commitment to the ideals of the patriot
opposition of the late 1770s is apparent in their first letters, in which
Louisa commiserates with Eliza because she has missed the opportunity
of seeing the famous parade of Volunteer soldiers on College Green
(4 November 1779). Ostensibly a demonstration of loyalty to the British
Crown, the Volunteer parade was more accurately an assertion of Irish
rights, particularly to free trade: the equestrian statue of William III before
which the soldiers marched was decorated with political slogans such as 'A
FREE TRADE: OR ELSE' (p. 179 n.). Eliza's response demonstrates how
their friendship is predicated on shared political loyalties, both to Ireland
and to the proto-feminist ideal of female education:

> you may find, in the most glorious times of Greece and Rome, the women
> were just as warm in their country's cause, as the men: and history has
> applauded them for it; though now people affect to think those things above
> our capacity, and indeed the present mode of education for our sex is so very
> trifling, that I fear there is some truth in the supposition. (p. 36)

Elsewhere, Eliza notes that both of their families have supported their
acquisition of knowledge and learning, granting them the intellectual
respect in which they can become proud citizens of Ireland and rational
friends whose mutual love and esteem is based on shared principles, both
moral and political (p. 88).

Mary O'Dowd has shown how women's involvement in patriot politics in the late 1770s and early 1780s can be seen as a brief interlude, before greater restrictions over female propriety took hold, and political debates shifted to parliamentary reform and the extension of the franchise, rather than the 'buy' and 'wear' Irish campaigns in which women had been such a significant presence.[38] In Louisa Mortimer's explicitly 'patriot' discourse, the allegory of relations between Ireland and England becomes an attack on England as possessive, controlling, and jealous:

> if we do not watch her [England] with unremitting attention, she will, by some artifice, the first convenient opportunity, contrive to render every thing she grants of no effect, for they are selfish, illiberal people, and look with a jealous eye on every advantage enjoyed by their fellow subjects, either envying their prosperity, or looking on it as so much taken from them. (p. 85)

Louisa adds that such faults are yet worse when they characterise the 'temper of a whole nation', as the ill effects are so much worse, with 'millions of people ... sure to be oppressed'. But England does have a specific counterpart or character type within the frame of the novel itself: the wicked Englishwoman Caroline Freeman, whose desire for Eliza's fiancé causes her to create a mutual jealousy which results in their separation, and whose actions must be exposed before the lovers can marry and the plot reach its resolution.

Elizabeth Sheridan's portrayal of Caroline Freeman can also be seen as a revisiting of her mother's portrayal of Miss Burchell, whose desire for Orlando Faulkland cast him as her seducer so as to prevent marriage to Sidney. Elizabeth Sheridan's novel overlays the representation of female sexual perfidy and enmity with considerable political bite and shows how conventional tropes can be adapted, as we will see, to suit different political contexts. However, the gender politics of female homosociality are also significantly different in the two novels and might be considered first, before turning to the question of the novel's use of political allegory.

In Frances Sheridan's *Memoirs of Miss Sidney Bidulph*, the friendship of Sidney and Cecilia remains the only constant element beyond Sidney's exemplary piety and obedience to the cultural mores of her context, including absolute fidelity to her mother. But the novel also interrogates an unthinking allegiance to women. Both Lady Bidulph and Sidney are led to make mistakes because of their sympathy for Miss Burchell, who manipulates Lady Bidulph's partiality to her own sex in particular, to secure her marriage to Orlando. Only belatedly is Miss Burchell revealed to be an arch-manipulator, a 'sly rake in petticoats' (p. 387). Misled by their 'finer feelings' of compassion and emotionalism, Lady Bidulph and her daughter become not only victims of her scheming but unwitting architects of it. Sidney's paean to the importance of having one, special friend only – 'We can have but *one friend* to share our heart, to whom we have no reserve, and whose loss is irreparable' (p. 121) – permits the novel both to eulogise female–female friendship in ways not dissimilar to the romantic friendship of poetic tradition, and to warn of the perils of internecine female enmity, in which female homosocial relations are structurally warped by sexual rivalry.

In Elizabeth Sheridan's *The Triumph of Prudence over Passion*, friendship acts as a bulwark against female enmity – Louisa deftly manages to thwart Caroline Freeman's plans, having seen through her from the very first (p. 131) – and against the disadvantages of life as a woman in this period compared to that of 'the lords of the creation', in Louisa's characteristically facetious phrase (p. 39). Louisa and Eliza are as 'unreserved' in their letters to each other as Sidney and Cecilia and, as Ian Campbell Ross and Aileen Douglas, the editors of the modern edition, note, it is the 'wit and irreverence' with which they write, as much as what they say to each other, that demonstrates the value of rational female friendship (p. 11). Many of these witticisms bind the friends together in knowing solidarity against the restrictions they suffer as women. For example, both Louisa and Eliza write daringly of their disapproval of a mutual friend's husband and their relief, for her sake, that she is now a widow, their exchanges culminating in Louisa's reflection that 'it is shocking enough to date a woman's happiness from the death of her husband; but if husbands will be brutes, they must expect both their wife and her friends will wish them dead' (p. 39). Such acerbity retains its force today, but it is notable that the tone of these fictional exchanges is identical to that of the Bluestockings when they commiserate with Elizabeth Vesey on her separation from them in Ireland and on the hurt and ignominy caused by her openly philandering husband.[39]

The idea that the constancy and intensity of female friendship might pose a challenge to the ideal of the companionate marriage appears to have hardened as the century progressed. Louisa Mortimer's commitment to a single life echoes that of Richardson's Anna Howe and of Frances Sheridan's Dolly, one of two sisters in *Conclusion of the Memoirs of Miss Sidney Bidulph* (1767), but is now inflected with the political tenor of Irish patriot politics in the early 1780s. Louisa's repeated assertions of independence, her refusal to be dictated to by a husband, become synecdoches of Irish sovereignty. Unlike Mrs O'Neil, she would not wait for her husband's permission to stay later than him at a wedding party, 'for', she writes, 'I would not submit to be treated like a child' (p. 123). Unlike Eliza, she could not speak the marriage vows, with their promise to 'obey' a husband (p. 173). When the novel ends with Louisa's continuing commitment to the life of an 'old maid', in defiance of generic and cultural expectations, it signals a correspondence between singlehood and political independence and creates a fictional allegory strikingly at odds with the 'national tale' of marriage and political union characteristic of Romantic-period Irish fiction. This chapter's final section turns to the ways in which national allegories of sisterhood were invoked in the eighteenth century, as a context for Elizabeth Sheridan's novel in particular, and the poems and fictions of female friendship more generally.

Sister Kingdoms

The most famous exponent of Irish political and legislative equality in the eighteenth century was William Molyneux, who argued that Ireland's relationship to England was not that of colony but 'sister kingdom', equal and distinct, though bound together under the one crown. Molyneux himself, however, never used the term which is often invoked to explain his position. That idea would first find popular expression in a 1753 satirical pamphlet, *The True Life of Betty Ireland*, in which the history of Ireland, specifically of its relationship with England, is allegorised as that of sisters.[40] Betty is now less dependent than formerly on her elder sister's cast-off clothes, the pamphlet argues, although she continues to attempt to gain her sister Blanche's favour, sending her gifts (exports) and permitting pensions to be given to her former servants (English placemen in Ireland). The pamphlet concludes with the hope that the sisters will come to a better understanding, since their bickering is of advantage to neither. In this regard, the pamphlet draws upon conventional views of female squabbling:

> But their Manners and Disposition are so different, that it's next to impossible they should ever love one another, tho' for mutual Interest, and to make that Figure in the Eye of the World which two *Ladies* of their Distinction and Fortune ought to assume, their Friends may agree to promote *jointly* their Interests, and never heed how peevish and untoward *either* of them may be, or pay any Regard to the *fanciful Aversions*, and ungrounded Jealousies, which are always inseparable from a female Breast.[41]

The sister allegory was particularly useful in the mid-century period when, as Jacqueline Hill has noted, anti-Union feeling in Ireland needed to be balanced with loyalty to George II.[42] There is clearly no idealisation of female friendship here, and Betty and her sister Blanche are sketched as contrasting, but by no means ideal, personalities. Blanche is proud, reserved, and parsimonious; Betty is vain, open, and prodigal. Blanche is cautious and hides her faults; Betty is not conscious of any faults and thus constantly displays them. Blanche is the more censorious sister; Betty the greater liar. The sisters are thus related, but differentiated, bound historically by shared 'stewards' (in an obvious pun on 'Stuarts') and other monitors but not by affection. 'Sisterhood' is a relational position, not a feeling.

After this satire's depiction of the acrimony between Ireland and England, the idea of political 'sisters' would disappear until the 1770s and 80s, when the term 'sister-kingdom' became suddenly common.[43] Now it referred to respectful, equal relations, on the part of both sisters and nations. This chapter has traced the ways in which increasing numbers of women writers across the eighteenth century engaged with the ideal of 'sisterhood' or, rather, the female friendship for which it often acted as synecdoche. Such works show how female friendship came to be valorised. Sheridan's *The Triumph of Prudence over Passion* reflects the celebration of female–female affection typical of the late century, but it is also written at a particular moment when Irish patriot discourse called the existence of a 'loving' relationship between the sister kingdoms of Ireland and England into question. Female amity between Louisa and Eliza is thus grounded in their shared political principles, but only enmity can explain the relationship with England.

One year after the publication of Elizabeth Sheridan's novel, Ireland was granted a degree of legislative independence with the amendment of Poynings' Law, repeal of the Declaratory Act, and other legislative concessions. In the brief flourishing of what came to be known as 'Grattan's Parliament', more positive depictions of the 'sister kingdoms' of Ireland and Britain became possible in Ireland, including Charlotte Brooke's claim to Ireland being the 'elder' sister (because of her greater antiquity):

> The British muse is not yet informed that she has an elder sister in this isle; let us then introduce them to each other! together let them walk abroad from their bowers, sweet ambassadresses of cordial union between two countries that seem formed by nature to be joined by every bond of interest, and of amity.[44]

Brooke's allegory of sisterhood was possible only in the very particular moment of the later 1780s: when the existence of Grattan's Parliament gave

Irish patriot discourse a new, but short-lived, confidence in which claims to political equality (and, even, longer heritage) could be claimed and when, largely under the aegis of sensibility, the affection between sisters could be celebrated. Such feelings and attitudes would not suddenly disappear in the 1790s, when political volatility would give way to political Union and distrust of female collective agency would resurface. But they would not feature in this particular formation again, in which 'sisterhood' in its many manifestations – as female friendship (in the domain of feelings), female homosociality (in terms of agency), and female solidarity (in those of politics) – could be a wide-ranging figure of idealism.

Conclusions

In *The Sexuality of History* (2014), Susan Lanser argues that early modern print traditions of sapphism effected subversive possibilities of many kinds: those of a levelling which undermines hierarchies; the erasure of models of dominance; the exploration of a collective subjectivity; proto-feminist critique; the emergence of women as a self-conscious constituency; and the constitution of women as political subjects, as persons who have claims to rights. Not all of these are necessarily evident in the case studies explored here. The deference to female patrons evident in the poetry of Philips and Barber, for example, prevents a number of their poems from articulating the kind of class critique implicit in claims to 'levelling' in female homosociality. But many of these political effects continue, if in attenuated form. In none of these texts do the writers speak as wives or daughters; poetry and fiction alike experiment with gender-switching; and calls for female friendship and assembly retain their provocation in a culture which often seeks to prohibit or curtail them.

This chapter has returned to the feminist debates of the 1970s, debates which have not been applied to the body of Irish women's writing of this period because of our own cycles of salience, historical and theoretical. With relatively little interest in the writings of Irish women until the 1990s, female friendships and societies have remained relatively unexamined.[45] Susan Lanser and Penelope Anderson have recently argued that female friendship in the eighteenth century loses its earlier political frisson, lacking the clearer provocations of early modern writings.[46] However these specific examples of Irish writing suggest instead that representations of 'sisterhood', in its many and overlapping senses, offered a space for women beyond domesticity,

heterosexuality, and the relationships of family, which was both imaginative and imagined, aspirational and lived. The frequency with
which intense female friendship came to be represented within poetry
and fiction by women writers is itself a remarkable event. Writing on
the eve of the departure to England of her friend, Lady Anne Bligh,
Letitia Bushe hoped that the intensity of her feelings for her friend
might settle instead into a 'quiet' form of friendship, like that 'such as
Mrs Allen and Mrs Grey have for each other for ought I know; or the
woman who frys Pancakes on the Bridge feels for her friend who touts
stockings at the opposite corner'.[47] As Bushe herself concedes, she can
only guess at the nature of these friendships. In the continued and
future absence of ever knowing, it seems more just to keep the many
possibilities of 'sisterhood' open.

Notes

1. Jonathan Swift, 'Letter to a Very Young Lady on her Marriage', in *Miscellanies*,
   2 vols (London, 1727), II, p. 326.
2. See, for example, [Edward Ward], *A Trip to Ireland* ... ([London], 1699), p. 9;
   John Waldron, *A Satyr Against Tea* (Dublin, 1733); and Aindrias Mac Craith's
   poem, 'Éigsíní Ban Agus Tae' (On Tay-Drinking Poetesses), in *The Field Day
   Anthology of Irish Writing*, Vols IV/V: *Irish Women's Writing and Traditions*, ed.
   Angela Bourke et al., 2 vols (Cork University Press, 2002), IV, pp. 440–41;
   *A True Explanation of the Humours of the Cheating Age: Or, a Brief Account of the
   Behaviour of the Town-Misses* ... (Dublin, *c.* 1740–70), pp. 3–4.
3. See, for example, *Thoughts on Friendship: By Way of Essay, for the Use and
   Improvement of the Ladies* (London, 1725), p. 13; James Fordyce, *Sermons to
   Young Women*, 2 vols (London, 1766), I, pp. 160–72 (p. 173).
4. Alicia LeFanu, *Memoirs of the Life and Writings of Mrs Frances Sheridan* (London,
   1824), p. 4. See also William Congreve's *The Way of the World* (1700), IV, v, in
   which Mirabell's conditions of marriage include that Millamant have 'no sworn
   confident, or intimate of your own sex'; and note 39 below. On the increasing
   suspicion of female friendships, see Janet Todd, *Women's Friendship in Literature*
   (New York: Columbia University Press, 1980); Betty Rizzo, *Companions without
   Vows: Relationships among Eighteenth-Century British Women* (Athens, GA:
   University of Georgia Press, 1994); and Paula Backscheider, *Eighteenth-Century
   Women Poets and Their Poetry: Inventing Agency, Inventing Genre* (Baltimore,
   MD: Johns Hopkins University Press, 2005), pp. 184–85 (p. 188).
5. [William King], *The Toast* (Dublin, 1732), pp. 16, 85. The author was the
   college head and Jacobite sympathiser, William King, who was embroiled in
   a legal case to recover the loan from his uncle and his wife, the former Countess
   of Newburgh.

6. Henry Rowlands, *Mona antiqua restaurata* (Dublin, 1723), p. 81; Capt. Charles Walker, *Authentick Memoirs of the Life, Intrigues and Adventures of the Celebrated Sally Salisbury* (Dublin, 1723), p. 47; *An Epistle to the Fair-Sex, on the Subject of Drinking* (Dublin, 1744), p. 26; Jonathan Swift, *Directions to Servants* (Dublin, 1745), p. 67; *The History of My Own Life* (Dublin, 1757), p. 148; Henry Brooke, *Juliet Grenville*, 3 vols (Dublin, 1774), I, p. 129; Frances Brooke, *The Excursion*, 2 vols (Dublin, 1777), II, p. 16.

7. 'The Basket', in *Miscellaneous Poems, by Several Hands, published by D. Lewis* (1730), p. 233; Sarah Scott, *A Description of Millenium Hall* (London, 1762), pp. 85, 86.

8. Adrienne Rich, 'Compulsory Heterosexuality and Lesbian Existence', *Signs: Journal of Women in Culture and Society* 5.4 (Summer 1980), 631–60.

9. See Sharon Marcus, *Between Women: Friendship, Desire, and Marriage in Victorian England* (Princeton University Press, 2007), pp. 9–14, 29–32.

10. Eve Kosofsky Sedgwick's argument in *Between Men: English Literature and Male Homosocial Desire* (New York: Columbia University Press, 1985) that female homosociality (unlike its male counterpart) is contiguous with, rather than opposed to, female homosexuality is also pertinent here.

11. See Backscheider, *Eighteenth-Century Women Poets*, pp. 175–232.

12. Marie-Louise Coolahan, *Women, Writing, and Language in Early Modern Ireland* (Oxford University Press, 2010), pp. 203–06, 209–10.

13. 'Philo-Philippa', 'To the Excellent *Orinda*', in *Verse in English from Tudor and Stuart Ireland*, ed. Andrew Carpenter (Cork University Press, 2003), pp. 367–73 (p. 370).

14. See Thomas Thornton, *A Catalogue of Books, to be sold by Auction at Dick's Coffee-House, &c.* [Dublin], [1730?], p. 2; *Flin's Sale Catalogue of Books. For the year 1764 . . .* ([Dublin], [1764]), p. 49; W. R. Chetwood, *A General History of the Stage; (more particularly the Irish Theatre) . . .* (Dublin, 1749), pp. 52–53; Robert Hitchcock, *An Historical View of the Irish Stage . . .*, 2 vols (Dublin, 1788–94), I, pp. 43–44.

15. *Memoirs of Laetitia Pilkington*, ed. A. C. Elias, Jr, 2 vols (1748; Athens, GA: University of Georgia Press, 1997), I, pp. 58–59, 227–28 (p. 228).

16. Mary Barber, *Poems on Several Occasions* (London, [1735]), pp. 40, 51–53, 73–76, and 169.

17. See Mary Barber, 'To the Honourable Mrs Percival' (pp. 122–23); 'The Prodigy. A Letter to a Friend in the Country' (pp. 22–27); and the collection's final poem, 'To a Lady, who commanded me to send her an Account in Verse, how I succeeded in my Subscription' (pp. 275–81), in Barber, *Poems on Several Occasions*.

18. Charlotte McCarthy, *The Fair Moralist, or, Love and Virtue . . . to which is added Several Occasional Poems* (London, 1745). McCarthy's poems were included in the two London editions (1745, 1746), but not the first Dublin edition of her novel (1747), and only a few poems are published in the later Dublin edition (1783).

19. See Charlotte McCarthy, 'On Delia and Silvia' (pp. 190–91) and 'On Two Sisters' (p. 201), in *The Fair Moralist* (1746); and Margaret Goddard, 'A Translation from a Translation of the Ninth Ode of Horace', *Poems on Several Occasions* (Dublin, 1748), pp. 60–61.

20. McCarthy, *Fair Moralist* (1746), pp. 218–20, and Goddard, *Poems on Several Occasions*, pp. 5–6.

21. McCarthy, *Fair Moralist* (1746), p. 83: 'To a Friend, Who Took It Ill I Never Wrote in Her Praise'.

22. Ibid., p. 80: 'Written in Mrs V – t's Fair Circassian, on Her Asking Me How I Lik'd the Poem', and Goddard, *Poems on Several Occasions*, pp. 49–51.

23. *The Poems of Olivia Elder*, ed. Andrew Carpenter (Dublin: Irish Manuscripts Commission, 2017). Subsequent quotations are from this edition and are cited in the text.

24. Lillian Faderman, *Surpassing the Love of Men: Romantic Friendship and Love between Women from the Renaissance to the Present* (New York: William Morrow, 1981).

25. Harriette Andreadis, *Sappho in Early Modern England: Female Same-Sex Literary Erotics, 1550–1714* (University of Chicago Press, 2001), p. 54.

26. Anna Maria Edwards, *Poems on Various Subjects, by the author of The Enchantress* (Dublin, 1787), pp. 33–40.

27. Future references to *The Fair Moralist* are from the first London edition (1745) and are cited parenthetically in the text. For an account of McCarthy's efforts to be published, see Toby Barnard, *Brought to Book: Print in Ireland, 1680–1784* (Dublin: Four Courts Press, 2017), pp. 337–40.

28. Frances Sheridan, *Eugenia and Adelaide*, 2 vols (London, 1791), II, pp. 4, 6.

29. Ibid., II, p. 29.

30. Samuel Richardson, *Clarissa, or The History of Young Lady*, ed. Angus Ross (Harmondsworth: Penguin, 1985), p. 40.

31. Ibid., p. 873.

32. [Sarah Fielding], *Remarks upon Clarissa, Addressed to the Author* (London, 1749), p. 46.

33. *An Abridgment of Clarissa . . .* (Dublin, 1756).

34. Barnard, *Brought to Book*, pp. 235–36; Tom Keymer, *Richardson's* Clarissa *and the Eighteenth-Century Reader* (1992; Cambridge University Press, 2004), pp. 214–28.

35. On the significance of Cecilia to the novel, see Jane Spencer, 'Women Writers and the Eighteenth-Century Novel', in *The Cambridge Companion to the Eighteenth-Century Novel*, ed. John Richetti (Cambridge University Press, 2006), pp. 212–35; and, especially pertinent to this chapter, Susan S. Lanser, *The Sexuality of History: Modernity and the Sapphic, 1565–1830* (University of Chicago Press, 2014), pp. 178–79.

36. Frances Sheridan, *Memoirs of Miss Sidney Bidulph*, ed. Patricia Köster and Jean Coates (Oxford University Press, 1999), p. 266. Further references are to this edition and will be cited in the text. Notably, Sheridan's sequel novel – *Conclusion of the Memoirs of Miss Sidney Bidulph* (London, 1767) – dramatises

the story of two sisters (Dolly and Cecilia), the daughters of Sidney, who fall in love with the same man, Orlando, son of their mother's failed suitor.

37. See the modern edition, in which the authorship of Sheridan is identified: Elizabeth Sheridan, *The Triumph of Prudence over Passion*, ed. Ian Campbell Ross and Aileen Douglas (Dublin: Four Courts Press, 2011). Further references are to this edition and will be cited in the text.

38. Mary O'Dowd, 'Women and Patriotism in Eighteenth-Century Ireland', *History Ireland* 14.5 (2006), 25–30.

39. See, for example, *Thraliana: The Diary of Mrs Hester Lynch Thrale, 1776–1809*, ed. Katharine C. Balderston, 2 vols (Oxford: Clarendon Press, 1942), I, p. 361 (20 January 1779), and *Letters from Mrs Elizabeth Carter to Mrs Montagu, between the years 1755 and 1800*, 3 vols (London, 1817), III, pp. 241–50. Elizabeth Griffith opened her novel *The History of Lady Barton* with an important defence of female friendship against its depreciation by Louisa Barton's husband, Sir William: see Elizabeth Griffith, *The History of Lady Barton: A Novel, in Letters*, 3 vols (London, 1771), I, pp. 2, 50. The opening section of the novel consists of letters exchanged between Louisa in Ireland and her sister Frances in England (I, pp. 1–102). I am grateful to Clíona Ó Gallchoir for drawing this novel to my attention.

40. *The True Life of Betty Ireland. With Her Birth, Education, and Adventures. Together with Some Account of Her Elder Sister Blanch of Britain* ([Dublin], 1753). For the identification of Sir Richard Cox as the author of this pamphlet, see Jacqueline Hill, '"Allegories, Fictions, and Feigned Representations": Decoding the Money Bill Dispute, 1752–6', in *Eighteenth-Century Ireland / Iris an dá chultúr* 21 (2006), 66–88 (pp. 75, 86). See also the satirical letter from 'Helen O'Roon' in Dublin to her female friend in London, in which the relationship of England to Ireland is described as that of 'our Mother-Sister-Country': *The Pr[ima]te Vindicated, And The Affairs of I[relan]d set in a true Light. In a Letter from the Honourable Hellen O'Roon, to the Right Honourable Lady Viscountess ****** in London* (Dublin Printed; repr. London, 1754), p. 11.

41. *The True Life of Betty Ireland*, pp. 33–34.

42. See Hill, '"Allegories, Fictions, and Feigned Representations"', p. 74, and Jarlath Killeen, *The Emergence of Irish Gothic Fiction: History, Origins, Theories* (Edinburgh University Press, 2014), pp. 108–12.

43. The phrase is invoked in the prologue to Richard Cumberland's *The West Indian* (1771) but becomes increasingly common in the 1780s: see, for example, *Flora's Banquet* (Belfast, 1782), p. 144; Felix McCarthy, *A Serious Answer to Lord George Gordon's Letters to the Earl of Shelburne* ([London], 1782), pp. 8, 19; *The Book of Seven Chapters* (London, 1785), p. 145; *Short Observations on the Necessity of Admitting Dublin to Participate in the Corn Export Bounties* (Dublin, 1785), p. 19; *Thoughts on the Kingdom of Ireland* ([Bath], [1785]), pp. 3, 5; Joseph Richardson, *A Complete Investigation of Mr. Eden's Treaty* (London, 1787), p. 120.

44. Charlotte Brooke, ed., *Reliques of Irish Poetry* (Dublin, 1789), pp. vii–viii.

45. For notable exceptions, see S. J. Connolly, 'A Woman's Life in Mid-Eighteenth-Century Ireland: The Case of Letitia Bushe', *The Historical Journal* 43.2 (2000), 433–51, and Lisa L. Moore, 'Queer Gardens: Mary Delany's Flowers and Friendships', *Eighteenth-Century Studies* 39.1 (Fall 2005), 49–70.

46. Penelope Anderson, *Friendships Shadows: Women's Friendship and the Politics of Betrayal in England, 1640–1705* (Edinburgh University Press, 2012); Lanser, *Sexuality of History*, pp. 134–35.

47. Quoted in Connolly, 'A Woman's Life', p. 448.

PART V

Transcultural Contexts

The Popular Criminal Narrative and the Development of the Irish Novel

Joe Lines

In eighteenth-century Britain and Ireland, public fascination with crime was fed by bestselling biographies of robbers and murderers. These texts are studied today as influences on key works of English literature such as Daniel Defoe's *Moll Flanders* (1722) and John Gay's *The Beggar's Opera* (1728). Less considered has been their role in Irish literary history, despite the fact that criminal biographies were published and read in Dublin throughout the eighteenth century. This chapter will argue that these texts, with their combination of biography with fiction, Irish with English and continental sources, and crude national stereotyping with innovative characterisation, became an important subtext for the eighteenth-century Irish novel. Criminal biographies present challenges to interpretation, as they alternate between claims to truth and flagrant invention. Lincoln B. Faller has distinguished two types of biography: texts about murderers which were modelled on spiritual autobiographies, and tended to be didactic and to emphasise their accuracy, and lives of thieves which were less moralistic and more fanciful, taking inspiration from the Spanish picaresque novel.[1] An example of the latter is George Fidge's *The English Gusman* (1652), which is based on the life of the highwayman James Hind, but alludes in its title to Mateo Aleman's novel *Guzmán de Alfarache* (1599).[2] *Guzmán* had been translated into English by James Mabbe in 1622 as *The Rogue*, a text which elicited a trend for what J. A. Garrido Ardila has dubbed 'Guzmanian imitations'.[3] The most popular of these, Richard Head's *The English Rogue* (1665), had an afterlife of its own in subsequent volumes and abridged editions.[4] Due to this proliferation of fictional, fictionalised, and biographical rogue tales in the seventeenth century, the term 'criminal narrative' has been used to discuss texts about real and invented criminals alongside one another.[5]

Many criminal narratives from this era featured Irish subjects. The Ordinary of Newgate's *Accounts*, which began publishing in 1679, recorded

the histories and offences of the condemned. Peter Linebaugh has calculated that 14 per cent of those memorialised in the Ordinary's *Accounts* were
born in Ireland.[6] After the death of the Irish highwayman Redmond
O'Hanlon in 1681, a pamphlet-length biography was published in
Dublin.[7] From the early eighteenth century, individual biographies were
compiled together into larger collections such as Alexander Smith's *The
History of the Lives of the Most Noted Highway-Men* (1714), which featured
tales such as that of 'Patrick Flemming, an Irish Murderer and Highwayman'.[8] Smith's collection was one source for a compendium published in
Dublin, John Cosgrave's *A Genuine History of the Lives and Actions of the
Most Notorious Irish Highwaymen, Tories and Rapparees* (1747).[9] This
collection and the contemporaneous highwayman's memoir *The Life and
Adventures of James Freney* (1754) acquired a wide readership in Ireland,
disseminating as chapbooks and entering the oral tradition.[10]

Criminal narratives would become an enduring part of Irish popular
culture, but the printed texts of the early to mid-eighteenth century also
have something to tell us about the origins of the Irish novel. This chapter
reconsiders Cosgrave's *Irish Highwaymen* in the context of the earlier
narratives from which much of its content was drawn, and as itself
a possible influence on the early novel in Ireland. Niall Ó Ciosáin has
highlighted this collection's positive representation of its subjects, which
differs strikingly from the anti-Catholic and xenophobic tone of London-
published biographies of the Irish.[11] I will argue instead that, taken
together, both English and Irish criminal narratives possess conventions
of plot and characterisation which enable them to elude the national
prejudices of the era. In these texts, an association between Ireland and
criminality is often confounded by a recurring interest in geographical
mobility and hybrid nationality which is ultimately derived from picaresque fiction. This potential to upend expectations is present in early
English criminal narratives, as will now be demonstrated.

Nationality and Travel in *The Irish Rogue* (1690)

Criminal narratives often emphasised the nationality of their subjects, treating them as figures for their country – either because a foreign setting added
to the tale's novelty, or because an 'English rogue' could be marketed as
a native version of the Spanish picaresque model. Head's *The English Rogue*,
however, begins not by defining, but by complicating its subject's nationality, as the rogue is born to English parents in Carrickfergus, County
Antrim, and attributes his crimes to an early exposure to Irish culture or

'Clymate', rather than to 'the disposition of the Parent'.[12] The success of *The English Rogue* elicited a trend for titles such as *The Dutch Rogue* (1683) and *The French Rogue* (1694) which, according to Leah Orr, 'combine an English version of the picaresque tradition with English nationalism'.[13] It is thus unsurprising that a work titled *The Irish Rogue; or, The Comical History of the Life and Actions of Teague O Divelley* appeared in London in 1690. This fiction narrates the upbringing, exploits, and robberies of the titular rogue, at first in rural Ireland, then in Spain and France. *The Irish Rogue* has been treated dismissively in studies of early Irish literature, and it can be faulted for displaying little knowledge of Ireland, relying instead on durable English preconceptions. But a detailed reading of *The Irish Rogue* reveals an unexpectedly positive representation of the Irish central figure. Like *The English Rogue*, this text makes manifest a tension between national types and the protean individual who can embody several different nations. And in this regard, *The Irish Rogue* establishes patterns in the representation of Irish nationality which are echoed in later fiction.

Derek Hand's assessment of *The Irish Rogue* can stand for critical consensus on the text, being both brief and inaccurate on details such as the subtitle: 'Novels such as the anonymously written *The Irish Rogue: or the Further Adventures of Teague O'Divelly* [sic] (1690) reproduce negative attitudes towards Ireland and Irishness from the vantage point of British metropolitan power.'[14] Certainly, the author of *The Irish Rogue* makes full use of the available stereotypes, beginning when O Divelley informs us that his father was a 'Tory, living by the length of his Sword'.[15] 'Tory' is here used in its original sense to mean a robber or bandit, derived from the Irish '*tóraighe*' or 'wanted'. Many tories in Restoration Ireland, such as Redmond O'Hanlon, were descended from Gaelic families dispossessed in the Elizabethan or Cromwellian conquests.[16] *The Irish Rogue* also refers to the 1641 rising in grotesque imagery designed to highlight the savagery and sectarianism of the Catholic rebels, referring to 'the Grand Rebellion of 1640' as a time 'when the massacred Protestants fat served for Consecrated Candles to light the Shrines of the Popish Saints' (p. 69). The text also includes a section on 'the Inclination of the Irish', who apparently delight 'in Branglings and War', 'are naturally Contemners of all other Nations, and carry a kind of an Irreconcilable hatred to the English' (pp. 109–10). The Irish were often accused of national pride and unfriendliness towards other nations in the late seventeenth century, as David W. Hayton has argued.[17] The text's reliance on stereotype rather than first-hand knowledge is evidenced when its views on the Irish national character are said to be derived from 'an old author, *viz. Stainhurst*'

(p. 109), the sixteenth-century travel writer Richard Stanihurst.[18] At such points, *The Irish Rogue* imagines Irish national characteristics as absolute and ineluctable. The lawlessness of past tories and rebels is perpetuated by the career of the rogue protagonist, and can stand for the whole nation, who are imagined as an unremittingly hostile people.

The Irish Rogue locates the source of crime in Ireland's conflicted history, feeding into existing English prejudices. But the framing of the criminal as typical of his nation is difficult to sustain. As the narrative develops, O Divelley's advertised Irishness becomes sublimated, particularly when he leaves Ireland. The rogue is a fugitive from justice after a robbery and a daring escape from jail. Boarding a ship to Spain, he reasons, 'all the World being my Home, I knew not but my Adventures might prove as successful there as any where' (p. 102), imagining himself as a citizen of the globe, rather than of any specific country. He makes himself at home when he arrives in Cadiz, speedily learning Spanish: 'I soon ... could understand most words in the *Donish* Discourse' (p. 120). He also acquires new clothes and poses as a Spanish nobleman: 'I appeared a Don at all points, Mounted and Armed.' This persona is convincing enough to fool the natives, as he is accosted by Spaniards 'desirous to be entertained with the News of the Court' (pp. 137–38). O Divelley's skilful assimilation is an example of how he contradicts, rather than reinforces, Irish stereotypes, an inconsistency which is admitted in the preface: 'you may be apt to imagine, a Native of Ireland (considering those people by nature are dull) could not be guilty of so much Ingenuity'.[19] Later, he travels to Paris, where 'I changed what Silver I had into Gold and Jewels ... and feasted nobly, entertaining the Sparkish Ladies, and trying the difference of Nations' (p. 176). His passing as Spanish and French is unexpected given the text's earlier claims that the Irish are unreceptive to other cultures, being 'naturally Contemners of all other Nations'. O Divelley's skill at 'trying the difference of Nations' might not accord with Irish stereotypes, but it is characteristic of criminal literature. A similar transformation is effected in the biography *Don Tomazo, or the Juvenile Rambles of Thomas Dangerfield* (1680). The informer and petty criminal Dangerfield 'was by birth of English parents' but has, we are told, 'put his name into the Spanish garb, to which he was most accustom'd in his travels'.[20] The criminal narrative was characterised by an 'awareness of the insecurity of personal identity, of the permeability and multiplicity of the self', according to Hal Gladfelder, who attributes such 'hybridity or shifting between extremes' to the form's status as a compound of biography and picaresque fiction.[21] O Divelley's skilful adaptation to other cultures is thus to be expected in criminal narratives, but it also complicates the singular definition of his nationality set up in the text's title and references to 'the Irish'.

Taking account of the influence of the picaresque on *The Irish Rogue* complicates readings of it as straightforwardly anti-Catholic. O Divelley's travels take in only Catholic nations, and as such, his journey might be taken as exemplary of the religious, economic, and military connections between Ireland, France, and Spain in this period. Migratory and trade routes between Ireland's west coast and ports such as Cadiz were well-established by the seventeenth century, and significant numbers of young men travelled to study for the priesthood at continental Irish colleges.[22] In 1690, the French army recruited three regiments from Ireland, thereby establishing the Irish Brigades.[23] Given this context, O Divelley's travels could be read as underlining the association between Irish Catholics and Britain's rivals in Europe, thus implying treachery or sedition from the text's perspective. However, the choice of Spain as a destination may not have been politically motivated in this way. Translations of the Spanish picaresque were popular at this time, and were cited as influences in such biographies as *Don Tomazo*: 'The Cheats and cunning Contrivances of *Gusman* and *Lazarillo de Tormes* have been made *English*, out of the *Spanish* Language, as well to instruct as to delight.'[24] *The Irish Rogue* betrays its knowledge of *Lazarillo* by copying an episode from that picaresque novel about a pardoner selling fake papal indulgences. In both versions, an accomplice of the pardoner pretends to doubt his wares, and then to be stricken by divine vengeance, in order to impress a watching crowd.[25] For the writer of *The Irish Rogue*, a sojourn in Spain, a country popularly associated with amusing tricksters, may have been simply part of the protagonist's picaresque education. The '*Donish*' O Divelley is readable as a treacherous and mobile Catholic Irishman, but also as a hybrid rogue produced by the popularity of the picaresque in English fiction at this time.

Teague O Divelley probably takes his name from an Irish character who featured in two plays by Thomas Shadwell. Comparing the plays with the fiction reveals that the latter presents the Irish more positively, even though the works emerged from similar English and anti-Catholic contexts. Shadwell's plays *The Lancashire Witches* (1682) and *The Amorous Bigot* (1690) both featured 'Tegue O Divelly', a villainous Irish priest. The earlier play ends with O Divelly being arrested as a conspirator in the 'Popish Plot' which had panicked the nation in 1678, after Titus Oates's allegations about a Catholic conspiracy to raise rebellions on both sides of the Irish Sea.[26] Fears of revolt in Ireland remained high throughout the 1680s, although Hayton's study of English attitudes to the Irish in this decade identifies an 'ongoing process by which dread was being gradually replaced by derision'.[27] Fittingly, Shadwell's plays exemplify both outlooks. The title of *The Amorous Bigot* sums up O Divelly's double significance: he is a menacing religious 'bigot', but also a laughable 'amorous' priest whose desires for women are thwarted at every turn. In *The Lancashire Witches*, he conspires to rape the heroines, Theodosia and Isabella, declaring, 'fait and trot I have a great need too, it is a venial Sin, and I do not care'. But under cover of darkness, the priest mistakes an old witch for 'de pretty Wenches', and is left crying 'O phaat have I done?'[28] His nefarious intentions and comic failure distinguish this scene from the later fiction. In *The Irish Rogue*, O Divelley is more attractive to women than Shadwell's priest, and thus overcomes the binary of 'dread' and 'derision' in the anti-Irish discourse of the time. For example, when posing as a Spanish Don in a noblewoman's castle, he reveals a hitherto-unsuspected refinement, discoursing at length on the merits of her collection of paintings. Her passions are aroused: 'finding me thus free and discerning, she came closer, leading me into her Closet, and there discovering her Wants' (pp. 139–43). In stark contrast to Shadwell's plays, O Divelley in *The Irish Rogue* is a rakish seducer who is allowed to possess the 'discerning' tastes of a gentleman. The rogue derives his more positive aspects from the expectations of the criminal narrative. The seventeenth-century 'Stage-Irish' plays of Shadwell and others, with their British settings, position Irish characters as outsiders and relegate them to the roles of villain or butt of jokes.[29] The criminal narrative, in contrast, allows the Irish to occupy the central role, affording room for character development. Criminal lives style their protagonists as cautionary figures, but there is an extent to which they also glamorise rogues because of their intelligence and freedom from moral and legal restraints, as John Richetti acknowledges.[30] This ambivalence in criminal literature allows *The Irish Rogue* to represent the Irish in a more complex way than is possible in contemporary drama.

The Irish Rogue reiterates contemporary English prejudices when it presents the Irish as violent and primitive, but its protagonist exceeds this crude definition of Irishness. O Divelley's intelligence, attractiveness, and refinement make him a more positive figure than would seemingly be allowed by the text's view of his nation. His European travels and facility for languages and disguise estrange him from stock ideas of the Irish as savage, 'dull', or risible. Existing assessments of *The Irish Rogue* as a crude production, then, pay insufficient attention to its representation of identity within the frame of a picaresque criminal narrative. Moreover, the xenophobic aspects of the text did not prevent it gaining a readership in Ireland, where it was reissued in 1740. The tale evidently required some editing to fit the tastes of mid-century Irish readers; the rogue's name, which combines the anti-Catholic slur 'Teague' with the satanic 'O Divelley', was altered to 'Darby O Brolaghan'. A claim in the original that the Irish are 'the most superstitious of all nations' (p. 5) was excised; and when the rogue falls in love with a young girl, a footnote in the Dublin edition reads, 'Here the author very judiciously describes the Irish beauties, who are perhaps in general the most lovely creatures on earth.'[31] But the bulk of the text, including the travels of the rogue through Spain and France, was left unchanged. This picaresque travel plot, I am arguing, enables the rogue's identity to be presented as contingent and outside the restrictive terms of anti-Irish prejudice. Also characteristic of the criminal narrative tradition is a blurring between biography and fiction. We can see this in a short tale which was bound with the 1740 Dublin edition of *The Irish Rogue*: 'The Gold-Merchant; or, the Notorious Cheats of Turlough, and his Man Patrick'.[32] This humorous story about a hoax involving a treasure-trove would later reappear with a slightly different title in Cosgrave's collection of criminal biographies, and is of a piece with the other stories in *Irish Highwaymen* as a story of a trickster.[33] As I will show, the strategies of plotting and characterisation observed in these criminal narratives are notable also in later Irish fiction. But Cosgrave's use of pre-existing sources and representation of Irish nationality will be examined more closely before turning to the ways in which the criminal narrative and the emerging novel extend the ideas and procedures of prose fiction.

Rogue Fiction in Mid-Eighteenth-Century Dublin: Cosgrave's *Irish Highwaymen* (1747)

Criminal literature was read as avidly in Dublin as it was in London between 1680 and 1750. Local and newsworthy crimes were retailed through broadside-length crime reports and gallows speeches.[34] Longer biographies, some derived from the Ordinary of Newgate's *Accounts*, were also available to readers.[35] Unlike the reports and speeches, most of the criminal biographies to appear in Dublin were reprints of London-published texts, not original works.[36] In 1735, the Dublin publisher George Golding advertised for sale texts including 'English Rogue', 'Spanish Rogue', and 'French Rogue'.[37] Around 1740, an increase in the publication of original criminal narratives is observable, going hand in hand, James Kelly argues, with the dwindling popularity of the court reports and speeches.[38] Cosgrave's *Irish Highwaymen* is thought to have been first published in the 1730s or 40s, though the earliest surviving edition, the third, dates from 1747.[39] The last page of this edition lists under 'Books printed for Country Dealers' both 'ENGLISH Rogue, or Witty Extravagant' and '*Jonathan Wild* and his Accomplices' (p. 166), two titles which further suggest the availability of criminal narratives in eighteenth-century Ireland (the latter text evidently concerned the famous London thief-taker, executed in 1725). Little is known about Cosgrave himself, who appears to have authored or published no other works. His Irish nationality is implied by asides such as 'as it is customary with my Countrymen' (p. 91), as well as the fact that his text takes a more sympathetic view of the Irish than the London-published texts analysed earlier.

Cosgrave's collection was frequently reprinted, reaching its tenth Dublin edition in 1782. Ó Ciosáin argues that such texts maintained a wide readership because they represent 'tories' and 'rapparees' as heroic figures of resistance to an imposed, colonial justice system.[40] *Irish Highwaymen* highlights the aristocratic descent of bandits such as O'Hanlon, connecting their actions to the dispossession of their forebears: 'The ideological context of these texts, therefore, and the principle which legitimises a challenge to authority, is nobility of blood and the rightful ownership of land.'[41] The popular success of texts like *Irish Highwaymen* is undoubtedly explained by their conjoined themes of ancestral injustice and resistance to the law. However, the interpretation of Cosgrave's protagonists as figureheads for an oppositional culture ignores some of the vexed and troublesome aspects of the criminal biographies, their 'shifting between extremes' of characterisation in Gladfelder's phrase. Such incoherency is legible in the biography of Redmond O'Hanlon, as he veers between usurping the role of the 'Justices of the Peace' in County Armagh, styling himself 'chief Ranger of the Mountains', and being given 'the Kings Protection for three years' (pp. 9–10). During this period, O'Hanlon remained 'very inoffensive in the Country, and kept company with some of the best Gentlemen in the Kingdom, who not only took great Pleasure in hearing him relate his Exploits, but caressed and made much of him' (p. 16). O'Hanlon is thus represented both as resisting the imposition of state power, and accommodating himself strategically to it. His status as a gentleman makes him popular with the people, but also in elite circles. Such unpredictability of character and identity is general to the biographies in Cosgrave's collection.

'The Goldfinder' is a different kind of narrative to most of the biographies in *Irish Highwaymen*, as its subject is neither a robber nor based on a real person; but it manifests a similar tendency to complicate national stereotypes. The protagonist, Manus Mac Oneil, resembles a character type identified by Faller in the criminal biography, 'the buffoon', who typically 'either plays tricks or has tricks played upon him'.[42] The Irish were stereotypically seen as buffoons in the latter sense, as ignorant and gullible; but in 'The Goldfinder', Manus is represented as outwitting everyone he meets. He 'passed upon the World as a stupid innocent Bum[p]kin, incapable of forming the least Design or Intrigue, which gave him the Advantage of carrying on his Cheats successfully for a long Time without being in the least suspected' (pp. 129–30). After claiming to discover a treasure-hoard in Kildare, he swindles those who attempt to buy his gold, selling them fake ingots made of brass. We see him duping an '*English* Countryman', who 'hearing the fellow talk'd so simply, verily imagined that he was a meer Ignoramus, and thought all that he had said was . . . true' (pp. 131–32). Hearing his brogue-inflected speech, the 'Countryman' assumes that Manus is too ignorant for any subterfuge; but the joke, this time, is not on the Irishman, but on the Englishman, who swallows the fable and tells his friends. Consequently, 'People that had Money came privately from all Parts to seek *Manus* in hopes of making their Fortunes' (p. 133). The satire of this story targets the credulity of 'People that had Money', as Manus defrauds an inn-keeper, a merchant's son, and 'an eminent Banker' (pp. 135–38). The middling-sort readership of the criminal narrative might have felt themselves being mocked here, but perhaps they were amused nonetheless.[43] The comic poten-tial of 'The Goldfinder' for the urban middle class is literally enacted when Manus is put on trial in Dublin, as his witty replies to the prosecutor 'filled the Court with Surprize and Laughter, to see how artfully he could evade the Force of the Law, tho' in Appearance he seemed like a Fool' (p. 141). Tellingly, he escapes court unpunished, and is still at large by the end of the narrative, making 'The Goldfinder' the only biography in *Irish Highwaymen* not to conclude with a hanging. The licence granted to Manus distinguishes 'The Goldfinder' from biographies of tories such as O'Hanlon. Manus is less capable of provoking larger anxieties about sedition (he never resorts to violence, for instance), and his crimes thus require no correction by state-administered justice. Although it lacks the political edge of the O'Hanlon biographies, 'The Goldfinder' complicates the stock figure of the Irish buffoon, transferring the charge of credulity from the rustic to his respectable victims.

Irish Highwaymen can be compared to seventeenth-century fictions like *The Irish Rogue* in its invocation of nationality (most obviously in its title), and the tension that then develops between supposedly national qualities and the individual personalities of characters. Cosgrave adapted many of the lives featured in *Irish Highwaymen* from earlier publications, including several London-published collections.[44] Smith's 1714 compilation, for exam-ple, provided Cosgrave with Richard Balf's story, and the 1719 second edition was the source of William Macquire's life.[45] Ó Ciosáin has compared the English originals with Cosgrave's versions by drawing upon Faller's typology of fictional criminals, which featured the violent and savage 'brute' and the gallant 'hero' alongside the buffoon. Smith and Cosgrave treat the Irish in opposing fashions, with the former representing Irishmen as brutes, whereas in *Irish Highwaymen*, the hero is 'by far the dominant figure'.[46] Both collections, then, attempt to make the Irish rogue into a national exemplar. But this agenda is undercut by the fact that, as Faller notes, 'few . . . criminals are consistent enough to be all of one type; they shift from one to another quite freely'.[47] In *Irish Highwaymen*, Flemming is a case in point, 'having the name of . . . a violent Rogue and barbarous Murderer', but then becoming more heroic when he robs 'the Primate and Bishop of Raphoe': 'because they made no Resistance, he used them very honourably, doing no further Damage, after borrowing what Money and Bills they had' (pp. 45–46). The dichotomy of savagery and civility, so often invoked to define the Irish, is present in the brutes and heroes of these biographies. But if the same rogue can act both honourably and savagely, then these qualities lose their exemplarity. Thus, *Irish Highwaymen* takes on the conventions of earlier criminal biographies, which problematise the notion of the criminal as a national archetype.

Cosgrave's collection follows its English models by utilising travel narratives which sideline the Irish origins of the rogue. This can be seen in the life of the highwayman James Butler, which closely resembles that found in the London-published collection *A Full and Compleat History of the Lives, Robberies, and Murders, of all the Most Notorious Highwaymen* (1742). Butler's mobility makes him hard to interpret as a representative 'Irish' rogue. In Cosgrave's account, he enlists in 'Lord Galway's regiment' and travels to Spain, then deserts to fight for 'the Spaniards' (p. 64). But his allegiances are temporary, as he leaves the military and drifts between various employments, becoming a 'Mountebank', a 'Conjuror', and then joining a company of '*Banditti*' or Italian robbers (pp. 64–65). His wandering takes in Italy, France, and Holland before ending in London, where he is eventually executed for highway robbery (pp. 66–68). The Irishman passes easily between various countries and underworlds, finding accomplices everywhere he goes, as with the Italian '*Banditti*', or in 'Paris, where he soon found Means to introduce himself into *Cartouch's* Gang' (p. 66). Butler learns to speak European languages, 'both Spanish and Italian' in Cosgrave's version, emerging as a cosmopolitan figure.[48] His travels reflect the form's impulse to exoticise and hybridise criminals. They also return the rogue to his picaresque roots in Spain. Butler's ability to acquire languages and operate with equal success in many countries makes him comparable to the protagonist of *The Irish Rogue*. Though, unlike O Divelley, Cosgrave's Butler is based on a real person, his resourceful and mobile character is indebted to the picaresque tradition. Even as Irish rogues are made into figures for their nation in criminal narratives, their nationality is obscured beneath other associations as a consequence of their itinerant histories, during which they seem to belong more to an international criminal stratum than to one specific country.

Two further biographies illustrate the prevalence of travel in *Irish Highwaymen*. James Carrick and John Mulhoni were accomplices who, like Butler, both fought in European wars and robbed in London. The Dublin-born Carrick joins the army as an ensign and is posted to Spain, where 'he indulged himself in all the Extravagancies of the Country, rioting in Wantonness and Debauchery' (p. 77). When the war ends, he goes to England and takes up highway robbery – until, 'another of his Comrades being taken, he withdrew himself to France for more Safety. Here he also pursued the old Sport' (p. 78). For his part, Mulhoni joins the navy and 'served several years in the Mediterranean' (p. 69). He then returns to Ireland and 'in Conjunction with *James Carrick*, they committed a Number of Robberies' (p. 70). In this account, Mulhoni and Carrick migrate to London together and become part of a gang. These two biographies are both clearly based on the same 1742 London-published collection from which Cosgrave's life of Butler is derived.[49] In both accounts of Mulhoni, for example, he dies 'very penitent according to the Principles of his Religion', which is '*Roman Catholick*' (p. 76).[50] However, Cosgrave's few additions are revealing. The 1742 collection relates how 'the daily Instances of the Seizures of Highwaymen, and the constantly hanging them, so discouraged' Mulhoni and Carrick that they abandon the highways around London.[51] Cosgrave renders the passage as follows:

> But the daily Instances of the Seizures of Highwaymen, and constantly hanging them, together with the small favour *Irishmen* are shown by *English* Juries, insomuch that it became a Proverb, *An* Irishman's *Name is enough to hang him*, I say, all this, considered together, discouraged our *Irish* Heroes so much that they no longer adventured to survey the high Roads on horseback. (p. 72)

This account adds a critical reference to '*English* Juries' and also signals an awareness of its Dublin readership by referring to Mulhoni and Carrick as 'our *Irish* Heroes'. Even as settings shift and narratives are borrowed from earlier texts, then, these biographies occasionally reveal a specifically Irish perspective – here, when addressing the treatment of migrants in England.

Such patriotic asides in *Irish Highwaymen* distinguish it from the main-stream of criminal narrative. Yet equally, it is also a digest of pre-existing material from that tradition. It adapts biographies from several different English collections, as well as materials originally published in Dublin, such as 'The Goldfinder', which originally appeared in the 1740 reprint of *The Irish Rogue*. Emerging from this intertextual background, the collection manifests recurring tendencies such as the plot of travel and the fluidity of the criminal's identity and nationality. The European itineraries of Butler, Carrick, and Mulhoni all evoke the Spanish picaresque, and echo English fictions such as *The Irish Rogue*. The three editions of *Irish Highwaymen* by 1747 clearly indicate an appetite for local crime stories in mid-eighteenth-century Dublin. It makes sense, then, that the Irish rogue began to figure in novels written in Ireland at around this time. The most prominent of these is *The History of Jack Connor* (1752) by William Chaigneau, a writer of French Huguenot descent who worked as an army agent at Dublin Castle. A tale of an Irish orphan's progress from beggary to the landowning elite, *Jack Connor* has justly been compared to the novels of Alain-René Le Sage, Tobias Smollett, and Henry Fielding. But as Ian Campbell Ross points out, it might have been first read as 'rogue fiction or even criminal biography', given that at least one copy of the third Dublin edition of the novel was bound with the memoirs of James Freney.[52] Jack Connor's life features conspicuous similarities to Irish criminal narratives of the time, such as his European travels, which include Paris and Cadiz – frequent destinations for Irish migrants in this era, and places featured in *The Irish Rogue*. Jack travels in Europe as a result of military service, as in the biographies of Butler, Carrick, and Mulhoni. And beyond its travel narrative, *Jack Connor* is also centrally concerned with the mutability of national identity, with its hero undergoing several changes of name, beginning when he migrates to London and takes the more English-sounding alias of 'John Conyers' to avoid prejudices against his nation.[53]

Even a brief sketch of the plot and geography of *Jack Connor* suggests parallels with criminal narratives printed in Dublin in the preceding decades. The impact of criminal literature on the Irish novel has mostly been noted in relation to the cultural afterlife of tories such as O'Hanlon. Of all Cosgrave's biographies, O'Hanlon's was 'the most successful and seems to have been the only one to have been taken up and reprinted singly and outside Ireland'.[54] After 1800, tories would become appealing subjects for novels such as William Carleton's *Redmond Count O'Hanlon, the Irish Rapparee* (1862).[55] But in the mid-eighteenth century, the depredations of rapparees were still too proximate and worrying for them to be acceptable subjects for a writer of the Protestant establishment like Chaigneau (James Freney, for instance, was still at large until 1749).[56] For the Irish novelist at this time, the most attractive aspect of the rogue seems to have been his mobility and protean character, rather than his outlaw status or origins in a dispossessed aristocracy.

The tropes of travel and variable identity present in the biographies in *Irish Highwaymen* are widespread in earlier rogue fictions which imitated the picaresque. This broader tradition was also known to Irish readers, judging by advertisements for *The English Rogue, French Rogue*, and *Spanish Rogue* in Dublin print of the 1730s and 40s. These narratives style the rogue as the representative of a nation, and often highlight their subjects' nationality as the explanation for their crimes. However, qualities which are constructed as nationally characteristic, such as violence (in English narratives about the Irish), are freely discarded and controverted during these unpredictable tales. Tropes of the rogue tale, such as travel, social mobility, and the rogue's wit and adaptability, challenge stock definitions of nationality. This is observable in the refashioning of Thomas Shadwell's Stage Irishman O Dively into a more complex and attractive figure in *The Irish Rogue*. This text was published in 1690, several decades before the 'earliest conscious contradiction of traditional stage-Irish attributes' on the English stage, Thomas Sheridan's *The Brave Irishman* (1746).[57] The criminal narratives studied here thus imply that early Irish fiction is an illuminating context and comparison for histories of Irish drama already mapped by Hayton, Joep Leerssen, and others. In eighteenth-century Ireland, criminal narratives were not only popular, but were reshaped into new forms, establishing a set of conventions which was available to novelists such as Chaigneau. In the 1750s and 60s, *Jack Connor* was joined by several more novels which focused on the travels and adventures of Irishmen.[58] Irish novelists were still exploiting this pattern in the 1780s, as can be seen from the Limerick-born Charles Johnston's *The History of John Juniper* (1781), a bawdy tale of an Irish rake who refuses to mend his ways.[59] Such texts demonstrate that the criminal narrative remained a productive resource for Irish fiction throughout the eighteenth century.

Notes

1. Lincoln B. Faller, *Turned to Account: The Forms and Functions of Criminal Biography in Late Seventeenth- and Early Eighteenth-Century England* (Cambridge University Press, 1987), pp. 3–4, 12.
2. George Fidge, *The English Gusman; or The History of that Unparallel'd Thief James Hind* (London, 1652).

3. J. A. Garrido Ardila, 'The Picaresque Novel and the Rise of the English Novel', in *The Picaresque Novel in Western Literature: From the Sixteenth Century to the Neopicaresque*, ed. Garrido Ardila (Cambridge University Press, 2015), pp. 113–39 (pp. 124–25).

4. Leah Orr, '*The English Rogue*: Afterlives and Imitations, 1665–1741', *Journal for Eighteenth-Century Studies* 38.3 (2015), 361–76.

5. For relevant discussions, see John Richetti, *Popular Fiction before Richardson: Narrative Patterns, 1700–1739* (Oxford: Clarendon Press, 1969), pp. 38–47, and Hal Gladfelder, *Criminality and Narrative in Eighteenth-Century England* (Baltimore, MD: Johns Hopkins University Press, 2001), pp. 33–44.

6. Peter Linebaugh, *The London Hanged: Crime and Civil Society in the Eighteenth Century*, 2nd edn (London: Verso, 2003), pp. 91–92, 288.

7. *The Life and Death of the Incomparable and Indefatigable Tory Redmond O Hanlyn* (Dublin, 1682).

8. Alexander Smith, *The Second Volume of the History of the Lives of the Most Notorious Highway Men* (London, 1714), pp. 207–19.

9. Niall Ó Ciosáin, *Print and Popular Culture in Ireland, 1750–1850* (Basingstoke: Macmillan, 1997), pp. 88–89.

10. Ray Cashman, 'The Heroic Outlaw in Irish Folklore and Popular Literature', *Folklore* 111.2 (2000), 191–215 (p. 191).

11. Ó Ciosáin, *Print and Popular Culture*, pp. 84–99; Niall Ó Ciosáin, 'The Irish Rogues', in *Irish Popular Culture, 1650–1850*, ed. James S. Donnelly and Kerby A. Miller (Ballsbridge: Irish Academic Press, 1997), pp. 78–96.

12. Richard Head, *The English Rogue Described, in the Life of Meriton Latroon* (1665; London, 1667), p. 7.

13. Orr, '*The English Rogue*', p. 366.

14. Derek Hand, *A History of the Irish Novel* (Cambridge University Press, 2011), p. 29. The text's title is also inaccurately given as '*Teague O'Divelly, or The Irish Rogue*' in Garrido Ardila, 'The Picaresque Novel', p. 124.

15. *The Irish Rogue, or the Comical History of the Life and Actions of Teague O Divelley* (London, 1690), p. 3. Further references to this work are given after quotations in the text.

16. Ó Ciosáin, 'The Irish Rogues', pp. 80, 84.

17. D. W. Hayton, *The Anglo-Irish Experience, 1680–1730: Religion, Identity and Patriotism* (Woodbridge, Suffolk: Boydell Press, 2012), p. 14.

18. See, for example, the following: 'The [Irish] people are thus enclined, religious, franke, amorous, irefull … delighted with wars', in Richard Stanihurst, 'The Description of Ireland', in *Holinshed's Irish Chronicle, the History of Ireland from the First Inhabitants Thereof, unto the Yeare 1509*, ed. Liam Miller and Eileen Power (Dublin: Dolmen Press, 1979), pp. 3–116 (p. 112). This passage compares closely with *The Irish Rogue*: 'The Inclination of the Irish, says he, is to be superstitiously Religious, Frank, Amorous, Ireful … delighting in Branglings and War' (pp. 109–10).

19. 'To the Reader', in *The Irish Rogue*, initial pages unnumbered (p. 1 of 3).

20. *Don Tomazo, or the Juvenile Rambles of Thomas Dangerfield* (London, 1680), p. 4. On Dangerfield and *Don Tomazo*, see also Kate Loveman, '"Eminent Cheats": Rogue Narratives in the Literature of the Exclusion Crisis', in *Fear, Exclusion and Revolution: Roger Morrice and Britain in the 1680s*, ed. Jason McElligott (Aldershot: Ashgate, 2006), pp. 108–22.

21. Gladfelder, *Criminality and Narrative*, p. 35.

22. See Samuel Fannin, 'The Irish Community in Eighteenth-Century Cadiz', in *Irish Migrants in Europe after Kinsale, 1602–1820*, ed. Thomas O'Connor and Mary Ann Lyons (Dublin: Four Courts Press, 2003), pp. 135–48; and Patricia O'Connell, 'The Early-Modern Irish College Network in Iberia, 1590–1800', in *The Irish in Europe, 1580–1815*, ed. Thomas O'Connor (Dublin: Four Courts Press, 2001), pp. 49–64 (pp. 49–50).

23. Ian McBride, *Eighteenth-Century Ireland: The Isle of Slaves* (Dublin: Gill and Macmillan, 2009), p. 185.

24. 'Preface', *Don Tomazo*, initial pages unnumbered (pp. 2–3 of 5).

25. See *The Irish Rogue*, pp. 172–75. The same episode appears in the contemporary *The Pleasant Adventures of the Witty Spaniard, Lazarillo de Tormes* (London: J. Leake, 1688), pp. 109–15.

26. Thomas Shadwell, *The Lancashire Witches*, in *The Complete Works of Thomas Shadwell*, ed. Montague Summers, 5 vols (London: Fortune Press, 1927), IV, pp. 99–188 (pp. 187–88); John Gibney, *Ireland and the Popish Plot* (Basingstoke: Palgrave Macmillan, 2009), pp. 5–6. Shadwell's play was first performed in 1681 and first printed the following year.

27. Hayton, *The Anglo-Irish Experience*, p. 7.

28. Shadwell, *The Lancashire Witches*, pp. 168–69.

29. Joep Leerssen, *Mere Irish and Fíor-Ghael: Studies in the Idea of Irish Nationality, Its Development and Expression Prior to the Nineteenth Century*, 2nd edn (Cork University Press, 1995), pp. 94–97.

30. Richetti, *Popular Fiction*, p. 59.

31. *The Irish Rogue, or the Comical History of the Life and Actions of Darby O Brolaghan* (Dublin, 1740), pp. 3, 13. The editing of the text is piecemeal, however, with references to the Irish as 'naturally mistrustful' and 'thievish' retained, along with the material taken from Stanihurst's 'Description of Ireland'. See pp. 38, 43, 60–65.

32. *The Irish Rogue* (1740), pp. 101–15.

33. 'The Goldfinder, or the Notorious Cheats of Manus Mac Oneil, and His Man Andrew', in John Cosgrave, *A Genuine History of the Lives and Actions of the Most Notorious Irish Highwaymen, Tories and Rapparees* (Dublin, 1747), pp. 129–50. Further references to this edition are given after quotations in the text.

34. James Kelly, 'Introduction', in *Gallows Speeches from Eighteenth-Century Ireland*, ed. Kelly (Dublin: Four Courts Press, 2001), pp. 11–69.

35. For example, Paul Lorrain, *A Narrative or, the Ordinary of Newgate's Account of What Passed between Him and James Sheppard* (Dublin, 1718), or *A Narrative of all the Robberies, Escapes, &c. of John Sheppard* (Dublin, 1724). The second of these is thought to be by Daniel Defoe.

36. The Irish book trade relied upon reprints of imported English texts at this point; a text like the 1682 biography of O'Hanlon is exceptional. See Mary Pollard, *Dublin's Trade in Books, 1550–1800* (Oxford: Clarendon Press, 1989), pp. 1–17, 224.

37. See the closing advertisements in [Voltaire], *The History of Charles XII. King of Sweden. In Eight Books* (Dublin, 1735), p. 162.

38. Kelly, 'Introduction', pp. 37–38.

39. Ó Ciosáin, *Print and Popular Culture*, pp. 87–88.

40. The term 'rapparee' was 'roughly synonymous' with tory, denoting an outlaw in eighteenth-century Ireland: see Cashman, 'The Heroic Outlaw', p. 193.

41. Ó Ciosáin, *Print and Popular Culture*, p. 93.

42. Faller, *Turned to Account*, p. 129.

43. On the price and likely readership of criminal biographies, see Faller, *Turned to Account*, p. 47, and Philip Rawlings, *Drunks, Whores and Idle Apprentices: Criminal Biographies of the Eighteenth Century* (London: Routledge, 1992), pp. 1–35 (pp. 3–4). Ó Ciosáin, 'The Irish Rogues', concludes that the first readers of Cosgrave were probably Catholic gentry and middle-class tenant farmers, though the book became more cheaply available later in the century (pp. 91–92).

44. Ó Ciosáin provides a helpful table of the sources of Cosgrave's collection in 'The Irish Rogues', p. 84.

45. Smith, *Second Volume of . . . Highway-men* (1714), pp. 133–44 ; Alexander Smith, *A Compleat History of the Lives and Robberies of the Most Notorious Highway-men*, 3 vols (London, 1719), II, pp. 236–42.

46. Ó Ciosáin, *Print and Popular Culture*, pp. 88–89.

47. Faller, *Turned to Account*, p. 144.

48. The same biographical details feature in the London-published collection, with the exception of Butler's learning Spanish and Italian. See 'J. W.', *A Full and Compleat History of the Lives, Robberies, and Murders, of all the Most Notorious Highwaymen* (London, 1742), pp. 123–26. Cartouche was a notorious Parisian criminal executed in 1721. See *The Life and Actions of Lewis Dominique Cartouche* (London, 1722). An earlier biography of Butler appears in Smith, *A Compleat History of the . . . Highwaymen* (1719), II, pp. 341–52. But the 1742 collection was more likely to have been Cosgrave's source, as its biography features specific details not included in Smith, which Cosgrave reuses, such as 'Lord Galway's Regiment' and Butler teaming up with Cartouche. See 'J. W.', *A Full and Compleat History of . . . the most Notorious Highwaymen*, pp. 123–24.

49. See *A Full and Compleat History of . . . the most Notorious Highwaymen*, pp. 155–62. Mulhoni's life was first published in James Carrick, *A Compleat and True Account of all the Robberies Committed by James Carrick, John Malhoni, and their Accomplices* (London, 1722), as Ó Ciosáin has noted ('The Irish Rogues', p. 86). However, Cosgrave's biography more resembles that of 1742 in its abbreviated style, eliding much of the detail present in the original, as well as in its wording.

50. *A Full and Compleat History of . . . the most Notorious Highwaymen*, p. 157.
51. Ibid., p. 155.
52. See Ian Campbell Ross, 'Introduction', in William Chaigneau, *The History of Jack Connor*, ed. Ross (Dublin: Four Courts Press, 2013), pp. 11–34 (p. 14), and Ian Campbell Ross, 'Novels, Chapbooks, Folklore: The Several Lives of William Chaigneau's Jack Connor, now Conyers; or, John Connor, alias Jack the Batchelor, the Famous Irish Bucker', *Eighteenth-Century Ireland / Iris an dá chultúr* 30 (2015), 60–86 (pp. 69–70).
53. Chaigneau, *Jack Connor*, ed. Ross, p. 93. National identity in *Jack Connor* is discussed in Ian Campbell Ross, 'An Irish Picaresque Novel: William Chaigneau's *The History of Jack Connor*', *Studies: An Irish Quarterly Review* 71 (1982), 270–79, and Catherine Skeen, 'Projecting Fictions: *Gulliver's Travels, Jack Connor*, and *John Buncle*', *Modern Philology* 100.3 (2003), 330–59.
54. Ó Ciosáin, 'The Irish Rogues', pp. 84, 92.
55. Daniel J. Casey, 'Carleton and the Count', *Seanchas Ardmhacha: Journal of the Armagh Diocesan Historical Society* 8.1 (1975/76), 7–22.
56. Bridget Hourican, 'Freney, James', in *The Dictionary of Irish Biography* (Cambridge University Press, 2009): http://dib.cambridge.org/ [accessed 2 April 2017].
57. *The Brave Irishman* was first performed under this title in 1746, and not published until 1754. Leerssen, *Mere Irish and Fíor-Ghael*, p. 116.
58. See, for example, *The Adventures of Dick Hazard* (London, 1754); Edward Kimber, *The Juvenile Adventures of David Ranger*, 2 vols (London, 1756); Thomas Amory, *The Life of John Buncle, Esq.* (1756), ed. Moyra Haslett (Dublin: Four Courts Press, 2011); and [Thomas Amory], *The Life of John Buncle, Esq.*, Vol. II (London, 1766).
59. [Charles Johnston], *The History of John Juniper* (Dublin, 1781).

CHAPTER 16

Gaelic Influences and Echoes in the Irish Novel, 1700–1780

Anne Markey

This essay explores the nature, extent, and significance of Gaelic influences and echoes in a range of Irish novels published between 1700 and 1780. Significantly, all such novels were written in English. While eighteenth-century authors including Seán Ó Neachtain (1655–1728) and Micheál Coimín (1676–c. 1760) produced a handful of fictional works in Irish that circulated in manuscript form, the stories they wrote were prose romances that had little in common with the new species of writing known as the novel. Cathal G. Ó Háinle argues that *Stair Éamainn Uí Chléirigh* (The History of Eamon Cleary), written by Ó Neachtain before 1719, exhibits 'a realism of the kind that was so important in the emerging novel in English'.[1] Nevertheless, as Ó Háinle acknowledges, the realism of Ó Neachtain's allegory about a man who battles with the evils of drink and gambling before finding redemption is 'limited by the incomplete realisation' of the titular character, so that the story is best categorised as a proto-novel.[2] During the eighteenth century, and indeed for several decades afterwards, factors including lack of access to printing technology, increasing literacy in English along with the demise of spoken Irish, and a limited urban readership, militated against the emergence of the Irish-language novel. Given the paucity of printed material available in the Irish language in the period, it is unsurprising that the ability to read was, as Niall Ó Ciosáin has observed, a skill 'usually acquired in English'.[3] Children in Charter Schools established over the course of the eighteenth century by the Incorporated Society for Promoting English Protestant Schools in Ireland were taught to read using English-language primers, catechisms, psalters, and prayer books.[4] English-language textbooks, as well as chapbooks and versions of several novels such as *The Vicar of Wakefield*, *Tristram Shandy*, and *Sandford and Merton*, were being used in hedge schools around Ireland in the early years of the nineteenth century.[5] Indeed, it was not until 1904 that *Séadna*, a story rooted in Gaelic storytelling traditions and generally regarded as 'the first "novel" in Irish' was published.[6]

Although Ian Watts's account of *The Rise of the Novel* (1957) has been persuasively challenged on various grounds, its linkage of the development of novels in English with the spread of Protestantism has been echoed in more recent criticism.[7] As Aileen Douglas points out, 'most eighteenth-century Irish fiction was produced by Irish Protestants, either the descendants of early Norman settlers (the Old English) or more recent arrivals'.[8] Notwithstanding what Joep Leerssen describes as 'an Ascendancy context of spreading interest in Ireland's Gaelic past', the majority of early Irish novelists, whose first language was English, had limited, if any, access to primary sources in the Irish language.[9] In addition, many Irish novels were published, at least initially, in London and frequently addressed to English readers with little knowledge of Irish history or contemporary affairs. Consequently, much eighteenth-century fiction written by English-speaking authors who were born or spent time in Ireland shows little influence of, and little interest in, Gaelic culture. Nevertheless, there are notable exceptions, as some Irish novels published before 1780 draw on beliefs and traditions associated with Irish-language culture in ways that illuminate both the diversity and the particularity of early Irish fiction. The ensuing examination of Gaelic echoes and influences in *Vertue Rewarded* (1693); *Irish Tales* (1716); *Gulliver's Travels* (1726); *The Life of John Buncle, Esq.* (1756); and *The Fool of Quality; or, The History of Henry, Earl of Moreland* (1765–70) aims to expand understandings of the early novel in general and the early Irish novel in particular. Direct reference and oblique allusion to Irish history, traditions, and culture within these novels not only facilitated the correction of Anglophone misapprehensions about Ireland and the Irish but also illuminate interactions between the worlds of the Irish-speaking majority and the Protestant elite in eighteenth-century Ireland.

Those interactions counter Daniel Corkery's presentation of Gaelic Ireland as a hermetically sealed cultural unit. In *The Hidden Ireland* (1924), Corkery claimed that Irish-language culture stretched back almost two thousand years and remained largely untouched during the eighteenth century by what previous English-language commentators had regarded as the progressive forces of modernity and anglicisation. Finding evidence of this Gaelic world view preserved in the work of a group of Munster poets living in reduced circumstances amongst the oppressed and impoverished Catholic peasantry of the Penal Law period, Corkery constructed a division between what he termed 'Gaelic' and 'Planter' Ireland, and so by association between Irish-language literature and Irish writing in English.

Interestingly, however, he detected similarities between Gaelic and continental literature by writers including Villon and Rabelais, although he argued that these parallels were unconscious correspondences rather than evidence of actual cultural or literary interchange.[10] *The Hidden Ireland*, as Patrick Walsh points out, 'was initially warmly received, being seen as a necessary corrective to Anglo-Irish history toward which the surviving English-language sources were naturally skewed', and remained highly influential during the early decades of the Irish state.[11] However, with the advent of historical revisionism in the 1960s, Corkery's views began to be challenged on various grounds.[12] In 1962, for example, Vivian Mercier, referring to texts in both English and Irish, claimed that 'an unbroken comic tradition may be traced in Irish literature from approximately the ninth century down to the present day'.[13] In 1969, Louis Cullen called for a reassessment of Corkery's concept of a hidden, Gaelic Ireland, presenting in its place a more politically nuanced and empirically based account of eighteenth-century Irish society. Almost two decades later, Joep Leerssen convincingly demonstrated how Protestant antiquarian and linguistic research over the course of the eighteenth century created a 'traffic between the Gaelic "sub-culture" and the Ascendancy' which transcended the type of linguistic, religious, and social barriers constructed by Corkery.[14] As Leerssen astutely observed, those types of interactions resulted in the emergence of new forms of Irish national identity, 'as the Anglo-Irish now begin to regard Ireland's Gaelic history as their own'.[15] Subsequent critical investigations of Irish-language texts and bilingual scribal activity have continued to draw attention to cultural and linguistic interactions between Irish and English, and so persuasively undermine the notion of eighteenth-century Gaelic Ireland as untouched by external influences.[16] Similarly, some critics have investigated how Irish writing in English illuminates issues relating to nuanced constructions of national identity in the period.[17] This essay draws on and develops those investigations through a detailed analysis of the significance of Gaelic influences and echoes in the early Irish novels selected for discussion.

The earliest example of novelistic recourse to Irish-language narrative traditions occurs in *Vertue Rewarded; or, The Irish Princess* (1693), an anonymously authored fiction published in London that announced itself as 'A New Novel' on the title page. The main narrative, set with considerable precision in Clonmel during the summer of 1690 in the immediate aftermath of the Battle of the Boyne, tells how Marinda, a young Irishwoman, having resisted all attempts at seduction by the Prince of S——g, a foreign commander in the army of King William III, finally has her virtue rewarded by marriage to her royal suitor. Early in the story, when the Prince is resting near a spring in a shaded copse, the narrator introduces an anecdote allegedly taken from 'an ancient Irish chronicle' about a pre-Norman Gaelic princess, 'Cluaneesha, the only child of Macbuain, King of Munster'.[18] The Irish princess's honour is besmirched when her stomach mysteriously swells and malicious rumours about her lack of chastity are circulated by her rivals. However, Cluaneesha's virtue is eventually vindicated when she drinks water from the spring beside which the European Prince is resting centuries later. The clear water causes the swelling of Cluaneesha's stomach to subside and her beauty to increase. As both her detractors and an adulterous woman had previously drunk water from the same well only to swell grotesquely before dying in agony, Cluaneesha's right to succeed her father is acknowledged by the people. Critics have suggested that the interpolated story of Cluaneesha in *Virtue Rewarded* invites Jacobite readings of the novel. Siobhán Kilfeather, for example, contends that the tale 'recalls accusations against the integrity of the former Queen Mary', the wife of James II, who was deposed by their daughter Mary and her husband, William III, while Derek Hand claims that it 'suggests a moment ripe for the kind of vision that a Gaelic Aisling (vision) poem might offer'.[19] Elsewhere, it has been argued that Cluaneesha's story 'is used to promote a positive view of the civility of ancient Irish society, possibly unique in English-language fiction of the late seventeenth century'.[20] Despite the narrator's claim, the story of Cluaneesha is an original, authorial fiction that never appeared in any Irish chronicle.[21] Nevertheless, the author of *Virtue Rewarded* knew enough about the Gaelic tradition of *dinnseanchas*, which links the Irish landscape with both historical and legendary events and people, to invent a story that highlights recourse to anecdote in the development of the early Irish novel. Equally significantly, the anecdote about Cluaneesha not only complicates the Protestant, pro-Williamite politics of the main narrative, but also anticipates sympathetic representations of Gaelic and, by extension, contemporary Ireland in later eighteenth-century novels.

While the author of *Virtue Rewarded* feigned familiarity with an Irish-language manuscript, Sarah Butler, the author of *Irish Tales: or, Instructive Histories for the Happy Conduct of Life* (1716), had demonstrable and extensive knowledge of one such source.[22] As Ian Campbell Ross has revealed, Butler drew deftly and comprehensively on *Foras Feasa ar Éirinn* (written *c.* 1634) by Seathrún Céitinn (Geoffrey or Jeoffrey Keating) for its account of Ireland's resistance to successive Viking invasions from the late ninth to the early eleventh centuries, culminating in the defeat of the invaders at the Battle of Clontarf in 1014.[23] The work aimed, *inter alia*, to counteract the many hostile accounts of Ireland written by English authors involved in the settlement of Ireland. Given that the story of Cluaneesha has no basis in Gaelic culture, Leerssen's claim that *Irish Tales* represents 'the first instance of post-bardic Gaelic antiquarianism influencing English literature' is verifiably and intriguingly correct.[24] In 1716, when *Irish Tales* was published in London, *Foras Feasa ar Éirinn* was only available in manuscript form. Consequently, Sarah Butler must have had access to a scribal version of Keating's text, available not only in Irish but also in Latin and English translation. Echoing Keating, Butler presents a predominantly positive representation of pre-Norman, Catholic Ireland, downplaying internecine struggles for supremacy between provincial kings and insisting instead on Ireland's ability to withstand foreign corruption. By drawing on Keating's account of Irish resistance to Viking colonisation, the author of *Irish Tales* uses the distant past to make a political point about the present, so what may be the earliest example of a Catholic novel can be read as a political allegory, sympathetic to the Jacobite cause.

Nevertheless, the principal narrative about the doomed love affair between Dooneflaith, the daughter of Maolseachelvin, King of Meath, and Murchoe, son of another provincial Irish king, Brian Boru, is, as the author acknowledges, an invention. The virtuous lovers' mutual desire to marry is thwarted not only by the lust of Turgesius, a Viking leader captivated by Dooneflaith's beauty, but also by the thirst of the young couple's fathers for power and supremacy. Although the Irish defeat the Danes at the end of the novel, the prospect of continued Irish self-governance is considerably clouded by the death of Brian Boru and of the virgin lovers. Maolseachelvin succeeds Brian Boru as High King of Ireland, but the closing pages reveal that he was the last monarch of the Milesian race. *Irish Tales*, then, draws on *Foras Feasa* to produce an amatory fiction, which functions as a warning tale that is as much about the demise of the old, Gaelic Catholic order as it is about the defeat of foreign invaders.

In the 'Preface' to the novel, the author recalls how the Irish were once renowned for their learning and piety, while lamenting that bondage resulting from subjugation has now bowed their spirits and damaged their reputation. This vindication of native Irish civility is supported not only by allusion to *Foras Feasa ar Éirinn* but also by astute reference to such hostile, English-language accounts of Ireland and its people as St Bede's *The Ecclesiastical History of the English People* (731 AD), Meredith Hanmer's *The Chronicle of Ireland* (written 1572; published 1633), William Camden's

Britannia (1586), Edmund Spenser's *A View of the Present State of Ireland* (written 1596; published 1633), and Peter Heylin's *Cosmographie* (1652), as well as to more recent, sympathetic sources such as Peter Walsh's *A Prospect of the State of Ireland from the Year of the World 1756, to the Year of Christ 1652* (1682) and Roderick O'Flaherty's *Ogygia: seu, Rerum Hibernicum Chronologia* (1685). The range of sources referenced testifies to the diversity of conflicting views of the value and significance of Gaelic culture available to authors of early Irish novels. Intriguingly, Irish proper names are presented in eccentric and inconsistent forms throughout *Irish Tales*; for example, Maolseachelvin, who appears in most manuscript forms of *Foras Feasa* as Maolseachluin, is also referred to as Moalseachelvin in *Irish Tales*. The unusual forms of names evident in the novel highlight not only the difficulties of representing Irish orthography in English-language texts but also the unfamiliarity of Irish historical material to an English readership.

While little is known about the author of *Irish Tales*, Jonathan Swift has long been acknowledged as one of the foremost writers of his time. At least since the 1970s, there has been an increasing recognition that Swift's Irish background is an important context for an appreciation of his work.[25] That is clearly the case with his pseudonymous pamphlets relating to Irish affairs published in the 1720s, but it is equally, if not so obviously, relevant to *Travels into Several Remote Nations of the World. In Four Parts. By Lemuel Gulliver* (1726). Indeed, various critics from the late nineteenth century onwards have identified and examined parallels between the first two parts of Swift's enduringly popular fantasy and elements of Gaelic tradition. In 1895, Joseph Jacob commented on similarities between 'A Voyage to Brobdingnag' and 'How Fin Went to the Kingdom of the Big Men', a folktale drawn from the Fenian cycle of Irish mythology. In Part II of Swift's satire, the shipwrecked Gulliver finds himself dwarfed by the Brobdingnagians before coming to royal attention and living at court; in the Irish tale, the legendary hero travels by sea from Howth, in north County Dublin, to a land of giants, where he 'was brought to the palace of the king, whose worthies and nobles assembled to see the little man'.[26] Jacobs suggested that Swift had been inspired by a variant of this folktale told to him during his childhood in Ireland: 'The voyage to Brobdingnag will occur to many readers, and it is by no means impossible that, as Swift was once an Irish lad, *The Voyage* may have been suggested by some such tale told him in his infancy.'[27] Given that Swift reported that he was in the habit of riding along the beach to Howth on the advice of his physician during his first years as Dean of St Patrick's Cathedral in Dublin, it is also possible that he heard a version of the story as an adult.[28] Acknowledging the superficial similarities between the Irish folktale collected by Jacobs and Part II of *Gulliver's Travels*, Arthur C. L. Brown in 1904 pointed out more 'striking resemblances to Swift's Brobdingnag' in another Irish story, '*Aidedh Ferghusa* or The Death of Fergus', which recounts visits made by the chief poet and king of the *Luchrupán*, or legendary little people, to Fergus, King of Ulster. These resemblances include the small visitors being cared for by intermediary figures who bring them to the royal palace; the larger natives' lack of personal hygiene; and the small visitors' misadventures at the royal table with the little man falling into a bowl of porridge in the Irish tale and into a bowl of cream in Swift's story.[29] Later critics also drew attention to similarities between elements of the first two parts of *Gulliver's Travels* and aspects of these two Irish stories.[30] Alan Harrison, however, rejected 'the influence of *Aededh Ferghusa* on *Gulliver's Travels* because it is a rare text', with which Swift, or his Irish-speaking friend, Anthony Raymond, was unlikely to have been familiar.[31] Margaret R. Grennan, meanwhile, pointing out that Swift's friends included other Irish speakers, demonstrated with numerous examples that the languages of both the Lilliputians and the Brobdingnagians contain several words that 'are very close to the Gaelic; others at least suggest it; and more are compounded of Irish roots'.[32] Harrison, in turn, argues that Swift, in common with 'most English speakers who regularly moved around Ireland in the early eighteenth century' was likely to have acquired 'some competence in the Irish language'.[33] This acknowledgement makes it seem even more likely that Gulliver's attempts to make sense of the languages he hears on his travels reflect his creator's experience of living in Ireland.

Derek Hand's observation that 'Irish readings of *Gulliver's Travels* focus on the depiction of the Yahoos in Book 4' reflects a tendency among postcolonial critics to examine similarities between the debased slaves of the apparently civilised and enlightened Houyhnhnms and the inhabitants of Swift's Ireland.[34] Gearóid Ó Cléirigh not only argues that these similarities were intentional on Swift's part but also suggests that the name of the enslaved species may be an anglicisation of 'Each-ó, Each-ó', an encouraging cry used by Irish horse riders (each being an Irish word for horse).[35] In Ó Cléirigh's view, Swift, as a member of the Protestant Ascendancy, viewed the native Irish with the same disdain and fear as the Houyhnhnms felt in relation to the Yahoos, while also being aware that he was viewed with similar disdain by the English, who made little distinction between the native Irish and the descendants of English settlers in Ireland. Additionally, Ó Cléirigh draws attention to 'Mianta Uí Dhoirnín' [The desires of Ó Doirnín], an undated poem in which Peadar Ó Doirnín (*c.* 1700–1769) bemoaned the present state of

Ireland. Two lines in the final stanza describe a chaotic disordered world where a horse mounts its rider ['Ach ó chuaidh an saol fó seach is gur éirigh / An t-each ar chléith an mharcaigh].[36] In Ó Cléirigh's view, the striking correspondences between this description and the final section of *Gulliver's Travels* suggest that either Swift was aware of the poem or that Ó Doirnín was familiar with the book.[37] Although it is not possible to prove either scenario, the intriguing similarities between the visions of the two writers point to cultural interchange between Gaelic and Planter Ireland.

Establishing convincing, albeit superficial, connections between *Gulliver's Travels* and the Irish language and its associated storytelling and literary traditions was in itself a significant scholarly achievement. Some critics, however, have also considered the significance of these similarities. As early as 1930, Mary Colum made the important point that it is 'vain to try and judge the work of any Irish writer without a knowledge of the Gaelic inheritance which has influenced everybody born in Ireland'.[38] Fifteen years later, Margaret R. Grennan drew on her knowledge of that inheritance to propose that 'there is a delicate suggestion of the Irish manner in Book 1'. That suggestion was subsequently developed by Vivien Mercier, who argued that 'Swift displays all the most strongly marked features of the Gaelic comic tradition. In *Gulliver's Travels* he shows himself a master of fantasy.'[39] In Declan Kiberd's view, Swift's invocation of Irish storytelling traditions in *Gulliver's Travels* 'is an early instance of the empire "writing back", engaging in reverse anthropology, sitting in judgment on an England that liked to sit in judgment of others'.[40] Be that as it may, Swift's recourse to Gaelic material in a work that defies easy categorisation underlines the malleability of the concept of genre at a time when the new species of writing known as the novel was still emerging. Michael McKeon argues that early novels characteristically drew on a variety of narrative traditions, including history and romance.[41] Few early novelists had any access to or knowledge of Irish narrative traditions, so Swift's incorporation of Gaelic material added to the strangeness of a work that caused a sensation when first published and that continues to vex the world while diverting it.

Swift's exposure to Irish-language culture was enhanced by his frequent visits to the house of his friend, Thomas Sheridan, in Quilca, County Cavan, where he wrote sections of *Gulliver's Travels*. Sheridan, who ran a school for boys, was one of the earliest teachers of Henry Brooke, who went on to become a dramatist, poet, antiquarian, novelist, and miscellaneous writer. In 1744, Brooke published a prospectus for a work to be entitled: 'The History of Ireland. From the Earliest Times. Wherein are set forth the Ancient and Extraordinary Customs, Manners, Religion, Politics, Conquests, and Revolutions, of that once Hospitable, Polite, and Martial Nation; Interspersed with Traditionary Digressions, and the Private and Affecting Histories of the most celebrated of the Natives'.[42] This history, which was to be largely based on translations of Gaelic material provided by Charles O'Conor of Belanagare to Brooke's cousin, Robert Digby, never appeared. However, Brooke's ongoing interest in Gaelic Ireland and respect for aspects of its culture is evident in *An Essay on the Antient and Modern State of Ireland* (1759), in which he 'eulogized Gaelic customs'.[43] The *Essay*, Brooke announced, was written in vindication 'of the honour and advantage of *Ireland*', a kingdom whereof he declared himself, 'without vanity, proud of being a Native'.[44] Dividing Irish history into three periods (the ancient Milesian period; the early Christian period; and the Norman conquest onwards), in common with other eighteenth-century Protestant antiquarians as well as Catholic historians, he found much to praise in pre-Norman, Gaelic Ireland. For example, he extolled the Milesian devotion to learning of all sorts and, echoing Charles O'Conor in *Dissertations on the Ancient History of Ireland* (1753), applauded the ancient adherence to 'a popular Right of Election [...] extremely consistent with the Essence and Genius of True Liberty'.[45] In expressing his approbation for the ancient Irish practices of electing rulers, Brooke was rejecting the disapproval of commentators such as Sir James Ware who bemoaned that by 'the Law of Tanistry [...] the hereditary right of succession was not observed'.[46]

Brooke also drew favourable attention to the 'naturally civil, generous and hospitable' character of the Irish peasantry, while lauding the system whereby sons of noble families were fostered by sages who educated them in the principles of 'Religion, Political wisdom, Law, History &c.'.[47] In Brooke's view, it was particularly commendable that:

> the education of the Landed Gentry, when Luxury, with its wasted Catalogue of Vices had not rendered Property so mutable and wavering as in modern Ages, was provided for; whether by the immediate Care of Parents or essential attention of Guardians, by the Laws of the Land; in order that Gentlemen should, to the Antiquity of Birth and Possession, add the important Dignity of Learning.[48]

Fostering, less in the sense of entrusting an older child's education to a trusted guardian but more in terms of sending an infant away from the parental home to be nursed, was not unknown in England. Nevertheless, it was generally regarded as a particularly Irish custom, which had long disturbed and alarmed the English in Ireland because of its apparent threat to systems of inheritance based on primogeniture. In 1612, Sir John Davies, describing fosterage as a practice tending towards 'the utter ruine of a Commonwealth' and the cause of 'mischiefe in this Realm', avowed: 'But such a generall Custome in a Kingdome, in giving and taking children to Foster, making such a firme Alliance as it doth in Ireland, was never seene or heard of, in any other Countrey of the world besides.'⁴⁹ As early as 1571, Edmund Campion declared of the Irish: 'They love tenderly their foster children, and bequeathe to them a childes portion', adding: 'They love and trust their Foster Brethren more then their owne.'⁵⁰ In 1596, Edmund Spenser was even more vociferous in his condemnation of the Irish practice of fostering, denouncing it as an 'infection' that militated against the anglicisation of the country, because 'the childe that sucketh the milke of the nurse, must of necessity learne his first speach of her [. . .] So that the speach being *Irish*, the heart must needes bee *Irish*'.⁵¹ In *An Essay on the Antient and Modern State of Ireland*, Brooke not only offers a positive presentation of his native country that counters earlier hostile accounts of pre-Norman Ireland, but also suggests that some of the Gaelic customs he eulogises could usefully be adapted in modern times.

That suggestion is borne out by Brooke's account of the childhood education and early adulthood of the second son of an English nobleman in *The Fool of Quality, or, The History of Henry, Earl of Moreland* (1765–70). Effectively this 'sprawling and heterogenous novel' is a private and affective history of an exemplary individual, interspersed with narrative digressions.⁵² Hence, both its tone and form echo Brooke's earlier approach to the history of Ireland. Although Mr Meekly, a friend of the titular hero's father, briefly but convincingly defends the Irish against charges of laziness and indigence in the fifth and final volume of Brooke's sentimental novel, Ireland does not feature as a location and no Irish characters appear in the story. Nevertheless, the author's respect for Gaelic culture is an important source for and feature of the early volumes of a work that critics agree was heavily influenced by Rousseau's *Emile* (1762).⁵³ In *Emile*, Rousseau deplored the contemporary predilection of upper- and middle-class women for sending children out to wet-nurses, arguing that they cared little for the children in their care, and implored mothers to take responsibility for what he regarded as their sacred duty of breastfeeding so that modern society might be reformed: 'But let mothers deign to nurse their children, morals will reform themselves, nature's sentiments will be awakened in every heart, the state will be repeopled.'⁵⁴ The hero of *The Fool of Quality*, young Harry Clinton, is sent away from home as an infant to be nursed by a robust but poor woman, who loves, rather than indulges, her charge, whose parents never enquire for him until he is five years old. As a result, Harry grows into a hardy boy with no knowledge of fashion and no taste for luxury. By contrast, his elder brother, Richard, is cared for by his doting mother, who panders to the young heir's every whim, with the result that he becomes a spoilt child. That young Harry's early upbringing has more in common with the type of fosterage that was a feature of Gaelic Ireland than with Rousseau's educational system is evidenced not only by the mutual affection between the child and his surrogate family but also by the length of his stay with them. Indeed, when Mr Fenton, a benevolent, well-educated stranger, to whose attention Harry comes when he is aged five and a half, asks his carers if they are his parents, they reply: 'we are but his Fosterers'.[55] The mysterious Mr Fenton, who later turns out to be Harry's paternal uncle, abducts the boy whom he educates largely by means of didactic stories, including the kind of fable critiqued by Emile's tutor as being beyond the comprehension of a child. Harry's wise protector, whom the boy addresses as 'Dada', has more in common with the sage guardians who fostered the sons of the Gaelic nobility than he does with Rousseau's fictional alter ego. When Richard Clinton dies of smallpox in Paris, his younger brother, Harry, who has been raised in liberal principles by his uncle, becomes reconciled with his father whom he succeeds as Earl of Moreland: 'Our Hero was now the Master of Millions, approaching to the Prime of Youth, glowing with Health, Action and Vigour, of Beauty incomparable, beloved of All who knew him, and the Attraction and Admiration of every Eye where he passed.'[56] Here, Brooke's distaste for primogeniture and approval of the Gaelic law of tanistry is expressed through the approved and happy succession of a second son to an English title. Consequently, Brooke's advocacy throughout the novel of social reform through education rests on covert recourse to his knowledge of Irish history and culture.

Despite unfavourable early reviews, *The Fool of Quality* proved enduringly popular, being reprinted several times in both Britain and America as well as being abbreviated by John Wesley in 1781 and edited by Charles Kingsley in 1859. By contrast, *The Life of John Buncle, Esq.*, written by Thomas Amory and published in two parts in London in 1756 and 1766, was an experimental novel that faded largely into obscurity after its initial success. Though little read, it was nevertheless the subject of an essay, 'On John Buncle', by William Hazlitt in *The Round Table* (1817) and was edited by Ernest A. Baker in 1906. It has also featured regularly in late twentieth- and early twenty-first-century accounts of early Irish fiction.[57] Although born in England, probably in the 1690s, Amory spent much of his childhood and early adulthood in Ireland, principally in counties Clare and Dublin, before settling in London in the 1750s. The preface to *John Buncle* not only reveals that the hero of this first-person narrative similarly moved as an infant from England to Ireland, but also that the strangeness of the ensuing narrative in which improbable stories are presented as true is attributable to his familiarity with Gaelic culture: 'as to the difference of my life, from that of the generality of men, let it only be considered, that I was born in London, and carried an infant to Ireland, where I learned the Irish language, and became intimately acquainted with its original inhabitants'.[58] Ian Campbell Ross has drawn attention to the significance of the Irish dimensions of the novel, arguing persuasively that Amory's reliance on anecdote reveals his recourse to the tradition of *seanchas* (local, oral, popular lore), in which often fantastic tales are guaranteed as being truthful by a storyteller who declares that he witnessed or participated in the implausible events described.[59] More recently, Moyra Haslett has drawn attention to the amount of largely unacknowledged 'borrowed' material, ranging from short phrases to long page spans of material quoted verbatim from other sources in *John Buncle*, pointing out that some mid-eighteenth-century critics argued that such borrowings were not incompatible with originality.[60] It is also significant that the concept of plagiarism, defined as 'literary theft', is alien to the oral tradition of *seanchas*, within which the notion of original authorship is oxymoronic as material is repeated, sometimes with variations designed to appeal to particular audiences, by different tellers and so passes from one generation to the next.[61] A similar process is evident in Amory's apparently cavalier appropriation of existing texts, which 'would have been recognised by the educated reader whom *Buncle* so evidently addresses'.[62] Both Amory's reliance on anecdote and his frequent repetitions of material likely to be familiar to his audience testify to the novel's indebtedness to Irish oral narrative.

That Amory's knowledge of Gaelic culture extended beyond a palpable familiarity with its storytelling traditions is clear in a passage recalling a pleasant journey by Buncle and some acquaintances in southern Ireland:

> As I travelled once in the county of Kerry in Ireland, with the White Knight, and the Knight of the Glin. We called at Terelah O Crohanes, an old Irish gentleman, our common friend, who kept up the hospitality of his ancestors, and shewed how they lived, when Cormac Mac Cuillenan, the Generous, (from whose house he descended) was king of Munster and Archbishop of Cashel, in the year 913. There was no end of eating and drinking there, and the famous Downe Falvey played on the harp. For a day and a night we sat to it by candle-light, without shirts or cloaths on; naked,

excepting that we had our breeches and shoes and stockings on; and I drank
so much burgundy in that time, that the sweat ran of a red colour down my
body.[63]

As Ian Campbell Ross observes, this unambivalently celebratory description
of the hospitality and lifestyle of the Gaelic aristocracy 'has no obvious
fictional precedent' but has much 'in common with contemporary descriptions in Irish of life in the big houses, whether Gaelic or Planter in Gaelic
areas, in the work of such 18th-century poets as Aodhagán Ó Rathaille or
Seán Clárach Mac Domhnaill'.[64] Moyra Haslett's observation that the
Knight of Glin referenced by Buncle is likely to have been the eighteenth
Knight, Thomas Fitzgerald (c. 1675–1735), whose home was frequented by
Gaelic poets, including Ó Rathaille, adds credence to the argument that the
affinities between Amory's positive views of the Irish aristocracy and those
expressed by contemporary Irish-language poets are not coincidental.[65] That
Buncle's claim to have enjoyed Fitzgerald's hospitality reflects Amory's own
experience is rendered very likely by the reference to the famous Downe
Falvey. Fame can be fleeting, but around 1755 the melodious Donn
O Failbhe's astounding talents were extolled in two quatrains attributed to
the blind Munster poet, Donnchadh Caoch Ó Mathghamhna, while in
1779, Echlin Keane, another Irish harpist, described 'Dunflavie' from 'the
County of Limerick' as 'a Celebrated performer & a Gentleman'.[66] However
unlikely red sweat may be, Amory's account of Irish generosity as experienced in mid-eighteenth-century Munster seems rooted in truth.

To reinforce the point made in the passage that Irish liberality can be
traced back over the centuries, Amory includes two lengthy footnotes
that take up more space than the anecdote itself. He claims that the
information provided in these notes, which stress the civility and hospitality of pre-Norman Ireland, was drawn from a range of sources,
including the medieval Psalters of Cashel and Tara, as well as more
recent works, including Roderick O'Flaherty's *Ogygia: seu, Rerum
Hibernicum Chronologia* (1685) and Hugh McCurtin's *A Brief
Discourse in Vindication of the Antiquity of Ireland* (1717), that sought
to refute hostile colonial accounts of Ireland. Although the information
provided by Amory appears to be gleaned entirely from *The General
History of Ireland* (1723), Dermot O'Connor's translation of Geoffrey
Keating's *Foras Feasa ar Éirinn* (c. 1634), his references to other sources
underline the extent of his desire to convince the reader that Ireland is,
and always has been, a place where strangers are welcomed and generously entertained. This section of *The Life of John Buncle, Esq.* not only

highlights friendly interactions between Gaelic and Planter Ireland but also celebrates Gaelic customs, culture, and cordiality.

The preceding section, in which Buncle recalls an encounter with a community of women living in the English countryside, has affinities with other earlier and contemporary literary representations of female societies, including *Párliament na mBan*. This text, composed by Domhnall Ó Colmáin in the late seventeenth century, purports to be an account of the proceedings of a parliament of women held in 1697 in Cork city. In essence, it is, as Brian Ó Cuív, its twentieth-century editor remarks, a didactic work which deals primarily with prayer and sin, subjects that are also discussed by Buncle with Azora, the leader of the group of English women he encounters.[67] The first section of *Párliament na mBan* is largely a loose translation of Erasmus's 'Assembly or Parliament of Women', demonstrating that the similarities between Gaelic and continental literature viewed as unconscious and accidental by Corkery were in fact intentional and deliberate. Significantly, Ó Colmáin departs from his source to advocate the education of girls, as his parliamentarians decree that their daughters should attend school until the age of twelve and that the more intelligent amongst them should continue to study the liberal arts, including arithmetic and geometry. Tellingly, Buncle is impressed by the quickness of the younger English women 'in answering very hard arithmetical questions' and by Azora's mastery of algebra and 'geometric figures'.[68] Both *Párliament na mBan* and *John Buncle* can be viewed as 'writings that engaged with, revised and adapted Enlightenment views on women's education'.[69] Consequently, both texts reveal affinities not only between Irish-language literature and Irish writing in English but also convincing links between those two strands of Irish cultural production and European thought.

Vivien Mercier argues that Irish writers in English have been influenced at least since the early eighteenth century by Gaelic traditions of which most were barely aware.[70] The feigned and verifiable recourse of the early Irish novelists considered in this essay to Irish-language material or other sources sympathetic to Ireland's enduring traditions and past cultural glory shows how very aware they were of this heritage. To varying degrees, their knowledge of Gaelic Ireland, past or present, is openly acknowledged or covertly interwoven in narratives presented to readers unlikely to know anything positive about the country's history or its current inhabitants. In each case, Gaelic echoes and influences set their work apart from that of other contemporary writers of English fiction. Through explicit reference to Irish history or implicit evocation of Irish-language traditions, these novels present a positive view of Ireland and the Irish that challenged less favourable colonial accounts of the country and its inhabitants. Although they provide persuasive evidence that undermines Daniel Corkery's view of the complete division between Gaelic and Planter culture in eighteenth-century Ireland, they effectively prefigure his postcolonial reclamation and revaluation of Irish culture, past and present.

Notes

1. Cathal G. Ó Háinle, 'The Novel Frustrated: Seventeenth- to Nineteenth-Century Fiction in Irish', in *Unity in Diversity: Studies in Irish and Scottish Gaelic Language, Literature and History*, ed. Ó Háinle and Donald E. Meek (School of Irish, Trinity College Dublin, 2004), pp. 125–52 (p. 141); see also Philip O'Leary, *The Prose Literature of the Gaelic Revival, 1881–1921: Ideology and Innovation* (University Park, PA: Pennsylvania State University Press, 1994), pp. 5–6.
2. Ó Háinle, 'The Novel Frustrated', p. 142; Alan Titley describes *Stair Éamainn Uí Chléirigh* as 'the closest thing we can get to a novel in Irish in 18th-century Ireland'. See Titley, 'Writing in Irish': www.dublincityofliterature.net/wp-content/uploads/Irish-Language-Writing.pdf [accessed 2 August 2017].
3. Niall Ó Ciosáin, *Print and Popular Culture in Ireland, 1750–1850* (Basingstoke: Macmillan, 1997), p. 154.
4. Aileen Douglas, *Work in Hand: Script, Print, and Writing, 1690–1840* (Oxford University Press, 2017), pp. 78–80.
5. Antonia McManus, *The Irish Hedge School and its Books, 1695–1831* (Dublin: Four Courts Press, 2004), pp. 245–53.
6. Brian Ó Conchubhair and Philip O'Leary, 'The Canon in Irish Language Fiction', *Dublin Review of Books* (1 June 2015): www.drb.ie/essays/the-canon-in-irish-language-fiction [accessed 2 August 2017].
7. See, for example, Jarlath Killeen, *The Emergence of Irish Gothic Fiction: History, Origins, Theories* (Edinburgh University Press, 2014), p. 53.
8. Aileen Douglas, 'The Novel before 1800', in *The Cambridge Companion to the Irish Novel*, ed. John Wilson Foster (Cambridge University Press, 2006), pp. 22–38 (p. 22).
9. Joep Leerssen, *Mere Irish and Fíor-Ghael: Studies in the Idea of Irish Nationality, its Development and Expression prior to the Nineteenth Century* (Amsterdam and Philadelphia: John Benjamins, 1986), p. 339.
10. Daniel Corkery, *The Hidden Ireland: A Study of Gaelic Munster in the Eighteenth Century* (1924; Dublin: Gill and Macmillan, 1967), p. 170.
11. Patrick Walsh, 'Daniel Corkery's *The Hidden Ireland* (1924) and Revisionism', *New Hibernia Review* 5.2 (2001), 27–44 (p. 27).
12. For an account of how revisionist historians challenged what they perceived to be nationalistic accounts of Irish history, see Kevin Whelan, 'The Revisionist Debate in Ireland', *boundary 2* 31.1 (2004), 179–205.

13. Vivien Mercier, *The Irish Comic Tradition* (Oxford University Press, 1962), p. vii.

14. Louis M. Cullen, *The Hidden Ireland: Reassessment of a Concept* (1969; Dublin: Lilliput Press, 1988); Leerssen, *Mere Irish and Fíor-Ghael*, p. 370.

15. Leerssen, *Mere Irish and Fíor-Ghael*, p. 376.

16. See, for example, Alan Harrison, *The Dean's Friend: Anthony Raymond, 1675–1726, Jonathan Swift and the Irish Language* (Dublin: Caisleán an Bhúrcaigh, 1999); Lesa Ní Mhunghaile, 'An Eighteenth-Century Gaelic Scribe's Private Library: Muiris Ó Gormáin's Books', *Proceedings of the Royal Irish Academy* 110.C (2010), 239–76; Lesa Ní Mhunghaile, '"My comparatively feeble hand": Charlotte Brooke agus *Reliques of Irish Poetry* (1789)', in *Aistriú Éireann*, ed. Charlie Dillon agus Ríona Ní Fhrighil (Belfast: Queen's University Press, 2008), pp. 68–82; and Charles Dillon, '*An Ghaelig nua*: English, Irish and the South Ulster Poets and Scribes in the Late Seventeenth and Eighteenth Centuries', in *Irish and English: Essays on the Irish Linguistic and Cultural Frontier, 1600–1900*, ed. James Kelly and Ciarán Mac Murchaidh (Dublin: Four Courts Press, 2012), pp. 141–61.

17. See, for example, Katherine O'Donnell, 'The Image of a Relationship in Blood: Párliament na mBan and Burke's Jacobite Politics', *Eighteenth-Century Ireland / Iris an dá chultúr* 15 (2000), 98–119; Jarlath Killeen, *Gothic Ireland: Horror and the Irish Anglican Imagination in the Long Eighteenth Century* (Dublin: Four Courts Press, 2005); Ní Mhunghaile, '"My comparatively feeble hand"'.

18. *Vertue Rewarded; or, The Irish Princess*, ed. Ian Campbell Ross and Anne Markey (Dublin: Four Courts Press, 2010), p. 62.

19. Siobhán Kilfeather, 'Sexuality, 1685–2001', in *The Field Day Anthology of Irish Writing*, Vols IV/V: *Irish Women's Writing and Traditions*, ed. Angela Bourke et al., 2 vols (Cork University Press, 2002), IV, pp. 766–68 (p. 767); Derek Hand, *A History of the Irish Novel* (Cambridge University Press, 2011), p. 19.

20. Ian Campbell Ross and Anne Markey, 'From Clonmel to Peru: Barbarism and Civility in *Vertue Rewarded; or, The Irish Princess*', *Irish University Review* 38.2 (2008), 179–202 (p. 184).

21. Ibid.

22. Sarah Butler, *Irish Tales: or, Instructive Histories for the Happy Conduct of Life*, ed. Ian Campbell Ross, Aileen Douglas, and Anne Markey (Dublin: Four Courts Press, 2010).

23. Ian Campbell Ross, '"One of the Principal Nations in Europe": The Representation of Ireland in Sarah Butler's *Irish Tales*', *Eighteenth-Century Fiction* 7.1 (1994), 1–16.

24. Leerssen, *Mere Irish and Fíor-Ghael*, p. 378.

25. See, for example, Ann Cline Kelly, 'Swift's Explorations of Slavery in Houyhnhnmland and Ireland', *PMLA* 91.5 (October 1976), 846–55; Carole Fabricant, *Swift's Landscape* (Baltimore, MD: Johns Hopkins University Press, 1982); Ian Campbell Ross, *Swift's Ireland* (Dublin: Easons, 1983); Robert Mahony, *Jonathan Swift: The Irish Identity* (New Haven, CT

and London: Yale University Press, 1995); Joseph McMinn, *Jonathan's Travels: Swift and Ireland* (Belfast and New York: Appletree Press, 1994); and Brean Hammond, *Jonathan Swift* (Dublin: Irish Academic Press, 2010).

26. Joseph Jacobs, *More Celtic Fairy Tales* (London: D. Nutt, 1895), p. 196.

27. Ibid., p. 233.

28. Thomas Sheridan, *The Life of the Rev. Dr. Jonathan Swift, Dean of St. Patrick's Dublin* (London, 1784), p. 212.

29. Arthur C. L. Brown, 'Gulliver's Travels and an Irish Folk-Tale', *Modern Language Notes* 19.2 (1904), 45–46 (p. 45).

30. See, for example, Aodh de Blacam, 'An Anglo-Irish Reading Programme: The 18th Century', *Irish Monthly* 47.558 (1919), 666–73 (p. 669); Gerard Murphy; *The Ossianic Lore and Romantic Tales of Medieval Ireland* (Dublin: Colm O Lochlainn, 1955), pp. 31–32; Mary Colum, 'Jonathan Swift', *The Saturday Review of Literature* (22 November 1930): http://marycolum.com/articles/jo nathan-swift/ [accessed 2 August 2017]; and Mercier, *Irish Comic Tradition*, pp. 29–31.

31. Harrison, *The Dean's Friend*, p. 158.

32. Margaret Grennan, 'Lilliput and Leprecan: Gulliver and the Irish Tradition', *ELH* 12.3 (September 1945), 188–202 (pp. 197, 200).

33. Harrison, *The Dean's Friend*, p. 154; see also Andrew Carpenter and Alan Harrison, 'Swift's "O'Rourke's Feast" and Sheridan's "Letter": Early Transcripts by Anthony Raymond', *Proceedings of the first Münster Symposium on Jonathan Swift*, ed. H. Real and H. Vienken (München: W. Fink, 1985), pp. 27–46.

34. Hand, *A History of the Irish Novel*, p. 35.

35. Gearóid Ó Cléirigh, 'Ó Sheacaibítigh go Houyhnhnms', *Feasta* 64.7 (2011), 19–26 (p. 26).

36. Breandán Ó Buachalla, ed., *Peadar Ó Doirnín: amhráin* (Dublin: An Clóchomhar, 1969), p. 35.

37. Ó Cléirigh, 'Ó Sheacaibítigh go Houyhnhnms', p. 26.

38. Colum, 'Jonathan Swift'.

39. Grennan, 'Lilliput and Leprecan', p. 202; Mercier, *Irish Comic Tradition*, p. 188.

40. Declan Kiberd, *Irish Classics* (London: Granta, 2000), p. 88.

41. Michael McKeon, *The Origins of the English Novel, 1600–1740*, new edn (Baltimore, MD and London: Johns Hopkins University Press, 2002), pp. 25–64.

42. See Leerssen, *Mere Irish and Fíor-Ghael*, p. 377.

43. D. George Boyce, *Nationalism in Ireland*, 3rd edn (London and New York: Routledge, 2003), p. 117.

44. Henry Brooke, *An Essay on the Antient and Modern State of Ireland* (Dublin, 1759), p. 5.

45. Ibid., p. 7. For Brooke's reliance on O'Conor, see Clare O'Halloran, *Golden Ages and Barbarous Nations: Antiquarian Debate and Cultural Politics in Ireland, c. 1750–1800* (Cork University Press, 2004), p. 224, and Colin Kidd, 'Gaelic Antiquity and National Identity in Enlightenment Ireland and

Scotland', *The English Historical Review* 109.434 (November 1994), 1197–214 (p. 1201).

46. Sir James Ware, *Enquiries Concerning Ireland and Its Antiquities* (Dublin, 1705), p. 21.

47. Brooke, *An Essay*, pp. 8, 36.

48. Ibid., p. 10.

49. Sir John Davies, *A Discovery of the True Causes Why* Ireland *Was Never Entirely Subdued, and Brought under Obedience of the Crowne of* England, *untill the Beginning of His Majesties Happy Raigne* (London, 1612), pp. 178, 180.

50. Edmund Campion, *Campion's Historie of Ireland*, in James Ware, *The Historie of Ireland, Collected by Three Learned Authors, Viz. Meredith Hanmer, Doctor in Divinitie; Edmund Campion Sometime Fellow of St Johns College in Oxford; and Edmund Spenser* (Dublin, 1633), pp. 14, 19.

51. Edmund Spenser, *A View of the State of Ireland*, in Ware, *Historie of Ireland*, pp. 47, 48.

52. Markman Ellis, *The Politics of Sensibility: Race, Gender and Commerce in the Sentimental Novel* (Cambridge University Press, 1996), p. 130.

53. See, for example, Ian Campbell Ross, 'Prose in English, 1690–1800: From the Williamite Wars to the Act of Union', in *The Cambridge History of Irish Literature*, ed. Margaret Kelleher and Philip O'Leary, 2 vols (Cambridge University Press, 2006), I, pp. 232–81 (p. 271); Dinah Birch and Katy Hooper, eds., *The Concise Oxford Companion to English Literature*, 4th edn (Oxford University Press, 2012), p. 256.

54. Jean-Jacques Rousseau, *Emile, or On Education*, trans. Allan Bloom (New York: Basic Books, 1979), p. 46.

55. Henry Brooke, *The Fool of Quality, or, The History of Henry, Earl of Moreland*, Vol. I (Dublin, 1765), p. 46.

56. Henry Brooke, *The Fool of Quality*, Vol. V (Dublin, 1770), p. 243.

57. See, for example, Ian Campbell Ross, 'Fiction to 1800', in *The Field Day Anthology of Irish Writing*, ed. Seamus Deane, Andrew Carpenter, and Jonathan Williams, 3 vols (Derry: Field Day, 1991), I, pp. 682–769; Ian Campbell Ross, 'Irish Fiction before the Union', in *The Irish Novel in the Nineteenth Century*, ed. Jacqueline Belanger (Dublin: Four Courts Press, 2005), pp. 34–51 (pp. 47–48); and Douglas, 'The Novel before 1800', pp. 30–32.

58. Thomas Amory, *The Life of John Buncle, Esq.* (1756), ed. Moyra Haslett (Dublin: Four Courts Press, 2011), p. 46.

59. Ian Campbell Ross, 'Thomas Amory, *John Buncle*, and the Origins of Irish Fiction', *Éire-Ireland* 18.3 (1983), 71–85.

60. Moyra Haslett, 'Introduction', in Thomas Amory, *The Life of John Buncle Esq.*, pp. 11–40 (pp. 23–26).

61. For the definition of plagiarism, see *Oxford English Dictionary Online*: www-oed-com.queens.ezp1.qub.ac.uk/ [accessed 2 August 2017].

62. Haslett, 'Introduction', p. 23.

63. Amory, *John Buncle*, pp. 174–76.

64. Ross, 'Thomas Amory, *John Buncle*, and the Origins of Irish Fiction', pp. 74–75.
65. Haslett, in Amory, *John Buncle*, p. 307.
66. Colm O'Baoill,'Donn Ó Fáilbhe', *Éigse* 19.1 (1982), 172–73; J. L. Campbell, 'An Account of Some of the Eminent Harpers in Ireland within the Last Two Centuries as Given by Echlin O'Kean Harper, Anno 1779', *Éigse* 6 (1948–52), 146–48 (p. 148).
67. Brian Ó Cuív, ed., *Párliament na mBan* (Dublin Institute for Advanced Studies, 1977), p. xxxi.
68. Amory, *John Buncle*, pp. 167, 169.
69. Gerardine Meaney, Mary O'Dowd, and Bernadette Whelan, *Reading the Irish Woman: Studies in Cultural Encounter and Exchange, 1714–1960* (Liverpool University Press, 2013), p. 36.
70. Mercier, *Irish Comic Tradition*, pp. 238–39.

CHAPTER 17

New Beginning or Bearer of Tradition? Early Irish Fiction and the Construction of the Child

Clíona Ó Gallchoir

While the eighteenth century is routinely identified as the period in which ideas about children and childhood acquired a distinctive and distinctively modern quality, for reasons which are closely connected with the rise of enlightenment thought in the same period, it is only very recently that we have had any discussion of how those ideas were articulated in the Irish context.[1] In this essay I focus on two relatively little known but significant early Irish novels, William Chaigneau's *The History of Jack Connor* (1752) and Henry Brooke's *The Fool of Quality* (1765–70), in order to explore the ways in which their representations of childhood reflect both broader enlightenment ideas about childhood, and the specific socio-political conditions pertaining in Ireland in this period. Appearing only three years after the publication of Rousseau's *Emile* (1762), and clearly influenced by it, Brooke's *The Fool of Quality* has been identified as 'the first extended portrayal of childhood in English-language fiction'.[2] The earlier and less well known *The History of Jack Connor* is however also notable for its depiction of childhood and its foregrounding of education as a theme. This essay argues that Irish social and economic conditions created a heightened awareness of the significance of children as potential sources of social change, and this awareness is reflected in an important subgenre of Irish fiction that includes the later works of Maria Edgeworth. Before turning to the novels, however, I want to address some of the specific ways in which children and childhood were the focus of attention in eighteenth-century Ireland, in the period immediately following the Williamite settlement.

The religious and sectarian character of the Williamite conflict meant that in the first half of the century in particular, ideas of 'improvement' were invariably associated with Protestant beliefs and practices. The unavoidably sectarian character of Irish society and institutions in the aftermath of the Williamite wars, coupled with a commitment to improvement that derived from the mainstream of enlightenment thought, together produced a distinctive construction of the child in Ireland. Influenced by

Locke and later by Rousseau, Anglican improvers eagerly embraced the idea of the child as a blank sheet and an innocent point of origin. This construction of the child from the point of view of Protestant improvement was however intensified by the perception of Catholicism as degenerate and irredeemable, resulting in a sometimes alarming insistence on preserving the child's 'innocence' by a brutal separation from the home and family environment.

The very specific value attached to children in early eighteenth-century Ireland can be gauged by the fact that within the minority of those in the Church of Ireland who argued for a concerted effort to convert the Catholic population, those who focused on the conversion of adults were in an even more insignificant minority. The only systematic conversion programme to gain state support was the system of Charter Schools, in which children would receive instruction in English, in Protestant principles, and in useful skills that, it was hoped, would make them more employable and productive; in a variety of ways, therefore, it was hoped that first the charity schools and then the Charter Schools would contribute to Ireland's moral and economic improvement. The Charter Schools were, in their design if not in their execution, a project that reflected enlightenment principles: those who promoted them were convinced of the power of education to effect significant change on an individual and societal level. A pamphlet of 1748, for instance, extols the potential of the schools to effect great changes in Ireland, 'not by Force or Terror, not by Penal Laws and Prosecutions, which can only make Hypocrites; but by the innocent and gentle means of enlightening and instructing the innocent Minds of Children in the pure Truths of the Gospel'.[3]

The optimism expressed in the ability of the Charter Schools to effect social change is based on the idea that children are educable and malleable, and that children born within Catholic families and communities nonetheless have the potential to become enlightened and industrious Protestants. Thus the project of the Charter Schools was partly shaped by Lockean epistemology and psychology, and partly by the specifically sectarian nature of the state in eighteenth-century Ireland. What is less well known is that the question of whether to focus conversion programmes at children or adults was a matter of controversy, and that the campaign led by Archbishop Boulter to gain state funding for Charter Schools signalled a rejection of any real attempts to convert adults.[4]

Canvassing among colleagues and friends for financial support for the Charter Schools, Archbishop Boulter framed the need for such a system in terms of the need to target children given the impossibility of converting or reforming the adult population. Writing to the Duke of Newcastle in 1730, he stressed that 'the ignorance and obstinacy of the adult papists is such, that there is not much hope of converting them'.[5] In a letter to the Bishop of London in the same year, he likewise lamented 'the obstinacy with which they [Irish Catholics] adhere to their own religion', a circumstance which 'occasions our trying what may be done with their children to bring them over to our church'.[6] The rhetorical construction of Irish children as the material on which a future of enlightened progress could be based thus derives in part from a construction of the native Irish as intractable and uneducable. Boulter's sense of the hopelessness of effecting any meaningful change among the adult population and his corresponding promotion of schemes involving children are highlighted by his inclusion of a despondent observation about the incidence of Protestants converting to Catholicism: 'instead of converting those that are adult, we are daily losing several of our meaner people, who go off to popery'.[7]

Further insight into the reluctance to engage with the adult population can be gained from considering attitudes towards the Irish language in this period. For reasons that are self-evident, any attempts at the conversion of adults would have to involve the use of the Irish language, and the extreme reluctance to adopt Irish as a language of preaching and religious instruction seems to be the chief explanation for the abandonment of any programmes directed at adults. The hostility provoked by the idea of using Irish is very vividly captured in John Richardson's *A Proposal for the Conversion of the Natives of Ireland* (1711). Richardson was a passionate advocate both for a programme of conversion and for using Irish, and he incorporated into his *Proposal* 'Answers' to the 'Objections' made against it, thus giving some understanding of contemporary Protestant attitudes to the Irish language. One of the objections Richardson addresses is '*that keeping up a difference in Language, will keep up a difference in Religion, so that by Preaching in* Irish, *we shall rather confirm the Natives in* Popery, *than convert them to the* Protestant *Religion*'.[8] In answer to this somewhat irrational hostility Richardson articulates the view of language as a means for the communication of ideas, and asserts that truth does not depend on the specific means whereby it is communicated:

> the different manner of communicating our Thoughts of any Thing to others, doth neither alter the Nature of the Thing, nor our Thoughts and Notions of it: Otherwise different Languages would be the causes of Mens [sic] having different conceptions of other Things, as well as of Religion; whereas altho' there be great Variety of Languages in the world, yet we have Reason to believe, that all Men agree in their Apprehensions and Conceptions of many

Things; and on the other side we find, that Men speaking the same Language, have different Thoughts of the same Thing.[9]

Richardson's detractors apparently see the Irish language as a barrier through which truth cannot penetrate; in effect, the Irish language functions as a symbol of the location of native Irish Catholics beyond the reach of enlightenment and beyond the reach of the truth of the Gospel. This view is of course incompatible with the vision of Ireland as a field for Protestant-led improvement and is ultimately threatening to the self-image of the improvers. The almost exclusive focus on children and on Charter Schools in the place of Irish-language conversion programmes can therefore be understood as a way to maintain the belief in progress and in the supposedly irresistible appeal of the 'pure Truths of the Gospel', while at the same time accommodating the colonial constructions of the native Irish which characterised earlier phases of conquest and settlement.

The recourse to children as a means either to overcome or accommodate ideological contradiction is by no means unique to the elite of eighteenth-century Ireland. According to Jacqueline Rose, Rousseau's *Emile*, the eighteenth century's most influential text about childhood, is fundamentally characterised by just such a use of children.[10] The view of children as offering a point of access to uncorrupted Nature, and thus as a source for the renewal of a degenerate world, finds its most famous expression in Rousseau's text. The educational process he describes is therefore not simply for the benefit of the child: by showing how to safeguard the uncorrupted nature of the child, Rousseau also offers the adult reader access to this same quality. The project of the Charter Schools, that of 'enlightening and instructing the innocent minds of children in the pure Truths of the Gospel', is similarly promoted in a context in which the 'obstinacy' of the Catholic population and the phenomenon of converts to Catholicism cast doubt both on the supposedly self-evident superiority of reformed religion and on the ability of the Anglican elite to bring about the social reform to which they were apparently committed.

The improvers' concerns around language and its relation to truth also find an echo in Rousseau. In *Emile*, Rousseau famously advised against reading as a means of educating children, preferring direct engagement with and experience of nature, and seeing language as inevitably compromised by the corrupt civilisation in which it had arisen. According to Rose, Rousseau's view of the uncorrupted child is associated with what she calls 'an ideal form of language', 'uncontaminated by the intrusion of the verbal sign'.[11] Rose argues that when adults write about and indeed for children, they express their own desires, and this, she says, lies at the root of his construction of the child. What Rousseau is really looking for, she argues, is an ideal form of language: 'in *Emile* […] the child is being asked not only to retrieve a lost state of nature, but also to take language back to its pure and uncontaminated source in the objects of the world'.[12] The fear of a contaminated language is starkly expressed in the fear felt by many within the Anglican church that to preach and instruct in Irish would not – in fact *could not* – communicate religious truth, but would instead simply confirm the native people in their superstitious beliefs. In this context, the promotion of programmes aimed at children suggests not so much an optimistic reforming zeal as an apprehension as to the degenerate nature of Irish society, as well as uncertainty about the whole project of 'improvement'.

Whereas Rousseau's ideal course of education was entirely theoretical, the advocates for social and moral improvement in Ireland had to attempt to realise their programmes, and this proved difficult. In fact, the gap between the rhetoric about the 'grand project' of Charter Schools and what was actually achieved was stark. Far from enabling children to become enlightened and productive subjects, the Charter Schools were characterised by 'immense cruelty and squalor'.[13] The schools were condemned in a report of 1782 which recommended closure, although the system was not in fact dismantled until 1825.[14] For those in the eighteenth century who were convinced that such schools offered the only real hope of transforming Ireland, however, the chief obstacle was that although children in theory offered the promise of a blank sheet ready to receive the imprint of truth and light, children in practice were embedded in a network of familial and social relationships. The leaders of the charity schools that pre-dated the Charter Schools attempted to mitigate the perceived negative effects of these relationships in a number of ways: parents were for instance obliged to sign declarations giving the school managers authority over their children and guaranteeing not to interfere in their religious formation. The impracticability of these measures was acknowledged in the formal Charter School scheme that replaced the charity schools, in that a key feature of the scheme was the removal of children from their families. The pamphlet-writer of 1748 confirms that 'the Effects of this Charter could not be obtained in their full Latitude, without keeping the Children apart from their Parents, and maintaining them in Meat, Drink, and Cloathing, and erecting Houses for their Accommodation'.[15] This practice mirrored the approach already taken in the foundling hospitals and workhouses, whereby women who were detained for begging were separated from any children they had, and the children were then 'transplanted' to a different part of the country.

The numbers of Catholic parents prepared willingly to place their children in these institutions was unsurprisingly low, and often driven by extreme financial necessity. In 1757 the managers of the schools acknowledged the problem of insufficient numbers: they proposed to set up a nursery to encourage poor and indigent women to give up their infant children, who could then be sent to the schools when they were older. In effect, only the abandoned orphan could function as the 'ideal' child and offer the promise of a new beginning. A telling historical detail, however, reveals that the vision of the child as a pure and uncontaminated point of origin for an improved future was impossible to sustain: the exchange of foundling children from one part of the country to another was written into law in 1735, such a measure being deemed necessary in order 'to prevent the improper interference of parents'.[16] This interference even took the form of what was described as 'collusion', whereby Catholic mothers would offer their services as wet-nurses to workhouses and orphanages in order to re-establish contact with their own children.[17]

The combination of enlightenment ideas and the sectarian character of eighteenth-century Irish institutions together resulted in a discourse in which children were constructed as ideal vehicles of enlightenment. In addition, however, the specific emphasis on children as 'not adults' and the need to imagine 'innocent' children as distinct from the contaminated adult world meant that the only children that offered the possibility of realising this potential were those that were separated from their parents and families. The attempt to educate children according to these ideological demands resulted in institutions that were both cruel and ineffective. In the context of the early novel, however, the figure of the orphan (*Tom Jones*) and the individual cut off from family (*Pamela*) and community (*Robinson Crusoe*), offered scope for fictional narratives in which ordinary people experienced challenges and adventures that resonated with a growing readership. The novels of Chaigneau and Brooke, both of which feature central characters who are separated for extended periods from their natural families, therefore belong to an extent within a broad Anglophone tradition (and particularly in Chaigneau's case, a wider European tradition). The incorporation into their novels of the themes of education and childhood, lost or abandoned children, and separated families has, however, a distinct resonance given the socio-political context just described. It seems undeniable, given the very particular significance accorded to children in early eighteenth-century Ireland, that the interest of both Chaigneau and Brooke in representing childhood and the effects of education resulted from their own engagement with various projects of improvement. Their novels however are not simple mirrors of the ideological constructs of the established church in Ireland. In these texts some of the specific social and historical conditions of eighteenth-century Ireland are reimagined in a dynamic engagement with the central intellectual currents of the day, producing original reflections on some key concerns of the period – heredity, environment, education, and the relationship between the family and the state.

Chaigneau, *The History of Jack Connor* (1752)

At a number of points in *The History of Jack Connor*, a novel that concerns the life and adventures of its eponymous orphan hero, the narrator explicitly acknowledges the influence of Henry Fielding, whose *The History of Tom Jones, a Foundling* was published only three years previously in 1749. Chaigneau thus claimed no specific originality in his creation of a flawed but fundamentally virtuous orphan making his way in the world. His creation of an orphan protagonist was also, however, clearly motivated by his enthusiastic support of the Charter School system, about which he had written an essay originally published anonymously in *The Daily Gazetteer* (1748) under the title *Stultus versus Sapientem; in Three Letters to the Fool*. The thematic and generic connections between Chaigneau's novel and pamphlets on Protestant education are underlined by the fact that this essay was subsequently included in the fourth edition of the novel published in Dublin in 1766; even more pointed is the narrator's extensive digression, within the novel, in praise of the '*noble Charity*' 'now known by the Name of the *Incorporated Society, for Promoting of English Protestant Schools in Ireland* '.[18]

In the opening chapters in particular, those concerned with Jack's parentage and early life, Chaigneau's novel in fact reflects the concerns of contemporary pamphlet literature on a range of topics, not just Charter Schools. Jack Connor is the illegitimate child of Dolly Bright, a Catholic laundry maid, and Sir Roger Thornton, her master. When Dolly falls pregnant, Sir Roger arranges for her hasty marriage to one of his Protestant employees, Jeremiah Connor, formerly a soldier in the Williamite army. When Dolly and Jerry fall on hard times and are evicted from their farm, they are forced to turn to begging as their only means of supporting themselves. This turn of events prompts the narrator to remark satirically that 'The Transition from an *Irish Farmer* to a *Beggar*, is very *natural* and common in the Country' (p. 45). Chaigneau here aligns himself very clearly with the many patriotic and improving writers, including Robert

Molesworth, David Bindon, Samuel Madden, and of course, Swift, who devoted a great deal of time and ink to describing Irish economic problems and potential solutions to them.

The spectacle of beggary was a common starting point for these pamphlets, and such was its currency as a rhetorical strategy that it was savagely satirised by Swift in his *Modest Proposal* (1729). It is therefore significant that the first description of Jack is of this stereotypical symbol of Irish poverty and underdevelopment: 'About the Age of Five Years, Jack remembers his daily sitting on a Ditch with his *Father* and *Mother*, industriously employed in that *most antient* and *most noble* Profession of *Begging*' (p. 48). The frontispiece to the 1766 Dublin edition captures this well-worn trope in a visual image of Irish beggary (Fig. 6). That Jack is not the stereotypical ragged urchin of the pamphlets, but has instead been accorded the privilege of being an individual, is suggested in the use of the verb 'remembers', with its gesturing towards an interior consciousness reflecting on his own experience. This is amplified by the reference to Jack's ability to read and his father's gift to him of Richard Allestree's *The Whole Duty of Man*; so enamoured is he that he asks '*if there was any more Books in the World, for he would read them all*' (p. 49). The true transformation not only in his fortunes but in his status from undifferentiated stereotype to novelistic hero comes about, however, when he is abandoned by his mother, who runs away with a lecherous priest following the death of her husband. Jack is rescued from the roadside by Mr Kindly, the steward to Lord Truegood. Truegood is an exemplary improving landlord whose establishment of a charity school is described at length in a passage which incorporates the commendation of Charter Schools already referred to, and he benevolently provides for Jack's care and education.

Read in this way, Chaigneau's novel appears to mirror very closely the ideological constructions sketched in the first part of this essay. Jack's development as an individual is predicated on his removal from his family and his experience of a specifically Protestant education provided under the auspices of a member of a benevolent and improving landed class. Moreover, his Catholic origins are depicted overwhelmingly negatively in that his mother, it appears, chooses her immoral relationship with the repulsive Fr. Kelly over her own child. Chaigneau also explicitly endorses the policy of 'transplantation' in order to prevent contact between parents and children. In *Jack Connor* he refers to unsuccessful attempts 'to pervert' the children in Lord Truegood's school 'and make them return to their Parents, and consequently to *Sloth, Ignorance* and *Filth*' (p. 62). In the ironic *Stultus versus Sapientem*, meanwhile, the foolish letter-writer complains bitterly that:

Fig. 6 William Chaigneau, *The History of Jack Connor*, 2 vols (Dublin, 1766), I, Frontispiece. Reproduced courtesy of the National Library of Ireland (LO 13227/1)

these subtile protestants take from them the tools they work with, by transplanting the innocent children many miles distant from their native parishes; by which contrivance, their parents, or priests, are prevented from frightening them with purgatory or hell, or keeping them firm in the cause of indolence and rags.[19]

In spite of these ideological and thematic parallels, however, *The History of Jack Connor* is far from being standard pamphlet literature in novel form. On its original publication, the text was, as Ian Campbell Ross has pointed out, received both as a 'truly moral tale' and as an entertaining if disreputable narrative.[20] These contrasting judgments, Ross observes, can be understood in the context of 'the still contested status' of the novel form, in which Chaigneau's incorporation of both the discourse and the subject matter of improving pamphlets reflected the shifting generic boundaries that pertained at the time. Significantly, however, the ideological position that Chaigneau appears to uphold so wholeheartedly in *Stultus versus Sapientem* is undermined rather than supported in *Jack Connor*.

Jack is by no means an 'exemplary' product of charitable schemes of education and improvement. His journey from childhood to maturity involves a series of often comical blunders and moral lapses, though his fundamental good nature is never in doubt. His arrival at maturity, moreover, is signalled by an unexpected return to his apparently shameful origins. As the novel reaches its conclusion, Jack learns that his mother Dolly is in Cadiz, the wealthy widow of a trader named Magragh. Dolly is overjoyed to see her son again, and accepts with equanimity the difference in their religious faiths:

> Tho' we are, unhappily, of different religions, yet, believe me, I am not so bigotted to mine as to desire a Change in your's. I have learnt by Experience the true *End* and *Use* of *Religion*, is to make us *good*, *virtuous*, and *charitable*. – Since your Religion has taught you the practice of those great Duties, why should I wish you to alter? No, my dear *Jack*, keep strictly to, and be faithful in it. My Religion did not make me wicked, it was my *Weakness* and my *Ignorance*. Thank *God*, I am now wiser. (p. 223)

Dolly's redemption, in spite of a highly irregular life in which she was at one time the mistress of two different priests, indicates a far from doctrinaire moral viewpoint. Although Chaigneau's novel at first appears to shape a plot around the fantasy of new beginnings that motivated the Charter School system, by ultimately reuniting mother and son and allowing for Dolly's moral growth and development, it abandons the insistence on the child as defined by their otherness to a degenerate adult world that cannot be reformed or improved. The joyful reunion of mother and son, and the discovery that Dolly had been tricked and coerced into leaving Jack behind, recall the determination of Catholic mothers and parents not to relinquish their children to institutions, rather than the 'official version' in which children were either enthusiastically offered as pupils, or heartlessly abandoned by negligent mothers.

The redemption of Dolly and the reintegration of Jack's Catholic origins are moreover signalled in subtle but significant details in the early chapters of the novel. Dolly herself is more than usually intelligent and it is her ability to read that initially attracts the attention of Sir Roger Thornton. Although her learning is initially the cause of her downfall, it is later of considerable benefit to Jack, whom she teaches to read when her husband loses his sight. Jack reads to his father from *The Whole Duty of Man*, and later it is his ability to read passages from the book fluently that disposes Mr Kindly in his favour. The ability to read is passed from mother to son in a manner that is *not*, as the Anglican reformers had feared, contaminated by her Catholicism. The language he learns is transparent, in that it enables him to read and understand the quintessentially Protestant lessons contained in *The Whole Duty of Man*. As Ian Campbell Ross has noted, a feature of the novel is that Jack is always aware that he is the son of a Catholic mother and a Protestant father, 'and so an embodiment of one of the principal social fissures in contemporary Irish society'.[21] In this he anticipates the Earl of Glenthorn, hero of Maria Edgeworth's *Ennui* (1809), who is also the Protestant son of a Catholic mother.

Brooke, *The Fool of Quality* (1765–70)

Henry Brooke's *The Fool of Quality* is in many ways also an important forerunner of Edgeworth's fiction, though it has retained a place in literary history chiefly for being one of the earliest responses to Rousseau's *Emile*. It is also known to have influenced Thomas Day, who was himself an enthusiast for Rousseau and who, in *The History of Sandford and Merton*, drew on *The Fool of Quality* for his narrative of the contrasting upbringing of the over-indulged gentleman's son, Tommy Merton, and the hardy and industrious farmer's son, Harry Sandford. In spite of the fact that it has such striking thematic similarities with *Jack Connor*, there has to date been no extended discussion of the two novels in relation to one another. Like William Chaigneau, Henry Brooke was an active participant in the culture of improvement, and the author of a large number of essays and pamphlets relating to Irish affairs, as well as contributions to *The Public Register; or, Freeman's Journal*. In one of the few critical discussions of the text, Markman Ellis very usefully identifies that Brooke incorporates into his novel what are effectively two quite lengthy extracts from a 1759 essay, *The Interests of Ireland Considered [...], particularly with respect to Inland Navigation*, and notes that the inclusion of this material, which in its original form was entirely focused on Ireland, in a novel which is primarily set in England and makes only very fleeting references to Ireland, amounts to a 'transposition of location between the canal tract and the novel'.[22] Ellis reads this 'transposition of location' in the context of Brooke's relationship to the patriot movement in Ireland and as 'evidence of the stress produced within the Protestant ascendancy by the complex negotiation of being British in Ireland'.[23] Ellis's concern is with the novel's use of the sentimental in order to negotiate a transition from an aristocratic to a commercial social system, but there is clearly ample scope to pursue the novel's representation of childhood and education according to the same logic.

The extent to which Brooke focuses on childhood in *The Fool of Quality* is, in the context of the period, genuinely unusual and arresting. The whole of the first volume is given over to often minutely detailed representations of Harry and his experiences, but these are interspersed with political and philosophical commentary in a way that indicates the author's own awareness of the importance of education as a subject. His imaginary reader, however, with whom he enters into periodic dialogues, is less impressed, and objects that: 'you are extremely unequal and disproportioned; one Moment you soar where no Eye can see, and strait descend with Rapidity to creep in the vulgar Phrase of Chamber Maids and Children'.[24] Brooke here seems to be following Rousseau in his minute attention to what the conventional reader regards as 'vulgar'; Rousseau, for instance, asserts that 'Childhood is unknown' and advises educators to 'begin, then, by studying your pupils better. For most assuredly you do not know them at all'.[25]

Brooke's depiction of childhood and his ideas on education were, however, not derived exclusively from Rousseau, and in some respects they differ considerably. Brooke was deeply religious and explicitly states that the source of human goodness and virtue is divine (II, p. 232). Positing Nature and therefore the child as inherently good, Rousseau proposes that children need not be disciplined, punished, or rewarded in any way other than through a process of natural consequences: 'one ought not to get involved with raising a child if one does not know how to guide him where one wants by the laws of the possible and the impossible alone'.[26] Brooke also rejects conventional systems of discipline but he does not replace them with a regime of 'natural' experience – instead the drivers of his pedagogical programme are benevolence and sensibility: 'he [Mr Fenton] never proposed any Encouragement or Reward to the Heart of our Hero, save that of the Love and Approbation of Others' (I, p. 47). Rousseau by contrast does not address what he calls social virtues until Book IV, when Emile is fifteen, stating that children are until then incapable of sharing in the feelings of others and that to expect otherwise is to encourage falseness and affectation.

Given these quite fundamental philosophical differences, the significant areas of common ground between Rousseau and Brooke are all the more striking. The most obvious similarity is an emphasis on physical hardiness that is closely related to a critique of aristocracy and is inflected by primitivism in both cases. Rousseau was explicit in saying that 'The body must be vigorous in order to obey the soul. [...] The weaker the body, the more it commands; the stronger it is, the more it obeys', and in order to promote this physical health he advocated early exposure to physical hardship and the demands of the environment: 'Experience teaches that even more children raised delicately die than do others. [...] Exercise them, then, against the attacks they will one day have to bear. Harden their bodies against the intemperance of season, climates, elements; against hunger, thirst, fatigue. Steep them in the water of the Styx.'[27]

Brooke advocates a very similar regime, and makes his disdain for the childrearing practices of the aristocracy abundantly plain when he outlines the different experiences of Richard, the eldest son of the Duke of Moreland, and his younger brother Harry. As the heir to the title and estate, Richard is physically pampered and morally indulged. The narrator tells us that '*Richard*, who was already entitled my little Lord, was not permitted to breathe the Rudeness of the Wind' (I, p. 34) and 'the whole Family conspired, from the Highest to the Lowest, to the Ruin of promising Talents and a benevolent Heart' (I, p. 35). The contrast with his younger brother could not be greater:

> Young *Harry*, on the other Hand, had every Member as well as Feature exposed to all Weathers, would run about, Mother-naked for near an Hour, in a frosty Morning; was neither physicked into Delicacy, nor flattered into Pride; scarce felt the Convenience, and, much less understood the Vanity of Clothing; and was daily occupied, in playing and wrestling with the Pigs and two mungril [sic] Spaniels on the Dunghil [sic]; or in kissing, scratching, or boxing with the Children of the Village. (I, p. 35)

For readers familiar with representations of rural life in eighteenth- and nineteenth-century Ireland, this passage, and particularly the reference to the 'Dunghil' is a highly localised version of the primitive. As David Lloyd observes, 'no traveller in Ireland failed to note the ubiquity of the peasant's dunghill and its immediate proximity to the cabin door'.[28] What stands out about Brooke's reference to the dunghill is that (in contrast to the implication in Lloyd's comment) it is resoundingly positive. There is a fascinating contrast here with the description of Jack Connor as a stereotypical ragged urchin begging on a ditch. Whereas in Chaigneau's text, the hero must emerge from this reductive stereotype and be drawn into an idealised process of education in order to become a fully formed individual, in Brooke's novel, the hero is marked out as a hero because he has been spared the excessive refinement that has damaged his brother – his position on the dunghill symbolises his freedom from artificial and corrupt ideas and behaviours. In this portrayal of Harry's childhood, Brooke incorporates Rousseauvian primitivism with details suggestive of an Irish location in such a way as to challenge the received view of the Irish peasantry as uncivilised subjects in need of elite Protestant leadership. Elsewhere, there is evidence in the novel that Ireland's political and social history prompted Brooke to question one of Rousseau's central tenets, maternal breastfeeding.

The aristocratic nature of Harry's family is underlined by the fact that he is sent as an infant to a wet-nurse; moreover, because he is a second son and not the heir he also has diminished value in the eyes of his parents and is left in the care of his wet-nurse until long past infancy. As we have seen, however, Harry ultimately benefits from the benign neglect of his parents and Brooke celebrates the advantages that he derives from the 'primitive' environment in which he spends his early childhood. Harry is reintegrated into his family when he is eight, and his parents learn to love him, thus apparently model-ling the growth of the bourgeois ideal of family along Rousseauvian lines. But whereas Rousseau claims that one of the evils of wet-nursing is that the inevitable dismissal of the nurse teaches the child to be ungrateful, and to regard his nurse as a servant, Brooke represents Harry's bond with his nurse and foster father as real and lasting. The joyful scenes with which the novel ends include Harry's introduction of his bride to 'his Fosterers, his very dear Daddy and Mammy' (V, p. 344). This endorsement of the idea of fostering and relationships that extend beyond the bourgeois family is highly signifi-cant in the context of the Anglo-Irish population, in which contact with the Catholic Irish, initially through fostering and later through wet-nursing, was seen to have particularly deleterious consequences for a community that feared religious and moral contamination. Brooke effectively turns this discourse on its head, and presents Irish peasant life in an overwhelmingly positive way, as the ideal 'nursery' for his hero.

Writing of *Ennui*, Katie Trumpener describes it as 'the work that initiates the nationalist reclamation of the fostering system' in which Edgeworth 'undertakes a groundbreaking redaction of seventeenth-cen-tury Anglo-Irish polemics about Ireland'.[29] My discussion of *The Fool of Quality* however indicates that reclamations of fostering from an Anglo-Irish perspective begin with Brooke, rather than Edgeworth. Brooke's interest in the trope of fostering pre-dates Edgeworth's by nearly forty years and as such it does not fully map on to Trumpener's broader argument as to the emergence of nationalist literary cultures within the British empire in the late eighteenth and early nineteenth centuries. Instead, Aileen Douglas's observation that 'ostensibly committed to a domestic ideal, [*The Fool of Quality*] also insists that domestic space be ruptured for true social health' offers a way of reading Brooke's repeated insistence on complicating and disrupting the bourgeois family.[30] Although Harry's return to his parents seems at first to signal the consolidation of the bourgeois ideal, the family is once again fractured when he is abducted by his uncle and taken away from his distraught family 'for his own good', specifically as a means to broaden his experience of the world. Brooke's positive representation of the relationship between child and wet-nurse, and of a fostering relationship more generally, is thus amplified by a plot in which Harry's capacity for social leadership demands awareness of social and economic structures outside of his own family unit.

The contrast with *Emile* is striking, in that Rousseau condemns the practice of wet-nursing not only because it weakens the emotional bonds within families, but because a reformed family unit is in his view the point from which to build a reformed state:

> More depends on this one [subject] than is thought. Do you wish to bring everyone back to his first duties? Begin with mothers. You will be surprised by the changes you will produce. [...] [L]et mothers deign to nurse their own children, morals will reform themselves, nature's sentiments will awaken in every heart, the state will be repeopled. This first point, this point alone, will bring everything back together.[31]

Brooke's view of the relationship between the family and the health of the state thus differs significantly from Rousseau's, and the origins of this difference could be argued to lie in his view of history in Ireland.

In his *Tryal of the Roman Catholics of Ireland* (1761), Brooke offers a brief look at Irish history and at the ways in which recurrent violence and conflict militated against the growth of the population, observing that 'Want as naturally withheld them from the Propagation of their Species, which was further abridged and thinned by the Waste of frequent Wars.'[32] He also notes that 'the Custom of settled Peace, with the Assurance of domestic Quiet and Family-Enjoyments, are necessary to the Encouragement of matrimonial Establishments'.[33] The issue of population growth was one of intense concern for the Anglo-Irish elite, from William Petty onwards. Although this type of analysis has been critiqued as a form of colonial control, in Brooke's case we see a difference in emphasis, and an acknowledgement that the domestic and the political are interlinked. Whereas Rousseau suggested that a reformed motherhood could 'repeople' the state, Brooke's location in Ireland and his knowledge of Irish history lead him to a very different conclusion, namely that the state plays a critical role in enabling family life to flourish.

Brooke's awareness of Irish history also informs his thinking on education and its importance. In addition to concerns with and ideas for

economic development, Brooke's pamphlets offer evidence of his awareness of the revolution in land ownership which had occurred as a result of
English settlement and which was completed in the aftermath of the
Williamite wars and the introduction of the Penal Laws. Consider, for
instance, his comments on why Catholics in Ireland might reasonably have
been expected to rise in support of the Jacobite cause in 1745:

> The *French* invasion of *Great Britain*, was headed by a Person who was, by
> Birth, Education, Principle, and Interest, an Enemy to the Freedom and
> Rights of a Constitution that was established on the Dispossession of his
> Ancestors; and he was, consequently, an Enemy to the general Change, of
> Privilege and Property, that ensued on said Establishment. The said Change,
> as we all know, was to the Disadvantage of *Roman Catholics*. Had the Invader
> prevailed; a Change would, again, have ensued, in their Favour.[34]

The difficulty apparent here in differentiating between a 'Change' that results
in an 'Establishment' and a further 'Change' that might upset that very
Establishment suggests that Brooke's position as an Irish patriot who supported the Glorious Revolution creates a distinct and split consciousness. A
similar awareness of the casualties and beneficiaries of cycles of change is
evident in *The Fool of Quality*. In its numerous interpolated stories of virtuous
distress and selfless benevolence it contains 'many tales of cyclic and hyper-
bolic impoverishment and wealth', which Markman Ellis regards as a sort of
proxy for representations of the economic and commercial.[35] In spite of the
fact, however, that most of these tales of impoverishment concern commercial
matters rather than issues of land, I would contend that Brooke's awareness
precisely of *cycles* of impoverishment and wealth was evidently heightened by
his knowledge of Irish history, in particular the history of dispossession. In *The
Fool of Quality*, furthermore, specific reference is made to the extent of the
changes in land ownership in Ireland. Mr Fenton laments that 'there is no
Place, on Earth, wherein Property can be said to be fixed or ascertained' (II,
pp. 176–77), and in spite of the fact that the British constitution is agreed to be
the 'best calculated for the Security of Liberty and Property', Britain is by no
means immune from these 'Convulsions and Changes' (II, p. 177): 'Think,
what a general Change of Property has been made, in *Great Britain*, during
the two very late Revolutions; I am told that, in a neighbouring Country, the
Alienation has been nearly universal; perhaps a third Revolution is also at
Hand' (II, p. 177).

It seems clear that Brooke's position as an Anglo-Irish patriot gave
him a heightened sense of the instability of property and social position, and I would argue that this in turn contributed to his interest in

education. This is something that he shares with Rousseau, who argues explicitly that the programme of education he outlines in *Emile* is essential in order to be prepared for social and financial instability, or as he describes it, 'the unsettled and restless spirit of this age which upsets everything in each generation'.[36] The extraordinary vicissitudes experienced by Brooke's protagonists also anticipate those of Maria Edgeworth, not only in *Ennui*, but also, for instance, in *Madame de Fleury* (1809), a novella set at the time of the French Revolution, where it is observed that:

> In these times, no sensible person will venture to pronounce that a change of fortune and station may not await the highest and the lowest; whether we rise or fall in the scale of society, personal qualities and knowledge will be valuable. Those who fall, cannot be destitute; and those who rise, cannot be ridiculous or contemptible, if they have been prepared for their fortune by proper education. In shipwreck, those who carry their all in their minds are the most secure.[37]

Viewed from this perspective, Edgeworth's tales of personal transformation and social reform inherit and adapt a tradition that starts with Chaigneau and Brooke. In their texts we find the trope of mothers and children lost and found, the exchange of aristocrat and peasant, the creation of hybrid identities, and the heir who inherits according to meritocratic notions of worth. As this discussion has indicated, these plots and tropes were shaped both by enlightenment constructions of childhood and by the reality of violence, economic underdevelopment, and sectarian division in Ireland, where for instance the separation of parents and children was deemed socially necessary, and war had resulted in the sudden loss of wealth and status. The novels of Chaigneau and Brooke thus suggest that Ireland's social conditions in the eighteenth century, often characterised as backwards, resulted in an early and radical response to the developing discourses of childhood and education.

Notes

1. For a discussion of the eighteenth century as a watershed in terms of ideas about childhood, see Hugh Cunningham, *Children and Childhood in Western Society Since 1500* (London: Longman, 1995), pp. 58–68. For recent work on the literature of childhood in eighteenth-century Ireland, see Anne Markey, 'Childhood and the Early Irish Novel', *Journal of the History of Childhood and Youth* 9.2 (2016), 247–60, and 'Irish Children's Fiction, 1727–1820', *Irish University Review* 41.1 (2011), 115–32.

2. Ian Campbell Ross, 'Prose in English, 1690–1800: From the Williamite Wars to the Act of Union', in *The Cambridge History of Irish Literature*, ed. Margaret Kelleher and Phillip O'Leary, 2 vols (Cambridge University Press, 2006), I, pp. 232–81 (p. 271).

3. Anon., *A Brief Review of the Rise and Progress of the Incorporated Society of Dublin, for Promoting English Protestant Schools in Ireland* (Dublin, 1748), p. 10.

4. See Kenneth Milne, 'Irish Charter Schools', *Irish Journal of Education* 8.1 (1974), 3–29 (p. 12).

5. Hugh Boulter, *Letters written by His Excellency Hugh Boulter, D. D. Lord Primate of All Ireland, &c.*, 2 vols (Oxford, 1769–1770), II, pp. 12–13.

6. Ibid., II, p. 10.

7. Ibid., II, pp. 11–12.

8. John Richardson, *A Proposal for the Conversion of the Natives of Ireland to the Established Religion* (Dublin, 1711), p. 16.

9. Ibid., p. 17.

10. See Jacqueline Rose, *The Case of Peter Pan, or the Impossibility of Children's Literature* (Philadelphia, PA: University of Pennsylvania Press, 1993), pp. 42–65.

11. Ibid., pp. 47, 46.

12. Ibid., p. 47.

13. Milne, 'Irish Charter Schools', p. 4.

14. For a highly critical account of the Charter Schools, see W. E. H. Lecky, *A History of Ireland in the Eighteenth Century*, 5 vols (London: Longman, Green & Co., 1913), I, pp. 232–38.

15. Anon., *A Brief Review*, p. 5.

16. William Dudley Wodsworth, *A History of the Ancient Foundling Hospital of Dublin* (Dublin, 1876), p. 4.

17. Ibid., p. 4. See also Lecky, *History of Ireland*, I, p. 232. George Nicholls's *A History of the Irish Poor Law* (London, 1856), pp. 42–45, details the provisions of this law and condemns parents who abandon their children but with 'unreasoning inconsistency' seek to interfere in their religious instruction (p. 45).

18. William Chaigneau, *The History of Jack Connor*, ed. Ian Campbell Ross (Dublin: Four Courts Press, 2013), p. 62. Further references to this novel are given after quotations in the text.

19. William Chaigneau, 'Stultus versus Sapientem; in Three Letters to the Fool', in *The History of Jack Connor*, 2 vols (Dublin, 1766), II, pp. 345–46.

20. Ian Campbell Ross, 'Introduction', in Chaigneau, *The History of Jack Connor*, ed. Ross (Dublin: Four Courts Press, 2013), pp. 11–34 (p. 11).

21. Ibid., pp. 18–19.

22. Markman Ellis, *The Politics of Sensibility: Race, Gender and Commerce in the Sentimental Novel* (Cambridge University Press, 1996), p. 158.

23. Ibid., p. 159.

24. Henry Brooke, *The Fool of Quality, or, The History of Henry, Earl of Moreland*, 5 vols (Dublin, 1765–70), I, p. 220. Further references are given after quotations in the text.

25. Jean-Jacques Rousseau, *Emile, or On Education*, trans. Allan Bloom (New York: Basic Books, 1979), pp. 33, 34.
26. Ibid., p. 92.
27. Ibid., pp. 54, 47.
28. David Lloyd, 'Nomadic Figures: The "Rhetorical Excess" of Irishness in Political Economy', in *Back to the Future of Irish Studies: A Festschrift for Tadhg Foley*, ed. Maureen O'Connor (Oxford: Peter Lang, 2010), pp. 41–64 (p. 56).
29. Katie Trumpener, *Bardic Nationalism: The Romantic Novel and the British Empire* (Princeton University Press, 1997), p. 214.
30. Aileen Douglas, 'The Novel before 1800', in *The Cambridge Companion to the Irish Novel*, ed. John Wilson Foster (Cambridge University Press, 2006), pp. 22–38 (p. 36).
31. Rousseau, *Emile*, p. 46.
32. Henry Brooke, *Tryal of the Roman Catholics of Ireland* ([London], 1761), p. 18.
33. Ibid., p. 20.
34. Henry Brooke, *The Farmer's Case of the Roman Catholics of Ireland* (Dublin, 1760), p. 9, Letter I.
35. Ellis, *Politics of Sensibility*, p. 139.
36. Rousseau, *Emile*, p. 42.
37. Maria Edgeworth, *Madame de Fleury*, in *The Novels and Selected Works of Maria Edgeworth*, Vol. V, ed. Heidi van de Veire and Kim Walker, with Marilyn Butler (London: Pickering & Chatto, 1990), p. 253.

PART VI

Retrospective Readings

Re-Imagining Feminist Protest in Contemporary Translation: Lament for Art O'Leary and The Midnight Court

Lesa Ní Mhunghaile

Certain texts have an enduring quality that continues to capture the imagination of countless generations.[1] This is irrespective of the distance in time from when they were first composed and the fact that the text's significance in its original context is no longer known. Such texts retain their appeal because, in the words of Seamus Heaney, they 'subsume into [themselves] the social and intellectual preoccupations of different periods and ... answer them by divulging new and timely meanings'.[2] The eighteenth-century Gaelic literary tradition provides two fine examples of such texts, namely Eibhlín Dhubh Uí Laoghaire's lament for her husband, *Caoineadh Airt Uí Laoghaire* (The Lament for Art O'Leary), and Brian Merriman's long narrative poem, *Cúirt an Mheán Oíche* (The Midnight Court).[3] Composed at a time of both cultural and linguistic transition, these powerful expressions of female defiance, within what was a male-dominated tradition, give voice to a number of concerns including domestic violence, sexual frustration, arranged marriages, unions between partners of disparate age, and English oppression.[4] Despite the various questions that continue to surround the original Gaelic poems, not least those relating to the authorship of *Caoineadh Airt Uí Laoghaire* and possible influences on *Cúirt an Mheán Oíche*, their popularity has endured, a fact demonstrated by the large number of editions and translations of both which were published during the twentieth century.[5]

While it is generally acknowledged that 'no culture can be represented completely in any literary text, just as no source text can be fully represented in a translation', this has not deterred the large number of translators who have been drawn to these two texts since the nineteenth century. Indeed, each of these translators has provided not only 'a reading accessible to the time in which it is produced' but also readings that have differed widely from one another.[6] This chapter will take as its starting point an understanding that literary translation is the 'adaptation of a work of literature to a different audience, with the intention of influencing the way in which that audience reads the work'.[7] It will consider the most recent English renderings of *Caoineadh Airt Uí Laoghaire* and *Cúirt an Mheán Oíche* – those by Vona Groarke and Ciaran Carson – and will interrogate the role translation has played in the transition of these two key eighteenth-century Gaelic texts to a twenty-first-century English-language context. Taking cognisance of the poets' reflections on their own translations, it will consider the new and timely meanings these poets have brought to the fore in their translations and assess their reimagining of eighteenth-century Gaelic female protest.

Translation from one language to another is not only about negotiation between two different languages and cultures but also entails a process of both discovery and recovery.[8] The discovery of the Irish-language literary tradition began in earnest towards the end of the eighteenth century and since then it has provided a rich source of inspiration for English-speaking writers in Ireland. Three early anthologies of Irish-language poetry translated into English – Charles Henry Wilson's *Poems translated from the Irish language* (1782), *Select Irish Poems translated into English* (n.d.), and Charlotte Brooke's *Reliques of Irish Poetry* (1789) – sought not only to preserve a tradition they believed to be in terminal decline and to provide wider access to material in the Irish language, but also to vindicate Gaelic culture.[9] While Wilson and Brooke's volumes were compiled in a colonial context, Carson and Groarke's translations have been produced in a postcolonial setting, one in which a language shift from Irish to English has taken place. Translations undertaken in this situation present their own specific challenges for English-speaking Irish writers and, as Seamus Heaney has noted, it 'usually involves considerations other than the strictly literary'. As a consequence, he argues, additional historical, cultural, and political contexts need to be taken into consideration:

> as when a native American author turns to material in one of the original languages of the North American continent. In each case, a canonical literature in English creates the acoustic within which the translation is going to be heard; an overarching old colonial roof inscribed 'The land was ours before we were the land's' is made to echo with some such retort as 'You don't say!'.[10]

Carson and Groarke's translations are aimed at both a domestic and an international audience and, unlike Wilson and Brooke, their objective is not primarily one of preservation. Instead, they draw on their own experiences as poets in order to fashion new versions in English that are stand-alone poems. In doing so 'while they have the original to serve as detailed ground-plan and elevation, they are trying to build themselves a robust home in a new country, in its vernacular architecture, with local words for its brick and local music for its mortar'.[11] Carson and Groarke's approach is consistent with that taken by the author and literary translator Umberto Eco, who believes that a translation should render 'not necessarily the intention of the author (who may have been dead for millennia), but the *intention of the text* – the intention of the text being the outcome of an interpretative effort on the part of the reader, the critic or the translator'. He regards the impact that a translation has upon its own cultural milieu as having more importance 'than an impossible equivalence with the original'.[12] Taking this approach enables translators to continue discovering elements within the original texts that have evolved since their creation, thereby facilitating the transition process. The following section will consider the new elements discovered or emphasised by Vona Groarke during her transposition of *Caoineadh Airt Uí Laoghaire* into a timeless setting.

Caoineadh Airt Uí Laoghaire and Vona Groarke's *Lament for Art O'Leary*

Caoineadh Airt Uí Laoghaire has been described as 'one of the great laments and one of the great love poems in the Irish language'.[13] Attributed to Eibhlín Dhubh Ní Chonaill, aunt of the famous nineteenth-century politician Daniel O'Connell, it tells the tale of the life and death of her husband, Art Ó Laoghaire in County Cork in 1773. His demise at the age of twenty-six was the culmination of a feud with his Protestant neighbour, Abraham Morris, magistrate and former High Sheriff of Macroom. The events surrounding the poem should be considered in the general context of Catholic oppression under the Penal Laws and sectarian tension in Munster during the 1760s and 1770s.[14] A number of allegations had been made about Ó Laoghaire, a Catholic, in the two years prior to his death, as a result of which he had been declared an outlaw. On the fateful day in May 1773, according to tradition, Ó Laoghaire was on his way to ambush Morris, when he himself was ambushed and shot dead by a 'one-eyed soldier'.[15] The mare he had been riding made her way back to Ó Laoghaire's home, where Eibhlín Dhubh on seeing the horse, immediately jumped on its back and rode to where Art lay dead. There, according to the lament, she spontaneously composed the first part of the poem in which she recounts how they had first met and states that she drank his blood from the ground in her cupped hands without waiting to clean it.[16] The remaining parts of the lament deal with a number of topics including the couple's life together with their children, an account of the last time she saw Art, her defence of allegations that she had fallen asleep during his wake, Art's alleged adultery, and curses placed on Abraham Morris, Seán Mac Uaithne, and James Baldwin for their involvement in Art's death and the confiscation of his horse. In some versions of the lament, found in both the oral and manuscript traditions, Eibhlín Dhubh refers to Art having hit her with a stick, but justifies his violence by blaming herself for having argued with him.[17]

Caoineadh Airt Uí Laoghaire was transmitted orally in a number of different versions in Munster during the eighteenth and nineteenth centuries. The best-known version was written down on two occasions, perhaps fifty years apart, from the recitation of the professional keener, Nóra Ní Shíndile (Norry Singleton), who died in 1873. The verses taken down on the first occasion formed the basis of Seán Ó Tuama's 1961 edition, which was the standard text until the publication of Angela Bourke's edition and translation in 2002.[18] Bourke's new edition was based on the version taken down on the second occasion from Ní Shíndile by Domhnall Mac Cába of Banteer, County Cork. This version is contained in a manuscript written by the Kerry scribe Pádraig Feirtéar in 1894, who had copied the text from a manuscript belonging to Mac Cába and had also appended to it a number of lines of *Caoineadh Airt Uí Laoghaire* he had heard from his kinswoman, Mairéad Ní Fhionnagáin in 1893.[19] No contemporary manuscript copies of the poem are extant, but some later nineteenth-century copies have been preserved, some of which include an English translation.[20]

Caointe (sing. *caoineadh*), or laments, in the Gaelic tradition were composed extempore by keening women, *mná caointe*, and were chanted or sung. They were formulaic, comprising of a group of short rhymed lines with two or three stresses, each group beginning with a formulaic opening line such as 'Druidigí thart, a mhná' (Gather round me, women) or 'Mo ghrá go daingean tú' (My constant love).[21] They were performed by a lead keening woman, usually a close relative of the dead person or, failing that, a professional keening woman was employed. The lead keener was assisted in the chorus by a group of women who chanted refrains such as 'och, ochón'. It was a communal effort in which women collaborated with one another. Lamenters, according to Angela Bourke, were 'grief therapists, as well as inciters of public outrage'.[22] The *caoineadh* usually contained the following themes: praise of the dead person's beauty, generosity, home, and lineage and criticism of their enemies, exhortations to rise up and follow the lamenter home, and descriptions of the lamenter's grief.[23] The performance was generally accompanied by wailing, tearing of hair, and hand clapping.[24] Drawing attention to its performative aspect, Bourke has also noted the potentially subversive nature of the *caoineadh* and has argued that it may be read as a form of feminist utterance, as it offered women 'a license to speak loudly and without inhibition, and frequently to defend their own interests against those of men'.[25] The messages conveyed in laments could be coded. They could 'make political points under the guise of personal grief, or protest publicly at domestic situations for which no other remedy was available'.[26]

Much debate surrounds *Caoineadh Airt Uí Laoghaire* and this has primarily centred on its authorship and its oral folk nature.[27] Sarah McKibben has succinctly summed up the poem's problematic nature: 'In *Caoineadh Airt Uí Laoghaire* we thus have a complex, multiply mediated work at odds with various official discourses, whose original form(s) we cannot know, whose precise oral and performance history we may only surmise, echoing with masterful shared locutions and deliberate repetition, and which simultaneously served very different functions as a matter of course.'[28] Angela Bourke has noted that in the very act of committing to print a text that has originated in the oral tradition a considerable amount is lost, as the process necessarily 'entails the suppression of much that is not text in what was originally said or sung – and in the suppression of what it meant'.[29] Thus, she argues, by means of a 'triple process of appropriation', *Caoineadh Airt Uí Laoghaire* has become 'a degendered literary text in English' that has been removed from its oral origins.[30] However, Breandán Ó Buachalla has challenged *Caoineadh Airt Uí Laoghaire*'s oral origin and has posited instead a literary origin that subsequently had Eibhlín's name attached to it.[31] Another area of debate surrounding the text is whether more than one voice can be discerned within it and whether it can be divided into different time frames. Seán Ó Tuama's edition attributes various sections of the text to different personages – Eibhlín Dhubh Art's sister and father – and claims that it was composed extempore and in five stages: while Art was lying dead on the ground, during his wake, at his funeral and afterwards, and six months after his burial when he was re-interred in Kilcrea.[32] Ó Buachalla, however, has disagreed with this presentation of the text, arguing instead that it was not a spontaneous composition and that only Eibhlín Dhubh's voice can be heard. He argues further that the narrative in *Caoineadh Airt Uí Laoghaire* ranges across the full time spectrum and moves seamlessly back and forth. The narrator, he posits, appears to occupy a timeless, liminal position.[33]

This timeless liminal position is reflected in Vona Groarke's English rendition of *Caoineadh Airt Uí Laoghaire*. Her starting point was a desire to offer a version 'that tried to nail how much Eileen really *fancied* her husband', as she felt that most English versions failed to 'capture completely the extremes of Eileen's rage and desire'.[34] As a consequence, her translation does not allude to the allegations of adultery or domestic abuse that are present in some Irish-language versions of the lament. Acutely aware of the challenges posed by transposing a text from one tradition to another, particularly with regard to capturing tone and register, her response has been to focus on three key timeless elements: Eibhlín Dhubh's grief at her husband's death, her rage at those who brought it about, and her desire for him. Though cognisant of the lament's public dimension and aware of Bourke's suggestion that the *caoineadh* can be read as feminist utterance, Groarke chooses to emphasise the private nature of Eibhlín Dhubh's suffering and the impact Art's death had on both her and her children. This emphasis is predicated on an understanding that the deep emotions expressed by Eibhlín Dhubh are ones that any audience can identify with regardless of whether they encounter the text in the eighteenth or twenty-first centuries:

> But insofar as we can ever enter a moment in lives that are not our own, or a language that many of us no longer practise; insofar as we can inhabit any other person's grief or grievance; insofar as poetry can ever speak to us across the ditches of centuries, Eileen's lament allows us. It turns the here and now around to face another time and place, so that we almost stand beside her and feel the heat of her outrage on our cheeks. The urgency, passion and elegance of Eileen's utterance throw themselves against a darkness we can't fail to recognize. (p. 18)

Margaret Mills Harper has argued that, in taking this approach, Groarke has created a version that is located in an 'imaginary space that is not defined by colonialist/nationalist politics, or a social space that is much concerned with reproducing faithfully the milieu or generic contexts of the powerful originals'.[35] This imagined space is one that is contemporary and 'engages with grieving, as well as historical remembering and memorializing, through a sensibility that questions how these qualities exist in multiple cultures and times, and what may be felt by engaging in the act of moving between them'.[36]

By approaching the text in this manner, questions of faithfulness to the original lose their importance. Indeed, Groarke's version is not based on any one Irish-language edition of the text but rather on as many English translations as she could find, due to her desire to undertake a version 'that admits it considers English translations as much as it concentrates on the original' (p. 10).[37] Her initial approach was to read and study as many versions of the poem as she could and while working on her translation she consulted those of Bourke, Frank O'Connor, Ó Tuama, and Thomas Kinsella. Though enjoying O'Connor's version and appreciating 'Bourke's more matter of fact scholarly translation' which 'values faithfulness to the original Irish above all', she found something lacking in all of the translations: 'if I had found in any one of them absolutely everything I wanted in a translation I wouldn't have persisted with my own' (p. 11). As a result, the poem benefits from the insights and experience she brings to bear on it, incorporating, as Lucy Collins has noted, 'the subtle, penetrative detail that is so much a part of Groarke's own original work'.[38] Groake admits to having sacrificed accuracy for passion and notes that her decision for doing so was based on the understanding that her version was 'an attempt to capture the *tone*, as opposed to the exact *content*, of the original Irish' (p. 12). She confesses, however, that sometimes her 'translation' of lines 'had squeezed the life out of them'. At other times she added 'an image or a metaphor to try to give a passage an inkling of the elegance or music' that she had identified in the Irish original (p. 14). In order to make her version 'new' she dispensed with previous translations of the term of endearment 'Mo ghrá go daingen tú' ('My love and my delight' or 'My steadfast love'), which she believed sounded 'phony' and 'lavish' to her ear and chose the term 'Husband' instead for its simplicity. In doing so she has given a more contemporary feel to her version. More radically, she rejected the metre of the original lament which consists of short rhymed lines of three stresses, as she felt that it 'became monotonous and stale' when employed over prolonged stanzas.[39] Maintaining it, she believed would demand 'a sacrifice of drama and sincerity' that she felt was 'too high a price to pay' (p. 15). The result of this decision, however, is that the intrinsically rhythmic, chanting nature of the original has been lost, one that is fundamental to its performative aspect. In the absence of this, the pace of the poem is slower than the original and, as Collins has noted, Groarke favours a more meditative style throughout: 'I knew I would have you / if it meant / stepping out of my whole life, / carrying nothing with me.'[40]

Groarke also admits to having taken licence with the various voices that have been identified by Ó Tuama in the lament. Although, as noted above, there is uncertainty as to the attribution of parts of the lament to Eibhlín Dhubh or members of Art's family, she re-attributes a number of stanzas to Art's sister and dispenses altogether with the two stanzas attributed in

Ó Tuama's edition to Art's father, re-attributing them instead to Eibhlín Dhubh. These changes were made, she argues, so as not to distract from the drama and tension of verbal contests between Eibhlín Dhubh and Art's sister (p. 15). Thus, by focusing on the figure of the grieving widow and her love for her dead husband and dispensing with the three-beat metre of the Irish texts, with its strongly performative aspect, Groarke's reimagining of *Caoineadh Airt Uí Laoghaire* removes it from its eighteenth-century politico-historical context and transforms Eibhlín Dhubh and her story into one with a universal, timeless appeal. As a consequence, however, Eibhlín Dhubh's participation in 'a communal women's performance tradition', which formed one of the lament's original functions, has been downplayed.

Cúirt an Mheán Oíche and Ciaran Carson's *The Midnight Court*

Cúirt an Mheán Oíche, a long poem of over one thousand lines by Brian Merriman (1749–1805), is believed to have been composed in rural County Clare sometime in the mid- to late eighteenth century. It became instantly popular within the Gaelic literary tradition and was soon translated into English. Since the early nineteenth century at least twelve complete English-language translations have been produced.[41] It is regarded as 'one of the masterpieces of Irish literary tradition' and 'one of the greatest comic works of literature, and certainly the greatest comic poem ever written in Ireland'.[42] Composed at a time when fewer original works of this nature were being produced in the Irish language: 'it is arguably the last true masterpiece of poetic creation in the language'.[43] Its radical engagement with Enlightenment ideas about human nature mark it out from other Gaelic poems composed at that time and, as Ní Dhonnchadha argues, it may have been at the forefront of the emergence of a new mind-set among Gaelic writers, were it not for the fatal blow dealt to the literary tradition in the nineteenth century by events such as the Great Famine and the consequent acceleration in the language shift from Irish to English.[44]

The subject matter of the poem has been regarded as subversive, ranging as it does over a vast array of topics such as 'clerical celibacy, concealed pregnancy, free love, illegitimacy, infidelity, casual sex, marriages between partners of disparate ages, the superiority of bastards and foundlings, promiscuity, seduction, sexual frustration, the utility of marriage as a social institution, and the social value of virginity'.[45] Alan Titley has argued, however, that Merriman was a bawdy writer, 'not smutty, sexy, dirty, or sly and definitely not erotic, impure, indecent, immodest, or salacious. He was just bawdy, Rabelaisian, ribald, and racy.'[46] As Heaney has noted, rather than concentrating on the contemporary political situation in Ireland, the poem 'is more psycho-sexual than national-patriotic'.[47] It is presented as a dream vision that is structured in three parts: prologue, three dramatic monologues, and an epilogue. In the prologue the poet falls asleep and encounters a female bailiff who summons him to a court in Feakle, County Clare, presided over by Aoibheall, the fairy queen of Munster. The bailiff criticises the state of the country and complains that men are failing to marry or mate with the available women. Three lengthy monologues make up the main body of the poem. The first is by a young woman who complains of having been sexually neglected and boasts of her own sexual attributes. The second is by an old man who rages against his own situation in which he was tricked into marrying a young woman who was already pregnant. He argues that marriage should be abandoned and that children born out of wedlock are more healthy and vigorous. The third monologue is by the young woman again, in which she castigates the old man for his sexual inadequacies and asks why are clergymen not allowed to marry? The verdict is given by Aoibheall at the end of the poem, in which she decrees that unmarried men of twenty-one or over are to be tied to a tree beside a headstone in Feakle graveyard and whipped, and that sexually inadequate husbands should allow their wives to take younger lovers. She declares that a time will come when Catholic priests will be allowed to marry. The poem ends with the poet waking from his dream just as the women are about to carry out Aoibheall's decree.

Like *Caoineadh Airt Uí Laoghaire*, the poem has been subject to much debate and has attracted 'competing and conflicting critiques'.[48] Scholars have attempted to ascertain whether it was influenced by European literature and political thought or whether it is a product of native originality, with some suggesting that it expresses an older mode of realism, while others argue that it offers a reworking of existing modes of presentation or expression in the Irish language such as the sovereignty myth.[49] A further reading suggests that it is a witty satire on contemporary literary conventions.[50] The poem's subversive nature has drawn criticism, much of which has been 'motivated more by ideological and moral agendas then aesthetical or literary concerns'.[51] Frank O'Connor's deliberatively provocative English translation, which was banned in 1945, drew much of that criticism and also helped add to the text's notoriety. He used it to attack the puritanical position regarding sexuality taken by the Catholic church in Ireland during the early decades of the twentieth century.[52] Often departing from the literal sense of the original, he lent an anti-clerical tone to the text and emphasised the poem's bawdiness. *Cúirt an Mheán Oíche* played an important role in the first half of the twentieth century, therefore, because it advocated liberal social values in the face of the repressive social conditions and censorship that prevailed at that time.[53]

Ciaran Carson is the most recent prominent Irish poet to attempt an English translation of *Cúirt an Mheán Oíche*, drawing on his wide experience of translating the Irish-language works of Seán Ó Ríordáin, Nuala Ní Dhomhnaill, and Gearóid Mac Lochlainn. Neal Alexander regards his translation work as 'a process through which to explore the productive estrangements and transactions that take place in the junctures between language and the cultures they express'.[54] An accomplished traditional Irish musician, songs and musical allusions feature prominently in Carson's poetry as does the reproduction of traditional music metres.[55] He states that he was drawn to the 'internal rhymes and four strong beats to the line' of *Cúirt an Mheán Oíche*, which reminded him of the jig tune 'Larry O'Gaff' and the song 'Paddy's Panacea'. As a result, he decided to adopt the 6/8 jig rhythm as a basis for his translation.[56] Though raised an Irish speaker, the greatest challenge he faced in translating the poem was in dealing with its language. He notes that 'the language itself is continually interrogated' in the poem and he compares Merriman to an illusionist, 'continually spiriting words into another dimension' (p. 14). Among the challenges he faced was finding 'English equivalents for Merriman's abundant lexicon of vilification, for his numerous double entendres, for the gorgeousness of his verbal music' (p. 14). He describes the feelings of inadequacy he experienced in working with the English and Irish languages, both of which were familiar to him and yet strange, and compared his translation work to being in a foreign country as he 'wandered the boundaries between them' (p. 14). At one point, he likens it to entering the otherworld at nightfall, like the heroes of the Fianna, and making his way through a dark wood alone, finally 'emerging into a mountainy region where a few lights glimmer on the hillside. These are the houses where the word-hoards are concealed' (p. 14).

Clearly aware of the problematic nature of translation, therefore, Carson's solution is to adopt a 'foreignising' approach, one that does not attempt to domesticise the text by minimising its strangeness.[57] As a consequence, his translations 'illuminate the inevitably incomplete and troubled relationship between original and translation'.[58] He tries to retain the complexities of the original language and metre and to echo Merriman's couplets and quatrains as closely as possible. However, in order to do so he is sometimes forced to transpose lines and couplets and at times feels that he has no choice but to depart from the literal meaning of Merriman's words. He acknowledges that this is:

the inevitable fate of any verse translation. One is forced to look askance at the first words that enter one's mind; and seeking alternatives, with different metrical weights and different sonorities, one usually arrives at a more elegant – and, somehow, a more *right* – frame of words. Of course the original is changed in the process – how could it be otherwise? – but so is one's mind, one's understanding of what the words might mean; and that is how it should be. One must enter that foreign country, and learn its language anew. (pp. 14–15)

One of the features of Merriman's original poem is the richness of its language and the expression of a number of different meanings in one word or phrase. Gregory Schirmer has praised Carson's sensitivity to this aspect of the poem, which allows 'Merriman's eighteenth-century Irish a strong presence in his translation'.[59] And Neal Alexander has noted that Carson's 'rollicking, high-spirited translation seems very much in keeping with the tradition of the carnivalesque', and draws attention to his recreation of Merriman's 'abundant lexicon of vilification' in the following extract:

> By the CROWN of Craglee, if I don't admit
> That you're doting, decrepit, and feeble of wit –
> And to treat this assembly with all due respect –
> I'd rip off your head from its scrawny wee neck,
> And I'd knock it for six with the toe of my boot,
> And I'd give the remainder no end of abuse,
> And I'd pluck such a tune from the strings of your heart,
> I'd consign you to Hell without halo or harp.   (p. 45)[60]

A further feature of the Gaelic original is the concreteness of language employed. Schirmer has drawn attention to Carson's 'overtranslation of Merriman's concrete language' and has argued that Carson's sensitivity to this concreteness 'is particularly forceful in his versions of the many passages in the poem having to do with sexuality'. In fact, Carson loads his version with sexual suggestiveness by introducing specific images not found in the original:

> And many's the girl who had set out her stall
> Found it heaving with goods, from a clerical call.
> It's well I remember their members being praised
> For the wonderful families their efforts have raised.[61]

In a comparison of Heaney's partial translation of *Cúirt an Mheán Oíche* with Carson's version, Alexander notes that Heaney moderates some of the poem's 'earthiness and vernacular energy' by focusing on 'the text's exposure of male anxieties over suppressed female power' and also 'by excising its central exchanges and opting to read this eighteenth-century Irish poem "within the acoustic of classical myth"'. In contrast, Carson's version 'effects a more thoroughgoing imbrication of high rhetoric and vulgar comedy, and also paints a vivid portrait of contemporary Ireland's "calamitous state" through anachronistic references to "hush money, slush funds", "upstarts and gangsters", and a "climate" that has "worsened of late"'.[62] In effect, Carson's sensitivity to the poem's original language and rhythm and his attempt to introduce orality and music into his translation have assisted the poem's transition to a contemporary context.

Conclusion

It is worth recalling Octavio Paz's claim that 'every translation, up to a certain point, is an invention and it constitutes a unique text'.[63] This chapter has examined the role played by translation in the transition of literary texts from one culture to another and from one time period to another with a specific focus on the unique (and deliberately contemporary) texts produced by Vona Groarke and Ciaran Carson. In doing so, it has drawn attention to various aspects that have been gained or lost during the translation process. A translator can sometimes enrich or clarify the source language text during this process and, as Susan Bassnett has argued, what can often be seen as lost from the 'source language' can be replaced in the 'target language' context.[64] Both Carson and Groarke have brought their own experience as English-language poets to bear on their versions, and have succeeded in identifying or drawing out elements in the original poems that resonate with a twenty-first-century audience. In the case of Groarke, she was working with a text that had already undergone one form of transition, namely from the oral tradition to the printed word. Her version chooses not to highlight this oral origin in order not to detract from the poem's drama, but in dispensing with its original three-beat metre she has also changed the poem's tone. Carson, on the other hand, has introduced anachronistic elements to his translation that resonate with a contemporary audience who are disenchanted with the current political landscape.

For some contemporary poet/translators such as Gabriel Rosenstock there is no 'real substantial difference between personal creative work and literary translation' as 'it springs from the same creative source'. Rosenstock regards the process of translating into Irish from other languages as one that enables him to enrich his own poetic imagination: 'There's something mysteriously alive in a real poem and you take that life and it's a responsibility, a sacred responsibility, to handle that life, and to give it as it were another life on the page, in another language. Translator as midwife. By so doing, you are also enriching your own imaginative and spiritual life in immeasurable ways.'[65] Thus, through this means, the original text serves as a source of inspiration, enabling it to transition to multiple contexts and time periods. A successful translation of eighteenth-century Irish-language literature to a twenty-first-century audience must engage with a number of issues, in particular gender, colonial and cultural politics, voice/performance and print. In their role of 'translator as midwife', Carson and Groarke have successfully transitioned *Caoineadh Airt Uí Laoghaire* and *Cúirt an Mheán Oíche* for a new era.

Notes

1. The author gratefully acknowledges The Gallery Press (www.gallerypress.com) for permission to quote from Vona Groarke's *Lament for Art O'Leary* (Oldcastle: Gallery Press, 2008) and Ciaran Carson's *The Midnight Court: A New Translation of* Cúirt an mheán oiche *by Brian Merriman* (Oldcastle: Gallery Press, 2005). Further references to these two poems are given after quotations in the text.
2. Seamus Heaney, *The Redress of Poetry* (New York: Farrar, Straus & Giroux, 1995), p. 53.
3. Eibhlín Dhubh Uí Laoghaire is most usually referred to by her maiden name in the critical literature – Eibhlín Dhubh Ní Chonaill – and this form will be used hereafter in the chapter.
4. For a discussion of Gaelic literature in transition during the period 1780–1830, see Lesa Ní Mhunghaile, 'Gaelic Literature in Transition, 1780–1830', in *Irish Literature in Transition, 1780–1830*, ed. Clare Connolly (Cambridge University Press, 2020), pp. 37–51. For a feminist approach to Irish lament poetry, see Angela Bourke, 'More in Anger than in Sorrow: Irish Women's Lament Poetry', in *Feminist Messages: Coding in Women's Folk Culture*, ed. Joan Newlon Radner (Urbana and Chicago, IL: University of Illinois Press, 1993), pp. 160–82.
5. *Caoineadh Airt Uí Laoghaire* first appeared in print in Mrs Morgan John O'Connell's *The Last Colonel of the Irish Brigade* (1892). It was followed by a number of other editions, the standard text of which for many years was Seán Ó Tuama's edition, *Caoineadh Airt Uí Laoghaire* (Dublin: An Clóchomhar, 1961). The definitive text and translation is now considered to be that of Angela Bourke in the chapter 'Lamenting the Dead', in *The Field Day Anthology of Irish Writing, Vols IV/V: Irish Women's Writing and Traditions*, ed. Bourke et al., 2 vols (Cork University Press, 2002), IV, pp. 1372–84. At least twelve complete translations of the poem have been undertaken: Eleanor Hull (1912), Frank O'Connor (1932, 1940, 1959), K. H. Jackson (1951), Eilís Dillon (1971), John Montague (1974), Thomas Kinsella (1981), Brendan Kennelly (1989), P. L. Henry (1991), Malachi McCormick (1994), Angela Bourke (2002), and Vona Groarke (2008).

6. Maria Tymoczko, 'Post-Colonial Writing and Literary Translation', in *Post-Colonial Translation: Theory and Practice*, ed. Susan Bassnett and Harish Trivedi (London and New York: Routledge, 1999), pp. 19–40; Susan Bassnett, *Translation Studies*, 3rd edn (London and New York: Routledge, 2002), p. 102.

7. André Lefevere, 'Mother Courage's Cucumbers: Text, System and Refraction in a Theory of Literature' (1982), in *The Translation Studies Reader*, ed. Lawrence Venuti (London and New York: Routledge, 2000), pp. 233–49 (pp. 234–35).

8. For an understanding of these concepts in relation to translation in India, see the work of Sujit Mukherjee: *Translation as Discovery and Other Essays on Indian Literature in English Translation* (New Delhi: Allied, 1981) and *Translation as Recovery* (New Delhi: Pencraft International, 2004).

9. For Wilson, see Mícheál Mac Craith, '"We Know all these Poems": The Irish Response to Ossian', in *The Reception of Ossian in Europe*, ed. Howard Gaskill (London: Thoemmes Continuum, 2004), pp. 91–108. For Charlotte Brooke, see Lesa Ní Mhunghaile, *Charlotte Brooke's* Reliques of Irish Poetry (Dublin: Irish Manuscripts Commission, 2009).

10. Seamus Heaney, *Finders Keepers: Selected Prose, 1971–1991* (London: Faber & Faber, 2002), p. 63.

11. Don Paterson, *Orpheus: A Version of Rilke's 'Die Sonette an Orpheus'* (London: Faber & Faber, 2006), p. 73.

12. Umberto Eco, *Mouse or Rat?: Translation as Negotiation* (London: Weidenfeld & Nicolson, 2003), p. 5.

13. Seán Ó Tuama, ed., *An Duanaire, 1600–1900: Poems of the Dispossessed*, trans. Thomas Kinsella (Dublin: Dolmen Press, 1981), p. 199.

14. L. M. Cullen, 'The Contemporary and Later Politics of "Caoineadh Airt Uí Laoire"', *Eighteenth-Century Ireland / Iris an dá chultúr* 8 (1993), 7–38.

15. Seán Ó Tuama, *Repossessions: Selected Essays on the Irish Literary Heritage* (Cork University Press, 1995), p. 85.

16. Ibid., p. 86.

17. *An Lóchrann* (June 1926), p. 50. See also Ó Tuama, *Caoineadh*, p. 85. For an example from the manuscript tradition, see Peadar Ó Muircheartaigh, 'Muintir Longáin agus Caoine Airt Uí Laoire: Fianaise Nua-Aimsithe ar a Ról i Seachadadh an Dáin', in *Eighteenth-Century Ireland / Iris an dá chultúr* 28 (2013), 148–69 (p. 152).

18. Bourke, *Field Day Anthology*, IV, pp. 1372–84.

19. University College Dublin Library, Special Collections, Ferriter MS., no. 1.

20. For a discussion of a copy of the poem with an English translation probably penned by the Cork scribe Seosamh Ó Longáin sometime during the period 1849–65, see Ó Muircheartaigh, 'Muintir Longáin'.

21. Bourke, 'More in Anger than in Sorrow', p. 168.

22. Bourke, 'Lamenting the Dead', IV, p. 1366.

23. Ibid., IV, p. 1366.

24. Bourke, 'More in Anger than in Sorrow', pp. 162–68.

25. Bourke, 'Lamenting the Dead', IV, p. 1366.

26. Ibid., IV, p. 1367.

27. See, for example, Breandán Ó Madagáin, *Gnéithe den Chaointeoireacht* (Dublin: An Clóchomhar, 1978); Angela Bourke, 'Performing – Not Writing', *Graph* 11 (1991–92), 28–31; Seán Ó Coileáin, 'The Irish Lament: An Oral Genre', *Studia Hibernica* 24 (1984–88), 97–117; and Breandán Ó Buachalla, *An Caoine agus an Chaointeoireacht* (Dublin: Cois Life, 1998).

28. Sarah E. McKibben, *Endangered Masculinities in Irish Poetry, 1540–1780* (University College Dublin Press, 2010), p. 101.

29. Angela Bourke, 'Performing, Not Writing: The Reception of an Irish Woman's Lament', in *Dwelling in Possibility: Women Poets and Critics on Poetry*, ed. Yopie Prins and Maeera Shreiber (Ithaca, NY and London: Cornell University Press, 1997), pp. 132–46 (p. 133).

30. Ibid., p. 132.

31. Ó Coileáin, 'The Irish Lament', pp. 105–06; Ó Buachalla, *An Caoine agus an Chaointeoireacht*, pp. 50–53.

32. See Seán Ó Tuama's edition of *Caoineadh Airt Uí Laoghaire*.

33. Ó Buachalla, *Caoine agus an Chaointeoireacht*, pp. 23–27.

34. Groarke, *Lament for Art O'Leary*, p. 12.

35. Margaret Mills Harper, '"Carolina Hat": Vona Groarke's *Lament for Art O'Leary*', *Irish University Review* 43.2 (2013), 274–87 (p. 275).

36. Ibid., p 275.

37. For an account of the translation history of *Caoineadh Airt Uí Laoghaire*, see Ríóna Ní Fhrighil, '*Caoineadh Airt Uí Laoghaire* agus stair a aistrithe', in *Aistriú Éireann*, ed. Charlie Dillon and Ríóna Ní Fhrighil (Belfast: Cló Ollscoil na Banríona, 2008), pp. 49–67.

38. Lucy Collins, 'Review of *Lament for Art O'Leary* by Vona Groarke; *Spindrift* by Vona Groarke', *Irish University Review* 40.2 (2010), 217–220 (p. 217).

39. See Seamus Heaney, 'Title Deeds: Translating a Classic', *Proceedings of the American Philosophical Society* 148.4 (2004), 411–26 (pp. 425–26).

40. Collins, 'Review', p. 218.

41. Liam P. Ó Murchú, 'Aistriúchán/-áin Frank O'Connor de *Chúirt an Mheonoíche*', in *Aistriú Éireann*, ed. Charlie Dillon and Ríóna Ní Fhrighil (Belfast: Cló Ollscoil na Banríona, 2008), pp. 131–45. Translations of *Cúirt* were undertaken by Denis Woulfe (1880), Michael C. O'Shea (1897), Arland Ussher (1926), Frank O'Connor (1945, 1959), Lord Longford (1949), David Marcus (1953), Patrick C. Power (1971), Cosslett Ó Cuinn (1982), Thomas Kinsella (1981), Seamus Heaney (1993) (partial), and Ciaran Carson (2005).

42. Máirín Ní Dhonnchadha, 'Review of Gregory A. Schirmer, *The Midnight Court: Eleven Versions of Merriman* (Lilliput Press)', *History Ireland* (March/ April 2016), 59; Ó Tuama, *Repossessions*, pp. 63–77.

43. Cullen, 'Contemporary and Later Politics', p. 8.

44. Ní Dhonnchadha, 'Review', p. 59.

45. Brian Merriman, *The Midnight Court / Cúirt an Mheán Oíche: A Critical Edition*, ed. Brian Ó Conchubhair, trans. David Marcus (Syracuse, NY: Syracuse University Press, 2011), p. xv. Five different Irish-language editions, the most definitive of which is Liam P. Ó Murchú's *Cúirt an Mheon-Oíche le Brian Merríman* (Dublin: An Clóchomhar, 1982), have been produced. See also L. Chr. Stern, 'Brian Merriman's *Cúirt An Mheadhóin Oidhche*', in *Zeitschrift für Celtische Philologie* 5 (1905), 193–415; *Cúirt An Mheadhon Oidhche*, ed. Risteárd Ó Foghludha (Fiachra Éilgeach) (1912; Dublin: Hodges Figgis, 1949); and *Cúirt An Mheán Oíche*, ed. Daithí Ó hUaithne (Dublin: Dolmen Press, 1968).

46. Alan Titley, '*Cúirt an Mheán Oíche*: A Wonder of Ireland', in *The Midnight Court*, ed. Ó Conchubhair, pp. 47–58 (p. 56).

47. Heaney, *Redress of Poetry*, p. 41.

48. Ó Conchubhair, *Midnight Court*, p. xvii.

49. Art Ó Beoláin, *Merriman agus Filí Eile* (Dublin: An Clóchomhar, 1985), pp. 7–23; Gearóid Ó Crualaoich, 'The Vision of Liberation in *Cúirt an Mheán Oíche*', in *Folia Gadelica: Essays Presented by Former Students to R. A. Breatnach* ed. Pádraig de Brún, Seán Ó Coileáin and Pádraig Ó Riain (Cork University Press, 1983), pp. 95–104.

50. Alan Titley, 'An breithiúnas ar Cúirt an mheán oíche', *Studia Hibernica* 25 (1989–90), 105–33 (p. 132).

51. Ó Conchubhair, *Midnight Court*, p. xvii.

52. Gregory A. Schirmer, *The Midnight Court: Eleven Versions of Merriman* (Dublin: Lilliput Press, 2015), p. 33.

53. Heaney, *Redress of Poetry*, p. 53.

54. Neal Alexander, *Ciaran Carson: Space, Place, Writing* (Liverpool University Press, 2010), p. 179.

55. Seán Crosson, 'Performance and Music in the Poetry of Ciaran Carson', *Nordic Irish Studies* 3.1, *Special Issue: Contemporary Irish Poetry* (2004), 101–11.

56. Carson, *The Midnight Court*, p. 11.

57. For the 'foreignisation' approach to translation, see Lawrence Venuti, *The Scandals of Translation: Towards an Ethics of Difference* (London and New York: Routledge, 1998).

58. Schirmer, *The Midnight Court*, p. 98.

59. Ibid., p. 106.

60. See Alexander, *Ciaran Carson*, p. 205.

61. Schirmer, *The Midnight Court*, p. 105. A literal translation of the corresponding lines reads as follows: 'Often have cattle and gifts been gained / The contents of a churn and a rick from a visit of the clergy, / Often in my memory their qualities were praised / And a great number of their always-clever deeds of lust.'

62. Alexander, *Ciaran Carson*, p. 206. See also Carson, *Midnight Court*, pp. 21, 33.

63. Octavio Paz, 'Translation: Literature and Letters' in *Theories of Translation*, ed. Rainer Schulte and John Biguenet (University of Chicago Press, 1992), pp. 152–62 (154).

64. Bassnett, *Translation Studies*, p. 36.

65. Gabriel Rosenstock in interview with Lesa Ní Mhunghaile, Glenageary, County Dublin, 2 July 2013. For a full transcript of this interview, see http://roghaghabriel.blogspot.ie/2013/07/the-rejection-of-early-morning-dew.html [accessed 27 March 2017]. See also Lesa Ní Mhunghaile, 'Gabriel Rosenstock: "The Rejection of the Early Morning Dew"', in *Cultural/Literary Translators: Selected Irish-German Biographies II*, ed. Sabine Egger (Trier: Wissenschaftlicher Verlag, 2015), pp. 195–210.

CHAPTER 19

'Our Darkest Century': The Irish Eighteenth Century in Memory and Modernity

James Ward

'Irish literature', as the introduction to this collection maintains, is a term that cannot be applied during the period 1700–80 without careful attention to the complexity and variety it denotes. This closing chapter echoes Marie-Louise Coolahan's opening contribution by applying a similarly restive logic to the boundaries of the period itself. Recent work in literary studies has challenged the methodological assumption that historical periods function as 'bounded containers' which serve to confine culture within temporal limits.[1] Work on the eighteenth century in particular has identified forms and practices of advanced capitalism through which our own modernity, both consciously and unwittingly, 'extends or inherits the eighteenth [century] by intensifying it'.[2] Informed by these arguments, the following chapter traces the persistence in present times of two texts from near the beginning and the end of the period covered by this volume: George Farquhar's *The Recruiting Officer* (1706) and Oliver Goldsmith's *The Deserted Village* (1770).

While Goldsmith's poem dramatises a traumatic rupture between tradition and modernity in memorable and haunting verse, Farquhar's play uses knockabout comedy for ideological ends that amount, as Kevin J. Gardner notes, to rendering 'certain death more palatable'.[3] Focusing on characters uprooted from rural lifestyles by transnational capitalism and global conflict, both texts have historically been read, remembered, and performed to mark change. *The Deserted Village* went on to influence the 'idyllic vision of a rural, self-sufficient republic' propounded by Éamon de Valera, while a tradition of using *The Recruiting Officer* to launch new venues and ventures continues today.[4] The afterlives of these texts therefore encompass much more than their authors' posthumous fame and canonical status. A striking early example comes in the experiences of marine officer Watkin Tench in the penal colony of New South Wales. Arriving as part of the first group of colonists to make landfall in January 1788, Tench knew *The*

Deserted Village by heart and he used Goldsmith's *A History of the Earth and Animated Nature* (1774) to identify as emus the large flightless birds that could outrun the colony's greyhounds.⁵ He was also one of two eyewitnesses who left written accounts of a performance staged by convicts in the colony of *The Recruiting Officer* on 4 June 1789. The performers, as the other witness observed, 'professed no higher aim than "humbly to excite a smile," and their efforts to please were not unattended with applause'.⁶

   In the present, as in the penal colony, Farquhar and Goldsmith's texts act at once to alleviate and enforce the shock of cultural transition through the forces of memory and modernity. While memory inheres in a break between a remembered past and a lived present, modernity experiences this past through accumulation and acquisition: its defining action, as Marc Augé says, is the incorporation of the 'past in a present that supersedes it but still lays claim to it'.⁷ Like modernity, memory has been theorised in diverse and exciting ways. A concise characterisation of personal memory, which has wider application to collective and textual dimensions of cultural memory, can be found in Eavan Boland's poem 'We Are Always Too Late'. It opens with the declaration 'Memory / is in two parts', 'the revisiting' and 'the re-enactment'.⁸ Boland's own 2011 poem 'Re-Reading Oliver Goldsmith's "Deserted Village" in a Changed Ireland' exemplifies this double process. In addition to the re-reading of Goldsmith's text signalled in the title, the poem re-enacts and revisits *The Deserted Village*, with the real locale of Dundrum taking the place of the fictional village of Auburn. Through the construction of Ireland's largest retail complex, Dundrum Town Centre (opened 2005), Boland's poem replays the privatisation and repurposing of formerly communal space depicted in *The Deserted Village*. While offering comparable meditations on the original's themes of accelerated social change, consumption, and luxury, Boland re-reads *The Deserted Village* as a record of complicity rather than protest. At its centre is the accusation that Goldsmith uses an aesthetics of nostalgia to intensify and accelerate loss under the cover of commemoration. The poem therefore extends Boland's longstanding critique of the eighteenth century as a period of both catastrophic and insidious change, which has been a persistent feature of Boland's poetry since its decisive turn to historical subject matter in the 1990s.⁹ As evidenced by its recent placement in a sequence of poems about re-reading texts and revisiting historic scenes, from the seventeenth-century colonial poet Anne Bradstreet to Boland's own arrival in New York in 1956, Goldsmith's poem remains a singularly problematic memorial presence, not least because of the ways in which it is seen to exemplify its wider period.[10] The eighteenth is, in the words of another of the poems that contribute to this critique, 'our darkest century' (p. 279).

Re-reading Goldsmith

Boland's poetry places strong emphasis on the connotative and evocative power of material things and physical spaces. 'Small things / make the past' (p. 295), she writes, and these things, along with the space they inhabit, occasion her poems: the book as object, the writer's pen, engraved silver, a wedding spoon, the room which contains all of these things and the changing townscape it looks out on. And, as with many Dublin writers, the city's Georgian architecture, memorably characterised as 'that zest for air and proportion which was the mask of an Augustan oppressor', contributes a sense of the eighteenth century as a visible, permanent, and obvious feature of the everyday.[11] In keeping with this material focus, Boland's poem on Goldsmith is occasioned by an object, specifically a volume containing *The Deserted Village*, left for many years unread on a shelf. The action of the poem is folded into a momentary interval between the speaker registering the presence of the book and taking it down to read. She reflects on the transformation of Dundrum from historic village to branded 'Town Centre', passing these thoughts through the thematic and stylistic filters of Goldsmith's poem. However, the poem asserts a difference between origin and source, identifying Goldsmith's native townland of Lissoy as only the first of these, in a clear insistence against easy assumptions of authenticity and inheritance that also reflects Boland's own relation to canonical poets and poetics. Opening with the remark 'I never took it down', the poem engages the long-held status of Goldsmith's work as an object of institutional and public memory, taught in schools and, as Norma Clarke notes, habitually learned by heart.[12]

Despite its traditional significance as instrument and object of memory, Goldsmith's poem becomes, in Boland's re-reading, a work of forgetting. The eighteenth-century poet is conjured at work committing his subjects not to memory but to oblivion. The speaker describes her effort:

> ... to summon his face,
> To see his pen work the surface,
> To watch lampblack inks laying phrase after phrase
> On the island, the village he is taking every possible care to erase.   (p. 65)

This encounter breaks the conventional link between writing and memorial preservation captured in Roger Chartier's observation that 'the mission of the written was to dispel the obsession with loss'.[13] Indeed, the animating distinction in Chartier's theory of textuality between inscription and erasure is dissolved: the poet witnesses inscription *as* erasure.

Western literary and philosophical traditions generally present writing as memory's 'most important metaphor and [...] medium', as Aleida Assmann observes; however, as she goes on to note, a counter-tradition established in Plato's *Phaedrus* portrays writing 'as an aid not to memory but to reminiscence [...] not truth but only the semblance of truth'.[14] According to this distinction, writing cannot meaningfully preserve knowledge or transmit it to others. It can function to awaken memory in 'someone who already knows', but to those who do not, it purveys only semblances and fictions. Beyond its purview there remains a 'dynamic, productive and inaccessible part of memory', *anamnesis*, which 'cannot even be touched by writing, let alone replaced by it'.[15] Of Plato's contrasting mnemonic modes, one true but untouchable in writing, one ersatz but amenable to textual transmission, the second applies in Boland's reading to Goldsmith's idealisation of village life, which in turn prefigures the privatisation, redevelopment, and rebranding of communal spaces at the turn of the twenty-first century. Boland recalls that she wrote the poem between 2002 and 2004, 'a time when there was building everywhere', when 'the old place was being turned into the fiction of the new place [...] the new place erased the old one as it [...] does in Oliver Goldsmith's poem'. Foreshadowing such transformations, Goldsmith becomes an alchemist who alters the substance of his personal memories, replacing truth with semblance. 'Lissoy', Boland asserts, 'the real village that Oliver Goldsmith came from, is somehow transmuted in his language and his lines into a much more idealised English village'.[16] *The Deserted Village* stands in this re-reading for a rapidly advancing and specifically anglicising modernity, which in turn is identified as prototypical of the operation of transnational capital in the twenty-first century.

Wiping and warping memory as it 'work[s] the surface', Goldsmith's pen is conceived as an agent of traumatic loss. This it shares with engraving tools in Boland's two poems on eighteenth-century silverwork. In 'Bright-cut Irish Silver', having been extracted by 'wounding an artery of rock', the metal is said to bear in its engraved surface a 'cicatrice of skill'.[17] The later poem, 'In Which Hester Bateman, Eighteenth-Century English Silversmith, Takes an Irish Commission', describes how its subject:

> ... made a marriage spoon
> And then subjected it to violence.
> Chased, beat it. Scarred it and marked it.
> All in the spirit of our darkest century.   (p. 279)

Through dual-purpose verbs which work, as several critics have noted, as terms both of art and punishment, these lines assert a hidden connection between eighteenth-century art and colonial violence.[18] Reversing conventional associations between the period and enlightenment, Boland's dark eighteenth century mixes the bleakness of trauma and the obscurity of forgetfulness. One reason for this persistent association is that the period marks a tipping point in the historic transition whereby Ireland became a predominantly Anglophone culture. Along with other textual and material artefacts, Boland indicts the familiar, memorable, and well-loved verse of *The Deserted Village* in this transition; the poem compounds a series of losses in which '[t]he final one is through language' (p. 66). Her own poem 'My Country in Darkness', attempts to add substance to what has been blotted out. Set '[a]fter the wolves and before the elms', it imaginatively recreates the end of the Irish bardic tradition ('a dead art in a dying land'), upon which, in the poem's final line, 'Darkness falls' (p. 245). Along with Thomas Moore, whose poem 'Dear Harp of My Country' supplies this poem's title, an important source-text for Boland's recurring association of eighteenth-century memory with enveloping darkness is Daniel Corkery's *The Hidden Ireland* (1924). This is a text which, as Boland's reflections on her Goldsmith poem make clear, partially restores to view the lives and poetic traditions erased by the anglicising modernity for which *The Deserted Village* stands.

Corkery's book, a key text of post-independence cultural nationalism and, later, of revisionist controversy, has more recently been discussed in terms that move beyond claims about its status as empirical history and towards an assessment of its author as 'a sophisticated cultural theorist'.[19] In a similar vein, Boland regards *The Hidden Ireland* as an exercise in cultural memory which presents, in her words, 'poets from another world, most of them lost to time and history'.[20] This recuperative vision contrasts with the treatment of this world offered by Goldsmith, whom she describes as 'astonished and put off [. . .] by the Irish bards of the time. Those were Corkery's poets, historically adrift, Irish-speaking, and disinclined to take the slightest interest in London.'[21] As this last remark shows, Boland's reflections on Corkery sometimes come close to reproducing *The Hidden Ireland*'s powerful but partial myths of cultural dichotomy and mutual indifference. Along with the work of James Kelly, Ciarán Mac Murchaidh, and Lesa Ní Mhunghaile, Anne Markey's chapter in the current volume challenges such myths and their basis in an underlying notion of eighteenth-century Gaelic Ireland as a hermetically sealed unit that was cut off from the public sphere of Anglophone culture.[22] While acknowledging its

mythopoeic dimension, Corkery described his own project in more historiographical terms as a corrective to W. E. H. Lecky's *History of England in
the Eighteenth Century* (1878–90). Introducing a recurring opposition
between light and darkness, he sets out *The Hidden Ireland*'s mission as
'lighting up the period it deals with' through a focus on 'that side of Irish
life, the Gaelic side, which to [Lecky] and his authorities was dark'.[23] This
darkness was for Corkery an historical fact as well as a cultural symptom.
Contrasting the vibrant poetic culture of eighteenth-century Munster with
its material conditions, he writes that 'to see it against the dark world that
threw it up, is to be astonished, if not dazzled'.[24] Readers are dazzled by
poets who wrote and dwelt in smoky, insanitary darkness and who,
Corkery writes, often went blind as a result. While Boland's poetry
draws heavily on this poeticised notion of a dark eighteenth century, her
work does not follow Corkery in opposing it with light. Viewed almost
incidentally through objects and artefacts of a successor culture, the hidden
Ireland remains so, obscure and irrecoverable even though, when its
memory surfaces on book- and antique-lined shelves of well-appointed
homes in Dublin suburbs, it sometimes hides in plain sight.

A further distinct quality of darkness is its pairing with sweetness.
Goldsmith's lampblack inks cause his native village to disappear in 'sweet
Augustan double talk'. Similarly, in Boland's depiction of Bateman, the
smith remains 'oblivious' to 'grape shot and tar caps' as 'she pours out /
And lets cool the sweet colonial metal'. This invocation of ritual punish-
ments and ballistic technologies deployed by Crown forces against the 1798
rebellion helps explain the poem's insistence on the darkness of the eighteenth century. Boland's repeated linking of darkness to sweetness is itself
a dismantling and reassembly of an enlightenment coinage, 'sweetness and
light'. As taken up by Matthew Arnold in *Culture and Anarchy* (1869),
Jonathan Swift's phrase comes to stand for 'the idea of beauty and of
a human nature perfect on all its sides, which is the dominant idea of
poetry'.[25] The recoupling of sweetness to darkness reflects postcolonial and
memory studies' critique of 'commodified human experience' in which,
rather than perfection, 'beauty is coextensive with pain'.[26] In Boland's
Bateman poem, silver, which in Western iconography represents betrayal
as well as wealth, forges this connection. The metal, as Toby Barnard has
argued, had a symbolic value in eighteenth-century Ireland that went
beyond its monetary worth. It was a durable investment commodity in
a context of failing banks. Ascent within society and the professions was
marked by 'commissions for grandiose silver services'. Theft, of silver
spoons in particular, was an offence regularly punished by transportation

to the colonies, and decorative work was not just a marker of status but also a security measure. Engraving, Barnard writes, 'especially with the crest and arms of the owner, assisted identification and recovery. It also increased the show it made when displayed in buffets or on sideboards.' Boland's poem is therefore occasioned by an artefact which marks a point of both demarcation and contact between the 'quickening consumerism of eighteenth-century Ireland', as Barnard calls it, and its hidden history of judicial and economic violence.[27]

Silver bears witness to Bateman's 'craft of hurt' but it also separates the English smith from her Irish commission. She remains 'oblivious', a word that ambiguously pivots between historic and modern meanings of 'forgetful' and 'unaware'. The metal itself takes on this awareness, acting as a medium of memory, performing a 'mediation / Between oppression and love's remembrance' (p. 279). In the poem on Goldsmith, whose name itself recalls Boland's juxtaposition of metallurgy with colonial violence, the eighteenth-century poet is clearly and actively implicated in erasure and loss. Like the silversmith, Goldsmith is seen to 'work the surface' of the page, a conventionally planar superficies which memory invests with depth. The work undertaken, however, is to obfuscate the surface and shut off such depths as may otherwise appear, much as Dundrum's 'little river was paved over with stone' to become a surface over which shoppers now pass 'the way souls are said to enter the underworld' with 'no one remembering'. When Goldsmith's own words make an appearance in Boland's poem they do so as interference, as surface noise which blocks an effort at retrieval:

> Would any of it come back to us if we gave it another name?
> *(Sweet Auburn loveliest village of the Plain.)*   (p. 66)

Forming a metrically awkward rhyming couplet with Boland's rhetorical question, the opening line of *The Deserted Village* intrudes here upon the speaker's memory to occlude the possibility of other pasts. Together with the following stanza's image of unremembering shoppers crossing paved-over rivers 'the way souls are said to enter the underworld', such dialogic interpolation invokes the first section of T. S. Eliot's *The Waste Land* (1922). Though it chooses metaphors of ruin, rubbish, and fragmentation, rather than Corkery's iconography of darkness and light, *The Waste Land*, like *The Hidden Ireland* (first published two years after it), is a modernist memory-text which strives to preserve vestiges of artistic inheritance in the wake of cultural apocalypse. Similarly, in Boland's poetry the eighteenth century is a cataclysm which brings darkness and loss on a national scale comparable with the devastation visited across Europe by the First World War and commemorated in *The Waste Land*. 'Re-Reading Oliver Goldsmith' further asserts that twenty-first-century capitalism accelerates and refines the homogenising, flattening, and commodification of experience which eighteenth-century artworks like those of Goldsmith and Bateman initially brought to the cultural realm. But as objects which bear on their material surfaces impressions and traces of complex historical relations that are legible in unexpected ways, these works paradoxically act as windows onto a world they once erased, serving to make eighteenth-century darkness visible.

Rehearsing Farquhar

In contrast with Boland's poetic rendering of a modernity paradoxically but indelibly marked by a darkly irrecoverable past, *The Recruiting Officer* renders the process of memory-making transparent. Farquhar's play shows how political institutions acquire longevity and continuity, and how political violence acquires legitimacy, from the ability of culture to make and remake memory in ways that combine repetition with change. Tracing the global consolidation of the British fiscal-military state, the histories of the play's performance, reception, and adaptation have gone on to re-enact these processes. In addition to the convict performance in New South Wales in 1789, *The Recruiting Officer* was also the first documented drama staged in two locations in colonial America – New York in 1732 and Charleston in 1736 – as well as Kingston, Jamaica in 1750. The Australian 1789 performance, however, acquired a particular resonance in cultural memory after being fictionalised by Thomas Keneally in his 1987 novel *The Playmaker*, which in turn was adapted for the stage by Timberlake Wertenbaker as *Our Country's Good* and premiered at the Royal Court Theatre in 1988. Farquhar's play functioned throughout the eighteenth century to export a political modernity that harnessed populist sentiment to state violence. But, as modern appropriators have demonstrated, beginning with Bertolt Brecht's adaptation *Trumpets and Drums* (1955), the play presents these subjects in ways that enable critique as well as endorsement.

Farquhar's play adds a performative dimension to the inscriptive processes of memory which this chapter has so far discussed. 'In the course of migrations, wars, and conquests', Assmann writes, 'an earlier memory is extinguished by "overwriting"'.[28] Strikingly presenting paper as a material that can quench flame, this palimpsestic metaphor also suggests a relationship between superscription and violence that is, as I have suggested, a recurrent feature of Boland's approach. A comparable figure is also present in Keneally's novel about the performance of *The Recruiting Officer* in New South Wales in 1789. In his epilogue to *The Playmaker*, Keneally calls the performance a 'flicker of a theatrical intent' that 'would consume in the end the different and serious theatre of the tribes of the hinterland'.[29] With a complexity comparable both to Assmann's metaphor of overwriting as extinguishment and Boland's figure of inscription as erasure, Keneally uses unstably figurative language in which theatre is both agent and object of obliterative force. This uneasy imputation of theatricality across boundaries of culture, subjection, and power also applies in the novel itself, where it meets images of superscription and supersession comparable to those discussed in Boland's work. In a moment of comic anti-climax, Caesar, a Madagascan slave, bursts onto the stage in the middle of the performance and is said to have 'out-theatred' the company (p. 352). Theatre also enables Arabanoo, an Indigenous Australian captured by the colonists and partially integrated into their society, to feature in fantasies of cultural overlap entertained by the novel's title character, Marine Lieutenant Ralph Clark. Watching rehearsals along-side Arabanoo, Clark speculates that the captive 'seemed to take some comfort' from them and muses on the possibility that Arabanoo 'consid-ered the reading of the lines and the rehearsal of actions to have religious meaning' (p. 160). As this passage suggests, Keneally uses *The Recruiting Officer* to give meaning and shape to novel experience in unfamiliar territory. In the words of Annalisa Pes, the play is 'reframed by the new spatial and temporal context' where its 'captivating effects' supersede the penal colony's 'public rituals of authority' and expose them as theatrics which are no less performative for being real.[30] During the eighteenth century more generally, theatre helped to produce and reinforce new realities rather than simply present fictive ones. It was a familiar, mobile, adaptable technology with which to manage cultural transitions and cement territorial acquisitions. It served, as Joseph Roach observes, to extend the global reach of Anglophone culture by working 'to canalize specified needs, desires, and habits in order to reproduce them'.[31] The concept of surrogation is central to this project. Proceeding from the observation that 'repetition is change', Roach states how institutions' geographical mobility and temporal continuity depend on their ability to be taken up by different people in different places so that in the process of transmission new 'traditions may [...] be invented and others overturned'.[32] Conscription in Farquhar's play is an obvious analogue for this system of surrogation. Its reliance on mechanisms of reproduction is

literalised in its title character's declaration of intent, following the successful conclusion of its romance plot, to leave the military and 'raise recruits
the matrimonial way'.[33]

Elsewhere in the play Captain Plume describes recruitment in terms
which explicitly connect key enterprises in the project of colonial modernity. 'A baker, a tailor, a smith, and a butcher. I believe', he says, 'the first
colony planted at Virginia had not more trades in their company than
I have in mine' (V, iv, ll. 1–3, p. 120). The word 'company', because it can
refer to organisations in the commercial, military, and theatrical spheres,
invests this line with a concentrated awareness of connections between
power, performance, and capital. The line also invokes Farquhar's home
city as a historic point of intersection between military conquest and
private finance. Derry, re-founded as Londonderry in 1609 by companies
of tailors, fishmongers, and ironmongers, commemorates the British state's
outsourcing of its own expansion. Like the first colony planted at Virginia
or, indeed, the penal colony of New South Wales, it was a testing ground,
a site of experiments in accelerated modernity. 'You could hardly say that
capitalism was invented in early modern Ireland', writes John Kerrigan,
'but the liquidization of traditional landholding [. . .] induced premature
modernization. Derry was an epicentre of this process because of the
plantation of 1609.'[34] As a work in which Irish speech, characters, and
references are almost completely absent, *The Recruiting Officer* conspicuously does not memorialise such Irish contexts in specific or easily recognisable ways. Rather, the play dramatises processes of surrogation and
transformation through which anywhere can be anywhere else, a fact
which helps account for the play's geographical mobility and adaptability
in performance throughout the eighteenth century. Memory-texts of the
1789 performance highlight rehearsal, a process which allows anyone to be
anyone else, as a display of this surrogative function.

The Playmaker and, to an even greater extent, Wertenbaker's dramatisation *Our Country's Good*, follow a well-established pattern of representing
dramatic performance in fiction by focusing on the rehearsal period and
climaxing with the opening night. The depiction of rehearsal in these texts
is anachronistic and idealised, however: it reflects a more general habit, as
Tiffany Stern remarks, of 'unwittingly imposing present theatrical practice
onto the past'.[35] Group rehearsal superintended by a director, and even the
very role of director, did not feature in pre-nineteenth-century theatrical
practice. Preparations for the 1789 performance are therefore unlikely to
have taken the form depicted in Keneally and Wertenbaker's fictions.
Moreover, as Robert Jordan argues, Keneally's decision to make Ralph

Clark the driving intelligence behind the production is based on another suspect assumption – that theatre was an essentially genteel activity in which the lower orders as represented by the convicts would have had to be guided and instructed.[36] Such observations, drawn from research that was not available to the authors of *The Playmaker* and *Our Country's Good*, do not render these texts' premise invalid or their content obsolete. Rather they draw attention to the ways in which rehearsal features not just as animating metaphor but as commentary on the workings of cultural memory, revealing it to be a process founded on invention and intervention as much as recollection and reconstruction. To the extent that these texts are allegories of the making of memory, rehearsal performs what Carol B. Bardenstein calls 'the *active* nature of the construction of memory, articulated in the notion of "acts of memory"'.[37] This active quality, however, represents only one half of a dual process in which conscious, provisional rehearsal meets unthinking repetition: revisiting and re-enactment, as Boland's bipartite model of memory puts it. In an influential discussion of concepts which have since become central to the discipline of memory studies, Pierre Nora differentiates between 'true memory' which inheres in 'gestures and habits, in skills passed down by unbroken traditions, in the body's inherent self-knowledge, in unstudied reflexes and ingrained memories', and historical memory, 'which is nearly the opposite: voluntary and deliberate, experienced as a duty, no longer spontaneous'.[38] Also recognisable, as previously discussed, in Plato's *Phaedrus*, a version of this distinction applies to the rehearsal watched by Ralph Clark. The officer finds it remarkable that the convict actors 'somehow had a gift for the exact theatrical emphasis to place on a line' and believes that 'if he had had to find his players from amongst the officers and the better wives of the Marines they would have brought to Farquhar none of the instinctive touch which seemed to be there' (p. 157).

In such moments where convict-actors embody the 'true memory' of bodily self-knowledge, Keneally's novel finds an escape from history. By minimising the finality of performance, the novel, like Wertenbaker's adaptation, posits rehearsal as a temporary suspension of otherwise oppressive penal and colonial contexts. This effect is reproducible beyond fiction: 'Rehearsing is the only time you're not in prison', remarked a Wormwood Scrubs inmate preparing for a production of Wertenbaker's play.[39] Through comparable moments of temporary displacement and erasure, fictions of the 1789 performance offer relief from the memory of expropriation and oppression in which the performance is implicated. Robert Baker-

White has argued more generally of rehearsal that its depiction onstage enacts 'a vision of potentiality and freedom' which shows 'theater as a disjunctive, fragmented, incoherent, contradictory, interrupted, and interruptable enterprise'.[40] This vision is temporary, however, and limited in scope. The following scene from Wertenbaker's play underlines the provisionality of rehearsal's release:

Sideway *turns to* **Liz** *and starts acting, boldly, across the room, across everyone.*

SIDEWAY What pleasures I may receive abroad are indeed uncertain; but this I am sure of, I shall meet with less cruelty among the most barbarous nations than I have found at home.

LIZ Come, Sir, you and I have been jangling a great while; I fancy if we made up our accounts, we should the sooner come to an agreement.[41]

The bold acting of the two convicts is an attempt to drown out the activity of Major Robbie Ross who intrudes on the rehearsal, taunting and sexually humiliating the convict-actors. The relief they seek is undercut by the dialogue they rehearse. Farquhar's words, freighted at the time of writing with the violence of European war from which the action of the play forms a brief interlude, acquire new and intensified weight through reframing. His characters' references to cruelty and barbarous nations, typical hyperboles of comedy-of-manners couples, acquire obvious and disruptive resonance through their utterance in the penal colony. In performance, *Our Country's Good* can restore concrete referents to these abstract terms. During a 2011 production of the play for BBC Radio, for example, a sound effect was faded up on the word 'jangling' to remind listeners that Liz, at Major Ross's insistence, goes through the rehearsal in chains.[42]

Through such reminders of context, the liberatory power of rehearsal meets an opposite discourse where directed performance is a figure for constraint. In a reversal of the ontological primacy of rehearsal over performance familiar from everyday speech, to rehearse can mean to re-enact, often laboriously, something that has already been performed. Apposite in this context is Judith Butler's account of the performative, as initially outlined in an essay published the same year *Our Country's Good* was first staged. Butler theorises gendered social identity as 'an act which has been rehearsed', 'a performative accomplishment which the mundane social audience, including the actors themselves, come to believe and to perform in the mode of belief'.[43] This idea of rehearsal as a not wholly volitional repetition of historically accreted acts might in turn be connected to broader questions of historical memory and trauma, some of which are encoded in the etymology of the word 'rehearse'. The term, as Susan Letzler Cole points out, means 'to harrow again', and comes from the motion of a *herce*, a harrow, being 'dragged over already ploughed land in order to break up clods of earth'.[44] The image contained in this figure of territory repetitively inscribed and re-inscribed is one that recurs in discussions of the 1789 performance in cultural memory.

In *The Playmaker*, as Jim Davis writes, 'theatre's ability to "possess" becomes one of the novel's central metaphors', through which it 'allegorically explores the imposition of colonial power'; indeed, 'the play itself is something that colonizes [...] imposing an order, a pattern, a structure on intractable material'.[45] Such critical framing of Farquhar's play within a modern fiction, against the historical context of the 1789 performance, and through the broader ideological uses of theatre, is also found in Linda Hutcheon's discussion of the original touring production of *Our Country's Good*, which ran on alternating nights with *The Recruiting Officer*, with actors taking the parts in Farquhar's play they had previously 'rehearsed' on stage. To experience these successive performances was for Hutcheon an object lesson in irony, where 'said and unsaid meanings rubbed together through mutual contextual framing' to produce 'disturbing continuities, not differences'.[46] Reframing Farquhar's works was not, however, a twentieth-century invention. Jason Shaffer details performance histories in colonial and revolutionary America during the 1760s and 70s, where the plays 'found new life and acquired new meanings'. In May 1765, amid rising anti-British antagonism, a New York theatre staging Farquhar's *The Twin Rivals* was attacked and burnt. But Farquhar's work was also co-opted in opposite ways: a colonel in Washington's army wrote to his sister in 1778 of a proposed performance of *The Recruiting Officer* by the revolutionary troops, which he hoped would be set aside in favour of 'the more agreeable Entertainment of taking possession of Philadelphia'.[47] Brecht deployed the same historical setting as a backdrop for his adaptation *Trumpets and Drums*. During the action of the play, news reaches Shrewsbury of the fall of Boston, causing Justice Balance to remark that the 'sun is setting on the British Empire' – reframing, as Joel Schechter notes, Farquhar's comic heroes as counter-revolutionaries and their war as a lost cause.[48]

By contrast, in the Australian penal settlement, founded after the loss of the American colonies created a pressing need for new territory to accommodate transported convicts, the play's morale-boosting properties were noted. Watkin Tench, the Goldsmith-reading officer referred to at the start of this chapter, provides the most detailed account of the 1789 performance:

[T]he play of 'The Recruiting Officer' was performed by a party of convicts, and honoured by the presence of his excellency, and the officers of the garrison. That every opportunity of escape from the dreariness and dejection of our situation should be eagerly embraced, will not be wondered at. The exhilarating effect of a splendid theatre is well known: and I am not ashamed to confess, that the proper distribution of three or four yards of stained paper, and a dozen farthing candles stuck around the mud walls of a convict-hut, failed not to diffuse general complacency on the countenances of sixty persons, of various descriptions, who were assembled to applaud the representation.[49]

One striking aspect of this account is its apprehension of the performance's affective power through the physical space and material objects that housed and surrounded it. He thinks not in terms of theatre in the abstract but 'the exhilarating effect of a [...] theatre', and lists, with a hand clearly used to drawing up inventories, the modest fittings which produce an effect of splendour. David Collins, the other officer who wrote about the performance, also had his eye on how the hut was 'fitted up for the occasion'.[50] These brief accounts enact processes of mediation, context, and distancing, which have been theorised collectively by Erving Goffman as a single process of framing. In *Frame Analysis*, Goffman notes that a well-known play can not only 'be presented in various versions [...] but also one of these versions can be satirized, guyed, camped, or played broad, the persistent purpose being to use a traditional presentation as a substance in its own right, as something in itself to work upon'.[51] Discussing their centrality to the representation of conflict, Butler argues that frames have the effect of 'instrumentalizing certain versions of reality'. She presents a frame not as an inert surround but an active force, 'always throwing something away, always keeping something out, always de-realizing and de-legitimating alternative versions of reality'.[52] Both accounts of framing conceive the process through acts of transformation, preservation, and erasure which reflect and extend the functions and effects of memory discussed in this chapter. Memory-texts, I have suggested, 'frame' the Irish eighteenth century through predecessor texts in the double sense of re-contextualising them through historic trauma and implicating them in it. Both the satirical possibilities of framing advanced by Goffman and the more serious work of exclusion described by Butler apply to the presentation of war and the memory of war in *The Recruiting Officer*.

Farquhar frames conflict through contrasting modes of memory, personified in the two characters who discharge the office of the play's title. For

Captain Plume, usually seen as the sole title character of the play, warfare is a succession of repeated and virtually identical actions. '[A]ll I know of the matter', he says in response to Justice Balance's request for an account of the Battle of Höchstädt, 'is, our General commanded us to beat the French, and we did so, and if he pleases to say the word we'll do't again' (II, i, ll. 16–18, p. 31). Brecht's adaptation renders this principle of functional repetition in more tersely epigrammatic terms: 'One battle is very much like another.'[53] In the play's other recruiting officer this reductive discourse meets an opposite mode of elaboration through sentimental fiction. Captain Brazen, the effusive counterpart to the studiedly nonchalant Plume, misconstrues the epithet 'laconic' as a surname upon which to construct an anecdote larded with poignant detail: 'Poor Jack Laconic: he was killed at the Battle of Landen! I remember truly that he had a blew riband in his hat that very day, and after he fell, we found a piece of neat's tongue in his pocket' (III, i, ll. 215–18, p. 62). Much as with the rural types who populate Goldsmith's *Deserted Village*, individuating narrative detail is a mnemotechnic device which lends emotional impact and verisimilitude to fictionalised 'memories'. In claiming to 'remember truly' what is a blatant fiction, Brazen presents a satirically heightened version of memory as an effect which can be staged, a histrionic performance that contrasts with Plume's portrayal of war as perpetual rehearsal. His sentimentality works alongside Plume's mundane repetition in a dynamic that is mutually sustaining rather than deconstructive. By combining clear-sighted recognition of the banality of military violence with its necessary elaboration through sentimental heroics, *The Recruiting Officer* lays bare the mechanics of memory-making. Raised in the play's successor texts from subtext to major theme, this process overlays mundane repetition with ostentatious, staged effects. This kind of double process, I have argued, typifies the cultural and affective persistence of literary texts from the Irish eighteenth century.

Conclusion

In her discussion of modern Irish memory, Emilie Pine notes that phenomena of cultural memory are 'not unique to late modernity'. Rather, 'memory achieves a high cultural value whenever "there is a perceived or constructed break with the past"'.[54] The continuing presence of Goldsmith and Farquhar's texts inheres in such breaks. Boland revisits Goldsmith's text as one that conceals and elides other, deeper fractures with and within its poetic fictions. The symbolic violence of the poem compares with the incipient horrors of modern global warfare, always just offstage in *The Recruiting Officer*. Both texts' impact on an individual agent of British state power, Watkin Tench, show how literature provided more than mere abstract or theoretical underpinning for specific political and territorial transitions that contribute to the general themes of this volume. Instead, Irish writing played a concrete and dynamic part in giving meaning and value to colonial modernity and assisting its global spread. This much said, the texts also give complexity and depth to the experience. In counter-memorial echoes which the successor-texts discussed here have done much to amplify, they also, crucially, preserve negative impressions of what was left behind, dismantled, and wiped out.

Notes

1. Caroline Levine, *Forms: Whole, Rhythm, Hierarchy, Network* (Princeton University Press, 2015), p. 54; Eric Hayot, *On Literary Worlds* (Oxford University Press, 2012), pp. 147–61.

2. Ian Baucom, *Specters of the Atlantic: Finance Capital, Slavery and the Philosophy of History* (Durham, NC: Duke University Press, 2005), p. 22.

3. Kevin J. Gardner, 'George Farquhar's *The Recruiting Officer*: Warfare, Conscription, and the Disarming of Anxiety', *Eighteenth-Century Life* 25.3 (2001), 43–61 (p. 48).

4. Michael Griffin, *Enlightenment in Ruins: The Geographies of Oliver Goldsmith* (Lewisburg, PA: Bucknell University Press, 2013), p. 151; Tiffany Stern, 'Introduction', in George Farquhar, *The Recruiting Officer*, ed. Stern (London: Methuen, 2010), p. vii. The play was staged to launch Lichfield Garrick Theatre in 2003.

5. Tom Keneally, *The Commonwealth of Thieves* (London: Vintage, 2007), p. 235.

6. David Collins, *An Account of the English Colony of New South Wales* (London, 1804), p. 61.

7. Marc Augé, *Non-Places: An Introduction to Supermodernity*, trans. Jon Howe (1995; London: Verso, 2008), p. 61.

8. Eavan Boland, *New Collected Poems* (Manchester: Carcanet, 2005), p. 186.

9. Boland's major poems on this topic are: 'Bright-cut Irish Silver' (1990), 'The Death of Reason' (1994), 'My Country in Darkness' (1998), and 'In Which Hester Bateman, Eighteenth-Century English Silversmith, Takes an Irish Commission' (2001). All of these poems were subsequently printed in *New Collected Poems* (2005). Future references from these poems will be from this edition and will be cited in the text.

10. Eavan Boland, 'Edge of Empire', in *A Woman without a Country* (Manchester: Carcanet, 2014), pp. 55–69.

11. Eavan Boland, *Object Lessons: The Life of the Woman and the Poet in Our Time* (1995; Manchester: Carcanet, 2006), p. 4.

12. Eavan Boland, 'Re-Reading Oliver Goldsmith's "Deserted Village" in a Changed Ireland', in *A Woman without a Country* (Manchester: Carcanet, 2014), pp. 64–67 (p. 64). Further references to this collection are given after quotations in the text. The poem was first published in *PN Review 198* 3.4 (February–March 2011). Norma Clarke, *Brothers of The Quill: Oliver Goldsmith in Grub Street* (Cambridge, MA: Harvard University Press, 2016), p. 2.

13. Roger Chartier, *Inscription and Erasure: Literature and Written Culture from the Eleventh to the Eighteenth Century*, trans. Arthur Goldhammer (University of Philadelphia Press, 2007), p. vi.

14. Aleida Assmann, *Cultural Memory and Western Civilization: Arts of Memory* (Cambridge University Press, 2011), pp. 174, 175.

15. Ibid., p. 175.

16. Illuminations Maynooth, 'Eavan Boland Talks about "Re-Reading Oliver Goldsmith"': https://soundcloud.com/illuminationsmaynooth/eavan-boland-talks-about-re-reading-oliver-goldsmith [accessed 20 September 2016].

17. Boland, *New Collected Poems*, p. 173.

18. Rajeev S. Patke, *Postcolonial Poetry in English* (Oxford University Press, 2006), p. 26; William Logan, *The Undiscovered Country: Poetry in the Age of Tin* (New York: Columbia University Press, 2005), p. 222.

19. S. J. Connolly, 'Eighteenth-Century Ireland: Colony or *Ancien Regime*?', in *The Making of Modern Irish History: Revisionism and the Revisionist Controversy*, ed. D. George Boyce and Alan O'Day (London and New York: Routledge, 1996), pp. 15–33 (p. 18).

20. Eavan Boland, 'A Light by Which We May See', *Michigan Quarterly Review* 54 (2015), http://hdl.handle.net/2027/spo.act2080.0054.301 [accessed 21 September 2016].

21. Ibid.

22. James Kelly and Ciarán Mac Murchaidh, 'Introduction: Establishing the Context', in *Irish and English: Essays on the Irish Cultural and Linguistic Frontier, 1600–1900*, ed. Kelly and Mac Murchaidh (Dublin: Four Courts Press, 2012), pp. 15–42; Lesa Ní Mhungaile, 'Bilingualism, Print Culture in Irish and the Public Sphere, 1700–c. 1830', in *Irish and English*, ed. Kelly and Mac Murchaidh, pp. 218–42.

23. Daniel Corkery, *The Hidden Ireland: A Study of Gaelic Munster in the Eighteenth Century* (1924; Dublin: Gill and Macmillan, 1984), p. 6.

24. Ibid., p. 154.

25. Matthew Arnold, *Culture and Anarchy*, ed. Stefan Collini (Cambridge University Press, 1993), p. 67; Jonathan Swift, 'The Battel of the Books', in *The Cambridge Edition of the Works of Jonathan Swift*, Vol. I: *A Tale of a Tub and Other Works*, ed. Marcus Walsh (Cambridge University Press, 2010), pp. 141–64 (p. 152).

26. Elizabeth Kowaleski Wallace, *The British Slave Trade and Public Memory* (New York: Columbia University Press, 2006), p. 105.

27. Toby Barnard, *Making the Grand Figure: Lives and Possessions in Ireland, 1641–1770* (New Haven, CT: Yale University Press, 2004), pp. 135, 139, 122.

28. Assmann, *Cultural Memory*, p. 287.

29. Thomas Keneally, *The Playmaker* (London: Hodder & Stoughton, 1987), p. 359. Further references will be given after quotations in the text.

30. Annalisa Pes, 'A Restoration Drama at the Antipodes: George Farquhar's *The Recruiting Officer* in Thomas Keneally's *The Playmaker*', in *Rehearsals of the Modern: Experience and Experiment in Restoration Drama*, ed. Susanna Zinato (Naples: Liguori, 2010), pp. 149–58 (p. 150).

31. Joseph Roach, *Cities of the Dead: Circum-Atlantic Performance* (New York: Columbia University Press, 1996), pp. 27–28.

32. Ibid., pp. 29–30.

33. George Farquhar, *The Recruiting Officer*, ed. Tiffany Stern (London: Methuen, 2010), V, vii, l. 155, p. 144. Further references will be given after quotations in the text.

34. John Kerrigan, *Archipelagic English: Literature, History, and Politics, 1603–1707* (Oxford University Press, 2008), pp. 300–01.

35. Tiffany Stern, *Rehearsal from Shakespeare to Sheridan* (Oxford: Clarendon Press, 2000), p. 4.

36. Robert Jordan, *The Convict Theatres of Early Australia, 1788–1840* (Strawberry Hills, NSW: Currency House, 2002), pp. 6, 30.

37. Carol B. Bardenstein, 'Trees, Forests, and the Shaping of Palestinian and Israeli Collective Memory', in *Acts of Memory: Cultural Recall in the Present*, ed. Mieke Bal, Jonathan Crewe, and Leo Spitzer (Hanover, NH: University Presses of New England), pp 148–71 (p. 148).

38. Pierre Nora, 'Between Memory and History: *Les Lieux de Mémoire*', *Representations* 26, Special Issue: *Memory and Counter-Memory* (1989), 7–24 (p. 13).

39. Philip Roberts and Max Stafford-Clark, *Taking Stock: The Theatre of Max Stafford-Clark* (London: Nick Hern, 2007), p. 157.

40. Robert Baker-White, *The Text in Play: Representations of Rehearsal in Modern Drama* (Lewisburg, PA: Bucknell University Press, 1999), p. 16.

41. Timberlake Wertenbaker, *Our Country's Good* (London: Methuen, 2003), p. 65, citing *The Recruiting Officer*, V, iii.

42. BBC Radio 4, *Our Country's Good*, dir. Sally Avens, broadcast 17 December 2011.

43. Judith Butler, 'Performative Acts and Gender Constitution: An Essay in Phenomenology and Feminist Theory', *Theatre Journal* 40.4 (1988), 519–31 (pp. 526, 520).

44. Susan Letzler Cole, *Directors in Rehearsal: A Hidden World* (London: Routledge 1992), p. 4.

45. Jim Davis, 'A Play for England: The Royal Court Adapts *The Playmaker*', in *Novel Images: Literature in Performance*, ed. Alan Reynolds (London: Routledge, 1993), pp. 175–90 (pp. 175, 187).

46. Linda Hutcheon, *Irony's Edge: The Theory and Politics of Irony* (London: Routledge, 1994), pp. 22–23.

47. Jason Shaffer, *Performing Patriotism: National Identity in the Colonial and Revolutionary American Theater* (Philadelphia, PA: University of Pennsylvania Press, 2007), pp. 103, 88, 61.

48. Bertolt Brecht, *Trumpets and Drums*, trans. Rose and Martin Kastner, in *Collected Plays*, Vol. IX (New York: Vintage, 1973), p. 297; Joel Schechter, 'Eighteenth-Century Brechtians', *Studies in Theatre and Performance* 33 (2013), 187–209 (p. 194).
49. Watkin Tench, *A Complete Account of the Settlement at Port Jackson in New South Wales* (London, 1793), p. 25.
50. Collins, *An Account of the English Colony*, p. 61.
51. Erving Goffman, *Frame Analysis: An Essay on the Organization of Experience* (Boston, MA: Northeastern University Press, 1986), p. 81.
52. Judith Butler, *Frames of War: When Is Life Grievable?*, rev. edn (2009; London: Verso, 2016), p. xiii.
53. Brecht, *Trumpets and Drums*, p. 267.
54. Emilie Pine, *The Politics of Irish Memory: Performing Remembrance in Contemporary Irish Culture* (Basingstoke: Palgrave, 2011), p. 6, citing Nora, 'Between Memory and History'.

Index

Addison, Joseph, *Cato*, 136, 137
aisling, 12, 19, 38, 265, 327
Aleman, Mateo, *Guzmán de Alfarache*, 307
Amory, Thomas
  The Life of John Buncle, Esq., 57, 123, 334–37
  Memoirs of Celebrated Ladies of Great Britain, 6
ancien regime, 5, 8
Anglicanism, 51, 63
Anglophone literary tradition
  Dublin English, 40–41
  European literary trends and, 202
  introduction to, 7–12, 15–16, 18
  linguistic hegemony, 32
  national tale, 19
  New English and, 39
  patriotism in, 217
  sentimental writing and, 195
Arnold, Matthew, *Culture and Anarchy*, 387
atheism, 73–74, 79, 92, 99, 102, 121
Atkinson, Joseph, 158
Australia, 21, 389, 390, 394–95
autobiographical writing, 39, 41–42

Barber, Mary, *Poems on Several Occasions*, 17–18,
  153, 227–41, 287–88
Barret, George, 165
Barry, Spranger, 58, 59, 172
beggary in fiction, 350
Belfast, 106, 189, 268
Berkeley, George (Bishop), 49, 93–94, 96–97,
  104–6, 115, 116–20
  Alciphron, 51–52
  An Essay towards a New Theory of Vision, 116
  The Querist, 52
  Siris, 52
  *Three Dialogues between Hylous and
    Philonous*, 51
  *Treatise Concerning the Principles of Human
    Knowledge*, 51
Blacklock, Thomas, 123
blasphemy, 99

boat trips on lakes in poetry, 158–59
Boland, Eavan, 21, 384–89
  'My Country in Darkness', 386
  'We Are Always Too Late', 383
Bolg an tSolair (journal), 62
Boorde, Andrew, 35f
  Fyrst Boke of the Introduction of Knowledge, 34
Boyle, Henry, 244
Boyle, Robert, 118
Brecht, Berthold, *Trumpets and Drums*, 389, 394
Brooke, Charlotte, *Reliques of Irish Poetry*, 62, 366
Brooke, Frances, 190, 193
Brooke, Henry, 12, 13, 60–62, 178–80, 331–32,
  333–34
  *Betrayer of his Country (The Earl of
    Westmoreland)*, 61
  'Constantia, or the Man of Law's Tale', 61
  The Earl of Essex, 61
  *The Farmer's Six Letters to the Protestants of
    Ireland*, 61
  *The Fool of Quality, or, The History of Henry,
    Earl of Moreland*, 333–34, 343, 353–59
  Gerusalemme Liberata (Tasso), 60
  *Gustavus Vasa; or, the Deliverer of his Country
    (The Patriot)*, 60
  Jack the Giant Queller, 12, 61
  *Ogygian Tales: or a curious collection of Irish
    Fables, Allegories, and Histories from the
    relations of Fintane the Aged*, 61
  The Spirit of Party, 61
  The Tryal of the Roman Catholics of Ireland, 61
  Universal Beauty, 60
Brown, John, *An Estimate of the Manners and
  Principles of the Times*, 254
Browne, John, *Seasonable Remarks on Trade*, 104
Browne, Peter, *A letter in answer to a book entitled,
  Christianity not mysterious*, 95
Bryskett, Lodowick, *Discourse of civill life*, 38–39
Burke, Edmund
  Catholic rights and, 13
  critique of Irish stage, 173–74

401

Burke, Edmund (cont.)
  Letter to Sir Hercules Langrishe, 63
  Molyneux Problem and, 123–24
  national identity and, 62–63
  A Philosophical Enquiry into the Origin of Our
    Ideas of the Sublime and Beautiful, 123–24
  prejudice, campaign against, 94
  Reflections on the Revolution in France, 63
  toleration and, 92–93, 97–98, 101–2
Burnell, Henry, *Landgartha*, 40
Bury, Catherine Maria, 199
Butler, Eleanor, 245, 290
Butler, Sarah, 56, 327–28
  Irish Tales, 266

Campion, Edmund, 333
Carrick, James, 317
The Case of the Stage in Ireland (pamphlet),
    172–73
Catholicism
  audiences/readers, 6, 38, 52, 103
  authors, 2, 54–55, 62, 100–1, 122–23, 367–72
  Charter Schools and, 343–49
  fictional character, 1–3, 9, 56–57, 60, 74, 81,
    271, 308–19, 327–29, 349–53
  introduction to, 10, 13, 14–15
  national identity and, 37
  Penal Laws and, 54, 61, 101, 102–3, 215–16, 367
  Protestantism and, 51, 53–55, 63, 80–81, 101,
    138, 178–79, 309–10
  religious discrimination and, 102, 103
  support of Jacobite cause, 358
  toleration and, 100–1, 142
Céitinn, Seathrún, *Foras Feasa ar Éirinn*, 327–28
Chaigneau, William, *The History of Jack Connor*,
    18, 56–57, 263–68, 271–80, 276f, 318–19, 343,
    349–53, 351f
Chamberlayne, Walter, 'A Poem occasion'd by
    a view of Powers-court House', 165
Chambers, Ephraim, *Cyclopaedia*, 50
chapbooks, 160
charity in poetry, 233–34, 236
Cheselden, William, 'An Account of some
    Observations made by a young Gentleman,
    who was born blind', 119–20
children/childhood in fiction
  aristocratic childhood, 356
  Charter Schools and, 343–49
  fosterage customs, 20, 333, 334
  orphan protagonist, 349–53, 351f
  political and philosophical commentary in,
    353–59
  Rousseau and, 354–55
  wet nursing, 20, 356
Christian charity, 92

Christian faith, 100, 101
Christ's divinity, 124–25
Churchill, Charles, 247, 251–56
  The Rosciad, 245–46, 253
Cibber, Theophilus, 171, 185
civic awareness, 174
civic virtue, 105–6
'Classical Irish' period, 35–36
Clonmel, Tipperary, 6, 56, 210, 214, 326
Collins, David, *An Account of the English Colony*
    of New South Wales, 395
Colman, George, 136, 198
colonialism in fiction, 212–13, 215, 216, 220
colonisation in literature, 5, 212–13, 265, 328
comedy of manners, 12
comic poetry, 237, 365–66, 367–76
Concanen, Matthew, *Miscellaneous Poems*
    Original and Translated, 152, 153
Condillac, Étienne Bonnot de, 120–21
Connaught, 20, 177
copyright legislation, 12
Cork, 189, 337
Cork County, 31, 33, 39, 63, 113–14, 115,
    155, 368
Corkery, Daniel
  The Hidden Ireland, 21, 36, 325–26, 337–38,
    386–88
Cosgrave, John, *Genuine History of the Lives and*
    Actions of the Most Notorious Irish
    Highwaymen, Tories and Rapparees, 308,
    313–19
cosmopolitanism, 16, 196, 202, 269,
    271–77
Counter-Enlightenment forces, 110
Counter-Reformation history, 38
country estate landscapes in poetry, 155–59
country festivities in poetry, 160
Crabbe, George, 'To His Grace the Duke of
    Rutland', 166–67
crime biographies
  introduction to, 307–8
  A Genuine History of the Lives and Actions of the
    Most Notorious Irish Highwaymen, Tories
    and Rapparees, 308, 313–19
  The Irish Rogue; or, The Comical History of the
    Life and Actions of Teague O Divelley, 308–13
crime narratives
  identity tropes in, 319
  savagery *vs.* civility in, 316
  travel tropes in, 319
Culloden, battle of (1746), 3, 274, 275
cultural exchange through translation, 197–201
cultural memory in literature, 386, 389,
    391–94
cultural transmission, 36

d'Arnaud, François de Baculard, *Les Époux Malheureux, ou histoire de Mr et Mme de Bédoyère*, 193

Daviel, Jacques, 122

Day, Thomas, *The History of Sandford and Merton*, 353

Defoe, Daniel, *Moll Flanders*, 307

Delacourt, James, 'To Mr Thomson, on his Seasons', 164

Delamayne, Thomas, 'To Francis Bindon Esq.', 163

Delany, Patrick, 'On Longford's Glin', 165

Denham, John, 'Cooper's Hill', 154

Derham, William, 118

Diderot, Denis, 121–22, 123–24
    Lettre sur les aveugles, 121

dissenters, 3, 8, 69, 78, 80, 94, 102, 266

divine mystery, 95

Dobbs, Arthur, *Essay on the Trade and Improvement of Ireland*, 104

Dobbs, Francis, *The Patriot King; or Irish Chief*, 60

domestic relationships in poetry, 236–38

Don Tomazo, or the Juvenile Rambles of Thomas Dangerfield (Anon.), 310–11

'Dromineann donn dílis' ('My dear Droimeann Donn'), 4

Drought, James, 124–25

Du Bois, Dorothea, 56

duanaire (poem-book), 36–37

Dubh, Caitilín, 36–37

Dublin Castle, 22, 40, 176, 177, 318

Dublin English, 40–41

Dublin Journal, 132

Dublin Philosophical Society, 116

The Dublin University Magazine, 129–30

Dunkin, William
    The Murphaeid, 55
    The Parson's Revels, 1–4, 22–23, 55

East India Company, 220

Edgeworth, Maria, 247
    Belinda, 18, 245–46, 257–60
    Ennui, 353, 356
    Madame de Fleury, 359

education and literacy, 54, 130–33, 272–73, 343–49

educational writing, 135

Edwards, Anna Maria, 'Female Friendship. A Tale. Founded on fact', 290

Elder, Olivia, 8, 9, 19, 56
    Poems, 164, 288–89

Eliot, T.S., *The Waste Land*, 388

Elrington, Thomas, *Sermons Preached in the Chapel of Trinity College, Dublin*, 124–25

English-language/literary modes, 20–21, 40, 50, 167, 370–71

Enlightenment in Ireland
    campaign against prejudice, 94–98
    Christ's divinity and, 124–25
    Counter-Enlightenment forces, 110
    improvement, 104–6
    introduction to, 5, 14–15, 91–94
    national identity and, 51
    radical engagement with, 372
    toleration / intolerance, 92, 98–104, 106

environment, 8, 44, 247, 344, 349, 355, 356

epistolary fiction, 58, 77, 196–97, 292, 294–95

European travel writing, 208

exile and national identity, 37

famine, 4, 163, 219–20, 372

farming in poetry, 161–62

Farquhar, George, 396–97
    The Recruiting Officer, 382–84, 389–96

Faulkner, George, 1, 84, 292

female friendship poems, 286–90

female intimacy, 288–89

feminisation of Ireland, 265

feminist debate over sisterhood in fiction, 299–300

feminist protest in literary translation
    Caoineadh Airt Uí Laoghaire, 365–66, 367–72
    Cúirt an Mheán Oíche, 365–66, 367–76
    introduction to, 365–67
    summary of, 376–77

fiction. *see also* children/childhood in fiction; foreign territories in fiction; novels; sisterhood in fiction
    beggary, 350
    Catholic characters, 1–3, 9, 56–57, 60, 74, 81, 271, 308–19, 327–29, 349–53
    epistolary fiction, 58, 77, 196–97, 292, 294–95
    feminist debate over sisterhood in, 299–300
    foreign territories in, 17
    lesbianism in, 244–47, 285–86, 290–91
    national identity in, 56–57, 273–74
    transplantation policy in, 350–51

Fidge, George, *The English Gusman*, 307

Fielding, Henry, 198, 201
    The Adventures of David Simple, 284

Fielding, Sarah, 284

Fitzgerald (née Butler), Eleanor, Countess of Desmond, 40

Fitzgerald, Thomas, 336

Fitzmaurice, Anastacia, 189

foreign territories in fiction, 17

fosterage customs, 20, 333, 334

Foucault, Michel, *The History of Sexuality: The Will to Knowledge*, 249–50

Franciscan order, 37
freethinkers, criticism of, 93–94, 96–97
French books in Ireland, 190–91, 199–200, 202
French language
  abridgment, 111, 113
  plays, 141
  prose, 32, 41
  sentimental novels, 190–97, 199–200, 202
  speech, 32
  translations, 50

Gaelic influences
  in Irish novels, 324–38
  keening women, 368–69
  in poetry, 21, 367–76
  sexual topics in Gaelic poetry, 373, 375
  of Swift, Jonathan, 329–32
Gardiner, Luke, 140
Garrick, David, 251–56
  The Fribbleriad, 252–53, 253f, 255
Gay, John, *The Beggar's Opera*, 307
gay experiences. *see* queer studies
gay historiography, 244–47
genres, literary, 12
Georgic poetry, 167
Goddard, Margaret, *Poems on several occasions*, 287–88
Golding, George, 313
Goldsmith, Oliver, 161, 197–98, 396–97
  The Deserted Village, 162, 382–89
  The Vicar of Wakefield, 190
gothic novels, 11, 57–58
Graffigny, Françoise de, 190
  Lettres d'une Peruvienne / Letters of a Peruvian Princess, 193
Grant, Roger, 117
Grattan, Henry, 129
Grierson, Constantia, 229–30, 231–33, 240
Griffith, Elizabeth, 57–58, 59, 190–91, 196, 200
Groarke, Vona, 21, 366
  Lament for Art O'Leary, 370–72
Gulliver's Travels (Swift)
  conception of, 82
  epistolary exchanges preceding, 77
  Gaelic influences in, 329–32
  human beings *vs.* non-humans, 69
  imperialism in, 207–8
  introduction to, 10–11
  Molyneux Problem, 118

Head, Richard, *The English Rogue*, 307
Heaney, Seamus, 21, 365, 366, 372, 375–76
The Hibernian Journal, 141
The Hibernian Magazine, 138–40, 139f
Hiberno-English, 1–2, 10, 34–41, 50, 55

Hill, Aaron, 132, 135
Hitchcock, Robert, *Historical View of the Irish Stage*, 174, 175–76
homosexuality in literature. *see* queer studies
Huguenots, 56, 136, 189, 199–200, 273, 318
Hume, David, 91, 97
hunting in poetry, 161
Hutcheson, Francis, 51, 118, 119, 239
  A System of Moral Philosophy, 103

identity. *see also* national identity
  Gulliver's Travels, 214–18
  The History of Arsaces, Prince of Betlis, 208, 218–21
  introduction to, 207–9
  summary to, 222
  Vertue Rewarded; or, the Irish Princess, 208, 209–14
improving pamphlets, 351
Irish Anglican theology, 115
Irish antiquarianism, 62
Irish Enlightenment. *see* Enlightenment in Ireland
Irish feasts, 1–4, 153, 310
Irish Gaelic texts. *see* Gaelic influences
Irish hospitality, 3, 60
Irish-language culture, 43, 325, 331
Irish literature. *see also* masculinity in Irish literature; queer studies
  colonisation in, 5, 212–13, 265, 328
  cultural memory in, 386, 389, 391–94
  defined, 10–11
  memory in, 384–85, 386, 392, 395
  misogynistic satire, 285
  paternal affections in, 277–78
  patriarchy in, 277–78
  satire in, 137, 235, 297–99
  teleology in, 32, 36, 41–42
Irish parliamentarians, 141, 177
Irish peerage, 268–69
The Irish Rogue; or, The Comical History of the Life and Actions of Teague O Divelley (Anon.), 308–13
Irishness, 9, 10, 12, 13, 59, 157, 208, 215, 247, 257, 264–65, 309–10, 312
Italian opera, critique of, 256
Italian Renaissance, 43

Jacobite Rebellion (1745), 52, 61, 274, 358
Jacobitism
  allegiance to, 21
  Catholicism and, 358
  defeat of, 3
  links to France, 189
  in novels, 9, 56, 80, 266, 269, 274, 327

in poetry, 12
in song, 4
in theatre, 2
in Tory ministry, 68, 78, 80
James II, King, 269
Johnson, Samuel, 173, 251–52
Johnston, Charles, 63
  Chrysal, or the Adventures of Guinea, 218
  The History of Arsaces, Prince of Betlis, 208,
    218–21
  The History of John Juniper, 319
Jones, Henry, 56
  'On a fine Crop of Peas being spoil'd by
    a Storm', 161
Jones, William, 117
Jonson, Ben, 70, 77
  The Irish Masque at Court, 34

Keating, Geoffrey. *see* Céitinn, Seathrún
keening women in Gaelic culture, 368–69
Kelly, Dominick, 55
  *The History of Mr. Charles Fitzgerald and
    Miss Sarah Stapleton*, 2
Kelly, Hugh, 59–60, 190, 198
Kelly riots (1747), 181–82. *see also* theatre/theatre
    riots
Keneally, Thomas, *The Playmaker*, 21, 389–90,
    392, 394
Kerry, 35, 55, 57, 153–55, 198, 335, 368
Kilkenny, 40, 115, 189, 230
King, William, 2, 326–27
  Divine Predestination and Fore-knowledge, 115

landscape poetry. *see* Gaelic influences; poems/
    poetry about landscapes
language. *see also* feminist protest in literary
    translation
  bi-lingualism, 5
  Dublin English, 40–41
  English-language/literary modes, 20–21, 40, 50
  French language, 199–200
  literary transition and, 34–41, 35*f*
  in poetry, 1–2, 165
Latin, 1–2, 8, 10, 11, 32, 37–38, 40, 41, 44, 50, 55,
    155, 237, 253–54, 328
Leland, Thomas
  *The History of Ireland from the Invasion of
    Henry II*, 103
  Longsword, 57–58
lesbianism in fiction, 244–47, 285–86, 290–91
Leslie, John, 158
letters and accounts by women. *see* women
    writers/writing
libertarianism, 75
Licensing Act (1737), 60

life writing, 39, 41–42
Limerick, 57, 122, 189, 218, 319
literacy and education, 272–73
literary canonicity, 50
literary criticism, 8, 13
literary culture, 5, 8, 12, 14, 35, 37, 38, 41, 356
literary imagination, 22
literary transition
  defined, 32–33
  introduction to, 12–23, 31–34
  languages and, 34–41, 35*f*
  scholarship and, 41–45
Locke, John, 94–95, 99–100, 111–13
  An Essay concerning Humane Understanding, 111
  Of the Conduct of the Understanding, 99
  Some Thoughts Concerning Education, 272
Londonderry/Derry, 40, 60, 189, 391
Louis XIV, King, 209–10
Lucas, Charles, 132–38, 181
'Lucasia.' *see* Owen, Anne

Mac Bruaidín, Tadhg (Mac Bruaideadha), 34–35
Mac Gabhráin, Aodh, 'Pléaráca na Ruarcach',
    3, 4
Mace, William, 118
Madden, Samuel, *Reflections and Resolutions
    Proper for the Gentlemen of Ireland*, 266
Madden, William Balfour, 156–57, 166
Magazin à La Mode, 189
Mahomet Riots (1754), 182–83. *see also* theatre/
    theatre riots
male homosexuality, 245
Mandeville, Bernard, *The Fable of the Bees*, 105
'Marinda.' *see* Monck, Mary
masculinity in Irish literature. *see also* soldiers
  introduction to, 263–68
  martial cosmopolitanism and, 271–77
  as omnipresent and invisible, 264
  stabilising concept of, 255–56
  in Swift, 268–71
  as system of politeness, 279
McCarthy, Charlotte, 287, 288
  The Fair Moralist, 290–91
Mercier, Louis-Sébastian, *L'Habitant de la
    Guadeloupe: Comédie en trois actes*, 201
Mérian, Jean-Bernard, 122
Merriman, Brian, *Cúirt an Mheán Oíche*
    (The Midnight Court), 365–66,
    367–76
Mettrie, Julien Offray de la, 120–21
migration, 4, 22, 39, 164, 207, 389–90
Milton, John, *The Masque of Comus*, 129,
    135–36
misogynistic satire, 285
Molesworth, Robert, 232

Molyneux, William, 92
  The Case of Ireland Stated, 178, 207, 297
  Dioptrica nova, 111, 112
Molyneux Problem
  alternative solution to, 113–17
  Christ's divinity and, 124–25
  experimental developments, 117–20
  French connections to, 120–24
  overview of, 111–13
Monck, Mary, 152, 232
Montesquieu, *The Spirit of the Laws*, 103
The Monthly Review, 190–91
Moore, Edward, *The Foundling*, 198
Moore, Thomas, 129, 140, 386
Mulhoni, John, 317
Munster, 7, 20, 33, 41, 325, 336, 367, 387
Murphy, Arthur, 59–60, 198

national identity
  Catholicism and, 37
  Enlightenment in Ireland, 51
  exile and, 37
  poetry and, 55–56
  in prose fiction, 56–57, 273–74
  writing and, 49–64
Newton, Isaac, 118
Ní Bhriain, Fionnghuala, 36–37
novels (prose fiction). *see also* fiction; *Gulliver's
    Travels*; women writers/writing
  colonialism in fiction, 212–13, 215, 216
  Franco-Irish transnational novels, 189–202
  Gaelic influences in Irish novels, 324–38
  gothic novels, 11, 57–58
  introduction to, 6–7, 20
  national identity and, 56–57
  sentimental novels, 190–91, 199–200, 202
  translation of, 197–201
Nugent, Richard, *Cynthia*, 39, 42

Ó Briain, Donnchadh (Donough Ó Brien),
    34–35
Ó Coimín, Mícheál, 324
Ó Colmáin, Domhnall, *Parliament na mBan*, 337
O'Connor, Morrough
  'The County of Kerry. A Poem', 55, 154–55
  'Eclogue in Imitation of the first Eclogue of
    Virgil', 154–55
O'Conor, Charles, 61, 142, 332
  The case of the Roman-Catholics of Ireland, 91,
    100–1
  *Seasonable Thoughts Relating to our Civil and
    Ecclesiastical Constitution*, 91, 100–1
O'Halloran, Sylvester, 122–23
  *A New Treatise of the Glaucoma, or
    Cataract*, 122

O'Hanlon, Redmond, 314
Ó Neachtain, Seán, *Stair Éamuinn Uí Chléirigh*,
    3, 324
Ó Ruairc, Brian na Múrtha (Brian Ballach
    Moore Ó Rourke), 4
O'Sullivan Beare, Philip, 38
oral culture, 9, 36
orphan protagonist, 349–53, 351*f*
Ovidian myth, 31
Owen, Anne, 286–87

paternalism, 277–78
patriot politics and women writers, 294–95
patriotic engagement, 53
peasant class, 135, 159–63, 167, 325, 332, 355,
    356, 359
Penal Laws, 101, 102–3, 215–16, 367
Philips, Katherine, 40
  'To the Excellent *Orinda*', 286–87
Philips, William
  Hibernia Freed, 6, 60
  St. Stephen's Green, 60
Pilkington, Laetitia, 156, 230
  Memoirs, 233, 287
Pilkington, Matthew, *Poems on Several
    Occasions*, 230
Plato, 385, 392
Plunket, Mary Bridget, 189
poems/poetry
  'Classical Irish' period and, 35–36
  comic poetry, 237, 365–66, 367–76
  Dublin English, 40–41
  farming in, 161–62
  female friendship poems, 286–90
  Gaelic poetry, 21, 367–76
  hunting in, 161
  introduction to, 1–4
  labourers in, 159–63
  national identity and, 55–56, 273–74
  religious topics in, 160
  women poets/poetry, 17–18, 36–37, 39, 227–41,
    286–90
poems/poetry about landscapes
  country estate landscaping, 155–59
  future politics and, 166–67
  introduction to, 151
  labourers and, 159–63
  natural *vs.* contrived, 152–53
  perception of landscape, 164–66
  weather impact on, 163–64
Ponsonby, Elizabeth, 292
Ponsonby, Sarah, 245, 290
Pope, Alexander, 230, 238–39
  Epistle to Dr Arbuthnot, 255
popery laws, 102

popular culture, 10, 19–20
postcolonialism, 50
Poynings' Law, 298
Presbyterians, 2, 9, 51, 54, 79, 151, 215, 216, 268, 288
Prévost, Antoine-François, *Manon Lescaut*, 192–93
priestcraft, 94
Prior, Thomas, *List of the Absentees of Ireland*, 53, 104
private theatricals, 15, 144
Proast, Jonas, 99–100
prose fiction. *see* novels
Protestant Ascendancy, 4–5, 53, 61, 138, 142, 207, 208, 330–31
Protestantism
  Berkeley and, 99
  Catholicism and, 51, 53–55, 63, 80–81, 101, 138, 178–79, 309–10
  Charter Schools and, 343–49
  imperialist fiction and, 207–9
  Irish identity and, 9–10, 13
  masculinity in literature, 266–67
  paternalism and, 278
  potential threats to, 268
  Presbyterians, 79, 151, 215, 216, 268
  rise of, 103, 130

Quakers, 1, 13
Quayle, Francis, 114
queer studies
  Freke in *Belinda*, 245–46, 257–60
  Fribble in *The Rosciad*, 245–46, 251–56
  introduction to, 17–19, 244–47
  lesbianism in fiction, 244–47, 285–86, 290–91
  yahoo creatures in *Gulliver's Travels*, 245, 247–51

Radcliffe, Stephen, 99
rationality, 58, 77, 98, 135
realism in fiction, 217
Reformation period, 38
religious persecution, 101, 102, 103
religious topics in poetry, 160
Revocation of the Edict of Nantes (1685), 189
Riccoboni, Marie-Jeanne, 191–97, 198–99, 200, 201
Richardson, John, *A Proposal for the Conversion of the Natives of Ireland*, 345–46
Richardson, Samuel, 193–94, 201
  Clarissa, or the History of a Young Lady, 284, 291–93
Robinet, J. B. R., 200–1

romantic friendship between women, 289–90
Romantic nationalism, 50
Romanticism in poetry, 165
Rousseau, Jean-Jacques, 193, 354
  Emile, 343, 353, 357, 359
Rycaut, Paul, *The Royal Commentaries by the Inca Garcilasso de la Vega*, 210, 213

satire in literature, 137, 235, 297–99
Saunderson, Nicholas, 121–22, 123
scholarship and literary transition, 41–45
Scott, Sarah, 190
  A Description of Millenium Hall, 285
Scott, Walter, 218
sectarianism, 3, 101
sentimental novels, 190–97, 199–200, 202
sexual desire, 273–74
sexual topics in Gaelic poetry, 373, 375
Shadwell, Charles, 10, 60
Shadwell, Thomas
  The Amorous Bigot, 311, 312
  The Lancashire Witches, 311, 312
Shakespeare, William, 134
  Coriolanus, 279
  Henry V, 34, 178
  Macbeth, 138–44, 139*f*
Shepherd, Samuel, 'Leixlip', 166
Sheridan, Alicia, 143
Sheridan, Elizabeth, *The Triumph of Prudence over Passion*, 6, 58, 294–95, 296–97
Sheridan, Frances, 57, 130–31, 190–97, 200–1, 284, 295–96
  The Discovery, 192
  The Dupe, 192
  Eugenia and Adelaide, 290–91
  The History of Nourjahad, 192
  The Memoirs of Miss Sidney Bidulph, 16, 57, 192, 194, 195–96, 292–94, 295–96
  Conclusion of the Memoirs of Miss Sidney Bidulph, 192, 296
Sheridan, Richard Brinsley, 5, 6, 59, 183
Sheridan, Thomas, 11, 15, 16, 53, 55, 59, 131, 156, 171–86, 279, 331
  The Brave Irishman, 319
Sidney, Philip, *Arcadia*, 39–40
sister kingdoms, 297–99
sisterhood in fiction. *see also* fiction
  female friendship poems, 286–90
  feminist debate over, 299–300
  introduction to, 284–86
  overview of, 290–97
  sister kingdoms, 297–99
Smart, Christopher, 'The Temple of Dulness', 164

Smith, Alexander, *The History of the Lives of the Most Noted Highway-Men*, 308
Smith, Charles, 167
Smock Alley riot (1754), 131, 133–34, 137. *see also* theatre/theatre riots
sociability in poetry, 228
social constructivism, 244, 249
social customs, 20
social welfare, 174
soldiers, 34, 189, 263–68, 270, 271, 274, 277, 294
sonnets, 39, 41, 42, 43
Southwell, Anne, 39
spas in poetry, 158
Spence, Joseph, 123
Spenser, Edmund, 33, 39, 333
   Colin Clouts Come Home Againe, 33
   'Mutabilitie Cantos', 31–32, 33
Stage Irishman, 13, 18, 22, 58–60, 153, 196, 263–64, 267–68
Stanihurst, Richard, 38
Steele, Richard, 264
Sterne, Laurence, 121–22, 123–24
   The Life and Opinions of Tristram Shandy, Gentleman, 190
   A Sentimental Journey Through France and Italy, 190
Stone, George, 244
Swift, Jonathan. *see also Gulliver's Travels*
   Argument against the abolishing of Christianity, 71–72
   beggary in fiction, 350
   bibliography and textual studies, 81–84
   biography of, 70–77
   'Carberiae Rupes', 155
   Description of a City Shower, 55
   Description of the Morning, 55
   The Drapier's Letters, 52
   Gaelic influences on, 329–32
   imperialist writing of, 207–8
   and improvement, 105–6
   introduction to, 10–11, 13–14, 68–70
   Irish studies on, 77–81
   landscape poetry, 155
   The Legion Club, 55
   masculinity and, 268–71
   A Modest Proposal, 217, 350
   Molyneux Problem, 118
   national identity and, 52–55
   Ode to the King, 55
   O'Rourke's Feast, 56
   poetry by, 55
   prejudice, campaign against, 95–96
   A Proposal for the Universal Use of Irish Manufacture, 52
   on propriety of Barber, 230–31, 240

The Story of the Injured Lady, 214
A Tale of a Tub, 3, 105
'To Charles Ford, Esq. On his Birthday', 55
Synge, Edward, 101
   An Appendix to a Gentleman's Religion, 113–17

Temple, John, *The Irish Rebellion*, 57
Tench, Watkin, 394–95
'The Goldfinder' (Cosgrave), 314–15
theatre, 6, 40, 59–60, 131, 133–34, 137
   audience rebellion/riots, 180–83
   'Bon Ton Theatricals', 133–38
   dramatic productions, 59–60
   licensing of, 12
   managers/management, 11, 16, 140, 172, 177, 180
   national theatre in the eighteenth century, 171–86
   'pop-up' theatres, 6
   private theatricals, 15, 144
   Theatre Royal, Smock Alley, 174, 176, 185
   wage inflation in, 176
Thomson, James, 167
Toland, John, 62, 97, 100
   Christianity not Mysterious, 50–51, 94
   Letters to Serena, 94–95
   Molyneux Problem, 115
Touchet, Mervin, 244–45
transition. *see* literary transition
translation, 197–201, 376–77. *see also* feminist protest in literary translation
Travels into Several Remote Nations of the World (Swift). *see Gulliver's Travels*
Treaty of Limerick (1691), 189
Trinity College, Dublin, 1, 51, 58, 60, 62, 95, 115, 124–25, 154, 176, 199–200, 288
The true life of Betty Ireland (pamphlet), 297–98

Uí Laoghaire, Eibhlín Dhubh, *Caoineadh Airt Uí Laoghaire* (The Lament for Art O'Leary), 365–66, 367–72
Ulster-Scots, 8, 10, 50, 215

Vendermere, John, 140
ventriloquism in poetry, 237
Vermaasen, John, 118
Vertue Rewarded; or, the Irish Princess (Anon.), 2, 6–7, 17, 20, 208, 209–14, 325, 326–28
Victor, Benjamin, 184–85
   History of the London and Dublin stages, 175–76
Virgil, *Aeneid*, 153
Voltaire, 91, 120, 182, 199
   Élemens de la philosophie de Neuton, 120
   Letters concerning the English Nation, 120
   Mahomet, 182
   Treatise on Toleration, 101

War of the Austrian Succession, 274
War of the Spanish Succession, 82, 269
Waterford, 189, 278
weather in poetry, 163–64
Wertenbaker, Timberlake, *Our Country's Good*,
    21, 389, 391–94
West of Ireland, 152–53
Westmeath, 2, 39, 132, 161–62
wet nursing in childhood, 20, 356
Wheatley, Francis, 166
Whyte, Laurence, 161–62
    *A Poetical Description of Mr. Neal's new musick-
    Hall in Fishamble-street, Dublin*, 55–56
Whyte, Samuel
    'Bon Ton Theatricals', 133–38
    A Collection of Poems on various subjects, 129
    *A Didactic Essay including an idea of the
    Character of Jane Shore as performed by
    a Young Lady in a Private Play*, 129
    Grafton Street school, 130–33
    introduction to, 15, 19, 129–30

prologues and epilogues, 134
Wilkes, Wetenhall, 'Bellville: a poem', 157–58
William III, King, 209–10
Williamite wars (1690–91), 209, 210, 212–13, 358
wit in poetry, 235
Wollstonecraft, Mary, 97
women writers/writing. *see also* queer studies;
    individual women writers
    feminist debate over sisterhood in fiction,
    299–300
    French language access and, 199–200
    letters and accounts, 37
    patriot politics and, 294–95
    poets/poetry, 17–18, 36–37, 39, 227–41,
    286–90
    sentimental novels, 190–91, 199–200, 202
    translation of novels, 197–201

Yeats, W. B., 21, 49
Young, Arthur, 102
Young Ireland movement, 50